Religion i

WITHDRAWN

0 7 MAY 2021

D0293447

RELIGION AND MODERNITY

Series Editors: Paul Heelas, Linda Woodhead; Editorial Advisor:
David Martin; Founding Editors: John Clayton and Ninian Smart.
*Lancaster University, Lancaster University, University of Boston,
University of California – Santa Barbara*

The **Religion and Modernity** series makes accessible to a wide
audience some of the most important work in the study of
religion today. The series invites leading scholars to present clear
and non-technical contributions to contemporary thinking about
religion in the modern world. Although the series is geared
primarily to the needs of college and university students, the
volumes in **Religion and Modernity** will prove invaluable to
readers with some background in Religious Studies who wish
to keep up with recent thinking in the subject, as well as to
the general reader who is seeking to learn more about the
transformations of religion in our time.

Published:

Don Cupitt – *Mysticism after Modernity*
Paul Heelas (ed.), with the assistance of David Martin and
Paul Morris – *Religion, Modernity and Postmodernity*
Linda Woodhead and Paul Heelas – *Religion in Modern Times*

Forthcoming:

Nancy McCagney – *Religion and Ecology*
Juan Campo – *Pilgrimage and Modernity*
David Smith – *Hinduism and Modernity*

Religion in Modern Times

An Interpretive Anthology

Edited by
Linda Woodhead and
Paul Heelas

YORK ST. JOHN
COLLEGE LIBRARY

BLACKWELL
Publishers

Copyright © Blackwell Publishers Ltd 2000

Editorial matter and organization copyright ©
Linda Woodhead and Paul Heelas 2000

First published 2000

2 4 6 8 10 9 7 5 3 1

Blackwell Publishers Ltd
108 Cowley Road
Oxford OX4 1JF
UK

Blackwell Publishers Inc.
350 Main Street
Malden, Massachusetts 02148
USA

All rights reserved. Except for the quotation of short passages for the
purposes of criticism and review, no part of this publication may be
reproduced, stored in a retrieval system, or transmitted, in any form
or by any means, electronic, mechanical, photocopying, recording or
otherwise, without the prior permission of the publisher.

Except in the United States of America, this book is sold subject to
the condition that it shall not, by way of trade or otherwise, be lent, resold,
hired out, or otherwise circulated without the publisher's prior
consent in any form of binding or cover other than that in which it
is published and without a similar condition including this condition
being imposed on the subsequent purchaser.

British Library Cataloguing in Publication Data

A CIP catalogue record for this book is available from the British Library.

Library of Congress Cataloging-in-Publication Data

Religion in modern times / edited by Linda Woodhead and Paul Heelas.
p.   cm. — (Religion and modernity)
Includes bibliographical references (p.   ) and index.
ISBN 0-631-21073-3 (alk. paper) — ISBN 0-631-21074-1 (pbk. : alk. paper)
1. Religion.   I. Series.   II. Woodhead, Linda.   III. Heelas, Paul.
BL48.R425   2000
200'.9'04 21—dc21   99-041199

Typeset in 10 on 12½ pt Meridien
by Graphicraft Limited, Hong Kong
Printed in Great Britain by MPG Books, Bodmin, Cornwall

This book is printed on acid-free paper.

To those who suffered most in the making of this book:
our spouses, Alan and Anna-Marie,
our children, Guy and Sebastian,
our dogs, Lily, Daisy, Murphy, Magnus and Bella,
and the photocopier on C Floor, Furness College

contents in brief

contents

acknowledgements

The authors and publishers gratefully acknowledge the following for permission to reproduce copyright material:

Ahlstrom, Sydney, E., *A Religious History of the American People* (Yale University Press, New Haven and London, 1972); Beckford, James A., *Religion and Advanced Industrial Society* (Unwin Hyman [Routledge] London, Boston, Sydney and Wellington, 1989); Bellah, Robert, Religious Evolution. *American Sociological Review*, 29, June, 1964 (American Sociological Association, Washington, D.C.); Berger, Peter, *The Heretical Imperative. Contemporary Possibilities of Religious Affirmation* (Copyright © 1979 Peter L. Berger. Used by permission of Doubleday, a division of Bantam Doubleday Dell Publishing Group, Inc., New York); Casanova, José, *Public Religions in the Modern World* (The University of Chicago Press, Chicago and London, 1994); Comaroff, Jean and Comaroff, John, Introduction from Jean Comaroff and John Comaroff (eds), *Modernity and Its Malcontents. Ritual and Power in Postcolonial Africa* (The University of Chicago Press, Chicago and London, 1993); Emerson, Ralph Waldo, *Essays & Lectures* (The Press Syndicate of the University of Cambridge, 1983); Giddens, Anthony, Introduction, from Max Weber, *The Protestant Ethic and the Spirit of Capitalism* (Unwin Hyman [Routledge], London, Boston and Sydney, 1985); Hunter, James Davison, *Evangelicalism. The Coming Generation* (The University of Chicago Press, Chicago and London, 1987); Juergensmeyer, Mark, *The New Cold War? Religious Nationalism Confronts the Secular State* (University of California Press, Berkeley and Los Angeles, 1993. Copyright © 1993 The Regents of the University of California); Roof, Wade Clark and William McKinney, *American Mainline Religion. Its Changing Shape and Future* (Copyright © 1987 Rutgers, The State University. Reprinted by permission of Rutgers University Press); Taylor, Charles, *Sources of the Self. The Making of the Modern Identity* (Cambridge University Press, Cambridge 1989. Reprinted by permission of the publisher from

Sources of the Self by Charles Taylor, Harvard University Press, Cambridge, Mass. Copyright © 1989 Charles Taylor); Troeltsch, Ernst, *The Social Teaching of the Christian Churches* (Routledge [Unwin Hyman] London, 1931); Weber, Max, *The Protestant Ethic and the Spirit of Capitalism*, trans. Anthony Giddens (Routledge [Unwin Hyman], London, Boston and Sydney, 1985); Wilson, Bryan, Secularization: The Inherited Model, from Philip Hammond (ed.), *The Sacred in a Secular Age. Toward Revision in the Scientific Study of Religion* (University of California Press, Berkeley, Los Angeles and London, 1985. Copyright © 1985 The Regents of the University of California).

The publishers apologize for any errors or omissions in the above list and would be grateful to be notified of any corrections that should be incorporated in the next edition or reprint of this book.

introduction to
the volume

This book began life as two separate projects: a book *and* an anthology. In the end it proved impossible to keep the two apart, and the finished product combines both. It is made up of a large number of short readings linked by introductory comments and organized within an original framework. It can be read either as a book with long quotations, or as an anthology with extensive commentary and interpretation.

The reason it proved impossible to offer a conventional book on religion in modern times was that we were aware of so many important and informative writings in the area, and of our debt to them. The reason it proved impossible to put together a straightforward anthology of readings was the absence of an agreed framework for the subject. Unlike established disciplines like systematic theology or even the sociology of religion, religion in modern times remains relatively uncharted territory.

This volume has three main aims: first, to introduce a wide range of the most important, influential and incisive writings on religion in modern times; second, to place these readings within a framework which can help the reader make sense of the field; and third to offer a new interpretation of religion in modern times, and a new language for speaking about the topic. In pursuing the third aim, we have also sought to relate wider theories about modern culture and society to the religious realm. Theories of individualization, consumerization and dedifferentiation can illuminate the study of religion; equally, the study of religion can illuminate these and other theories.

The volume brings together some three hundred readings. Some of these are theoretical, others empirical or illustrative. Some are by academics, others by poets, theologians, or practitioners. Theoretical contributions range from Karl Marx to Robert Bellah; empirical studies from Nancy Ammerman to Godfrey Lienhardt; examples from Karl Barth to Sai Baba.

The picture of religion in modern times that emerges from these pages is one which is both more interesting and less uniform than is often assumed. It is a picture of variety and coexistence. Thus, to give just a few examples from many which appear in the volume, old faiths and new spiritualities *both* appear to be doing well, though the former worship a transcendent God and the latter seek a god within. Likewise, both secularization *and* sacralization appear to be occurring in different parts of the world. Finally, in some parts of the world religion today is more politically militant than ever before; in others its political significance is rapidly shrinking.

Distinctive Approach

So far as we know, this is the first attempt to bring together the existing literature on religion in modern times. It differs from anthologies and books in the sociology of religion like those by Steve Bruce ((ed.), 1995a); Michael Hill (1973); and Meredith McGuire (1997), because it deals exclusively with the modern period, draws on the writings of participants as well as theorists, and pays little attention to some of the more general topics and debates which have come to dominate the sociology of religion. Equally, this volume differs from collections like the fundamentalisms project (Marty and Appleby, 1991–5), which draw together reflections on a single topic in the study of religion in modern times, because it attempts to survey a wider religions field.

This book also differs from tradition-based surveys of religion in modern times such as those by Mary Pat Fisher (1997) or John Hinnells (1997). Whilst it is tradition-informed, it does not use a tradition-based classification of the 'world's religions' (Hinduism, Judaism, Christianity, etc.) as its starting point. Instead, it attempts to identify the main varieties of religion in modern times – varieties which can be found in and across all the traditions.

Part One of the volume surveys these different varieties of religion. It identifies three as having particular historical and classificatory importance, and names them *religions of difference, religions of humanity*, and *spiritualities of life*. These different types of religion can be thought of as three points on a spectrum of understandings of the relationship between the divine, the human, and the natural order. At one end of the spectrum, religions of difference distinguish sharply between God and the human and natural. At the other, spiritualities of life adopt a 'holistic' perspective and stress the fundamental identity between the divine, the human and the natural. And in the middle of the spectrum, religions of humanity attempt to keep the three elements in balance,

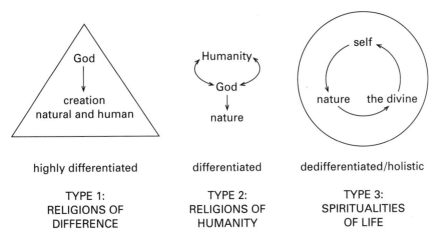

The spectrum of religion in modern times

resisting a subordination of the human to the divine or the natural. Represented in visual form, this spectrum has become known to our students as 'the triangle and the blob'.

Whilst our typology owes much to theorists such as Robert Bellah, we do not view the different varieties of religion from an evolutionary perspective. Instead, we present a picture of religion in modern times in which these different forms of religion coexist. This coexistence takes place on a global, national, local and personal level. Sometimes it may be conflictual or even violent, at other times harmonious or creative. It may also lead to the formation of new varieties of religion. Of these, we regard what we call *experiential religions of difference* and *experiential religions of humanity* as the most important. The former combine characteristics of a spirituality of life (such as a strong stress on the authority of individual experience) with elements of a religion of difference (such as an equally strong stress on the authority of scripture). The latter combine a stress on the authority of experience with a strong humanitarian emphasis. The most important example of an experiential religion of difference in the twentieth century is Charismatic Christianity, which combines a belief in the authority of the Bible and a biblical ethic with an emphasis on the importance of powerful and intensely-felt experience of God as Holy Spirit. Whilst perhaps numerically less significant, experiential religions of humanity continue to be visible in both eastern and western cultures as, for example, in the teaching of the current Dalai Lama and the work of some contemporary liberal Christian theologians.

As well as offering a new framework for understanding the varieties of modern religion, this volume is also distinctive in the way it understands and handles 'modernity' and 'modern times'. Its title, *Religion in Modern Times*, has been deliberately chosen in order to refer simply to a time-period: the eighteenth, nineteenth and twentieth centuries (though particular emphasis falls on the twentieth century, with events and developments in preceding centuries considered only insofar as they continue to influence the shape of religion today). 'Modern Times' is deliberately broader than 'modernity'. The former designates simply a period of time; the latter the sociocultural attributes of the so-called 'developed' societies distinctive of the West (and now, increasingly, of other parts of the world as well). Whilst there is no clear agreement about these attributes, most discussions of modernity appeal to a range of economic, political and cultural processes including, for example, industrialism, capitalism, rationalization, bureaucratization, democratization, and the 'turn to the self'.

The assumption behind much talk of 'modernity' and of its distinctive trends is an assumption which we do not share, namely that the period is a relatively homogeneous one characterized by universal, unilinear processes, and that a sharp divide can be drawn between modern and 'pre-modern' or 'traditional' societies, with modernity representing a more complex and advanced state of development. Whilst we reject these assumptions, however, we are not hostile to all attempts to generalize about religion and modernity, or to discern trends within them. On the contrary, one of the aims of this volume is to discern such trends, and to relate theories of modern culture and society to what is happening in the religious field. What is distinctive about our approach is that instead of viewing these trends as uniform, unilinear and exceptionless, we present a picture of variety and coexistence. We resist an understanding of either religion or modernity as unitary or evolutionary.

The characterization of religion in terms of a range of potentially conflictual types in **Part One** is therefore closely bound up with the attempt of the volume as a whole to characterize modernity as a complex and sometimes contradictory set of social and cultural trends, values and assumptions, contexts and varieties. As well as examining the *varieties* of religious and modern culture in **Part One**, **Part Two** is therefore dedicated to a consideration of the different *contexts* of religion in modern times: economic, political, gendered and ethnic. Equally, whilst literature on unilinear *trends* and processes is included in **Part Three**, we also include counter-arguments and counter-evidence, and suggest ways in which these trends may not be uniform or homogeneous, and may be qualified by each other as well as by the different varieties and contexts of religion in modern times.

The concern with contexts takes us from the more cultural in **Part One** to the more concrete and sociocultural in **Part Two**. The readings included here reveal the different ways in which religion shapes and is shaped by the worlds it inhabits. Three particular contexts are singled out as particularly important: the rise of capitalistic market economies (see the chapter entitled Economic); the rise of the modern state (Political); and the rise of difference (Difference: Gendered and Ethic). Under the heading of Difference we include at least two phenomena characteristic of modern times: the assertion of strong, exclusive prescriptive difference, and the articulation of more open, tolerant, and 'postmodern' forms of difference. All these contexts are viewed in terms of their interactions with religion in modern times.

Part Three returns us to texts that delineate the most important trends in religion in modern times. We identify four: secularization, detraditionalization, universalization, and sacralization. The former has long been a central preoccupation of the sociology of religion. The last, sacralization, has found advocates only more recently. Essentially both have to do with the quantity of religion. By contrast, theories of detraditionalization and universalization are less prominent in the literature, and have to do with transformations of religion. Detraditionalization names a turn from the authority of the past and of external institutions and authority figures to the authority of the self, whilst universalization names a turn from the differentiated, exclusivistic, and divisive to the inclusive, perennial, universal and ecumenical. Whilst we include literature which portrays these trends as inexorable, uniform and unilinear, we ourselves suggest a different understanding. By relating them to the varieties of religion outlined in **Part One** as well as to the different contexts surveyed in **Part Two**, we offer a more complex and differentiated account of these trends, and view them not as mutually exclusive but as coexistent.

Together, then, the three parts of this volume build up a picture of religion in modern times as a product of the complex interaction and interplay of different types of religion with different contexts, in which different trends become visible. These interactions take place in different ways and at different speeds in different parts of the globe. Whilst it may be both possible and helpful to generalize about various trends in religion in modern times, these also appear to be influenced by a wide range of factors and to take different forms in relation to different types of religion. They are not inevitable, and they may not be irreversible. Secularization, for example, seems to affect some varieties of religion more than others. It operates at a different pace and in different ways in different contexts. It is both effected and affected by a wide variety of factors. It seems characteristic of some so-called 'pre-modern' as well as many modern societies. And in some places in the world today it appears to be eclipsed by the opposite process of 'sacralization'.

In short, whilst this volume is interested in theory and in general perspectives, as well as in the more concrete and empirical, it is wary of over-generalized treatments of religion and modernity. It is particularly resistant to grand periodizations of pre-modernity and modernity, and to the idea that there are distinctive and homogeneous forms of religion which correspond to each. (For the same reasons, it is also critical of the general periodization 'postmodernity' – on this topic see Frequently Asked Questions (pp. 8–9) below, and comments in the conclusion to the volume.)

If this book's approach were to be summed up in just a few sentences they might be:

- *religion is not one thing; modernity is not one thing*
- *diversity and coexistence, not uniformity*

The Readings

On the whole the readings in this volume are short – under a page long. We have picked passages that offer striking formulations and which articulate key ideas about religion in modern times. Sometimes these passages are presented in full, sometimes abbreviated. Where we have cut a passage which is longer than a sentence we always indicate this by [. . .].

By using a large number of short passages the volume attempts to cover as much of the existing literature as possible. The shape of the book has not, however, been dictated solely by the literature – if it had been more than half would have been on secularization! Instead we have tried to balance coverage with our other aim of presenting an original and informative interpretation of religion in modern times.

In presenting this interpretation of religion in modern times at least four types of material have been used: analytical and theoretical reflections, historical studies, empirical studies, and concrete examples. We have particularly favoured readings that combine some historical or empirical research with more general, theoretical reflections, and have tended to avoid very specific case studies which do not make more general points. Where suitable theoretical material has not been available, a concrete example of the sort of religion or development we are trying to illustrate has often been used. Concrete examples have also been employed in order to illustrate more abstract theoretical points.

The material presented in this book is drawn from across the disciplines. The criterion for inclusion has been the quality of the reading itself, not its provenance. Readings come from history, theology, cultural studies, sociology, anthropology, women's studies and gender studies, politics, economics, social theory, philosophy and religious studies. Examples are from sources as various as papal encyclicals, self-help manuals, poems and, in one case, a Valentine's card. Obviously it has not been possible to include everything. Some omissions are due to contingent factors: our own ignorance; our inability to locate a book; the prohibitive cost of a permission. But we have tried hard to ensure as wide a coverage as possible.

The volume also aims at global coverage. Whilst it has proved impossible to include readings on religious developments in every part of the globe, we have tried at least to *represent* and *illustrate* what is going on in religion in modern times on a global scale. Sadly the volume does not include as many readings on non-western as on western religions; this is due not only to the limitations of our own knowledge, but to the lack of suitable material. With some honourable exceptions, there seems a dearth of theoretical reflection and empirical research available in the English language on religion in many areas outside the west. In area terms, the greatest single omission in this volume is probably in relation to religion in communist (or formerly communist) countries, particularly China. Another area the volume does not cover as fully as we would have liked concerns indigenous (particularly small-scale) pre-modern religions and their encounter with modernity.

Inevitably then the selection of readings offered in this volume reflects the literature available. Despite a serious attempt at global coverage, those topics and areas about which most has been written are over-represented. The biases which result will be discussed further in the Conclusion. The most obvious weights the volume towards the West, particularly the United States, and its dominant form of religion, Protestant Christianity. One further point about the 'weighting' of readings which is worth making at the outset is that the three main historical varieties of religion surveyed in **Part One** are each given equal space, whilst the 'combined varieties' (experiential religions of difference and experiential religions of humanity) are treated more briefly. This is in no way intended to reflect the actual numerical weight of these forms of religion in modern times.

FAQ (Frequently Asked Questions)

The general approach of this book has been tested out both on our students and on more general audiences. Important modifications have resulted. We have also become aware of some recurring questions which the book seems to raise.

Question: Are there only three varieties of religion in modern times?

Answer: No! As the figure on p. 3 suggests, these are merely three points on a theoretical spectrum. As the chapter on Combinations at the end of **Part Three** shows, in practice these three types coexist, interact, conflict, merge and modify one another in many different ways. The two further varieties of religion in modern times to which the volume draws attention (experiential religions of difference and experiential religions of life) are the best illustration of this.

Question: What is your definition of religion?

Answer: We don't define it, for the simple reason that one of our main aims (as explained above) is to get away from monolithic understandings of religion. For those who are interested, there is an extensive literature on this topic, which is reviewed in almost all introductions to the sociology of religion.

Question: What about postmodernity?

Answer: Postmodernity means many things. A movement in arts and architecture. A form of literary criticism. A school(s) of philosophy. And a distinct sociocultural era. In relation to religion in modern times it is the latter – the idea that we are entering a new postmodern era – which is the most relevant. To the extent that this hypothesis is part and parcel of a unilinear, periodizing way of thinking, we are obviously critical. Used in a more nuanced way to suggest certain important shifts in recent times, however, some of the literature on postmodernity may be helpful for understanding religion. Indeed, religion may be a good test of the whole idea of postmodernity. Some of the developments highlighted by theorists of postmodernity (such as globalization; the dissolution and decentering of self; the transformation of time and space; the de-essentializing of gender) have not yet proven their worth in terms of their ability to advance our understanding of religion in modern times (perhaps they are just waiting for the right theorists to come along or for religion to change in appropriate fashion). Others, on the other hand – most notably the idea that our times are characterized by a new understanding and evaluation of difference – seem much more illuminating. These issues are discussed further in the section on Difference in **Part Two**, and in the Conclusion.

How to Use this Book

This volume has been designed so that it can be read as a book, starting at the beginning and working through systematically, or as a reference work where one dips into particular sections. Like a book it has unifying themes and cross-linkages, which will become most apparent if it is read from beginning to end. For those who are just dipping in, however, cross-references are supplied so that it is possible to follow up major themes without too much difficulty.

If it works as intended, this volume will allow readers to identify the books and articles which they would like to study in greater depth, and of which only a taste can be given here. These in turn contain bibliographies which can lead readers even deeper into particular areas of interest. Suggestions for further reading are included only occasionally: sometimes these highlight a publication from which no reading has been included, but which is germane to the subject under consideration, and sometimes these direct readers to anthologies which offer an introduction to literature in a related area.

The Authors

On the surface at least, the authors of this book have little in common – besides the fact that they both teach in the Department of Religious Studies at Lancaster University. Linda Woodhead lectures in Christian Studies, Paul Heelas on Religion and Modernity, and particularly on the New Age. Linda was originally trained as a theologian, Paul as an anthropologist. Linda is a child of the 1980s, Paul of the 1960s. Linda describes herself as a moderately conservative Christian, Paul as an 'optimistic humanist'. In terms of the figure on p. 3, Linda is thus at the triangle end, with Paul having distinctly blobish leanings.

Yet both authors are fascinated by religion in modern times, and were drawn together by this common interest. Both have been shaped and

influenced by the interdisciplinary approach to Religious Studies characteristic of the Lancaster Department. Both are interested in the rise of
alternative forms of spirituality in modern times, and by the Indian
dimensions of such spirituality (Paul has written a book on *The New Age
Movement* (1996), and Linda is currently writing on *Rabindranath Tagore
and the Rise of Modern Spirituality*). Equally, both are interested in liberal,
'relational' and humanistic forms of religiosity in popular as well as more
theoretical manifestations (they have recently written on the religiosity
of Princess Diana and her admirers for the collection *Diana: The Making of
a Media Saint*, edited by Jeffrey Richards, Scott Wilson and Linda Woodhead,
1999). Paul has also edited books on *Detraditionalization* (with Scott Lash
and Paul Morris, 1996) and, most recently, on *Religion, Modernity and
Postmodernity* (with the assistance of David Martin and Paul Morris, 1998).

Religion, Modernity and Postmodernity and *Religion in Modern Times* are
published in the recent Blackwell series on 'Religion in the Modern
World', of which Linda and Paul are the editors. Both books are intended to set an agenda for that series, and to carry forward its stated
aim of publishing accessible work on all aspects of religious life and
thought in modern times. We would welcome correspondence on this or
related matters. Your reactions to this volume would also be appreciated.
We can be contacted at:

The Department of Religious Studies
Lancaster University
Lancs LA1 4YG
UK

e-mail: relstud@lancaster.ac.uk
or via the departmental web page: http://www.lancaster.ac.uk/vsers/
religstudies/

Thanks to . . .

Stephan Chambers at Blackwell Publishers, who had the idea of a volume
on religion and modernity in the first place. Alex Wright, Clare Woodford,
Joanna Pyke, and others at Blackwell Publishers who have seen this
book through to publication; Ginny Stroud-Lewis for seeking permissions;
and Anthony Grahame for copy-editing so superbly. All our colleagues
at Lancaster, to whom we are indebted in all sorts of different ways for
ideas, inspirations, criticisms and kindnesses, and in particular to Deborah
Sawyer for her support whilst Head of Department, to Richard Roberts

for encouraging us to develop **Part Two**, together with David Waines and John Sawyer for their advice on Islam and Judaism. Our students, who have had a major influence on this volume. The readers of our proposal, who made many helpful suggestions at an early stage in its evolution. The library staff at Lancaster who have sourced almost all the material used here. Ninian Smart for founding the Department at Lancaster in the first place, and so providing the institutional space for the sort of study of religion which this volume exemplifies. The Department of Religious Studies at Santa Barbara – a sister 'West Coast' department close in spirit to Lancaster whose members are well represented in the pages which follow. Steve Bruce and David Martin, both of whose comments have had a significant influence on the shape of this volume, and whose work and friendship have proved an inspiration and a blessing to us. And finally, all those scholars and practitioners whose writings are extracted in what follows, and to whom we are greatly indebted. More intimate debts are acknowledged in the dedication.

part one

varieties

introduction to
part one

The primary aim of **Part One** is to introduce the reader to the main forms of religion influential in modern times. There are, of course, many ways in which this could be done. Rather than examining different religions tradition by tradition, we have attempted to identify the broader categories in terms of which these religions can be understood. Building on previous attempts (a number of which are included in chapter one, on Mapping Cultures), we have identified three main – but by no means mutually exclusive – varieties of religion in modern times: 'religions of difference', 'religions of humanity' and 'spiritualities of life'. These have an historic and paradigmatic priority in the modern religious field.

Religions of difference emphasize the importance of the transcendent, a realm which lies over and above anything of a this-worldly nature. Religions of humanity attribute considerably greater authority and goodness to what the human has to offer, in particular the exercise of reason. Spiritualites of life locate the sacred within the self and nature, rejecting the idea that the spiritual is essentially different from what lies within the very order of things.

Very rarely do particular traditions fall into just one of these categories. Typically, all three of our varieties are present in any one 'major' tradition. Christianity, for example, embraces religions of difference (such as conservative Roman Catholicism and fundamentalist Protestantism), religions of humanity (the more liberal denominations), and spiritualities of life (practised, for example, by many Quakers). In practice, too, the different varieties interact and combine. Two of the most important combinations in the twentieth century (discussed in chapter five, on Combinations, at the end of **Part One**) are what we call 'experiential religions of difference' and 'experiential religions of humanity'. Whereas the former combine elements typically associated with religions of difference and spiritualities of life, the latter combine elements typical of religions of humanity with elements more normally associated with spiritualities of life.

As well as being used as a useful hermeneutical framework for exploring the diverse beliefs and practices of religions on the ground, the varieties are addressed in terms of their relationships with the modern world. Religions of difference, religions of humanity and spiritualities of life relate to modern times in quite different ways, not least in the ways in which they oppose, affirm and articulate more general social and cultural phenomena. Each of the chapters which follow therefore considers explanations of the relation between these different varieties and modernity.

Attention is also paid to the future. Informed by consideration of how each variety has been faring during modern times, the aim is to give some idea of what could lie in store.

Part One closes with discussion of relationships between religions of difference, religions of humanity and spiritualities of life. As well as illustrating conflicts, the readings also illustrate the ways in which the varieties converge or otherwise interplay. The last consideration is especially important. For it must not be thought that the three varieties always operate as essentialized 'wholes'. Far from it. Religious life and thought is often 'messy', transgressing the neat divisions of the academic. The three varieties certainly exist in pure form. Equally certain, though, they very often interplay.

With regard to the links between **Part One** and the rest of this volume, **Part Two** serves to complement the more cultural orientation of **Part One** by attending to specific ways in which religions operate in particular social settings. **Part Three** serves to complement explanations introduced in **Part One** by exploring general trends and processes affecting religion in modern times.

CHAPTER ONE

mapping cultures

Introduction

Chapter One presents several of the most influential portrayals of cultures in the modern world. These portrayals provide languages and categories for discussing diversity within the cultural realm as a whole, as well as for exploring the relationships between religious and more secular territories. As will become clear, our identification of varieties of religion – religions of difference, religions of humanity and spiritualities of life – has been strongly influenced by the following endeavours to make sense of the complexities of modern times.

1.1 Taylor's 'moral sources'

Charles Taylor, 1989: *Sources of the Self. The Making of the Modern Identity*. Cambridge: Cambridge University Press (pp. 495–8).

Summarizing themes central to his magnum opus, *Sources of the Self*, Charles Taylor identifies three primary 'moral sources': theism, disengaged reason and Romantic expressivism. Although these three sources – close to our varieties of religion – are clearly different from one another, Taylor serves to alert us to complexity: the 'lines of battle' are multiple; so are the ways in which the three domains 'are continually borrowing from and influenced by each other'.

> I started with an attempt to encapsulate the moral imperatives which are felt with particular force in modern culture. These emerge out of the long-standing moral notions of freedom, benevolence, and the affirmation of ordinary life, whose development I traced at some length from the early modern period through their Deist and Enlightenment forms. We as inheritors of this development feel particularly strongly the demand for universal justice and beneficence, are peculiarly sensitive to the claims of equality, feel the demands to freedom and self-rule as axiomatically justified, and put a very high priority on the avoidance of death and suffering.

But under this general agreement, there are profound rifts when it comes to the constitutive goods, and hence moral sources, which underpin these standards. The lines of battle are multiple and bewildering, but in these pages I have been sketching a schematic map which may reduce some of the confusion. The map distributes the moral sources into three large domains: the original theistic grounding for these standards; a second one that centres on a naturalism of disengaged reason, which in our day takes scientistic forms; and a third family of views which finds its sources in Romantic expressivism or in one of the modernist successor visions. The original unity of the theistic horizon has been shattered, and the sources can now be found on diverse frontiers, including our own powers and nature.

The different families of modern views draw on these frontiers in different ways, and they combine what they take from our powers and from nature in characteristic fashion. The disengaged view obviously leans heavily on our powers of disengaged reason. This is the source which powers the austere ethic of self-responsible freedom, the courageous ethics of belief. But a conception of nature also enters into its ethic of benevolence – albeit this is hard to avow openly – if only in the rather minimal way, as we saw with E. O. Wilson, of enthusiasm at man's 'evolutionary epic'. Romantic or modernist views make more of our powers of creative imagination and generally draw on a much richer conception of nature, which has an inner dimension. [...]

Of course, my map is overschematic. For one thing, the three domains don't stay the same; they are continually borrowing from and influenced by each other. For another, there have been attempts to straddle the boundaries and combine more than one. I mentioned Marxism as a marriage of Enlightenment naturalism and expressivism. But third, we need to see the map in a temporal dimension. Not everyone is living by views which have evolved recently. Many people live by pre-modernist forms of Romantic expressivism. In some respects, the actual goals which inspired the students' revolt of May 1968 in Paris, for all the borrowing of modernist forms from Situationism, Dada, Surrealism, avant-garde cinema, and the like, were closer to Schiller than to any twentieth-century writer. The picture of a restored harmony within the person and between people, as a result of 'décloisonnement', the breaking down of barriers between art and life, work and love, class and class, and the image of this harmony as a fuller freedom: all this fits well within the original Romantic aspirations. The basic notions could have been drawn from the sixth of Schiller's *Aesthetic Letters*. This picture comes close at times to a pre-Schopenhauerian perspective.

Then again, many of the ideas of 'human potential' movements in the United States also go back to the original expressivism, partly through the indigenous American line of descent, including Emerson and Whitman. These movements often incorporate post-Freudian psychology, but frequently (as Europeans often remark) without the tragic sense of conflict which was central to Freud. Their notion of expressive fulfilment is very much 'pre-Schopenhauerian'. Consider this personal credo:

> BE GENTLE WITH YOURSELF. You are a child of the Universe no less than the trees and the stars. You have a right to be here. And whether or not it is clear to you, no doubt the universe is unfolding as it should. Therefore be at peace with God, whatever you conceive Him to be. And whatever your labors and aspirations, in the noisy confusion of life, keep peace in your soul. With all its sham, drudgery and broken dreams, it is still a beautiful world.

Or again, there are strands of American evangelical Protestantism which in some respects are continuous with the spirituality of the Great Awakening. This is not to say that there have not been important changes: predestination has been forgotten, modern technology has been fully mobilized for revival – in all sorts of ways this religion has been contaminated by the modern world. But there has been no willing and express acceptance of Romantic expressivism or modernism. The emphasis is still on the saving power of grace and on the order which this alone can put in one's life.

My point here is not at all to depreciate these views, as though the later ones were bound to be better; only to show how understanding our society requires that we take a cut through time – as one takes a cut through rock to find that some strata are older than others. Views coexist with those which have arisen later in reaction to them. This is to oversimplify, of course, because these rival outlooks go on influencing and shaping each other. Born-again Christians in the United States cannot help being somewhat influenced by expressive individualism. Indeed, some of them went through the latter, during the 1960s, for instance, and ended up joining a strict evangelical church. Something had to rub off. But the outlooks are *defined* in polar opposition.

1.2 Tipton's fourfold analytical scheme

Steven Tipton, 1984: *Getting Saved from the Sixties. Moral Meaning in Conversion and Cultural Change*. Berkeley, Los Angeles and London: University of California Press (pp. 282–4).

Distinguishing between four ideal 'styles' of ethical evaluation – the authoritative, regular, consequential (or utilitarian) and expressive – Steven Tipton provides a systematic analysis of the exercise of authority and judgement. A good illustration of the analytical scheme in action is provided by Robert Bellah et al. (1985, esp. ch. 9). The scheme, it is surely safe (if controversial!) to add, can be used in any cultural context: religious or not; western or non-western.

These four styles constitute a taxonomy along the following dimensions:

A General Orientation and Mode of Knowledge
1 The authoritative style is oriented toward an authoritative moral source known by faith.
2 The regular style is oriented toward rules or principles known by reason.
3 The consequential style is oriented toward consequences known by cost-benefit calculation.
4 The expressive style is oriented toward the quality of personal feelings and of situations known by intuition.
B Form of Discourse
In posing the moral question, 'What should I do?'
1 The authoritative style asks, 'What does God command?' and answers with which act is 'obedient' and 'faithful.'
2 The regular style asks, 'What is the relevant rule or principle?' and answers with which act is 'right' or 'obligatory' according to the rules.
3 The consequential style asks, 'What do I want? What act will most satisfy it?' and answers with which act will be most 'efficient' or 'effective' in producing the consequences that satisfy a given want.
4 The expressive style asks, 'What's happening?' and answers with which act is most 'fitting' in response.
C Right-making Characteristic of an Act
1 Authoritative: an act is right because the authoritative source commands it.
2 Regular: an act is right because it conforms to the relevant rules and principles.

3 Consequential: an act is right because it produces the most good consequences; that is, maximizes satisfaction of wants.

4 Expressive: an act is right because it constitutes the most fitting response to the situation and the most appropriate or honest expression of one's self.

D Cardinal Virtue

1 Authoritative: obedience to moral authority makes a person most worthy of praise.

2 Regular: rationality in discerning and enacting moral principles makes a person most worthy of praise.

3 Consequential: efficiency in maximizing the satisfaction of his wants makes a person most worthy of praise.

4 Expressive: sensitivity of feeling and situational response makes a person most worthy of praise.

E Resolution of Disagreement

1 Authoritative: moral disagreement is resolved by literal exegesis of scripture and increased familiarity with it; and, ultimately, by conversion.

2 Regular: moral disagreement is resolved by reasoning dialectically (from problem to solution to generalized, consistent principles to other problems, and so on) to increasingly abstract principles consistently generalizable to the most cases.

3 Consequential: moral disagreement is resolved by review of the pertinent empirical evidence; and, ultimately, by social-scientific explanation of alternative perceptions of the facts.

4 Expressive: moral disagreement is resolved by exchanging discrepant intuitions within the context of ongoing social interaction, thereby reshaping the situation (or community), and the agents' consciousness as formed by the situation.

F Degree of Specificity of Prescription (ranked from most to least specific)

1 The authoritative style yields the greatest possible specificity of prescription or proscription of particular acts by means of commandments and regulations that can be casuistically applied to particular cases.

2 The regular style provides less specific prescription of acts by ruling out certain acts because they fail to meet prior fixed criteria of right conduct – regardless of their consequences.

3 The expressive style yields still less specific prescriptions of right acts, derived from the intuited moral sense of the relevant

(reference) group or community regarding the most fitting feeling within a given situation and the most fitting act in response to it.

4 The consequential style yields the least specific prescriptions regarding right acts, since it judges acts solely by their effectiveness in producing given consequences or achieving given goals. It does not judge acts qua acts, viewing them as instrumental procedures for effecting desired consequences.

1.3　Durkheim: humanity

Emile Durkheim, 1973 (orig. 1898): Individualism and the Intellectuals. In Robert N. Bellah (ed.), *Emile Durkheim. On Morality and Society*. Chicago and London: University of Chicago Press, pp. 43–57 (pp. 44–7).

Durkheim begins this famous essay with harsh things to say about 'the strict utilitarianism and the utilitarian egoism of Spencer and the economists', continuing, 'It is indeed easy game to denounce as an ideal without grandeur this crass commercialism which reduces society to nothing more than a vast apparatus of production and exchange. For it is exceedingly clear that all communal life is impossible without the existence of interests superior to those of the individual' (p. 44). Given this last point, he goes on to write of 'another sort of individualism' (p. 44) which he sees as lying at the very heart of modern life. The ethic of humanity, it can be added, is closely bound up with religions of humanity – a consideration developed later in **Part One**, as well as in the chapter on Universalization in **Part Three**.

It has been professed, for the past century, by the vast majority of thinkers: this is the individualism of Kant and Rousseau, of the idealists – the one which the Declaration of the Rights of Man attempted, more or less happily, to formulate and which is currently taught in our schools and has become the basis of our moral catechism. They [critics] hope to deal a blow to this form of individualism by striking instead at the former [utilitarian] type; but this one is profoundly different, and the criticisms which apply to the one could hardly suit the other [utilitarian form]. Far from making personal interest the objective of conduct, this one sees in all personal motives the very source of evil. According to Kant, I am sure of acting properly only if the motives which determine my behavior depend not on the particular circumstances in which I find myself, but on my humanity in the abstract. Inversely, my actions are bad when they can be logically justified only by my favored position or by my social condition, by my class or caste interests, by my strong passions, and so on. This is why immoral conduct can be recognized by the fact that it is closely tied to the actor's individuality and cannot be generalized without manifest absurdity. In the same way, if, according to Rousseau, the general will, which is the basis of the social contract, is infallible, if it is the authentic expression of perfect justice, it is because it is the sum of all individual wills; it follows that it constitutes a sort of impersonal average from which all individual considerations are eliminated, because, being divergent and even antagonistic, they neutralize each other and cancel each other out. Thus, for both these men, the only moral ways of acting are those which can be applied to all men indiscriminately; that is, which are implied in the general notion of 'man.'

Here we have come a long way from that apotheosis of well-being and private interest, from that egoistic cult of the self for which utilitarian individualism has been rightly criticized. Quite the contrary, according to these moralists, duty consists in disregarding all that concerns us personally, all that derives from our empirical individuality, in order to seek out only that which our humanity requires and which we share with all our fellowmen. This ideal so far surpasses the level of utilitarian goals that it seems to those minds who aspire to it to be completely stamped with religiousity. The human person (*personne humaine*), the definition of which is like the touchstone which distinguishes good from evil, is considered sacred in the ritual sense of the word. [. . .]

For this eighteenth-century liberalism which is at bottom the whole object of the dispute is not simply a drawing-room theory, a philosophical construct; it has become a fact, it has penetrated our institutions and our mores, it has blended with our whole life, and if, truly, we had to give it up, we would have to recast our whole moral organization at the same stroke.

1.4   Voll: 'styles of action' in Islam

John Obert Voll, 1982: *Islam. Continuity and Change in the Modern World*. Boulder: Westview Press; Essex: Longman (pp. 29–31).

John Voll identifies four styles in Islamic religion, the adaptationist, conservative, fundamentalist and personal. With much in common with the classificatory schemes introduced above, the extract serves to make the point that internal differences in Islam can be mapped in much the same fashion as in Christianity and western culture.

Throughout this discussion, four styles of action have been noted, and they provide the network for the interaction of continuity and diversity within the Islamic experience. These four styles are the framework of social action in the Islamic dimension of this study.

The first of these styles is the adaptationist, which represents a willingness to make adjustments to changing conditions in a pragmatic manner. This style is clearly visible in the political realism of the early rulers of the community, who adopted many ideas and techniques in creating the early empires and the later sultanates. It is also manifested in the intellectual tradition by those thinkers who have adapted the Greek philosophical traditions in explaining Islamic positions. The religious syncretism of Akbar in Moghul India and the open flexibility of the popular Sufi teachers are other examples of this style.

This style of action in the Islamic tradition opened the way for the great syntheses that have given a great deal of dynamism to the development of the Islamic community. It has made it possible for the Muslims to cope with a wide variety of challenges, such as the tensions resulting from the first conquests, the problems associated with the collapse of the early imperial unity, and the intellectual problems of integrating new ideas into the basic framework of the Islamic faith.

The success of Islam brought achievements that are worth preserving, which is the motivation behind the second style, the conservative. As a great synthesis emerged, much of the learned community hoped to preserve the gains that had been made. From the very beginning, the perfection of the revelation has been seen by Muslims as requiring a reserved attitude about change that is too rapid. The opposition of the early companions to Ali may have been an attempt to preserve the type of community that had been created in Medina by the Prophet. Later ulama undertook to preserve the system of Islamic law once it had been defined. In this style, a mistrust of innovation tends to be the keynote.

The efforts of the conservatives have served the Islamic community well in times of turmoil, and they have helped to keep the compromises of the adaptationists within the bounds of what has become accepted as Islamic. In the long run, the conservative style of action has avoided supporting stagnation of the community by gradually accepting new circumstances as they have become established. It has provided a basis for the tolerant acceptance of diversity on both the doctrinal and the popular levels.

The third style is the fundamentalist. The scriptures of religions that accept the concept of the recording of divine revelations provide a basis for a common, permanent standard to use in judging existing conditions. In Islam, the Quran represents such an unchangeable standard, and the fundamentals of the faith as presented in the Quran have a universally accepted validity within the Islamic community. The fundamentalist style of action insists upon a rigorous adherence to the specific and the general rules of the faith as presented in that generally accepted record of revelation. When additional elements are also accepted as authoritative, they may also be included among the fundamentals. Thus, within Sunni Islam, the Sunnah or path of the Prophet, as defined by the *hadith* literature, is also used as a basis for evaluating Islamic practices, as are the collections of the traditions of Ali and the imams within Shi'i Islam.

From early times, there have been Muslims who have insisted on an uncompromising adherence to the rules of the faith, such as the Kharijites. By Abbasid times, this rigorism was being espoused by some of the Sunni ulama, and a careful study of the life of the Prophet and *hadith* scholarship became the focus of attention for those who demanded that the Islamic community act strictly in accord with the Quran and the Sunnah. A leading figure in this style of action was Ahmad ibn Hanbal (780–855), whose rigorism set the tone for the strict Hanbali *madhhab* and for later Sunni fundamentalists, including Ahmad ibn Taymiyyah (d. 1328) and the eighteenth-century revivalist, Muhammad ibn Abd al-Wahhab.

The distinction between the fundamentalist and the conservative styles is important. Fundamentalists are unwilling to accept compromises and are more often critics than defenders of existing conditions. They utilize a literal and rigorous interpretation of the Quran and the Sunnah as a basis for judging existing practices. They frequently are political activitists, and they often are disturbing elements and upset social stability.

The fundamentalist style serves as a corrective adjustment mechanism. In the context of change and adaptation, fundamentalists work to keep the basic Islamic message in full view of the community. When adjustments to local conditions or the adoption of new ideas and techniques threaten to obliterate the unique and authentically Islamic elements, fundamentalist pressure begins to build. In one sense, the mission of Islamic fundamentalism is to keep adjustments to change within the range of those options that are clearly Islamic.

Such efforts can be seen in the work of the Naqsh-bandiyyah during Moghul times in India.

The fourth Islamic style places emphasis on the more personal and individual aspects of Islam. Although all Muslims recognize the communal implications of the revelation, there is a style that tends to subordinate legal structures and communal institutions to the personal aspects of piety and the leadership of charismatic, divinely guided individuals. The Shi'i conception of the imamate and the popular belief in the Mahdi are broad, political manifestations of this style. It is also seen in the Sufi tradition of personal piety and the importance of the local spiritual guide. This style of action permeates the whole Islamic experience, and in a general sense, the resistance of the Islamic tradition to the creation of a formal church structure and an ordained clergy is a product of this individualized spirit.

These styles are not formal, separate movements within the Islamic community but represent orientations for action within the broader Islamic experience as a whole. In any specific group or individual, the styles are combined with varying degrees of emphasis, and they can be used as an analytical framework for understanding the dynamics of Islamic history.

The Islamic dimension of this study includes the historical experience of the community. In that history, there is a dynamic interaction among the elements of continuity and diversity, including the interplay between the challenge of changing conditions and the steady adherence to the fundamentals of the faith. The way these elements interact is described by observing the various styles of Islam. The heritage of the Islamic community is the foundation of the modern history of Islam.

CHAPTER TWO

religions of difference

Introduction

The 'difference' which characterizes this important variety of religion is manifest at a number of levels. It is perhaps most immediately evident in a tendency to differentiate clearly between the divine and the human. Religions of difference attribute authority first and foremost not to human beings nor to nature, but to the transcendent. They locate the source of all goodness and truth in the transcendent, maintaining that humans are saved by a God outside rather than a God within. In this they can be distinguished from the two other main varieties of religion in modern times identified in **Part One**: religions of humanity (which attribute greater authority and goodness to the human), and spiritualities of life (which locate divinity within self and nature).

Steven Tipton refers to the moral style typical of religions of difference as 'authoritative': 'The authoritative style asks, "What does God command?" and answers with which act is "obedient" and "faithful"' (reading **1.2**). Since God exceeds the grasp of limited human beings, however, religions of difference characteristically recognize mediating authorities through which the divine is revealed. This is normally a sacred text or collection of texts which give access to a past time in which the divine is thought to have been disclosed more perfectly than in the present. Whilst some religions of difference attribute authority to the very words of scripture, others also look behind them to the authoritative person(s) or revelation(s) they uniquely represent. Additionally, some religions of difference attribute authority to tradition – the more diffuse body of teachings, laws, rituals and practices which maintain continuity between a community's past and present.

The practical implications of belief in divine–human difference in modern times are varied. Generally, a world-rejecting asceticism seems to have given way to a this-worldly asceticism which treats this life and its activities as preparation for the next. Typically, religions of difference place great stress upon the importance of worship, that cluster of activities in which human beings draw close to God whilst also maintaining their proper distance. For religions of difference the good life consists not in trying to abolish this distance, but in maintaining correctly structured relationships with God and fellow-creatures. Morality is about learning and respecting differences – differences not only between the divine and the human, but between male and female, between children and parents, and between those in and those under authority. Such difference, which is explored further in the readings on Difference in **Part Two**, may be referred to as 'prescriptive difference' since it prescribes what is right and good rather than leaving this open to individual decision. The ideal of sacrifice also tends to be important within the moral economy of religions of difference, since it is necessary to renounce one's own will and desire in order to give way to that of God and God's representatives. Obedience is therefore valued more highly than freedom; humility than self-assertion; self-control than self-expression.

Whilst religions of difference tend not to be dualistic in the sense that they postulate two opposed metaphysical realities, one good and one evil (for they insist that ultimately the divine is the only reality), they manifest a duality insofar as they lay emphasis on the sinfulness, weakness, incompleteness, imperfection or corruption of the human race and the world. Whereas spiritualities of life view the world as basically good, and suffering as the result of ignorance, religions of difference believe in the reality of sin. This stress serves to heighten the contrast they draw between the human and divine, and to make it clear that redemption can come only through the intervention of the latter. Applied in a temporal dimension, this logic of redemption translates into the belief that we are living in an era which has fallen away from the past golden age to which text and tradition alone now give access. Only the decisive interruption of God can now redeem this world: religions of difference are often characterized by expectant anticipation of a coming age in which divine intervention will bring evil and suffering to an end and redeem the faithful.

Difference also exists at the sociological level. Characteristically religions of difference take the form of tightly-bounded communities which differentiate themselves both from other religious communities and from 'the world'. These communities function to create and sustain societies of godly and enlightened people who maintain a critical distance from wider society. Such communities are generally exclusivistic in the sense that they believe themselves to be sole possessors of the truth. As several of the readings below reveal, however, the degree of exclusivity and 'set-apartness' may vary considerably. What Troeltsch calls the 'church' type of community is inclusive in wanting to bring all humankind within its portals, and is willing to accommodate itself to worldly institutions in order to do so. By contrast the 'sect' type is more fully exclusivistic, demanding voluntary commitment from its members and adopting a critical stance towards those people and institutions who remain outside. At whatever point along this spectrum, however, the maintenance of a significantly different culture, ethos and life-style remains important. As many of the readings in **Part Two** on religion in social contexts reveal, religions of difference can therefore play an important role in political mobilization by undergirding ethnic and national identities. Differentiated communities may also take different organizational forms internally. Whilst some are characterized by clear internal differentiation – often of a hierarchical kind – others are more egalitarian, and others again recognize only the authority of charismatic individuals.

Despite predictions that religions of difference would be most susceptible to the acids of modernity, they remain a significant force in modern times. A common expectation was that they would inevitably liberalize (see, for example, James Davison Hunter, reading **1.27**). In fact we can observe both a liberalizing and a 'differentiating' tendency evolving together since at least the nineteenth century, with the differentiating tendency becoming increasingly confident and – in many instances – increasingly extreme throughout the course of the twentieth. This differentiating tendency is evident in an accentuation of divine–human difference, in the drawing of a sharp distinction between those within and those outside the religious community, in extreme and exclusivistic claims to possession of truth, in an identification of the written word of scripture with absolute truth, and in a heightened emphasis upon the evil of the present age and the imminence of a new order. Very often such highly differentiated religion appears when religions of difference are revitalized in the face of a serious threat from their socio-political or cultural environments. In the vocabulary we are proposing here, these more differentiated and exclusivistic forms of twentieth-century religion can be termed 'religions of heightened difference'. In addition, we can discern the rise of yet another variation within the broad category 'religions of difference' during the course of the twentieth century – what we term 'experiential religions of difference'. Whilst retaining features typical of religions of difference, such as a stress on divine–human difference and on scriptural authority, these religions also give an important place to experience. The most important example of an experiential religion of difference, Charismatic Christianity, is considered in more detail in the chapter on Combinations which closes **Part One**.

In **Part Two** the reader will find more extended discussion of the social, economic and political contexts which have both helped and hindered the growth of religions of difference in modern times. The political force of religions of difference and, most strikingly, of religions of heightened difference, are examined here. **Part Three** contains further readings on the fate of religions of difference in modern times. Whilst the section on secularization reminds us that these were the religions which were often thought to be most threatened by the forces of moderniza-tion, the section on sacralization reveals how their survival and in some cases their revitalization in recent times have led some commentators to reassess their resiliance and resourcefulness.

Cognate Terms

Traditional religion, conservative religion

Though both of these terms are often used in relation to what we call 'religions of difference', we tend to avoid them in this volume. The terms work by drawing attention solely to religions' respect for the past. By concentrating on this one feature, however, they risk becoming reductionist. They also have a polemical edge, having been formed and shaped in Enlightenment and post-Enlightenment contexts in which conservatism (taken to be typical of religion) was contrasted unfavourably with more mature, rational and 'modern' attitudes. Talk of 'conservative' religion may also mislead by implying that such religion is always polit-ically conservative – as **Part Two** will illustrate, religions of difference actually have extremely varied political manifestations.

Rigid religion, strict religion

These too are terms which we avoid in this volume, but which appear in some extracts. Thus Dean Kelley speaks of 'conservative' and 'strict' forms of Christianity in an influential article in which he argues that such religion is inherently stronger and more enduring than liberal religion (see extract **3.94**). To call religion strict implies a number of things: that it makes great demands on its adherents, that it will not countenance any relaxation of its standards, and that these standards may well be at odds with those of the wider society. As some of the readings below will indicate, however, these characteristics seem more typical of the 'sect' than the 'church' type of differentiated religious community.

Evangelical, Charismatic, and Pentecostal religion

These terms appear throughout this book. Since they refer only to Christianity, they have a much narrower reference than 'religions of difference'. They are used not only by scholars but, quite often, by adherents of the form of Christianity in question. Evangelical Christianity takes its name from its concern with 'evangelization' – conversion through bringing people into contact with the saving message of the Christian gospel, particularly through the scriptures. With roots in the Reformation of the sixteenth century, Evangelicalism flowered in the eighteenth, nineteenth and twentieth centuries, particularly in the West. (For a fuller definition of Evangelical Christianity see David Bebbington, extract **1.81**.) Charismatic Christianity is a more recent, twentieth-century phenomenon. Pentecostalism is generally regarded as the first movement to demonstrate charismatic characteristics. Today the terms 'Charismatic' and 'Pentecostal' tend to be used interchangeably, and this volume follows this practice. Whilst Charismatic Christianity has evangelical roots and shares a strong evangelical emphasis, it places greater emphasis on the power and reality of the Holy Spirit. As a result it often has a strongly experiential emphasis. In its more extreme manifestations, this emphasis can eclipse that on holy scripture. Whilst we treat Evangelical Christianity under the heading of religions of difference, we consider Charismatic Christianity in the separate section on Combinations at the end of **Part One**, because we categorize it as an experiential religion of difference.

Experiential religions of difference

We have identified three main historic types of religion in modern times. These by no means exhaust the varieties of religion in the contemporary world. In practice many religions combine elements from different types, as the section on Combinations shows. One of the most successful combinations today is that which draws on the moral strictness and authoritative approach of religions of difference, together with the stress on the importance of experience more typical of a spirituality of life. In this section we name religions marked by this mix 'experiential religions of difference', and consider them in more detail in the section on Combinations at the end of **Part One**. One of the best examples of an experiential religion of difference is Charismatic Christianity.

Fundamentalism

The term 'fundamentalism' has become increasingly common in both academic and popular discourse in recent decades. Those who accept the term do so because they believe that it is possible to identify movements of religious resurgence with common 'fundamentalist' features in all the world's major religious traditions. (See, for example, two of the most important recent studies of fundamentalism, Bruce Lawrence's *Defenders of the Faith* (1995), and the multi-volume 'Fundamentalism Project' edited by Martin E. Marty and R. Scott Appleby (1991–5).) Generally, the defining features of fundamentalism are said to include a desire to return to the fundamentals of a religious tradition and strip away unnecessary accretions; an aggressive rejection of western secular modernity; an oppositional minority group-identity maintained in an exclusivistic and militant manner; attempts to reclaim the public sphere as a space of religious and moral purity; and a patriarchal and hierarchical ordering of relations between the sexes. It is generally acknowledged that fundamentalism is a distinctively modern, twentieth-century movement, despite historical antecedents.

Those who oppose the term 'fundamentalism' tend to do so because they claim that it is used by western liberals to refer to a broad spectrum of religious phenomena which have little in common except for the fact that they are alarming to liberals! Opponents point out that to bracket together religions like resurgent Islam in Iran and South American Pentecostalism as 'fundamentalist' is to obscure the very important differences between them (not least that the former wishes to dominate the public and political arenas, whilst the latter withdraws from these areas). Few so-called fundamentalists themselves accept the term, and many regard it as insulting.

The debate about the legitimacy of the term fundamentalism will no doubt continue. There seems little doubt that it is beset by dangers and temptations. One temptation, which we have strongly resisted, is to identify the whole of the spectrum of religions of difference as fundamentalist (or, to put it another way, to label all religion which does not come under the categories of either religions of humanity or spiritualities of life as fundamentalist). As the readings below reveal, religions of difference encompass a wide range of different forms of belief, practice and organization. Some of these fit most of the criteria of fundamentalism just outlined. Some do not. Because of this, we have decided to avoid the term fundamentalism. In its place we use the term 'religions of heightened difference' to refer to more extreme and differentiated forms of religion. We believe that this term is more effective in signalling both the distinction and the connections between this and other forms of religions of difference. We use the term fundamentalism only in relation to those who first used it: the fundamentalist Christians in the United States who issued their manifestoes at the beginning of the twentieth century, and who were – and continue to be – concerned to defend certain 'fundamental' doctrines, including that of Biblical inerrancy, against the inroads of secular modernity.

Religions of Difference: overview

1.5 Bellah's characterization of religions of difference

Robert Bellah, 1964: Religious Evolution. *American Sociological Review* 29: 358–74 (pp. 366–8).

In his influential essay on religious evolution, Robert Bellah offered a characterization of five stages of religious development: 'Primitive', 'Archaic', 'Historic', 'Early Modern' and 'Modern'. Whether or not one accepts the thesis of evolution, Bellah's typology is helpful in making sense of the richness and variety of religions. In the extract below Bellah delineates Historic Religion, and in so doing offers a succinct overview of many of the most salient features of religions of difference. Bellah contrasts Historic Religion with Archaic Religion on the one hand, and Early Modern on the other. Both the latter are less differentiated than Historic Religion. Though more differentiated than Primitive Religion, Archaic Religion is still basially monistic: it tends to 'elaborate a vast cosmology in which all things divine and natural have a place'. Likewise, Early Modern Religion (which in all cases derives from the Protestant Reformation) once more collapses the hierarchical, differentiated structuring of this world and the other world, bringing the human and the divine back into more direct, unmediated relationship than is typical of Historic Religion. (This is, of course, a somewhat controversial reading of the Reformation: other interpretations emphasize the opposite: that *increased* differentiation took place at this time.) Extracts from Bellah's characterization of the final stage of religious evolution (Modern Religion) can be found at **3.25**.

> The next stage in this theoretical scheme is called historic simply because the religions included are all relatively recent; they emerged in societies that were more or less literate and so have fallen chiefly under the discipline of history rather than that of archaeology or ethnography. The criterion that distinguishes the historic religions

from the archaic is that the historic religions are all in some sense transcendental. The cosmological monism of the earlier stage is now more or less completely broken through and an entirely different realm of universal reality, having for religious man the highest value, is proclaimed. The discovery of an entirely different realm of religious reality seems to imply a derogation of the value of the given empirical cosmos: at any rate the world rejection discussed above is, in this stage for the first time, a general characteristic of the religious system.

The *symbol systems* of the historic religions differ greatly among themselves but share the element of transcendentalism which sets them off from the archaic religions: in this sense they are all dualistic. The strong emphasis on hierarchical ordering characteristic of archaic religions continues to be stressed in most of the historic religions. Not only is the supernatural realm 'above' this world in terms of both value and control but both the supernatural and earthly worlds are themselves organized in terms of a religiously legitimated hierarchy. For the masses, at least, the new dualism is above all expressed in the difference between this world and the life after death. Religious concern, focused on this life in primitive and archaic religions, now tends to focus on life in the other realm, which may be either infinitely superior or, under certain circumstances, with the emergence of various conceptions of hell, infinitely worse. Under these circumstances the religious goal of salvation (or enlightenment, release and so forth) is for the first time the central religious preoccupation. [. . .]

Religious action in the historic religions is thus above all action necessary for salvation. Even where elements of ritual and sacrifice remain prominent they take on a new significance. In primitive ritual the individual is put in harmony with the natural divine cosmos. His mistakes are overcome through symbolization as part of the total pattern. Through sacrifice archaic man can make up for his failures to fulfill his obligations to men or gods. He can atone for particular acts of unfaithfulness. But historic religion convicts man of a basic flaw far more serious than those conceived of by earlier religions. According to Buddhism, man's very nature is greed and anger from which he must seek a total escape. For the Hebrew prophets, man's sin is not particular wicked deeds but his profound heedlessness of God, and only a turn to complete obedience will be acceptable to the Lord. For Muhammad the *kafir* is not, as we usually translate, the 'unbeliever' but rather the ungrateful man who is careless of the divine compassion. For him, only Islam, willing submission to the will of God, can bring salvation.

The identity diffusion characteristic of both primitive and archaic religions is radically challenged by the historic religious symbolization, which leads for the first time to a clearly structured conception of the self. Devaluation of the empirical world and the empirical self highlights the conception of a responsible self, a core self or a true self deeper than the flux of everyday experience, facing a reality over against itself, a reality which has a consistency belied by the fluctuations of mere sensory impressions. Primitive man can only accept the world in its manifold givenness. Archaic man can through sacrifice fulfill his religious obligations and attain peace with the gods. But the historic religions promise man for the first time that he can understand the fundamental structure of reality and through salvation participate actively in it. The opportunity is far greater than before but so is the risk of failure.

Perhaps partly because of the profound risks involved the ideal of the religious life in the historic religions tends to be one of separation from the world. Even when, as in the case of Judaism and Islam, the religion enjoins types of worldly participation that are considered unacceptable or at least doubtful in some other historic religions, the devout are still set apart from ordinary worldlings by the massive collections of rules and obligations to which they must adhere. The early Christian solution, which, unlike the Buddhist, did allow the full possibility of salvation to the layman, nevertheless in its notion of a special state of religious perfection idealized religious withdrawal from the world. In fact the standard for lay piety tended to be closeness of approximation to the life of the religious.

Historic religion is associated with the emergence of differentiated religious collectivities as the chief characteristic of its *religious organization*. The profound dualism with respect to the conception of reality is also expressed in the social realm. The single religio-political hierarchy of archaic society tends to split into two at least partially independent hierarchies, one political and one religious. Together with the notion of a transcendent realm beyond the natural cosmos comes a new religious elite that claims direct relation to the transmundane world. Even though notions of divine kingship linger on for a very long time in various compromise forms, it is no longer possible for a divine king to monopolize religious leadership. With the emergence of a religious elite alongside the political one the problem of legitimizing political power enters a new phase. Legitimation now rests upon a delicate balance of forces between the political and religious leadership. But the differentiation between religious and political that exists most clearly at the level of leadership tends also to be pushed down into the masses so that the roles of believer and subject become distinct. Even where, as in the case of Islam, this distinction was not supported by religious norms, it was soon recognized as an actuality. [. . .]

The *social implications* of the historic religions are implicit in the remarks on religious organization. The differentiation of a religious elite brought a new level of tension and a new possibility of conflict and change onto the social scene. Whether the confrontation was between Israelite prophet and king, Islamic ulama and sultan, Christian pope and emperor or even between Confucian scholar-official and his ruler, it implied that political acts could be judged in terms of standards that the political authorities could not finally control. The degree to which these confrontations had serious social consequences of course depended on the degree to which the religious group was structurally independent and could exert real pressure. [. . .]

Religion, then, provided the ideology and social cohesion for many rebellions and reform movements in the historic civilizations, and consequently played a more dynamic and especially a more purposive role in social change than had previously been possible. On the other hand, we should not forget that in most of the historic civilizations for long periods of time religion performed the functions we have noted from the beginning: legitimation and reinforcement of the existing social order.

Religions of Difference: themes

Theme: divine–human difference

1.6   Otto: 'the idea of the holy'

Rudolph Otto, 1958 (orig. 1917): *The Idea of the Holy*. London, Oxford and New York: Oxford University Press (pp. 9–10).

In the previous extract Bellah highlights 'duality' as an important characteristic of religions of difference. These religions are 'transcendental' and view the human and natural worlds from the perspective of transcendence. Here Otto describes the experience of transcendence. In *The Idea of the Holy* he argues that it constitutes the core of all true religion. (See also Otto in extract **3.56**.)

It may perhaps help [. . .] if I cite a well-known example, in which the precise 'moment' or element of religious feeling of which we are speaking is most actively present. When Abraham ventures to plead with God for the men of Sodom, he says (Gen. xviii. 27): 'Behold now, I have taken upon me to speak unto the Lord, which am but dust and ashes.' There you have a self-confessed 'feeling of dependence', which is yet at the same time far more than, and something other than, *merely* a feeling of dependence. Desiring to give it a name of its own, I propose to call it 'creature-consciousness' or creature-feeling. It is the emotion of a creature, submerged and overwhelmed by its own nothingness in contrast to that which is supreme above all creatures.

1.7   Chesterton commends metaphysical difference

G. K. Chesterton, 1961 (orig. 1908): *Orthodoxy*. Glasgow: Collins Fontana Books (pp. 127–8).

Religions of difference assert not only divine–human difference, but difference within the world and between its inhabitants. God has created a world in which difference is real and not a mere epiphenomenon of some more ultimate unity. In this extract from his spirited defence of conservative Christian orthodoxy, Chesterton celebrates the metaphysical difference which he sees as central to Christianity's world-view. He did so in conscious opposition to forms of inner spirituality like Theosophy which were popular in his day and which proclaimed the monistic message that 'all is one'. Chesterton's work is thus revealing of the way in which religions of difference have sometimes gained new impetus in the modern period through opposition to inner spiritualities, a theme which is explored at the end of **Part One** in the section on Combinations. (see also Chesterton, reading **1.90**.)

We come back to the same tireless note touching the nature of Christianity; all modern philosophies are chains which connect and fetter; Christianity is a sword which separates and sets free. No other philosophy makes God actually rejoice in the separation of the universe into living souls. But according to orthodox Christianity this separation between God and man is sacred, because this is eternal. That a man may love God it is necessary that there should be not only a God to be loved, but a man to love Him. All those vague theosophical minds for whom the universe is an immense melting-pot are exactly the minds which shrink instinctively from that earthquake saying of our Gospels, which declare that the Son of God came not with peace but with a sundering sword. The saying rings entirely true even considered as what it obviously is; the statement that any man who preaches real love is bound to beget hate. It is as true of democratic fraternity as of divine love; sham love ends in compromise and common philosophy; but real love has always ended in bloodshed. Yet there is another and yet more awful truth behind the obvious meaning of this utterance of our Lord. According to Himself the Son was a sword separating brother and brother that they should for an æon hate each other. But the Father also was a sword, which in the black beginning separated brother and brother, so that they should love each other at last.

1.8   McGuire on dualism in the Roman Catholic Church

Meredith B. McGuire, 1982: *Pentecostal Catholics. Power, Charisma, and Order in a Religious Movement*. Philadelphia: Temple University Press (pp. 38–9).

In her study of contemporary American Pentecostal Catholics, Meredith McGuire also found that 'dualism' was an important feature of their lifeworlds. She uses the word broadly to embrace dualism between God and world, flesh and spirit, good and evil. In the following extract McGuire explores such dualism and reveals the ways in which it is both continuous and discontinuous with more traditional forms of Catholicism.

Dualism reshapes members' interpretations of events of everyday life – including their own roles – and it gives significance to events that formerly seemed meaningless. Dualism assigns meaning to human failure, suffering, social problems, personal difficulties, and death. Events that once appeared to be random, haphazard, or disorderly, now are seen as part of a clear pattern. Believers' sense of ambiguity and insecurity is resolved by seeing their role as part of 'something big' – a cosmic struggle in which one gains power and purpose by siding with the forces of Good. Dualism creates order out of chaos. The external chaos of the disordered social world is not the only source of threat; intra-group problems also constitute a threat. Problems of disorder are inherent in the establishment of the prayer group itself, because there is much ambiguity during the early development of a movement, especially when members perceive their new belief system to be a departure from their previous religious tradition. The participants resolve problems of uncertainty and ambiguity by emphasizing their role in a cosmic dualistic order.

The dualistic theodicy supports the biographical security of individual believers. One of the fundamental concerns expressed by recruits to the Catholic pentecostal movement is a strong desire to know for sure where they 'stand' before God. This desire for certainty is fulfilled by a secure framework of order positing a distinct duality between the forces of Good and Evil and showing a clear-cut path for the believer who would side with Good. Such simplified course of action informs the member that one is safe and secure by siding with the Good. This personal sense of security is expressed in the belief that 'I am saved already.' Fichter's survey found that over 50 percent of the Catholic pentecostal respondents believe that they are already saved. This assuredness is not merely a peculiar characteristic, accidentally borrowed from Protestant pentecostals; rather, it is very important as an appeal to Catholic pentecostals.

This discussion of the movement's emphasis on dualistic interpretations of reality has focused on the foundation of a new order. It should be noted, however, that the old framework of order of pre-Vatican II Catholicism was, for many believers, essentially a dualistic scheme as well. The imagery and concreteness of the pentecostal dualism is more potent than that of pre-Vatican II Catholic dualism, but many members of the movement were probably exposed to a number of dualistic interpretations in early religious socialization. For example, the Baltimore Catechism taught the following ideas, among others, about angels and devils:

95   Not all the angels remained faithful to God; some of them sinned.
101 The good angels help us by praying for us, by acting as messengers from God to us, and by serving as our guardian angels.
103 Our guardian angels help us by praying for us, by protecting us from harm, and by inspiring us to do good.
107 The chief way in which the bad angels try to harm us is by tempting us to sin.
111 Besides tempting us, the devils are sometimes permitted by God to plague persons from without, and this is called obsession, or even to dwell in them and exercise power over their faculties and this is called possession.

112 Sometimes God permits obsession and possession to punish wicked persons; and sometimes He permits these attacks of the devil in the case of good persons to afford them an opportunity of practicing virtue.

114 The commands used by the Church against the attacks of the devils are called exorcisms.

In the years immediately preceding Vatican II, as well as during and after the Council, the salience of these images appears to have declined. For example, O'Connor notes, 'Even more than the doctrine of the Holy Spirit, the doctrine of the evil spirit has been discarded by the sophisticated theology that has sprung from the Enlightenment and demythologizing.' A renewed emphasis on a dualistic world view, therefore, may have had the functions both of positing a strong new framework of order while relating that new order to elements of the lost one, and of providing a sense of continuity with tradition.

Theme: communities of difference

1.9 Troeltsch's distinction between church and sect

Ernst Troeltsch, 1931: *The Social Teaching of the Christian Churches*. 2 vols, trans. Olive Wyon. London: George Allen and Unwin Ltd; New York: MacMillan (pp. 338–9).

Troeltsch's distinction between three types of Christianity – church, sect, and mysticism – has long been influential within the sociology of religion, with a number of sociologists moving beyond Troeltsch's original intention by treating them as ideal types applicable to religion in general and not merely to historic Christianity. Troeltsch's 'mystical type' conforms closely to what we refer to in this book as 'spiritualities of life', and is discussed in reading **1.59**. Here we consider Troeltsch's church and sect types, since these forms of community seem characteristic of Christian religions of difference. As Troeltsch explains in the following reading, the sect is a voluntary form of organization which demands strict loyalty from its members and maintains a clear distinction from other forms of social organization. By contrast, the church dispenses grace to its members in the objective form of the sacraments, and requires a far lower degree of commitment. It is a compulsory, sometimes coercive, monopolistic institution which strives to dominate the public and political as well as the more narrowly religious sphere. The sect tends to be exclusive in the sense that it believes that only those within its ranks *are* saved, the church exclusive in the sense that it believes that only those within its ranks *can be* saved, but inclusive in the sense that it happily accepts that in this world it will be a refuge for both saints and sinners.

The essence of the Church is its objective institutional character. The individual is born into it, and through infant baptism he comes under its miraculous influence. The priesthood and the hierarchy, which hold the keys to the tradition of the Church, to sacramental grace and ecclesiastical jurisdiction, represent the objective treasury of grace, even when the individual priest may happen to be unworthy; this Divine treasure only needs to be set always upon the lampstand and made effective through the sacraments, and it will inevitably do its work by virtue of the miraculous power which the Church contains. The Church means the eternal existence of the God-Man; it is the extension of the Incarnation, the objective organization of miraculous power, from which, by means of the Divine Providential government of the world, subjective results will appear quite naturally. From this point of view compromise with the world, and the connection with the preparatory stages and dispositions which it contained, was possible; for in spite of all individual inadequacy the institution remains holy and Divine, and it contains the promise of its capacity to overcome the world by means of the miraculous power which dwells within it. Universalism, however, also only becomes possible on the basis of this compromise; it means an actual domination of the institution as such, and a believing confidence in its invincible power of inward influence. Personal effort and service, however fully they may be emphasized, even when they go to the limits of extreme legalism, are still only secondary; the main thing is the objective possession of grace and its universally recognized dominion; to everything else these words apply: *et cetera adjicientur vobis*. The one vitally important thing is that every individual should come within the range of the influence of these saving energies of grace; hence the Church is forced to dominate Society, compelling all the members of Society to come under its sphere and influence; but, on the other hand, her stability is entirely unaffected by the fact of the extent to which her influence over all individuals is actually attained. The Church is the great educator of the nations, and like all educators she knows how to allow for various degrees of capacity and maturity, and how to attain her end only by a process of adaptation and compromise.

Compared with this institutional principle of an objective organism, however, the sect is a voluntary community whose members join it of their own free will. The very life of the sect, therefore, depends on actual personal service and co-operation; as an independent member each individual has his part within the fellowship; the bond of union has not been indirectly imparted through the common possession of Divine grace, but it is directly realized in the personal relationships of life. An individual is not born into a sect; he enters it on the basis of conscious conversion; infant baptism, which, indeed, was only introduced at a later date, is almost always a stumbling-block. In the sect spiritual progress does not depend upon the objective impartation of Grace through the Sacrament, but upon individual personal effort; sooner or later, therefore, the sect always criticizes the sacramental idea. This does not mean that the spirit of fellowship is weakened by individualism; indeed, it is strengthened, since each individual proves that he is entitled to membership by the very fact of his services to the fellowship. It is, however, naturally a somewhat limited form of fellowship, and the expenditure of so much effort in the maintenance and exercise of this particular kind of fellowship produces a certain indifference towards other forms of fellowship which are based upon secular interests; on the other hand, all secular interests are drawn into the narrow framework of the sect and tested by its standards, in so far as the sect is able to assimilate these interests at all. Whatever cannot be related to the group of interests controlled by the sect, and by the Scriptural ideal, is rejected and avoided. The sect, therefore, does not educate nations in the mass, but it gathers a select group of the elect, and places it in sharp opposition to the world. In so far as the sect-type maintains Christian universalism at all, like the Gospel, the only form it knows is that of eschatology; this is the reason why it always finally revives the eschatology of the Bible. . . .

1.10   The Doctrine of Papal Infallibility, 1870

The Doctrine of Papal Infallibility, 1870. In Henry Bettenson (ed.) 1989: *Documents of the Christian Church*. Oxford: Oxford University Press (pp. 273–4).

As Troeltsch points out in the extract above, the differentiated communities characteristic of religions of difference are often themselves vested with authority (particularly where the church type is concerned). This authority may inhere in some aspect of the institution, for example in its teachings, rituals, sacraments, members or official representatives. The assertion of papal infallibility in 1870 furnishes an interesting example of the way in this sort of claim to possession of truth has intensified as well as declined in the modern context. By the 1960s Vatican II offered a very different picture of the authority of the church, an authority which was now said to be vested in 'the holy people of God' as well as in their priestly representatives. In many ways the pontificate of John Paul II has been characterized by a reassertion of clerical and papal authority.

We [i.e. Pope Pius IX], adhering faithfully to the tradition received from the beginning of the Christian faith – with a view to the glory of our Divine Saviour, the exaltation of the Catholic religion, and the safety of Christian peoples (the sacred Council approving), teach and define as a dogma divinely revealed: That the Roman Pontiff, when he speaks *ex cathedra* (that is, when – fulfilling the office of Pastor and Teacher of all Christians – on his supreme Apostolical authority, he defines a doctrine concerning faith or morals to be held by the Universal Church), through the divine assistance promised him in blessed Peter, is endowed with that infallibility, with which the Divine Redeemer has willed that His Church – in defining doctrine concerning faith or morals – should be equipped: And therefore, that such definitions of the Roman Pontiff of themselves – and not by virtue of the consent of the Church – are irreformable. If any one shall presume (which God forbid!) to contradict this our definition; let him be anathema.

1.11 Heilman: the authority of tradition in ultra-orthodox Jewry

Samuel Heilman, 1992: *Defenders of the Faith. Inside Ultra-Orthodox Jewry*. New York: Schocken Books (pp. 203–4).

As well as being constituted by their claim to a unique relationship to absolute truth, differentiated communities are constituted by their continuity with the past. The nature of their respect for the past differs, however. As the readings below on authoritative text (**1.12–1.14**) show, some religions of difference locate authority primarily in a sacred text and a 'golden age' to which it gives access, but have little interest in intervening eras. By contrast, other communities have a greater sense of an on-going and unfolding connection with the sacred past, and a greater respect for 'tradition'. Ultra-orthodox Judaism belongs to the latter category; it is, as Heilman discovers, a community which continually relates past to present.

In a community that gives the highest value to yesterday and sees tradition as the great teacher, the need to repeatedly demonstrate that there is nothing so ancient and archaic in the Jewish past that it does not have its place in the Jewish present is constant. I call this process 'traditioning.' It means never seeing the past as beyond retrieval but rather experiencing it as an ongoing reverberation in the present.

In a sense, traditioning was embedded in everything the children learned about the past, and especially about the Bible. For them there really was no history, for history sees the past as discrete but ultimately not recoverable, while the haredim were always dipping into the past as if it were still present. To them the Bible was not just an account of the dawn of Israelite peoplehood but a code book for Jewish behavior. The lives of its heroes were not simply the stuff of stories but archetypes for contemporary behavior. Similarly, the rabbis were not simply ancient lawmakers, figures of Jewish history; they were living mentors for contemporary existence. The stories and lessons teachers repeated were thus not just moral tales or archaic codes; they were the necessary ingredients of recipe knowledge, the information needed for everyday life as a Jew. In short, there was nothing so old that it was meaningless today. As if to hammer this home, haredim often stressed precisely those elements of Jewish life that seemed to be most out of tune with the times. They reveled in anachronism, asserting its timeliness. This was of course the polar opposite of the modern attitude that valued novelty above all.

Theme: authoritative text

1.12 Heilman: the authority of text in ultra-orthodox Jewry

Samuel Heilman, 1992: *Defenders of the Faith. Inside Ultra-Orthodox Jewry.* New York: Schocken Books (pp. 20–1).

Even those religions of difference like ultra-orthodox Judaism which maintain the highest respect for the past often find it difficult to maintain continuity with the past in the modern context. As Heilman observes in the reading below, the consequence is inevitably a greater reliance upon text and textual experts than would once have been the case.

In the wholly traditional world, people knew what Judaism demanded of them. They did not have to check code books and texts to know what was right and wrong. Instead, they relied on cultural competence that came from their living in an environment governed by a relatively stable tradition over which there was little or no debate. But the modern world was increasingly undermining stability and severing continuity with the past. With the break-up of the ghetto and the seemingly ceaseless change that accompanied it, people felt increasingly removed from the norms of the Jewish street. How could one know what exactly to do? What was insignificant custom and what unalterable law?

In this new atmosphere those who wanted to remain true to the tradition had either to improvise or go 'by the book.' [. . .]

Code books were always important in the life of Jews, particularly in times of cultural transition. Now, when mass production made them widely available, they filled the social and cultural vacuum left by the demise of traditional norms. Studying these books that articulated every jot and tittle of law and custom became the absolute prerequisite for religious behavior throughout the traditionalist world.

All 'this opened the way for individuals and groups to compete, as it were, among themselves on the degree of stringency and intransigency, within the range of alternatives found' in the code books. But many of these stringencies were paradoxically new, representing radical continuity and radical change at one and the same time.

1.13 Antoun: Muslim fundamentalism rejects tradition in favour of text

Richard T. Antoun, 1989: *Muslim Preacher in the Modern World. A Jordanian Case Study in Comparative Perspective*. Princeton, New Jersey: Princeton University Press (pp. 236–7).

Some modern religions of heightened difference attribute exclusive authority to a sacred text rather than to tradition. They may even regard the tradition with hostility – as a distraction from the true Word of God. In these cases, the sacred past shrinks to occupy only that space to which scripture gives access and ceases to include the longer history of the community and its practices, teachings, laws and scriptural interpretations. In the extract below Richard Antoun notes this tendency in contemporary Islamic fundamentalism (the 'Voll' to whom Antoun refers is the Islamic scholar John Voll whose work can be found in readings **1.4**, **1.18** and **2.76**). A related phenomenon is that whereby religions which do not historically have a single authoritative text 'textualize' themselves in modern times. An example would be Hinduism, which insisted on the canonical status of 'Vedanta' (usually said to comprise Vedas and Upanishads) after the eighteenth century.

Muslim individuals and groups, particularly since the eighteenth century, have called for socio-moral reconstruction on the basis of a return to Holy Scripture, the Quran, and the Traditions of the Prophet. Fundamentalists aim 'to rediscover the original meaning of the Islamic message without historic deviations and distortions and without being encumbered by the intervening tradition. . . .' In this regard, Voll in particular has stressed that Islamic fundamentalism emerges out of 'traditional' Islamic institutions such as the study of the hadith and the practice of Islamic mysticism interpreted in an activist sense.

And yet, as the above-mentioned quotation indicates, fundamentalism is incompatible with the conservative, traditional stance of many
Muslim scholars since it regards the intervening 1300-year cumulative
tradition of Islamic scholarship as an encumbrance. It is not accidental,
therefore, that in the twentieth century Islamic fundamentalism has
been spread by teachers and preachers such as Hasan al-Banna, Shaykh
Kishk, and Shaykh Luqman, and by emotionally and morally intense
lay Muslims such as Ali Shariati rather than by professionally committed Muslim scholars such as Ayatollah Khomeini (the exception).
Fundamentalism, then, represents a sharp break with established
religious tradition at the same time that it calls for a return to the past.
But it is to be a past reaffirmed in a different light, a past dispensing
with significant traditions of law, theology, and mystical practice.

1.14   Toumey on science, creationism and the Bible

Christopher P. Toumey, 1994: *God's Own Scientists. Creationists in a Secular World.* New
Brunswick, New Jersey: Rutgers University Press (p. 261).

The word 'fundamentalism' was first used by conservative Protestants in the
USA in the early part of the twentieth century. They wished to return to Christian 'fundamentals', and insisted on the unique authority and literal truth of
scripture. Here Toumey shows how this programme is often bound up with
what might be called a 'scientification' of the Bible. Toumey argues that creationists
(who reject the theory of evolution as incompatible with the Biblical account of
creation) want the Bible to be scientific and science to be Biblical. Far from being
simply anti-modern and anti-science, fundamentalism may thus be influenced
by science in significant ways.

Creationism's model of reality, in its most general form, is the not so
contentious idea that God has given us a framework of morality
within which our lives make sense. Indeed, this is a central assumption of Judeo-Christian thought. But in the United States in the
twentieth-century, it seems to conservative Christians that this reality
has not been presented realistically enough, for if it is stated just a
little too abstractly, then it becomes vulnerable to multiple interpretations by liberal Christians, theistic evolutionists, and other supposedly soft headed people. To make that reality less hazy, more like a
solid rock, the theological conservatives wrap it in their epistemology
called biblical inerrancy, wherein it becomes both lucid and tangible.
If Noah traveled in a wooden boat, like one we can touch, over a

stormy sea, like one we can feel, eventually to reach a solid patch of ground, like one we can stand on, then his story has a plain authenticity that, presumably, can be extended to the rest of the Bible's contents. Scientific creationism contributes to this assumption of authenticity by fine-tuning it, making Bible stories as tangible as test tubes. This way, the grace of scientific sanctification enhances the scriptural basis of conservative morality.

Theme: sin, evil and redemption

1.15   Barth on the wrath of God

Karl Barth, 1963 (orig. 1921): *The Epistle to the Romans*, 6th edn. London: Oxford University Press (pp. 43–4).

Religions of difference characteristically view the world and the human condition as tainted by sin, evil and suffering. Christianity has tended to place particular emphasis upon such themes, and this emphasis has been carried into the twentieth century by its more differentiated forms. In the following passage the neo-orthodox theologian Karl Barth (1886–1968) offers a commentary on Paul's words in Romans 1.18 about 'the wrath of God' which is 'revealed against all ungodliness and unrighteousness of men'. For Barth, the ungodliness of man consists in man's taking the place of God.

The wrath of God is the judgement under which we stand in so far as we do not love the Judge; it is the 'No' which meets us when we do not affirm it; it is the protest pronounced always and everywhere against the course of the world in so far as we do not accept the protest as our own; it is the questionableness of life in so far as we do not apprehend it; it is our boundedness and corruptibility in so far as we do not acknowledge their necessity. The judgement under which we stand is a fact, quite apart from our attitude to it. Indeed, it is the fact most characteristic of our life. Whether it enters within the light of salvation and of the coming world depends upon the answer we give to the problem of faith. But it is a fact, even should we choose the scandal rather than faith. That time is nothing when measured by the standard of eternity, that all things are semblance when measured by their origin and by their end, that we are sinners, and that we must die – all these things ARE, even though the barrier be not for us the place of exit. Life moves on its course in its vast uncertainty and we move with it, even though we do not see the great question-mark that is set against us. Men are lost, even though they know nothing of salvation. Then the barrier remains a barrier and does not become a place of exit. The prisoner remains a prisoner and does not become the watchman. Then is waiting not joyful but a bitter-sweet surrender to what is inevitable. Then is the contradiction not hope, but a sorrowful opposition. The fruitful paradox of our existence is then that which consumes it like a worm. [...]

Our relation to God is *ungodly*. We suppose that we know what we are saying when we say 'God'. We assign to Him the highest place in our world: and in so doing we place Him fundamentally on one line with ourselves and with things. [...]

We confound time with eternity. This is the *ungodliness* of our relation to God. And our relation to God is *unrighteous*. Secretly we are ourselves the masters in this relationship. We are not concerned with God, but with our own requirements, to which God must adjust Himself. [...]

Our devotion consists in a solemn affirmation of ourselves and of the world and in a pious setting aside of the contradiction. Under the banners of humility and emotion we rise in rebellion against God. We confound time with eternity. That is our *unrighteousness*. – Such is our relation to God apart from and without Christ, on this side of resurrection, and before we are called to order. God Himself is not acknowledged as God and what is called 'God' is in fact Man. By living to ourselves, we serve the 'No-God'.

1.16 Hal Lindsey: escaping this evil age

Hal Lindsey, 1983: *The Rapture. Truth or Consequences.* Toronto, New York, London, Sydney: Bantam Books (pp. 175–6).

The expectation of an imminent divine intervention which will bring this world to an end is characteristic of many religions of difference (and particularly of religions of heightened difference) in modern times. In best-selling books like *The Late Great Planet Earth* and *The 1980's: Countdown to Armageddon*, the Evangelical Christian Hal Lindsey offers one version of such expectation, cataloguing the evils of our age and predicting a coming 'Tribulation', followed by Christ's millenial rule (hence the term 'millenial' is sometimes attributed to religious movements characterized by vivid expectation of the end of the world). According to Lindsey, believers will be spared the Tribulation by being raptured from the earth before its onset. This sort of expectation would seem to stimulate evangelization and a quest for moral purification at the individual rather than the social or political level. In the case of other religions of difference, however, dissatisfaction with the present state of affairs and belief in a Golden Age, whether past or future, may have greater socio-political implications – as it does in contemporary Shi'ite Islam, for example (see Arjomand, 1984, pp. 196–7; Sivan, 1985, pp. 186–7).

> I have never been more thankful to God for the personal hope of the Lord's return for the believer before the coming world holocaust. I had unwittingly begun to take this wonderful truth for granted.
>
> It breaks my heart as I daily pour over world events and see how rapidly the world as we know it is moving toward a catastrophic end. [. . .]
>
> The hope of the Rapture is a very practical force in my life at this point in history. It motivates me to gain a combat knowledge of the Bible in order to be able to face the perilous times that precede the Tribulation. It motivates me to win as many to Christ as possible before it's too late. I want to take as many with me as I can. Although I grieve over the lost world that is headed toward catastrophe, the hope of the Rapture keeps me from despair in the midst of ever-worsening world conditions.
>
> The one who knows that Jesus Christ is in his heart and has the sure hope of the Lord's coming for him before the Tribulation is the only one who can face today's news and honestly be optimistic.
>
> My prayer is that this book has helped you to have a certain and sure hope of the Lord's 'any moment' return to take you to His Father's house.
>
> I'll see you at His feet!
>
> HAL LINDSEY

Religions of Difference: explanations

Explanation: reaction to modernity

1.17 Hallencreutz and Westerlund: fundamentalism as a revolt against the modern age

Carl F. Hallencreutz and David Westerlund, 1996: Introduction: Anti-Secularist Policies of Religion. In David Westerlund (ed.), *Questioning the Secular State. The Worldwide Resurgence of Religion in Politics*. London: Hurst and Company, pp. 1–23 (pp. 6–7).

The idea that religions of difference – and in particular religions of heightened difference – are primarily reactionary was popularized by writers like Richard Hofstadter (1962) who, in *Anti-Intellectualism in American Life*, painted a picture of American fundamentalists as belonging to increasingly marginalized social groups and protesting against having to give up their long-established privileges and way of life. A related explanation of the rise of evangelical religion in America views it as a reaction to liberalism: to liberal Christian theology and Biblical studies in the early part of the twentieth century, and to the more extreme liberalism of counter-cultural movements from the 1960s onwards (see, for example, Martin (1983) and Robert Wuthnow, reading **1.89**). Many explanations of the rise of Islamic fundamentalism likewise view it as a reaction to the forces of western modernity. In the following reading Carl Hallencreutz and David Westerlund discuss such explanations. Like Bruce Lawrence (1995), whose work they consider, they distinguish between fundamentalists' rejection of modernism (the material and technological achievements of the modern world) and their acceptance of modernity (the secular ideology associated with the Enlightenment).

In many works, 'fundamentalism' has been contrasted to modernism or what is conceived of as modern. For instance, the subtitle of Bruce B. Lawrence's book *Defenders of God*, in which he deals with Christian, Muslim and Jewish 'fundamentalists', is *The Fundamentalist Revolt against the Modern Age*. Similarly, Thomas Meyer writes about 'fundamentalism as "the world-wide insurrection against the modern"'. Here it is important to stress the distinction between the concepts of modernism and the modern, which are sometimes confused. It is not modernity as such which is opposed by so-called 'fundamentalists' but *secular modernity* or *modernism*. They reject the idea that consensual norms and ultimate values can be located in a secular or non-religious source. In Christian contexts the term 'modernism' was originally associated with a reform movement which started within the Catholic Church at the end of the nineteenth century. Because it supported historical critical research on the Bible and evolutionist ideas, it was condemned in 1907 in a papal encyclical. This denunciation of modernism was supported by the integrist movement – the Catholic dichotomy of modernism/integrism corresponding roughly to the Protestant dichotomy of liberalism/fundamentalism.

Within, and particularly outside, religious contexts modernism is associated with the philosophical values of the Enlightenment, which are regarded as anti-religious and are thus naturally refuted by Muslim 'fundamentalists'. However, they are clearly not against modern technological and scientific achievements. They do not see an opposition between reason and religion – many Muslim 'fundamentalists' are students at or alumni of faculties of science and medicine. They do not aim to reestablish some form of medieval society, although the earliest period of Islamic history is an important source of their inspiration. Their goal is to 'Islamize' the modern world, not to reject it. This can be achieved by practising *ijtihad*, that is, an independent interpretation or analysis of the Quran and Sunna. In this they differ from more traditionally oriented Muslims who believe that 'the gates of *ijtihad*' were closed more than 1,000 years ago. Reformist movements that champion the principle of *ijtihad* have appeared time and again in Islamic history. Hence one should be careful not to over-emphasize the issue of 'fundamentalism v. modernism'.

1.18 Voll explains Islamic fundamentalism as a reaction to the failure of the West

John Voll, 1987: Islamic Renewal and the 'Failure of the West'. In Richard T. Antoun and Mary Elaine Hegland (eds), *Religious Resurgence: Contemporary Cases in Islam, Christianity, and Judaism*. New York: Syracuse University Press, pp. 127–44 (pp. 141–2).

The Islamic scholar John Voll is critical of the view that religions of heightened difference can be explained simply as a reaction to the triumph of the modern West. He offers a more multi-layered explanation which pays attention to the continuities of such religions with earlier strands of Islam, and which views them as a reaction to the perceived failure and inadequacy rather than success of the modern West.

The evaluation of the experience of the West is an important dimension of the modern Islamic experience. Many of the major movements of modern Islamic thought were based on an assumption of the success of the West, at least in certain key aspects of human life. However, by the beginning of the fifteenth Islamic century, the concept of the failure of the West emerged as an important assumption. The perception of the West's failure liberated Muslim intellectuals from certain limitations that had bound earlier Muslim modernists. Although this factor does not fully explain the nature of the current resurgence of Islam, it is one dimension of the contemporary situation. It is not a measurable factor, such as class origin or age of participants in movements; it is, however, an important part of the logical framework and intellectual context of contemporary Islamic renewal.

The concept of the failure of the West has helped to liberate Muslims from concern about the invisible jury of foreigners watching events in the Islamic world. It has opened the way for a significant dialogue within the Islamic world, among Muslims, as to the authentic nature of Islam. In a second area of liberation, this Islamic discussion is no longer hindered by constraints imposed by the concept of secularism as a necessary part of modernization. In this way, affirmation of

religious positions was no longer seen as being reactionary by definition. A third aspect of liberation is that the perceived failure of the
West makes it possible to distinguish between Western and modern
and, in this way, opens the door for the creation of an authentically
Islamic modernity.

Muslims are not the only people to perceive a failure of the traditional Western models of modernity. There is a great global effort to
achieve liberation from at least some aspects of the consequences of
Western-dominated and Western-oriented modernization. This effort
can be seen within the West itself. The postmodern theology described
by the Christian theologian Harvey Cox, for example, is a clear statement concerning the end of the old Western-dominated styles of
'modernity.'

Explanation: refuge from pluralism, atomization or anomie

1.19   Ammerman explains fundamentalism as a refuge from change and chaos

Nancy Tatom Ammerman, 1987: *Bible Believers. Fundamentalists in the Modern World*. New
Brunswick and London: Rutgers University Press (p. 192).

Many sociologists from Durkheim onwards have characterized the social relations
which hold together complex modern societies as impersonal, superficial, transitory and segmented – in contrast to the more affective, settled and committed
social relations of pre-modern and rural society. The contrast is encapsulated by
Ferdinand Tönnies's famous distinction between *gemeinschaft* and *gesellschaft*.
Following on from this theory, the success of religions of difference in modern
times is sometimes explained in terms of their ability to provide a refuge from
atomization, pluralism and anomie. Quite often these concepts are not clearly
defined or distinguished, and they may be used singly or in combination to
designate a range of conditions from moral normlessness to social isolation. The
following extract from Nancy Ammerman's study of an American fundamentalist
church reveals how wide-ranging this sort of explanation can be, and how it
may have both psychological and sociological dimensions. This sort of explanation of the appeal of religions of difference is the negative version of the more
positively put argument that religions of difference offer social, moral and cultural
capital (see readings **1.21–1.23**).

Fundamentalism provides a coping strategy for those who find themselves adrift in the world that seems untrustworthy and unforgiving.
There are, in addition, social dimensions to these psychological
needs. The world seems far more untrustworthy when it is changing

than when it remains stable. In an age when mobility and divorce have contributed to a feeling that many relationships are impermanent, when rapid technological change exceeds our ability to respond, feelings of lostness are to be expected. At such times, growth in Fundamentalism can also be expected. Fundamentalism has its greatest appeal in times and places where values and ways of life are changing. Those who are relatively new to the middle class, for instance, may find it disconcerting to see the rules by which they achieved their status declared no longer operative. Having been hard working and respectable, they are especially unhappy to see the rules bent for others. Likewise, those who grew up in small towns or on farms but have moved to the city know firsthand the chaos that characterized the transition to modernity. And, for the college-educated, home-owning sons and daughters of immigrant laborers, change is a personal reality. They belong neither to their parents' world nor fully to the postindustrial middle class. For people like these, caught between two worlds, Fundamentalism provides an attractive alternative.

These observations suggest that membership in a church like Southside is the result of a complex combination of social and psychological factors. It is not merely a response to some inner conflict nor a simple product of social forces.

1.20 Hegland challenges the anomie thesis

Mary Elaine Hegland, 1987: Conclusion: Religious Resurgence in Today's World – Refuge for Dislocation and Anomie or Enablement for Change? In Richard T. Antoun and Mary Elaine Hegland (eds), *Religious Resurgence. Contemporary Cases in Islam, Christianity, and Judaism*. New York: Syracuse University Press, pp. 233–56 (pp. 242–4).

In the following extract Mary Hegland marshalls evidence against the thesis that modern Islamic resurgence can be explained as a reaction to alienation and anomie. Far from alienating and isolating modern individuals, she argues, modern processes like urbanization and the spread of education have provided new opportunities for a wider range of people to avail themselves of social and cultural resources. Fundamentalism is an integral part of this process and of the political mobilization which results. (An interesting angle on this debate is offered by Said Amir Arjomand (1984, p. 22) who points out that there is no logical link between atomization and anomie, and argues that whilst Middle Eastern Islamic militants are not atomized, they do suffer normative disturbance and are reacting to an alien social world whose norms are felt to be subversive of traditional values.)

Noting the new environment with exposure to a different style of life, the 'disruption of traditional bonds,' and the often less than adequate living conditions of urban migrants, some analysts have assumed that a related disorientation, anomie, and dislocation are prompting the urban working class into participating in the Islamic resurgence. The evidence for such a conclusion is insufficient, however, and remains to be questioned along the following lines:

1. Assumptions of anomie and social isolation in urban settings appear to be exaggetated. In their 1970-71 study of migarnts and native women of Isfahan (Iran), John and Margatet Gulick found an even higher percentage of native women reporting very frequent contact with relatives (79.7%) than did migrant women (76.5%). According to the data gathered by the Gulicks, contact among relatives increases with the number of generations a family lived in Isfahan. The researchers conclude that 'city living, far from bringing about less association with relatives, is compatible with it and may even reinforce and encourage it.' [. . .]

2. The lower middle classes were not marginal or alienated from society, but, on the contrary, were experiencing increased incorpora-tion into society – and perhaps most important, they were receiving an education. [. . .]

3. Inadequate evidence is available to support assumptions of anomie, disorientation, uprootedness, and social isolation supposedly suffered by urban migrants. Quite to the contrary, Farhad Kazemi, in his study of the migrant poor of Tehran, discovered that migrants had extensive contact with friends and relatives, both in the home village and the city; did not feel lonely; assisted each other; and found their incomes to have met or exceeded their expectations.

4. Research among leaders and members of religious movements has not found socially isolated, deprived, or anomic individuals. Rather, participants are upwardly mobile, educated, normal, socially engaged persons, who enjoy much better than average opportunity in life. Ibrahim, for example, found members of militant Islamic groups to be 'model young Egyptians.'

5. Some analysts blame the 'disruption of social bonds' and the destruction of the social fabric caused by migration and recent social change for the alienation and anomie that have supposedly led vic-tims to return to the comfort and security of religion. However, such 'traditional social bonds' have not always affected individuals positively, and could in fact have resulted in social isolation and deprivation

through forced acquiescence to an economic, political, and ideological structure that did not serve the individuals' best interests.

With the advent of the great expansion in economic opportunities formerly bound individuals – and even more so, their offspring – could escape the constraints of these repressive bonds. They were no longer politically captive, or forced to accept the dominant inter- pretation of religion and ritual. Aspects of the old structure *did* break down, but the result for affected individuals was not anomie or social isolation, but rather the freedom to engage in political struggle on their own and to use religious symbolism in resistance to the system and in presenting their own grievances – or to be available to the political manipulation of persons and groups outside of the village. The new economic opportunities thus appeared to disrupt repressive vertical bonds while allowing horizontal bonds of mutual assistance and support to continue.

The new-found strength, resources, and freedom from constraint of the rural migrants and commuters to urban areas and urban working classes is paralleled by the situation of another, overlapping group: the youth. The latter have also experienced a recent tre- mendous expansion both in relative numbers and in the resources available to them. They have also broken free from traditional bonds and constraints. The jobs and educational opportunities available to young people at present mean that they are no longer beholden to their elders for financial resources and economic opportunities. [. . .]

The involvement of the young, because of their great numbers and their virtual monopoly over the eagerly sought after modern educa- tion, has lent great force to the religious resurgence in recent years.

Explanation: provision of social, moral, cultural and transcendent capital

1.21 Greeley on social capital

Andrew M. Greeley, 1990: *The Catholic Myth. The Behaviour and Beliefs of American Catholics.* New York: Charles Scribner's Sons (pp. 154–5).

Whilst the 'anomie thesis' focuses on the negative fact of social, moral and cognitive dislocation driving people to take refuge in religions of difference, a related cluster of explanations place more emphasis upon the positive goods which such religions may supply. One variant points out that religions of difference may play an important role in marking, defining and sustaining the identity of threatened or rivalrous groups (see, for example, reading **3.91** in which Steve Bruce argues that religions of difference flourish when they become markers of threatened political, cultural and ethnic identities). It is highly doubtful whether liberal religions and inner spiritualities, which both downplay difference, could operate in the same way. Another variant of this form of explanation – illustrated by this reading from Andrew Greeley – draws attention to the 'social capital' provided by the strong communities characteristic of religions of difference. Greeley's point is supported by Warner (1990), Roof (1978), and Ammerman (1997), who all discover that the American congregations which are flourishing are those which cater for what Warner calls 'localism'. Although (or because) modern Americans are frequently mobile and migratory they seem to desire the strong local communities which religions of difference may be uniquely placed to provide. Warner calls the phenomenon 'elective parochialism'. A different but related cluster of explanations of the appeal of religions of difference focus on their ability to help individuals achieve social and economic advancement. See, for example, Bernice Martin on charismatic Christianity in South America (reading **2.23**). This theme of religion as a source of 'capital' of various kinds recurs throughout the volume.

> The American neighborhood parish is one of the most ingenious communities that human skill has ever created. Its overlapping network of religious, educational, familial, social, and political relationships has created what my colleague James S. Coleman (who is not Catholic) calls 'social capital,' a social resource in the strict sense of the word because it comes not from individual investments but from relational patterns. To call the overlapping networks of human relationships 'capital' is to say that, as with any capital, more can be accomplished because the relationship networks exist (just as more can be done if you build a new steel mill than if you don't). Coleman contends that it is precisely the social capital in Catholic schools which enables them to be more effective educational institutions than public schools.
>
> Social capital is the extra energy generated by overlapping networks of relationships. It is the economic result of a community shaped by the Sacramental Imagination. Coleman's insight reinforces what Catholic theory used to believe about the parish. Oddly enough, just at the time when one of America's most distinguished sociologists discovers the importance of the neighborhood parish, Catholic theorists seem to have abandoned their faith in it.

1.22 Ammerman on moral and spiritual capital

Nancy Tatom Ammerman, 1997: *Congregation and Community*. New Brunswick, New Jersey: Rutgers University Press (pp. 367–8).

In his famous explanation of 'Why Conservative Churches are Growing' (1977) and 'Why Conservative Churches are Still Growing' (see extract **3.94**), Dean Kelley argued that the churches which succeed are those which are 'strict' and 'serious' and 'make life meaningful in ultimate terms'. In her study of twenty-three American congregations, Nancy Ammerman also found that a religion's ability to provide meaning was an important part of its appeal. In the passage below she suggests that religious congregations' ability to provide moral meanings imbued with sacred significance is an important part of their enduring appeal. Though Ammerman herself does not make this suggestion, and believes that religions of humanity as well as religions of difference are capable of providing moral capital, others (like John Voll explaining Islamic resurgence in Esposito, 1983) argue that religions of difference are particularly adept at providing moral capital because they offer clearer and more objective ethicalities than other forms of religion in modern times.

Congregations create some kinds of social capital, then, that differ from the contributions of other associations. More than any other organizations, congregations are expected to represent the community's moral order, to hold up the best human values while condemning human fault. When politicians indulge in idealistic moral rhetoric, we are never quite sure that it represents anything beyond their own partisan interests. We expect religion, on the other hand, to hold up the highest ideals for their own sake. This becomes especially important in the upbringing of children. The tie between congregational membership and family formation remains strong in U.S. culture. Those who sow wild oats as young adults often return to the fold when their children reach school age. At least since the Halfway Covenant, in the seventeenth century, parents have sought the protection of faith and the good graces of the Church for their children – even when they themselves were less than enthusiastic believers. Many adults see religious training for their children as part of their obligation to the world. They would not be doing good or making the world a better place if their children were denied the training provided by the church. While other institutions may participate in the moral upbringing of children, none take on this task quite so explicitly as do religious bodies.

This concern for inculcating moral standards does not end with children. Congregations also want their adult members to live by the principles of the faith. Even members who are less than orthodox in their beliefs are encouraged by congregations to practice the faith by living the Golden Rule. In these twenty-three congregations, we often heard from adults who especially valued worship each week as a time for reflection and priority setting. The set-aside time, the sacred space of the church, perhaps the inspiration of the music reminded them of what should be most important in their lives, almost regardless of the preacher's message. For others the teachings and doctrines are much more thoroughly and articulately incorporated into everyday life. But for both the theologically well versed and the theologically inept, congregational membership had been consciously sought out as a way to support virtuous living.

1.23   Hefner on transcendent capital and the potency of difference

Robert W. Hefner, 1993: Introduction: World Building and the Rationality of Conversion. In Robert W. Hefner (ed.), *Conversion to Christianity: Historical and Anthropological Perspectives on a Great Transformation*. Berkeley: University of California Press, pp. 3–44 (pp. 34–5).

In this extract Robert Hefner argues that the appeal of religions of difference lies in their ability to enlarge moral vision and recast community. For Hefner, the remarkable persistence of such religions can be explained by the fact that they continue to proclaim transcendence and to reorder lives and communities in the light of this ideal.

All the world faiths relativize received social ways by announcing a Truth without which, they claim, human existence has no real meaning. This foundational belief legitimates doctrines and rites to which, in principle, all people are to be drawn. It may also mandate the organization of institutions for the propagation of the faith and the sustenance of 'imagined communities' unlike any previously seen. For a social science that recognizes that problems of morality and self-identification are central to all social life, this aspect of the world religions places them among the most remarkable achievements of human culture.

Indeed, these religions are without parallel in human history. Political empires and economic systems have come and gone, but the world religions have survived. *They are the longest lasting of civilization's primary institutions.* Their genius lies in their curious ability to renounce this world and announce another, more compelling and true. They relocate the divisive solidarities of language, custom, and region within a broader community and higher Truth. They do so ideally, of course, and it goes without saying that the ideal may be, and routinely is, ignored or violated by those who would use the Truth for other ends. At times, of course, redemptive ideals may lose their appeal. History is not linear, and communities once thrust into expansive world orders may suddenly turn inward. Alternately, as in the modern West, secular idioms may provide a non-spiritual alternative to the ideals of religious transcendence, or the give and take of self-interested exchange may narrow moral vision and erode popular interest in projects of ethical transcendence.

But history suggests that the ideal of transcendence will endure. The message carries well in a world of expansive horizons and ethical challenge. In such contexts the world religions offer the promise of community recast according to a divine plan. It goes without saying that the promise is never fully realized. But the ideal survives. The very generality of its ethic allows this ideal to exert powerful influence on the most diverse human affairs and provides living testimony to one of the most enduring responses to the challenges of identity and morality in our complex world.

Explanation: sustaining plausibility

1.24   Berger: 'plausibility structures'

Peter L. Berger, 1969: *A Rumour of Angles*. London: Allen Lame/The Penguin Press (pp. 18–19; 31–2).

Developing insights in the sociology of knowledge, Peter Berger argues that 'knowledge' is reinforced by other people believing the same thing, and undermined by other people believing different things. Berger goes on to suggest that the pluralism which he believes to be a defining feature of modern times therefore undermines supernaturalist belief-systems which claim to possess absolute truth (see reading **3.17**). In the extract below he argues that religions of difference nonetheless survive in the modern world by virtue of their strongly bounded and differentiated communities, which serve to bring believers together and so reinforce their beliefs. This argument can in fact be stated in two ways: (1) because religions of difference have clear teachings which are not open to a range of interepretations (unlike religions of humanity and spiritualities of life), they engender solidarity and (2) because religions of difference engender solidarity, it is easier for their members to believe the same thing. The first version of the argument can be found in Warner (1990, p. 292). Here Berger articulates the second.

Today the supernatural as a meaningful reality is absent or remote from the horizons of everyday life of large numbers, very probably of the majority, of people in modern societies, who seem to manage to get along without it quite well. This means that those to whom the supernatural is still, or again, a meaningful reality find themselves in the status of a minority, more precisely, a *cognitive minority* – a very important consequence with very far-reaching implications.

By a cognitive minority I mean a group of people whose view of the world differs significantly from the one generally taken for granted in their society. Put differently, a cognitive minority is a group formed around a body of deviant 'knowledge'. The quotation marks should be stressed here. The term 'knowledge' used within the frame of reference of the sociologist of knowledge always refers to what is *taken to be* or *believed as* 'knowledge'. In other words, the use of the terms is strictly neutral on the question of whether or not the socially held 'knowledge' is finally true or false. [. . .]

For better or for worse, men are social beings. Their 'sociality' includes what they think, or believe they 'know' about the world. Most of what we 'know' we have taken on the authority of others, and it is only as others continue to confirm this 'knowledge' that it continues to be plausible to us. It is such socially shared, socially taken-for-granted 'knowledge' that allows us to move with a measure of confidence through everyday life. Conversely, the plausibility of 'knowledge' that is not socially shared, that is challenged by our fellow men, is imperilled, not just in our dealings with others, but much more importantly in our own minds. The status of a cognitive minority is thus invariably an uncomfortable one – not necessarily because the majority is repressive or intolerant, but simply because it refuses to accept the minority's definitions of reality *as* 'knowledge'. At best, a minority viewpoint is forced to be defensive. At worst, it ceases to be plausible to anyone. [. . .]

The fundamental option [for religion] is simple: it is a choice between hanging on to or surrendering cognitive deviance. [. . .]

Only in a countercommunity of considerable strength does cognitive deviance have a chance to maintain itself. The countercommunity provides continuing therapy against the creeping doubt as to whether, after all, one may not be wrong and the majority right. To fulfil its function of providing social support for the deviant body of 'knowledge', the countercommunity must provide a strong sense of solidarity among its members (a 'fellowship of the saints' in a world rampant with devils) and it must be quite closed vis-à-vis the outside ('Be not yoked together with unbelievers!'). In sum, it must be a kind of ghetto.

Explanation: dependence and equality

1.25 Warner on 'the culture of public humbling'

R. Stephen Warner, 1990: *New Wine in Old Wineskins. Evangelicals and Liberals in a Small-Town Church.* Berkeley, Los Angeles and London: University of California Press (pp. 293–4).

Whilst there is an obvious tendency towards hierarchialism in religions of difference, they can also be surprisingly egalitarian. In part, as Stephen Warner explains below, this is due to the willingness of adherents to admit their common dependence on God. Protestant forms of religion are particularly likely to acknowledge the equality of all believers before God ('the priesthood of all believers'), to empower all believers with their promise of the holy spirit poured out on all, and to insist that every believer can and should interpret God's word for him or herself. (Not surprisingly some scholars have credited Protestantism with a major role in the rise of liberal democracy in the West – see Troeltsch and Parsons in readings **2.44** and **2.45**.) Given the pervasiveness of anti-elitist sentiment and suspicion of authority in modern times, the egalitarian agenda of religions of difference has an obvious appeal. Equally, the licence to admit weakness and dependence may exercise a powerful appeal in modern cultures in which the pressure to perform and to succeed can be so strong (see Durkheim's description of utilitarian individualism in reading **1.3**). Warner's account of equality in dependence in an evangelical church recalls Steven Tipton's account of a similar phenomenon in the revivalist Christian sect he studied in *Getting Saved from the Sixties* (1982). Tipton writes, '[the sect] rejects stratification itself, insisting with milennial urgency on the universality of love and the absolute value of the individual soul before God . . . High and low standing will be levelled by the Second Coming, and to prepare for this even [the sect] pledges itself to utter social equality and unity in the present. But the sect does not simply reject conventional social status. It also shifts the bases of status from economic, educational, and political success to moral and spiritual perfection. In doing so it makes social acceptance invulnerable to circumstantial reverses or social-structural barriers . . .' (pp. 71–2).

There is an inherent, though implicit, interpersonal bridge in the very nature of the evangelicals' confession of faith, which is the admission of personal spiritual need. In effect, evangelicalism recognizes that it can be as difficult to receive as to give, and its culture is built around a demand for receptivity and a confession of dependence. [. . .] Catholic charismatics 'place a high value on openness, emotional intensity, and childlike characteristics.' Contrast this ideal with the sixties liberal ideal expressed by Harvey Cox:

We speak of God politically whenever we give occasion to our neighbor to become the responsible adult agent, the fully posttown and posttribal man God expects him to be today. . . . We do not speak to him of God by trying to make him religious but, on the contrary, by encouraging him to come fully of age, putting away childish things.

It is the culture of public humbling that is most characteristic of evangelicals in contrast to liberals. When one is willing to acknowledge his or her own religious neediness, the possibility is opened for religious exchange to occur within the fellowship itself, and the fellowship need not search out the needy as recipients of religious benevolence. Hence evangelical groups are parochial; hence they are more likely to be groups. Other things being equal, we should expect to find more vital evangelical than liberal church communities.

Religions of Difference: prospects

1.26   Roof and McKinney: the growth of heightened difference

Wade Clark Roof and William McKinney, 1992: *American Mainline Religion. Its Changing Shape and Future*. New Brunswick, NJ: Rutgers University Press (p. 150).

As the sections on Secularization and Sacralization in Part Three reveal, religions of difference have both confirmed and confounded predictions of decline in modern times. In relation to Christianity – the religion for which figures are most readily available – many long-established 'mainline' churches have declined during modern times, but their decline has been variable. In Europe the rate of this decline has varied from country to country and from denomination to denomination. In America decline has been less marked, and has occurred only relatively recently (since the late 1960s). On the other hand, forms of Christianity characterized by heightened difference have grown since the last war on a world-wide scale. This growth has also been evident in Islamic, Hindu and Jewish religions of heightened difference over the same period, as well as in highly differentiated 'new' religious movements like those of the Seventh-Day Adventists, Jehovah's Witnesses, and Mormons. The following table from Roof and McKinney shows how in America Protestant denominations of heightened difference have flourished relative to mainline, more moderate and liberal denominations. If one simply extrapolates from these figures, the implications for the future of religions of moderate and heightened difference are clear: decline in the former case, growth in the latter.

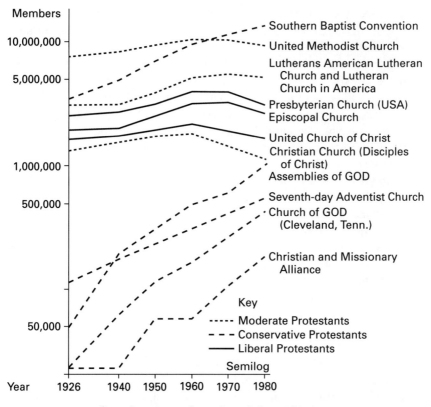

Growth patterns for selected denominations

1.27 Hunter on the inevitable liberalization of religions of difference

James Davison Hunter, 1987: *Evangelicalism. The Coming Generation*. Chicago and London: The University of Chicago Press (pp. 182–5).

Despite the apparent success of religions of difference in recent times (see above), James Davison Hunter's research amongst college age Evangelicals in America led him to conclude that the boundaries of one influential religion of difference – Evangelical Protestantism – are being inexorably eroded. In the passage below he offers an explanation which identifies at least three features of modernity as responsible: an 'ethic of civility' (characteristic of democracy); the undermining of Evangelical teachings by new knowledges; and the corrosive power of pluralism. Later in his book Hunter offers examples of the liberalizing, de-differentiating process at work in all the world's major religious traditions; the process, he believes, is as universal as modernity itself.

Conservative Protestantism has changed in significant ways since the beginning of the century and, from all appearances, it is continuing to change! [. . .]

Though these changes may level off, the process is likely to continue, for the simple reason that the symbolic boundaries of Protestant orthodoxy are not being maintained or reinforced. To be sure, there is good reason to believe that conservative Protestantism may be *incapable* of adequately reinforcing these boundaries. This is so for three important reasons. The first has to do with the 'ethic of civility.' Evangelicals generally and the coming generation particularly have adopted to various degrees an ethical code of political civility. This compels them not only to be *tolerant of others*' beliefs, opinions, and life-styles, but more importantly to be *tolerable to others*. The critical dogma is not to offend but to be genteel and civil in social relations. While their adoption of this ethic expresses itself politically, it expresses itself as a religious style as well. In this latter sense, it entails a deemphasis of Evangelicalism's more offensive aspects, such as accusations of heresy, sin, immorality, and paganism, and themes of judgment, divine wrath, damnation, and hell. Anything that hints of moral or religious absolutism and intolerance is underplayed. Indeed there is enormous social pressure to adapt to this code of civility. As one national opinion survey showed, the predominant image of conservative Protestantism is still negative. They are very often viewed as 'overly strict on moral issues,' 'closed minded,' 'intolerant of others' religious views,' and 'fanatical about their own beliefs' and are believed to place 'too harsh an emphasis on guilt, sin or judgement' and to be 'too rigid and simplistic.' This kind of characterization cannot help but create tremendous social constraints to be less strict, less fanatical, more open-minded, and so on. [. . .]

The second reason can only be inferred, but the logic and the evidence are compelling. It is that an increasing number of Evangelicals no longer really believe in the sanctity of these symbolic boundaries. A deep, compulsive, organic faith in the eternal and transcendent verities that emerge out of a quiet, taken-for-granted certainty is disappearing. It is not as though these Evangelicals no longer believe in God, his authority, or the authority of Scriptures, or the divine sanction of the traditions. It is that they have difficulty believing in these things simply and literally, the way a person would say that his neighbor exists. Once the belief that the central facts (carried by the traditions and taught by churches) are facts in the most literal and absolute sense is weakened, traditional religion begins to disintegrate. The most important case in point is the place of Scriptures. When it is allowed, as it is increasingly so in Evangelicalism, to interpret the Bible subjectivistically and to see portions of the Scripture as symbolic or nonbinding, the Scriptures are divested of their authority to compel obedience. They may still inspire but they are substantially disarmed. The same is true for codes of behavior and belief traditionally held to be biblically inspired. When these lose a sense of divine origin or divine sanction, or when they are seen as having a human and temporal origin, the believer's conviction is enfeebled.

The modern world order, then, not only creates conditions which constrain modifications in the belief system of orthodoxy but also undermines the disposition of the orthodox to believe unequivocably. [. . .]

The third reason Evangelicalism may not be capable of reinforcing the boundaries is the simplest of all. It is that there is no longer any abiding consensus as to what many of the boundaries are. This is so among ordinary laymen and clergy, but it appears to be particularly true for the coming generation. From all indications the pluralism of opinion over theological, moral, familial, and political issues in Evangelicalism (already wide-ranging) is expanding and not coalescing into a new consensus.

1.28 Martin: the difficulty of sustaining heightened difference

David Martin, 1982: Received Dogma and New Cult. *Daedelus*, Winter 1982, pp. 53–71 (pp. 67–8).

Here David Martin reviews the advantages and disadvantages of maintaining a 'sharp edge to the world'. He has in mind highly differentiated 'cultic' forms of religion like the Moonies (Unification Church), Children of God, and Hare Krishna, all of which have displayed a considerable potential for growth in recent times. In many ways his conclusions are compatible with those of Hunter in relation to evangelicalism in the above reading. (On the growth of such religions see also Rodney Stark, reading **3.100**).

Since these movements present such a sharp edge to 'the world,' and draw the young into comprehensive, total loyalties, they experience certain gains and losses. The main advantage is their capacity to attract the idealists who seek a purpose to life, and even to history. Like the evangelicals, but to an even greater extent, they mobilize those who seek a wider meaning and a deeper service than self can provide. By running in parallel to evangelicals, at a more acute angle to society, they are unlikely to draw many of those young idealists who have already been drawn to evangelical religion. The only exchange between evangelicals and the cults has been a tendency at the margin for some of the more experimental evangelicals to adopt certain items from the 'alternative' life-styles, the better to 'save' the young from the appeal they might otherwise exercise.

On the debit side, the extreme demands they make are likely to ensure a following as small as it is totally committed and unremittingly enthusiastic. Only as the 'edge' presented to society dulls somewhat is a wider expansion likely, and this indeed is what is happening in some degree. Categories of commitment are allowed which permit believers to sojourn partway between the religious universe and the wider secular world. Until that happens there will be a spiral of suspicion, and of claim and counterclaim between the media and the organs of the new movement, especially where young people are taken out of their families of origin into the wider fellowship of faith.

1.29 Troeltsch on the necessary transformation of religions of difference

Ernst Troeltsch, 1931: *The Social Teaching of the Christian Churches*, 2 vols, trans. Olive Wyon. London: George Allen and Unwin Ltd; New York: MacMillan, (pp. 1007–10).

In this rich passage Ernst Troeltsch draws out the implications of his great study of the Christian churches for Christianity's future. Writing at the beginning of the twentieth century, he observes a Catholic church clinging desperately to the church model and a Protestant church abandoning this model in favour of sectarianism on the one hand and mysticism on the other. In the broadest terms, Troeltsch's prediction/proposal for the future is that Christianity must reconcile church, sect and mysticism if it is to survive (for a definition of these types of Christianity see Troeltsch, reading **1.9**). Troeltsch believes that religions of difference have the best chance of survival in modern times, but that they must become less coercive and authoritarian. Given this view, the success of fundamentalist Christianity would no doubt have dismayed him. Would he, however, have viewed the upsurge of Charismatic Christianity as an acceptable reconciliation between church, sect and mysticism? In our view, expounded in the conclusion to the volume, experiential religions of difference like Charismatic Christianity which combine an emphasis on transcendence and authoritative truth with a positive evaluation of individual experience, may prove one of the most successful forms of religion in the future.

Unless it is organized into a community with a settled form of worship, Christianity cannot be either expansive or creative. Every kind of reaction to a mere 'freedom of the Spirit' in the hope that it will grow and thrive without organization, is a Utopian ideal which is out of touch with the actual conditions of life, and its only effect is to weaken the whole.

[. . .] [Yet] the days of the pure Church-type within our present civilization are numbered. Ideas which the modern world accepts as natural and obvious do not agree with the views of the Church. Compulsion is no longer a defence of the whole against individual disturbance; it only means the forcible restraint of currents of real vitality. Either completely or partially the civil power has retired into the background, and soon it will cease to have any influence at all.

In countries where the religious situation contains many different elements, the various ecclesiastical systems constitute a large body of opinion, in which each particular communion claims to possess the sole Truth, thus neutralizing the religious influence of all. The churches are losing their hold on the spiritual life of the nations, and many of their functions are now being exercised by educationists, writers, administrators, and by voluntary religious associations. Under these circumstances the Catholic Church-type has been forced to exercise an increasingly powerful and external dominion over the consciences of men. The Protestant churches, on the other hand, have not exercised the same influence. This is due to two causes: (1) because they are not sufficiently vigorous to be able to do this; and (2) because their subjective interpretation of the idea of the Church contains strong tendencies which are directly opposed to a development of this kind. Thus they have not been able to withstand the influence of the sect-type and mysticism, both of which are tendencies which have a close affinity with the modern world. The Protestant Church-type, therefore, has persisted with the aid of sectarian ideas and the relativism of idealism and mysticism. Protestantism no longer represents the pure Church-type, although the ecclesiastical spirit of conformity has raised indignant enough protests against this irresistible development, and either secretly or openly casts longing glances at Catholic ideals. Protestantism is developing at present along the following lines: separation between Church and State; suspension of the endeavour to form new churches; the independence of the individual congregation; the transformation of State churches into popular churches in which there is a united system of administration, while the individual congregations are left a free hand to manage their own affairs; by this very fact, however, these churches contain a certain amount of high explosive which is a continual menace to their existence. Even beneath the veil of an apparently stable united confessional Church, the lack of denominational principle on the part of most of the members has produced this situation. More and more the central life of the Church-type is being permeated with the vital energies of the sect and of mysticism; the whole history of Protestantism reveals this very clearly. While Catholicism does all it can to hinder the development of these tendencies, they are both becoming stronger and stronger within the Protestant churches. In the mutual interpenetration of the three chief sociological categories, which must be united with a structure which will reconcile them all, lie its future tasks, tasks of a sociological and organizing kind, which are more pressing than all doctrinal questions. Along this path all efforts to achieve a reconciling unity have failed. An 'Ecclesiastical Protestant system of dogma' no longer exists. Thus it is evident that union and cohesion must be sought in some other sphere than in that of dogma. This will only be possible on the assumption that the churches which have been created by compulsion, on a basis of authority and rigid conformity, may become homes within which Christians of very varying outlook can live and work together in peace.

1.30   Voll: religions of difference wax and wane

John O. Voll, 1982: *Islam. Continuity and Change in the Modern World*. Boulder, Colorado: Westview Press; Harlow: Longman (pp. 356–7).

In his influential studies of Islam, Voll adopts a long perspective. As we have seen in extract **1.4** he views Islam as composed of many different 'styles', and argues that Islamic fundamentalism represents not an unprecedented new development, but the revitalization of one of these styles. When he looks to the future in the extract below, he adopts a similar approach. Depending on future political and social events, religions of heightened difference may wax or they may wane. If they wane, other 'styles' of Islam will take their place. In neither case will Islam cease to be a potent force in the modern world.

History is not a predictive science, and the social scientists have had little success in devising an accurate means of foretelling the future. However, it is possible to speculate about the future of the Islamic revival on the basis of its continuities with the past.

At the beginning of the fifteenth Islamic century, Islamic communities are engaged in a vigorous reaffirmation of the Islamic message, frequently utilizing a fundamentalist style. In the revival of the 1970s, a new type of fundamentalism was emerging, and it combined traditional themes with radical approaches. It has sometimes clashed with the more traditional fundamentalism in which much of the 1970s revival is expressed.

If the more traditional fundamentalism of the current revival proves inadequate, there are alternative ways for the continuing assertion of the validity of the Islamic message. Some Muslims have expressed the fear that if the current Islamic movement does not make rapid progress in solving the problems of Muslim societies, there will be many who will turn away from Islam. However, if past experience is any guide, the future will not include the demise of Islam even if the current experiments fail. What will happen is that there will be a shift in the dominant style.

If the current fundamentalism is discredited, it could be replaced in many different ways, depending on local and global conditions. If the failure leads to social collapse, the emerging dominant style might be a militant messianic Islam or the emerging radical fundamentalism. It could also mean a reversion to a more pragmatic adaptationism. Whatever happens, it is clear that with its unity and variety, its consensus and conflict, its continuity and change, Islam will continue in its fifteenth century to be a vital force in the world.

CHAPTER THREE

religions of humanity

Introduction

Whereas religions of difference exalt the divine over the human, religions of humanity shift the locus of authority from transcendent to human. Whilst the human is not as closely identified with the divine as it is in spiritualities of life, God and humanity are nevertheless brought into closer ontological and epistemological relationship with one another than in religions of difference. Rather than being viewed as awesome, fearful, and set-apart, the deity is seen as much more approachable, tolerant, compassionate. The human is like the divine, an image of the divine – it can even participate in the divine. Indeed, many religions of humanity insist that it is *only* by starting with the human and human experience that one can come to know something of God.

In their dependence on the category of humanity, liberal religions are clearly linked to the wider cultural shift towards 'the human' noticed by Durkheim in reading **1.3**, and discussed in the chapters on Detraditionalization and Universalization in **Part Three**. As such they are part and parcel of the Enlightenment movement – at least in their modern origins. Their Enlightenment heritage can also be seen in a characteristic confidence in the powers of human reason. For some religions of humanity, such as Deism (see reading **1.34**), reason is indeed the defining characteristic of humanity and the highest authority (it is the rational, 'regular' approach of this cultural and religious 'style' which theorists like Charles Taylor and Steven Tipton emphasize in readings **1.1** and **1.2**). Some religions of humanity, however, have been equally inspired by Romanticism, and tend to place more emphasis on the importance of some combination of human intuition, feeling, or experience. As such they share key characteristics with what Taylor and Tipton refer to above as the 'expressive' style of modern culture. In both cases, religions of humanity tend to be critical of competing authorities. Religious institutions, scriptures, traditions, rituals, sacraments, and specialists are all approached with a measure of suspicion. Often they are lumped together under the catch-all term 'tradition', and are viewed as the external, fossilized remnants of once-living forms of human religious life and experience. Though religions of humanity may accept that tradition can continue to inform the present (and in general tend to be less eclectic in their use of tradition than spiritualities of life), they nevertheless refuse to regard it as an absolute and unquestioned authority. Religions of humanity are generally willing to subject what they see as the un-questioned dogmas of previous ages to historical scrutiny. Likewise, they tend to be respectful of modern science more generally, and to argue that religious truth can never be allowed to contradict scientific truth. The human, human experience, and human reason become the meas-ure of truth. Since individuals must be free to chose, decide, believe, and make up their own minds where matters of religion are concerned, both *tolerance* and *freedom* are key values.

Whilst they may understand the human in either an individual or a social sense, it is rare to find the social dimension entirely absent in religions of humanity. Often they are characterized by a strong sense of the importance of the collective dimension of human existence and by active ethical and political concern. Whilst religions of difference are equally unlikely to understand the human apart from the social, they are more likely to think of the latter in terms of communities of believers. By contrast, religions of humanity understand human communities, including other religions, in much more inclusive terms. Their loosely bounded and inclusivistic communities are often termed 'denominations' by sociologists in contrast to the 'churches' and 'sects' of religions of difference. Religions of humanity tend to view the only true boundaries of community as coterminous with those of the human race itself. Where religions of difference thus place their emphasis on building up a com-munity of believers, liberal religions hope to transform human society as a whole. As such, they are both an example and a powerful driving force of the process of universalization which is discussed in the chapters on Universalization and Detraditionalization in **Part Three**.

The humanitarian and cosmopolitan goals of religions of humanity, together with their suspicion of 'traditional' religion, imbue them with deeply ethical intent. They argue that doctrine and dogma are secondary to action. What counts are good deeds, not fine words; compassionate actions, not doctrinal correctness; active love, not empty rituals. Not surprisingly, such religions view service of humanity as the highest duty and the essence of true religion. The best deeds are those which aid one's fellow human beings, respect their rights, and exemplify kindness and compassion. Such deeds help build up the this-worldly kingdom of God which is the goal of religious liberalism and which replaces eschatological and other-worldly hopes. Religions of humanity are characteristically optimistic both in their belief in the fundamental goodness of human nature and in the possibility of building the perfect human society here on earth. Often they are strongly progressivist, and may draw on the evidence of biological evolution to undergird their confidence in the inevitable dawning of a new godly society.

In sum, religions of humanity shift the locus of authority from the transcendent to the human as the two are brought into closer epistemological and ontological relation. Tradition is seen as a potential barrier between the two, and as an impediment to the creation of a new, improved human society. Such religions believe in human ability to judge so-called higher authorities and to make responsible choices. They stress the value of freedom. They are open and tolerant. And they believe that deeds are at least as important as words, creeds, and doctrines.

Many of the most characteristic features of religions of humanity appear in pre-modern times, and in a number of different cultures (in ancient Greece and Rome; in some pre-modern forms of Judaism, Buddhism, Hinduism and Islam; and in the Renaissance, for example). Whilst it would therefore be inaccurate to view religions of humanity as unique to modern times, certain of their characteristics have clearly been shaped by modern contexts. Their debt to the Enlightenment and their role in the wider cultural 'turn to the human' is noted above, and is explored further in **Part Three**. Their appropriation of many insights of the modern sciences – historical, biological, psychological and social-scientific – is another example. Likewise, key events of modern times like the French and American revolutions, key thinkers like Kant and Rousseau, and key discourses like that of 'human rights', have fed (and been fed by) religions of humanity. Given this closeness to modern culture, some commentators below suggest that recent changes, including a greater suspicion of science and a waning optimism, will inevitably weaken religions of humanity. Yet, as other readings point out, in some ways religions of humanity remain uniquely well adapted to modern times – not least in their espousal of the values of freedom and tolerance, and in their support for a humanitarian ethic.

The ways in which the turn to the human characteristic of this variety of religion weakens the authority of religious texts, traditions and institutions is discussed in **Part Three** under the heading of Detraditionalization. Likewise, the unifying and cosmopolitan implications of an emphasis on the common deliverances of natural reason are further considered in the chapter on Universalization. Given the fact that the boundaries between religions of humanity and religions of difference and spiritualities of life are often so fluid, it is also useful to read this chapter alongside what precedes and what follows it. There is clearly a spectrum running from religions of difference on the one hand to spiritualities of life on the other. Religions of humanity stand between them, and themselves cover a spectrum from more differentiated forms at one end (the religion of the current Pope, where he emphasizes that the church is an 'expert in humanity', see reading **3.69**), to very open and tolerant forms of detraditionalized liberalism at the other (the religion of the Dalai Lama, see reading **1.39**). Just as we have spoken of experiential forms of religions of difference, so there are also experiential religions of humanity. These combine a humanitarian ethic with a stress on the importance of experience and self-realization, and are further considered in the chapter on Combinations at the end of **Part One**. Spiritualities of life, it seems, take religions of humanity to an extreme: experience becomes the *sole* authority; the human is *identified* with the divine; loyalty to a tradition is *wholly* abandoned; and belief in the unity of humanity is replaced with belief in the unity of *all* life.

Cognate Terms

Liberal religion/liberal christianity

Liberal Christianity is the best known and probably the most influential example of a religion of humanity. In part this can be explained by the fact that Christianity has at its centre a human being (Jesus of Nazareth) who is also divine, and in part by the fact that it has been so inescapably bound up with the forces of modernization in the West. The adjective liberal can, of course, be extended to religions besides Christianity, and a term like 'liberal religions' would be closely cognate to 'religions of humanity'. Whilst the latter focuses upon the way in which these religions exalt the human, the former places more emphasis on their characteristic emphasis on (human) freedom. In this volume the terms 'religions of humanity' and 'liberal religions' are used interchangeably.

Modernism

Again applied primarily to Christianity, 'modernism' describes those mainly nineteenth and early twentieth century forms of Christianity which deliberately set out to bring the church and its thinking into closer relation with modern culture and society. Whilst such an aim has been important in many religions of humanity, it would be misleading to suggest that it was always their central motivation. To do so would be to assume that such religions were no more than derivative religious renderings of secular culture. In fact, as some of the readings which follow show, religions of humanity have played a more central, constructive and independently creative role at the heart of modern culture.

Experiential religions of humanity

In the previous section we introduced the category 'experiential religions of difference' to characterize religions like Charismatic Christianity. One can equally speak of experiential religions of humanity in the case of religions which retain a liberal and humanitarian stress, but combine this with reliance on the authority of experience. Since many liberal religions are in any case open to the deliverances of experience, this step is an easy one to take. Experiential religions of humanity are considered in more detail in the chapter on Combinations at the end of **Part One**.

Denominationalism

This term is widely used to refer to the institutional and creedal openness thought to be characteristic of liberal religion. Unlike a church or a sect, a denomination is permeable both to its wider society and to other forms of religion, and may seek rapprochement with them.

Religions of Humanity: overviews

1.31   Ahlstrom introduces Christian liberalism

Sydney E. Ahlstrom, 1972: *A Religious History of the American People*. New Haven and London: Yale University Press (pp. 779–81).

In the reading below, the religious historian Sydney Ahlstrom offers an overview of liberal Christianity which captures many of the most salient features of religions of humanity more generally. Though his focus is on Christianity, his remarks apply to religious liberalism elsewhere in the world. Ahlstrom speaks of the nineteenth century as the 'Golden Age' of liberal religion, whilst noting that its roots stretch much further back.

Liberalism was, first of all, a point of view which, like the adjective 'liberal' as we commonly use it, denotes both a certain generosity or charitableness toward divergent opinions and a desire for intellectual 'liberty.' Liberal theologians also wished to 'liberate' religion from obscurantism and creedal bondage so as to give man's moral and rational powers larger scope. In this broad sense, liberals could be linked with a long Christian tradition extending from Abelard and Erasmus through Locke and Paley to Channing and the Transcendentalists. Actually, however, the 'liberalism' of the nineteenth century was a positive and structured movement, not merely a vague tendency or an indefinite state of mind. Whether it was called the New Theology, Progressive Orthodoxy, Modernism, or some other name, it had a fairly definite doctrinal content.

In the language of historical theology, liberals were Arminian or Pelagian. With regard to human nature, they emphasized man's freedom and his natural capacity for altruistic action. Sin, therefore, was construed chiefly as error and limitation which education in morals and the example of Jesus could mitigate, or else as the product of underprivilege which social reform could correct. Original Sin or human depravity was denied or almost defined out of existence. As their predecessors of the Enlightenment had done, liberals tried to avoid deterministic conclusions by arguments for the creative and autonomous nature of the human spirit.

A strong emphasis on ethical preaching and moral education accorded with the liberal view of man. Ethical imperatives became central to the Christian witness, and the Sermon on the Mount was often regarded as the heart and core of the Bible. On the other hand, liberals tended to slight traditional dogma and the sacraments. Baptism came to be considered as an initiatory formality or as a dedicatory rite for parents, while the Lord's Supper was usually given only memorial significance and its importance to public worship was minimized. [. . .]

Because of their revised estimate of man's nature and their tendency to interpret the entire evolutionary process as ultimately for mankind's benefit, liberals were fervently optimistic about the destiny of the human race. Supported by the apparent success of democratic governments and the evidence of scientific and technological advances, their confidence in the future outran even that of the Enlightenment's apostles of progress. The Kingdom of God was given a this-worldly interpretation and viewed as something men would build within the natural historical process. For them, in Reinhold Niebuhr's striking phrase, 'History was the Christ.'

Their interest in history caused the liberals to go even farther, radically altering the meaning and significance of revelation. The Old Testament was interpreted chiefly as a record of Jewish history, religiosity, and growing moral earnestness that culminated in the life and message of Jesus. The New Testament was placed in the same context, and the main aim of scholarship was to clarify the religion of Jesus. Because the New Testament consists exclusively of the history and testimony of the post-Easter church, it created many problems for liberals. Paul the Apostle became a very troublesome saint. On the divinity of Jesus and the inspiration of the Scriptures, therefore, widely divergent views arose. The dominant tendency was in the direction of a benign naturalism, although it was veiled by an extremely pious and time-honored vocabulary. Hence Jesus' divinity sprang from the fact that he spoke the most sublime truths and proclaimed the highest and (probably) the final religion. Creeds and dogmas about these matters were 'human constructions' subject to evolutionary development and interpretation. Time had purged them of much error, and the process was still going on. The Bible thus had authority because, judged by standards outside of it (historical, philosophic, scientific, and experiential), it deserved to be so regarded.

Liberals tended strongly to monistic ways of construing many traditional problems of theology and philosophy. Wishing to see unity in all things rather than disjunction, they preferred to combine or merge the romantic inclination to see man and nature as alike infused with divinity and the Darwinian tendency to relate man to the natural world in a scientific way. Similarly, man and God were brought together. Liberals dwelt much more on the immanence of God than on his transcendence. As Bushnell had argued, the natural and the supernatural were consubstantial, observable in almost all forms of being. The supernatural and the spiritual tended to be identified; and the spiritual in turn was identified with consciousness – the conative, intellectual, emotive side of man. Finally, the ancient disjunctions between the subjective and objective, between the mental world and the 'real' or 'objective' world, were minimized philosophically by theories of reality which stressed the ideal nature of things and by intuitional or idealistic theories of knowledge. Not all liberals, by any means, believed that such matters were crucial, but when they did venture into philosophical realms, they usually regarded Plato, Kant, Hegel, Schleiermacher, Coleridge, and various mystical philosophers as very important and reliable guides.

1.32 Kopf on 'rational faith' in India

David Kopf, 1979: *The Bramo Samaj and the Shaping of the Modern Indian Mind*. Princeton, New Jersey: Princeton University Press (p. 3).

This extract reminds us that religions of humanity are not confined to the West. David Kopf is known for his studies of liberal religion in India, particularly Bengal, and has demonstrated how much mutual influence there was between liberals in India and the West from the late eighteenth century onwards. Here he describes how Unitarianism, a pioneering and influential universalist religion of humanity with Western, Protestant origins, came to exercise an influence in early nineteenth-century India where new religious movements like the Brahmo Samaj were emerging out of a desire to reform Hinduism by bringing its rational, ethical, and humanitarian elements to the fore and supressing its more 'traditional' and 'superstitious' accretions.

Though Unitarianism was never a mass movement, the implications of its protest had far-reaching effects among the modernizing intelligentsia in India. Three simple though radical ideas for the time (1815 to 1835) provided the link between the enlightened few in Calcutta and the enlightened few in England and the United States.

The first was liberal religion, or the substitution of a rational faith for the prevailing popular religions of the world, which, they thought, increasingly curtailed the freedom of human beings by enslaving them to mechanical rituals, irrational myths, meaningless superstitions, and other-worldly beliefs and values. The second was the idea of social reform, or emancipation in which all known penalized classes and groupings such as workers, peasants, and women were to be elevated through education and the extension of civil rights to participate fully in the benefits of modern civilization. Finally, there was the idea of universal theistic progress, or the notion that the perfectability of mankind could be achieved by joining social reform to rational religion.

1.33 Ammerman on 'Golden Rule' Christianity

Nancy T. Ammerman, 1997: Golden Rule Christianity. Lived Religion in the American Mainstream. In Donald G. Hall (ed.), *Lived Religion in America: Toward a Theory of Practice*. Princeton, NJ: Princeton University Press, pp. 196–216 (pp. 197–206).

The liberalism discussed by Ahlstrom and Kopf in the readings above was in many ways a religion of cultural elites. Liberalism has always had a strong theological dimension and can in some ways be viewed as the attempt to forge a religion with intellectual credibility within the modern context. In the following extract, however, Nancy Ammerman explores liberalism as a popular as well as an elite religion. Her discovery of the importance of what she calls 'Golden Rule' Christianity ('do unto others as you would be done by') in contemporary America also reveals the continuing influence of liberalism into the late twentieth century. Ammerman's findings are based on her research in 23 Christian congregations across the US, and on survey responses from 1,995 individuals in these congregations. The results of this research have been published in full in *Congregation and Community* (Ammerman, 1997).

The first step in describing the religiosity of 'lay liberals' is to recognize what these people believe and practice. Their religiosity is not just a paler reflection of evangelical fervor, but different in kind. For that reason, I will not call them 'lay liberals.' Religious liberalism is usually taken to indicate the opposite end of a scale that is anchored by evangelicalism. That, in turn, indicates that the primary differences we should observe are differences in the certainty with which people hold traditional beliefs: evangelicals are relatively certain, whereas liberals have rejected or reinterpreted traditional ideas about the Bible, Christ's divinity, the second coming, and the like. What I want to suggest, however, is that this category of religious persons is best defined not by ideology, but by practices. Their own measure of Christianity is right living more than right believing. What Hoge, Johnson, and Luidens found, in fact, was that these Christians are characterized by a basic 'Golden Rule' morality and a sense of compassion for those in need. It is those practices of doing good and caring for others that we highlight here.

As we looked at the interviews from our study, across all the demographic and ideological categories, the most frequently mentioned characterization of the Christian life was that people should seek to do good, to make the world a better place, to live by the Golden Rule. A smaller group of people – mostly those in evangelical churches – defined the Christian life in terms of being saved, but even those people also talked about the importance of living by the principles taught in the Bible, chief among them the Golden Rule.

In our surveys, we also asked people to tell us how important various practices were to 'living the Christian life,' as well as what they thought their church's top priorities ought to be. Taking those two lists together, one can identify three clusters of responses. The largest (51 per cent of the total of 1,564 respondents for whom we have complete information) we might call 'Golden Rule Christians.'

It includes people who say that the most important attributes of a Christian are caring for the needy and living one's Christian values every day. The most important task of the church, they say, is service to people in need. They can be distinguished from two other groups. On one side stand more evangelically oriented respondents, comprising 29 per cent of the total. They emphasize prayer, Bible study, and witnessing as key Christian practices and, correspondingly, want their churches to give attention to evangelism and helping them resist the temptations of this world, while preparing for the world to come. On the other side are the activists, 19 per cent of the total, who emphasize social action and working for justice. [. . .]

What I am describing may in fact be the dominant form of religiosity among middle-class suburban Americans. It certainly is among the middle-class suburban Americans in our study. It is their form of 'lived religion.'

[Its] guiding moral philosophy is not unrelated to traditional religious beliefs and texts. For Golden Rule Christians, it is grounded in the Bible, but certainly not in a literal reading of it. [. . .]

Nearly half of the activists and Golden Rule Christians said that the Bible's 'stories and teachings provide a powerful motivation as we work toward God's reign in the world.' Another quarter of the Golden Rule Christians (and a higher proportion of activists) said the Bible is a 'useful guide for individual Christians in their search for basic moral and religious teachings.' Almost no one was ready to throw the Bible out as 'irrelevant.' Among the interviews we analyzed, about one-quarter, spread equally across different types of respondents, specifically mentioned the Bible as important to their own lives and to what they think their children should learn. Just because they do not accept traditional definitions of inspiration or inerrancy does not mean that they have no use for Scripture. Like the rest of their religious life, their use of Scripture is defined more by choices and practice than by doctrine. They draw from Scripture their own inspiration and motivation and guidance for life in this world. Their knowledge of Scripture may not be very deep, but they have at least some sense that the Bible is a book worth taking seriously, especially as a tool for making one's own life and the life of the world better. [. . .]

What is this good life for which Golden Rule Christians aim? Most important to Golden Rule Christians is care for relationships, doing good deeds, and looking for opportunities to provide care and comfort for people in need. Their goal is neither changing another's beliefs nor changing the whole political system. They would like the world to be a bit better for their having inhabited it, but they harbor no dreams of grand revolutions. [...]

This emphasis on caring also defines their picture of God. Just as our interviewees' most common description of the Christian life was living by the Golden Rule, so the most common description of God was as a protector and comforter. God was experienced most often in moments of need. Even beyond times of crisis, these church members talked about seeing God's presence in the ways 'things just work out' or feeling more confident about everyday challenges because they know God will care for them. Among the survey respondents, preferred images of God included savior, comforter, and father. These pictures of God as loving, caring, comforting, and protecting largely transcended ideological lines. They are characteristic of Golden Rule Christians, but they are by no means alien to the evangelicals and activists in our study. [...]

Golden Rule Christianity seems to have at least some impact on the other domains Golden Rule Christians inhabit. Religiosity is not, for them, utterly 'private.' In business and in the community, they value honesty, believing that good people give an honest day's work and do not try to cheat others. They say that their faith also means that they treat their co-workers and clients with more care than do others who are not religious. [...]

While they may not be eager to talk about religious issues while they are at work, and they might find it hard to articulate any coherent theological sense of 'vocation,' they claim that the practices they put at the center of the Christian life inform their everyday economic and civil activities. [...]

What I have described so far is a set of caregiving practices that extends from family to neighborhood to larger community. They are practices based in a generalized Christian ethic that calls for people to 'love one another' and treat others as they would wish to be treated. Among Golden Rule Christians, these practices are explicitly nonideological, and those two factors taken together lead to another of the characteristics of this mode of religiosity – its tolerance.

... Less than half of all our Golden Rule-style respondents say they ever participate in 'seeking converts or new members' for their church. Indeed, members of both Carmel and St. Lawrence specifically mentioned tolerance for diversity as a virtue of their faith tradition. Methodists noted that Methodism (at least in their view) does not impose a rigid creed on its members, and Catholics talked about the diversity of spiritual experience among Catholics – from visions of Mary to charismatic renewal to ordinary Mass-going. They like being part of a church that leaves room for people with different beliefs and experiences.

The basis for unity, then, is an ethic rather than dogma, a principle long acknowledged by ecumenical organizations. In the early years of the Federal Council of Churches, leaders chose to emphasize 'the Fatherhood of God and the brotherhood of man,' to concentrate on achieving a kind of pragmatic unity through the pursuit of 'social gospel' reforms, rather than any doctrinal unity or actual church union. More recently, theologian Leo Lefebure has noted that efforts toward interreligious dialogue seem to be helped by the assumption that 'there is a fundamental ethical structure on which very diverse religions can come to at least limited agreement apart from special claims of revelation.' Citing the declaration 'Toward a Global Ethic' issued by the 1993 Parliament of the World's Religions, he notes that at its center 'is the Golden Rule, a principle of wisdom found in various forms in different religions.' Those who work from such 'principles of wisdom' (practices) rather than from explicit revealed dogma have ground on which to meet.

Religions of Humanity: themes

Theme: demythologization

1.34   Gay and early rationalist criticisms of 'tradition'

Peter Gay, 1968: *Deism: An Anthology*. Princeton, NJ, Toronto, Melbourne, London: D. Van Nostrand Co. (p. 13).

The attack on 'tradition' which would become a defining mark of modern liberalism began as early as the seventeenth century in the West when a group of English religious reformers and radicals known as the Deists began to attack 'historic' religion, particularly Christianity. The 'father of Deism', Lord Herbert of Cherbury (1583–1648), wrote 'Every religion which proclaims a revelation is not good, nor is every doctrine which is taught under its authority always essential or even valuable . . . The supreme Judge requires every individual to render an account of his actions in the light, not of another's belief, but of his own'. Deism may have been a small and elite movement but, in Peter Gay's words, it 'reflected and articulated a critical transition in religious consciousness, [and] by reflecting and articulating it so plainly, so coarsely, it hastened the transition' (1968, p. 10). As Gay makes clear, the Deists' criterion of truth was reason and reason alone. They advocated a rational religion cut loose from dogmatic superstition which would be able to unite and liberate a Europe ravaged by religious wars. Their central emphasis was on the freedom of the individual to think and act for himself.

All deists were in fact both critical and constructive deists. All sought to destroy in order to build, and reasoned either from the absurdity of Christianity to the need for a new philosophy or from their desire for a new philosophy to the absurdity of Christianity. Each deist, to be sure, had his special competence. While one specialized in abusing priests, another specialized in rhapsodies to nature, and a third specialized in the skeptical reading of sacred documents. Yet, whatever strength the movement had – and it was at times formidable – it derived that strength from a peculiar combination of critical and constructive elements. Deism, we might say, is the product of the confluence of three strong emotions: hate, love, and hope. The deists hated priests and priestcraft, mystery-mongering, and assaults on common sense. They loved the ethical teachings of the classical philosophers, the grand unalterable regularity of nature, the sense of freedom granted the man liberated from superstition. They hoped that the problems of life – of private conduct and public policy – could be solved by the application of unaided human reason, and that the mysteries of the universe could be, if not solved, at least defined and circumscribed by man's scientific inquiry. The deists were optimists about human nature: they rejected the Fall and thought that man could be at once good and wise. Had they only hated, they would have been cranks. Had they only loved, they would have been enthusiasts. Had they only hoped, they would have been visionaries. They were something of all this, but since they combined these qualities, they were something more and something better as well. They were powerful agents of modernity.

1.35 Bultmann on demythologization

Rudolph Bultmann, 1964 (orig. 1958): *Jesus Christ and Mythology*. London: SCM Press (pp. 15; 17–18).

The term 'demythologization' was made famous by the liberal Christian theologian Rudolph Bultmann (1884–1976). By regarding much of the Bible as 'mythological', Bultmann opened the possibility of reinterpretation in order to get at its 'deeper meaning'. Such a project has been typical of religions of humanity since the Enlightenment (see the reading which follows). Like Bultmann, these religions believe that sacred texts and traditions should be judged by the light of human faith and reason, and reinterpreted or discarded where they prove incompatible with these higher authorities. The project of demythologization marked a new stage in the relationship between history and religion.

The whole conception of the world which is presupposed in the preaching of Jesus as in the New Testament generally is mythological; i.e., the conception of the world as being structured in three storeys, heaven, earth and hell; the conception of the intervention of super-natural powers in the course of events; and the conception of mir-acles, especially the conception of the intervention of supernatural powers in the inner life of the soul, the conception that men can be tempted and corrupted by the devil and possessed by evil spirits. This conception of the world we call mythological because it is different from the conception of the world which has been formed and devel-oped by science since its inception in ancient Greece and which has been accepted by all modern men. In this modern conception of the world the cause-and-effect nexus is fundamental. Although modern physical theories take account of chance in the chain of cause and effect in subatomic phenomena, our daily living, purposes and actions are not affected. In any case, modern science does not believe that the course of nature can be interrupted or, so to speak, perforated, by supernatural powers. [. . .]

For modern man the mythological conception of the world, the conceptions of eschatology, of redeemer and of redemption, are over and done with. Is it possible to expect that we shall make a sacrifice of understanding, *sacrificium intellectus*, in order to accept what we cannot sincerely consider true – merely because such conceptions are suggested by the Bible? Or ought we to pass over those sayings of the New Testament which contain such mythological conceptions and to select other sayings which are not such stumbling-blocks to modern man? In fact, the preaching of Jesus is not confined to eschatological sayings. He proclaimed also the will of God, which is God's demand, the demand for the good. Jesus demands truthfulness and purity, readiness to sacrifice and to love. He demands that the whole man be obedient to God, and he protests against the delusion that one's duty to God can be fulfilled by obeying certain external command-ments. If the ethical demands of Jesus are stumbling-blocks to modern man, then it is to his selfish will, not to his understanding, that they are stumbling-blocks.

What follows from all this? Shall we retain the ethical preaching of Jesus and abandon his eschatological preaching? Shall we reduce his preaching of the Kingdom of God to the so-called social gospel? Or is there a third possibility? We must ask whether the eschatological preaching and the mythological sayings as a whole contain a still deeper meaning which is concealed under the cover of mythology. If that is so, let us abandon the mythological conceptions precisely because we want to retain their deeper meaning. This method of interpretation of the New Testament which tries to recover the deeper meaning behind the mythological conceptions I call *de-mythologizing* – an unsatisfactory word, to be sure. Its aim is not to eliminate the mythological statements but to interpret them. It is a method of hermeneutics. The meaning of this method will be best understood when we make clear the meaning of mythology in general.

1.36   Woodhead: demythologization on the basis of 'experience'

Linda Woodhead, 1997: Spiritualising the Sacred: A Critique of Feminist Theology. In *Modern Theology*, vol. 13, no. 2, April 1997: 191–212 (p. 194).

Whilst Deists in the seventeenth and eighteenth century criticized 'traditional' religion on the basis of natural reason, and scholars like Bultmann criticized it on the basis of historical and scientific reason, it is has become equally common in the twentieth century to criticize it on the basis of 'experience'. In recent feminist critiques of 'traditional' religion, it is 'women's experience' which becomes the criterion of truth. As Linda Woodhead shows in the following extract, the result is that the religious scriptures and creeds which were once regarded as authoritative become relegated to the status of 'myth'.

In tracing back the authority of Christian belief to the self-interested strategies of patriarchal clerics, the feminist construal of Christianity is of course inherently critical. It undermines Christian dogma's constitutive claim to be true and revelatory and suggests that it is in fact nothing more than what Ruether refers to as 'codified collective experience'. As she says in *Sexism and God-Talk*, 'What have been called the objective sources of theology; Scripture and tradition, are themselves codified collective experience'. Lift the veil on scripture and tradition, remove the rhetoric of clerics, and you find only experience.

For this reason, feminist theologians argue, it is best to drop mystifying terms like 'dogma' and 'revelation', and speak instead of 'myths', 'symbols', 'models', 'metaphors', and 'parables'. Interestingly, these terms tend to be used almost interchangeably by feminist theologians, usually with little or no attempt at definition or discrimination. Their meaning, it seems, is bestowed simply by the way in which they are used in opposition to the alternative (and similarly undifferentiated) cluster of terms, 'dogma', 'absolute truth', 'revelation'. In other words, it seems that if something is said to be 'mythical' or 'symbolic', it is precisely its refusal to make a claim to absolute truth which is signalised. Not that feminist theologians want to deny the importance and value of religious 'symbols' – rather they want to stress their provisionality and revisability and their subordination to the individual religious 'experience' they inadequately express. To quote Ruether again: 'If a symbol does not speak authentically to experience, it becomes dead or must be altered to provide a new meaning'.

1.37 Berger on subjectivization

Peter L. Berger, 1969: *The Social Reality of Religion*. London: Faber and Faber (p. 166).

In the following extract Peter Berger suggests that the liberal demythologization which relegates religious truth to the status of 'myth' or 'symbol' also involves a subjectivization, psychologization and privatization of religion (see other readings on these themes in chapter on detraditionalization in **Part Three**). Berger has in mind particularly late twentieth-century forms of liberal Christian theology. It is possible to argue that Berger here identifies a process by which religions of humanity may transmute into spiritualities of life: an emphasis on the authority of the human leads to the belief that it is in the depths of one's own experience that one touches the divine, which in turn leads to the belief that the Self is itself divine (see next section on spiritualities of life).

The new liberalism 'subjectivizes' religion in a radical fashion and in two senses of the word. With the progressive loss of objectivity or reality-loss of the traditional religious definitions of the world, religion becomes increasingly a matter of free subjective choice, that is, loses its intersubjectively obligatory character. Also, religious 'realities' are increasingly 'translated' from a frame of reference of facticities external to the individual consciousness to a frame of reference that locates them *within* consciousness. Thus, for example, the resurrection of Christ is no longer regarded as an event in the external world of

physical nature, but is 'translated' to refer to existential or psychological phenomena in the consciousness of the believer. Put differently,
the *realissimum* to which religion refers is transposed from the cosmos
or from history to individual consciousness. Cosmology becomes
psychology. History becomes biography. In this 'translation' process,
of course, theology adapts itself to the reality presuppositions of
modern secularized thought – in fact, the alleged necessity to so
adapt the religious traditions (to make them 'relevant') is commonly
cited as the *raison d'être* of the theological movement in question.

Various conceptual machineries have been employed in this
enterprise. The concept of 'symbol,' as developed in neo-Kantian
philosophy, has been useful. The traditional religious affirmation can
now be regarded as 'symbols' – what they supposedly 'symbolize'
usually turns out to be some realities presumed to exist in the 'depths'
of human consciousness. A conceptual liaison with psychologism and/
or existentialism makes sense in this context and, indeed, characterizes
most of contemporary neo-liberalism.

Theme: humanity and human freedom

1.38   Passmore: 'the perfectibility of man'

John Passmore, 1970: *The Perfectibility of Man*. London: Duckworth (pp. 169–70).

The subjectivization which Berger identifies as characteristic of religions of
humanity in the reading above is only possible because of their exaltation of
the subject, the human. Whilst such religions (unlike spiritualities of life) do not
generally identify human beings with the divine, they are nonetheless defined
by their high doctrine of humanity. Thus the Unitarian William Channing (1780–
1842) entitled a famous essay on the glory of human nature 'Likeness to God',
and the Pittsburgh Platform of 1885, the foundation document of liberal ('Reform') Judaism, spoke of 'the indwelling of God in man'. Far from being hope-
lessly estranged from God, human beings are understood as naturally open to
divine influence. As John Passmore shows in the following extract, this view of
men as 'perfectible' has gained momentum throughout the modern period, and
become autonomous of religion.

Beginning with the Renaissance, but with increasing confidence in
the seventeenth century, men began to maintain that in their relationships to their fellow-men, rather than in their relationships to
God, lay their hope of perfection. 'Perfection' was defined in moral
rather than in metaphysical terms, and came gradually to be further

particularised as 'doing the maximum of good'. It was no longer supposed that in order to act morally men must abjure self-love; self-love was harnessed to the improvement of the human condition. 'Perfectibility' meant the capacity to be improved to an unlimited degree, rather than the capacity to reach, and rest in, some such ultimate end as 'the vision of God' or 'union with the One'. If men are to be able to perfect one another without divine assistance, however, it has to be presumed that they are not invincibly corrupt. Hence perfectibilists, following in Locke's footsteps, rejected original sin. Indeed, they agreed with Locke that men have no inborn moral tendencies, no innate tendency to act well or to act badly, but only a tendency to pursue pleasure and avoid pain.

This new 'moral psychology' opened the way to the suggestion that men could be to an infinite degree improved by the use of appropriate social mechanisms – in the first place, education. Education, Locke suggested, consists in forming moral habits in children by associating certain of their activities with pleasure, especially pleasure in the form of commendation, and others with pain, especially in the form of blame. Hartley developed Locke's innovations into a systematic perfectibilism by working out in detail an associationist psychology, according to which men could be not only educated but re-educated to any desired pattern.

In the twentieth century 'behavioural' psychologies have taken the place of associationism. But the fundamental assumptions remain. Innate differences are unimportant; men can be moulded to any desired shape by employing the appropriate psychological procedures. The road to infinite improvement lies open, on this view, to man: the only question is whether he is prepared to seize the opportunities which psychological science now offers him.

1.39   The Dalai Lama: 'human nature is basically good'

His Holiness the Dalai Lama, 1996: *Beyond Dogma. Dialogues and Discourses*. Berkeley, CA: North Atlantic Books (p. 39).

All the world's major religions have liberal forms. The version of Tibetan Buddhism promulgated by the current Dalai Lama is of this variety. In the following extract he articulates a characteristically liberal view of human nature. Like Ammerman's 'Golden Rule' Christians (see reading **1.33** above), the Dalai Lama believes that kindness is the highest virtue.

Given the fact that human nature is basically good, children, when they are still very young, do not really differentiate one person from another. Their love, their good-heartedness, are spontaneous. For example, they attach more importance to the smile of the person in front of them than to their race, nationality, or culture. I greatly appreciate the value of such an attitude, and it gives me great hope for the future.

In other respects, however, I am quite concerned. Children are naturally warm-hearted and kind, but certain aspects of the education they receive increase the divisions among them, and this has the effect of creating a gap between one child and others. It seems very important, therefore, that along with education this basic kindness, found in its natural state in children, must be fostered. By this I mean that education should be in harmony with the child's essentially kind nature. The most important element is that children be raised in a climate of love and tenderness. Although from an ideal perspective human qualities ought to be developed in conjunction with kindness, I often say that if I had to choose between important general qualities and kindness, I believe I would choose kindness.

1.40   Radford Ruether: 'the promotion of the full humanity of women'

Rosemary Radford Ruether, 1983: *Sexism and God-Talk. Toward a Feminist Theology*. London: SCM Press Ltd (pp. 18–19).

Even though the doctrine of human perfectibility has sometimes been applied only to white western males, its universalist implications have been seized upon by individuals and groups wishing to assert their equality. The following extract by Rosemary Radford Ruether shows how a liberal feminist theologian can use the doctrine in this way.

The critical principle of feminist theology is the promotion of the full humanity of women. Whatever denies, diminishes, or distorts the full humanity of women is, therefore, appraised as not redemptive. Theologically speaking, whatever diminishes or denies the full humanity of women must be presumed not to reflect the divine or an authentic relation to the divine, or to reflect the authentic nature of things, or to be the message or work of an authentic redeemer or a community of redemption.

This negative principle also implies the positive principle: what does promote the full humanity of women is of the Holy, it does reflect true relation to the divine, it is the true nature of things, the authentic message of redemption and the mission of redemptive community.

Theme: ethicization and politicization of religion

1.41   Rammohun Roy: an ethical religion to unite mankind

Rammohun Roy, 1934: *The Precepts of Jesus. The Guide to Peace and Happiness, Extracted from the Books of the New Testament Ascribed to the Four Evangelists.* London: John Mardon (pp. vi–vii).

In the following passage the pioneering Bengali religious reformer Rammohun Roy (1772–1833) introduces a book in which he has extracted Jesus' ethical teachings from the rest of the New Testament. Best described as a Hindu-Unitarian, Rammohun believed that the world could be united in brotherhood and equality by following an ethical religion based on these teachings (the reading by Kopf at **1.32** above helps contextualize Rammohun's reformed Hinduism).

I feel persuaded that by separating from the other matters contained in the New Testament, the moral precepts found in that book, these will be more likely to produce the desirable effect of improving the hearts and minds of men of different persuasions and degrees of understanding. For, historical and some other passages are liable to the doubts and disputes of free-thinkers and anti-christians, especially miraculous relations, which are much less wonderful than the fabricated tales handed down to the natives of Asia, and consequently would be apt at best to carry little weight with them. On the contrary, moral doctrines, tending evidently to the maintenance of the peace and harmony of mankind at large, are beyond the reach of metaphysical perversion, and intelligible alike to the learned and to the unlearned. This simple code of religion and morality is so admirably calculated to elevate men's ideas to high and liberal notions of one GOD, who has equally subjected all living creatures, without distinction of caste, rank, or wealth, to change, disappointment, pain, and death, and has equally admitted all to be partakers of the bountiful mercies which he has lavished over nature, and is also so well fitted to regulate the conduct of the human race in the discharge of their various duties to GOD, to themselves, and to society, that I cannot but hope the best effects from its promulgation in the present form.

1.42   Esack: Islamic Liberation Theology

Farid Esack, 1997: *Qur'an, Liberation and Pluralism. An Islamic Perspective of Interreligious Solidarity against Oppression.* Oxford: Oneworld (p. 261).

Whilst some liberals (like Rammohun), have understood religious morality as primarily directed at the individual, others (often influenced by Hegel) have understood it in more social and/or political terms. This is true of the nineteenth- and twentieth-century 'social gospel' movement in Christianity and, more recently, of the liberation theology which originated in Latin America in the late 1960s, but which has since become influential in many other parts of the world (in Korea as Minjung Theology, and in India as Dalit Theology, for example). Drawing on a Marxist analysis as well as on liberal ideas of human equality and freedom, liberation theologians argue that religion must be an agent in the liberation of the poor and oppressed (see Levine's description of Liberation Theology in reading **2.39**). In the following extract Farid Esack concludes a book in which he articulates an Islamic version of liberation theology.

What we do know is that our world has become small and the dangers threatening it, multifarious. There is no conspiracy directed specifically against Islam; there are frightening mechanisms available to ensure the destruction of humankind. Humankind, especially the marginalized and oppressed, need each other to confront these dangers and the challenges of liberation. Let us hope that, because of, and not despite, our different creeds and worldviews, we are going to walk this road side by side. Let us hope that we will be able to sort out some of the theological issues whilst we walk the road. If not, then at least we will get another opportunity after we have ensured our survival and that of our home, the earth.

   In the midst of all of this praise of tentativeness and heurism there is a certainty that I embrace. The struggle for justice, gender equality and the re-interpretation of Islam so that it legitimates and inspires a comprehensive embrace of human dignity is one to which I am deeply committed. My own humanity is intrinsically wedded to this struggle in its various forms. While the struggle for gender equality is about justice and human rights for women, it cannot be regarded as a women's struggle any more than the battle against anti-Semitism is a Jewish struggle, or that of non-racialism a struggle belonging to Blacks, or that of religious pluralism one belonging to Western academics. All of us, whether in our offices, bedrooms, kitchens, mosques or boardrooms participate in the shaping of the cultural and religious images and assumptions that oppress or liberate the Other, and thus ourselves.

Theme: optimism

1.43 Young on evolutionary optimism

Robert M. Young, 1970: The Impact of Darwin on Conventional Thought. In Anthony Symondson (ed.), *The Victorian Crisis of Faith. Six Lectures by Robert M. Young, Geoffrey Best, Max Warren, David Newsome, Owen Chadwick, R. C. D. Jasper.* London: SPCK, pp. 13–35 (pp. 27–8).

In the influential essay extracted below, Robert Young argues that far from undermining Christianity, science, particularly evolutionary theory, helped re-shape it and gave it a new confidence in the inevitability of moral, spiritual and social progress, and in human perfectibility.

Having argued that the evolutionary debate produced an adjustment within a basically theistic view of nature rather than a rejection of theism, I now want to go on to say that what evolution took away from man's spiritual hopes by separating science and theology and making God remote from nature's laws, it gave back in the doctrine of material and social and spiritual progress.

Far from justifying the fears of the more conventional objectors to evolution, the authors of the theory were believers in a most compassionate philosophy which absorbed pain and struggle into a sanguine belief in progress which was as optimistic as the most extreme hopes of the faithful. Belief in progress was not new in the nineteenth-century evolutionists, nor did they have a monopoly of it. They yielded to none in their faith, and their version of the doctrine of unlimited progress had the additional support of being guaranteed by the laws of nature. Lyell, an anti-evolutionist until 1869, had said in his first defence of uniformitarian geology, in 1827,

> If there be no attribute which more peculiarly characterizes man than his capability of progressive improvement, our estimate of the import-ance of this progressive power is infinitely enhanced by perceiving what an unlimited field of future observations is unfolded to us by geology, and by its various kindred sciences.

If Lyell could say this on the basis of the new geology, how much more could Spencer say in 1857, on the basis of his own theory of evolution (two years before Darwin's theory was published) that progress was not merely a fact about man. In his essay on 'Progress: Its Law and Cause', he said,

It will be seen that as in each phenomenon of to-day, so from the beginning, the decomposition of every expended force into several forces has been perpetually producing a higher complication; that the increase of heterogeneity so brought about is still going on, and must continue to go on; and that thus Progress is not an accident, not a thing within human control, but a beneficent necessity.

... John Burrow has argued in his excellent work on *Evolution and Society* that this was the main point of embracing evolution: it provided a guarantee of progress, where the utilitarians had only been able to hope that they could engineer it.

1.44 Nehru's religion of progress

Jawaharlal Nehru, 1983: *The Discovery of India.* New Delhi: Oxford University Press (pp. 513–14).

Though Nehru is often thought of as the founder of secular democracy in India he was much influenced by religion and, as the following extract reveals, retained a residual religiosity. Stripped bare of traditional elements, all that remains of religion for Nehru is faith in progress itself.

Even if God did not exist, it would be necessary to invent Him, so Voltaire said – 'si Dieu n'existait pas, il faudrait l'inventer.' Perhaps that is true, and indeed the mind of man has always been trying to fashion some such mental image or conception which grew with the mind's growth. But there is something also in the reverse proposition: even if God exists, it may be desirable not to look up to Him or to rely upon Him. Too much dependence on supernatural factors may lead, and has often led, to a loss of self-reliance in man and to a blunting of his capacity and creative ability. And yet some faith seems necessary in things of the spirit which are beyond the scope of our physical world, some reliance on moral, spiritual, and idealistic conceptions, or else we have no anchorage, no objectives or purpose in life. Whether we believe in God or not, it is impossible not to believe in something, whether we call it a creative life-giving force or vital energy inherent in matter which gives it its capacity for self-movement and change and growth, or by some other name, something that is as real, though elusive, as life is real when contrasted with death. Whether we are conscious of it or not most of us worship

at the invisible altar of some unknown god and offer sacrifices to it
– some ideal, personal, national or international; some distant objective that draws us on, though reason itself may find little substance
in it; some vague conception of a perfect man and a better world.
Perfection may be impossible of attainment, but the demon in us,
some vital force, urges us on and we tread that path from generation
to generation.

Religions of Humanity: explanations

Explanation: capitulation or accommodation to secular culture

1.45   Berger: 'an immense bargaining process with secular thought'

Peter L. Berger, 1980: *The Heretical Imperative. Contemporary Possibilities of Religious Affirmation.*
London: Collins (pp. 158–9).

Several of the readings above indicate that religions of humanity are closely
entwined with modern culture, not least with the turn to 'the human' as a key
conceptual and evaulative category. Equally, they are influenced by the rise of
science – by scientific method and discoveries. Thus religions of humanity may
be understood as the religious dimension of developments in secular culture.
One extreme version of this explanation views such religions as nothing more
than a capitulation to modern secular culture, as the following account of modern
liberal Protestant theology by Peter Berger illustrates. As in Berger's case, this
explanation of liberal religion is often favoured by critics of such religion, particularly those who favour religions of difference. (See also readings on the 'turn
to the self' in the chapter on Detraditionalization in **Part Three**, and the readings
on the development of the ethic of humanity in the chapter on Universalization
in **Part Three**.)

This defensive attitude ('apologetic' in the modern sense of the word,
as against the classical meaning of 'apologetics' in the church) continued as a crucial characteristic of the 'liberal century' that followed
Schleiermacher in Protestant theology. This theology can, indeed, be
described as an immense bargaining process with secular thought –
'We'll give you the miracles of Jesus, but we'll keep his ethics'; 'You
can have the virgin birth, but we'll hold on to the resurrection'; and
so on. Figures like Kierkegaard, who were unwilling to follow these

lines, remained marginal to the theological situation and only came into their own after the end of the 'Schleiermachian era.'

We cannot possibly try to discuss the development of Protestant liberal theology in its (often fascinating) historical details. We would only point to what, pretty much beyond doubt, can be regarded as the infrastructural foundation of Protestant liberalism – the period of capitalist triumphs in economy and technology, of Western expansion, and of bourgeois cultural dominance – in sum, the 'golden age' of bourgeois capitalism. This was a period of profound confidence in the cultural, political, and economic values of Western civilization, a confidence fully reflected in the optimistic *Weltanschauung* of Protestant liberalism. The compromises of the theologian, consequently, were not negotiated under duress, but in the confrontation with a secular culture deemed eminently attractive and praiseworthy, not just materially but in its values. Put crudely, it paid to sell out on certain features of the tradition. It should not surprise us that the dominance of Protestant liberalism coincided with the period during which this bourgeois world retained its attractiveness and, indeed, its credibility.

Explanation: the cultural logic of Protestanism

1.46   Troeltsch: Luther as the founder of religious subjectivism

Ernst Troeltsch, 1966: *Protestantism and Progress. A Historical Study of the Relation of Protestantism to the Modern World*. Boston: Beacon Press (pp. 192–7).

Ernst Troeltsch understood the rise of non-dogmatic, subjectivist forms of Christianity as the outgrowth of developments inadvertantly set in train by the Reformer Martin Luther (1483–1546) when he made subjective conviction of faith more central to salvation than the external authorities of the Christian church.

If to the Catholic it was precisely the external authority and the substantiality of grace which seemed to guarantee salvation, for Luther's feeling it was just that authority which was uncertain and alien, and that substantiality which was unintelligible and elusive. He needed for the personal life something purely personal. The means was therefore faith, *sola fides*, the affirmation, by the complete surrender of the soul to it, of that thought of God which has been made clear and intelligible to us in Christ. The assurance of salvation must be based on a miracle in order to be certain; but this miracle must be one occurring in the inmost centre of the personal life, and must be clearly intelligible in its whole intellectual significance if it is to be a miracle which guarantees complete assurance. Religion is completely transferred from the sphere of the substantial sacramental communication of grace, and of ecclesiastical, sacerdotal authority, to the psychologically intelligible sphere of the affirmation of a thought of God and of God's grace, and all the ethico-religious effects arise with psychological clearness and obviousness from this central thought. The sensuous sacramental miracle is done away with, and in its stead appears the miracle of thought, that man in his sin and weakness can grasp and confidently assent to such a thought. That is the end of priesthood and hierarchy, the sacramental communication of ethico-religious powers after the manner of a sensible substance, and the ascetic withdrawal from the world, with its special merits.

In all this Luther's sole object was the attainment of complete assurance of grace, which for him, while he followed the way of merit and the monastic life, of sacraments and sacerdotal authority, had threatened to become ever more alien and external, more human and conditional, and therefore more uncertain. The goal was the same as before, but the way to it was entirely new. But with this set of ideas it happened as it often does happen – that the new way to the old goal became more important than the goal itself; from that which was at first a new means there developed a new end and a new association of ideas. When, with the growth of Confessional wrangling, the tyranny of authoritative dogma became unbearable, and consequently dogma itself suspect, the centre of gravity was shifted from the doctrine of salvation and justification, which was closely bound up with the main Trinitarian and Christological doctrines, to personal subjective conviction, to the emotional experience of a sense of sin and of peace of heart. That, however, gave free scope for the establishment of the idea of faith on a purely subjective inward foundation, and consequently also for the possibility of its taking various forms not bound up with any official dogma. The Bible became, instead of the infallible rule of faith, a spiritual entity and power of a more fluid character, a witness to historical facts from which psychologically mediated religious energies streamed forth.

Explanation: detraditionalization and the flight from authority

1.47   McLeod: Freemasonry and social change

Hugh McLeod, 1981: *Religion and the People of Western Europe 1789–1970*. Oxford and New
York: Oxford University Press (p. 44).

It is possible to explain the rise of religions of humanity in modern times as due
to their congruence with modern liberal values like freedom and equality and their
easy alliance with the forces of democratization. Such religions can be seen as
anti-elitist: as the natural home for those who opposed 'traditional' religion because
of their alienation from the clerical, social, political or cultural elites supported
by such religion. Thus, for example, the religion of humanity espoused by liberal
feminist theologians like Rosemary Radford Ruether in reading **1.40** above can be
understood as a reaction by women against patriarchal forms of religion. Likewise,
the liberal Hinduism discussed by David Kopf in reading **1.32** can be understood as the reaction of a new educated Indian middle class against brahminical
(Indian priestly) control of Hinduism – as well as against racially and culturally
exclusive forms of an imperialist Christianity. Religions of humanity are thus fed
by a typically modern suspicion of exclusivistic authority and of external structures and institutions which is considered in **Part Three** in the chapter on
'Detraditionalization'. Here Hugh McLeod reflects on the political and social
significance of one of the most influential religions of humanity: Freemasonry.

> The cult of reason in 1793 was the first of many attempts to build a
> new religion of humanity on the ruins of the old supernaturalism.
> In practice, though not in original intention, Freemasonry was to
> be among the most important of these. While in Britain it had no spe-
> cial religious or political significance, in many Catholic countries it
> became 'the International of the revolutionary middle classes in their
> struggle against feudal and religious institutions'. Though the masons'
> religious doctrine had little specific content, their emphasis on tolera-
> tion and on morality as the essence of good living, was in itself an
> implicit challenge to the increasingly dogmatic and exclusive Catholic-
> ism of the nineteenth century. Throughout the period of the Third
> Republic in France the influence of the Masonic lodges was quite
> disproportionate to their small membership. From Gambetta to Léon
> Blum probably a majority of the leading figures on the Left were
> masons. Links were closest with the Radicals; but they included many
> Socialists too. The lodges provided a pressure group on behalf of
> republican causes; a rival to the church in its charitable work, and
> even in its rituals and rites of passage; and a means by which repub-
> lican politicians could make contacts and establish their credentials.

Explanation: clerical protest

1.48   Hofstadter: Christian liberalism as social protest by clergy

Richard Hofstadter, 1955: *The Age of Reform*. New York: Vintage Books (pp. 151–2).

Another explanation of the rise of humanitarian religion in modern times (and particularly of liberal Christianity) focuses on the appeal of its social criticism to clergy whose social status has been gradually eroded by forces of modernization. The following extract from the historian Richard Hofstadter offers this explanation, as does Jeffrey Hadden (1969). The latter sees the disjunction between clerical liberalism and lay conservatism as a major factor inhibiting the progress of liberal Christianity.

The clergy were probably the most conspicuous losers from the status revolution. They not only lost ground in all the outward ways, as most middle-class elements did, but were also hard hit in their capacity as moral and intellectual leaders by the considerable secularization that took place in American society and intellectual life in the last three decades of the nineteenth century. On one hand, they were offended and at times antagonized by the attitudes of some of the rich men in their congregations. On the other, they saw the churches losing the support of the working class on a large and ominous scale. Everywhere their judgments seemed to carry less weight. Religion itself seemed less important year by year, and even in their capacity as moral and intellectual leaders of the community the ministers now had to share a place with the scientists and the social scientists. [. . .]

In the light of this situation, it may not be unfair to attribute the turning of the clergy toward reform and social criticism not solely to their disinterested perception of social problems and their earnest desire to improve the world, but also to the fact that as men who were in their own way suffering from the incidence of the status revolution they were able to understand and sympathize with the problems of other disinherited groups. The increasingly vigorous interest in the social gospel, so clearly manifested by the clergy after 1890, was in many respects an attempt to restore through secular leadership some of the spiritual influence and authority and social prestige that clergymen had lost through the upheaval in the system of status and the secularization of society.

Explanation: the quest for human unity

1.49   Seager: religions of humanity as a response to colonial difference

Richard Hughes Seager, 1995: *The World's Parliament of Religions. The East/West Encounter, Chicago, 1893*. Bloomington and Indianapolis: Indiana University Press (pp. 95–7).

As the chapter on Universalization in **Part Three** reveals in more detail, a trend in modern times has been to stress what religions have in common rather than what differentiates them. One of the most effective ways of doing this is by appealing to a common humanity which transcends differences. Obviously this is a strategy that comes naturally to religions of humanity, and one explanation of their success appeals to their ability to invoke the dream of a world united by a single religion and living in peace, and thus able to cope with difference. The success of religions of humanity in ethnically divided India furnishes one example. In the following extract, Richard Hughes Seager discusses another: the way in which eastern delegates to the World's Parliament of Religions held in Chicago in 1893 appropriated western religious liberalism in order to stress their unity with the West and to work towards a more unified and egalitarian global society. They were, of course, reacting against a colonial world which assumed both the difference and inferiority of non-western nations and races. (See also Bonney, reading **3.58**.)

The Parliament was meant to be a marker of progress into modernity, and given its delegations from around the world, its natural setting is the universal history of the modern period. Several broad developments help to set the East/West encounter in this important perspective.

One is 'the onset of global cosmopolitanism,' the spread of intellectual, political, and cultural values with European roots to many quarters of the globe. This process was irreversible by the mid-nineteenth century, when the traditional societies of Asia proved unable to stave off the West's military and industrial economy. Liberal ideals, democratic values, nationalism, individualism, and the critical spirit followed in the wake of trade and flag and began to transform Asian religions and societies, just as they were transforming the religions and societies of the West, in many ways. The global dissemination of a stock of general ideas and sentiments in the decades before the Parliament meant that a similarity of outlook existed among many delegates, despite the fact that their religious worldviews were formed in very different cultures and their aspirations were often expressed in incompatible theologies and philosophies. Yet, liberal ideals such as egalitarianism, the authority of science, the inspirational qualities of religion, universalistic ambitions and aspirations, and toleration were common property, which helped in ways unexpected by many in the West to level the playing field on which the contest between East and West was played. [. . .]

The Asian at the Parliament set out to accomplish a number of things – to check Christian missionaries, counter western aggression, assert the integrity of their own religious traditions, and gain public support for their objectives. Leading Asian delegates also answered the call sent out by the Department of Religion to forge a common religious discourse for an emerging global society. Their contribution to the liberal quest for unity was decisive because, as the drive for unity arose on the side of the West, it found complements, albeit cast in alien terms and unauthorized theologies, among delegates from the East. The liberal inclusivism of Howe, Hirsch's vision of a coming religion, and the virtuosi performances by liberals like Rexford and Boardman, with their eclectic, free-form theologies, were mirrored by the equally compelling and dramatic visions of modern Asian inclusivities. The end result was the apparent creation of a global religious discourse forged in the ambiguous realm of religious ideas in the interstices of the great religions of the world. The Parliament, many could reasonably think, had accomplished its stated goals by becoming the harbinger of a global community of religious sentiment for the twentieth century.

Religions of Humanity: prospects

1.50   Roof and McKinney: declining numbers, steady influence

Wade Clark Roof and William McKinney, 1987: *American Mainline Religion. Its Changing Shape and Future*. New Brunswick and London: Rutgers University Press (pp. 86–7).

As Wade Clark Roof and William McKinney point out in their study of American mainline religion, it is the liberal Christian denominations which have declined fastest since the 1960s (see reading **1.26**). Yet this decline in numbers can mask the continuing influence of liberal Protestantism in American cultural life: does decline in churchgoing mask the fact that religions of humanity are still a potent cultural and religious influence?

Declines in institutional membership and support and a diminished influence since the 1960s point to a significant loss of vitality, more so for this sector of American religion than for any other. The self-confidence and aggressiveness with which they once engaged the culture is now missing. Optimism about the country and democratic faith, and belief that American progress and prosperity are linked with the work of God in history – once marks of liberal theology – have all faded. Commitment to social action has remained important, yet not without exacting a spiritual price; concerns for personal faith and the cure of souls are judged by many to be neglected in the pursuit of other causes. Having made more accommodations to modernity than any other major religious tradition, liberal Protestantism shows many signs of tired blood: levels of orthodox belief are low, doubt and uncertainty in matters of faith common, knowledge of the Scriptures exceedingly low. A loss of morale and mission shows up in both its public demeanor and its corporate life.

Congregational life has especially suffered, considering that the corrosive acids of modern individualism have taken a greater toll on the liberal churches than on any others. Twenty years ago Stark and Glock pointed to the weakness of socioreligious group bonds in these churches. They concluded that the liberal churches were 'religious audiences' rather than communities – a description even more true now than when they wrote. Levels of church attendance for liberal Protestants are well below average: 39 per cent attend regularly, 24 per cent attend occasionally, and 37 per cent attend less often than once or twice a year. Episcopalians attend less than Presbyterians or United Church of Christ members. Liberal Protestants have weaker denominational loyalties and are less likely to be members of church-related groups. Drawing off upper-middle-class constituencies, their clienteles are the most exposed to the currents of modern individualism and the pursuits of self-fulfillment. Boundaries between the religious community and the larger culture are often vague, and commitment to the church as a gathered community of believers in which faith is shaped and nurtured is noticeably lacking.

Liberal Protestantism's cultural influence is greater than its lack of religious vitality suggests. Known for its close ties historically with the northern and eastern establishment, it still is a power and presence of some significance though less so than in the first part of the twentieth century. Persons within this tradition are disproportionately represented among the nation's civic and corporate elite. Kit and Frederica Konolige's description of Episcopalians is fitting: 'the wealthiest, most eastern, best educated, and most highly placed professionally of any Christian denomination in the United States.' Politically the power of liberal Protestants continues to be fairly strong despite the gradual erosion of WASP influence throughout this century: all three religious groups have far more members in the U.S. Senate and House of Representatives than would be expected based on their aggregate sizes. Relatively speaking, the old-line liberal Protestant community accounts for slightly less than 10 percent of the American population. Membership rolls at present show the Episcopal Church numbering about 2.8 million, the recently reunited Presbyterian Church (U.S.A.) slightly more than 3 million, and the United Church of Christ 1.7 million.

1.51   Bruce: liberalism cannot sustain itself

Steve Bruce, 1990: *A House Divided. Protestantism, Schism, and Secularisation*. London and New York: Routledge (pp. 152–3).

The assumption that the decline of religions of humanity will be faster than that of religions of difference is widespread in the sociology of religion. As the previous reading by Roof and McKinney illustrates, it is often bound up with the belief that both its doctrines and social bonds are weak. Here Steve Bruce offers a version of this argument. He takes issue with Stark and Bainbridge, who argue that the decline of religions of humanity is due to their inability to satisfy fundamental human needs and desires. His alternative explanation is that such religions (in particular liberal Christianity) are well able to meet these needs, but are so close to the culture that they are unable to sustain an independent identity. This is the other side of Berger and Kelley's argument about why religions of difference flourish – because their clear and common doctrines undergird their separated communities, and their separate existence makes beliefs more plausible (see readings **1.24** and **3.94**). Bruce in effect runs the argument the other way: because religions of humanity do not have such clear creeds or demarcated boundaries they are unable to sustain themselves. It is also possible to take the premises of this argument and reach a completely opposite conclusion. In **Part Three** we see that the most important trends of religion in modern times include detraditionalization, privatization, and universalization. The fact that religions of humanity typify all these trends may equally suggest that they will not disappear into the wider culture, but that they are well adapted to modern times, and that their chances of survival are enhanced thereby.

The reasons for the decline of liberal Protestantism can be stated briefly. In their various ways, Stark and Bainbridge, Kelley, and others have explained the weakness of liberal Protestantism as a result of its failure to satisfy the customers. The contentious compensator notion of Stark and Bainbridge can be replaced with the observation that liberal Protestantism demands very little from its adherents and offers little in return. The problem with comparing the rewards and costs of different belief-systems is that it is not the objective outsider's evaluation which explains whether such belief-systems are maintained: it is the views of believers and potential believers which are important. While I take the view that conservative Protestantism is both more demanding and more satisfying, I am an outsider. Given the ability of one culture to maintain beliefs which another finds fanciful, it is dangerous to suppose that liberal Protestantism is intrinsically unsatisfying (independently of the believers showing us, by their actions, that this is the case). Hence there is a need for caution in attributing the decline of liberalism to its failure to satisfy fundamental needs and desires.

It is possible that Stark and Bainbridge and others have missed an alternative explanation of the decline of liberalism: that it is too successful. Those liberals who feel satisfied with the belief-system are likely to maintain and perhaps exaggerate, but certainly transmit to their children, the liberal ethos, with its tolerance, its implicit universalism, and its faith in the social gospel and in vaguely moral behaviour. In the end, the extreme liberal has no reason to remain active in a liberal Protestant denomination. In the absence of a large increase in the support for conservative Protestantism, the decline of liberal Protestantism suggests that, far from having failed, it has done its job so well that those who accepted it feel no further need for it.

1.52   Roof: evolution of liberalism

Wade Clark Roof, 1978: *Community and Commitment. Religious Plausibility in a Liberal Protestant Church*. New York: Elsevier (pp. 215–17).

Despite the impression that may have been given by the previous readings, not all those who observe religions of humanity discern or predict decline. In reading **1.33** above Nancy Ammerman finds liberalism to be flourishing in contemporary American congregations. Likewise James Davison Hunter discerns and predicts the inevitable liberalization of religions of difference worldwide as the forces of secular modernity take hold (see reading **1.27**). Though he is less positive about the strength of liberalism than either Ammerman or Hunter,

Wade Clark Roof does not assume that the demise of religions of humanity is inevitable. In the following reading he offers four predictions concerning such religion in the USA, focusing on future transformation as well as decline. One of his predictions is that such religion may become *less* liberal and more differentiated as it attains minority status.

We offer four predictions concerning liberal Protestantism:

1. *These churches may experience even further declines in the years ahead, but they should persist indefinitely as cognitive-minority institutions.* Despite whatever new surges of life may come from the recent evangelical revival in some quarters, this will not likely alter trends in liberal church decline. At some point in the foreseeable future, however, the declines should stabilize as the churches adapt themselves to new social realities and concern themselves with preserving their theological heritage. Though they are likely to function increasingly as cognitive-minority institutions; this need not imply a sectarian conception of the church necessarily. Given their theological heritage and middle-class clientele it is doubtful these institutions would become anything like sects in the classical meaning of the term. More likely is the possibility that groups of highly committed traditionalists within the churches will come to resemble *ecclesiolae* – that is, small bands of strict and faithful believers amidst a larger congregation of casual, lukewarm members. The imagery of *ecclesiolae in ecclesia* (little churches within the church) is suggestive. It points to a situation not only of high levels of traditional commitment on the part of some, but to the institutionalization of alternative levels of commitment within the church.

2. *Among committed members, communal ties should strengthen.* A growing Protestant minority consciousness will encourage within-group relations such as closer friendship patterns, organizational participation, and shared activities. Many members will begin to appreciate more deeply their relations with fellow believers and to discover common bonds with one another. As this happens, local community ties should increasingly overlap with the religious, thus serving to mutually reinforce one another and to provide a firm plausibility structure for traditional believers.

3. *As the active members of these churches become more traditional in outlook, they will likely espouse more conservative and provincial cultural attitudes.* Increasing proportions of traditional, locally oriented members will encourage a culturally conservative and defensive posture. As a result there could be growing signs among rank-and-file members of

intergroup prejudice, intolerance, and other forms of closed-mindedness. If this happens it will follow, of course, not from theology or even from the churches as such, but from the intensification of commitment to traditional values and ideology. Accordingly, the stance toward the church's role in public affairs will likely lean on the side of retreat and withdrawal rather than active involvement.

4. *Even though religious and cultural homogeneity may increase, liberal churches will continue as conflict-ridden institutions.* There are several reasons for thinking that conflict is endemic to these institutions. Because of their theological heritage and established social position, they draw into their ranks many who are disillusioned with other denominations and who seek a more relevant faith. This should continue as an attraction, though perhaps less so in the future as the churches become more conservative in character. Nonetheless, the cosmopolitan outlook on the part of many will continue to encourage the search for meaning as well as a liberal social ethic. Modern, secular influences will also continue to prompt reformulations of belief and to undermine traditional ways of believing. Ironically, these modernizing influences result in stronger instrinsic commitments to religious values but at the same time undercut commitment to the church as an institution. The churches are left with conservatives as their most active participants, but even so the potential for conflict is always present – as, for example, with controversies currently over abortion, homosexuality, and women's ordination. Both the clergy and progressive-minded laity are committed to liberal concerns, and hence conflicts are likely to surface whenever passions run high in the society and polarizations develop over issues of great importance.

These, then, are our predictions. Whether they prove to be correct or not, the fact is that liberal Protestantism's future will continue in the years ahead as a topic of considerable importance, and one that is closely linked to the American future. To a considerable extent, the future of this religious tradition depends on how successfully the churches can retain, and capitalize upon, a distinctive theological heritage in a time when the winds of change are blowing in a more conservative direction. If they can do this, there is the possibility of forging a new cultural synthesis attractive to larger segments of contemporary society, which might perhaps disprove our predictions. But if they cannot, the future as we have described it may be upon us sooner than we realize.

1.53 Gaustad: religions of humanity undermined by the collapse of modernist assumptions

Edwin Scott Gaustad, 1982: Did the Fundamentalists Win? In Mary Douglas, Steven Tipton (eds), *Religion and America. Spiritual Life in a Secular Age.* Boston: Beacon Press, pp. 169–78 (pp. 176–7).

It is often argued that religions of humanity have declined in modern times because they allied themselves too closely with late nineteenth-/early twentieth-century assumptions about the goodness of humanity, the inevitability of progress, and (in the case of American liberalism) the superiority of WASP (White Anglo-Saxon Protestant) culture. As Gaustad suggests in the following passage, the questioning of these assumptions in the post-war period would seem to lead to the decline of religions of humanity – unless they can reinvent themselves. The increasing weight afforded a 'postmodern' critique of modernity has made Gaustad's points even more pertinent, since many of the elements of modernity which are attacked are central to religions of humanity. To give the most obvious example: postmodernism attacks talk about humanity as 'essentializing', and substitutes deconstructive readings of the self. (See the chapter on Difference in **Part Two.**)

In the 1970s the accumulation of guilt grew too heavy to bear. Much was wrong with American society; much was unlovely in the American past. Had Protestantism been so closely identified with the nation's culture, so involved in its major moral decisions, that all ills and hypocrisies could properly be charged to its account? The treatment of the Indian, the development of slavery, the exploitation of the environment, the inequities of class, race, and gender, the nativism and the anti-Semitism, the moralism and 'social control,' the imperialism and colonialism – were all these integral parts of that Protestant empire once envisioned? WASP had become a four-letter word, and liberal Protestant leaders were obliged to admit that they were indeed mostly white, mostly Anglo-Saxon (or Teutonic, if that helped at all), and indubitably Protestant. They were also mostly male and middle class. Even in the midst of civil rights efforts on behalf of the blacks, 'White Christian Churches . . . and All Other Racist Institutions' were assaulted in 1969 by a black manifesto that demanded repentance and reparation. The WASP-ness of liberal Protestantism had somehow become akin to the racial and religious attitudes of the Ku Klux Klan. Traditional Protestant morality was dismissed as bourgeois, patronizing, and obsolete. Protestantism's habitual involvement in social and political affairs was characterized as elitist and patriarchal. Its maleness was chauvinistic and exploitative. All that guilt eroded self-confidence and left leadership flaccid.

If and when a liberal Protestant did lift his or her voice in the early 1980s, it was with little assurance that anyone was listening. Such Protestants did not appear to be determining destinies in this world or the next. What in American society would be left undone, what vacuum in private life left unfilled, if liberal Protestantism were suddenly to disappear? Any unfinished business could be quickly polished off by a presidential commission or the community chest.

1.54   Gee: can religions of humanity adapt to marginalization and pluralization?

Peter J. Gee, 1992: The Demise of Liberal Christianity? In Bryan Wilson (ed.), *Religion: Contemporary Issues*. London: Bellew, pp. 135–42 (pp. 141–2).

Taking issue with Berger's assumption that religions of humanity accommodate to modern culture, whilst the more resilient religions of difference resist it (see reading **1.45**), Gee argues that liberal Christianity's willingness to dialogue with contemporary culture is both responsible and typical of traditional Christian practice in previous ages. Gee tends to view liberal Christianity's openness to the wider culture as a strength rather than a weakness; its real weakness, he argues in the following extract, is its reluctance to adjust to a world in which Christianity is no longer hegemonic. In Gee's view it is liberal Christianity's ability to adapt to a more pluralistic world which will determine its future prospects.

As the Christian churches have increasingly become marginal social institutions with diminished social functions, theologians have sought to maintain the intellectual respectability of Christian faith in terms consistent with contemporary culture, so that even if the objective of retaining control over the total society has been lost, it has remained possible for Christians to be part of the mainstream culture while retaining their intellectual integrity.

I am not therefore convinced by arguments put forward by sociologists and others that complex diffuse systems of belief cannot be sustained in the contemporary era. Difficulties certainly face those who attempt to popularize the more sophisticated and abstract intellectualized theologies. But there are many layers of belief in all Christian denominations. A survey of many supposedly 'liberal' congregations would reveal a wide diversity of perspectives from the extreme conservative to the incoherent radical. In reality, liberal Christianity has often been the preserve of intellectuals, and it has always been parasitic upon orthodox 'conservative' Christianity. It emerges whenever religious people encounter secular belief systems and political perspectives and endeavour to achieve some degree of synthesis between them. In so far as they consider it to be necessary, individuals will always be able to construct their own idiosyncratic modes of reconciling their religious commitment with secular philosophies.

But in another respect the prognosis is not so good. However well the churches have adapted institutionally to marginalization and pluralization, they have not done so very effectively at the level of core belief. So much of Christian theology, and this applies even more to 'liberal' theology, was fashioned in a context in which Christian social power and influence could be taken for granted. So, for example, the recommendations of reports like the Church of England's *Faith in the City* are dependent on precisely the types of power and influence that changes in British society are sweeping away. And Christian radicals who feel compelled to apply the insights of their faith to the national and international political scene are increasingly coming up against this problem. Religious change and fragmentation make politicized interpretations of the gospel easier, but there are fewer people ready to be influenced by it. [. . .]

The real challenge facing liberal Christianity will be to find a creative and effective response to marginalization, and the progressive severing of its former effective links to social power. Instead of looking nostalgically for ways to re-create lost social and cultural power, will liberal Christians find new ways to respond to the religious needs of a post-modern culture and the imperatives of their faith? If not, the fate of liberal Christianity may be sealed, in England at least.

1.55 Larson on the continuing influence of the liberal ideal in India

Gerald James Larson, 1995: *India's Agony over Religion*. Albany, New York: State University of New York Press (pp. 201–3).

Most of the predictions made about the future of religions of humanity are made in relation to the West and, in particular, to liberal Christianity. At the close of this section on the prospects of religions of humanity it is worth remembering that such religions continue to exist and, in some cases to flourish, outside the West. In extract **3.70**, for example, Robert Hefner draws attention to the importance of liberal Islam in parts of Southeast Asia. The importance of a religion of humanity in modern India should also be noted. Beginning with reformers like Rammohun Roy (see reading **1.41**) and continuing in the work of Indians like Rabindrananth Tagore (see reading **1.85**), a tolerant, liberal and humanistic rendering of Hinduism has proved highly influential in India and in the development of liberal democracy in that country. It has been utilized by the Congress Party to argue against the forces of religious separatism. Here Larson argues that Gandhi and Nehru also belonged to this tradition, and that it constitutes an 'Indic civil religion' which has helped undergird Indian national unity and political democracy. (See readings **2.41** and **2.42** for definitions of civil religion.) Larson's argument is criticized by Madan (1997) on the grounds that it attributes more unity and influence to this humanistic tradition than actually exists, and that it underestimates its supremicist and anti-pluralist tendencies.

The Gandhian-Nehruvian Neo-Hindu multinational civilisation-state is not just a political or national entity. I am inclined to think that it is also important to realize that it is a religious entity as well, a religious entity that might be called simply the Gandhian-Nehruvian Indic civil religion. In other words, the hybrid discourse of modernity in India is not simply a political idiom wherein such notions as 'secular state,' 'socialism,' 'persistent centrism,' 'non-alignment,' and 'democracy' have a strong Neo-Hindu coloring and provenance. The hybrid discourse of modernity in India is also symptomatic of a new kind of religion. [. . .]

There is, in other words, I wish to argue, a Gandhian-Nehruvian Indic civil religion that exists in India alongside the various particular religious traditions. Its cognitive base or belief system is the loose conglomeration of Neo-Hindu notions and liberal-democratic-cum-socialist ideas already discussed above. Its creation-narrative is partition, as celebrated on Independence Day, 15 August, and its sustaining myth is the fashioning of the all-inclusive Neo-Hindu 'socialist' and 'secular state,' as celebrated on Republic Day, 26 January. Its exemplary prophets are Gandhi and Nehru, and in good Neo-Hindu fashion it recognizes and celebrates with national holidays the founders of all the great religions of the world (Gautama the Buddha, Mahāvīra, Jesus, Muhammad, Guru Nanak, and others) as well as such Hindu figures as Kṛṣṇa, Rāma, and so forth. *Mutatis mutandis*, when Indians speak about their respect for all religions and their 'secular' traditions of tolerance, non-violence, non-attachment (non-alignment), self-reliance, commitment to the life of the nation, abhorence of 'communalism,' and their desire to share the spiritual riches of the Indic heritage with the ('materialist') West, it is not unlike Americans speaking about the

'American way of life' and the 'religion of the Republic' or about America as the promised land and the American people as a chosen people with a special 'mission' in the world. In both instances one is dealing with much more than rhetoric or a political idiom with a religious tint. One is also dealing with the religious idiom of an institutionalized civil religion.

CHAPTER FOUR

spiritualities of life

Introduction

Whereas religions of difference, and – in lesser measure – liberal religions of humanity, hold that the divine ultimately exists over-and-above anything which this world has to offer, spiritualities of life focus on what already lies within the order of things. Teachings and practices dwell on the intrinsic spirituality of the person or the intregral spirituality of the natural order as a whole. Some focus on transforming and healing personal life; others on putting spirituality to practice in connection with environmentalism, the women's movement, education, relationships, community life and responsibilities, and the arts and crafts. There are even those prosperity teachings (discussed in the chapter entitled Economic in **Part Two**) which apply and find the spiritual within the manufactured order of work, commerce, consumerism and manufacture.

Those pursuing the quest within typically adopt a dualistic understanding of what it is to a person. On the one hand, there is that which belongs within, the 'Higher Self' or, simply, 'inner spirituality'; on the other, there is what has been acquired from without, that 'lower self' or 'ego' which has been instilled by way of the institutional, farbricated order. Given its spiritual nature, the former alone provides the basis for the true, perfect, life. (See Tipton, reading **1.2**, on the expressive style of ethical evaluation, where ethicality is taken to be informed by what lies within life.) In contrast, the lower self, formed by institutions such as the family, schools, capitalism or religious traditions, is not to be trusted: it is the product of institutions which themselves are taken to owe a great deal to unenlightened – lower self – operations. Accordingly, those intent on the quest within practice rituals designed to *liberate* themselves from the hold of the unenlightened order, from the limitations of their lower selves.

In relation to time, religions of difference typically draw on the past as containing wisdom for the present; and religions of humanity aim to bring about a better world in the future by way of ethical reform. In contrast to these relationships with the past and the future, religions of life dwell on the here and now. The perfect life is already, inherently, present; the only thing that is necessary is to 'work' with rituals, meditations, 'psychotechnologies' (etc.) in order to make that transformative contact which involves the manifestation of the divinity of life itself. Spiritual *experience* is all that ultimately matters.

Spiritualities of life – or inner spiritualities – are to be found in many parts of the world, most especially in countries practising eastern mystical traditions. As well as introducing such traditions, attention is focused by the readings which follow on 'western' manifestations: on that 'under-current' or 'counter-current' running through the Romanticism of the eighteenth and earlier nineteenth centuries (itself influenced by the East) through movements like Theosophy during the late nineteenth century, to those contemporary renderings know as 'New Age' or 'Paganism/ Neo-Paganism' (for example).

Inner spiritualities typically emphasize the unitary, the 'same', the perennial spirituality which lies at the heart of all religions, indeed the natural order as a whole. The reader may therefore find it useful to draw on what follows by turning to the chapter on Universalization in **Part Three** which elaborates the theme of the diminuation of different creeds and traditions in favour of an emphasis on what is held in common. Another important characteristic of spiritualities of life is associated with the fact that authority is taken to lie within rather than without. The reverse side of the crucial importance attached to one's own, spiritually-informed experience is that those involved do not believe in simply relying on the dictates of tradition. Albeit to varying degrees, spiritualities of life are detraditionalized forms of religiosity. So forcefully do some reject tradition that they may be 'genuinely' post-traditional. (Readers of this volume will find more on this theme in the chapter on Detraditionalization in **Part Three**.)

Whilst spiritualities of life are certainly expanding in many cultures (see chapters on Detraditionalization and Sacralization in **Part Three**), it cannot readily be claimed that they are numerically important enough – in most contexts – to add up to being a major rival to other forms of religiosity. This said, however, it is noteworthy that there are clear signs of developments taking place within religions of difference,

religions of humanity, and, in particular, experiential religions of difference, which point in the direction of spiritualities of life. (See the readings by Miller on a form of experiential religion of difference (**3.34**, **3.87**,
3.97).) What can be thought of as 'the cultural elevation of the self' is
associated with shifts – within many religions – towards those teachings
to do with the immanence of the divine which are exemplifed by
spiritualities of life. (See Detraditionalization in **Part Three**.) It would
be rash to deny that there is a widespread trend towards the 'inner'
and the valorization of 'life'. However, it should be born in mind that
some have argued that spiritualities of life are of little consequence. By
virtue of the fact that such spiritualites emphasize experience, they are
seen as providing a 'product' – namely experiences – for consumers.
Accordingly, they are seen as having little – if any – existential, political
or spiritual significance. (See readings **3.20** to **3.22** in the section on
Seculárization.)

Spiritualities of life might be dismissed as being consumeristic, fashionable and self-indulgent. However, readings elsewhere in this volume raise other possibilities. Thus New Age management trainings
are making a significant impact in the world of 'big' business (see
extracts in the Economic chapter in **Part Two**). Furthermore, and
much more importantly, it should not be forgotten that revolutionary
religious leaders, like Gandhi, have been inspired by this kind of spirituality (see reading **3.64**). Indeed this is the spirituality of many of the
great mystics.

Cognate Terms

New Age, New Age Movement

Perhaps the most frequently encountered term in this area of religious
activity is 'New Age' (or 'The New Age Movement'), a term which has
been used since the nineteenth century, if not before, and which has
become common currency since the 1960s. (One reason for its prevalence
being its adoption by journalists.) This popular term does indeed overlap
with what we are here calling 'spiritualities of life'. However, we do not
favour the term 'New Age' or 'The New Age Movement' in this volume,
not least because many of those involved with the quest within have
come to associate the term with what they take to be consumeristic,
trivial, 'Hollywood spirituality'. It therefore seems better to use a less
emotionally charged term.

Expressive Spirituality

Although not in common usage, the formulation 'expressive spirituality' serves to capture the broader cultural current of which spiritualities of life are but one manifestation. It derives from Charles Taylor's talk of 'Romantic expressivism' (see reading **1.1**), and from Tipton who speaks of the 'expressive style of ethical evaluation' (**1.2**) (see also reading **3.26** by Bellah and associates on 'Sheilaism', and Troeltsch, reading **1.59** on mysticism). Its usefulness is that it draws attention to the great importance attached by those pursuing the inner quest to *freedom* and *self-expression*: to expressing what one truly is; to living life as the expression of one's authentic nature; to affirming oneself as bound up with the natural or authentic order as a whole. It should be noted, however, that the term does not capture the more instrumentalized, utilitarian wing of spiritualities of life. (For discussion of this wing see entries on prosperity religion in the section entitled Economic in **Part Two**.)

Paganism/Neo-Paganism

These terms direct attention to a particular variety of resource drawn upon by some of those involved with the quest within. Pagans or neo-Pagans draw on pre-modern inner spiritualities, associated with such 'ancient traditions' as witchcraft, Celtic/Druidic spirituality, shamanism, and (for pagans in Brazil) the Amerindian. It should be noted, however, that some pagans are polytheistic, and to that extent may have more in common with religions of difference than with spiritualities of life. Likewise, some pagans organize themselves in more differentiated communities that is typical of those pursuing spiritualities of life.

New Religious Movements

The term 'NRMs' became popular in academic discourse after the 1960s because – being relatively imprecise – it can encompass *all* new forms of 'alternative' religion in the 'West'. More strictly defined, however, there are (relatively) few NRMs teaching the inner quest. This is because the authoritative nature of well-organized NRMs means that they do not appeal to those following the inner path, who tend to place considerably more value on 'freedom'. Given this value, it is not surprising that the great bulk of the activities associated with spiritualities of life take the form of (relatively) non-authoritative workshops, events, courses (etc.).

Such new 'spiritual outlets' (nSOS), as they might be called, are very different from the NRM, with its hierarchy, committed membership, exclusivism, and its prescription of determinate steps to be followed in order to obtain enlightenment.

Spiritualities of Life: overviews

1.56   Bloom's portrayal

William Bloom, cited in Michael Perry, 1992: *Gods Within. A Critical Guide to the New Age.* London: SPCK (pp. 33–5).

William Bloom is one of Britain's leading advocates of the inner quest. As well as providing a comprehensive overview of spiritualities of life, this extract serves to draw attention to universalistic or holistic assumptions (that the same reality lies at the heart of all religions) and the importance which is attached to spiritually authoritative 'private experience' (compare with the authority of text and community in religions of difference and that of humanity and reason in religions of humanity). The characteristics of the 'Age' which is experienced as dawning are also introduced.

- All life – all existence – is the manifestation of Spirit, of the Unknowable, of that supreme consciousness known by many different names in many different cultures.
- The purpose and dynamic of all existence is to bring Love, Wisdom, Enlightenment . . . into full manifestation.
- All religions are the expression of this same inner reality.
- All life, as we perceive it with the five human senses or with scientific instruments, is only the outer veil of an invisible, inner and causal reality.
- Similarly, human beings are twofold creatures – with:
    (i)   an outer temporary personality and
    (ii) a multi-dimensional inner being (soul or higher self).
- The outer personality is limited and tends towards materialism.
- The inner being is infinite and tends towards love.
- The purpose of the incarnation of the inner being is to bring the vibrations of the outer personality into a resonance of love.
- All souls in incarnation are free to choose their own spiritual path.
- Our spiritual teachers are those souls who are liberated from the need to incarnate and who express unconditional love, wisdom

and enlightenment. Some of these great beings are well-known and have inspired the world religions. Some are unknown and work invisibly.

- All life, in all its different forms and states, is interconnected energy – and this includes our deeds, feelings and thoughts. We, therefore, work with Spirit and these energies in co-creating our reality.
- Although held in the dynamic of cosmic love, we are jointly responsible for the state of our selves, of our environment and of all life.
- During this period of time, the evolution of the planet and of humanity has reached a point when we are undergoing a fundamental spiritual change in our individual and mass consciousness. This is why we talk of a New Age. This new consciousness is the result of the increasingly successful incarnation of what some people call the energies of cosmic love. This new consciousness demonstrates itself in an instinctive understanding of the sacredness and, in particular, the interconnectedness of all existence.
- This new consciousness and this new understanding of the dynamic interdependence of all life mean that we are currently in the process of evolving a completely new planetary culture.

Essentially the New Age movement is concerned with individual spiritual experience. It is in many ways a liberation movement, seeking to free and to empower the individual's private experience of spiritual realities – freedom from religious dogma and authority, and empowerment in the face of a mainstream intellectual culture which at best patronises and at worst disdains spiritual realities.

New Age culture respects experience. It honours the divine in all life and is filled with enthusiasm for any path or tool that leads to and strengthens people in their experience of the divine. New Age culture believes that we live in an interdependent local and cosmic environment, and that for various reasons humanity as a whole is currently passing through a transformation of consciousness. This transformation is manifest in a new sense of personal divinity and in a new sense of the spiritual interdependence of all existence. This, in turn, is reflected in what is being recognised as a general paradigm shift away from a predictable Newtonian billiard-ball model of life to a more open-ended and intuitively understood model.

1.57   Heelas's portrayal

Paul Heelas, 1996: *The New Age Movement. The Celebration of the Self and the Sacralization of Modernity*. Oxford and Cambridge, Mass.: Blackwell (pp. 28–9).

This brief summary of the main characteristics of spiritualities of life ranges from popular culture (lines from a song by the Waterboys) to a formulation couched in more analytical terms.

New Agers see the person divided into that which belongs to artifices of society and culture and that which belongs to the depths of human nature. Inspired by spiritual disciplines or practices rather than by dogmas, beliefs or codified moralities, participants become aware of what they *are*. A song by the Waterboys, surely one of the best New Age bands in Britain, serves to capture the virtues of this shift:

> Man gets tried/Spirit don't/Man surrenders/Spirit won't/
> Man crawls/Spirit flies/Spirit lives when Man dies.
> Man seems/Spirit is/Man dreams/Spirit lives/
> Man is tethered/Spirit is free/What Spirit is man can be.

More comprehensively, the New Age is a highly optimistic, celebratory, utopian and spiritual form of humanism, many versions . . . also emphasizing the spirituality of the natural order as a whole. Ultimacy – God, the Goddness, the Higher Self – lies within, serving as the source of vitality, creativity, love, tranquility, wisdom, responsibility, power and all those other qualities which are held to comprise the perfect inner life and which, when applied in daily practice (supposedly) ensure that all is utopian. By definition – and recalling Shirley MacLaine's 'It all starts with self' – New Agers universally suppose that it is crucial to 'work' on what it is to be a person. A new *consciousness*, and all that it brings with it, is essential. This alone opens the way to experiencing the spirituality of other people or the natural order; this alone provides the resources for fulfilling the potential of the planet.

And more analytically, as an *internalized* form of religiosity, the New Age is (albeit to varying degrees) *detraditionalized*. That is to say, *autonomy* and *freedom* are highly valued; and *authority* lies with the *experience* of the *Self* or, more broadly, the *natural realm*. This means that New Agers attach great importance to the *Self-ethic*, which includes emphasis on the exercise of *Self-responsibility* and which, more generally, serves as a 'meta-"narrative"' operating at the *experiential* level. Detraditionalization is also associated with the Movement's *perennialized* outlook, namely that the same wisdom can be found at the heart of all religious traditions.

1.58   Anon: 'love yourself'

Anon: 'love yourself' (unpublished Valentine's card).

Without wishing to imply that spiritualities of life are only about the self and one's own life – for a great number strongly emphasize the interfusing spirituality of the natural order as a whole – the fact remains that the celebration of what it is to be alive is an absolutely central pursuit: as this anonymous Valentine's card to one's self illustrates.

> love yourself
>
> for no one
> can be closer
> or share more time
> with you
>
> be patient
> and kind to yourself
>
> value your attributes
> appreciate your gifts
>
> let go of the past
> retaining only
> its wisdom
>
> remain aware
> for you are now
>
> new

1.59   Troeltsch: inner spirituality in historical context

Ernst Troeltsch, 1931: The Social Teaching of the Christian Churches, vol. II. London: George Allen & Unwin; New York: Macmillan (pp. 793–5).

Troeltsch identified the phenomenon we are categorizing as 'spiritualities of life' long before many academic commentators had become aware of its significance.

What he refers to as 'religious Romanticism' has played a crucial role in the maintenance and development of immanentist spirituality in the West. Tracing some of the key themes of what he also calls 'the newer mysticism', Troeltsch is especially interesting on how Christian teachings and practices can be transformed into a form of inner spirituality: Christ coming to be seen as a figure who evokes that 'spark' which belongs to all humans; the church and public worship dropping from sight. (See Hanegraaff (1996) for a comprehensive historical account of spiritualities of life.)

Everyone who has read Schleiermacher's *Discourses* knows that there is clearly proclaimed in them the 'spiritual' idea of a direct revelation of religious feeling, and a mutual understanding of all Spirit-filled men and of all revelations, and that the sociological conclusions are also drawn quite definitely from these ideas: a system of loosely connected groups, varying from time to time, gathered round particularly strong leaders and prophets, serves to unite the faithful in ever new groupings for mutual fellowship, in order to awaken the spiritual consciousness which all possess; the 'spirit' is not tied to the historic Christian community, but, reaching out beyond its borders, it can allow religious feeling, which is in itself everywhere the same, to form ever new concrete groups. The prophets and seers, Christ Himself included, are merely those who arouse and enkindle that spark of direct religious life which is the possession of every human being. [. . .]

The general outlook is determined by the main features of the modern view of the world, and the whole tendency towards inwardness and immediacy is intimately connected with the personality of Schleiermacher. However, whether this is simply an analogy or one which is based on history, the whole idea is very closely related to Protestant mysticism. In Novalis, Moravian Christ-mysticism was also placed within this setting; later on, Schleiermacher developed this idea still farther; here, too, it is, however, a genuine Christ-mysticism, i.e. the view which regards the whole of life as full of a power which is only concretely incarnate in Christ; the Lord's Supper means that the believer is fed with the materialized and concrete Divine Spirit, who indwells the universe; the whole rite is a symbol of the unity between the Spirit and Nature, between the prophet and the community.

This religious Romanticism possessed two most important new features: (1) On the one hand, under the influence of modern conceptions of law and world unity, the dualistic opposition between the flesh and the spirit disappears, and with that the asceticism which was so characteristic of the older Protestant mysticism. Whereas the latter had scarcely reconciled its ascetic Dualism with the idea of Divine Immanence by means of the Neo-Platonic theory of Emanations, and further, within this framework, had made room for the freedom of the creature, the new Protestant mysticism tended absolutely and directly towards Immanence and Determinism. Where this was not the case, freedom is still only the principle of an ascending and victorious evolution, not that of an ascetic and dualistic opposition between the redeemed soul and the flesh which is tainted with sin. Hence the mystical religious philosophy of the present day has a strong affinity with the Pantheistic idea of Immanence, and the ancient idea of the opposition between the flesh and the Spirit is transformed into the idea of progress through the stages of an evolutionary process. (2) The second important change is the coalescence of the fully developed religious 'inwardness' and individuality with the aestheticism of individuality, with the differentiation of the altogether individual artistic feeling. This far transcends the aestheticism of Platonism which still always clings to the universal, of which we hear echoes from time to time in the Christian mysticism of the Ancient World, and which reappeared at the Renaissance. Under the influence of Christian thought and of modern life, this is an extremely differentiated aesthetic of entirely individualistic feeling. With that it is only too easy to combine that whole aesthetic relativism which regards everything as right in its own place, and as contributing to the harmony of the whole. Although Schleiermacher, Novalis, Fichte, Schelling, and Hegel all strenuously opposed this tendency, it has continued to grow and increase down to the present day, combined with the growth of an aesthetic world-outlook, and under the impression of the extreme variety in history. This double combination, however, signifies a most important complement to pure Christian 'inwardness'. Whereas the older mysticism had absorbed the Neo-Platonic doctrine of deification, and natural philosophy, the newer mysticism now drew into itself the modern conception of humanity and aesthetic individualism. This meant that it was now able to play its part in the practical tasks of modern life.

This religious romanticism, together with the aesthetic differentiation and the mysticism which is connected with the philosophical idea of Immanence, is the source of that which the modern German Protestant of the educated classes can really assimilate – his understanding of religion in general. This is the secret religion of the educated classes. Mystical and spiritual literature, therefore, celebrates to-day its resurrection. Lutheranism, in particular, provides a very fertile soil for these ideas, since from the outset Lutheranism had certain affinities with this type of spirituality in its most genuine form. This kind of spirituality meets with far less understanding in Anglo-Saxon countries and among Calvinistic peoples; to them it appears unpractical, anti-social, non-ecclesiastical, and unethical. Yet from the literature of the Emerson group, and in the works of Carlyle – (Carlyle's spirit was, it is true, actively ethical and not aesthetic) – even there (among the Anglo-Saxon peoples) this line of thought had been pursued for a long time: History is a symbol; thought wells forth eternally, only reaching special intensity in the heroes of mankind. Finally the aesthetic spiritual temper entered into English life through Ruskin and his school; this has rightly been described as the end of Puritanism.

The sociological consequences of this fundamental position soon became evident. The religious community – both the Church and the conventicle – had lost all significance. Public worship had become entirely unnecessary, and without any meaning for religion. The historical element had simply become a symbol, a means of stimulus, while some went farther and regarded it with great suspicion. The historical element had almost entirely lost any connection with public worship; instead it had become a theme for scientific treatment, a subject for the free play of the imagination, or a means of stimulating certain moods according to one's own private fancies. Literature, poetry, and the old Philadelphianism, the formation of small groups governed by personal impressions, took the place of the old fellowship in worship, just as Schleiermacher describes in his *Discourses*, only usually with much less earnestness.

In the meantime also the Naturalistic Monism of modern nature philosophers, and Brahmanic and Buddhist ideas, added their quota to this confused mingling of ideas; moreover, all relation to Christian history, and indeed to Christian Personalism in general, was thrown into great confusion, or even into a complete break with the past and passionate opposition to it. But even where this complete severance from the spirit of Christianity had not take place, or had not done so consciously, in these romantic ideas the tendency was to identify Christianity with an entirely personally differentiated and entirely inward spiritual religion.

Spiritualities of Life: themes

Theme: immanence

1.60 Wordsworth and nature

William Wordsworth, 1911: Lines. Composed a Few Miles above Tintern Abbey. (orig. 1798) *Lyrical Ballads* Ed. Thomas Hutchinson. London, New York, Toronto, Melbourne: Oxford University Press, pp. 205–7 (p. 207).

As Troeltsch points out in the extract above, the Romantic movement was an important constitutive ingredient in the development of spiritualities of life. The following famous lines by Wordsworth do not simply evoke the indwelling spirituality of nature and the senses; they also portray this spirituality as the source of 'purest thoughts' and morality. (For more on immanence, holism and nature, see Albanese (1977, 1990).)

> And I have felt
> A presence that disturbs me with the joy
> Of elevated thoughts; a sense sublime
> Of something far more deeply interfused,
> Whose dwelling is the light of setting suns,
> And the round ocean and the living air,
> And the blue sky, and in the mind of man:
> A motion and a spirit, that impels
> All thinking things, all objects of all thought,
> And rolls through all things. Therefore am I still
> A lover of the meadows and the woods,
> And mountains; and of all that we behold
> From this green earth; of all the mighty world
> Of eye, and ear, – both what they half create,
> And what perceive; well pleased to recognise
> In nature and the language of the sense
> The anchor of my purest thoughts, the nurse,
> The guide, the guardian of my heart, and soul
> Of all my moral being.

1.61 Farmer and the Self

Carry Farmer, 1910: How I Discovered the Great Self within the Little Self. *Bibby's Annual* 5 (summer), pp. 40–2 (pp. 40–1).

Earlier this century Bibby's Annual – run out of Liverpool by Theosophical magnate Joseph Bibby – was the foremost New Age 'glossy' of Britain. Influenced, among others, by Annie Besant, Rudolf Steiner and Vivekananda's Yoga Philosophy, Carry Farmer writes of the God that lies within us all, describing what it is to leave the 'little self' – by way of 'contemplation' – to experience 'spirit'.

It is largely by contemplation, by realising that the working power in us is *spirit*, and part of the great life of all, that God is found; we *come into Him*, as it were; we find a God 'Who draws and loves, and does not thunder,' and by meditating upon Him, we can keep near Him, and are safe in Him.

I cannot prove this to another; I have, so to say, *thought* myself into this great truth; found it by *looking inwards*; I know it intuitively; I *feel* it; I am *certain* of it; I have often *proved* this Presence to myself, especially in times of difficulty or danger. It is as if someone said, '*Be still* and *know* that I am God,' and being still, I realise that He is *in* me, and in us all. [. . .]

[The] Union of spirit is indescribable; it is not a state of excitement, of religious frenzy, or wild enthusiasm; but a feeling of intense calm; of *joy*, which no *pleasure* of the *senses* can give, or even be compared with; a feeling of *security*, a something quite as real as eating and drinking. It is not a state of ecstasy which passes away, but a perception of nearness to, and union with power. It brings strength, self-reliance, and takes away fear, and the inclination to 'worry;' the tension ceases, the strain is no more there. This sense of peace, of safety, of entire trust in Something higher than ourselves, the counterpart of which is *in* ourselves, and has been brought into communication with it by our conscious will, our 'Soul's sincere desire,' when once attained, rejuvenates, and gives an ever increasing joy in work, because it is so entirely restful. It must be actually experienced in order to be understood. No one can take it from us, neither can anyone give it to another, however greatly he may desire to do so. Each one must carve out the steps for his own feet, *do his own thinking*, make his own experiments, and discover the depths of his own soul; but there is 'a Divinity which shapes our ends' when we have rough hewn them. [. . .]

Says good George Herbert: –
       'By all means use sometimes to be alone,
       Salute thyself, see what thy soul doth wear,
       Dare to look in thy chest, for 'tis thine own;
       And tumble up and down what thou find'st there.'

1.62 Harding and 'the ultimate in Self-reliance'

Douglas E. Harding, 1986: *On Having No Head. Zen and the Re-Discovery of the Obvious.* London, Boston and Henley: Arkana (pp. 78–9).

When spirituality is taken to lie within the person, the only true, utterly reliable, source of authority becomes one's own spiritually-inspired experience. Organizations, exercising supra-Self authority and failing to recognize that 'we are all perfectly enlightened already', are counter-productive. Such is the argument of Douglas Harding, inspiration of the 'Headless Way'.

For a spiritual movement that's as alive and as distinctive as most others, the Headless Way is remarkably lacking in organization. It resembles the people who take it up in that it, too, is without a head – in the sense that it has no presiding authority, no governing council or headquarters, and no staff looking after a duly card-indexed and paid-up membership who meet regularly and try to follow certain guidelines.

The reason for this absence of structure doesn't lie in any lukewarmness, or reluctance to disseminate the experience this book is about. Rather the reverse. It arises from the nature of that experience itself – as the ultimate in Self-reliance. Or, in more detail, from the fourfold realization that the way really to live is to look in and see Who is doing so, that only you are in a position to see this 'Who', that this in-seeing establishes You as the authority on what matters supremely, and that accordingly your path will not conform to some set pattern laid down from above, by this or any other book or person or system. For example, though none of the eight stages described here can be bypassed, you may well find yourself negotiating the later ones in a different order, and certainly in a manner that's very much your own.

Looked at from outside, as a grouping of self-styled headless characters doing their thing, their apparent anarchy is at once a huge disadvantage (inasmuch as organization is necessary to get things off the ground) and something of an advantage (inasmuch as organizations spawn problems that obscure – if not undermine – those very things they were formed to advance). Looked at from inside, however, this worldly wisdom ceases to apply: our concern here isn't with things but with the No-thing they come from, with the Indefinable that reduces to nonsense all plans to put it on the map and make something of it. Why set up a Group or Faction – which at once splits humanity into us enlightened insiders and those endarkened outsiders – a Faction (if you please!) whose stated aim is to show there's *no* such split, that intrinsically they *are* us, and that we are all perfectly enlightened *already*? The truth is that the Headless Way isn't a way after all, a means of getting somewhere. Everything one's heart could possibly desire is freely given from the very start. This makes it strikingly different from those disciplines and courses which come in progress-ive instalments, with the real goods to be delivered some day: and meanwhile there has to be this Institution to lay down the rules and administer the whole business. Who, anyway, would join a set-up and pay good money to be given – when sufficiently trained – what he sees he already has, in full measure, pressed down and shaken together and running over?

Our overriding purpose, then – which is seeing into and living from Nothingness – is necessarily organization-resistant. [. . .]

But the headless one remains the Only One, and sees itself as the Alone, and faces its Solitariness. At this level there are no others.

Theme: eastern

1.63   Radhakrishnan: '*atmanam viddhi*'

S. Radhakrishnan, 1970: Foreword. In Arthur Osborne, *Ramana Maharshi and the Path of Self-Knowledge*. Bombay: Jaico Publishing House (pp. xi–xii).

Written by a Vice-President of the Republic of India, this extract could equally well have been written by a proponent of the 'New Age' in the West. Indian teachings and practices, of a powerfully detraditionalizing variety, have had a profound influence on cognate developments elsewhere.

We are given here a religion of the spirit which enables us to liberate ourselves from dogmas and superstitions, rituals and ceremonies and live as free spirits. The essence of all religion is an inner personal experience, an individual relationship with the Divine. It is not wor-ship so much as a quest. It is a way of becoming, of liberation.

The well-known Greek aphorism 'Know thyself' is akin to the Upanisad precept *atmanam viddhi*, know the self. By a process of abstraction we get behind the layers of body, mind and intellect and reach the Universal Self, 'the true light which lighteth every man that cometh into the world'. 'To attain the Good, we must ascend to the highest state and fixing our gaze thereon, lay aside the garments we donned when descending here below; just as, in the Mysteries, those who are admitted to penetrate into the inner recesses of the sanctuary, after having purified themselves, lay aside every garment and advance stark naked.' We sink into the measureless being that is without limitation or determination. It is pure being in which one thing is not opposed to another. There is no being to which the subject opposes himself. He identifies himself with all things and events as they happen. Reality fills the self as it is no longer barred by preferences or aversions, likes or dislikes. These can no more act as a distorting medium.

The child is much nearer the vision of the self. We must become as little children before we can enter into the realm of truth. This is why we are required to put aside the sophistication of the learned. The need for being born again is insisted on. It is said that the wisdom of babes is greater than that of scholars.

1.64 Sai Baba: 'bliss'

Sai Baba, cited in Samuel H. Sandweiss, 1975: *Sai Baba The Holy Man . . . and the Psychiatrist.* New Delhi: M. Gulab Singh & Sons (p. 116).

Sai Baba, the most influential of all contemporary Indian gurus, writes of the shift from the dull realm of delusion to what the 'Highest Self' has to offer.

Do not tell me that you do not care for that bliss, that you are satisfied with the delusion and are not willing to undergo the rigors of sleeplessness. Your basic nature, believe me, abhors this dull, dreary routine of eating, drinking and sleeping. It seeks something which it knows it has lost – *santhi*, inward contentment. It seeks liberation from bondage to the trivial and the temporary. Everyone craves for it in his heart of hearts. And it is available only in one shop: contemplation of the Highest Self, the basis of all this appearance.

1.65 Burbank's testimony

Luther Burbank, cited in Paramhansa Yogananda, 1969: *Autobiography of a Yogi.* London: Rider and Company (p. 297).

Earlier this century Swami Yogananda made a considerable impact in the West. Here, American scientist Luther Burbank praises the practicality of Yogananda's teaching. Note his emphasis on its 'scientific' credentials. Particularly during the last century and into the twentieth, the claim to be scientific was often made by adherents of inner spirituality, and contrasted with the prescientific and superstitous claims of older religions of difference.

LUTHER BURBANK
SANTA ROSA, CALIFORNIA
U. S. A.

December 22, 1924

I have examined the Yogoda system of Swami Yogananda and in my opinion it is ideal for training and harmonizing man's physical, mental, and spiritual natures. Swami's aim is to establish 'How-to-Live' schools throughout the world, wherein education will not confine itself to intellectual development alone, but also training of the body, will, and feelings.

Through the Yogoda system of physical, mental, and spiritual unfoldment by simple and scientific methods of concentration and meditation, most of the complex problems of life may be solved, and peace and good-will come upon earth. The Swami's idea of right education is plain commonsense, free from all mysticism and non-practicality; otherwise it would not have my approval.

I am glad to have this opportunity of heartily joining with the Swami in his appeal for international schools on the art of living, which, if established, will come as near to bringing the millennium as anything with which I am acquainted.

Luther Burbank

1.66 Herrigel: inner archery

Eugen Herrigel, 1953: *Zen in the Art of Archery*. London: Routledge and Kegan Paul (p. 18).

The Dane Eugen Herrigel spent many years in Japan acquiring the skills of archery. By 'working' at this 'sport' he in fact took himself to be 'working' on himself. Herrigel's book provides a pioneering account of what can be thought of as the 'Self-work ethic'. (For more on the Self-work ethic, see **2.21**, **2.22**.)

Zen Buddhism has struck out on paths which, through methodical immersion in oneself, lead to one's becoming aware, in the deepest ground of the soul, of the unnamable Groundlessness and Quality-lessness – nay more, to one's becoming one with it. And this, with respect to archery and expressed in very tentative and on that account possibly misleading language, means that the spiritual exercises, thanks to which alone the technique of archery becomes an art and, if all goes well, perfects itself as the 'artless art', are mystical exercises, and accordingly archery can in no circumstances mean accomplishing anything outwardly with bow and arrow, but only inwardly, with oneself. Bow and arrow are only a pretext for something that could just as well happen without them, only the way to a goal, not the goal itself, only helps for the last decisive leap.

Theme: women, essentialism and anti-essentialism

1.67 Christ: essential differences

Carol P. Christ, 1992: Why Women Need the Goddess. In Carol P. Christ and Judith Plaskow (eds), *Womanspirit Rising: A Feminist Reader in Religion*. San Francisco, New York and London: Harper & Row, pp. 273–87 (pp. 276; 277; 279; 282; 285; 286).

Among the many practical applications to which inner spirituality has been put, one of the most significant concerns gender. Following the first wave of 'gender-blind' feminism, where spirituality was put to work to affirm the essential 'same-ness' of all who are human, the second wave (developing with the 1960s) has responded to patriarchy in religions of difference (in particular) by deploying spirituality to affirm essential difference. Carol Christ is a leading figure of this development, stressing the uniqueness of women *qua* women. (For more on religion and gender see the chapter on Difference in **Part Two**.)

I will discuss four aspects of Goddess symbolism here: the Goddess as affirmation of female power, the female body, the female will, and women's bonds and heritage. [...]

The simplest and most basic meaning of the symbol of Goddess is the acknowledgement of the legitimacy of female power as a beneficient and independent power. A woman who echoes Ntosake Shange's dramatic statement, 'I found God in myself and I loved her fiercely,' is saying 'Female power is strong and creative.' She is saying that the divine principle, the saving and sustaining power, is in herself, that she will no longer look to men or male figures as saviors. [...]

A second important implication of the Goddess symbol for women is the affirmation of the female body and the life cycle expressed in it. Because of women's unique position as menstruants, birthgivers, and those who have traditionally cared for the young and the dying, women's connection to the body, nature, and this world has been obvious. [...]

A third important implication of the Goddess symbol for women is the positive valuation of will in a Goddess-centered ritual, especially in Goddess-centered ritual magic and spellcasting in womanspirit and feminist witchcraft circles. The basic notion behind ritual magic and spellcasting is energy as power. Here the Goddess is a center or focus of power and energy; she is the personification of the energy that flows between beings in the natural and human worlds. In Goddess circles, energy is raised by chanting or dancing. [...]

The fourth and final aspect of Goddess symbolism that I will discuss here is the significance of the Goddess for a revaluation of woman's bonds and heritage. As Virginia Woolf has said, 'Chloe liked Olivia,' a statement about a woman's relation to another woman, is a sentence that rarely occurs in fiction. Men have written the stories, and they have written about women almost exclusively in their relations to men. The celebrations of women's bonds to each other, as mothers and daughters, as colleagues and coworkers, as sisters, friends, and lovers, is beginning to occur in the new literature and culture created by women in the women's movement. [...]

The symbol of Goddess has much to offer women who are struggling to be rid of the 'powerful, pervasive, and long-lasting moods and motivations' of devaluation of female power, denigration of the female body, distrust of female will, and denial of the women's bonds and heritage that have been engendered by patriarchal religion. As women struggle to create a new culture in which women's power, bodies, will, and bonds are celebrated, it seems natural that the Goddess would reemerge as symbol of the newfound beauty, strength, and power of women.

1.68 Maeda on spirituality after deconstruction

Donna Maeda, 1977: The Other Woman: Irreducible Alterity in Feminist Thealogies. *Religion* 27 (2): 123–8 (pp. 123–4; 127).

Drawing on writers such as Trinh T. Minh-ha and Gayatri Spivak, Donna Maeda cogently criticizes the essentialized spirituality of the second wave of feminism. It remains unclear, however, as to how inner spirituality can operate with regard to the third wave of postmodern 'thealogies'. What is a Self-spirituality without a foundational self, a gendered spirituality without an essential gender? See also the reading by Starhawk (**2.83**).

Thealogical works of the feminist spirituality movement contain an 'ethical project' which begins with a critique of male-centredness in traditional theologies. Writers such as Mary Daly, Starhawk, Carol Christ and Judith Plaskow criticize the exclusion of women in religious histories, theological concerns and leadership. These writers recognize the relationship of sexism in religion to social powerlessness in the wider patriarchal context. From this ethical orientation, feminist thealogies have reworked religious language and symbolisms to incorporate femaleness into concepts of the sacred. Notions of self, consciousness and empowerment connect the revaluation of the sacredness of female being to broader social transformation. Yet feminist thealogies have also produced exclusions. When founded on essentialist notions of Woman and women's experience, feminist thealogies consider some women's lives to stand for all. In an early critique of Mary Daly's *Gyn/ Ecology: The Metaethics of Radical Feminism*, Audre Lorde rebuked this centering on some women's lives. Daly considered all women to be victims of cross-cultural variations of a misogynistic, sado-ritual syndrome. Lorde pointed out that in examining hatred of women as the source of all oppression, Daly ignored differences in race which place white women in advantaged positions, particularly in the United States.

Feminists have attempted to solve this problem by adding a variety of experiences in order to include more women. Yet women of color continue to criticize the reliance on white women's experience as the core to which 'other' women add nuances. Womanist, Mujerista and

Asian American groups have formed in order to investigate particular histories, cultures and sources of empowerment for thealogical work. Yet attempts to create bridges across differences have failed to discover an adequate response to problems of representation and the continued production of Otherness in feminist studies in religion. As Joan Martin notes, differences within a self as well as the specificities of historical conditions problematize any attempt at such representativeness. What is missing is an interrogation of conditions which create this situation.

Postmodern feminist theories which consider poststructuralist notions of subjectivity can lead to a deeper consideration of this problem. The ethical project of feminist thealogy notes that the male subject cannot represent humanity. Yet while critical of a rationalist, autonomous notion of the subject, feminist thealogies preserve a version of the modernist self, focusing on acquiring such subjectivity for female selves. Rather than examining the historical and social production of the subjectivity, feminist thealogy sustains a notion of coming to Self, a version of female subjecthood centered on a core being, expressive of self and identity. Starhawk's notion of power from within, Daly's Be-ing and Becoming of female Selves, and Christ's grounding of thealogy in women's experience all indicate the call on the subject as the location for transformation.

Postmodern theorists such as Trinh T. Minh-ha and Gayatri Spivak critique this modernist subject and its continued production of Otherness. Alternative subjectivities, eccentric to hegemonic discourse, disrupt and bring to crisis any assumed givenness. These theoretical perspectives point to strategic positionings necessary for sustained critique and change. [. . .]

Trinh [. . .] displaces marginalization along multiple axes of difference, disrupting any fixity or essence in subjectivity. Crossing multiple boundaries of self and other, re-writing the ethnic female subject, dislocates oppositions between otherness and sameness.

Like Trinh, Gayatri Spivak indicts the unified Subject of Western post-Enlightenment theory. Further, she calls into question any totalized discourse which seeks to narrate a unity of description or interpretation. She ruptures any totalized way of interrogating the subject.

Rather than seeking a firm Subject which might gain knowledge about the world, Spivak writes of a continual construction or narrativizing of present social reality. For Spivak, multiple positionalities of the subject disrupt any such construction. Differences between and within persons continually bring each narrativization to crisis. Noting the impossibility of finding one framework from which to articulate the totality, the subject operates from, but also disrupts, provisionally centered positions. Not only is the subject's position disrupted, but so also are multiple narrativizations viewed from that location. [. . .]

In contrast to the modernist autonomous, self-expressive, choosing Subject of knowledge, postmodern feminists espouse an ever-shifting multiple self. Rather than claiming an alternative, coherent stand-point from which to view social reality, as if particular identifiers might explain the views of a coherent Subject, such terms of 'iden-tity' indicate the multiple organized axes of difference which shift under and over the self.

Relying on a coherent Subject, many Western feminist theories reproduce exclusions of those whose lives cross boundaries of differ-ences other than gender. Feminist thealogies much be situated in this context which centers on individualist subjectivity. Feminist thealogical understandings of the situation of women have often reproduced Otherness through attempts to formulate a coherent totality against patriarchal oppression. Postmodern theory points out the partiality of positionings in the ethical project of feminist thealogies. By identify-ing such positionings, feminist thealogians can move beyond 'valuing difference' to an interrogation of what these fixities enact, rather than hoping for an inclusive, totalized narrative of oppression on which to ground practice.

Theme: technology

1.69   Rushkoff and 'technoshamanism'

Douglas Rushkoff, 1994: *Cyberia: Life in the Trenches of Hyperspace*. London: Flamingo (pp. 161–2).

Another development in spiritualities of life – which is surely set to expand from its current experimental basis – concerns the application of technology to the generation of experiences. It might well be said that technology is here replacing tradition. Computerized music, lighting, and images are brought to bear; so, often, are manufactured designer drugs. 'Cyberia', from the title of Rushkoff's book, evokes the 'ancient shaman' and the interconnected web of life – past and present. (See also Rushkoff's novel, *The Ecstasy Club* (1997) on technology, deprogramming, 'breaking through', and higher selves.)

The DJs consider themselves the technoshamans of the evening. Their object is to bring the participants into a technoshamanic trance, much in the way ancient shamans brought members of their tribes into similar states of consciousness. A DJ named Marcus speaks for the group:
    'There's a sequence. You build people up, you take 'em back down. It can be brilliant. Some DJs will get people tweaking into a real animal thing, and others might get into this smooth flow where everyone gets into an equilibrium with each other. But the goal is to hit that magical experience that everyone will talk about afterwards. Between 120 beats a minute and these sounds that the human ear has never heard before, you put them to music and it appeals to some primal level of consciousness.'

1.70   Taylor and 'terminal faith'

Mark C. Taylor 1998: Terminal Faith. In Paul Heelas (ed.) with the assistance of David Martin and Paul Morris, *Religion, Modernity and Postmodernity*. Oxford and Malden, Mass.: Blackwell, pp. 36–54 (pp. 52–3).

Drawing on Freud, Mark C. Taylor provides a more analytical and questioning account of technology and what it is to be divine.

Within this electronic economy, technology is the elixir for which we have always been searching.
    'These things that, by his science and technology,' Freud proceeds to explain, 'man has brought about on earth . . . not only sound like a fairy tale, they are an actual fulfillment of every – or of almost every fairytale wish':

Long ago [man] formed an ideal conception of omnipotence and omniscience, which he embodied in his gods. To these gods he attributed everything that seemed unattainable to his wishes, or that was forbidden to him. One may say, therefore, that these gods were cultural ideals. Today he has come very close to the attainment of this ideal, he has almost become a god himself. . . . Man has, as it were, become a kind of prosthetic God. When he puts on his auxiliary organs he is truly magnificent; but those organs have not grown on to him and they still give him much trouble at times. Nevertheless, he is entitled to console himself with the thought that this development will not come to an end precisely with the year 1930 AD. Further ages will bring with them new and probably unimaginably great advances in this field of civilization and will increase man's likeness to God still more.

The ancient dream of the alchemist is far from over. For those who have terminal faith, to become one with the matrix is to attain immortality by being transformed into the divine. The transformer is the electronic net in which we are already entangled. Freud could not, of course, begin to envision the radical changes that telecommunications would bring by the end of the century. The dream of the New Age is not only omnipotence and omniscience but, perhaps more important, the omnipresence that immortality bestows. 'Telepresence', Howard Rheingold insists, 'is a form of out-of-body-experience'. If carried far enough, sublimation creates a sense of the technological sublime in which even bliss becomes immaterial as the screen and I become one. Reflecting on the implications of the Gulf War, Paul Virilio comments:

> Curiously, telecommunications sets in motion in civil society the prop-
> erties of divinity: ubiquity (being present everywhere at every instant),
> instantaneousness, immediacy, omnivision, omnipresence. Every one of
> us is metamorphosed into a divine being here and there at the same time.

When every where is everywhere, a New Age approaches. Or so it seems.

The end is approaching . . . approaching without arriving from the ever-not-so-distant future. We are counting down or up to the end and the beginning of the new millennium. The New Age that many are proclaiming will, like all the new ages in the past, be repeatedly deferred. This non-arrival does not, however, deprive the New Age of its power. To the contrary, the very impossibility of realizing the end is what lends the apocalyptic imagination its force. Far from destroying faith, infinite deferral creates the distance that creates the time and space for faithful vision. Every faith is, in the final analysis, terminal faith.

Spiritualities of Life: explanations

Explanation: failures of the mainstream and the turn to the self

1.71   Berger, Berger and Kellner and the self as *the* source of significance

Peter Berger, Brigitte Berger and Hansfried Kellner, 1974: *The Homeless Mind. Modernization and Consciousness*. Harmondsworth: Penguin Books (pp. 73–5; 168).

Writing in 1909, Georg Simmel argued that 'The subjectivism of modern personal life . . . is merely the expression of [the fact that] . . . the vast, intricate, sophisticated culture of things, of institutions, of objectified ideas robs the individual of any consistent inner relationship to culture as a whole, and casts him back again on his own resources' (1976, p. 251). The basic idea is that mainstream institutions, not least those of traditional religion, fail to provide meanings and values of existential import. Those afflicted react; are forced to treat themselves, their own experiences, as the primary source of significance. Peter Berger and associates' *The Homeless Mind* provides an excellent account of the cultural dynamics behind the turn to the self and the associated quest for inner depth. Of particular note, 'homelessness' – whether generated by the relativization of social worlds or by the secularization of traditional religion – is 'hard to bear'. It is thus associated with the search for new 'homes' – or 'secondary institutions' – able to cater for self-exploration. And as is noted at various points in *The Homeless Mind* these new homes include mystical religions. (See also **Part Three**, on Detraditionalization, including the entry from Gehlen (**3.41**); Charles Taylor (1989, pp. 499–502) provides an excellent summary of those failures of the mainstream – in particular to do with the 'disengaged instrumental mode of life' (p. 499) taken to be associated with the turn to the self.)

Modern identity is *peculiarly differentiated*. Because of the plurality of social worlds in modern society, the structures of each particular world are experienced as relatively unstable and unreliable. The individual in most pre-modern societies lives in a world that is much more coherent. It therefore appears to him as firm and possibly inevitable. By contrast, the modern individual's experience of a plurality of social worlds relativizes every one of them. Consequently the institutional order undergoes a certain loss of reality. The 'accent of reality' consequently shifts from the objective order of institutions to the realm of subjectivity. Put differently, the individual's experience of himself becomes more real to him than his experience of the objective social world. Therefore, the individual seeks to find his 'foothold' in reality in himself rather than outside himself. One consequence of this is that the individual's subjective reality (what is commonly regarded as his 'psychology') becomes increasingly differentiated, complex – and 'interesting' to himself. Subjectivity acquires previously unconceived 'depths'. [. . .]

Modern identity is *peculiarly individuated*. The individual, the bearer of identity as the *ens realissimum*, quite logically attains a very important place in the hierarchy of values. Individual freedom, individual autonomy and individual rights come to be taken for granted as moral imperatives of fundamental importance, and foremost among these individual rights is the right to plan and fashion one's life as freely as possible. This basic right is elaborately legitimated by a variety of modern ideologies. It is all the more important to see its rootage in fundamental structures of modern society – institutional structures as well as structures of consciousness. [...]

The secularizing effect of pluralization has gone hand in hand with other secularizing forces in modern society. The final consequence of all this can be put very simply (though the simplicity is deceptive): *modern man has suffered from a deepening condition of 'homelessness'*. The correlate of the migratory character of his experience of society and of self has been what might be called a metaphysical loss of 'home'. It goes without saying that this condition is psychologically hard to bear. It has therefore engendered its own nostalgias – nostalgias, that is, for a condition of 'being at home' in society, with oneself and, ultimately, in the universe. [...]

Social life abhors a vacuum, probably for profound anthropological reasons. Human beings are not capable of tolerating the continuous uncertainty (or, if you will, freedom) of existing without institutional supports. Thus the underinstitutionalization of the private sphere has produced new institutional formations. These have been called 'secondary institutions'.

1.72   Tipton on addressing cultural conflict

Steven Tipton, 1983: Making the World Work: Ideas of Social Responsibility in the Human Potential Movement. In Eileen Barker (ed.), *Of Gods and Men. New Religious Movements in the West*. Macon: Mercer Press, pp. 265–282 (p. 281).

Whereas *The Homeless Mind* was specifically written with the '1960s' counter-culture in mind, Steven Tipton explores why people who had been involved with the counter-culture, but who have had to get jobs during the 1970s, should have turned to alternative forms of spirituality. Concentrating on influential movements like est, the argument is that such organizations are able to resolve tensions between counter-cultural values and expectations on the one hand, and work-requirements on the other. By turning to the self, one can truely live in the mainstream whilst handling its failures. A 'cultural contradiction of capitalism' – to use Daniel Bell's (1979) expression – is thereby addressed. (See also entries on the self-work ethic, **2.21** and **2.22**.)

Est's ethic responds to the predicament of 1960s youth strongly exposed to the expressive values of the counterculture and conventional private life, yet now faced with the instrumental demands of adult middle-class social and economic life. Its psychologized reintegration of expressive and utilitarian moral ideas also appeals, with differently felt emphases, to older graduates moved by the same contrary cultural impulse. *Est* defines what is intrinsically valuable in self-expressive categories consonant with countercultural ideals. Then it uses these personally fulfilling and expressive ends to justify the routine work and goal achievement of mainstream public life. 'Work hard and achieve your goals in order to feel alive and natural,' *est* advises in effect. This formula justifies 1960s youth in dropping back into middle-class economic and social life. And it motivates them to lead this life effectively, with an eye to inner satisfaction as well as external success. It also explains these youths' felt difficulty in continuing to be gratified by a countercultural life-style that did not fulfill residual middle-class expectations of social status, material comfort and stability, respectable work, emotional security, or the specifically ethical requirement that one must *deserve* feelings of well-being by virtue of first having achieved certain goals.

Explanation: the expectancies of the self

1.73 Taylor and 'the massive subjective turn of modern culture'

Charles Taylor, 1991: *The Ethics of Authenticity*. Cambridge, Mass. and London: Harvard University Press (pp. 14; 25–7).

Whereas many accounts of the appeal of spiritualities of life emphasize problems with traditional religion and life in the capitalistic mainstream of society, attention can also be drawn to the role played by the assumptions, expectations and values of those seeking 'self-fulfilment'. The argument – developed in readings **1.74** and **1.75** – is that those turning to inner spirituality are drawn from the ranks of those who already have faith in what lies within and who want to pursue their quest further, radicalizing it. In the extract which now follows, Charles Taylor summarizes the ethic of self-fulfilment. He writes of a

form of individualism, whose principle is something like this: everyone has a right to develop their own form of life, grounded on their own sense of what is really important or of value. People are called upon to be true to themselves and to seek their own self-fulfilment. What this consists of, each must, in the last instance, determine for him- or herself. No one else can or should try to dictate its content.

This is a familiar enough position today. It reflects what we could call the individualism of self-fulfilment, which is widespread in our times and has grown particularly strong in Western societies since the 1960s. [. . .]

One way of describing its development [the ethic of authenticity] is to see its starting point in the eighteenth-century notion that human beings are endowed with a moral sense, an intuitive feeling for what is right and wrong. The original point of this doctrine was to combat a rival view, that knowing right and wrong was a matter of calculating consequences, in particular those concerned with divine reward and punishment. The notion was that understanding right and wrong was not a matter of dry calculation, but was anchored in our feelings. Morality has, in a sense, a voice within.

The notion of authenticity develops out of a displacement of the moral accent in this idea. On the original view, the inner voice is important because it tells us what is the right thing to do. Being in touch with our moral feelings would matter here, as a means to the end of acting rightly. What I'm calling the displacement of the moral accent comes about when being in touch takes on independent and crucial moral significance. It comes to be something we have to attain to be true and full human beings.

To see what is new in this, we have to see the analogy to earlier moral views, where being in touch with some source – God, say, or the Idea of the Good – was considered essential to full being. Only now the source we have to connect with is deep in us. This is part of the massive subjective turn of modern culture, a new form of inwardness, in which we come to think of ourselves as beings with inner depths. [. . .]

[Rousseau's] great popularity comes in part from his articulating something that was already happening in the culture. Rousseau frequently presents the issue of morality as that of our following a voice of nature within us. This voice is most often drowned out by the passions induced by our dependence on others, of which the key one is 'amour propre' or pride. Our moral salvation comes from recovering authentic moral contact with ourselves. Rousseau even gives a name to the intimate contact with oneself, more fundamental than any moral view, that is a source of joy and contentment: 'le sentiment de l'existence.'

Rousseau also articulated a closely related idea in a most influential way. This is the notion of what I want to call self-determining freedom. It is the idea that I am free when I decide for myself what concerns me, rather than being shaped by external influences. It is a standard of freedom that obviously goes beyond what has been called negative liberty, where I am free to do what I want without interference by others because that is compatible with my being shaped and influenced by society and its laws of conformity. Self-determining freedom demands that I break the hold of all such external impositions, and decide for myself alone.

1.74 Shils and the 'uncontaminated self'

Edward Shils, 1981: *Tradition*. London and Boston: Faber and Faber (pp. 10–11).

Edward Shils deepens our understanding of those quite widespread cultural values and assumptions which – being 'quasi-secular' versions of the quest within – prime people to value the importance of seeking out deeper experiences of the 'really' significant in the here and now.

There is another, perhaps deeper, movement of the mind which, in the past century, has been inimical to the acceptance of what is offered by tradition. This is the metaphysical dread of being encumbered by something alien to oneself. There is a belief, corresponding to a feeling, that within each human being there is an individuality, lying in potentiality, which seeks an occasion for realization but is held in the toils of the rules, beliefs, and roles which society imposes. In a more popular, or vulgar, recent form, the concern 'to establish one's identity,' 'to discover oneself,' or 'to find out who one really is' has come to be regarded as a first obligation of the individual. Some writers on undergraduate education in the United States say that a college is a place where young persons can 'find out who they really are.' They suggest that the real state of the self is very different from the acquired baggage which institutions like families, schools, and universities impose. To be 'true to oneself' means, they imply, discovering what is contained in the uncontaminated self, the self which has been freed from the encumbrance of accumulated knowledge, norms, and ideals handed down by previous generations.

   The most recent refinements of the quest for the true self, to be attained not through contemplation but by allowing impulse to come to the surface and to be expressed in experience, may be traced back to the romanticism of the eighteenth and nineteenth centuries. The 'affirmation of life' at the end of the latter century went together with the sense of the unsupportability of 'artificial convention' and of the crippling restraints of Victorian morality. 'The century of the child,' announced by Ellen Key, the breaking of the hold of the super-ego offered by Freudian psychoanalysis, the release of the novelist's imagination from the discipline of the nineteenth-century novel, led by James Joyce, and the gratification of sexual impulses proposed by D. H. Lawrence were all phases of a great campaign of the *Zeitgeist* against the conventions and morals sustained by tradition. The muteness of tradition in the face of rational criticism weakened its position. The breaking of tradition opened the way for individuality to flourish.

There has been another, more recent change in the image of the world which has helped to reduce the weight of tradition. This is the increase in interest about the present. Of course, all human beings have always been concerned about the present state of affairs, their own affairs and conditions included. It could not have been otherwise. Yet the increase of interest in contemporaneity, proximate and remote in space, seems to be connected with a hedonistic concentration on the life-span of the individual and on the events which take place concurrently with it. This might be a consequence of the reduced confidence in personal survival; it might be a function of increased sensibility to sensual pleasures, increased intellectual alertness, and, in more recent decades, the much more profuse perception of contemporary events made possible through literacy and affluence and newspapers, radio, photography, and television.

1.75　Roof and Gesch: baby-boomers and nurturing the self

Wade Clarke Roof and Lyn Gesch, 1995: Boomers and the culture of choice. Changing patterns of work, family, and religion. In Nancy Ammerman and Wade Clark Roof (eds), *Work, Family, and Religion in Contemporary America*. New York and London: Routledge, pp. 61–80 (pp. 72–3).

Earlier in their article, Wade Clarke Roof and Lyn Gesch note that 'phrased in the language of sociology, and in keeping with the long-term Western trend described by numerous theorists, the shift broadly in American culture has been away from religion as collective-expressive toward more individual-expressive forms' (p. 63). This trend is explored in connection with the baby-boom generation, namely those 75 million (or so) people born between 1946 and 1964. Also earlier in their article, the authors report – on the basis of a survey – that some 55 per cent baby boomers are 'family attenders', engaging in religion collectively; and 45 per cent are 'religious individualists', saying that they make their own choices (p. 64). Given that religious individualists, with their faith in their own ability to chose, are the most likely to hold values to do with self-autonomy (of the kind explored in the preceeding two extracts) Roof and Gesch address the question: is the appeal of inner spiritualities associated with those holding expressivist values of a self-fulfilment variety? (See also Roof, 1993; Hammond, 1992.)

Boomers today are characterized generally by two, differing, religious styles, one described simply as 'religious' and the other 'spiritual.' The distinction is very real to members of this generation. To be religious conveys an institutional connotation, prescribed rituals, and established ways of believing; to be spiritual is more personal and experiential, and has to do with the deepest motivations of life for meaning and wholeness. The first is 'official' religion, standardized, and handed down by religious authorities; the second is 'unofficial,' highly individualistic, religion 'à la carte' as Reginald Bibby puts it. To many boomers, the religious and the spiritual have become disjointed, out of sync with one another in a world where institutions often seem cut off from people's inner feelings and experiences. Worse still, just going through the motions of religious involvement, if it is empty of meaning, smacks of hypocrisy to many who have felt estranged from institutions and activities that, in their judgment, lack authenticity and credibility. [. . .]

There is a close linkage between the family attenders and traditional religious styles. Compared with religious individualists, family attenders believe more in God, pray more frequently, are stronger church or synagogue members, and say grace at meals more often. Those who are Christian tend to hold a view of Jesus as a caring Shepherd, and insist that a person should 'stick to a faith' rather than 'explore many differing traditions.' This pattern of conventional beliefs, practices, and views is not surprising, especially the long-standing symbolic significance to family life of prayer and grace at meals.

Religious individualists, on the other hand, favor exploring religious alternatives; and those who are Christians are drawn to images of Jesus as 'liberator' and 'challenger.' Many of them are oriented to social justice causes, which in turn often places them in some conflict with the more conventional institutional belongers. They hold to a more expansive style of religious commitment, open and ready to enlarge their experiences, believing that faith – like life – is best thought of as a journey, a process rather than a finished product. If they relate at all to traditional belief systems and religious communities, it is in a somewhat detached manner, simply because they are less likely to commit themselves to the point of being controlled by any one way of believing. Consequently, many combine Judeo-Christian beliefs with reincarnation, astrology, and other 'New Age' beliefs and practices such as communicating with the dead, exploring psychic powers, and meditating. [...]

One half of the religious individualists holds to a deeply mystical conception of the Deity, and seemingly, a privatized faith largely cut off from, and presumably not dependent upon, organized religion. Though often having little or nothing to do with churches or synagogues, significant numbers of them report belonging to small gatherings, such as Twelve-Step groups, sharing groups, Goddess worship groups, women's groups, and men's groups, that allow them to share their lives and concerns in intimate, and yet often anonymous settings.

Spiritualities of Life: prospects

1.76   Bruce: insignificance

Steve Bruce, 1996: Religion in Britain at the Close of the 20th Century: A Challenge to the Silver Lining Perspective. *Journal of Contemporary Religion* 11 (3): 261–74 (pp. 272–3).

Steve Bruce summarizes evidence which suggests that interest in 'alternative religions' remains 'minute'. (See also Bruce (1995b), especially pp. 117–23.)

Elsewhere, I have considered at length the social significance of the 1970s new religious movements and the more recent New Age spirituality of what Heelas has called the 'self-religions'. Here, I will only observe that, given the millions who have been lost to the churches and, given the decline in the power of the Christian churches to stigmatise alternatives, the number of people who have shown any interest in alternative religions is minute, the commitment of most is slight, the most popular products are those which are most secular, those which have endured longest have become increasingly secular and most are consumed by people as a slight flavouring to their mundane lives. Interesting as they are for many other reasons, our contemporary new religious movements have nothing like the significance for the overall religious climate of, say, 19th century Methodism or 18th century Quakerism.

1.77   Luckmann: significance

Thomas Luckmann, 1990: Shrinking Transcendence, Expanding Religion? *Sociological Analysis* 50 (2): 127–38 (p. 138).

In contrast, Thomas Luckmann is convinced that modern religious themes, of an immanentist variety, have already become 'dominant'. (See also Luckmann in **3.99**.)

To sum up: The span of transcendence is shrinking. Modern religious themes such as 'self-realization,' personal autonomy, and self-expression have become dominant. More recently, they have fused either with the newly emerging mix of pseudo-science and magic or with certain rearticulations of the intermediate and great transcendences in the ecological components of the 'New Age.' The shrinking of transcendence thus does not mean a loss of the 'sacred.' The dominant themes in the modern sacred cosmos bestow something like a sacred status upon the individual himself by articulating his autonomy. As the transcendent social order and the great transcendences cease to be generally significant, matters that are important to the privatized, partly egoistic and hedonistic, partly ecological, symbolically altruistic individual become sacralized. And, of course, the offer of the traditional social constructions of the great transcendences on the part of the traditional universal religions still remains open.

1.78   Inglehart and postmaterialist values

Ronald Inglehart, 1990: *Culture Shift in Advanced Industrial Society*. Princeton: Princeton University Press (pp. 90–1).

The claim that immanentist spiritualities of life are set fair to become the new religion of the west is supported by the argument that the greater the loss of faith in traditional religion and mainstream institutions, and, conversely, the greater the turn to what the self has to offer, the more likely it is that people will adopt teachings and practices of inner spirituality. (See also **Part Three** on Detraditionalization; also reading **1.71** in this section.) Whilst not specifically attending to spirituality, Ronald Inglehart here provides evidence that 'postmaterialist values' – of an expressivist, 'authenticity', self-seeking, indeed *quasi*-sacred variety conducive to the spiritual quest within – have progressively become more significant among age cohorts: and are thus progressively more significant in the cultures under consideration.

[The following table] shows the inter-cohort differences in value priorities within each of the member nations of the European Community, based on the combined data from all surveys carried out from 1970 through 1986. Combining these surveys produces eight large samples of over 20,000 cases each, so that each of the seven cohorts averages nearly 3,000 cases, and three medium-sized samples of from 6,000 to 12,000 cases, with an average of more than 1,000 cases per cohort. The three medium-sized samples are from Greece, which has only been included in the European community since 1981, and from Luxembourg and Northern Ireland, in which relatively small samples of about 300 cases are interviewed in each Euro-Barometer survey. Finally, we also have two smaller samples, of about 2,700 cases each, from Spain and Portugal, respectively (both of which have been in the Community only since 1986). Each sample now displays a pattern almost completely free from anomalies. As we move from younger to older cohorts, the percentage of Materialists rises regularly and monotonically, whereas the percentage of Postmaterialists declines in similar fashion. Among the eleven large or medium-sized samples, we find only one anomaly, in which an older cohort is less Materialist than a younger one; this occurs in Belgium. [. . .]

Distribution of materialist and postmaterialist value types by age cohort in thirteen societies, 1970–86

Birth years of age cohort	Netherlands		West Germany		Great Britain		Denmark		Belgium	
	Mat	PM	Mat	PM	Mat	PM	Mat	PM	Mat	PM
1956–1965	20%	27%	22%	26%	22%	15%	24%	20%	30%	16%
1946–1955	23	23	26	19	27	14	25	19	29	16
1936–1945	26	19	34	12	29	10	32	12	34	12
1926–1935	33	13	41	9	31	9	35	9	37	10
1916–1925	35	12	42	9	35	7	38	6	42	7
1906–1915	42	8	49	6	40	6	46	4	46	5
1880–1905	43	6	53	5	45	4	49	2	51	4
N	(24,197)		(24,401)		(24,336)		(21,142)		(22,569)	

Birth years of age cohort	France		Italy		Repub. of Ireland		Luxem-bourg	
	Mat	PM	Mat	PM	Mat	PM	Mat	PM
1956–1965	26%	20%	30%	14%	31%	11%	22%	22%
1946–1955	28	18	34	13	37	8	28	14
1936–1945	35	14	48	8	44	5	34	9
1926–1935	42	9	51	6	45	5	40	9
1916–1925	46	8	55	4	51	3	42	6
1906–1915	54	4	57	3	53	3	45	5
1880–1905	54	3	58	3	53	3	49	6
N	(26,192)		(26,797)		(20,947)		(6,412)	

Birth years of age cohort	Northern Ireland		Greece		Spain		Portugal	
	Mat	PM	Mat	PM	Mat	PM	Mat	PM
1956–1965	28%	10%	31%	15%	27%	20%	41%	8%
1946–1955	42	5	40	13	40	15	47	4
1936–1945	47	5	49	7	53	6	55	5
1926–1935	48	6	51	6	60	3	60	3
1916–1925	50	5	55	6	62	3	70	2
1906–1915	55	4	60	3	72	2	72	1
1880–1905	56	4	62	4	67	2	74	0
N	(6,019)		(12,216)		(2,690)		(2,728)	

1.79   Heelas: exploring prospects

Paul Heelas, 1996: *The New Age Movement. The Celebration of the Self and the Sacralization of Modernity.* Oxford and Cambridge, Mass.: Blackwell (pp. 119–20).

Distinguishing between 'fully engaged New Agers' (for example, those who make their living by providing New Age practices), 'serious part-timers' (those living in the maintream who on occasion turn to New Age provisions to pursue their spiritual quest) and 'casual part-timers' (who tend to deploy provisions in a consumeristic fashion), Paul Heelas attempts to provide a summary of how far the New Age has developed to date.

It is abundantly clear that there are not many fully-engaged New Agers. Of the remainder, it is impossible to determine how many are serious part-timers and how many casual. It is not simply that the research has not been done; more fundamentally, it is difficult to see how really convincing research could be done. You are highly likely to get misleading replies if you go and ask a participant at a shamanic event (for example) 'are you here to enjoy yourself or because you are a spiritual seeker?' My overall impression, however, gleaned from a whole variety of sources, is that the serious part-timer is considerably more important than the casual variant: at least when it comes to those go along to activities to do with Self-actualization or healing. Certainly people who I have spoken to who run such events are pretty convinced that participants are not just there for the thrills and spills. Very often attracting the more expressivistic of the population – educationalists, people in the caring professions and so on – those concerned are seeking to handle life-crises, restore harmony, or to be more revealed as human beings. And they very often have to participate in quite gruelling and distressing (as well as uplifting) activities.

We can speculate about kinds (or degrees) of involvement with New Age teachings and practices; we can also speculate about how many might be partially New Age, and to what measure; we can attempt to gather statistics concerning numbers 'belonging' to movements or networks. What we cannot do is arrive at a determinate figure for the numbers involved (whatever 'involved' might mean). Thinking of the USA, however, it is safe to say that well in excess of 10 million people currently have *some* contact with what is on supply. But we neither know the total figure, nor the numbers – over the 10 million figure – for whom the contact is, to varying degrees, significant.

This said, we should not neglect the significance of what Talcott Parsons has called 'the expressive revolution'. Talk of a 'revolution' might be exaggerated, Inglehart claiming that only some 10 per cent of the populations of the USA and Britain are clearly expressivist (or 'pure' post-materialists, as he puts it.) But even this percentage means that considerable numbers – by virtue of being expressivist – will be thinking in terms of diluted, relatively secularized versions of the New Age outlook on life. And in some regions – to recall Don Lattin's finding that 62 per cent of those in the Bay area believe in the ideology of human potential – numbers swell to the extent that Luckmann's claim concerning the dominance of themes like 'self-realization' is validated.

1.80 Cupitt: self-spirituality without a self?

Don Cupitt, 1998: *Mysticism After Modernity*. Oxford and Malden, Mass.: Blackwell (pp. 1–3; 8–9; 11).

Whether or not inner spiritualities expand in significance in the future, they face a new challenge. Many academics, especially those of a postmodern persuasion, now claim that the 'self' is an artificial construction of modernity, the product of material interests and power-plays; the wholly cultural and provisional. How is it possible to have a spirituality of an immanentist nature if there is not an essentialized realm of selfhood to inform it? This is the issue addressed by Don Cupitt, who, it will be seen, shifts the focus of his spiritual-cum-'metaphysical' vision from the self to language. (See also Donna Maeda, **1.68**; the volume referred to in what follows is Taylor, 1984.)

To study what is happening to religion after modernity. In the past, all of people's ideas about reality and objectivity – their sense of life's basic *shape* – depended ultimately upon the authority of a deeply ingrained sense of religious law, and proximately upon a framework of shared philosophical assumptions. In modernity these assumptions especially concerned the human subject, consciousness, experience, reason, and language. But in postmodern times they have all broken down. Metaphysical realism has come to an end, and our whole world-view has become very much more pluralized, pragmatic, free-floating, and maintained by continual *bricolage*, or improvisation. In theological terms, this adds up (says Mark C. Taylor, in a very influential book) to the Death of God, the Disappearance of the Self, the End of History, and the Closure of the Book; the end therefore of all forms of realism and supernaturalism; the end of objective Truth, and of all forms of faith in some future and hoped-for totalization of the human world. [. . .]

The next step in clarifying what postmodernity is becoming will be to explain the new postmodern type of religious experience, now becoming available to us. I call this the mysticism of secondariness. It is a form of religious consciousness that actively rejoices in and affirms all the features of the postmodern condition that most shock and alarm the surviving Old Guard of the Enlightenment. [. . .]

The mysticism of secondariness, then, is thoroughgoing and free-floating relativism embraced with rapturous joy. The older 'platonic' kind of mysticism was usually claimed to be *noetic*, – by which I mean that people saw religious experience as a special supernatural way of knowing something Higher that was itself correspondingly supernatural. [. . .]

We give up the idea that mysticism is a special wordless way of intuitively knowing the things of another and higher world. We may discover that we no longer wish to go *beyond*. We do not hunger for 'absolutes,' and we are happy to give up the whole idea of equating blessedness with the gaining of a higher kind of knowledge. It is possible to be completely happy without either absolute knowledge or absolute Reality. The mysticism of secondariness is mysticism *minus* metaphysics, mysticism *minus* any claim to special or privileged knowledge, and mysticism without any other world than this one. We now get – you get, and I get – that feeling of eternal happiness, not by contrast with, but *directly off* everything that is merely relative, secondary, derived, transient, sensuous, and only-skin-deep. We have quite forgotten the old hunger for what is basic, rock-solid, certain, and unchangeable: we are content with fluidity and mortality. We very much like the fact that linguistic meanings are so imprecise, mobile, and constantly shifting, because it makes writing possible. We even like the transitoriness of our values, because it obliges us constantly to be reimagining our values, reaffirming them, and falling in love with them afresh. One of the most important philosophical insights that has precipitated us into postmodernity is the discovery that because we never come to any absolute beginning or last end, nothing is absolute or primary, nor even wholly independent. We are always in the midst of things, and everything is secondary. Everything becomes, and everything passes away. Relativism should not be a bogey to us: it is true, and religiously speaking it is good news. Nothing is substantial, everything is dependent and interrelated: and why not? Why shouldn't we just give up the idea that there's something *wrong* with being secondary and fleeting? [...]

Language goes all the way down; there is no meaningfulness and no cognition prior to language.

CHAPTER FIVE

combinations

Introduction

The three varieties of religion discussed in earlier chapters have a conceptual and historical priority within the map of religion in modern times. As chapter one on mapping cultures shows, they also relate in important ways to wider movements within modern culture, not least to the Enlightenment and Romantic movements. In practice, of course, religions on the ground rarely fall neatly into any one of these categories, but intersect and combine. There is a huge range of possible combinations, each of which is further complicated through interaction with wider political and economic contexts, as we shall see in **Part Two**. In the twentieth century, however, two combinations have become particularly prominent: experiential religions of difference, and experiential religions of humanity.

Experiential religions of difference combine aspects of a religion of difference with features more commonly associated with spiritualities of life. Currently the most notable example is provided by Charismatic Christianity, whose growth and vitality at the end of the century is matched only by resurgent Islam (see Martin, reading **1.84**). Charismatic religion is characterized by its strong stress on the importance of individual experience of God (as Holy Spirit). At the same time, however, it emphasizes the importance and authority of scripture, and of a strict 'Biblical' moral code. As the reading from Bebbington (**1.81**) explains, this combination of Biblicism with an emphasis on the authority of personal experience is part of the Evangelical heritage. Charismatic Christianity grows out of this Evangelical heritage, but intensifies the emphasis on direct, powerful and overwhelming experience in much the same way as spiritualities of life. The latter, however, lack Charismatic Christianity's communal dimensions, and its ability to provide clear norms and structures of living. It seems likely that the success of Charismatic groups often lies precisely in their ability to combine these different elements;

Biblical Pole		**Experiential Pole**
Scriptural Evangelicalism and Fundamentalism (religions of difference)		*Evangelical–Charismatic and Pentecostal (experiential religions of difference)*
Authority of the Bible higher than that of experience	Equal authority of Bible and experience	Authority of Experience higher than that of Bible

The Spectrum of Evangelical–Charismatic Christianity

in reading **1.82** Steven Tipton reflects on a Christian group in California whose ability to thus combine features of a religion of difference with those of religions of life has allowed it to attract many who had previously been associated with counter-cultural movements of the sixties.

The different forms of Evangelical–Charismatic Christianity may distinguished by the ways in which they handle the tension between scripture and experience. Viewed as a spectrum, those which place great authority on scripture may be placed at one end and those which place great authority on experience at the other. In the sector between the middle and the experiential end lie forms of Charismatic Christianity (an experiential religion of difference), with an increasing stress being placed on the importance of experience as one moves from right to left.

Experiential religions of humanity combine elements both of religions of humanity and spiritualities of life. In particular, they combine an emphasis on the authority of individual experience in the religious life with a humanistic ethic. Examples of such religiosity can be found from the nineteenth century onwards. Like Charismatic Christianity, such religiosity is by no means confined to the West, though it is most powerful in areas where both Enlightenment and Romantic culture have had an important influence, as in India. One of the early spokesmen for such religiosity, for example, was the Indian poet and spiritual teacher Rabindranath Tagore (see reading **1.85**). At the end of the twentieth century, that tradition is still carried to the West by spokesmen from Asia such as the Dalai Lama. Experiential liberal religion has also found powerful spokesmen and women in many other of the world's major religions. In Christianity, for example, the tradition of thought deriving from the theologian Paul Tillich is generally characterized by both a humanistic and an experiential emphasis (see reading **1.86** by John Robinson, for example). At a more popular level, Princess Diana and many of her admirers also appear to have been strongly influenced by an emotive and relational form of experiential liberal religion (see Woodhead, reading **1.87**).

A final influential combination in the modern religious field involves not two varieties of religion, but any one of the three varieties and that strand of modern culture which some commentators call 'utilitarian' or 'utilitarian individualism' (see Durkheim and Tipton in readings **1.2** and **1.3**). The result is the multi-faceted phenomenon of 'prosperity religion', which is discussed in chapter 6, Economic. As we shall see, prosperity religion in its many forms is as influential in Africa as in the United States. The so-called 'rationalization' of developed countries has by no means undermined the practice whereby people instrumentalize religion as a means to material, spiritual and physical well-being.

As well as combining in such constructive ways, different varieties of religion may also come together in conflict. Whilst such conflict can be violent, it may nevertheless help shape and define the religiosities which are involved. The most notable example of such conflict in modern times is that between religions of difference on the one hand, and liberal religion and/or spiritualities of life on the other. Such conflict is integral to many of the world's religions: liberal Christianity battles with conservative Christianity; reform Judaism attacks orthodox Judaism; liberal Hinduism opposes the rise of nationalist Hinduism – and so on. In reading **1.89**, Robert Wuthnow argues that contemporary America is divided by a 'great fracture' between cultural conservatives and liberals. This example furnishes a good example of the way in which even those in the most heated conflict can nonetheless be profoundly influenced by one another. Thus Christian conservatives and Christian liberals often construct their identities in opposition to one another, derive energy and impetus from their mutual excoriations, and structure their ideological debates in terms of binary oppositions and polarizations. Equally, such conflict often serves to reify, harden, and make more extreme the forms of religion or culture which do battle. Here conflict and co-creation often go hand in hand.

Not all contradictions between the varieties necessarily result in convergence or conflict, however. It also seems perfectly possible for an individual or a group to maintain two or more different and even contradictory styles of religious belief and practice simultaneously – to hold them, as it were, in parallel. In some cases this is possible because a sort of 'pillarization' occurs in which different beliefs and practices operate in different and self-contained spheres of social life. In other cases the different forms of religion may prove compatible because they are used in an instrumental fashion to achieve a common goal (e.g., the employment of a variety of religious techniques all aimed at healing). Here religion is primarily a matter of pragmatics; because it is judged by its effectiveness rather than its truth, logical contradiction becomes unimportant. Equally, metaphysical and logical incompatibility may simply go unnoticed or be regarded as unimportant in the religious sphere – a case of comfortable contradiction. Prince Charles's espousal of Prayer Book Anglicanism (religion of difference) and New Age religiosity (religion of life) provides a good example of such unacknowledged contradiction (see the Archbishop of Canterbury's comments on Charles's pillarization in reading **1.91**).

The readings in this chapter take us to the heart of the approach which we adopt in this book, and introduce one of its most distinctive themes: that of coexistence. The picture of religion in modern times which emerges from is not one of the triumph of one type of religion, nor of the universal sway of unilinear trends in modern religion, but of the colonization, polarization, tension, integration and union of different trends and different varieties of religion in different contexts, and at global, national, local and personal levels.

Experiential religions of difference (Evangelical–Charismatic)

1.81 Bebbington: scripture and experience as the twin authorities of Evangelicalism

David W. Bebbington, 1994: Evangelical social influence in North Atlantic societies. In Mark A. Noll, David W. Bebbington and George A. Rawlyk (eds.), *Evangelicalism: Comparative Studies of Popular Protestantism in North America, the British Isles, and Beyond, 1700–1900.* New York and Oxford: Oxford University Press, pp. 113–36 (pp. 129–30).

Evangelical Christianity, one of the most successful forms of religion in modern times, can be bracketed as a religion of difference because of its stress on the authority of scripture, but it also has a strong experiential stress. Here, the historian of evangelicalism David Bebbington defines Evangelicalism in terms of these two elements: belief in the authority of the Bible and in the authority of experience. Clearly these two may exist in some considerable tension, but the success of Evangelicalism would suggest that it is a creative tension.

A historian, whose task in these exercises is quite different from a theologian's, finds it relatively easy to define an essential evangelicalism in the social settings of the eighteenth and early nineteenth centuries. Differ as they certainly did in many particulars, still the individuals and groups that were recognized in their own settings as evangelical possessed a core of common characteristics. Two were most basic, and three others followed naturally. First, evangelicals throughout the

North Atlantic were determined Protestants who took with particular earnestness the historic Protestant attachment to Scripture. They could differ wildly among themselves on the meaning of the Bible, but the Scriptures remained a bedrock of authority. Second, evangelicals shared a conviction that true religion required the active experience of God. Again, evangelicals prescribed myriad norms for that experience and even more ways for accommodating the experience of God with reason, traditions, and hierarchies. But that experience remained a sine qua non for the type of religion that many contemporaries and more historians have labeled evangelical.

The three characteristics flowing from the biblical experientialism of evangelicals were nearly as important, especially since they shaped the lived reality of this biblical experientialism. First was a bias – whether slight prejudice or massive rejection – against inherited institutions. Since no inherited institution could communicate the power of God's presence as adequately as Scripture and personal Christian experience, no inherited institution enjoyed the respect accorded to experience and the Bible. Second, evangelicalism was, as a matter of principle, though often inarticulate principle, extraordinarily flexible in relation to ideas concerning intellectual, political, social, and economic life. Since such ideas possessed primarily instrumental value by comparison with the ultimate realities found in Scripture and the experience of Christ, they could be taken up, modified, discarded, or transformed as local circumstances dictated. Third, evangelicals practiced 'discipline,' to borrow a well-considered phrase from Daniel Walker Howe. Their experiential biblicism might lead along many different paths, and with contrasting conclusions, to principles of conduct for self and others, but however derived, those principles embodied a common evangelical conviction that the gospel compelled a search for social healing as well as personal holiness.

1.82 Tipton: order and ecstasy in counter-cultural Christianity

Steven Tipton, 1984: *Getting Saved from the Sixties. Moral Meaning in Conversion and Cultural Change.* Berkeley, Los Angeles and London: University of California Press (pp. 53–9).

Here Steven Tipton discusses a revivalist Christian sect in California, the Living Word Fellowship (LWF), which, by integrating Biblical and experiential emphases, has managed to win converts from the counter-cultural drug culture of the 1960s. The authoritative teaching of the group and its stress on Biblical norms provides a clear framework for adherents, whilst its charismatic stress on experience appeals to those already schooled in seeking after experiential 'highs'. Like Tipton, David Martin (1983) also notes that 'personal contact and subjective experience . . . was always an evangelical motif, but [in the sixties] it provided a point of overlap with the counter-culture. The sixties hungered and thirsted after subjective reality, and the evangelicals offered the bread of life and living water . . .' (pp. 62–3). Charismatic religion's ability to combine a stress on the importance of individual experience and participation with belief in a transcendent God and an authoritative scripture makes it compatible not only with the 'turn to the self' characteristic of modern times (see the chapter on Detraditionalization in **Part Three**), but also with traditional forms of spiritualism and healing, whilst its differentiated emphasis underpins the growth of strong, supportive communities with clear moral frameworks.

The high value attached to individual independence and discretion in American culture makes it difficult to accept an authority that enforces obligations and rules. Such rules, however, promise order to youth fed up with the predicament of 'doing your own thing' without knowing why, and being injured by others doing likewise. The failure of the countercultural dream and of an unregulated life within it motivates the rebellious convert to stay on. So does the fear of turning back for one who has already begun to burn her bridges behind her and to accept the threats of damnation aimed by sect doctrine at the defector. Positive motivation is provided by the sect's blessings for compliance with its norms. These blessings include: (1) an inner experience of personal efficacy, purpose, and meaning unified with an external moral authority; (2) social relations offering acceptance and love, friends and a spouse, within an intimate and stable community; (3) secure intrasect status and status superiority in relation to the larger society, both based on moral rectitude; (4) reconciliation to low-status work in the world and a sacred career to compensate for it; (5) millennial political power. Let us recount these blessings as facets of an applied ethic created by recombining the counterculture's expressive ideals with biblical authority and Christian love. [. . .]

In the LWF one looks to recognized authorities in order to find out which is the right way to live, but how does one come to recognize these authorities as true? This question remains at the root of the sect's moral style. The sect claims to enjoy a special relationship to God and to represent God's will; these claims become realities for its youthful members in two forms – ecstatic ritual experiences and communal relationships. These two forms resemble sect youths' earlier experience of psychedelic drugs and hippie communalism, yet each differs from its countercultural predecessor in telling ways.

The Christian's self-surrender to religious experience and then to authority recalls the drug user's self-surrender to psychedelic experience. Drug ideology counsels letting go of oneself completely in unmediated experience without concern for the consequences. So interpreted, the life of the senses is not mere hedonism. It has a self-transcendent character. Drugs flood the senses rather than simply gratifying them; this results in a blurring of and release from the categories of subject and object and a glimpse of monist truth. One woman compares this bohemian ethos with her parents' classic-become-conventional ideal of moderation in all things:

> I remember one thing I learned as a kid, from my family maybe, to do all things in moderation. [laughing] So I just figured I'd turn it upside down. That you'd be an acid head for awhile, a speed freak for awhile, an alcoholic. *The ultimate of every trip is when that trip controls you.* If you want to really understand any trip, you have to fall into it headfirst. [italics added]

The ultimate aim of life thus conceived is not to preserve or fortify the self, but to lose it, so that the drug 'does' the doer, just as in Pentecostal glossolalia the tongues 'speak' the speaker, or in Zen meditation the breathing 'breathes' the breather. The counterculture's drug ideology and its ecstatic or mystical religious successors similarly value self-surrender. The latter, however, insist more strongly on the related need for commitment to the object and practice of one's surrender, and from this experience they construct some form of cosmic and social authority. [. . .]

For many LWF youths 'getting high was like our control, our standard.' It became an experiential frame of reference for their daily lives, making the intensity and continuity of such altered states crucial to them. But the drug user must inevitably come down from intense highs to struggle with the everyday world of school, work, and personal relationships with nonusers. One ex-dealer reflects on tongue-speaking in light of these problems:

> When I began to speak in tongues I remember thinking it was a kind of Nirvana. [laughing] I was as high as I'd ever been on drugs, but it was a different kind of high, from a power outside myself, with a clearness and direction I'd never had before. The reality of it was what

was most beautiful. It was the reality of meeting God. I'd found something that was actually gonna take care of me and govern my life. It was something I could hold onto forever. It wasn't just a passing experience on a magical weekend.

With the Lord now, I have control of it. Whenever I want to speak to Him, I can. When I did drugs, I had a carefree feeling. I didn't worry about anything. It's the same way with God, that's how He wants us to be, only in a more real, responsible way. Don't worry about your job or where you're gonna eat. But God also says don't be lazy or just sit around, which is all I ever did before.

The carefree ecstasy of tongue-speaking compares with the hippie's psychedelic highs, Nirvana and all. But its divine agency, ritual control, and congregational context impart moral purpose and order to the convert's experience. If he follows this order, then his religious faith and community in turn reinforce the uplifting effects of the rite itself.

1.83   Griffith: therapeutic Evangelicalism

R. Marie Griffith, 1997: *God's Daughters. Evangelical Women and the Power of Submission.* California and London: University of California Press (p. 36).

In readings **1.27** and **3.42** James Davison Hunter argues that contemporary North American Evangelicalism is breaking away from the model of a strict religion of difference as it integrates experiential and expressive elements. R. Marie Griffith found the same thing to be true in relation to the influential movement of lay Evangelical women in the USA, 'Women's Aglow', which has drawn heavily on therapeutic culture. Here she reflects on this shift within American twentieth-century Evangelicalism more generally.

As evangelicals gradually ceased denouncing psychology outright, they shifted the battle lines, accepting the psychologists' diagnosis of modern dilemmas while asserting that the cure for emotional sickness was religious faith rather than secular therapies. Popular evangelical writers increasingly began to discuss problems in terms of 'anxiety' and 'inferiority complexes' and advised readers on heightening 'self-esteem' and fulfilling emotional 'needs,' however, and the boundary between religious and secular prescriptions steadily blurred. Religious writers quoted enthusiastically from psychotherapists and other 'positive thinkers' such as Dale Carnegie and Joshua Loth Liebman. Continuing to denounce liberal Protestants for accommodating and selling out to 'secular humanism,' evangelical authors devised an updated theology of their own, in which sin was often reconceptualized as sickness and concerns over salvation were replaced by concerns for earthly happiness, comfort, and health. Those who packaged their message most successfully, such as the well-known Christian pediatrician and psychologist James Dobson, tended to address a largely female audience and directed their concerns to marriage and family life, sex, and depression. [. . .]

It seemed irrefutable that a deep cultural shift 'from salvation to self-realization' had taken place.

1.84   Martin on the Charismatic upsurge

David Martin, 1996: *Forbidden Revolutions. Pentecostalism in Latin America and Catholicism in Eastern Europe*. London: SPCK (pp. 26–7).

The ability of Charismatic Christianity to combine a stress on authority with one of experience is by no means confined to its western manifestations. In his studies of Sicilian Pentecostalism, for example, Salvatore Cucchiari notes this same tendency, and relates it to an ability to unite the 'male' (authoritative/ Word) with the 'female' (experience/Spirit). (See, for example, Cucchiari, 1991, p. 691). Here David Martin reflects on the world-wide reach of Charismatic Christianity, and its vitality. (For more on the charismatic upsurge see readings **2.23**, **2.53**, **2.70**, **3.87**, **3.97**.)

Over the past thirty or so years the religious map of the world has changed dramatically. In the developed West, the liberal religious establishments have seen their constituencies shrink relative to the constituencies of the conservative evangelicals. In what used to be called the Third World, the World Council of Churches' share of the Protestant constituency has dropped, and a protean indigenous Christianity has emerged indifferent to the agenda of the Western theological intelligentsia. Jürgen Moltmann is not regular fare among South African Zionists or the vast crowds of pilgrims attending the Temple of La Luz del Mundo, Guadalajara.

More often than not, this shift is towards a Pentecostal faith in the gifts of the Holy Spirit – healing, speaking in tongues, exorcism, prophecy, holiness. Overall, depending on how you widen or narrow your definitions, perhaps a quarter of a billion persons are involved, making it comparable to the advance of a 'conservative' Islam. But Islam is about reintegrating whole societies behind a single religious

law, whereas this 'conservative' Christianity is a fissiparous movement undermining every kind of unifying ideology. You find it all
over non-Islamic Africa and even inside the Coptic Church. You find
it in South India, South Korea, the Philippines, Singapore, China and
the Caribbean (including Cuba). It is, above all, massively present in
Latin America; and in Southern and Eastern Europe you can detect
the ripples from Sicily to Kiev, with an outer ripple in Tiblisi. Its
world-wide reach was illustrated for me when I saw students preaching first in the main square of Santiago, Chile, and very similar
students in front of the Hanseatic town hall in Tallinn, Estonia. This
is what is meant by globalization.

Though Latin America is so far the most dramatic instance, the
pace of change is so fast that even larger numbers could soon emerge
elsewhere – for example, in China. Possibly quite soon, the forty million
and more evangelicals who make up 10 per cent of the population
of Latin America will be matched by a similar number in China, though
they would be no more than 3 per cent of the Chinese population.

Experiential religions of humanity

1.85 Tagore's experiential 'Religion of Man'

Rabindranath Tagore, 1961 (orig. 1931): *The Religion of Man*. London: Unwin Books
(pp. 10–11).

As the thought of the Indian poet and spiritual writer Rabindranath Tagore
(1861–1941) illustrates clearly, the liberal-humanistic and the expressive-
experiential varieties of modern religion and culture could be combined into a
new synthesis. In Tagore's message we thus find a strong emphasis on the ethical
and metaphysical importance of 'Man', together with a belief in 'an inner faculty
of our own' which alone brings us into contact with this humanity. (See also
Tagore in reading **3.61**.)

We have our eyes, which relate to us the vision of the physical universe.
We have also an inner faculty of our own which helps us to find our
relationship with the supreme self of man, the universe of personality.
This faculty is our luminous imagination, which in its higher stage is
special to man. It offers us that vision of wholeness which for the biological necessity of physical survival is superfluous; its purpose is to arouse
in us the sense of perfection which is our true sense of immortality.
For perfection dwells ideally in Man the Eternal, inspiring love for
this ideal in the individual, urging him more and more to realize it.

The development of intelligence and physical power is equally necessary in animals and men for their purposes of living; but what is unique in man is the development of his consciousness, which gradually deepens and widens the realization of his immortal being, the perfect, the eternal. It inspires those creations of his that reveal the divinity in him – which is his humanity – in the varied manifestations of truth, goodness and beauty, in the freedom of activity which is not for his use but for his ultimate expression. The individual man must exist for Man the great, and must express him in disinterested works, in science and philosophy, in literature and arts, in service and worship. This is his religion, which is working in the heart of all his religions in various names and forms. He knows and uses this world where it is endless and thus attains greatness, but he realizes his own truth where it is perfect and thus finds his fulfilment.

The idea of the humanity of our God, or the divinity of Man the Eternal, is the main subject of this book. [. . .]

On the surface of our being we have the ever-changing phases of the individual self, but in the depth there dwells the Eternal Spirit of human unity beyond our direct knowledge.

1.86   Robinson: God as 'the inter-personal'

John A. T. Robinson, 1967: *Exploration into God*. London: SCM Press (pp. 144–5).

Bishop John Robinson's *Exploration into God* was intended to 'dig deeper' into the ideas first explored in his best-selling *Honest to God* (1963). Robinson proposed that our out-dated image of a transcendent God must be replaced with an understanding of God who, as 'ground of our being' is existentially and experientially intimate with us, but who is also 'personal', and as such supports a 'personalist', love-based ethic. Here he explores the coming together of 'the All and the Personal' in true religion. The passage serves to illustrate the influence of a tradition of liberal-expressivism at the heart of twentieth-century popular and academic Christian theology. In recent times the tradition has fed the liberal wing of feminist theology: see Ruether, reading **1.40**.

Ultimately, in speaking of God all words are bound to fail. Yet rather than end in final aposiopesis, there is perhaps one more thing that can be said. One of the insights of our century is that the trans-personal character of God is better expressed by envisaging him not as a bigger and better Individual, nor as a sort of Hobbesian collective Personality *incorporating* all other persons, but in terms of the inter-personal.

This is the result of applying 'field' or relational thinking to persons as well as to things. For Buber has taught us that in the beginning – and in the end – is not the individual, the 'I' or the 'Thou', but the nexus 'I-Thou'. And the whole of reality, too, must ultimately be seen in terms, not of a God, a monarchical Being supreme among individual entities, but of a divine 'field' in which the finite 'Thous' are constituted what they are in the freedom of a wholly personalizing love. In the same vein, Berdyaev, summing up what he calls 'the pivotal idea' of his *Spirit and Reality*, says that the only justification of anthropomorphism is that 'God is like a *whole humanity* rather than like nature, society, or concept'. The pledge of ultimate Reality within this world, the sign of the Kingdom, is what Dumitriu described as 'that dense and secret undergrowth which is wholly composed of personal events'. But it is Teilhard de Chardin who has taken this idea to its most daring limits in the vision which closes *The Phenomenon of Man*. He sees the universe as pointing to 'the hyper-personal, beyond the collective', in which God is 'the Centre of centres' in an interlocking web of free spiritual relationship in which the All and the Personal are no longer exclusive.

1.87 Woodhead: Princess Diana's tender-hearted humanitarianism

Linda Woodhead, 1999: Diana and the Religion of the Heart. In Jeffrey Richards, Scott Wilson and Linda Woodhead (eds), *Diana. The Making of a Media Saint*. London: I. B. Tauris (1999), pp. 119–39 (pp. 127–32).

At the end of the twentieth-century the continuing influence of the liberal-experiential trajectory at the level of popular culture was influenced by the 'cult' of Princess Diana. Here Woodhead argues that the religiosity expressed by Diana and many of her admirers can best be described as a 'religion of the heart', and that it represents the union of a religion of humanity and a spirituality of life. Thus, its discourse of humanitarianism and its high valuation of the human is typical of a religion of humanity; its divinization of the human in self as well as others and prioritizing of emotional experience of a spirituality of life. Love, the central virtue of Diana's religiosity, is understood in affective terms – as a matter of the heart rather than of will or reason.

The claim that the religion which Diana articulated in the last years of her life was increasingly New Age . . . finds some strong grounds for support . . . Diana increasingly relied on the services of a very wide range of New Age and 'expressive' trainers, counsellors and therapists, and willingly embraced an expressive discourse of being true to self, loving self, and finding the 'real me'. Yet Diana never focused upon such goals to the exclusion of her other great concern: the giving of love to others. Or, to put it more accurately, she never saw the two goals as mutually exclusive. On the contrary, she believed that they informed one another. It was necessary to love self in order to love others; it was necessary to love others – and to be loved by others – in order to fulfil self. Diana's Religion of the Heart was not simply a religion of self: it was a religion of loving kindness directed to all needy human beings, self *and* others. It could be said that it drew on Christianity insofar as it stressed the importance of love and service to others, and on more expressive influences insofar as it stressed the importance of self [. . .] One of the salient features of humanitarian discourse has always been its universalism: as a universal category 'the human' transcends all differences, enabling humanitarians to affirm a mission in which each individual has equal claim. Diana's Religion of the Heart certainly adopted such universalism, and in doing so revealed another cultural debt: to the Enlightenment and to liberal Christianity. In addition, however, the Religion of the Heart adopted a newer form of universalism, a universalism which refuses to recognise a distinction between different *types* of love (such as eros and agape, for example). For the Religion of the Heart, there is only one form of love: the affective, engaged, reciprocal love . . . . It is this same love which is displayed in friendship, in romance, in parenthood, in compassionate care, in religious devotion [. . .] It is also to the discourse and conceptuality of humanitarianism that we must look in order to understand something of the metaphysical dimension of the Religion of the Heart. For, unlike traditional Christianity, such religion finds its ontological basis not so much in God as in the human. Where Christianity finds a wilful and sinful creature who is loved by God in spite of their sinfulness, the Religion of the Heart finds a uniquely precious individual who is inherently lovable. Where Christianity postulates original sin, the Religion of the Heart postulates original goodness [. . .] something of the reality and the value of the divine is transferred to the human. It is as if the human becomes brighter at the same time that the divine looses something of its radiance. Characteristics traditionally attributed to God begin to float across to the human. Instead of being understood as an earth-bound mortal creature of dust and ashes, the human becomes a spiritual being with supernatural capabilities.

1.88   Religious synthesis in *A Course in Miracles*

1985: *A Course in Miracles. The Text, Workbook for Students and Manual for Teachers.* London: Arkana, Penguin Books (p. 83).

Claimed to have been composed by direct supernatural dictation, and presented as a single volume of instruction for those wishing to learn the truth and to teach it to others, *A Course of Miracles* has become a best-seller. Its popularity may be partly attributable to the fact that it manages to integrate elements of differentiated Christianity with the humanitarianism and liberalism of a religion of humanity and the expressive stress of a spirituality of life – as the following extract reveals. It is also clear that many of the distinctive features of these original components are lost in the process – not least belief in the unique authority of Christ.

JESUS – CHRIST

There is no need for help to enter Heaven for you have never left. But there is need for help beyond yourself as you are circumscribed by false beliefs of your Identity, Which God alone established in reality. Helpers are given you in many forms, although upon the altar they are one. Beyond each one there is a Thought of God, and this will never change. But they have names which differ for a time, for time needs symbols, being itself unreal. Their names are legion, but we will not go beyond the names the course itself employs. God does not help because He knows no need. But He creates all Helpers of His Son while he believes his fantasies are true. Thank God for them for they will lead you home.

The name of *Jesus* is the name of one who was a man but saw the face of Christ in all his brothers and remembered God. So he became identified with *Christ*, a man no longer, but at one with God. The man was an illusion, for he seemed to be a separate being, walking by himself, within a body that appeared to hold his self from Self, as all illusions do. Yet who can save unless he sees illusions and then identifies them as what they are? Jesus remains a Savior because he saw the false without accepting it as true. And Christ needed his form that He might appear to men and save them from their own illusions.

In his complete identification with the Christ – the perfect Son of God, His one creation and His happiness, forever like Himself and one with Him – Jesus became what all of you must be. He led the way for you to follow him. He leads you back to God because he saw the road before him, and he followed it. He made a clear distinction,

still obscure to you, between the false and true. He offered you a
final demonstration that it is impossible to kill God's Son; nor can his
life in any way be changed by sin and evil, malice, fear or death.

   And therefore all your sins have been forgiven because they carried
no effects at all. And so they were but dreams. Arise with him who
showed you this because you owe him this who shared your dreams
that they might be dispelled. And shares them still, to be at one
with you.

   Is he the Christ? O yes, along with you.

Conflicts, explicit and implicit

1.89   Wuthnow on the 'great fracture' in American religion

Robert Wuthnow, 1995: *The Struggle for America's Soul. Evangelicals, Liberals, and Secularism.*
Grand Rapids, Michigan: William B. Eerdmans (pp. 21–3; 35–6).

Here the sociologist of religion Robert Wuthnow draws attention to a conflict
at the heart of American society: that between conservatives and liberals. He
shows how this cultural conflict is undergirded by social conflict, and notes that
attempts to bridge it (like that by liberal Evangelicals) have failed. In an earlier
book, *The Restructuring of American Religion (1988)*, Wuthnow also shows how
since the 1970s conflicts between different denominations in America have been
eclipsed by this wider conflict.

A great fracture runs through the cultural terrain on which the battles
of religion and politics are now being fought. It is a fracture that
deserves our attention. For it is of recent creation, a human construction, unlike the timeless swells of culture through which it has been
cut. It has become a mire of bitter contention, consuming the energies
of religious communities and grinding their ideals into the grime of
unforeseen animosities. At a broader level, this fracture also sym-
bolizes the unplanned developments in the larger terrain that did not
become evident until the battles themselves began to erupt. With the
advantage of hindsight, we can now discover the importance of these
developments. We can see how the present controversies in American religion were affected by broader changes in the society – the
consequences of which remained obscure at the time but have now
become painfully transparent. [. . .]

   Depending on whose lens we use to view it, we can describe this
fissure in any number of ways. Television evangelist Jimmy Swaggart

has described it as a gulf between those who believe in the Judeo-Christian principles on which our country was founded and those who believe in the 'vain philosophies of men.' On one side are the 'old-fashioned' believers in 'the word of Almighty God' who are often maligned as 'poor simpletons'; on the other side are the 'so-called intelligentsia,' those who believe they are great because they 'are more intelligent than anyone else,' 'socialists,' believers in 'syphilitic Lenin,' and the burdened masses who have nothing better to get excited about than football and baseball games. In contrast, a writer for the *New York Times* depicted it as a battle between 'churches and church-allied groups' who favor freedom, democracy, and the rights of minorities, on the one hand, and a right-wing fringe interested in setting up a theocracy governed by a 'dictatorship of religious values,' on the other hand.

Apart from the colors in which the two sides are portrayed, though, one finds general agreement on the following points: (a) the reality of the division between two opposing camps; (b) the predominance of 'fundamentalists,' 'evangelicals,' and 'religious conservatives' in one and the predominance of 'religious liberals,' 'humanists,' and 'secularists' in the other; and (c) the presence of deep hostility and misgiving between the two.

An official of the National Council of Churches summarized the two positions, and the views of each toward the other, this way: 'Liberals abhor the smugness, the self-righteousness, the absolute certainty, the judgmentalism, the lovelessness of a narrow, dogmatic faith. [Conservatives] scorn the fuzziness, the marshmallow convictions, the inclusiveness that makes membership meaningless – the "anything goes" attitude that views even Scripture as relative. Both often caricature the worst in one another and fail to perceive the best.' [. . .]

For a time, perhaps even as recently as 1976, it appeared that the gap between religious liberals and conservatives might be bridged by a significant segment of the evangelical community. Many of its leaders had participated in the educational expansion of the previous decade. They were exposed to the current thinking in higher education, had been influenced by their own participation in the civil rights movement and the antiwar movement, and had come to hold liberal views on many political issues, and yet retained a strong commitment to the biblical tradition, including an emphasis on personal faith.

Their voice, however, was soon drowned out by the more strident voices of the religious right. Television hookups and direct-mail solicitations replaced the evangelical periodical, seminary, and scholarly conference as more effective means of forging a large following and extracting revenue from that following. Issues such as abortion and feminism provided platforms on which the religious right could organize.

Educational differences continued to separate the more conservative from the more liberal. But other issues began to reinforce these differences. Issues arose that also reflected the experience of women in gaining higher education and becoming employed in professional careers, or the exposure one gained in college to the social sciences and humanities as opposed to more narrowly technical educations in engineering or business.

The religious right also borrowed the more activist style of political confrontation that the left had used during the 1960s. It began to renew the connection between values and behavior. Its commitment to personal morality remained strong, but it now urged believers to take political action, to organize themselves, to infuse their morality into the basic institutions of government. Each side developed special purpose groups to gain its objectives, either within more narrow denominational contexts or in the national arena.

Thus, deeper features of the social and cultural terrain underlie the present fracture between religious liberals and religious conservatives. Had it simply been, say, the Supreme Court's 1973 decision on abortion that elicited different responses from liberals and conservatives, we might well have seen a temporary flurry of activity followed by a gradual progression of interest to other matters. Instead, the religious environment is characterized by two clearly identified communities. Each has developed through the events spanning at least a quarter of a century. The two are located differently with respect to the basic social division that has been produced by the growth of higher education. Other bases of differentiation, such as regionalism, ethnicity, and denominationalism, that might have mitigated this basic division have subsided in importance. Each side has mobilized its recources around special purpose groups.

1.90   Chesterton defines Christian orthodoxy over against Theosophy

G. K. Chesterton, 1961 (orig. 1908): *Orthodoxy*. Glasgow: Collins Fontana Books (p. 130).

In reading **1.7** Chesterton describes and defends a highly differentiated form of Christianity. Here too we see how this religion was constructed in conscious opposition to the spirituality of life popularized by contemporaries like Annie Besant and her fellow Theosophists. Chesterton's Christian apologetic seems to offer a good example not only of polarization, but of the way in which conflicting forms of religion may reify and define themselves over against one another: the more Besant stresses that religion is about the universal, the more Chesterton wants to say that it is about difference, the more Besant stresses that it is about the inner, the more Chesterton wants to say it is about the outer. Peter Berger argues that the dominance of the market economy and the need to 'brand' and clearly define one's product in the religious marketplace accentuates the tendency to differentiate; see, for example, Berger (1969).

A short time ago Mrs. Besant, in an interesting essay, announced that there was only one religion in the world, that all faiths were only versions or perversions of it, and that she was quite prepared to say what it was. According to Mrs. Besant this universal Church is simply the universal self. It is the doctrine that we are really all one person; that there are no real walls of individuality between man and man. If I may put it so, she does not tell us to love our neighbours; she tells us to be our neighbours. That is Mrs. Besant's thoughtful and suggestive description of the religion in which all men must find themselves in agreement. And I never heard of any suggestion in my life with which I more violently disagree. I want to love my neighbour not because he is I, but precisely because he is not I. I want to adore the world, not as one likes a looking-glass, because it is one's self, but as one loves a woman, because she is entirely different. If souls are separate love is possible. If souls are united love is obviously impossible. A man may be said loosely to love himself, but he can hardly fall in love with himself, or, if he does, it must be a monotonous courtship. If the world is full of real selves, they can be really unselfish selves. But upon Mrs. Besant's principle the whole cosmos is only one enormously selfish person.

1.91 Runcie on the contradictions of Prince Charles's religion

Humphrey Carpenter, 1996: *Robert Runcie. The Reluctant Archbishop*. London: Hodder and Stoughton (p. 221).

In a conversation recorded in Humphrey Carpenter's biography of the Archbishop of Canterbury, Robert Runcie describes Prince Charles's religion as a contradictory mix of traditional Anglicanism and spirituality of life. Since there is no evidence that Charles himself feels his religion to be contradictory, one must conclude that this is a form of implicit conflict or contradiction. Princess Diana's religiosity, considered by Linda Woodhead in reading **1.87** furnishes an interesting contrast with that of her husband: a mix of liberal and experiential/expressive elements it appears to have been significantly more unified and harmonious. (Of those mentioned in the reading below, Laurens van der Post was one of Prince Charles's mentors and an advocate of an immanentist spirituality; the Greenham women were counter-cultural protestors against nuclear weapons.)

> [Prince Charles] didn't have a consistent view, because he would go in with the *Spectator* gang on 'the lovely language of the Prayer Book', but then he would say, 'Instead of interfering with politics, the church should be creating centres of healing in the inner cities – ought to be bringing together the spiritual, the intellectual and the architectural.' But these were only conversations in passing, not seriously sustained argument. [. . .]
>
> He was quite pious, and was cultivated by John Andrew [chaplain to Michael Ramsey], and was confirmed by Michael Ramsey, and had a sort of relationship there. When he came to Lambeth for his pre-marriage talk, I remember he said in a kind of nostalgic way, 'I came and served here sometimes.' But it was rather something that had passed away. And I think he was deeply into the Laurens van der Post spirituality. [. . .]
>
> Charles is highly sensitive – that's what everybody says. I could quote so many examples of personal letters or hidden acts of kindness to individuals in need, or unglamorous but worthwhile causes. But he is a mass of contradictions – almost as much as I am! He's punctilious in being Colonel-in-Chief of the Welsh Guards, but he also wants to be friends with the Greenham women. He's on about the grandeur of our cathedrals and the epic language of the Prayer Book, but he wants to be exploring Hinduism with people in inner cities. He hunts regularly, but is a great man about the environment. So that the public don't really know where they are. [. . .]

1.92 Berlin on ultimate and unresolvable value clash

Isaiah Berlin, 1991: *The Crooked Timber of Humanity. Chapters in the History of Ideas*, ed. Henry Hardy. London: Fontana Press (pp. 12–13).

Isaiah Berlin believes that conflict between ultimate values is a permanent and ineliminable feature of human life and culture. The hope that such values can ultimately be reconciled is illusory. If Berlin is right then conflict between different religions seems inevitable, and the final, perfect synthesis imagined in many of the readings on universalization in **Part Three** impossible. Obviously, the clash between religions which enshrine the most polarized values will be the greatest – as between religions which emphasize the value of compassion and those which emphasize the value of truth, or between those which emphasize the value of obedience and those which emphasize the value of liberty. For further reflections on the ultimacy of difference see the chapters on Difference in **Part Two**.

What is clear is that values can clash – that is why civilisations are incompatible. They can be incompatible between cultures, or groups in the same culture, or between you and me. You believe in always telling the truth, no matter what; I do not, because I believe that it can sometimes be too painful and too destructive. We can discuss each other's point of view, we can try to reach common ground, but in the end what you pursue may not be reconcilable with the ends to which I find that I have dedicated my life. Values may easily clash within the breast of a single individual; and it does not follow that, if they do, some must be true and others false. Justice, rigorous justice, is for some people an absolute value, but it is not compatible with what may be no less ultimate values for them – mercy, compassion – as arises in concrete cases.

Both liberty and equality are among the primary goals pursued by human beings through many centuries; but total liberty for wolves is death to the lambs, total liberty of the powerful, the gifted, is not compatible with the rights to a decent existence of the weak and the less gifted. An artist, in order to create a masterpiece, may lead a life which plunges his family into misery and squalor to which he is indifferent. We may condemn him and declare that the masterpiece should be sacrificed to human needs, or we may take his side – but both attitudes embody values which for some men or women are ultimate, and which are intelligible to us all if we have any sympathy or imagination or understanding of human beings. Equality may demand the restraint of the liberty of those who wish to dominate, liberty – without some modicum of which there is no choice and therefore no possibility of remaining human as we understand the word – may have to be curtailed in order to make room for social welfare, to feed the hungry, to clothe the naked, to shelter the homeless, to leave room for the liberty of others, to allow justice or fairness to be exercised. [. . .]

These collisions of values are of the essence of what they are and what we are. If we are told that these contradictions will be solved in some perfect world in which all good things can be harmonised in principle, then we must answer, to those who say this, that the meanings they attach to the names which for us denote the conflicting values are not ours. We must say that the world in which what we see as incompatible values are not in conflict is a world altogether beyond our ken; that principles which are harmonised in this other world are not the principles with which, in our daily lives, we are acquainted; if they are transformed, it is into conceptions not known to us on earth. But it is on earth that we live, and it is here that we must believe and act.

part two

contexts

introduction to
part two

Part One of this volume sought to examine the most influential varieties of religion in modern times. It was interested primarily in their content: their distinctive themes, values and promises. Whilst some note was made of the distinctive social forms, practices and possibilities of the different types of religion, the emphasis was on the cultural. **Part Two** moves to the more concrete conditions of social life. Religions are historically and materially defined. They occupy a concrete time and space. They are cultural, political and material enterprises. They involve individuals, social groups and social action. They interact with their economic and political contexts, and exercise a transforming or determinative role in relation to their social frame. In what follows we examine the interplay of religion with these contexts.

Modern times have been decisively shaped by a number of overlapping social transformations. Of these three seem to be of particular importance, particularly in relation to religion:

- the rise of the market economy,
- the rise of secular nation states, and
- the rise of difference.

Under the latter heading is included both the assertion of strong, 'prescriptive' forms of difference in modern times (perhaps most obvious in religions of heightened difference), and the articulation of new more 'open' forms of difference often associated with postmodernity and its advocates. (A fourth context which we would have liked to consider had there been space, would be that of the small-scale. It would range from intermediate and secondary institutions at one end, to private and intimate life at the other. Here one might have considered the changing forms of religious institutions (from church to the informal small group); schools and education; the rise of small self-help and discussion groups; leisure groups; intimate citizenships; the social forms of intimacy in modern times – all in relation to religion.)

Part Two is organized in terms of the three key contexts listed above. Chapter six, Economic, considers the most important economic contexts of religion in modern times. In particular, its readings reflect on the ways in which religion has shaped and been shaped by the increasing dominance of the market economy. Chapter seven, Political, considers political contexts of religion in modern times. Here major attention is given to the ways in which religion has served both to legitimate and to oppose the rise of the secular state, as well as offering alternatives. Chapter eight, Difference, considers the rise of difference in modern times, paying particular attention to gendered and ethnic difference. There are obvious and important overlaps between the chapters: the rise of religio-ethnic nationalisms, for example, is reviewed in chapter seven, but is also a major example of the rise of difference which is the subject of chapter eight.

The selection of readings in this part of the volume proved instructive. There is a relatively developed and sophisticated body of literature on the topic of religion and political contexts in modern times. By contrast, the topic of religion and economic contexts has attracted far less scholarly attention. The literature on religion and difference has barely begun to develop, especially at the level of general theoretical reflection. The specific topics of gendered and ethnic difference have, however, become growth topics in the academy since the late 1970s, and scholars of religion have begun to take them seriously for at least a decade. Nevertheless, a great deal more work remains to be done.

The state of scholarly investigation in relation to the various contexts considered in **Part Two** has inevitably affected the readings selected. We have tried throughout to select cases of 'religion in practice' only where these include some theoretical reflection on religion in modern times and make points of more general validity and interest. Because of the paucity of reflection on religion and economic contexts, however, we have inevitably had to include as many concrete examples as we have theoretical reflections. And in chapter eight, on Difference, we have had to select a number of general reflections on difference from the social sciences, and to draw out their implications for religion ourselves.

CHAPTER SIX

economic

Introduction

Few would dispute that the market economy has become a, if not the, dominant force in world affairs. Capitalism – seen by Peter Beger (1987) as 'production for a market by enterprising individuals or combines with the purpose of making a profit' (p. 19) – has evolved into a key agency of life. Money has come to matter. Whether by way of production or by way of consumption, it is widely assumed that wealth means success. But what has religion to do with this?

From the evaluative point of view, few topics concerning religion today arouse as much controversy as the relationship between religion and the quest for monetary profit. There are those who think that religion is properly concerned with other-worldly, spiritual salvation, and is bastardized if put to work to seek success in the world of mammon. Such people seek alternatives to the capitalistic mainstream, pursuing the path of renunciation. There are also those, however, who suppose that religion is very much to do with economic prosperity. Whether it be by motivating people to be more productive by instilling work ethics and positively evaluating capitalism, or by enabling people to be more effective producers by tapping them into sacred powers, religion is here clearly engaged in promoting success in this world.

From the more empirical point of view, in the pre-modern world religions typically played a key, and distinctive, role in organizing economic affairs. Today, the situation is much more complicated. Religious traditions have largely fragmented, with the consequence that it is rare for any one major tradition to speak with an authoritative voice about economic matters. And economic life itself has become considerably more variegated, with few if any national entities operating according to any one clearly defined set of economic principles like 'the free market' or 'socialism'.

As well as the relationship between religious and economic affairs becoming more complicated, it also has to be said that the relationship between the two spheres has tended to become much more tenuous. To varying degrees, the two spheres have become differentiated: the economic to be run according to its own principles, regulated by the secular state; the religious restraining its involvement on the grounds (amongst others) of respecting human liberty. (See chapter eight, Difference, in **Part Two** and chapter nine, Secularization, in **Part Three** for more on modernity and differentiation.) However, differentiation must not be over-emphasized: as a number of the readings which follow show, the voice and authority of religion is still called into play, serving to criticize the excesses of capitalism (if not capitalism itself), or serving to legitimate economic arrangements. Furthermore, attempts are still being made – in the spirit of the pre-modern – to develop religiously-informed ways of managing economic life: a point illustrated below by reference to Islamic economics (see reading **2.3**).

Another way in which differentiation between the religious and the economic is very much held in check concerns the operation of what can be thought of as *'prosperity religion'*. Unlike religions of difference, religions of humanity and spiritualities of life (as portrayed in **Part One**), this kind of religiosity does not form even a relatively distinct 'strand'. Instead, it is an aspect of, is resourced by, each of these three strands. For instance, prosperity teachings and practices – explicitly devoted to the creation of wealth – involve the instrumentalization of the sacred of religions of difference or of spiritualities of life, or some combination of the two, the sacred being put to use to obtain secular ends. Prosperity teachings may also draw on the resources of religions of difference, humanity and spiritualities of life to provide or legitimate work ethics, and to support positive evaluations of capitalism. As for how this holds differentiation in check, the point is simply that huge numbers of people, from all over the world, remain involved in forms of religion which are believed to contribute to this-worldly success. Even when the economy is regulated by the secular state, religion can very much 'spill over' to enter into the lives of those at work – to serve as a powerful force or resource.

Prosperity religion, of course, is bound up with what would appear to be an ever-more significant feature of modern times: the growth of consumer culture and the associated 'ethicality' – if that is the right term – of people intent on satisfying their consumeristically driven desires. It could well be the case that prosperity religion is (characteristically) about the sacralization of utilitarian individualism. Recall Tipton on this form of individualism in a reading at the beginning of the volume (**1.2**). Rather than the individual relying on secular means – in particular the exercise of reason – to obtain wealth, the person is resourced by those means, those powers or magical capacities, provided by the realm of the sacred. Such prosperity religion, then, is a way of empowering, indeed legitimating and giving *substance* to, the utilitarian self intent on enjoying the materialistic life.

As far as the study of the religious and the economic is concerned, the great master has to be Max Weber. (His classic thesis, summarized later in this chapter, is devoted to the role played by religion in the construction of capitalistic modern times.) Given the roles that religions continue to play in adjudicating between economic systems, in providing work ethics, in promising prosperity in the (North American, etc.) heartlands of modern times, in restraining the excesses of capitalism – indeed, given the fact that prosperity religion is arguably the most important (world-wide) application of what the religious realm has to offer – it is mystifying that so few academics since Weber have been tempted to explore the interplays between the domains of the religious and the economic. Of particular note, few have explored the fact that religion and capitalism have 'blended' in many cultures, sacralized capitalism very much holding its own in face of the supposedly secularizing forces of modernity. Given such neglect, there is relatively little theory concerning religion and the economic realm; hence the extensive use of illustrative material in this chapter.

Themes related to the current chapter are also to be found in readings to do with the (apparently) secularizing impact of capitalism and consumer culture (as in the reading by Bauman, **3.22**), the role played by what might be thought of as 'religious capital' in promoting advancement (see, for example, **1.21** and **1.22**), and the role played by political factors (see chapter seven). Given the impossibility of clearly distinguishing between economic and political aspects of sociocultural life, the links between what now follows and the chapter entitled Politics are especially close. And **Part Three** contains discussion of the argument that capitalism has contributed to significant change within religion, for example to do with universalization (or the development of 'the same') (see Gellner, **3.76** and Bruce, **3.77**).

The 'overviews' which now follow are designed to do two things. First, to draw on Weber to make the basic point that – at least traditionally – religion has been profoundly embedded in economic life and vice versa. (This should help counter the widely-held assumption that religion operates over and above, or in contrast to, 'mundane' worldly affairs.) And second, to introduce the key relationships between the religious and the economic in modern times: essentially, to do with praising, empowering, or seeking alternatives to, the mainstream of secular capitalism.

Economic: overviews

2.1   Weber on the importance of the economic in religion

Max Weber, 1966 (orig. 1922): *The Sociology of Religion*. London: Social Science Paperbacks in association with Methuen & Co Ltd (p. 1).

Weber wrote that 'At first the sacred values of primitive as well as of cultured, prophetic or non-prophetic, religions were quite solid goods of this world. With the only partial exception of Christianity and a few other ascetic creeds, they have consisted of health, a long life, and wealth' (1991, p. 277). In the following extract, Weber suggests that religion is rooted in the attempt to develop 'relatively rational' ways of obtaining concrete goals. Although scholars today are generally highly suspicious about seeking 'elementary forms of the religious life', the extract nevertheless serves to highlight the 'down-to-earth', indeed downright worldy, dimension of religious affairs.

> The most elementary forms of behavior motivated by religious or magical factors are oriented to *this* world. 'That it may go well with thee . . . and that thou mayest prolong thy days upon the earth' (Deut. 4:40) expresses the reason for the performance of actions enjoined by religion or magic. Even human sacrifices, uncommon among urban peoples, were performed in the Phoenician maritime cities without any otherworldly expectations whatsoever. Furthermore, religiously or magically motivated behavior is relatively rational behavior, especially in its earliest manifestations. It follows rules of experience, though it is not necessarily action in accordance with a means-end schema. Rubbing will elicit sparks from pieces of wood, and in like fashion the simulative actions of a magician will evoke rain from the heavens. The sparks resulting from twirling the wooden sticks are as much a 'magical' effect as the rain evoked by the manipulations of the rainmaker. Thus, religious or magical behavior or thinking must not be set apart from the range of everyday purposive conduct, particularly since even the ends of the religious and magical actions are predominantly economic.

2.2   Weber on 'economic ethics'

Max Weber, 1991 (orig. 1915): The Social Psychology of the World Religions. In H. H. Gerth and C. Wright Mills (eds), *From Max Weber: Essays in Sociology*. London: Routledge, pp. 267–301 (pp. 267–9).

Arguing that 'It is not our thesis that the specific nature of a religion is a simple "function" of the social situation of the stratum which appears as its character-istic bearer' (1991, p. 269), but rather has a more creative role to play, Weber here theorizes some of the 'practical impulses for action which are founded in the psychological and pragmatic contexts of religion'.

What is meant by the 'economic ethic' of a religion will become increasingly clear during the course of our presentation. This term does not bring into focus the ethical theories of theological com-pendia; for however important such compendia may be under certain circumstances, they merely serve as tools of knowledge. The term 'economic ethic' points to the practical impulses for action which are founded in the psychological and pragmatic contexts of religions. The following presentation may be sketchy, but it will make obvious how complicated the structures and how many-sided the conditions of a concrete economic ethic usually are. Furthermore, it will show that externally similar forms of economic organization may agree with very different economic ethics and, according to the unique character of their economic ethics, how such forms of economic organization may produce very different historical results. An economic ethic is not a simple 'function' of a form of economic organization; and just as little does the reverse hold, namely, that economic ethics unambiguously stamp the form of the economic organization.

No economic ethic has ever been determined solely by religion. In the face of man's attitudes towards the world – as determined by religious or other (in our sense) 'inner' factors – an economic ethic has, of course, a high measure of autonomy. Given factors of economic geography and history determine this measure of autonomy in the highest degree. The religious determination of life-conduct, however, is also one – note this – only one, of the determinants of the economic ethic. Of course, the religiously determined way of life is itself pro-foundly influenced by economic and political factors operating within given geographical, political, social, and national boundaries. We should lose ourselves in these discussions if we tried to demonstrate these dependencies in all their singularities. Here we can only attempt to peel off the directive elements in the life-conduct of those social *strata* which have most strongly influenced the practical ethic of their respective religions. These elements have stamped the most charac-teristic features upon practical ethics, the features that distinguish one ethic from others; *and*, at the same time, they have been important for the respective economic ethics.

2.3   Jomo summarizing 'Islamic economic alternatives'

K. S. Jomo, 1992: Introduction. In K. S. Jomo (ed.), *Islamic Economic Alternatives. Critical Perspectives and New Directions*. London: Macmillan, pp. 1–7 (pp. 1–2).

Whereas most of the major religious traditions are no longer associated with distinctive economic arrangements, some contemporary forms of Islam strive to retain their role as economic regulators. Islamicists discuss and debate how to run economic affairs in an 'Islamic' fashion – differing from both secular capitalism and secular communism. As is indicated in the reading which follows, and as is more clearly spelt out in the articles of the volume edited by K. S. Jomo, attention is paid to the very details of the economic realm: its ethical principles, interest rates, banking principles, and so on. The economic realm is not to be left as autonomous or *sui generis*, operating according to its own principles.

There has been growing interest in Islam and Islamic economic altern-atives in recent times, both within and outside the Muslim world. Even the International Monetary Fund (IMF) is reported to have publicly endorsed Islamic banking principles in the mid-1980s. [. . .]

Much of what claims or is taken to be Islamic economics falls into two main categories. First, there are the compilations, commentaries and elaborations on the Quran, the Sunnah (the Prophet's Traditions) as well as other texts by various Muslim scholars and authorities. More often than not, such efforts claim that these provide an adequate basis for a comprehensive Islamic economic framework superior to all other existing or even idealised economic systems.

Some proponents, especially from among the *ulama*, tend to em-phasise that economic aspects cannot be divorced from other aspects of human life, and hence, that economic reform is contingent on and consequent of spiritual transformation and commitment. Often, this approach asserts that worldly matters are ultimately determined by human intent, sacred or otherwise. Order or disorder, stability or instability, justice or injustice – all seem to be determined by the righteousness, or otherwise, of human motivation.

In this sense then, the impact, scope and significance of particular economic institutions or relations prescribed or proscribed by such interpretations of Islam do not pose much of a problem. Unless spe-cifically condemned, almost anything goes, as long as the intention (for God, for the faith) is alright. This *carte-blanche* implication of the apparently orthodox approach helps explain the considerable ambiguity and controversy in efforts to identify and elaborate Islamic economic alternatives.

The apparent inadequacies of the orthodox approach have given rise to attempts, mainly by Western-trained economists of the Muslim faith, to elaborate a more comprehensive Islamic economic system consistent with the Islamic prescriptions and proscriptions referred to earlier. In the main, the results of such efforts have involved the grafting or excision of these do's and don'ts respectively either on to an essentially pure market economy, i.e. liberal capitalism, or else on one combined with a welfare state said to be consistent with Muslim principles. Such perspectives often also imply a conservative neoclassical or marginalist economic perspective, or else a more liberal Keynesian one. Such approaches have caused some cynical observers to refer to the Islamic economic system as capitalism without *riba*, and perhaps, plus *zakat* and *niat* – a charge most would emphatically denounce, though usually by assertion, rather than persuasion.

There is also another – less common – caricature which equates the Islamic economic system with 'communism plus god', though this writer has yet to find any serious economic writing which even vaguely approximates such a position. Very common, however, is the view that Islam is unequivocally committed to justice, which can only be assured by essentially egalitarian economic institutions and relations, sometimes associated with some variety of socialism. For instance, socialist principles of distribution – in accordance with labour and need – are said to be prescribed by Islam. At the more theoretical level too, Islam is said to embody an essentially labour theory of value, rather than one based on subjective preference or marginal utility, as in neoclassical economics. The most common objections – i.e. that Islam favours commodity exchange and individual property rights – have been rebutted by reference to the 'market socialism' option, and by emphasising Islam's recognition of communal rights and state ownership.

2.4   Raban: Thatcher's capitalism

Jonathan Raban, 1989: *God, Man and Mrs Thatcher*. London: Chatto & Windus (pp. 12–13).

Attempts have been made, however, to apply Christianity to the specifics of the economic. Jonathan Raban here provides an extract from Margaret Thatcher's speech to the General Assembly of The Church of Scotland in 1988. Thatcher was then in full-flow in a moral-cum-religious crusade to construct an enterprise culture which would combat cultural forces undermining wealth creation. (See Wiener (1985) on the latter.) Wealth creation is here justified by reference to Biblical authority. And at the same time, Thatcher is attempting to bring about a form of capitalism which is legitimated by the fact that rather than money being loved 'for its own sake' it is invested in the future, used for charitable purposes, and so on. (For more on Christian evaluations of wealth creation see Wuthnow (ed.) (1995), including the essay by Marsha Witten (pp. 117–44); for a good illustration of a more general application of religion to honour capitalism, see Novak (1991), his argument also being that 'the life of the spirit' . . . 'makes democratic capitalism possible' (p. 14); for a summary of how spiritualities of life can serve to legitimate – indeed sacralize – the acquisition of riches, see Heelas (1996, pp. 95–6).)

The Old Testament lays down in Exodus the Ten Commandments as given to Moses, the injunction in Leviticus to love our neighbour as ourselves and generally the importance of observing a strict code of law. The New Testament is a record of the Incarnation, the teachings of Christ and the establishment of the Kingdom of God. Again we have the emphasis on loving our neighbour as ourselves and to 'Do-as-you-would-be-done-by'.

I believe that by taking together these key elements from the Old and New Testaments, we gain:

a view of the universe,
a proper attitude to work,
and principles to shape economic and social life.

We are told we must work and use our talents to create wealth. 'If a man will not work he shall not eat' wrote St Paul to the Thessalonians. Indeed, abundance rather than poverty has a legitimacy which derives from the very nature of Creation.

Nevertheless, the Tenth Commandment – Thou shalt not covet – recognises that making money and owning things could become selfish activities. But it is not the creation of wealth that is wrong but love of money for its own sake. The spiritual dimension comes in deciding what one does with the wealth. How could we respond to the many calls for help, or invest for the future, or support the wonderful artists and craftsmen whose work also glorifies God, unless we had first worked hard and used our talents to create the necessary wealth? And remember the woman with the alabaster jar of ointment.

2.5 Tawney and the religious critique of capitalism

R. H. Tawney, 1926: *Religion and the Rise of Capitalism. A Historical Study.* London: John Murray (pp. 282; 283–6).

Tawney's powerful prose serves to move us into diametrically opposed terrain: populated by those who draw on religion to criticize the capitalist project. He is critical of the (utilitarian) individualism of the market economy – an individualism which encourages everybody to seek out their own ends, thereby undermining those shared values essential for the communal good. (See also Parsons, 1968; Bellah et al., 1985.) Having written of the way in which religion is used to inform an economic ethic, and having introduced other (socialist, etc.) attempts to restore a moral culture to capitalism, he ends on a pessimistic note: the 'Church of Christ' cannot enter into dealing with 'the idolatry of wealth'. The 'idolatry' is too powerful. (For a critique of the economic from the point of view of spiritualities of life, see Schumacher (1980). Like Tawney, only more so, it is emphasized that work must serve the development of what it is to be a person.)

Few can contemplate without a sense of exhilaration the splendid achievements of practical energy and technical skill, which, from the latter part of the seventeenth century, were transforming the face of material civilization, and of which England was the daring, if not too scrupulous, pioneer. If, however, economic ambitions are good servants, they are bad masters. Harnessed to a social purpose, they will turn the mill and grind the corn. But the question, to what end the wheels revolve, still remains; and on that question the naïve and uncritical worship of economic power, which is the mood of unreason too often engendered in those whom that new Leviathan has hypnotized by its spell, throws no light. Its result is not seldom a world in which men command a mechanism that they cannot fully use, and an organization which has every perfection except that of motion. [...]

Economic efficiency is a necessary element in the life of any sane and vigorous society, and only the incorrigible sentimentalist will depreciate its significance. But to convert efficiency from an instrument into a primary object is to destroy efficiency itself. For the condition of effective action in a complex civilization is co-operation. And the condition of co-operation is agreement, both as to the ends to which effort should be applied, and the criteria by which its success is to be judged.

Agreement as to ends implies the acceptance of a standard of values, by which the position to be assigned to different objects may be determined. In a world of limited resources, where nature yields a return only to prolonged and systematic effort, such a standard must obviously take account of economic possibilities. But it cannot itself be merely economic, since the comparative importance of economic and of other interests – the sacrifice, for example, of material goods worth incurring in order to extend leisure, or develop education, or humanize toil – is precisely the point on which it is needed to throw light. It must be based on some conception of the requirements of human nature as a whole, to which the satisfaction of economic needs is evidently vital, but which demands the satisfaction of other needs as well, and which can organize its activities on a rational system only in so far as it has a clear apprehension of their relative significance. [. . .]

A reasonable estimate of economic organization must allow for the fact that, unless industry is to be paralysed by recurrent revolts on the part of outraged human nature, it must satisfy criteria which are not purely economic. A reasonable view of its possible modifications must recognize that natural appetites may be purified or restrained, as, in fact, in some considerable measure they already have been, by being submitted to the control of some larger body of interests. The distinction made by the philosophers of classical antiquity between liberal and servile occupations, the mediæval insistence that riches exist for man, not man for riches, Ruskin's famous outburst, 'there is no wealth but life,' the argument of the Socialist who urges that production should be organized for service, not for profit, are but different attempts to emphasize the instrumental character of economic activities, by reference to an ideal which is held to express the true nature of man.

Of that nature and its possibilities the Christian Church was thought, during the greater part of the period discussed in these pages, to hold by definition a conception distinctively its own. It was therefore committed to the formulation of a social theory, not as a philanthropic gloss upon the main body of its teaching, but as a vital element in a creed concerned with the destiny of men whose character is formed, and whose spiritual potentialities are fostered or starved, by the commerce of the market-place and the institutions of society. [. . .]

Compromise is as impossible between the Church of Christ and the idolatry of wealth, which is the practical religion of capitalist societies, as it was between the Church and the State idolatry of the Roman Empire.

Economic: examples

Example: work ethics

2.6 Giddens summarizing Weber's 'Protestant ethic' thesis

Anthony Giddens, 1985: Introduction (pp. vii–xxvi), to Max Weber, *The Protestant Ethic and the Spirit of Capitalism* (orig. 1904–5). London, Boston and Sydney: Unwin (pp. xii–xiv).

In one of the most debated theses in the study of religion, Weber argued that the construction of capitalism – and thus of the central dynamic of modernity itself – owed a great deal to various Puritan sects of the Reformation (themselves, it can be added, very 'strong' religions of difference). Rather than valuing work as a means to the end of consumption, the sects valued work and the accumulation of wealth as a means to the end of providing a sign that one was 'chosen'. Valuing work in this way, whilst being ascetic, Puritans were motivated to work hard, and to save and invest. Whilst far from being an intended of prosperity religion, the Protestant sects thus had an unexpected, unintended consequence. (See Larry Ray (1987) for critical discussion of the thesis.)

What explains this historically peculiar circumstance of a drive to the accumulation of wealth conjoined to an absence of interest in the worldly pleasures which it can purchase? It would certainly be mistaken, Weber argues, to suppose that it derives from the relaxation of traditional moralities: this novel outlook is a distinctively *moral* one, demanding in fact unusual self-discipline. The entrepreneurs associated with the development of rational capitalism combine the impulse to accumulation with a positively frugal life-style. Weber finds the answer in the 'this-worldly asceticism' of Puritanism, as focused through the concept of the 'calling'. The notion of the calling, according to Weber, did not exist either in Antiquity or in Catholic theology; it was introduced by the Reformation. It refers basically to the idea that the highest form of moral obligation of the individual is to fulfil his duty in worldly affairs. This projects religious behaviour into the day-to-day world, and stands in contrast to the Catholic ideal of the monastic life, whose object is to transcend the demands of mundane existence. Moreover, the moral responsibility of the Protestant is cumulative: the cycle of sin, repentance and forgiveness, renewed throughout the life of the Catholic, is absent in Protestantism.

Although the idea of the calling was already present in Luther's doctrines, Weber argues, it became more rigorously developed in the various Puritan sects: Calvinism, Methodism, Pietism and Baptism. Much of Weber's discussion is in fact concentrated upon the first of these, although he is interested not just in Calvin's doctrines as such but in their later evolution within the Calvinist movement. Of the elements in Calvinism that Weber singles out for special attention, perhaps the most important, for his thesis, is the doctrine of predestination: that only some human beings are chosen to be saved from damnation, the choice being predetermined by God. Calvin himself may have been sure of his own salvation, as the instrument of Divine prophecy; but none of his followers could be. 'In its extreme inhumanity', Weber comments, 'this doctrine must above all have had one consequence for the life of a generation which surrendered to its magnificent consistency . . . a feeling of unprecedented inner loneliness.' From this torment, Weber holds, the capitalist spirit was born. On the pastoral level, two developments occurred: it became obligatory to regard oneself as chosen, lack of certainty being indicative of insufficient faith; and the performance of 'good works' in worldly activity became accepted as the medium whereby such surety could be demonstrated. Hence success in a calling eventually came to be regarded as a 'sign' – never a means – of being one of the elect. The accumulation of wealth was morally sanctioned in so far as it was combined with a sober, industrious career; wealth was condemned only if employed to support a life of idle luxury or self-indulgence.

Calvinism, according to Weber's argument, supplies the moral energy and drive of the capitalist entrepreneur; Weber speaks of its doctrines as having an 'iron consistency' in the bleak discipline which it demands of its adherents. The element of ascetic self-control in worldly affairs is certainly there in the other Puritan sects also: but they lack the dynamism of Calvinism. Their impact, Weber suggests, is mainly upon the formation of a moral outlook enhancing labour discipline within the lower and middle levels of capitalist economic organisation. 'The virtues favoured by Pietism', for example, were those 'of the faithful official, clerk, labourer, or domestic worker'.

2.7   Estruch and a Catholic work ethic today

Joan Estruch, 1995: *Saints and Schemers. Opus Dei and its Paradoxes*. New York and Oxford: Oxford University Press (pp. 245; 240; 254).

Opus Dei, a Catholic quasi-monastic organization founded in 1939 by Escrivá da Balaguer and associated with many commercial enterprises, provides an example of an (apparently) efficacious work ethic in operation today. Among the contrasts with the traditional Protestant work ethic, work is here valued as a vehicle for self-sanctification. Joan Estruch's volume also serves to make the point that religious organizations can be very successful at wealth creation.

> The worldly asceticism of Opus Dei can be summarized in the words of its founder: 'To be holy means to sanctify work itself, to sanctify oneself in work, and to sanctify others with work'. [. . .]
>
> Manuel is a Catalan industrialist, father of an engineer who joined Opus Dei while still a student. After visiting one of the Work's centers and discovering its spirituality, Manuel said: 'Today I have discovered the best thing of my life; this suits me; *I have worked like a dog, frantically, doing nothing else, and now I discover that by working I can also sanctify myself. This is fantastic!'* [. . .]
>
> Earlier we observed that, unlike ascetic Protestantism, Opus Dei sees work as not so much man's contribution to the construction of a future Kingdom of God, as his collaboration in the establishment of 'Our Lord's true Kingdom,' here and now.
>
> 'Work, all work, is a testimony to the dignity of man, or his dominion over creation. It is the occasion for the development of one's own personality. It is the link joining a man with other human beings, the font of resources to sustain his own family; the means of contributing to the bettering of the society in which he lives, and to the progress of all humanity'.
>
> The two biblical texts which seem to provide the foundation for all the 'theology of work' of Msgr. Escrivá and his followers and which establish the origin of the divine commandment (vocation) to work are, first, 'Be fruitful and multiply; fill the earth and dominate it' (or subdue it, master it; Genesis 1:28); and second, the statement that God created man 'so he would work'.

2.8 Bellah and Japan

Robert N. Bellah, 1957: *Tokugawa Religion. The Values of Pre-Industrial Japan.* New York: Free Press; London: Collier-Macmillan (pp. 194–6).

Robert Bellah's general thesis is that Tokugawa religion must be given ' "credit" for contributing to the miraculous rise of modern Japan' (p. 196). Parallels are drawn with Weber's study of the role played by the (traditional) Protestant work ethic. It can also be noted that – as with Opus Dei – work is valued as providing an opportunity to engage in self-salvation.

Religion played an important role in the process of political and economic rationalization in Japan through maintaining and intensifying commitment to the central values, supplying motivation and legitimation for certain necessary political innovations and reinforcing an ethic of inner-worldly asceticism which stressed diligence and economy. That it may also have played an important part in the formation of the central values which were favorable to industrialization is at least a strong possibility.

Religion reinforced commitment to the central value system by making that value system meaningful in an ultimate sense. The family and the nation were not merely secular collectivities but were also religious entities. Parents and political superiors had something of the sacred about them, were merely the lower echelons of the divine. Fulfillment of one's obligations to these superordinates had an ultimate meaning. It ensured the continuation of future blessings and of that ultimate protection which alone could save the individual from the hardships and dangers of this transitory world.

Alternatively another set of religious conceptions was offered which also reinforced the central value system. This view accepted the structure of Japanese society and its values as in accordance with the nature of reality. Fully and wholeheartedly carrying out one's part in that society and living up to its values meant an identification with that ultimate reality. This losing the self and becoming identified with ultimate nature, a line of religious thought deriving from Mencius, also promised release from the basic frustrations of existence in a state of enlightenment. [. . .]

Finally, we must consider the relation of religion to that ethic of inner-worldly asceticism which is so powerful in Japan. The obligation to hard, selfless labor and to the restraint of one's own desires for consumption is closely linked to the obligations to sacred and semisacred superiors which are so stressed in Japanese religion, as also to that state of selfless identification with ultimate nature. As we have had repeated occasion to see, Japanese religion never tires of stressing the importance of diligence and frugality and of attributing religious significance to them, both in terms of carrying out one's obligations to the sacred and in terms of purifying the self of evil impulses and desires. That such an ethic is profoundly favorable to economic rationalization was the major point of Weber's study of Protestantism and we must say that it seems similarly favorable in Japan.

Example: magical empowerment

2.9 Schneider and Dornbusch: prosperity religion today

Louis Schneider and Standford M. Dornbusch, 1958: *Popular Religion. Inspirational Books in America*. Chicago: University of Chicago Press (pp. 38–9).

Presenting the main findings of a study of the forty-six best sellers of 'inspirational religious literature' published in the United States between 1875 and 1955, Louis Schneider and Standford Dornbusch make it clear that prosperity religion has not died out with the advance of modern times. The extract concerns theistic prosperity religion, 'surrender' to a God who 'exists objectively in his own right' being of crucial importance. At the same time, however, human nature is 'inherently good', positive 'thoughts' (etc.) also playing a key role in the quest for 'life-mastery'. We thus see interplay of the theistic with themes found in spiritualities of life.

1   The writers of the literature hold to the view that religion gives life meaning by providing a feeling of individual worth or significance.
2   Religious faith is said to ease the making of decisions: one needs only to surrender to God and the right decision will be forthcoming.
3   The writers insist that religion gives power to live by.
4   Religion promotes success, successful living, life-mastery.
5   It is true both that religious faith is asserted to bring happiness and satisfaction in this world and that man is said to be able to *expect* happiness in this world. It is further claimed that religion brings emotional security.
6   Religious faith is viewed as likely to bring *either* wealth or (emotional or physical) health.
7   The individual can make changes beneficial to himself by religious means.
8   There is small eschatological concern among Protestant writers. The notion of punishment in the next life is nearly absent among them, and they refer to a next life at all less than do the Catholics. A powerful stress on salvation in this life rather than the next prevails, and there is correspondingly slight preoccupation with the agencies of salvation in the next life.
9   God is averred to exist objectively in his own right, although an important undercurrent sustains the view that he exists since belief in him 'works.'

10   God is a God of good will toward man, liberal with rewards in this life, averse to punishments in the next. The conception of him as judge is given little attention.

11   The divinity of Christ is generally assumed.

12   The literature consistently sees man as inherently good.

13   Teleological or anthropomorphic views of nature are weak and subdued.

14   Although man in the literature is involved in *interpersonal* relations, within the family, on the job, and so on, he lives remarkably unaffected by institutional realities, in a world where his destiny is ostensibly largely remote from social, political, or economic circumstance.

15   The association of poverty with virtue is nearly absent.

16   Of some prominence in the literature is a technology of affirming positive thoughts, denying negative thoughts, denying the negative by affirming the positive. A corresponding stress on thought control is quite evident, and rather frequent emphasis is given to the view of the metaphysical primacy of the mental over the material.

17   Favorable mention of subjective religious experience is a strong general feature of the literature.

18   The literature has a pronounced antidogmatic strain (mitigated in recent years).

2.10   Peale's 'energy'

Norman Vincent Peale, 1952: *The Power of Positive Thinking*. Englewood Cliffs: Prentice-Hall (pp. 37–7; 40; 50–1).

Drawing on Biblical authority, this Christian minister – and the best-known of all prosperity teachers in the west – emphasizes 'self-surrender': giving oneself up to God and letting God's 'energy' do the work. Surrender is not taken to be a passive process. Inspired by the God which is 'in you', it involves the right – that is Christian – 'thought life'. Liberating the person from emotional and psychological disorders, positive thoughts also release power. As in the previous extracts, there are clear signs of 'New Age' thought in the work of Peale.

A friend in Connecticut, an energetic man, full of vitality and vigor, says that he goes to church regularly to 'get his batteries recharged.' His concept is sound. God *is* the source of all energy – energy in the universe, atomic energy, electrical energy, and spiritual energy; indeed every form of energy derives from the Creator. The Bible emphasizes this point when it says, 'He giveth power to the faint; and to them that have no might he increaseth strength.' (Isaiah 40:29)

In another statement the Bible describes the energizing and re-energizing process: '. . . in Him we live (that is, have vitality), and move (have dynamic energy), and have our being (attain complete-ness).' (Acts 17:28) [. . .]

A number of years ago I attended a lecture at which a speaker asserted before a large audience that he had not been tired in thirty years. He explained that thirty years before he had passed through a spiritual experience in which by self-surrender he had made contact with Divine power. From then on he possessed sufficient energy for all of his activities, and these were prodigious. He so obviously illustrated his teachings that everyone in that vast audience was pro-foundly impressed.

To me it was a revelation of the fact that in our consciousness we can tap a reservoir of boundless power as a result of which it is not necessary to suffer depletion of energy. For years I have studied and experimented with the ideas which this speaker outlined and which others have expounded and demonstrated, and it is my conviction that the principles of Christianity scientifically utilized can develop an uninterrupted and continuous flow of energy into the human mind and body. [. . .]

Every great personality I have ever known, and I have known many, who has demonstrated the capacity for prodigious work has been a person in tune with the Infinite. Every such person seems in harmony with nature and in contact with the Divine energy. They have not necessarily been pious people, but invariably they have been extraordinarily well organized from an emotional and psycho-logical point of view. It is fear, resentment, the projection of parental faults upon people when they are children, inner conflicts and obses-sions that throw off balance the finely equated nature, thus causing undue expenditure of natural force.

The longer I live the more I am convinced that neither age nor circumstance needs to deprive us of energy and vitality. We are at last awakening to the close relationship between religion and health. We are beginning to comprehend a basic truth hitherto neglected, that our physical condition is determined very largely by our emotional condition, and our emotional life is profoundly regulated by our thought life. [. . .]

The practice of . . . [Christian] principles will serve to bring a person into the proper tempo of living. Our energies are destroyed because of the high tempo, the abnormal pace at which we go. The conservation of energy depends upon getting your personality speed synchronized with the rate of God's movement. God is in you. [. . .]

One day Walter Huston, the actor, sat by Jack Smith's desk. He noted a big sign on the wall on which were penciled the following letters: A P R P B W P R A A. In surprise Huston asked, 'What do those letters mean?'

Smith laughed and said, 'They stand for "Affirmative Prayers Release Powers By Which Positive Results Are Accomplished."'

2.11   Ray: 'Let the Divine Plan of Your Life Manifest Itself'

Sondra Ray, 1990: *How to be Chic, Fabulous and Live Forever*. Berkeley: Celestial Arts (pp. 125–6; 130).

Although not all that far removed from Peale, Sondra Ray explicitly thinks of herself as 'New Age' rather than Christian. What matters is the fact that 'that you are already a spiritual Being'. By engaging in appropriate activities – including looking fabulous and helping others – the perfected life within comes to be manifested as success, even 'Physical Immortality'.

And how does Physical Immortality relate to being 'chic' and fabulous?

Well, to me, it is quite clearly related. When you feel wonderful, you're likely to look wonderful. This makes you *feel* even more wonderful. Looking fabulous raises your self-esteem and energy and makes you feel so much more alive. In this way, you attract more prosperity and fun to yourself – then you want to live more, and so it goes. [. . .]

Although it is true that the *soul* is what matters, and the exterior is not to be the top priority, it is also true that a person 'wears his mind.' And if you go around telling people you are an Immortalist and you want to live forever and you look like a slob or are very drab, people are going to wonder . . . who is he kidding? He does not even care about himself enough to iron his clothes.

Your actions and your looks should match up with your words so that you are in harmony, don't you think? And, in my opinion, Rebirthing and Immortality are *modern*. This *is* the New Age. Being chic is being fashionable, current, and doing it with *vitality*. [. . .]

You are fabulous. Include yourself fully in the *game* of life. You are one with the Creative Genius behind the original flow of life. You are valuable to the whole. Acknowledge the Presence (Great Spirit/God), and remember that you are already a spiritual Being. Embody that God has made you out of Himself, and you can now awaken to all the possibilities of the Life that is in you. Jesus said: 'It is done unto you as you Believe.'

Yes, you can be a fabulous person and have joy, happiness, love, friendship, health, success, and even Physical Immortality. But remember to have these thoughts and wishes for others. Jesus said, 'Give, and to you shall be given.' A fabulous person always helps others and sees God in everything. 'Life will be to you what you are to it.' (Ernest Holmes said that. He was the founder of Science of Mind and deserves our respect. He made great contributions to modern thought.)

And you, too, can make a contribution to this planet and humanity, and I salute you for figuring out what it is. Let the Divine Plan of Your Life Manifest Itself.

2.12   Sivananda: prosperity in India

Swami Sivananda, 1990: *Sure Ways for Success in Life and God-Realisation*. Tehri-Garhwal: The Divine Life Society (p. 22).

Numerically and perhaps existentially speaking, prosperity religion is almost certainly the most important form of religiosity in contemporary India. Among countless other teachers, Swami Sivananda, of the Divine Life Society, here illustrates this kind of religiosity by reference to what he calls the 'mind'. (McKean (1996) provides a good account of Indian 'sumptuary spirituality', including a chapter on the Divine Life Society; for a good example of prosperity religion from Japan, see Wilson and Dobbelaere (1994).)

SIGNS OF GROWING WILL

Unruffled state of the mind, poise, cheerfulness, inner strength, capacity to turn out difficult works, success in all undertakings, power to influence people, a magnetic and dynamic personality, magnetic aura on the face, sparkling eyes, steady gaze, powerful voice, a magnanimous gait, unyielding nature, fearlessness, etc., are some of the signs or symptoms that indicate that one's 'will' is growing.

BECOME AN EXPERT

You must become a Daksha (an expert) (refer Chapter XII, 16, Gita) in deciding a line of action when you are in a dilemma in the twinkling of an eye that can bring sure and positive success. You must keep the instrument (Buddhi) very, very subtle and sharp. See how smart and adept the Kshatriya kings were in olden days during warfares! A commander-in-chief is expected to have this faculty to a remarkable degree. Sivaji and Napoleon had this virtue.

DEVELOP FIRMNESS AND PATIENCE

Unwavering firmness and patience are needed to tide over critical situations and gain success. Dhriti and Dhairya (presence of mind), and Samata (balance of mind) develop the 'will' to a remarkable degree.

Example: responses to deprivation

2.13   Marx and Engels in critical mood

K. Marx and F. Engels, 1958 (orig. 1957): *K. Marx and F. Engels on Religion*. London: Lawrence and Wishart (pp. 42; 127–8; 297).

Religion can be used to legitimate inequality. Religion can be used to dull inequality (the 'opiate' thesis). Religion can be used to strive for equality or – much more typically – to simply become wealthy (by way of work ethics or by way of what today is often thought of in terms of the accumulation of 'cultural capital'). Religion can be used to legitimate acquired or established status. Religion can be used to enhance inequality by repressing the less well-off. Such functionalist theorizing – often articulated in terms of class categorization – owes a very great deal indeed to the blunt views of Marx and Engels. Unfortunately, it is not easy to extract from Marx and Engels whose arguments are generally bound up with intricate historical detail. The following three passages, however, serve to illustrate their ideas: the first concerning opiated compensation and remedial protest; the second how religion can be used to control the working class; the final paragraph (now by Engels) that feudal hierarchies had to be tackled by the bourgeoisie and the 'peasants' for them to progress economically.

Religious distress is at the same time the *expression* of real distress and the *protest* against real distress. Religion is the sigh of the oppressed creature, the heart of a heartless world, just as it is the spirit of a spiritless situation. It is the *opium* of the people.

The abolition of religion as the *illusory* happiness of the people is required for their *real* happiness. The demand to give up the illusions about its condition is the *demand to give up a condition which needs illusions*. The criticism of religion is therefore *in embryo the criticism of the vale of woe*, the *halo* of which is religion. [. . .]

The first measure of religious coercion was the Beer Bill, which shut down all places of public entertainment on Sundays, except between 6 and 10 p.m. This bill was smuggled through the House at the end of a sparsely attended sitting, after the pietists had bought the support of the big public-house owners of London by guaranteeing them that the license system would continue, that is, that big capital would retain its monopoly. Then came the Sunday Trading Bill, which has now passed its third reading in the Commons and separate clauses of which have just been discussed by commissions in both Houses. This new coercive measure too was ensured the vote of big capital, because only small shopkeepers keep open on Sunday and the proprietors of the big shops are quite willing to do away with the Sunday competition of the small fry by parliamentary means. In both cases there is a conspiracy of the Church with monopoly capital, but in both cases there are religious penal laws against the lower classes to set the consciences of the privileged classes at rest. The *Beer Bill* was as far from hitting the aristocratic clubs as the *Sunday Trading Bill* is from hitting the Sunday occupations of genteel society. The workers get their wages late on Saturday; they are the only ones for whom shops open on Sundays. They are the only ones compelled to make their purchases, small as they are, on Sundays. The new bill is therefore directed against them alone. In the eighteenth century the French aristocracy said: For us, Voltaire; for the people, the mass and the tithes. In the nineteenth century the English aristocracy says: For us, pious phrases; for the people, Christian practice.

The classical saint of Christianity mortified *his* body for the salvation of the souls of the masses; the modern, educated saint mortifies *the bodies of the masses* for the salvation of his own soul.

This alliance of a dissipated, degenerating and pleasure-seeking aristocracy with a church propped up by the filthy profits calculated upon by the big brewers and monopolizing wholesalers. [. . .]

The rising middle class was bound to come into collision with the established religion: first, that the class most directly interested in the struggle against the pretensions of the Roman Church was the bourgeoisie; and second, that every struggle against feudalism, at that time, had to take on a religious disguise, had to be directed against the Church in the first instance. But if the universities and the traders of the cities started the cry, it was sure to find, and did find, a strong echo in the masses of the country people, the peasants, who everywhere had to struggle for their very existence with their feudal lords, spiritual and temporal.

2.14   Bruce and the appeal of prosperity Christianity

Steve Bruce, 1990: *Pray TV. Televangelism in America*. London and New York: Routledge (pp. 159–61).

Although the traditional Protestant work ethic – as portrayed by Weber – has not fared well in the United States or elsewhere (see the extract from Bell, **2.19**, below, as well as Weber on the 'iron cage' (**3.12**), the same cannot be said of prosperity religions with their sacred or miraculous powers. Drawing on relative deprivation theory, Steve Bruce tackles the matter of explaining the appeal of the prosperity teachings of televangelism and the health and wealth gospel. So long as there is economic deprivation among those already holding certain basic conservative religious beliefs, it appears that the quest for 'miraculous solutions' will remain on the agenda. (For an application of deprivation theory to prosperity versions of spiritualities of life see Harris (1981).)

Some elements of the electronic church . . . [promise] that those who get saved will be rewarded *in this life* with health and wealth. And being rich is not only a good thing but it can come painlessly, without the effort of diligently striving. If you need something, just write it on the back of your Blessing Pact card and send it with your donation to Oral Roberts or make it one of your Seven Lifetime Prayer requests and accompany it by a suitably large donation and Pat Robertson will place it with thousands of others in a column in a prayer room in CBN headquarters where it will be promoted daily by the prayers of CBN employees until the Lord returns. [. . .]

There are still no good studies of just what sorts of people are attracted to the modern health and wealth teachings but a few general points can be made. What Max Weber neatly described as 'this-worldly asceticism' obviously fits best with the material interests of a social class which has the opportunity to better itself by diligence and such opportunities are not universally distributed. American blacks, for example, have been systematically denied opportunities and this is half of the explanation for the popularity of miracles in black pentecostalism. The other half is the greater presence in black Christianity of the expectation of miracles. One can appreciate why many poor whites would feel similarly unmoved by an ethos tailored to the situation of small businessmen, small farmers, or independent craftsmen. [. . .]

In the absence of good empirical material one is forced back on informed speculation but there seems little doubt that the health and wealth gospel and its slightly more moderate televangelism cousin appeals primarily to the working class and the lower middle class. Although it has rightly been criticized for failing to live up to its author's expectations of providing a general explanation of crime and deviance, Robert K. Merton's seminal 'Social structure and anomie' essay does point us in the right direction for understanding the appeal of prosperity theology to a particular section of the population who are already disposed to conservative Protestantism. The core of his essay is the simple but important point that there is a disjuncture at the heart of modern democracies. All members of our societies are encouraged to want and expect the same 'good things' out of life. That is, the goals are distributed universalistically. But the means to achieve these goals legitimately are not equally distributed. Some people have a long head start and others are patently handicapped. The result is a strong sense for many people of being *relatively deprived*. [. . .]

To simplify, there are two possible responses to relative deprivation. For a section of those people who are excluded from such conventional channels of social mobility as education, the response is the instrumental one of working ever harder, taking a second job, often in a DSO. Organizations such as Tupperware and Amway have a strong affinity with conservative Protestantism in two ways; indirectly in that the entrepreneurial ideology of DSOs is itself a 'secularized' form of some elements of the conservative Protestant tradition and directly in that the values found in conservative Protestant religion and in the direct selling economy combine to reinforce each other. But for reasons which are not yet clear (but which almost certainly stem from their position in the economy) some people do not produce that instrumental response but fall back instead on the magical promises of prosperity theology and 'name it and claim it'. The success in fund-raising of those television evangelists who make such promises demonstrates the demand, the need, which exists for miraculous solutions to socio-economic problems.

However, this should not be taken, as it is by Stark and Bainbridge in their grand theory of religion, as an explanation of why some people are attracted to religious belief. Where they argue that the persistence of needs that cannot be met in this world explains why people believe in a next world, I would argue that the faith comes first. It is because they are already disposed to believe that the Bible is the word of God, that there is a God who takes a direct interest in our lives, and that prayer works, that some people come to see solutions to their economic problems in religious activities.

2.15 Lewis: spirit possession as a 'war between the sexes'

I. M. Lewis, 1996: Spirit Possession and Deprivation Cults. *Man* 1 (3): 307–20 (pp. 318–20).

The world of spirit possession among the Tonga of Zambia – and in many other global settings according to Ioan Lewis – might seem far removed from the religions discussed by Bruce. But Lewis presents evidence which suggests that the dynamic of deprivation–compensation is also operative: now, though, in terms of the position of women.

It must now be clear, I think, that we are concerned here with a widespread use of spirit possession, by means of which women and other depressed categories exert mystical pressures upon their superiors in circumstances of deprivation and frustration when few other sanctions are available to them. [. . .]

I believe that the material I have so far presented on these peripheral cults supports my emphasis which is less on the conservative, *status quo* maintaining aspects than on the dynamic role of mystical sanctions in the war between the sexes. In short, my argument is that if in these traditionally male-dominated societies women are not always actually suffragettes, then they can readily become so when the circumstances are appropriate. I now refer for supporting evidence for this view to a recent study by Elizabeth Colson of the Tonga of Zambia. By contrasting the conservative, traditionalist, Valley Tonga with their more sophisticated and acculturated Plateau countrymen, and using historical evidence, Colson's material reveals what really is at stake in these women's deprivation cults.

Amongst the Plateau Tonga, increasingly involved in the modern market economy of Zambia since the 1930's, and with local opportunities for earning cash wages which do not require their menfolk to work extensively as absent migrant labourers, there has been a virtually parallel acculturation of men and of women. Moreover, the traditional pattern of relations between the sexes is one of equality rather than inequality. Thus, like men, whether unmarried or married, women participate freely in men's social activities and are not strongly hedged about with mystical or other restraints. In this situation possession by peripheral *masabe* spirits is today rare, and in so far as it exists, affects men and women equally.

Amongst the Valley Tonga the situation is altogether different. Here, for long, men have participated through labour migration in the wider European-orientated world, while women have remained at home fascinated by the town delights and mysteries from which they have been excluded. It is these secluded and excluded wives who are regularly subject to possession by spirits which today characteristically demand gifts that these women associate with their alluring urban counter-parts. As well as for gay cloths and luxury foods, one of the commonest demands of the spirits is for soap. This reflects a growing male sophistication and repugnance for the oil and ochre cosmetics which Valley women traditionally apply to their bodies, and a distinct preference by men for freshly bathed and fragrantly scented partners. It is in this cosmetic idiom that, through their possessing spirits, these rural women today call attention to their exclusion and neglect and seek to overcome it. In the past, their spirits desired men's garments and possessions.

Thus it is that these women's deprivation cults mirror the changing interests and desires of those who succumb to possession. [. . .]

Thus, contrasting this record of these cults among the Valley Tonga with the position on the Plateau, it is clear how in the former case much of the traditional inequality between the sexes continues and so the cults continue, with modifications in the cast of invading spirits corresponding to changing experience of the world. For the Plateau Tonga, with their more liberal treatment of women, such possession of this type as exists continues to affect men and women equally. This makes sense only if we acknowledge the at least potential dynamism which I have stressed in these cults.

2.16   Lienhardt and cargo cults

Godfrey Lienhardt, 1966: *Social Anthropology*. London, Oxford, New York: Oxford University Press (pp. 67–8; 135–6).

Cargo cults, most distinctively developed in Melanesia, and still operative today, provide evidence of another – arguably compensatory – response to economic deprivation. We say 'arguably' in that, as Godfrey Lienhardt suggests here, much more could well be involved than merely responding to economic problems: a 'moral regeneration', for example, which is not merely compensatory.

From towards the end of the last century, there have arisen in Melanesia many 'cargo cults' in which a prophet announces that the end of the world is near, and that the people will then get all the European goods they desire from some outside source. The millennium will have come:

> The people therefore prepare themselves for the Day by setting up cult-organizations, and by building store-houses, jetties and so on to receive the goods, known as 'cargo' in the local pidgin English. Often, also, they abandon their gardens, kill off their livestock, eat all their food and throw away their money.

Worsley has shown, with explicit reference to such studies as that of the Sanusi of Cyrenaica, how the leaders of these movements, religious preachers and prophets, represent a political response by the islanders to foreign wealth and foreign control. The prophet, speaking with a supposedly supernatural authority, is able to provide a focus of allegiance for people who otherwise would be divided and opposed, as members of different little communities each jealous of its neighbours and attached to its local gods and spirits. He is 'reshaping the world', to use an expression from a hymn by the Nuer prophet Ngundeng, as modern state authorities have sometimes tried to fashion the political order anew by more rational planning and action. [...]

K. O. L. Burridge, in *Mambu*, describes how

> participants ... engage in a number of strange and exotic rites and ceremonies the purpose of which is, apparently, to gain possession of European manufactured goods. ... Large decorated houses, or 'aeroplanes' or 'ships' made of wood, bark, and palm thatch bound together with vines, may be built to receive the goods, and participants may whirl, shake, chant, dance, foam at the mouth, or couple promiscuously in agitated attempts to obtain the cargo they want.

But something other than greed for material possessions is involved. Burridge says:

> The most significant theme in cargo movements seems to be moral regeneration: the creation of a new man, the creation of new unities, the creation of a new society. ... And both new man and new society are to be a true amalgam or synthesis, not a mixture of European and Kanaka forms and ideals.

These are religions largely created or initiated by charismatic leaders, as Max Weber called them, and bear the marks of consistency of a single dominating personality. But even then their coherence is not that of a logically thought out, rational scheme of ideas produced by one mind only. After the initial appeal of the leader's definition and interpretation of a particular social experience, others make their contributions to ritual and doctrine. The 'vision' of one man then becomes accepted by his followers as a source of their distinctive collective experience, of which their own visions are part. D. F. Pocock observes in *Social Anthropology*:

> These societies . . . were being subjected to a gathering flood of external experience which finally increased beyond the 'stretch' of the indigenous categories that might render it meaningful. . . . The social forms of communication appear inadequate. The society is as near to atomization as it could be. The last resort is a new stress upon the individual as that society conceives it, an emphasis upon history, upon individual possession by spirits, upon the individually inspired leader.

Messianic and millenarian cults arise in special historical circumstances, involving usually a strong sense of social deprivation in their adherents; but, eccentric in some details as these religions may be, we can see in them basic characteristics of other religions in which the historical factors affecting the growth of ritual and doctrine are more difficult to ascertain. In such religions, it is traditional teaching, more or less formalized according to the society, which establishes in the minds of believers a particular interpretation of cosmic order – a cosmogony, cosmology, and sometimes a cosmography – and a confidence in prescribed means of understanding and adapting to that order.

2.17   Levine and 'masterless men'

Daniel H. Levine, 1995: Protestants and Catholics in Latin America: A Family Portrait. In Martin E. Marty and R. Scott Appleby (eds), *Fundamentalisms Comprehended*. Chicago and London: University of Chicago Press, pp. 155–78 (p. 170).

Turning from Melanesia to South America, Daniel Levine summarizes some of the ways in which those who have become disembedded with regard to traditional economic activities, and who are seeking to enter new capitalistic economic orders, find religion a potent agent of change. The thesis is highly reminiscent of Lienhardt's on cargo cults. (See Martin (1990) for more on the general thesis that religion is called into play to serve economic ends when 'organic unities' are eroded (p. 3).)

Drawing on the experience of the Puritan revolution, many observers have pointed to the rise of 'masterless men,' individuals free of old constraints but not yet bound to definitive new arrangements. The marginal status of displaced peasantries, agroproletarians, new urban migrants, subordinate ethnic groups, or despite the gender-specific formulation, women, are often cited as making them especially critical audiences for and carriers of change.

The marginality in question is not just a matter of being on the 'wrong side' of lines of class, wealth, ethnicity, or gender. It is also not a question of social dislocation, anomic, or cultural loss. Marginality also characterizes aspiring classes whose experience of movement leaves them free from the old order but without a secure footing in the new arrangements being put together. Such masterless men and women are a prime source of new leadership and an avid clientele for innovations in religious discourse that underscore equality, identity, and an independent capacity to reason, judge, and act together.

Singly and in combination, these elements are apparent in Latin America. As with other great transformative moments of cultural and political history, contemporary Latin American experience has generated vast enthusiasms along with a sense of movement and openness. In such contexts, the creation of new cultural understandings and social movements through religion is best understood not as a defense against change, but rather as a creative effort to reunderstand the world and reorganize person, family, and community to deal more effectively with it. This is a meaningful and reflexive process, in which human agency plays a central role. Crafting identities that make sense for individuals and groups requires sustained efforts to create resources, to make them accessible and usable, and to open new social spaces where all these can be put to use.

2.18 Berger portraying '"schools" for social mobility'

Peter L. Berger, 1993: *A Far Glory. The Quest for Faith in an Age of Credulity*. New York: Doubleday (pp. 57–8).

The thrust of this extract from Peter Berger is that churches in North America have helped educate 'lower class people' (in particular) with regard to those values which will serve them well in the future. Changes in religious affiliation also serve to confirm progress, serving as 'badges' of higher class respectability.

Protestantism and its distinctive morality – which Weber called the 'Protestant ethic' – were crucial in creating American middle-class culture; indeed, for a long time – certainly well into the last decade of the nineteenth century – that culture was Protestant to the core. Protestant church membership was one of the most important badges of middle-class status. Equally important, the different Protestant denominations served not only as class indicators but, especially for the lower classes, as agents of upward mobility. Thus, say in a New England town around the turn of this century, membership in the Episcopal or Unitarian churches indicated upper-class status, delicately set off from the middle-class constituency of Congregationalists and Presbyterians, and sharply separated from the *hoi polloi* who went to a Baptist or Methodist chapel or remained obstinately unchurched. Again and again, an individual from the lower classes who wanted to make his way up took the first step by joining one of the Protestant churches catering specially to his kind. In a very tangible way these churches served as 'schools' for social mobility; they inculcated the bourgeois virtues without which social success was not possible. Thus, theologically speaking, an individual may now have been washed in the blood of the Lamb; speaking sociologically, in the same process he learned to wash his feet and also purge his speech of lower-class obscenities. American society has long been one of massive social mobility. As entire groups of people moved *en masse* into the middle class, their churches also attained respectability; at that point, other denominations took over their previous function as mobility training grounds. In this century, Pentecostal and Holiness churches have been the most important conduits for lower-class people into the 'Protestant ethic' and thus into the promised land of bourgeois respectability.

Economic: prospects

2.19   Bell and the fate of the Protestant work ethic

Daniel Bell, 1979: *The Cultural Contradictions of Capitalism*. London: Heinemann (pp. 21–2).

Producers need consumers. The traditional Protestant ethic might have been good for the realm of production, but the ascetic aspect of the ethic was hardly conducive for that of consumption. Given that producers have to sell their goods, it is hardly surprising, as Bell puts it, that the ethic was 'undermined . . . by capitalism itself'. The construction of consumer culture and its associated 'hedonism' has not only eroded asceticism; it has also meant that work has increasingly come to be valued as the means to the end of (secular) self-gratification. It is reasonable to infer from this extract that the application of consumer values to work does not bode well for attempts (such as Thatcher's, reading **2.4**) to restore traditional religious ethicality. (See also Campbell (1987) on the construction of consumer culture, seen as involving, somewhat counter-intuitively, Romanticism; and see reading **3.12** for Weber's account of the secularization of producer capitalism.)

In the early development of capitalism, the unrestrained economic impulse was held in check by Puritan restraint and the Protestant ethic. One worked because of one's obligation to one's calling, or to fulfill the covenant of the community. But the Protestant ethic was undermined not by modernism but by capitalism itself. The greatest single engine in the destruction of the Protestant ethic was the invention of the installment plan, or instant credit. Previously one had to save in order to buy. But with credit cards one could indulge in instant gratification. The system was transformed by mass production and mass consumption, by the creation of new wants and new means of gratifying those wants.

The Protestant ethic had served to limit sumptuary (though not capital) accumulation. When the Protestant ethic was sundered from bourgeois society, only the hedonism remained, and the capitalist system lost its transcendental ethic. There remains the argument that capitalism serves as the basis for freedom, and for a rising standard of living and the defeat of poverty. Yet even if these arguments were true – for it is clear that freedom depends more upon the historical traditions of a particular society than upon the system of capitalism itself; and even the ability of the system to provide for economic growth is now questioned – the lack of a transcendental tie, the sense that a society fails to provide some set of 'ultimate meanings' in its character structure, work, and culture, becomes unsettling to a system.

The cultural, if not moral, justification of capitalism has become hedonism, the idea of pleasure as a way of life. And in the liberal ethos that now prevails, the model for a cultural imago has become the modernist impulse, with its ideological rationale of the impulse quest as a mode of conduct. It is this which is the cultural contradiction of capitalism. It is this which has resulted in the double bind of modernity.

2.20   Hunter: Evangelicals and the secularization of work

James Davison Hunter, 1987: *Evangelicalism. The Coming Generation*. Chicago and London: The University of Chicago Press (pp. 72–4).

James Davison Hunter concentrates on conservative Protestantism in the United States. Even in this realm, it appears, widespread 'cultural trends' – not least to do with the nature and valorization of the self – have undermined 'traditional behavioral standards'; indeed, have resulted in the secularization of work. (See also the reading from Hunter (**3.42**) on the turn to the self in evangelical religion.)

Whatever remained of that constellation of values and sentiments [of conservative Protestantism] through midcentury has since lost most of its cohesiveness. The legacy has paled. It comes as little surprise, for example, to find out that industriousness, competitiveness, vocational discipline, and the like continue to carry only marginal moral value and virtually no spiritual meaning for the Evangelical. It is perhaps more surprising to discover that even as secular values, they have become marginal, deferring to values surrounding the private sphere (e.g., the importance of a creative life-style, of friends, family, and hobbies). By itself, however, this provides little cause for wonder. In the broader picture it does presage other developments.

Since mid-century the elaborate structure of prohibitions constituting the moral boundaries of Protestant orthopraxy has also weakened substantially, and parts of the structure have collapsed altogether. [. . .]

The culmination of this process is seen in the shifting presuppositions about the nature of the self. The traditional conception was a social-psychological precondition for an intense commitment both to success in vocation and to the building of moral discipline and fortitude. It undergirded, even made possible, the other core elements of inner-worldly asceticism. These traditional conceptions though have given way to a relatively novel conception, one that implicitly venerates the self. The meaning of this for inner-worldly asceticism is plain. At a purely practical level, how is self-denial or self-mastery for the purpose of developing moral character possible when that which is to be denied or mastered is under almost constant examination? How is the renunciation of the self possible if it is being 'improved,' or is being developed to its 'full potential,' or is needing stimulation by 'new experiences'?. [. . .]

It should not be forgotten that the life-ethic of asceticism was originally born out of religious conviction and devotion and not the reverse. This being so, it would be reasonable to assume that varying gradations of religious orthodoxy would still account for some variation among Evangelicals in their attitudes toward work, morality, and the self: namely, that the more intensely orthodox the Evangelical is, the more self-denying he or she will be. This is, in fact, the case: the more orthodox and dogmatic do tend to be more vocationally and morally ascetic in their orientation.

There are those among the younger generation who do, indeed, remain fairly strongly committed to traditional ideals of work and morality, and they are characterized by more than a high degree of theological orthodoxy. They also tended to be affiliated with the smaller, more sectarian denominations of the Holiness-Pentecostal tradition in conservative Protestantism. Finally there is just a slightly greater tendency for them to be from lower-middle-class and working-class families (with less educational achievement). But again these differences are statistically different but not substantially different. In the main, the demographic variations make only marginal differences in the degree to which Evangelicals have abandoned the old ethic.

In a word, the Protestant legacy of austerity and ascetic self-denial is virtually obsolete in the larger Evangelical culture and is nearly extinct for a large percentage of the coming generation of Evangelicals. The caricatures of Evangelicalism as the last bastion of the traditional norms of discipline and hard work for their own sake, self-sacrifice, and moral asceticism are largely inaccurate. Far from being untouched by the cultural trends of the post-World War II decades, *the coming generation of Evangelicals, in their own distinct way, have come to participate fully in them.*

2.21   Rose and the resacralization of work

Michael Rose, 1985: *Re-working the Work Ethic. Economic Values and Socio-Cultural Politics.* London: Batsford (pp. 54–5).

Michael Rose here explores what he calls 'the post-bourgeois pattern', a complex of assumptions and values, of an expressivistic variety, associated with the turn to the self. Tracing the doctrine of self-actualization back to the 'Young Marx before Marxism'. Rose provides the historical context of a development now making a significant impact within the world of management. (See also Maslow (1965) on the idea that work can be good both for self-development and the company; for more on what can be called the 'self-work ethic' – that work provides the opportunity to work on one's development – see Schumacher (1980); compare Bellah on Japan (**2.8**); and see **1.66**.)

[The] affirmative element in the post-bourgeois complex is a stress upon the right and need of people to develop to the full their personal abilities and talents (and even, for the more ambitious, to cultivate any inner 'spiritual' potentialities). Sometimes this principle has been stated so strongly that it almost takes on the form of a candidate central social value: anyone not disposed to develop his or her full potential could be left in no doubt as to what would be thought of them in the new social order. In its crudest and least appealing forms, it clearly deteriorates into simple indulgence of the ego and is thus hard to reconcile with those social obligations calling for altruism. But it is not our task to explore such ethical contradictions, which no doubt can be handled, to some extent, by applying principles of mutuality. A neutral label for this essential component is *self-actualisation*. As it is of unique importance for the possible evolution of work values, something must be said about the origins of the concept.

Intellectually, the doctrine of self-actualisation derives from philosophical marxism, or, more accurately, from the 'Young Marx before Marxism' whose philosophical concerns with identity and meaning in human life were occluded once marxism became an organised political force. In this original context, it is linked to the claim that existing institutions, and notably those associated with capitalist industrialism, block the greater part of innate human potentiality, and must therefore be supplanted by others that will permit the full growth of spontaneous creativity and sensuous enjoyment of existence. However, it need not be tied explicitly to this system of ideas, or, still less so, to an openly marxist political programme. In fact, a technical adaptation of these ideas, with most traces of Marx removed, was put forward forty years ago by the psychologist Abraham Maslow, in a doctrine of universal human needs. Maslow pictured these needs as arranged in a hierarchy, commencing with hunger, in such a way that once a 'lower' need has been satiated the next highest automatically governs behaviour. Self-actualisation becomes a pressing need only once all 'inferior' biological and social requirements have been met. Yet, once they have been, 'hunger' for self-actualisation may become as imperious as hunger for food. [. . .]

Personnel management doctrines derived from Maslow's scheme have been influential amongst organisation reformers in the last three decades. Management practices based on it are widely credited with improving employee morale and performance. Those individuals who adopt self-actualisation as a value will presumably seek work environments that actually do – or are believed to – maximise the expression and development of their inward potentialities. Some sacrifice of income or other rewards may be accepted in pursuance of this aim. It may be that changes in occupational structure will increase the number of work contexts where suitable changes in the content of work and in rewards can be made in order to meet such preferences. If so, this post-bourgeois stress can be accommodated in the existing economic order, and might even render it more stable and dynamic.

2.22 Thrift and New Age management trainings

Nigel Thrift, 1997: Soft Capitalism. *Cultural Values*, vol. 1 (2): 29–57 (pp. 45–7).

The application of inner spirituality to the business of being a manager is part of what Nigel Thrift calls 'soft capitalism'. Thrift helps us see why 'new ideas' – often of a radical, cutting-edge form – should exercise appeal. The fact that applied spirituality of the 'inner' variety has become (relatively) popular in the very heartlands of capitalistic modernity, it might be added, serves to indicate how prosperity teachings have adjusted with the times – rather than withering out as modernity progresses. (For an attempt to run a business according to the God within, see Heelas (1992) on The Bank of Credit and Commerce International.)

Managers want and need . . . new ideas. They need them to make their way in organisations, to solve particular company problems, to act as an internal motivational device, to guard against their competitors' adoption of new ideas, or simply to provide a career enhancer. In the latter case, 'the new idea' demonstrates to others that the manager is creative, up-to-the minute and actively seeing improvements; equally, though, the new idea can act as a defence, provide a quick-fix solution in a difficult period, or even simply reducing boredom (Huczynski). The management seminar not only acts to provide new knowledge but also to fix belief. For example:

> Managers may attend Tom Peters' seminars to become immersed to his personality. In fact, if he was not to say what they have already read, they would come away disappointed . . . 'managers may still pay repeated visits in their thousand to sit at [the guru's] feet, or buy his latest book.

One executive at a leading multinational talks of needing his "Drucker fix" every two years' (Huczynski).

Indeed, seminars may retail experiences of such intensity that they change the terms of what it means to be a person. Thus Martin documents how the initial cynicism of some participants in experiential seminars is gradually overtaken by the experience of the event. Huczynski has argued that managers search for three main qualities from management knowledge – predictability, empowerment, and esteem. [. . .]

In addition, managers seek self-development or growth. Thinking about the self has a long history in management. Kurt Lewin invented the so-called T-group, an early form of the encounter group which encouraged colleagues to expose their true feelings about each other, while Maslow's 'eupsychian' management, McGregor's 'Theory Y' and Herzberg's Motivation Theory all emphasised 'the need as a human to grow spiritually'. In other words, managers, like many other contemporary individuals, have, for some time, been enjoined

> to live as if running a *project* of themselves: they are to *work* on their emotional world, their domestic and conjugal arrangements, their relations of employment and the techniques of sexual pleasure, to develop a style of being that will maximise the worth of their existence to themselves. Evidence from the United States, Europe and the United Kingdom suggests that the implantation of such 'identity projects', characteristic of advanced democracies, is constitutively linked to the rise of a breed of new spiritual directors, 'engineers of the human soul'. Although our subjectivity might appear our most intimate sphere of experience, its contemporary intensification as a political and ethical value, is intrinsically correlated with the growth of expert languages, which enable us to render our relations with our selves and others into words and into thought, and with expert techniques, which promise to allow us to transform ourselves in the direction of happiness and fulfilment. (Rose)

The emphasis on self-belief as a function of personal growth is perhaps best exemplified by the growth of New Age training which attempts to import New Age ideas *via* techniques like dancing, medicine wheels, and the use of the *I Ching* (Heelas; Huczynski; Rifkin). New Age thinking has become popular in management for a number of reasons. Its world view, which draws on not only eastern and western spiritual traditions but also on quantum physics, cybernetics, cognitive science and chaos theory, chimes with the Genesis discourse. Then, its emphasis on personal development fits with the rise of 'soft skills' like leadership, intuition, vision and the like. In turn, New Age's stress on changing people works in with attempts to change the management (and workforce) subject, particularly because changing oneself or others seems a feasible and certain task compared with many others that management faces:

> Most generally, the idea is to transform the values, experiences and to some extent the practices of what it is to *be* at work. The New Age Manager is imbued with new qualities and virtues, new in the sense that they differ from those found in the unenlightened workplace. These have to do with intrinsic wisdom, authentic creativity, self-responsibility, genuine energy, love and so on. Trainings are held to effect this shift. Furthermore, work itself is typically seen to serve as a 'growth environment'. The significance of work is transformed in that it is conceived as providing the opportunity to work on 'oneself'. It becomes a spiritual discipline. (Heelas).

New Age training is a big business. In the United States $4 billion per year is spent by corporations on New Age consultants, according to Naisbitt and Aburdene. For example, the New Age think tank, Global Business Network, is underwritten by major companies like AT&T, Volvo, Nissan, and Inland Steel. Some companies like Pacific Bell, Procter and Gamble, Du Pont and IBM, offer, or have offered, their employees 'personal growth experiences' in-house. Thus, IBM provides 'Fit for the Future' seminars which introduce employees to the *I Ching*. It is claimed that this links internal intuitions with external events. IBM's manager of employee development is quoted as saying that 'it helps employees understand themselves better' (Huczynski).

2.23 Martin: Latin American Pentecostalism and 'new social capital'

Bernice Martin, 1998: From Pre- to Postmodernity in Latin America: the case of Pentecostalism. In Paul Heelas (ed.), with the assistance of David Martin and Paul Morris, *Religion, Modernity and Postmodernity*. Oxford and Malden, Mass.: Blackwell, pp. 102–46 (pp. 129–30).

Discussing the great surge of Pentecostalism in Latin America (see also **3.79**), Bernice Martin examines how the poor – and the middle – classes are served by a form of religion which is 'uniquely poised' to make the transition to postmodern capitalism. It can be added that Pentecostalism might currently be flourishing because it is serving this purpose, but could wane once – if ever – the function is completed.

> The current transformation of capitalism in Latin America, involves a postindustrial, post-Fordist labour force for whom assembly-line docility, deference to hierarchical authority or the clock-time disciplines of the factory would be anachronistic. What this postmodern economy requires from them is micro-entrepreneurial initiative, an individualized and more feminized psyche, a high level of self-motivation, and the flexibility with which to face insecure employment and self-employment, mobility, and the twenty-four-hour working day. This applies even, indeed especially, to the informal economy (in which Burdick and others have found Pentecostals over-represented) as well as to the new service occupations at the interface with information technology and modern communications (where middle-class Pentecostalism is currently fast expanding).
>
> Adjusting to all this is a very tall order indeed for a workforce catapulted into postmodern conditions out of a premodern, rural world, with no serious transition via industrial modernity. A cultural and social system based on patron–client relations within which the poor were of no political account and were socially defined by their ascribed roles, has rather suddenly given way to a system in which the opportunities and the costs fall ever more directly on the individual as an atomized unit of social as well as economic labour: as both the protections and the constraints of the old dispensation are stripped away. The need to operate *as an individual* at the level of the psyche, as well as in terms of social and economic roles, becomes ever more imperative and universal. Indeed, in some ways this affects the poor even more than the privileged, who are often able to transfer those aspects of the clientelist system which benefit them into the new structures – hence so much of the notorious corruption – while the poor are left to face the new economic dispensation as best they may.
>
> Pentecostalism is uniquely poised to effect this cultural transition, not least because its fundamental conception of the human person is as a unique, individual soul, named and claimed by God. Its business *is* the business of selfhood. As Salvatore Cucchiari expresses it, Pentecostal conversions are 'mythologies of the new self'. Furthermore, Pentecostalism simultaneously contains elements compatible with both the pre- and the postmodern. It carries forward enough of

the premodern and the local to enable it also to carry the global and radical possibilities of individualized self-consciousness without causing vertiginous confusion. It is able to re-package premodern religious sensibilities and to transform familiar elements of ethnic, familial and other habits of collective solidarity within a movement which also inaugurates new experiences of postmodern individualism, autonomy, mobility and self-determination.

The secret lies in the paradoxical combination of these contradictory elements. The new Protestantism offers converts a novel experience of *spiritual* autonomy which also makes for a deeper sense of the individualizing tendencies in the wider world; it energizes the irreducible human motivation to survive even in the most unpropitious circumstances, by harnessing that motivation to transcendent ends. At the same time it roots and supports the individual within a face-to-face, voluntary community of believers: the old ascribed solidarities may help to provide the template but it is the *voluntary* nature of belonging which is new. Within this voluntary community there have grown up practices of mutual help, the encouragement of education and modes of participation in the practical organization, in the pastoral work and in the evangelism of the church which serve to spread widely among the mass of believers the actual experience of individual responsibility and leadership. *Individualization* and the *voluntaristic, collective* creation of new social capital thus occur in tandem.

2.24   Gifford and prosperity in Africa

Paul Gifford, 1990: Prosperity: A New and Foreign Element in African Christianity. *Religion* 20 (4): 373–88 (pp. 382–3).

Paul Gifford here explores some of the reasons why the 'Gospel of Prosperity' is a significant component of the evangelical revival in Africa. An important factor is that Christian prosperity teachings are in tune with traditional religious beliefs (a point similar to that made by Bruce in reading **2.14**). It can be added that in Africa, as in many other parts of the world, the prospects for prosperity religiosity look promising.

> There is one group of Christians in Africa ... whose situation the Gospel of Prosperity suits perfectly. This group comprises the White Christians of South Africa and Zimbabwe. Among them it has a wide following. It is promoted in many White churches in South Africa, nowhere more so than in the flourishing Rhema Bible Churches

founded in South Africa by Ray McCauley who studied under Kenneth Hagin in Tulsa, Oklahoma. Among these Whites, the Gospel of Prosperity plays an important socio-political role. Any form of Christianity that insists that their disproportionate wealth is nothing to be guilty about, but on the contrary is the sign of a true Christian, provides considerable comfort – and some reassurance, in the face of the very real threat of losing that wealth. The Gospel of Prosperity assures them that wealth is their due and has nothing to do with the unjust structures with which Tutu, Hurley, Boesak and Naudé are continually confronting their churches. Again we see how the Gospel of Prosperity acts as a foil to any form of liberation theology. The reason for Black Africa's receptive response to the Gospel of Prosperity is different. It was always recognized that the appeal of Jim and Tammy Bakker with their Rolls, 50-foot walk-in closets, gold-plated bathroom fixtures and air-conditioned dog-kennels, lay in their embodying the wealth so many humbler viewers aspired to. Similarly, Copeland's $5000 watch and his stories about those Mercedes (given their function in Africa as status symbols) evoke a very natural reaction among many of Africa's poor. There is one factor which has increased Black Africa's receptivity to this Gospel of Prosperity. As Daneel has written: 'According to the traditional concepts of Africa, wealth and success are naturally signs of the blessing of God (or of the ancestors)'. This has often been given as one of the reasons for the appeal of Africa's independent churches; whereas Western churches have tended to restrict salvation to the things of the next world, independent churches to a far greater degree have included in the concept of salvation realities of everyday life like health, fertility, success and material goods. Africa has no tradition of asceticism. Africa's new Christians come to the Copelands, Ray McCauley, Kenneth Hagin and others from a tradition completely different from that influenced by the desert fathers, monasticism and Francis of Assisi.

There is another, almost accidental, factor helping the diffusion of the Gospel of Prosperity in Africa. Africa's debt crisis, with the consequent lack of hard currency, has affected the churches too. A Bible school in Liberia (and I suspect that this is far from an isolated case), having no foreign exchange to buy books, recently sent out a general appeal for help. Among the five or six who responded were Kenneth Copeland, Kenneth Hagin and Ed Louis Cole, with shipments of their own publications. Whatever the case before, that Bible school now teaches the Gospel of Prosperity, because it is taught in the only books available. So the Gospel of Prosperity is spreading because of these evangelists' attention to and investment in all areas of the media.

Africa's evangelical revival shows no loss of momentum. It has been estimated that every day in the West some 7500 people cease to be Christians; by contrast, each day in Africa some 16 000 people become Christians. These figures indicate the inexorable trend, and the rapidity with which the traditional face of Christianity is changing. If the Gospel of Prosperity continues to be a fairly standard part of the African evangelical revival, it will eventually be a significant element in world Christianity.

2.25   Tipton and Zen 'ectopia'

Steven Tipton, 1984: *Getting Saved from the Sixties. Moral Meaning in Conversion and Cultural Change*. Berkeley, Los Angeles and London: University of California Press (pp. 161–2; 172).

Outside the ranks of Islam, few today think that religion can overthrow the capitalistic market economy with its secularity. At best, it is widely thought, religion can endeavour to moderate its excesses, encourage charity. However, the hegemonic hold of capitalism (see Fukuyama (1992)) is still being contested – and will presumably continue to be so – even in the most capitalistically 'advanced' of nations. We are taken to the Pacific Zen Centre, a composite of Zen groups in the San Francisco Bay Area. Religion, it might be concluded, is here serving to provide one of the few places where people can find a 'genuine' alternative to, or escape route from, secular capitalism; a 'space' for constructing 'economic' alternatives.

Zen Center's monastic role offers sixties youth a definite alternative to bourgeois adulthood for the time being, with the possibility of working out a permanent alternative compounded of Zen's monastic and lay householder traditions, and countercultural motifs. This long-range ideal, which I will call *the monk in the world*, describes a figure who works quietly and calmly to take care of things or other people in some simple, direct occupation (farming, baking, carpentry, crafts, practical nursing), earning just enough to support his daily needs. He lives communally with other Zen students, often in the country, maintaining close relationships to a master and to nature. Conspicuously absent from this vision are the nuclear family, suburban home, and white-collar or professional career: in short, the hallmarks of middle-class life. The Zen student is a monk *in* the world, relatively uninsulated by the celibacy or cloister of the classic Christian contemplative. But his attitude toward the world in which he moves is mystically undriven, unattached yet all-accepting. The Puritan's this-worldly asceticism has given way to the Zen Buddhist's this-worldly mysticism. This attitude and its monk-in-the-world ideal usually remain with students who leave Zen Center. It also seems to have spread among Zen Center's lay friends, and perhaps beyond them, to others in the urban upper middle class. Few of these laypersons have dropped out, yet their understanding of what it means to stay in and do the world's work may be changing in ways related to Zen's mediation of countercultural values. [...]

In a world that may be headed toward eco-catastrophe Zen students see themselves exemplifying needed personal attitudes and inter-personal behavior. Furthermore, their ideal communities exemplify the cooperative lifestyle, social structure, and economy needed by the larger society – communities that feature small-scale, low-consumption and no-waste economies, which are labor-intensive and based on farming, trades, and crafts occupations aimed at self-support. They are localized, long-term communities with coresidential core groups, whose organization combines communal intimacy with monastic self-control. Ascetic labor in its monastic form gives rigor to the economic activity of self-support and the spiritual activity of self-realization. The social ethic of Zen Center assumes its greatest political and insti-tutional definition within this vision of 'Ecotopia.' Even at this extreme it is an exemplary ethic, not an aggressively activistic one. It consist-ently sees institutional change as arising from self-transformation. The Zen student may transform himself by practicing within a specially structured community, but that community is itself taken to be the creation of the master's and his disciples' state of consciousness.

CHAPTER SEVEN

political

Introduction

Politics is about the exercise of power, authority, and ultimately of violence. Normally when we speak of politics we have in mind the organized negotiations of power by political pressure groups, parties or states. Politics, Max Weber said, involves 'striving to share power or striving to influence the distribution of power, either among states or among groups within a state' (H.H. Gerth and C. Wright Mills, 1970, p. 78). David Martin (1997) explains that 'politics is the arena within which authority, violence, cohesion, and the maintenance of boundaries are conspicuously at play' (p. 166). Religion has always played a major part in politics; the oft-heard demand that religion and politics should be kept separate carries an implicit acknowledgment that they rarely are.

As the readings below reveal, the close relationship between religion and politics has been sustained in modern times, though the interplays between the two have been profoundly affected by the rise of secular states. Such states constitutionally oppose any official linkage with religion. In some cases (as in some communist states) the state may seek to abolish or emasculate religion altogether. In other cases (as in India and the United States) the state may distance itself from religion in order not to abolish it but to guarantee religious freedom within its territories. In yet other cases (as in England) a tenuous formal link between the state and a state religion (in this case the Church of England) remains. In all these cases, however, many social functions once performed by religious bodies are taken over by the state and state-controlled institutions. Thus responsibility for a range of public roles – including political, economic, educational, disciplinary, legal, welfare and health – is gradually lost. This process is known as 'social differentiation' or simply 'differentiation', and is the subject of a number of the readings below and in chapter nine on Secularization in **Part Three**. Differentiation is normally reinforced by the action of the market economy; indeed the rise of the modern state and the market economy are closely connected.

Despite the predictions of those who took the West's pattern of political and economic development to be normative, however, the rise of the modern secular state has by no means brought to an end attempts by religion to control political territory in all parts of the world. On the contrary, the latter part of the twentieth century has witnessed an upsurge of religious and religio-ethnic nationalism. The success of Zionism (the drive to establish a Jewish nation-state), the revolution in Iran, and the territorial wars in the former Yugoslavia illustrate only too well the continuing force of religion in politics (see readings on religious nationalism below; religio-ethnic mobilization is also treated in the chapter on Difference, which concludes **Part Two**). Religion in modern times has also played an important and sometimes decisive role in opposing various political regimes, as the extracts which follow on Islamic and Hindu opposition to colonialism, and on the part played by the churches in the recent overthrow of communism in eastern Europe, illustrate.

Whilst some forms of religion in modern times have thus opposed or sought to overthrow and supplant the modern nation-state, others have come to accept its legitimacy. This is particularly true in the West. Since the late nineteenth century even the Roman Catholic church, which had previously opposed the rise of the modern state fiercely, has come to accept it. In other cases religion has not merely resigned itself to the existence of the modern state, but has played an important role in bringing it into being and legitimating and supporting it thereafter. In reading **2.44**, for example, Ernst Troeltsch argues that modern democratic political freedoms derive from Protestantism, and in the reading which follows, Talcott Parsons suggests that modern democracy in the North American mould represents the institutionalization of Protestantism. In relation to legitimation, reading **2.43** discusses the way in which the *Deutsche Christen* legitimated the Nazi regime in Germany, and the readings which follow this discuss the phenomenon of 'civil religion' in the United States – an informal transdenominational civic religion which serves to undergird American democracy.

Even where religion accepts the diminished political role allowed by the liberal state and the associated process of differentiation, relegation to the purely private realm is not inevitable. The most obvious way in which religion can continue to play a role in political society is by sponsoring its own political parties. Reading **2.48**, for example, discusses the influence of the Christian Democratic parties in Europe. The rise of the Christian 'New Right' in America in the 1980s and its attempts to win political power provide a further example. Equally, religion may continue to have an active political role through its influence at the level of civil society and in the shaping of culture. In reading **2.53**, for example, David Martin draws attention to the huge social, economic and political significance of Latin American Pentecostalism despite its active refusal to become involved in formal politics. José Casanova's reflections on the continuing role of religion in public life in readings **2.29** and **3.80** reinforce Martin's point, reminding us that religion in modern times plays an important political role by shaping culture, creating alternative communities, contributing to a civil ethos, exercising pressure as a voluntary association, defending human rights, critiquing capitalism, and contributing to public policy debate. Casanova's argument is that in these various ways, religion remains significantly 'public' and that those who have predicted shrinkage to a purely private role and function have overstated their case. (The previous chapter has discussed a similar deprivatization and spill-over in relation to the economic realm.)

The insistence of theorists like Casanova that religion can continue to play an important public and political role even when its links with the state have been loosened is a reminder that politics is about more than state activity. As Alfred Stephan (1988, pp. 3–12) delineates it, the political it is made up of three arenas:

1 the state: the extensive and interconnected administrative, bureaucratic, legal, and coercive system which includes the apparatus of government and which serves to 'structure relations between civil and public power and to structure many crucial relationships within civil and political society'. (p. 3)
2 political society: the arena 'in which a polity specifically arranges itself for political contestation to gain control over public power and the state apparatus'. (Haynes, 1998, p. 7)
3 civil society: the arena of institutions and movements which are not explicitly political nor involved in state activities, but which can exercise profound political influence. The majority are voluntary. Religious groups, neighbourhood associations, interest groups, and

cultural and intellectual currents all operate at the level of civil society.

Whilst the readings below reveal that religion in modern times continues to play an important role in all three arenas, in the West religious activity appears to have become concentrated in the latter two and – in Casanova's view at least – in the civil arena in particular.

The readings in this chapter are arranged in a way which is designed to illustrate the range of religion's different orientations to the political order in modern times. Whilst the diversity of these orientations is clear, we also meet some general theories of religion and politics in modern times which seek to look beyond the diversity to discern general trends. These theories are considered further in **Part Three** where the chapter on Secularization, for example, contains readings which claim that the most salient feature of the relation between religion and politics is the way in which the latter has expanded independently of the former and taken over the roles religion once performed. To counterbalance these theories, chapter nine, on Sacralization, includes readings which suggest that though the political role of religion in modern times may have changed it has not diminished, and chapter eleven, on Universalization, considers how many religions and religious leaders continue to insist on religion's universal and global significance as a way of handling potentially disruptive forms of difference. It may therefore be helpful to read this chapter on political contexts, in conjunction with these broader reflections in **Part Three**.

Given the close and often inseparable relations between economic and political orders, this chapter should also be read in conjunction with the preceding chapter six, on Economic contexts. The story of the rise of the market economy is inseparably tied up with the story of the rise of the modern state, and there are many parallels in the ways in which religions have interacted with these developments. Equally, this chapter on Politics overlaps closely with the chapter on Difference which follows. Looked at in the most general terms, a great deal of politics has to do with the creation, maintenance, negotiation and defence of difference. The following chapter on Difference sharpens this topic. In particular, its consideration of ethnic difference complements readings included in this section on political contexts, and its consideration of gender difference is also a topic with a strongly political dimension – particularly if one agrees with the feminist extension of the political to include the personal.

2.26   Martin differentiates the religious and the political

David Martin, 1997: *Does Christianity Cause War?* London: Clarendon Press (pp. 135–6).

In this extract David Martin considers the relations between religious and political orders. Whilst some theorists view religion as no more than a form of proto-politics, Martin understands the spheres of religion and politics to be overlapping yet distinct.

The options which relate to social organization such as authority and equality naturally cut across the boundaries of religion and politics. Politics, like religion, is a field structured by different ways of relating authority and equality, closure and access, and so on. What remains deeply problematic is the relationship between their religious expression and their political expression. My own position is clear; it is that religion can prefigure the political realization of these options in the symbolic realm, but there remains an irreducible religious realm of transcendent possibilities that cannot be straightforwardly realized on the plane of politics. Religion erects symbolic platforms in consciousness, above all the protected sacred texts, and conducts miniature experiments in social living which anticipate and reflect (or are analogous to) realizations in politics. The Benedictine Order, for example, devised an early experiment in democracy; the Oneida Community conducted a late experiment in communal sexuality. In neither case was religion some illusory shadow merely waiting to acquire its true social substance. But why is the transcendent lake of religious power partly suspended behind a protective dam rather than released and dispersed along the irrigation channels of society?

For one thing, the plenitude of possibilities cannot all be realized at once: every alternative, even in the best of all possible worlds, imposes its opportunity cost. For another, there are conciliations and harmonies, and a vision of complete humanity, simply beyond the capacity of the political realm to deliver. They live in the sign language of liturgy. Above all, they live in the signs of the Presence which evoke the response of worship. Presence signifies Plenitude.

Yet, there is a common dynamic or pressure shared by the two realms which is the persistent human struggle to secure peace, to acquire access, to institute equality and ensure that communication takes place as far as possible between persons of equal worth and dignity. This presence provides the dynamic of successive transformations. But each transformation encounters its own specific, inbuilt opportunity costs and is by no means a simple possibility. It goes without saying that opportunity costs will be related to the social circumstances of the time and place. It is central to the whole project of the human sciences.

2.27   Hallencreutz and Westerlund: a typology of relations between state and religion

Carl F. Hallencreutz and David Westerlund, 1996: Introduction: Anti-Secularist Policies of Religion. In David Westerlund (ed.), *Questioning the Secular State. The Worldwide Resurgence of Religion in Politics*. London: Hurst and Company, pp. 1–23 (pp. 2–3).

This extract offers a schematic model of the different relationships which may pertain between the religious and the political. The authors' model is organized around the different stances which states may take towards the religions within their sphere of jurisdiction. These they refer to as 'policies of religion'. On 'Civil religion' see readings **2.41**; **2.42**; **2.43**.

In a comparative model of different policies of religion we can identify three main types, which may be further qualified in more detailed analyses. They can be illustrated in the following way:

POLICIES OF RELIGION: A COMPARATIVE MODEL

Confessional	Generally Religious	Secular
Strict/Modified		Liberal/Marxist

In countries with a confessional policy of religion, a certain religious tradition or community is politically established, with a more or less intimate interaction between religion and politics. This alternative is the predominant one in Muslim countries. In European history confessional policies of religion are a legacy from the time when there were national states that were uniform in religion. Religious states, which in some contexts may be considered as theocracies, pursue strictly confessional policies of religion. The Islamic Republic of Iran is an example of such a state: here the state apparatus is subordinate to Islam and religious leaders have a decisive say in political affairs. In other countries with a Muslim majority, as well as in some predominantly Christian and Buddhist countries such as Sweden and Thailand, there is a modified confessional policy. In countries with almost exclusively Muslim populations Islam is generally the state religion and is privileged in certain ways, but religious leaders and institutions are to some extent subordinate to the interests of the state.

The secular policy of religion evolved particularly after the American and French revolutions of the late eighteenth century and is now adopted in many countries all over the world. This alternative presupposes that there is at least a formal separation of religion and the state. There is a tendency to limit the role of religion to a 'religious' sphere of society. In liberal forms of the secular policy of religion, however, religion is seen as a societal resource. Individual as well as corporate religious freedom is provided for to a greater or lesser extent, and thus religion may in practice have a significant role in political life. In many such cases different types of 'civil religion' have developed, where religious symbols and practices are used politically to foster national integration. Marxist versions of the secular religious policy, established in the Soviet Union in 1917 and in China in 1949, are characterized by an ideologically-defined negative view of religion. Countries whose regimes are inspired by a Marxist critique of religion have a strong ideological divide between religion and politics, and corporate religions freedom may be subordinate to the prerogatives of political organizations.

The generally religious policy on religion is vaguer than the other alternatives. Here the state, while guided by religion in general, is not institutionally tied to any specific religious tradition. The best example of this middle option is Indonesia, where one of the five pillars of the state ideology, *Pancasila*, refers to belief in God as one of the bases on which the Indonesian nation should be built. This position, with its vague reference to belief in God, is very similar to 'civil religions' in other multi-religious states. However, whereas the generally religious policy of religion in Indonesia is an *official* policy, 'civil religion' is not *formally* recognized.

2.28   Douglas on disestablishment

Ann Douglas, 1978: *The Feminization of American Culture*. New York: Alfred A. Kopf (pp. 23–4).

Concomitant with the rise of the modern secular state is the process of disestablishment, the cutting of formal ties between religious and political power. Disestablishment is part and parcel of the process of social differentiation (on the latter see also reading **3.14**). Here Ann Douglas discusses disestablishment in North America. As she notes in a later passage, however, the effect of disestablishment on the church in America has not been wholly negative: 'because the American government had severed its formal connection with the church and yet wished to employ religious sanctions in justification of its claims, the secular authorities were unlikely to challenge or defy the spiritual authorities; energy on both sides was employed in preserving and strenghtening rather than in testing and redefining the links between them' (p. 26).

In 1775, just prior to the American Revolution, nine of the colonies had 'established' churches, comparable in status to the Anglican one in England. These were churches in which citizens were required by their governments to attend and maintain, and against which so-called dissenting sects like the Methodists or Baptists were allowed only very limited overt powers of competition. In Connecticut, for example, where the contest between established and non-established groups increasingly dominated the political scene between the Revolution and 1817, dissenters or non-Congregationalists could not meet in churches for worship until 1770; they were forced to pay taxes to support the Congregational Church until 1777. The Connecticut Assembly, dominated by Congregational interests, as late as 1812 refused to incorporate the fully qualified Episcopalian Cheshire Academy as a college. In the remaining New England states, Congregationalism was also the established church. Episcopalianism, a 'dissenting' sect in New England, was the official religion in the older southern states and New York. Predictably, the American Revolution brought disestablishment with it. New York went first in 1777; under Thomas Jefferson's urging, the Anglican Church in Virginia lost its official status in 1785; and, by 1833, when Congregationalism ceased to receive state support in Massachusetts, disestablishment was complete in the United States.

It must be stressed that official 'disestablishment,' wherever it occurred and whomever it affected, was a symbol rather than a cause. It conveniently marks and represents a gradual course of events by which certain groups of ministers were severed from their traditional sources of power; this process began long before disestablishment proper and was to make the formal act of disestablishment possible and finally inevitable. Disestablishment, in other words, typified and accelerated a historical process with complex roots in the general democratization and industrialization of American culture. The result of the disestablishment process was an apparent triumph for the competitive, commercial, and individualistic spirit: a 'voluntary' system in which no denomination had automatic precedence over any other and no person had any obligation to attend worship or to support religion beyond his or her own desire to do so. Between 1820 and 1875, the Protestant Church in this country was gradually transformed from a traditional institution which claimed with certain real justification to be a guide and leader to the American nation to an influential *ad hoc* organization which obtained its power largely by taking cues from the non-ecclesiastical culture on which it was dependent.

2.29   Casanova on the deprivatization of religion in modern times

José Casanova, 1994: *Public Religions in the Modern World*. Chicago and London: University of Chicago Press (pp. 220–2).

Focusing in particular upon religion in the West, José Casanova argues against the view that religion in modern times inevitably becomes privatized and loses political significance. Whilst he accepts that western society has become differentiated and that most churches have accepted disestablishment from the state and disengagement from political society, he shows that they continue to play an important public role – particularly within civil society. The latter may be defined as the sphere intermediate between political and intimate society. See also Casanova in reading **3.16**.

The age of secular-religious cleavages, of struggles over the historical process of modern secularization, has basically come to an end in the historical area of Western Christendom. As the Catholic church has finally accepted the legitimacy of the modern structural trend of secularization, that is, has accepted voluntarily disestablishment, and a mutual rapprochement between religious and secular humanism has taken place, the raison d'être of this type of mobilized political religion tends to disappear. As churches transfer the defense of their particularistic privilege (*libertas ecclesiae*) to the human person and accept the principle of religious freedom as a universal human right, they are for the first time in a position to enter the public sphere anew, this time to defend the institutionalization of modern universal rights, the creation of a modern public sphere, and the establishment of democratic regimes. This is what I call the transformation of the church from a state-oriented to a society-oriented institution. Churches cease being or aspiring to be state compulsory institutions and become free religious institutions of civil society. Insofar as the churches and their secular allies are successful in their struggles against authoritarian states, this type of mobilized political religion also loses its raison d'être – unless the churches resist full secularization and a new cycle of religious-secular cleavages, and mobilizations and countermobilizations begins. Of the case studies analyzed in this book, today such a scenario seems plausible, although unlikely, only in Poland.

The last cases of religion 'going public' or taking a public stand for the sake of defending the very right to a modern public sphere already constitute examples of what I term the deprivatization of modern religion. As used throughout this study, the term deprivatization has three different connotations, one polemical, the other two descriptive. The term is used first of all polemically against those versions of the theory of secularization and those liberal political theories that prescribe the privatization of religion as a modern structural trend necessary to safeguard modern liberties and differentiated structures. This study has shown that such an indiscriminate position against all forms of public religion is unfounded, that there are some forms of deprivatization of religion which may be justifiable and even desirable from a modern normative perspective.

I admit to a certain uneasiness in coining and using such an unrefined neologism as deprivatization. But the barbarism may be justified as long as the term maintains its polemical value, that is, as long as it is not widely recognized that religions in the modern world are free to enter or not to enter the public sphere, to maintain more privatistic or more communal and public identities. Privatization and deprivatization are, therefore, historical options for religions in the modern world. Some religions will be induced by tradition, principle, and historical circumstances to remain basically private religions of individual salvation. Certain cultural traditions, religious doctrinal principles, and historical circumstances, by contrast, will induce other religions to enter, at least occasionally, the public sphere.

Besides its polemical connotation, however, the term has been used in this study to describe two different kinds of move or relocation of religion. The active role of the Catholic church in processes of democratization in Spain, Poland, and Brazil marks the passage from a nonmodern etatist (Spain), representational (Poland), or corporatist (Brazil) form of publicity to the modern public sphere of civil society. In these cases the descriptive connotation is somewhat misleading since we are not dealing so much with a move from the private to the public sphere as with a change in the type of publicity. The descriptive connotation of the term deprivatization is properly speaking only appropriate for cases such as the public mobilization of Protestant fundamentalism or the public interventions of the American Catholic bishops, both of which represent a move by religion from the private to the public sphere.

Nonetheless, despite the possible misunderstandings that may result from using the same term somewhat inaccurately for such different connotations, I think that it is appropriate and valid to maintain the term in order to call attention to the fact that these three diverse connotations of the term deprivatization may also be viewed as interrelated aspects of the historically new phenomenon analyzed in this study. Namely, it is my contention that the rejection by certain religious traditions of the privatized role to which they were being relegated by secularist modernization theories and by liberal political theories, that the role of the Catholic church in processes of demo-cratization, and that the public interventions of religion in the public sphere of modern civil societies can no longer be viewed simply as antimodern religious critiques of modernity. They represent, rather, new types of immanent normative critiques of specific forms of institutionalization of modernity which presuppose precisely the acceptance of the validity of the fundamental values and principles of modernity, that is, individual freedoms and differentiated structures. In other words, they are immanent critiques of particular forms of modernity from a modern religious point of view.

Political: examples

Example: religious nationalism and theocracy

2.30   Gardell defines religious nationalism

Mattias Gardell, 1996: *Countdown to Armageddon. Louis Farrakhan and the Nation of Islam.* London: Hurst and Company (pp. 8–9).

Here Mattias Gardell offers a definition of religious nationalism. The cognate term 'theocracy' is usually used to delineate a broader phenomenon. Literally it means government by God, usually through priestly mediation. As such theo-cracy it is not necessarily nationalistic: it can, for example, be pan-national and/ or imperialistic.

Religious nationalism postulates that nations are divine creations with specific God-given purposes and features. The nation is often believed to stand in a unique relationship with the Creator(s), from which both specific obligations and exclusive rights are derived. Nations are thus ascribed certain roles in the grand divine design known as the history of mankind, the outcome of which frequently is revealed and included as central to the national identity. One's own nation is often regarded as the predestined leader of the nations of the earth. Frequently collateral to this thesis is the belief that members of the 'chosen nation' are themselves reflections of the divine. Here we encounter a mystic knowledge, a national gnosis, asserting that world history will conclude in the foundation of a nation of gods. Religious nationalists of this variety usually combine this notion with a vision of an apocalyptic battle, enacted between nations divine and diabolic.

2.31   Juergensmeyer on the rise of religious nationalism

Mark Juergensmeyer, 1993: *The New Cold War? Religious Nationalism Confronts the Secular State*. Berkeley and Los Angeles: University of California Press (pp. 1–7).

Mark Juergensmeyer argues that the rise of religious nationalism in the latter part of the twentieth century represents one of the most significant religious and political developments of recent times. In the book from which this extract is taken he discusses Islamic, Jewish, Hindu and Buddhist nationalisms, arguing that they represent a reaction to secular nationalism.

What appeared to be an anomaly when the Islamic revolution in Iran challenged the supremacy of Western culture and its secular politics in 1979 has become a major theme in international politics in the 1990s. The new world order that is replacing the bipolar powers of the old Cold War is characterized not only by the rise of new economic forces, a crumbling of old empires, and the discrediting of communism, but also by the resurgence of parochial identities based on ethnic and religious allegiances. Although Francis Fukuyama, among others, has asserted that the ending of the old Cold War has led to an 'end of history' and a world-wide ideological consensus in favor of secular liberal democracy, the rise of new religious and ethnic nationalism belies that assertion. Moreover, proponents of the new nationalisms hold the potential of making common cause against the secular West, in what might evolve into a new Cold War.

Like the old Cold War, the confrontation between these new forms of culture-based politics and the secular state is global in its scope, binary in its opposition, occasionally violent, and essentially a difference of ideologies; and, like the old Cold War, each side tends to stereotype the other. According to the major Islamic political strategist in Sudan, the post-Cold War West needs a new 'empire of evil to mobilize against.' Similarly, he and other religious politicians need a stereotype of their own, a satanic secular foe that will help them mobilize their own forces. Unlike the old Cold War, however, the West (now aligned with the secular leaders of the former Soviet Union) confronts an opposition that is nether politically united nor, at present, militarily strong. For that reason, it is often not taken seriously. This attitude, I believe, is a mistake. [. . .]

By characterizing the activists in this study as religious nationalists, I mean to suggest that they are individuals with both religious and political interests. To understand their perspective is an exercise in both comparative religion and comparative politics, for they appear– at least from our point of view – to be responding in a religious way to a political situation. Many of them, however, agree with the observation of a Palestinian leader, Sheik Ahmed Yassin, that there is 'no clear distinction between religion and politics' and that the distinction itself is a mark of Western ways of thinking. Rather, articulators of religious nationalism see a deficiency in society that is both religious and political in character, one that requires a response that is religious as well as political.

Although they reject secular ideas, religious nationalists do not necessarily reject secular politics, including the political apparatus of the modern nation-state. To show how this can be possible, I must explain how I use certain terms. By the *state*, I mean the locus of authority and decision making within a geographical region. By the *nation*, I mean a community of people associated with a particular political culture and territory that possesses autonomous political authority. A *nation-state* is a modern form of nationhood in which a state's authority systematically pervades and regulates an entire nation, whether through democratic or totalitarian means. The modern nation-state is morally and politically justified by a concept of *nationalism*, by which I mean not only the xenophobic extremes of patriotism but also the more subdued expressions of identity based on shared assumptions regarding why a community constitutes a nation and why the state that rules it is legitimate.

The new religious revolutionaries are concerned not so much about the political structure of the nation-state as they are about the political ideology undergirding it. They are concerned about the rationale for having a state, the moral basis for politics, and the reasons why a state should elicit loyalty. They often reject the European and American notion that nationalism can be defined solely as a matter of secular contract. At the same time, however, they see no contradiction in affirming certain forms of political organization that have developed in the West, such as the democratic procedures of the nation-state, as long as they are legitimized not by the secular idea of a social contract but by traditional principles of religion.

As a bhikkhu in Sri Lanka explained to me, what he despised was 'not democracy, but your idea of nationalism.' He and others like him reject the notion that what draws people together as a nation and what legitimates their political order is a rational compact that unites everyone in a geographical region through common laws and polit- ical processes. Such secular nationalism underlies both the parlia- mentary democracies of Europe and the Americas, and the socialist bureaucracies that once characterized Eastern European countries and the formerly Soviet republics of the Commonwealth of Inde- pendent States. This way of thinking about nationalism comes natur- ally to most Americans and Europeans, but it contains assumptions about the universal and secular nature of a moral social order that many religious people in the rest of the world simply do not take for granted.

I find it striking that the religious-nationalist point of view so strongly dismisses secular nationalism as fundamentally bereft of moral or spiritual values. How shocking this rejection would have been to some of the Western social scientists and other observers of global politics who proclaimed two or three decades ago that the advent of secular nationalism in the Third World was not only a triumph of Western political influence but also one of the West's finest legacies to public life throughout the world.

2.32 Martin outlines the circumstances under which faith and nation unite

David Martin, 1978: *A General Theory of Secularisation*. Oxford: Basil Blackwell (pp. 107–8).

In the course of exploring the conditions under which secularization does or does not occur in western Europe, David Martin notes how religion is vitalized in situations where it functions as the marker of a threatened nationality. He expands upon this point in his later study *Does Christianity Cause War?* (Martin, 1997). (See also Steve Bruce, reading **3.91**.)

An indissoluble union of church and nation arises in those situations where the church has been the sole available vehicle of nationality against foreign domination: Greece, Cyprus, Poland, Belgium, Ireland, Croatia. In such countries bishops have spoken for nations and in Cyprus actually led one in the independence struggle, as well as after it. If the struggle for independence becomes self-conscious at the time of romantic nationalism then the union is a peculiarly potent one, with overtones of a suffering Messianic role. Such one finds in Poland. As will be seen later all the countries mentioned remain areas of high practice and belief: the symbols must not only exist but be seen to be visibly tended. The Greeks must celebrate the Resurrection, the Irish climb St. Patrick's Mountain, and hundreds of thousands of Poles make a pilgrimage to our Lady of Czestochowa. In religion these are present facts. The myth of identity is strengthened further wherever the dominated group have been at the border with another faith: Spain, Austria, Malta, Greece and Poland (at different times) with Islam, Poland with Protestantism and Orthodoxy, Ireland with Protestantism. These are the unions of religion and nation based on suffering and threat. Indeed wherever there is a threat and a border situation the nation is pushed towards its historic faith, even sometimes when it is officially atheist but faced nevertheless with a threat from an atheist country: this is the contemporary situation of Roumania and Poland, and to a much lesser extent of Hungary and Czechoslovakia. Germany and Austria are also the defeated located at a border with atheist victors. And just as there are unions of faith and nation based on suffering so thare are unions, *less potent*, based on glory: notably the empires of Holland, Spain, Sweden, Austria and England. These unions are, *ceteris paribus*, much more relaxed: the symbols are less in need of being visibly tended. The most potent unions of all combine past glory and present suffering: once again, Poland.

Ambiguous or negative cases arise under the following circumstances. First, there is an ambiguity where domination restores a religion, as the Counter-Reformation restored Catholicism in Hungary and in Czech Lands, yet has to leave the myth in the hands of a beaten minority. Second, there is ambiguity where a revolution forces the nation to split into two and an old 'integrisme' confronts a new 'integrisme'. This is most likely to happen in Catholic countries since Catholicism is inherently an 'integriste' and organicist system. Third, there is ambiguity where the myths cannot be shared by the whole nation since different areas are dominated by differing religions.

This situation is exacerbated where delayed or historically 'late' unification finds these differences a nuisance, irrelevant or positively divisive: examples are Germany, Albania and Yugoslavia. Fourth, there is ambiguity if the ecclesiastical authority explicitly opposes national unification, as in Italy.

2.33 Abramov on Zionism

S. Zalman Abramov, 1976: *Perpetual Dilemma. Jewish Religion in the Jewish State*. Cranbury, New Jersey: Associated University Presses (pp. 60–1).

Zionism, the movement for the re-establishment of the Jewish nation in what is now Israel, is one of the most important examples of modern religious nationalism. In the following extract Zalman Abramov discusses the secular Jewish nationalism of the founder of Zionism, Theodor Herzl (1860–1904). Despite opposition from Jews who saw the demand for a Jewish nation-state as fundamentally secular, the Nazi-inspired massacres of Jews during the Second World War (the Holocaust) led to the setting up of the State of Israel in 1948. The perpetual dilemma to which Abramov's title refers concerns the extent to which the secular state of Israel can and should recognize the religion (Judaism) which underpins its identity.

In a pamphlet entitled *Der Judenstaat*, which was published in 1896, Herzl set forth his revolutionary views.

He conceived of Zionism, the movement he proposed to create, as a response to the challenge of anti-Semitism. The Jewish question existed wherever there were Jews in perceptible numbers, and since they naturally moved to places where they were not persecuted, they only succeeded in importing anti-Semitism through their migrations. They might perhaps be able to merge entirely with the nations surrounding them if they could only be left in peace for a few generations; but, Herzl believed, the nations would not leave them in peace. The Jewish problem 'is no more a social than a religious one, notwithstanding the fact that it sometimes takes that and other forms. It is a national question . . . we are a people, one people.' The solution he proposed was that the Jews be 'granted sovereignty over a portion of the globe large enough to satisfy the rightful requirements of a nation.' His definition of Jewish nationhood suggested that for him anti-Semitism was the primary problem. 'We are one people – our enemies made us one in our despair, as repeatedly happens in history. Distress binds us together, and thus united, we suddenly discover our strength.' It was the existence of a common enemy

that welded the scattered Jewish people into a nation. This was nationalism pure and simple, in itself devoid of any religious content. In
his attempt to give this nationalism a viable form, Herzl sought to
provide it with what it most obviously lacked, namely, a Jewish state.

2.34   Haynes: is Islam always theocratic?

Jeff Haynes, 1998: *Religion in Global Politics*. London and New York: Longman (p. 128).

For reasons which Jeff Haynes explains below, Islam is often thought of as
naturally theocratic. It is 'the unique case of a religion founded simultaneously
as both a religious charismatic community of salvation and as a political community'. But does this mean that it draws no distinction between the spheres of
religion and politics? Haynes summarizes both sides of the argument. On the
closely related debate about whether or not Islam is compatible with democracy
see Sisk (1992).

It is often suggested that religion and politics are inseparable in Islam.
It is said that the *umma*, the Islamic community, has traditionally seen
itself as simultaneously both religious *and* political community, that
is, the community of believers and the nation of Islam. The result is
that it is completely 'natural' for religious actors to seek to gain political
goals. Such a suggestion does not, however, go unchallenged; others
believe that it is quite inaccurate to argue that Islam has no differentiated religious and political spheres. Indeed, it is suggested, the history
of Islam is best viewed as the history of the various institutionalizations
of the dual religious and political charisma of Muhammad into bilateral
and differentiated religious and political institutions.

Certainly Islam's holy book, the Quran, depicts the faith as a belief
system encompassing both religion and politics. The Quran, divine
revelation received by Muhammad, and the *hadith*, prescriptions laid
down by him on the basis of his own reflections, are sacred texts for
Muslims. *Sharia* law, at least theoretically and in many cases practically,
also helps regulate Muslims' conduct. Partly as a result, it is widely
assumed, especially by non-Muslims, that politics and religion cannot
logically be separated in Islam. However, at the very least the all-
encompassing nature of this assumption can be strongly challenged.
As respected scholars have convincingly argued, Islam has a history
above all of pragmatism. And . . . there has never been a Muslim society
in which *sharia* law has governed more than a fragment of social life.
In practice, there is, on the one hand, very often separation between
the essence of the religious principles and institutions and those of
the temporal ruler and State. On the other, there has frequently

developed a pragmatic compatability between Islam's precepts and the very different imperatives of a world of secularizing states. The important point is that Islamic history contains innumerable examples of thought and action where *din* (religion) and *dawla* (State) have been sharply distinguished. What this amounts to is that the most spectacular recent example of Islam's political involvement – Iran's Islamic revolution of 1978–9 – is not the norm: actually it is historically novel. Further, there would appear to be no insurmountable obstacle of principle to a fair degree of compatability between 'Islamic' precepts and pragmatically modernizing State practice as regards citizenship and the nature of socio-political organization.

Example: opposition

2.35 1864: the Roman Catholic church condemns modern liberalism

The Syllabus of Errors, 1864. In Henry Bettenson (ed.), 1989: *Documents of the Christian Church*. Oxford: Oxford University Press, pp. 272–4 (pp. 273–4).

As readings **2.48** and **2.49** below reveal, the twentieth century has witnessed the gradual acceptance by the Roman Catholic church of the legitimacy of the modern liberal state. As these extracts from the *Syllabus of Errors* show, however, the Catholic church remained deeply opposed to the modern state and its usurpation of powers and privileges thought to belong to the church even as late as the nineteenth century. The *Syllabus of Errors* was a set of 80 theses condemned in earlier pronouncements of Pope Pius IX and collected together to form a comprehensive attack on modern errors.

5. ERRORS CONCERNING THE CHURCH AND HER RIGHTS

'That the Roman Pontiffs and Oecumenical Councils have exceeded the limits of their power, have usurped the rights of princes, and have even committed errors in defining matters of faith and morals. That the Church has not the power of availing herself of force, or of any direct or indirect temporal power. . . . That ecclesiastical jurisdiction for the temporal causes – whether civil or criminal – of the clergy, ought by all means to be abolished. . . . That National Churches can be established, after being withdrawn and separated from the authority of the holy Pontiff. That many Pontiffs have, by their arbitrary conduct, contributed to the division of the Church into Eastern and Western.' [. . .]

> 10. ERRORS RELATING TO MODERN LIBERALISM
>
> 'That in the present day, it is no longer necessary that the Catholic
> religion be held as the only religion of the State, to the exclusion of
> all other modes of worship: whence it has been wisely provided by
> the law, in some countries nominally Catholic, that persons coming
> to reside therein shall enjoy the free exercise of their own worship.
> . . . That the Roman Pontiff can, and ought to, reconcile himself to,
> and agree with, progress, liberalism, and modern civilization.'

2.36   Chaudhuri: the moral and religious basis of Gandhi's opposition to British rule in India

Nirad C. Chaudhuri, 1987: *Thy Hand Great Anarch! India 1921–1952*. London: Chatto and Windus (pp. 47–8; 274).

The power of religion to motivate and mobilize opposition to a political regime is well illustrated by Mahatma Gandhi's campaigns against British rule in India. Political commentators often gloss over Gandhi's religious motivation, or treat the latter as a cloak assumed for purely political purposes. As Nirad Chaudhuri argues in the following extract, nothing could be further from the truth: religion was the true basis of Gandhi's political activity. A one-time secretary of the Bengali politician Sarat Chandra Bose, Chaudhuri was in a position to observe Gandhi from close quarters. (See also reading **3.71** by Gandhi.)

Mahatma Gandhi did not regard his role as political in the true sense. Therefore political logic did not embarrass him. He was incapable of playing a political role unless he though it was at bottom moral and religious. On this score, there is a general misconception. It is thought that he brought religion into politics in order to raise it to a higher plane. On the contrary, the truth was that Mahatma Gandhi took politics into religion in order to become a new kind of religious prophet. He felt at home only in religion, and throughout his life showed no interest in politics *qua* politics, i.e. when it presented only secular political problems.

It was only when a political situation raised moral issues and faced him with a moral task that he would involve himself in it. Even then it had to present something more than a straightforward moral problem for which a solution could be suggested. It had to face him with a moral evil with such overwhelming temporal power behind it that for all practical purposes it was irremoveable by any kind of rational action, and could be met only by means of passive moral defiance and nothing more. As soon as even a moral evil became amenable to remedies, he lost interest in it. As to problems of government or even good government, no one could be more indifferent. So, after independence, and even from the moment it became a possibility in which he could believe, he took no further interest in Indo-British relations and turned himself to the ineradicable evil that the Hindu–Muslim hatred was, only to become a martyr to his cause.

2.37   Bennigsen: Sufi resistance to communism

Alexandre Bennigsen, 1981: Official Islam and Sufi Brotherhoods in the Soviet Union Today. In Alexander S. Cudsi and Ali E. Hillal Dessouki (eds), *Islam and Power*. London: Croom Helm, pp. 95–106 (pp. 95–8; 100–2).

Whilst the story of Christian opposition to communism told by Martin in the reading which follows this one is comparatively well known, the story of Islamic opposition told here by Alexandre Bennigsen is less often rehearsed. Bennigsen discusses the remarkable survival of the Muslim community in the USSR, a community consisting mainly of Sufi brotherhoods. Far less organized, ideological, and clericalized than revolutionary Islam of the sort seen in Iran or Pakistan, Bennigsen shows how such mass conservative Islam has powerfully resisted assimilation. Later in the article from which this extract is taken, Bennigsen remarks on the potential of such Sufism for more active political mobilization – a prediction which has been powerfully confirmed by events following the collapse of communism.

[This chapter] concerns 'forgotten Islam' – the Muslim community separated more or less completely from the rest of the Muslim world. This community resides in the Communist world. It is numerally important, numbering some 75 million believers: 45 to 50 million in USSR; 15 to 20 million in China; 3 to 4 million in Yugoslavia; 1.5 million in Albania with smaller Muslim colonies in Bulgaria, Rumania and Poland. [. . .]

All have survived as 'Islamic communities'. How? Why? And what are their attitudes toward the alien power? [. . .]

How did Muslims succeed in resisting assimilation? The answer is easy and everybody in the Soviet Union knows it: by remaining attached to Islam. [. . .]

Even Soviet specialists have finally understood that the 'religiosity' of a community does not depend on the number of 'working' mosques, nor on the theological competence of the believers, and that a 'corrupted' form of Islam more or less contaminated by various

Shamanistic rites and beliefs can be as 'fanatic', if not more so, as unadulterated official Islam (in the Checheno-Ingush Republic, the real bastion of Muslim conservatism, there was not a single working mosque between 1943 and 1978). [. . .]

[Islam's] impact may be summarised as follows:

1 By maintaining, or helping to maintain, a 'conservative public opinion' and by preserving various traditional customs and rites (especially the marital custom) it makes very difficult any *rapprochement* between Muslims and Russians;
2 It gives to political local nationalism a definitely religious colour by reinforcing among the believers (and also the unbelievers) the consciousness of belonging to a Muslim *umma*;
3 It makes impossible a new frontal attack against the official Muslim establishment;
4 It helps to maintain a climate of general xenophobia, 'us' versus 'them'.

Given the impact of the Iranian revolution, the general progress of fundamentalist trends in the entire Muslim world, and the fact that no Iron Curtain could nowadays protect completely Soviet Islam from the 'contamination' from abroad, one may wonder what policy or policies the Soviet government could devise to keep its Islam under control.

2.38 Martin on the role played by the churches in opposing communism in eastern Europe

David Martin, 1996: *Forbidden Revolutions. Pentecostalism in Latin America and Catholicism in Eastern Europe*. London: SPCK (pp. 14–15; 92–3).

Here David Martin shows how Christianity was able to oppose communist regimes in eastern Europe during the revolutionary changes of the late 1980s and early 1990s. In particular he draws attention to the power of Christian signs and symbols in this context.

What happened in Eastern (and Central) Europe has to do with a desire to recover and retain spaces not expropriated by the central powers of the state. There was a time when sacred spaces were themselves locked into the embrace of these powers, and their autonomy compromised, though one could always appeal to the deeper meanings they represented. That meant that a different rhetoric had to carry the burden of autonomy. But once sacred spaces were made marginal by edict of secular dogma, their meaning once more opened up for general use, and they became bases for symbolic challenges to the 'powers of this world'.

Sometimes a mere architectural presence was symbol enough, which is why Stalin systematically demolished so many cathedrals and why Ceausescu tore the heart out of Bucharest and proposed blocking the view of Timisoara Orthodox Cathedral. The point is that, at the very minimum, such buildings have an inalienable transcendental reference which is their sole raison d'être. If that transcendental reference could be compromised, nobody could take their stand on such a ground, literally or intellectually. As the tanks turned away in Timisoara, the Protestant pastor shouted 'God exists' – not because he had witnessed a miracle, but because in the face of triumphant evil one retains a faith that it does not have the last word.

2.39 Levine on liberation theology in Latin America

Daniel H. Levine, 1992: *Popular Voices in Latin American Catholicism*. Princeton, NJ: Princeton University Press (pp. 32–3; 37–8; 39–40).

The development and deployment of liberation theology, first in Latin America and then in other parts of the world, furnishes a good example of religion in the late twentieth century playing an active part in opposing socio-economic and political arrangements which are perceived as unjust. Here Daniel Levine describes the central features of liberation theology. Elsewhere in the same book he explains liberation theology's success in terms of its appeal to populations cut loose from previous social bonds by agrarian proletarianization, urbanization, and the growth of mass literacy and communications, and deprived of other political outlets by the repressive regimes of the 1970s. Levine concludes, however, that liberation theology's future is now threatened by political change in Latin America, and by the conservative and hierarchical leadership of John Paul II.

Liberation theology is part of a general Latin American response to the changes in Catholicism since the Second Vatican Council. Theologians and activists identified with this school share a concern with historical change, insist on the necessity and primacy of action to promote justice, and give place of preference to everyday experience as a source of religiously valid values. From these foundations, liberation theology has spurred and legitimized organizational innovation while undergirding a notable clerical populism throughout the region, which has sent sympathetic priests, sisters, and pastoral agents 'to the people.' Their notion of religious service embraces values of solidarity and shared experience and identifies strongly with people whose lives are deformed by oppressive structures. Phillip Berryman's definition points up the complexities at issue in liberation theology: (1) an interpretation of Christian faith out of the suffering and hope of the poor; (2) a critique of society and of the ideologies sustaining it; and (3) a critique of the activity of the church and of Christians from the angle of the poor.

Liberation theology comes together as a theory and a set of guidelines for action around issues of poverty and the poor. The theologians explain poverty in structural terms, using Marxist categories of class, conflict, and exploitation as the basis for a critical social analysis. They also insist on the need to see issues through the eyes of the poor, to share their conditions, and to live with them in ways that undercut long-established social and cultural distances between the church and average believers. Poverty is distinguished from misery. The former may have virtues of simplicity and lack of commitment to earthly things, but the latter has no virtues. Misery stunts human potential, making a fully Christian life impossible. Four closely related themes lie at the heart of liberation theology: first, a concern with history and historical change; second, the return to biblical sources; third, a stress on the poor, and a related emphasis on doing theology in a way that enhances the value of everyday experience and the insight of average people; and finally, close and complex relations with Marxism.

2.40   Nicholls: images of God may subvert *or* legitimate political authority

David Nicholls, 1989: *Deity and Domination: Images of God and the State in the Nineteenth and Twentieth Centuries.* London and New York: Routledge (pp. 233–44).

David Nicholls draws attention to the way in which images of God may have a positive, mutually reinforcing relationship with prevailing forms of political authority *or* a negative, subversive relationship: 'what functions as ideology in one context may be utopian in another'.

While the link between images of God and the state is sometimes difficult to trace, what emerges from our discussion is that dominant representations used of God are often positively related to the prevailing political rhetoric of the time, which in turn expresses a response to, or a reflection of, political movements and to changes taking place in the social structure.

Images of God and the civil government are sometimes *inversely* related, so that a picture of God becomes current which is in conscious or semi-conscious reaction to prevailing ideas about the state. Many of the religions of the poor and oppressed have seen the true God as identified with, and manifesting the idealised characteristics of, the *victims* of political authority rather than with the wielders of it. He is the suffering, crucified God of Studdert Kennedy, chaplain to British troops in the trenches of the First World War, and of the Japanese theologian Kitamori. A prayer book found on the body of a Haitian guerrilla leader, killed in 1920 during the struggle against the US occupation of his country, included a 'revolutionary prayer to our Saviour Jesus' and also a prayer to 'God who was born; God who died; God who came to life again; God who was crucified; God who was hanged'.

At other times the divine analogy has been explicitly *rejected*. . . . I noted how total claims being made by Nazi publicists led many German followers of Barth to reject the divine analogy and insist that the kind of ultimacy claimed for the race or the movement is appropriate only to God, whose sovereignty calls all human institutions into question. There is no earthly analogue to God. This is similar to the position taken by many Puritan parliamentary writers in seventeenth-century England.

Images of God frequently strengthen current political arrangements, giving some kind of legitimacy to the established order. This is true with welfare pictures of God and also with the 'democratic' conceptions of God which were popular among liberal Protestants in the USA. In an earlier period, the medieval picture of a God presiding over a feudal court, surrounded by ranks of angels and archangels, characterised by order, law and hierarchy, reflected the prevailing political structure of the day. There are indeed occasions when the divine analogy reinforces the status quo, but the heavenly model may also function as a criterion by which to judge and criticise current political procedures. Peter Brown observes:

> Christian writers did not mindlessly create a mirror in Heaven that reflected, in rosy tints, the hard facts of patronage and *prepotenza* that they had come to take for granted on the late Roman earth. The role of replication in late antiquity was subtly different: it enabled the

> Christian communities, by projecting a structure of clearly defined relationships onto the unseen world, to ask questions about the quality of relationships in their own society.

These projections, Brown goes on, allowed them to engage in 'muffled debates on the nature of power in their own world, and to examine in the light of ideal relationships with ideal figures, the relation between power, mercy and justice as practised around them'.

The replacement of monarchical by democratic and participatory images proposed by twentieth-century American writers must be perceived as reflecting developments which had already occurred at the political level, and as contributing to their legitimation. The adoption by Berdyaev of a similar range of divine pictures and concepts is, however, to be seen rather as a reaction to totalitarianism and as linked to demands for political changes based upon liberty and popular participation. To borrow Karl Mannheim's distinction, an image which functions as ideology in one context may be utopian in another.

Example: legitimation

2.41   Rousseau and civil religion

Jean-Jacques Rousseau, 1973: *The Social Contract and Discourses*. London and Melbourne: Dent (pp. 306–8).

What gives a state or a political regime legitimacy? What enables it to win the willing assent of the governed, rather than to rely simply on brute force? This problem becomes particularly acute for large-scale modern states where direct bonds between ruler and ruled disappear. One of the major contributions of the Romantic philosopher Jean-Jacques Rousseau (1712–78) was to draw attention to the crucial role which religion could – and in his view should – play in legitimation. Rousseau believed that Christianity was a religion of inward devotion – important for the individual, but ineffectual in relation to political society. For Rousseau the healthy functioning of the latter required in addition a second type of religion, 'civil religion'. In the following reading he explains what he means by this term. For a recent defence and fresh articulation of civil religion see Shanks (1995).

> But, setting aside political considerations, let us come back to what is right, and settle our principles on this important point. The right which the social compact gives the Sovereign over the subjects does not, we have seen, exceed the limits of public expediency. The subjects then owe the Sovereign an account of their opinions only to such

an extent as they matter to the community. Now, it matters very much to the community that each citizen should have a religion. That will make him love his duty; but the dogmas of that religion concern the State and its members only so far as they have reference to morality and to the duties which he who professes them is bound to do to others. Each man may have, over and above, what opinions he pleases, without its being the Sovereign's business to take cognizance of them; for, as the Sovereign has no authority in the other world, whatever the lot of its subjects may be in the life to come, that is not its business, provided they are good citizens in this life.

There is therefore a purely civil profession of faith of which the Sovereign should fix the articles, not exactly as religious dogmas, but as social sentiments without which a man cannot be a good citizen or a faithful subject. While it can compel no one to believe them, it can banish from the State whoever does not believe them – it can banish him, not for impiety, but as an anti-social being, incapable of truly loving the laws and justice, and of sacrificing, at need, his life to his duty. If any one, after publicly recognizing these dogmas, behaves as if he does not believe them, let him be punished by death: he has committed the worst of all crimes, that of lying before the law.

The dogmas of civil religion ought to be few, simple, and exactly worded, without explanation or commentary. The existence of a mighty, intelligent, and beneficent Divinity, possessed of foresight and providence, the life to come, the happiness of the just, the punishment of the wicked, the sanctity of the social contract and the laws: these are its positive dogmas. Its negative dogmas I confine to one, intolerance, which is a part of the cults we have rejected.

2.42 Bellah: civil religion in America

Robert Bellah, 1967: Civil Religion in America. *Daedalus*, vol. 96, no. 1, Winter: pp. 1–21 (pp. 7–9).

As the previous reading shows, civil religion in Rousseau's sense is a simple creed deliberately constructed and upheld by a sovereign or state in order to establish and maintain political legitimacy. For Robert Bellah, by contrast, civil religion is a less deliberate creation made up of an eclectic mix of religious and secular beliefs and symbols – though it has the same legitimating function. In the influential essay from which the following extract is taken, Bellah drew attention to the importance of such religion in the USA. Though he believed civil religion played a crucial role in sustaining American democracy, by the time he wrote *The Broken Covenant* in 1975 he feared that it had been undermined by individualism: 'Today the American religion is an empty and broken shell' (p. 142). The conclusion to 'Civil Religion in America' can be found at **2.58**. (See also Herberg in reading **3.51** who makes many similar points.)

The words and acts of the founding fathers, especially the first few presidents, shaped the form and tone of the civil religion as it has been maintained ever since. Though much is selectively derived from Christianity, this religion is clearly not itself Christianity. For one thing, neither Washington nor Adams nor Jefferson mentions Christ in his inaugural address; nor do any of the subsequent presidents, although not one of them fails to mention God. The God of the civil religion is not only rather 'unitarian,' he is also on the austere side, much more related to order, law, and right than to salvation and love. Even though he is somewhat deist in cast, he is by no means simply a watchmaker God. He is actively interested and involved in history, with a special concern for America. Here the analogy has much less to do with natural law than with ancient Israel; the equation of America with Israel in the idea of the 'American Israel' is not infrequent. What was implicit in the words of Washington already quoted becomes explicit in Jefferson's second inaugural when he said: 'I shall need, too, the favor of that Being in whose hands we are, who led our fathers, as Israel of old, from their native land and planted them in a country flowing with all the necessaries and comforts of life. Europe is Egypt; America, the promised land. God has led his people to establish a new sort of social order that shall be a light unto all the nations. [. . .]

What we have, then, from the earliest years of the republic is a collection of beliefs, symbols, and rituals with respect to sacred things and institutionalized in a collectivity. This religion – there seems no other word for it – while not antithetical to and indeed sharing much in common with Christianity, was neither sectarian nor in any specific sense Christian. At a time when the society was overwhelmingly Christian, it seems unlikely that this lack of Christian reference was meant to spare the feelings of the tiny non-Christian minority. Rather, the civil religion expressed what those who set the precedents felt was appropriate under the circumstances. It reflected their private as well as public views. Nor was the civil religion simply 'religion in general.' While generality was undoubtedly seen as a virtue by some, as in the quotation from Franklin above, the civil religion was specific enough when it came to the topic of America. Precisely because of this specificity, the civil religion was saved from empty formalism and served as a genuine vehicle of national religious self-understanding.

But the civil religion was not, in the minds of Franklin, Washington, Jefferson, or other leaders, with the exception of a few radicals like Tom Paine, ever felt to be a substitute for Christianity. There was an implicit but quite clear division of function between the civil religion and Christianity. Under the doctrine of religious liberty, an exceptionally wide sphere of personal piety and voluntary social action was left to the churches. But the churches were neither to control the state nor to be controlled by it. The national magistrate, whatever his private religious views, operates under the rubrics of the civil religion as long as he is in his official capacity, as we have already seen in the case of Kennedy. This accommodation was undoubtedly the product of a particular historical moment and of a cultural background dominated by Protestantism of several varieties and by the Enlightenment, but it has survived despite subsequent changes in the cultural and religious climate.

2.43 Nicholls on Christian legitimations of Nazism in Germany

David Nicholls, 1989: *Deity and Domination: Images of God and the State in the Nineteenth and Twentieth Centuries.* London and New York: Routledge (pp. 95–7).

The previous three extracts discuss relatively benign forms of legitimation. Here David Nicholls's discussion of the 'Deutsche Christen' in Nazi Germany reminds us that religious legitimation can be far from benign.

The 'Deutsche Christen' were not merely Christians who gave political support to the Nazi Party but Germans who generally portrayed the rise of Nazism in religious terms. The Führer was 'the redeemer in the history of the Germans'. Pastor Julius Leutheuser declared: 'Christ has come to us through Adolf Hitler. . . . We know today the Saviour has come.' It was perhaps the idea of a spiritual unity among Germans which attracted these Protestants, many of them coming from the liberal cultural-Protestant tradition, in which the church was seen as the religious aspect of the life of the *Volk*. The church must 'be co-ordinated into the rhythm of the National Revolution, it must be fashioned by the ideas of Nazism, lest it remain a foreign body in the unified German Nazi community'.

Example: religion at the origins of the modern state

2.44   Troeltsch on the religious origins of modern freedom

Ernst Troeltsch, 1966: *Protestantism and Progress. A Historical Study of the Relation of Protestantism to the Modern World*. Boston: Beacon Press (pp. 123–6).

As well as legitimating existing political arrangements, religion can play an even more fundamental role by helping bring such arrangements to birth. A number of the extracts above show how this can be true where religion infuses a religious nationalism. In the following extract Troeltsch shows how it can also be true in relation to more secular forms of polity, suggesting that liberal democracy itself is in part the product of religious forces. In particular, Troeltsch traces the origins of democracy to the sectarian Protestantism which first gained political ascendency in the English Revolution and later migrated to North America. George Jellinek (1979) confirms Troeltsch's observation by establishing that the modern principle of inalienable rights originated with the radical sects in America.

Liberty of conscience obtained only in Rhode Island, and this State was Baptist, and was therefore hated by all the neighbour States as a hotbed of anarchy. Its great organiser, Roger Williams, actually went over to Baptist beliefs, and thence passed to an undogmatic Spiritualism. And the second home of liberty of conscience in North America, the Quaker State of Pennsylvania, was also of Baptist and Spiritualist origin. In other places where the claim to toleration and liberty of conscience is found, it has political and utilitarian motives – in the end, indeed, the merchants of the Massachusetts theocracy yielded to this indifferentism. The parent of the 'rights of man' was therefore not actual Church Protestantism, but the Sectarianism and Spiritualism which it hated and drove forth into the New World. And this can surprise no one who understands the inner structure of orthodox Protestant, and of Baptist and Spiritualist, thought.

But at this point, now that our attention has been directed to these groups, there opens out before us a much wider range of vision. The North American Baptist and Quaker movements are derived from the great religious movement of the English Revolution, viz. Independency. This Independency was itself most strongly interpenetrated with Baptist influences, which, arising from the remnants of the earlier English Anabaptists, from Holland – the Continental asylum of the Anabaptists – and from the American refugees, reacted upon England.

Not less strongly did the mystical Spiritualism exercise an influence tending to disintegrate ecclesiastical systems and to strengthen the demand for liberty of conscience. It was now at last the turn of the step-children of the Reformation to have their great hour in the history of the world. Baptist Free-Churchism, democratic and communistic ideas, Spiritualistic non-Churchism, Pietistic Calvinism with a radical bent – all these tendencies entered into alliance with the consequences of the political catastrophe and the implications of earlier English Law. From this coalition arose, urged on by the army of the Saints, the demand for a Christian State, which should leave the form of the worship of God free to the different independent congregations, while securing Christian morality by strict regulations, and employing the civil power in the service of the Christian cause. The Cromwellian Commonwealth, which was avowedly intended to be a Christian State, for a short time realised this idea; short as was the time during which this grandiose edifice laid in the English Puritan Revolution. The momentum of its religious impulse opened the way for modern freedom.

2.45   Parsons: modern democracy as the institutionalization of Protestantism

Talcott Parsons, 1963: Christianity and Modern Industrial Society. In Edward A. Tiryakian (ed.), *Sociological Theory, Values, and Sociocultural Change*. London: Collier-Macmillan, pp. 33–70 (pp. 61; 65).

Talcott Parsons applies an argument like that developed by Troeltsch in the reading above to modern America. Far from viewing American liberal democracy as secular, he suggests, we should view it as the institutionalization of Protestant values. And far from representing a falling away from religion, democracy is for Parsons the embodiment and externalization of the 'voluntary principle' of Protestant Christianity.

A common view would agree with the above argument that the Reformation itself was not basically a movement of secularization but that, in that it played a part in unleashing the forces of political nationalism and economic development – to say nothing of recent hedonism – it was the last genuinely Christian phase of Western development and that from the eighteenth century on in particular the trend had truly been one of religious decline in relation to the values of secular society. [. . .]

Against this view I should like to present an argument for a basic continuity leading to a further phase which has come to maturity in the nineteenth and twentieth centuries, most conspicuously in the Untied States and coincident with the industrial and educational revolutions already referred to. From this point of view, the present system of 'denominational pluralism' may be regarded as a further extension of the same basic line of institutionalization of Christian ethics which was produced both by the medieval synthesis and by the Reformation. [. . .]

The denomination shares with the sect type its character as a voluntary association where the individual member is bound only by a responsible personal commitment, not by *any* factor of ascription. In the American case it is, logically I think, associated with the constitutional separation of church and state.

The denomination can thus accept secular society as a legitimate field of action for the Christian individual in which he acts on his own responsibility without organizational control by religious authority. But precisely because he is a Christian he will not simply accept everything he finds there; he will attempt to shape the situation in the direction of better conformity with Christian values. [. . .]

There is a tendency in much religiously oriented discussion to assume that the test of the aliveness of Christian values is the extent to which 'heroic' defiance of temptation or renunciation of worldly interests is empirically prevalent. This ignores one side of the equation of Christian conduct, the extent to which the 'world' does or does not stand opposed to the values in question. If one argues that there has been a relative institutionalization of these values, and hence in certain respects a diminution of tension between religious ideal and actuality, he risks accusation of a Pharisaic complacency. In face of this risk, however, I suggest that in a whole variety of respects modern society is more in accord with Christian values than its forebears have been – this is, let it be noted, a *relative* difference; the millennium definitely has not arrived.

2.46   Smart: Maoism as a religion

Ninian Smart, 1974: *Mao*. Glasgow: Fontana (pp. 83; 86).

In the preceding readings Troeltsch and Parsons argue that religion plays a vital role in the rise of democracy. Here Ninian Smart suggests that the rise of communism – particularly Maoism – should also be explained in relation to religion. Smart's suggestion is that religion shapes this form of totalitarian politics in an equally decisive way: for, according to Smart, Maoism is itself a religion.

The analogy between Maoism and religion has often been made. In one respect the matter is one of definition, but it can be illuminating to look into the comparison because it can help indirectly to explain certain aspects of the development of Mao's thought. So let us begin at the level of definition and then see how far the analogy applies. Here I rely on an analysis or religion which I have used elsewhere.

The analysis involves treating religion as a six-dimensional phenomenon. These six dimensions are: the doctrinal, the mythic, the ethical, the ritual, the experimental and the social or institutional. I will expand on these in turn, but one can note initially that the first three have to do with beliefs and values; the second three to do with human experience and behaviour. [. . .]

If we match Maoism against the religious grid it fits quite well. The reason why we may *not* think of it as a religion is that it is professedly anti-religious. But there are different ways of being anti-religious and – if I may be Irish about it – one way is the religious way. When the Conquistadors destroyed the Aztec power they destroyed their idols and system of religious practice. Naturally, they did this in the name of their own religion, but from an Aztec point of view Christianity was very far removed from their traditional conception of religion. The very militancy of Maoism in the face of the religions of China, culminating in the closing of temples, etc., during the Cultural Revolution, exhibited what I may call a religiously anti-religious zeal. This is very different from the humanist temper, which wants to replace religion by something which would certainly not match up to the grid which we have used. Sacred rituals, authoritative books, evangelical morality, all these would fade into non-existence in a humanist world. Maoism is not that world.

Moreover, Maoist eschatology provides a kind of substitute for the transcendental. If there is no heaven for the individual, there is a mysterious ultimate transformation of humanity. But typically, as with most eschatologies, no limit in time can be put on this, for the date is indefinitely in the future, perhaps infinitely.

Example: public roles of religion within liberal democracies

2.47   Martin: differentiation and the redistribution of secular and sacred space

David Martin, 1997: *Does Christianity Cause War?* London: Clarendon Press (pp. 40–1).

As discussed in the introduction to this chapter and extract **2.28**, the process whereby sets of social activities once performed by bodies like the church are split up between different institutions, many of which fall within the ambit of the modern state, is known by sociologists as differentiation (see also the chapter on Secularization in **Part Three**). The process of differentiation has affected all religious bodies within modern liberal states. Here David Martin describes the process of differentiation, but instead of concluding that it leads inevitably to the exclusion of the sacred from the political realm, he shows how it may lead to complex and often unpredictable redistributions of the sacred.

What differentiation does is to introduce a redistribution of secular and sacred space. Morally resistant social activities once carried on inside sacred space and under its umbrella appear in secular space outside that umbrella. In undifferentiated societies, councils of war were held and people carried on commercial activity even during the celebration of the Mass. In a differentiated society, however, sacred space is set aside for distinctively religious activities, while the autonomous secular dynamic of money and power occupies an entirely different sector.

And just as there is a 'secular' sector actually inside the sacred space of an undifferentiated society, so there is a sacred carry-over into secular sectors of a differentiated society. Thus the redistribution of the sacred in the course of transition from undifferentiated to differentiated societies is very complicated, and made more so because in a differentiated society the sacred acquires a life of its own outside both the ecclesiastical and the religious. The sacred may lodge itself in new structures of power, cohesion, identity, and legitimacy, particularly in relation to land and nation. The sacred can be attracted to the idea of land and nation without any reference to any specific Church or to any Church whatsoever. In the United States Church and State, Church and land are thoroughly differentiated but that does not inhibit a sacred aura from becoming attached to the United States, its people, its flag, and its territories. Wales has no established

Church but the RAF was unable to establish a bombing run on the Lleyn Peninsula on account of its sacred character. Political parties can attract elements of the sacred into their orbit, as well as reproducing patterns of behaviour supposed to inhere in religious bodies, such as rituals, creeds, dogmas, texts, coronations, priesthoods, gurus, charisma, exemplars, witch-hunts, exorcisms, and appeals to the original covenant. Marxist societies, putative heirs to the Enlightenment, have reproduced virtually every characteristic once thought to be the special property of religion.

2.48   Conway on the course of political Catholicism in Europe

Martin Conway, 1996: Introduction. In Tom Buchanan and Martin Conway (eds), *Political Catholicism in Europe, 1918–1965*. Oxford: Clarendon Press, pp. 1–33 (pp. 30; 33).

One of the most visible ways in which religions may continue to play a political role within modern liberal democracies is through the creation of political parties with a religious basis. The Christian Democratic parties of western Europe furnish perhaps the best example. Here Martin Conway describes these parties and their fate. In many ways they represent a transitional moment for political Catholicism. Most broke decisively from earlier Catholic opposition to the modern state (of the kind exemplified by the *Syllabus of Errors*, see reading **2.35**), but their explicitly religious programmes quickly faded (even though the parties remain). Today Catholic interests and agendas are more likely to be represented by voluntary associations, pressure groups, and lobbying bodies rather than by political parties. Casanova describes this shift in the mode of political activity in reading **2.29**.

With the gradual consolidation of the post-war political order and the integration of the states of Western Europe into Cold War alliances, so more traditional mentalities came to the fore and set the tone of Catholic political action during the late 1940s and the 1950s.

This was particularly evident in the course followed by the Christian Democrat parties of Western Europe. These marked in many respects a decisive new development in Catholic politics. The Christian Democrats of Germany and Italy, the CVP/PSC in Belgium, and, perhaps most strikingly, the Mouvement Républicain Populaire (MRP) in France were new political creations often founded by a younger generation of Catholic figures whose political attitudes had been forged by the experiences of the war years. They broke with both the defensive separatist mentality of the long-established Catholic parties and with the authoritarian Catholic temptations of the inter-war years in favour of a new personalist ideology which embraced a democratic political system and a social market economy of free enterprise combined with state intervention and enhanced welfare provision. In Germany, this change was all the more radical because the new Christian Democrat Party was a cross-confessional party, incorporating both Protestant and Catholic militants. This new political programme was accompanied by a new attitude towards the Catholic Church. Rather than presenting themselves as the defenders in the political sphere of the Catholic Church, the new parties consciously stressed their independence from clerical guidance and declared their wish to win the support of all voters regardless of their confessional or social background. [. . .]

Initial expectations that the Christian Democrats would be the agents of a programme of Catholic-inspired wide-ranging social and political reforms were . . . disappointed. Except in France, where the MRP went into rapid electoral decline after the elections of 1951, the Christian Democrat parties established themselves as parties of government, devoted to a Cold War political agenda of capitalist economics and defence of Western Europe against the Soviet Union. Only their commitment to the process of limited European integration, in which the Catholic political leaders De Gasperi, Adenauer, and Robert Schuman played a prominent though far from determinant role, remained as an indication of their initial reforming agenda. The momentum of domestic reforms rapidly evaporated, provoking a mood of often bitter disappointment among Catholic trade unions and other working-class Catholic organizations. Instead, in matters of domestic policy, the Christian Democrat parties of the 1950s became advocates of a moderate conservatism or came to rely on the traditional Catholic rallying-calls of the defence of the Church and its institutions against the supposed anticlerical ambitions of liberal and socialist parties. [. . .]

The political, social, and economic changes which took place during the 1960s brought about the demise of the model of political Catholicism which had developed in Europe since the late nineteenth century. The Church no longer sought to control Catholic political activities while the laity no longer saw any automatic connection between their Catholic faith and a particular political allegiance. This in no sense indicated that Catholicism had withdrawn from the political realm. The Church continued to speak out on matters of particular concern, such as legislation on birth-control, while Catholic political movements and individuals remained prominent in European political life. What did largely disappear was the notion of political parties devoted to the defence of the particular interests and values of Catholicism. Instead, a new – and perhaps more truly Christian democrat – vision emerged of Catholics working as an active influence within a range of non-Catholic parties and movements. A particular form of political Catholicism had gone but the intimate connection between Catholicism and politics remained.

2.49   Haynes: 'the new political Catholicism'

Jeff Haynes, 1998: *Religion in Global Politics*. London and New York: Longman (pp. 35–6).

Despite the influence of Catholic parties in the post-war period (documented in the previous reading), the closing decades of the twentieth century have seen Catholic political activity move from the realm of party politics to that of public debate. Here Jeff Haynes analyses this shift in relation to the USA, but questions its influence. Casanova also describes this shift in extract **2.29**. On Neuhaus see reading **2.52**.

Three discrete issues – abortion, nuclear weapons, and economic and social justice – exemplify the new type of public Catholicism. [. . .]

The most relevant aspect of the US bishops' pastoral letters and speeches is that the Catholic religious leaders have entered what Neuhaus calls the 'naked public square', probably not in order to establish their Church as the pre-eminent Church but to take part in public debate. By proposing their normative positions they contribute to rational public debate; there is no obvious reason why in America, notwithstanding the traditional fear of religious involvement in politics, religion should not contribute *as long as it plays by the rules of open public debate*, which the Catholic Church does. This is not to claim that Church leaders will necessarily have a great impact upon the debate; surveys indicate that Catholics in America resent being told what to do by their religious professionals and that the latter's powers of political mobilization are rather limited. For example, survey data released just before the November 1996 poll indicate that Catholics – notwithstanding their religious leaders' thundering denunciation of Clinton's abortion policy – were leaning to him rather than Dole by a margin of 10 points. The implication of this is that the Catholic religious leaders have less power of political mobilization than might be expected.

2.50   Wuthnow: the rise of the New
Christian Right

Robert Wuthnow, 1983: The Political Rebirth of American Evangelicals. In Robert C.
Liebman and Robert Wuthnow (eds), *The New Christian Right. Mobilization and Legitimation.*
New York: Aldine Publishing Company, pp. 167–85 (pp. 183–5).

Whilst Evangelicals have played significant political roles in the past, not
least in the anti-slavery movement in the nineteenth century, their relative
quiescence throughout much of the twentieth century seemed to count in
favour of the belief that religions of difference had increasingly withdrawn from
the political sphere. It therefore came as a surprise to many when Evangelicals
in North America became increasingly active in politics towards the end of
the 1970s. Not content with merely acting as a pressure group, coalitions of
Christian conservatives sought to enter and influence the political process by a
variety of means. In the 1980 elections, for example, state chapters of Christian
Voice and Moral Majority participated in a number of campaigns to oust
liberal congressmen. In the following reading Robert Wuthnow suggests that
the breakdown of the boundaries between morality and politics and religion
and morality in the 1960s and 1970s were partly responsible for the rise of this
'New Christian Right', and reflects on the significance of the phenomenon for
our understanding of religion and politics and the changing relations between
them.

What do we learn, in the end, from examining the symbolism that
formed so vital a part of the political rebirth among American
evangelicals? We learn, first, that religious systems are by no means
reducible to a few simple beliefs with inevitable political consequences.
Evangelicalism is a rich tradition of complex and varied symbolic
themes. These themes are themselves sufficiently differentiated to
permit highly specific responses to be undertaken in politics and in
other arenas under varying conditions. [. . .]

We also learn that religious systems are not closed, but interact with
the cultural climate in which they exist. The symbolic boundaries
demarcating the sacred and the profane, the moral and the political,
are subject to constant renegotiation in which symbols supplied both
by religious tradition and by events in the larger culture play a role.
This is especially the case in modern societies in which the availability
of mass communications permits the negotiation process to take place
on a highly visible society-wide scale.

As for the political rebirth of evangelicals, the major symbolic constructions that contributed to this development were the redefinition

of evangelicals themselves through symbolic episodes, such as the Carter Presidency, and the reconstruction of morality to include more public or institutional meanings rather than a purely private connotation. These developments took place within the limitations of public discourse about religion and politics that had been set within the evangelical tradition itself and within the broader understandings associated with American democracy. The effects of unplanned events such as Watergate, on the one hand, and those of carefully planned activities such as the organized efforts of political action groups, on the other, were to rearrange the symbolic boundaries among religion, morality, and politics sufficiently to make it thinkable for participation in all of these spheres to occur simultaneously and to affect one another. The fundamental religious assumptions of evangelicalism were not denied or overturned in the process. Nor was it necessary for evangelicals to experience severe anxieties, as a 'status politics' interpretation of these events would suggest, or to make use of vastly increased stores of political resources in order to mobilize themselves. The reconstruction of symbolic worlds created a domain in which participation simply became a sensible thing to do.

The political rebirth of evangelicals, contradicting what seemed to be the main patterns of several decades, is not testimony to the irrelevance or complete indeterminacy of religious convictions in the face of changing social circumstances. It is, instead, evidence of the capacity of religion to adapt to social conditions in ways yet little understood and to challenge not only the prevailing system of politics, but the prevailing views of academicians as well.

2.51 Roof and McKinney: the influence of black churches on American politics

Wade Clark Roof and William McKinney, 1987: *American Mainline Religion. Its Changing Shape and Future*. New Brunswick and London: Rutgers University Press (pp. 90–1).

As well as involving itself directly in the political process as in the two examples above, religion may play an influential public and political role in modern democracies through lobbying and campaigns. Here Roof and McKinney draw attention to the influence of the black churches in American in 'appealing to the conscience of white America', and in working for a more just and equal society by 'mobilizing religious values'.

Religion's functions in the black community have been diverse: a badly needed refuge from a hostile world, yet also a source of inspiration for social involvement. At times separatist interests have loomed large; in other times more inclusive themes have held sway. As the training ground for many black leaders – Nat Turner, Denmark Vessey, Martin Luther King, Jr., and more recently, Jesse Jackson – the black church has nurtured a vision of a just America in which blacks and whites alike could share in its bounty. The majority of participants in the black churches have promoted integration, and they have interpreted justice, liberation, love, suffering, and hope in light of the goal of creating a society in which blacks and whites could live together. Entry into the mainstream for blacks rests upon appeals to the conscience of white America and to overcoming the discrepancies between national ideals and continuing discriminatory practices. King was masterful in mobilizing religious values ('I have a Dream') as a means of breaking through to white America. Jesse Jackson's 1984 presidential candidacy represents the latest, and perhaps the most politically astute, effort yet at articulating an inclusive vision and program for the nation.

2.52 Neuhaus: putting religion back into the 'naked public square'

Richard John Neuhaus, 1984: *The Naked Public Square. Religion and Democracy in America.* Grand Rapids, MI: Eerdmans (pp. 258–60).

The proper role of religion in liberal democracy has become a matter of lively intellectual debate since the 1980s and the rise of the New Christian Right (see extract **2.50**). In *The Naked Public Square*, one of the most influential of the books to arise from this debate, Neuhaus argues that the survival of liberal democracy is endangered by the exclusion of religion from public debate. In particular, as the following reading makes clear, Neuhaus believes that only religions are really capable of legitimating the law on which a just society rests. As modern institutions which once exercised normative roles (such as the universities) have abdicated this responsibility, so religious traditions must fill the space created in the public square – so long, that is, as they play by the rules of open public debate and do not themselves become tyrannous.

This is the cultural crisis – and therefore the political and legal crisis – of our society: the popularly accessible and vibrant belief systems and world views of our society are largely excluded from the public arena in which the decisions are made about how the society should be ordered. As we have seen, critics such as Daniel Bell conclude, with some reluctance, that the answer lies in a more public role for religion. What they conclude with reluctance is the gravamen of this book. Specifically with regard to law, there is nothing in store but a continuing and deepening crisis of legitimacy if courts persist in systematically ruling out of order the moral traditions in which Western law has developed and which bear, for the overwhelming majority of the American people, a living sense of right and wrong. The result, quite literally, is *the outlawing of the basis of law*. When the moral sentiments and the traditions that have given them shape and voice are ruled out of order, even the most solemn questions are 'resolved' by mechanistic reduction to the lowest possible factor. [. . .]

There is in store a continuing and deepening crisis of legitimacy unless a transcendent moral purpose is democratically asserted by which the state can be brought under critical judgment, unless it is made clear once again that the state is not the source but the servant of the law. As we have paraphrased Spinoza, transcendence abhors a vacuum. Recall John Courtney Murray's cautions about the invitation extended when there is a vacuum in the public space of law and politics. The vacuum will surely be filled, as has so tragically happened elsewhere, by the pretensions of the modern state. As the crisis of legitimacy deepens, it will lead – not next year, maybe not in twenty years, but all too soon – to totalitarianism or to insurrection. The insurrection may be on the way to totalitarianism or on the way to what is described as authoritarianism, but after a period of either it is difficult to envision the resumption of the democratic experiment. Already figures such as Francis Schaeffer call for a reconsideration of justifiable revolution, and a good many less sober than he are in full-throated support of rebellion. They are in curious alliance with those on the left who, with very different analysis and intent, assert that there is no way out apart from revolution.

Meanwhile, the 'vital center' of liberal democratic faith is largely unattended. In the deepening night of 'cultural contradictions,' jurists and politicians go about their business of serving precedent and procedure, warding off the questions that break through 'the issues' of the moment. Yet others who fancy their philosophical indifference makes them pragmatists count on continued material prosperity to give everybody a stake in holding at bay the legitimacy crisis which threatens a system that 'works,' more or less, to the benefit of all, more or less. The American proposition is no longer proposed. The democracy that began as an experiment has become at best a habit, a temporary condition, perhaps a luxury that can no longer be afforded. The barbarians look less like a threat and more like some kind of answer.

2.53   Martin: Pentecostalism and the political significance of the apolitical

David Martin, 1996: *Forbidden Revolutions. Pentecostalism in Latin America, Catholicism in Eastern Europe*. London: SPCK (pp. 37–9).

It is possible for religion – whether under a democratic or non-democratic regime – to exercise a powerful political influence even when explicitly distancing itself from the political arena. In the following extract David Martin shows why this is true of the worldwide Charismatic upsurge, a form of religion superbly well adapted to modern, differentiated society. Interestingly, Martin's remarks on Pentecostalism tally with those of Levine on liberation theology (1992): 'one of liberation theology's most enduring contributions has been to demystify authority by giving the tools of association to everyone, and by making the effort legitimate in religious terms. The development of strong associational life provides underpinnings for a truly independent civil society. The resulting shift of power from resignation, fatalism, and silent powerlessness to equality, activism, organization, and voice is a cultural and political change of major proportions' (p. 351). See also Bernice Martin, reading **2.23**.

Such [evangelical] movements help erode all-embracing systems in politics or in religion and can best be understood through two frameworks. One is Halévy's argument that evangelical conversion assists peaceful cultural evolution rather than violent revolutionary upheaval. The other is De Tocqueville's argument about the way in which voluntary religious organizations build up 'social capital' through networks between the state and the individual. They mostly seek to bypass politics and the state and established religious bodies, and sometimes all three allied together. [. . .]

Pentecostals are an option of the poor rather than the liberationist 'option *for* the poor', and this option is most of all exercised by those who seek all-round betterment. In the long run they offer modest social mobility to most, and rapid mobility to a few. Naturally, many people find their beliefs and practices bizarre, but there is little that would have shocked the eighteenth-century Anglo-American evangelist George Whitefield, and rather a lot of that simply comes from taking the New Testament seriously. Another sign of this is their aversion to personal or political violence. Like the Quakers in England in 1661, they are 'the quiet in the land'; but they have also found out how to mobilize the power of marginality and of protective enclosure. They are people who show what can be done by actively attacking your immediate circumstances. They encounter limits, of course, but they also extend them.

2.54 Szerszynski: cultural politics

Bronislaw Szerszynski (forthcoming): Performing Politics: The Dramatics of Environmental Protest. In Larry Ray and Andrew Sayer (eds), *Culture and Economy: After the Cultural Turn*. London: Sage.

It is clear from many of the readings above that both religions of difference and religions of humanity continue to exercise a powerful political role in modern times. What of spiritualities of life? Because such spiritualities are often quite self-consciously privatized, emphasize the importance of the individual experience and the individual quest for God, and shun public, institutionalized forms of religion, their relative lack of political significance is perhaps to be expected. However, spiritualities of life have not been without political significance. As extract **2.36** above reminds us, Gandhi's spirituality (which exemplifies many typical characteristics of a spirituality of life) was highly politicized. Likewise, some contemporary social commentators claim that the so-called 'new social movements' (NSMs) of the late twentieth century, many of which have a strongly spiritual emphasis, represent a powerful new political force (on the similarities and overlaps between NSMs and NRMS (new religious movements) see Hannigan, 1990, 1991). Here Bronislaw Szerszynski develops such an argument in relation to the environmental movement, suggesting that the latter should be viewed as political as well as cultural – though it may be political in a new way. Compare this observation by Theodore Roszak (1979): 'We live in a time when the very private experience of having a personal identity to discover, a personal identity to fulfil, has become a subversive force of major proportions' (p. xxviii), and see extract **2.60** below in which Giddens introduces the idea of 'identity politics'.

Radical environmental protest is of interest because, while being a highly culturalised form of politics, it cannot easily be categorised under many of the theoretical labels used to understand such politics. Firstly, it cannot without distortion be simply seen as another example of the 'stylisation of life', as a simple instrumental display of cultural capital by one group in order to mark themselves out as superior to another. To do so would be to ignore the deep critique of contemporary society carried by such groups, or at least to regard this critique as nothing but another mark of distinction – as just another emblem of cultural membership, and as a weapon of *ressentiment* in the war for cultural superiority over others. [. . .]

Secondly, neither does radical environmental politics clearly belong to the category of 'identity politics', whereby a specific social grouping defends its rights to be recognised as a distinct subculture. Political activists such as those protesting against the construction of roads or runways do not simply want to be left alone to follow their way of life unhindered, or to have that way of life culturally valued and validated. Indeed, they go out of their way to put themselves in the way of society-as-usual, disrupting major construction projects and everyday traffic flow in order to communicate their message to society – and a message not on behalf of themselves as a group but on behalf of nature. This is a cultural politics which operates not simply by marking and performing the boundary of its own form of life. It does so in such a way that beckons those outside its boundary, hailing them with a moral claim that one *should* be on the *inside*. [. . .]

Thirdly, although following an alternative lifestyle is an integral feature of contemporary direct action, integral to the protest lifestyle is a purposive orientation, which also marks it out from – or at least marks it as a distinctive variant of – the politics of self-realisation and life decisions termed 'life politics' by Anthony Giddens. Individual self-realisation and the more communal pursuit of the good life are indeed features of radical environmental protest, but this is a self-realisation which is achieved through political effectiveness, and a good life which is always on the edge of being instrumentalised by the protest culture as simply a means to the higher end of the defence of nature. Constant self-monitoring in the name of individual responsibility is also characteristic of the protest subculture, but this is not simply felt as the demand to respond reflexively and responsibly to the choices that life lays before us, but as a call actively to pursue a project of societal transformation.

But apart from testing the adequacy of existing categories of contemporary politics, what light can radical environmental protest shed on the relation between culture and politics? [. . .]

What we are seeing in contemporary environmental protest, I would argue, is a new mode of performing the public sphere. . . . Although the Puritan mode of performing civic life has suffered a diminution, we may be witnessing the emergence of a new form of public ritual, one that is more plural and contestatory in its demands, and polysemic in its imagery and speech – one that weds authentic personal display with playfulness and irony. The cultural power of contemporary protests, I would suggest, lies at least partly in the polysemic and unstable nature of its symbolism, which draws us in as subjects and citizens in new and challenging ways, inviting society to redefine itself, its aspirations and priorities. As such, it perhaps hints at a way of performing politics otherwise.

Political: prospects

2.55 Casanova: religion before the juggernaut of modernity

José Casanova, 1994: *Public Religions in the Modern World*. Chicago and London: University of Chicago Press (p. 234).

As reading **2.29** reveals, José Casanova believes that religion in modern times is differentiated but not privatized. It continues to have public and political significance, even in the secular democracies of the contemporary West. In the following extract he reflects on one of religion's most important continuing political roles: critical reflection and protest at the excesses of the capitalist market and the modern state. It is, he believes, still an open question whether religion will be able to continue in this role, or whether it will be crushed by the forces of modernity.

Western modernity has lost some of its haughty self-assurance and is beginning to manifest some doubts about its arrogant attitude toward the other, precisely at a time when the attempt to transcend itself from within through socialism has apparently failed. Meanwhile the two dynamos of modernity, the capitalist market and the administrative state, continue their self-propelled march toward a world system, wrecking and challenging every premodern tradition and life form that stands in their way. Some of these traditions accommodate and accept the private niche reserved for them in the cultural marketplace, where they may even thrive in the modern or postmodern pantheon.

Others, particularly non-Western traditions, emboldened by modernity's self-doubts, are able to reaffirm their own identity against the modern West. If Weber was correct when he argued that ascetic Protestantism played some role in helping to shape the particular historical form which the institutionalization of modern differentiation and the privatization of religion assumed in the West, theories of secularization and modernization should be open to the possibility that other religions may also play some role in institutionalizing their own particular patterns of secularization.

Finally, there are those traditions which have maintained an uneasy relationship with modernity, partly accommodating, partly recognizing some of modernity's values as their own but refusing to accept the claims of the market and the state that moral norms ought not to interfere with their systemic logic of self-reproduction through the media of money and power. Through their ongoing critical encounter with modernity, those traditions may be in a position to further both the processes of practical rationalization and the unfinished project of modernity.

Western modernity is at a crossroads. If it does not enter into a creative dialogue with the other, with those traditions which are challenging its identity, modernity will most likely triumph. But it may end up being devoured by the inflexible, inhuman logic of its own creations. It would be profoundly ironic if, after all the beatings it has received from modernity, religion could somehow unintentionally help modernity save itself.

2.56 Fenn: the diffusion of the sacred

Richard K. Fenn, 1982: *Liturgies and Trials. The Secularization of Religious Language*. Oxford: Basil Blackwell (pp. 196–8).

Even though Casanova (see reading above) believes that religion continues to play a political role in the differentiated world of today, he is aware that this role is fragile and threatened. Many of those who uphold some version of secularization theory argue more forcefully than Casanova that religion in modern societies has ceased to play any significant political role (see, for example Bryan Wilson, reading **3.14** in the chapter on Secularization). Equally, those who argue that 'detraditionalization' better describes the process affecting religion in modern times than 'secularization' maintain that the public and political role of religion has diminished and that religion is increasingly confined to the private and domestic spheres. Both positions seem to imply that religion will play an increasingly insignificant political role in the future. The sociologist and theologian Richard Fenn does not deny the reality of secularization, and in the book from which this extract is taken finds evidence of secularization in the way in which religious and liturgical discourse is marginalized and undermined by hegemonic secular discourses like that of law and the courtroom. Like Casanova, however, he finds that religion continues to play important public roles, and that it is still uniquely able to challenge the invasive domination of the secular state and its discourses. He explores this continuing and important political role in the passage below. In his earlier book, *A Theory of Secularization* (1978), he also suggested that differentiation leads not to the exclusion of religion from the political sphere, but to its diffusion. 'The process of secularization', he says, 'increases the likelihood that various institutions and groups will base their claims to social authority on various religious grounds while it undermines

consensus on the meaning and location of the sacred' (p. 26). Compare Robert
Beckford's Comments on the diffusion of religion in **3.38**.

> Secular contexts may well find their rules for discourse broken more
> frequently in the future than in the past as individuals demand the
> right to testify to their religious convictions in the classroom, in the
> court, on the political campaign trail, and even in the hospital where
> matters of life and death have been the prerogative of only one
> profession to decide. Reflecting on the secularization of institutions in
> modern societies, Max Weber once argued that the spirit had left
> them and survived only in the private world of friendship and devo-
> tion. It is possible that Weber was premature in announcing the end
> of the Reformation, and instead we may expect to see the secularity
> and literalness of seminars and courtrooms increasingly interrupted
> by testimony concerning the things of the spirit.

2.57   Neuhaus: religion and the survival of liberal democracy

Richard John Neuhaus, 1984: *The Naked Public Square. Religion and Democracy in America.*
Grand Rapids, MI: Eerdmans (pp. 263–4).

In a look to the future which can in some ways be seen as an extension of the
argument made by several authors above that religion undergirds democratic
values (see, for example Troeltsch **2.44** and Parsons **2.45**), Neuhaus sees the
continued public vitality of religion as essential to the survival of liberal democracy. As we have seen in extract **2.52** above, Neuhaus believes that it is religion's
moral, legal, and generally *normative* role which is of particular importance.
Interestingly, however, he does not tie the survival of democracy to the survival
of Protestant Christianity, but seems to envisage the rise of a new, more embracing religious experiment – presumably one more suited to the pluralistic condition of modern times. On this latter point compare Bellah in the reading which
follows this one.

> Of the most militant majoritarians, often led by professed fundament-
> alists, we have perhaps said enough. They are making the most
> aggressive bid to become the new culture-forming elite in American
> religion. This author's sympathies and skepticisms should be evident
> by now. I do not think they will succeed. I hope not. At the same
> time, I am confident they will not go away. They have kicked a
> tripwire alerting large sectors of the society to the absurdities and
> dangers of the naked public square. The most hopeful prospect is
> that, if we and they have the imagination to move beyond present

polarizations, we will become partners in rearticulating the religious base of the democratic experiment.

Mainline, Jews, Catholics, Lutherans, Orthodox, Evangelicals, Fundamentalists – such religious taxonomy is of limited usefulness. He who said, 'Behold I am doing a new thing. Do you not perceive it?' no doubt has other surprises in store. We can engage in denominational and confessional classifications as we will, but it may have little to do with where that new thing comes from, with where it is perhaps already stirring and on the edge of its public debut.

But the new thing we are looking for may not come at all. The naked public square may be the last phase of a failed experiment, a mistaken proposition. We have no divine promise that a nation so conceived and so dedicated will endure any longer than it has. Afterward, there will still be laws, of that we can be sure. And the history books, if history books are allowed then, will record this strange moment in which a society was in turmoil over the connections between laws and the law, between law and life. Then the turmoil will seem very distant, for then no dissent will be permitted from the claim that the law is the law is the law.

This dour prospect is not alarmist. Surely something like it is what those thoughtful people must mean when they say that the day of liberal democracy is past. It makes little difference whether the successor regime is of the right or of the left or unclassifiable. By whatever ideology the idea, this audacious democratic idea, would be declared discredited. By whom, where, under what circumstances, by what conception and what dedication could it ever be tried again? Yes, of course, life would go on and God's purposes will not be defeated, not ultimately. But the world would be a darker and colder place. That it can happen is evident to all but the naive and willfully blind. That it will happen seems probable, if we refuse to understand the newness, the fragility, the promise, and the demands of religion and democracy in America.

2.58 Bellah hopes for an international civil religion

Robert Bellah, 1967: Civil Religion in America. In *Daedalus*, vol. 96, no. 1, Winter: 1–21 (p. 18).

At the end of his famous essay on civil religion (see reading **2.42**), Bellah acknowledges that whilst such religion may have served the American nation well, it is unsuited to a more global society (for Bellah the first 'time of trial' in

American history was the Revolution; the second the Civil War; and the third currently provoked by the demands of superpower status and an international role). In the following extract, taken from the end of the essay, he therefore looks forward in hope to the emergence of a more international civil religion. Bellah seems to suggest that the (peaceful) political future of the world depends upon the emergence of a sustaining global religion-cultural matrix. Pope John Paul II develops similar themes in reading **3.69**.

> Out of the first and second times of trial have come, as we have seen, the major symbols of the American civil religion. There seems little doubt that a successful negotiation of this third time of trial – the attainment of some kind of viable and coherent world order – would precipitate a major new set of symbolic forms. So far the flickering flame of the United Nations burns too low to be the focus of a cult, but the emergence of a genuine trans-national sovereignty would certainly change this. It would necessitate the incorporation of vital international symbolism into our civil religion, or, perhaps a better way of putting it, it would result in American civil religion becoming simply one part of a new civil religion of the world. It is useless to speculate on the form such a civil religion might take, though it obviously would draw on religious traditions beyond the sphere of Biblical religion alone. Fortunately, since the American civil religion is not the worship of the American nation but an understanding of the American experience in the light of ultimate and universal reality, the reorganization entailed by such a new situation need not disrupt the American civil religion's continuity. A world civil religion could be accepted as a fulfillment and not a denial of American civil religion. Indeed, such an outcome has been the eschatological hope of American civil religion from the beginning. To deny such an outcome would be to deny the meaning of America itself.

2.59   Juergensmeyer: the onward march of religious nationalism?

Mark Juergensmeyer, 1993: *The New Cold War? Religious Nationalism Confronts the Secular State*. Berkeley and Los Angeles: University of California Press (pp. 201–2).

In contrast to the hopes voiced by Bellah in the reading above, Mark Juergensmeyer's account of the rise of religious nationalisms at the end of the twentieth century (see reading **2.31**) raises the prospect of global political fragmentation. Here he speculates on whether this will in fact be the outcome of the process: should we expect 'a new cold war' between secular and religious nationalisms, or a more peaceful co-existence?

Because there is ultimately no satisfactory compromise on an ideological level between religious and secular nationalism, it is possible to imagine that the current situation could get far worse, and a global state of enmity could settle in, surpassing the hostility of the old Cold War. One can foresee the emergence of a united religious bloc stretching from Central and South Asia through the Middle East to Africa. With an arsenal of nuclear weapons at its disposal and fueled by American fear of Islam, it might well replace the old Soviet Union as a united global enemy of the secular West.

Such a conflict might be compounded by the rise of new religious radicals in Europe and the United States, including not only politically active Christians but also members of newly immigrant communities of Muslims, Hindus, and Sikhs who might support their religious comrades at home. A nascent cult of cultural nationalists in Japan and elsewhere in the Far East might also be in league with what could become the West's new foe.

Barring this apocalyptic vision of a worldwide conflict between religious and secular nationalism, we have reason to be hopeful. It is equally as likely that religious nationalists are incapable of uniting with one another, and that they will greatly desire an economic and political reconciliation with the secular world. In this event, a grudging tolerance might develop between religious and secular nationalists, and each might be able to admire what the other provides: communitarian values and moral vision on the one hand, individualism and rational rules of justice on the other. After all, both are responses to, and products of, the modern age. In Sri Lanka, India, Iran, Egypt, Algeria, Afghanistan, Mongolia, Central Asia, Eastern Europe, and other places where independent nations are experimenting with nationalism of a religious nature, they are doing far more than resuscitating archaic ideas of religious rule. They are creating something new: a synthesis between religion and the secular state, a merger between the cultural identity and legitimacy of old religiously sanctioned monarchies and the democratic spirit and organizational unity of modern industrial society. This combination can be incendiary, for it blends the absolutism of religion with the potency of modern politics. Yet it may also be necessary, for without the legitimacy conferred by religion, the democratic process does not seem to work in some parts of the world. In these places, it may be necessary for the essential elements of democracy to be conveyed in the vessels of new religious states.

2.60 Giddens: from emancipatory politics to identity politics

Anthony Giddens, 1991: *Modernity and Self-Identity. Self and Society in the Late Modern Age.* Cambridge: Polity Press (pp. 210–11; 214).

Anthony Giddens broadens our understanding of modern politics through his distinction between emancipatory and identity or 'life' politics. Elsewhere in the book from which this extract is taken he suggests that whilst life politics will never wholly supplant emancipatory politics, it is becoming the more dominant form of political activity at the end of the twentieth century. Whereas emancipatory politics seeks to eliminate differences in the quest for equality, Life politics actively promotes difference in the quest for self-actualization. Will this open up new possibilities for religion? The theme of difference is the subject of the following chapter.

Life politics does not primarily concern the conditions which liberate us in order to make choices: it is a politics *of* choice. While emancipatory politics is a politics of life chances, life politics is a politics of lifestyle. Life politics is the politics of a reflexively mobilised order – the system of late modernity – which, on an individual and collective level, has radically altered the existential parameters of social activity. It is a politics of self-actualisation in a reflexively ordered environment, where that reflexivity links self and body to systems of global scope. In this arena of activity, power is generative rather than hierarchical. Life politics is lifestyle politics in the serious and rich sense discussed in previous chapters. To give a formal definition: life politics concerns political issues which flow from processes of self-actualisation in post-traditional contexts, where globalising influences intrude deeply into the reflexive project of the self, and conversely where processes of self-realisation influence global strategies.

CHAPTER EIGHT

difference: gendered and ethnic

Introduction

Difference is, of course, nothing new. There has always been difference at every level of existence – from the biological to the social and cultural. Equally, religion has always interplayed and interacted with such difference, and has had to make sense of the existence of different religions and cultures. What may be new and characteristic of modern times, however, are the ways in which difference has come to be understood, asserted, activated, and valued.

One form of difference in which religions have always been implicated is strong, evaluative, exclusivistic, 'prescriptive' difference. This is particularly true of religions of difference. As we have seen in **Part One**, such religions are actively involved in the maintenance of their difference from other religions and communities. Clear initiation rites, defined dogmas, prescribed moralities, authoritative teachings, texts and traditions, clear social structures, and organized authority structures all help in the maintenance of difference. Strongly differentiated forms of religion are characteristically universalistic in the sense that they believe they have exclusive possession of universal truth. As a result they recognize but do not endorse divergence from their own norms. Communities and individuals that are different are simply wrong. They must be denied, destroyed, or assimilated, because in the end there is only one truth.

Prescriptive difference is also operative in such religions at other levels. It is very clear in the distinction which they draw between the divine and the created orders, between the saved and the damned, between priests and lay people, between male and female – and so on. Many of the differences which are defended are believed to be God-given and inscribed in the natural order of things. Such difference is strongest when it is thought to be prescribed by some power greater than human beings, and when it is conveyed by appointed guardians of the truth (see, for example, Pope Pius XI and Ayatollah Khomeni on male–female difference in readings **2.64** and **2.65**). In many cases such difference is hierarchical. In the Pauline 'household codes' in the New Testament, for example, women are to obey their husbands, children their parents, slaves their masters – and all their God.

The reassertion and reinscription of moralized, prescriptive difference is one aspect of the rise of difference in relation to religion in modern times. It is particularly obvious in the case of religions of heightened difference. As the previous chapter on political contexts has shown, such assertion is often bound up with national and ethnic mobilization. Because religions of difference maintain such clear boundaries, they are eminently well suited to the defence of threatened identies and the construction of communal ones.

The majority of the readings in this chapter consider the assertion of strong, prescriptive difference in modern times. Also important, however, is the rise of a second form of difference in the latter part of the twentieth century. Such difference has been articulated by a number of postmodern theorists, some of whose work is included in the 'overviews' below. One might refer to this second form of difference as 'postmodern difference'. Equally, one might call it 'open difference'. What is involved is an affirmatory, even celebratory, stance towards difference – in one's own life and in relation to the 'other'. Here difference is simply difference. Every individual and every group is thought to have the right, if not the duty, to be different. Difference, understood as good in itself, is open as regards its content and its authors. It is also open in the sense that it is not thought to be prescribed by God, nature, or by authoritative individuals, traditions or institutions. Instead, legitimate difference is thought of as self-determined by a group or individual. Likewise, difference is non-hierarchical and non-evaluative; difference, but not 'discrimination'. Any and all difference is treated as good – so long, that is, as it respects other differences and does not insist too dogmatically or violently on its own truth. Open difference is tolerant and provisional. It understands truth as a matter of perspective, relative to different standpoints and different narratives. It can embrace diversity, fragmentation and even – should such a thing be possible – contradiction.

What has led to this new emphasis on open difference? A number of different factors can be cited:

1 The spread, even the 'triumph', of democracy in the twentieth century, and the emergence of freedom, equality and the right of

self-determination as central values (see Berman, 1992). (On the other hand it can be argued that democracy has also played an important role in fostering universalism – see, for example, Alexis de Tocqueville, reading **3.73**.)

2 The refutation of universal narratives by historical events: for example, the failure of Enlightenment narratives of freedom and equality to enfranchise more than a privileged minority, and the manifest failure of universalist, modernizing narratives of 'development' to bring prosperity to all parts of the world.

3 The greater awareness of cultural, social and economic diversity consequent on improved communications and increased mobility.

4 Wide-ranging sociocultural changes associated with the late twentieth century including 'the end of organized capitalism' (Lash and Urry, 1987), the increased pace of globalization (see Hall, 1992), and the proliferation of philosophies of difference (see Harvey, 1990). Such changes are often classified under the general rubric of 'postmodernity'.

Before getting swept away by the rhetoric of the inexorable spread of postmodern difference, it is important to remember that even at the end of the twentieth century, essentialized, prescriptive difference remains a much more potent force in the religious field, and that difference continues to be limited, checked and contradicted by the survival (and even invention) of totalizing and universalist discourses and ideologies, as well as by the revitalization of religions of difference. The readings which follow reflect the relative weakness of open difference in the religious realm, the majority of them dealing with the relation between religion and the reinscription of prescriptive difference. Equally, the readings reflect the fact that the impact of the ideal of open difference on religion has tended to be greatest at the level of literary and academic reflection.

Despite the growing importance of discourses and strategies asserting difference (both open and prescriptive), it is interesting to note that the difference they advocate is itself understood differently. In particular, the *scale* of difference varies widely. At one extreme the assertion of difference and the rights of difference may be made by a whole religious or ethnic group, or even a whole gender. At the other extreme, the unit of difference is the individual, or even the individual discourses and strategies of power which construct the individual (the self on this postmodern account having been destabilized and decentred). Likewise, on the one hand men and women today lay claim to the identity of a unique individual; on the other to an identity constituted by belonging to a group. Difference is thus asserted simultaneously at a number of levels, often in conflictual or potentially conflictual ways.

The readings which follow consider two of the most important areas in which religion and difference interplay: gender and ethnicity. In some cases religion is itself the chief source of difference (both open and prescribed); in others it undergirds, reinforces and articulates pre-existing forms of difference (see, for example, reading **2.76** on the interactions between Islam and ethnic identity). Where religion acts to undergird difference, religion is often vitalized in the process (a point reinforced in chapter twelve, Sacralization, in **Part Three**). Religion may also be mobilized to fix or stabilize identities threatened by some of the forces of modernity: papal efforts throughout the twentieth century to insist upon women's natural childbearing, nurturing and domestic roles may, for example, be viewed as a reaction to economic and cultural changes which threaten to undermine the 'traditional' nuclear family, and with it a whole order of patriarchal authority (see reading **2.64**). As the latter example illustrates, and as the readings on women in Africa and Pakistan make explicit (**2.73** and **2.74**), gendered differences, like other differences, often take their place within wider symbolic universes, and in interlocking relation to other sets of differences. Thus the seclusion and obedience of Pakistani women symbolize not only the integrity of Islam, but the integrity of the nation.

Difference undergirded by religion does not merely serve conservative ends, however. As readings **2.66** and **2.67** remind us, religion may enable the construction, articulation and sanctification of new 'postmodern' differences – in these examples the construction of new forms of feminist and Black feminist spirituality which enable women to claim and celebrate a variety of ethnic and gendered differences. Equally it may undergird new religio-ethnic identities. Yet the mobilization of religion to undergird difference is always open to contestation by the opposing forces of universalization, which themselves often come in religious guise. In the late twentieth century the fashion is to celebrate difference and to gloss over religion's totalizing and universalizing tendencies. In situations of conflictual pluralism, however, such as in India, Indonesia, South Africa or the former Yugoslavia, an enlightenment narrative of universal humanity and united nations, or a Christian narrative of the one God who calls all men and women to worship him in a single peaceable kingdom, will continue to challenge ideologies of prescriptive difference. It remains to be seen whether such universalism will ultimately prove compatible with assertions of open difference (see, for example, reading **2.85**, and the readings on Universalization (chapter eleven) in **Part Three**).

As well as being read in conjunction with chapter eleven, chapter eight should be read in relation to **Part One**. The implications of the rise of difference for the varieties of religion explored there are interesting. The alliance between religions of difference and new assertions of gendered and ethnic difference has already been mentioned. In relation to religions of humanity, the undermining of universalizing metanarratives and the 'essentialist' category of the human by ideas of postmodern difference clearly constitues an important challenge. The implications of the rise of difference for spiritualities of life seem more complex. On the one hand, some varieties of such spirituality can be seen as taking open difference to its logical extreme where the individual becomes the 'consumer', arbiter and creator of his or her own religion (see the chapter on Detraditionalization in **Part Three**). On the other hand, many religions of life carry a strongly universalist and holistic message (see for example Emerson in reading **3.62**).

As we suggest in the Conclusion of this volume, the contradictions and interplays between universalization on the one hand, and difference on the other, seem to represent one of the most important tensions at the heart of contemporary religious life and thought.

Difference: overviews

2.61   Hall: open and prescriptive difference

Stuart Hall, 1992: The Question of Cultural Identity. In Stuart Hall, David Held and Tony McGrew (eds): *Modernity and Its Futures*. Cambridge: Polity Press in association with the Open University, pp. 274–316 (pp. 308–9).

In their respective ways both liberalism and Marxism imagined that difference and attachment to the local and particular would give way to more universalist and internationalist values and identities. It might also have been thought that the process of globalization which, aided by improved travel and communications, has gained pace in the twentieth century, would have led to an erosion of difference. Here Stuart Hall argues that such expectations of universalization have been confounded by the recovery of old identities and the production of new ones. Generally speaking, the older, wider identities of class and nation appear to be giving way to more particular, diverse and plural identities – including ethnic, gendered, and religious identities. The interesting point with which this reading concludes is that such identities can be *either* open *or* prescriptive.

Another effect [of globalization] has been to trigger a widening of the field of identities, and a proliferation of new identity-positions together with a degree of polarization amongst and between them. These developments constitute the second and third possible consequences of globalization I referred to earlier – the possibility that globalization might lead to a *strengthening* of local identities, or to the production of *new identities*.

The strengthening of local identities can be seen in the strong defensive reaction of those members of dominant ethnic groups who feel threatened by the presence of other cultures. [. . .]

It is sometimes matched by a strategic retreat to more defensive identities amongst the minority communities themselves in response to the experience of cultural racism and exclusion. Such strategies include re-identification with cultures of origin (in the Caribbean, India, Bangladesh, Pakistan); the construction of strong counter-ethnicities – as in the symbolic identification of second-generation Afro-Caribbean youth, through the symbols and motifs of Rastafarianism, with their African origin and heritage; or the revival of cultural traditionalism, religious orthodoxy and political separatism, for example, amongst *some* sections of the Muslim community.

There is also some evidence of the third possible consequences of globalization – the production of *new* identities. A good example is those new identities which have emerged in the 1970s, grouped around the signifier 'black', which in the British context provides a new focus of identification for *both* Afro-Caribbean and Asian communities. What these communities have in common, which they represent through taking on the 'black' identity, is not that they are culturally, ethnically, linguistically or even physically the same, but that they are seen and treated as 'the same' (i.e. non-white, 'other') by the dominant culture. It is their exclusion which provides what Laclau and Mouffe call the common 'axis of equivalence' of this new identity. However, despite the fact that efforts are made to give this 'black' identity a single or unified content, it continues to exist as an identity *alongside a wide range of other differences*. Afro-Caribbean and Indian people continue to maintain different cultural traditions. 'Black' is thus an example, not only of the *political* character of new identities – i.e. their *positional* and conjunctural character (their formation in and for specific times and places) – but also of the way identity and difference are inextricably articulated or knitted together in different identities, the one never wholly obliterating the other.

As a tentative conclusion it would appear then that globalization *does* have the effect of contesting and dislocating the centred and 'closed' identities of a national culture. It does have a pluralizing impact on identities, producing a variety of possibilities and new positions of identification, and making identities more positional, more political, more plural and diverse; less fixed, unified or trans-historical. However, its general impact remains contradictory. Some identities gravitate towards what Robins calls 'Tradition', attempting to restore their former purity and recover the unities and certainties which are felt as being lost. Others accept that identity is subject to the play of history, politics, representation and difference, so that they are unlikely ever again to be unitary or 'pure'; and these consequently gravitate towards what Robins (following Homi Bhabha) calls 'Translation'.

2.62 Said: the oriental 'other'

Edward Said, 1978: *Orientalism.* London: Routledge (pp. 300–2).

As Edward Said has shown in his pioneering work on 'orientalism', one of the most powerful examples of the assertion of difference in modern times has been the way in which a western imperialism constructed an oriential 'other' as the inferior mirror image of itself. The implications for religion have been considerable: in the West the so-called oriental religions came to be viewed as different from and inferior to their western counterparts; in the colonized East religions struggled to assert their equality (often in universalistic terms). The demise of western imperialism in the twentieth century has seen the revitalization and reassertion of these colonized religions with a strong assertion of their difference – this time a difference of superiority not inferiority. (On Islamic reassertion see, for example, Hunwick reading **2.81**.)

The principal dogmas of Orientalism exist in their purest form today in studies of the Arabs and Islam. Let us recapitulate them here: one is the absolute and systematic difference between the West, which is rational, developed, humane, superior, and the Orient, which is aberrant, undeveloped, inferior. Another dogma is that abstractions about the Orient, particularly those based on texts representing a 'classical' Oriental civilization, are always preferable to direct evidence drawn from modern Oriental realities. A third dogma is that the Orient is eternal, uniform, and incapable of defining itself; therefore it is assumed that a highly generalized and systematic vocabulary for describing the Orient from a Western standpoint is inevitable and even scientifically 'objective.' A fourth dogma is that the Orient is at bottom something either to be feared (the Yellow Peril, the Mongol hordes, the brown dominions) or to the controlled (by pacification, research and development, outright occupation whenever possible).

2.63   Heelas: religion and postmodern difference

Paul Heelas, 1998: Introduction: On Differentiation and Dedifferentiation. In Paul Heelas (ed.) with the assistance of David Martin and Paul Morris, *Religion, Modernity and Postmodernity*. Oxford and Malden, Mass.: Blackwell, pp. 1–18 (pp. 4–7).

Here Paul Heelas offers a characterization of postmodern or open difference, and relates it to religion.

James Beckford, in a succinct characterization of postmodernity which deserves full citation, notes the following features:

1   A refusal to regard positivistic, rationalistic, instrumental criteria as the sole or exclusive standard of worthwhile knowledge.
2   A willingness to combine symbols from disparate codes or frameworks of meaning, even at the cost of disjunctions and eclecticism.
3   A celebration of spontaneity, fragmentation, superficiality, irony and playfulness.
4   A willingness to abandon the search for over-arching or triumphalist myths, narratives or frameworks of knowledge.

Combining the first and the last of his four points, the claim is that truth provided by the exercise of reason and the transmission of tradition is – at least in measure – weakened, even abandoned. Differences, we can go on to add, become *deregulated* or unpoliced. The different becomes 'simply' the different, this in the sense that this mode of distinction has, become liberated from 'strong' distinguishing features. That is to say, detraditionalization, as well as the (relative) abandonment of what reason can ascertain, serves to ensure that people no longer know what – in some cultural or absolute sense – is true or what is false; is legitimate or not; is to be valued or not. Or so it is claimed. [. . .]

  Thinking of the significance of this for religion, postmodern religion – as a number of scholars have called the development – is very much in the hands of the 'free' subject (again, assuming that the subject has not disintegrated into a series of discourses or cultural processes). The deregulation of the religious realm, combined with the cultural emphasis on freedom and choice, results in intermingled, interfused, forms of religious – or 'religious'-cum-'secular' – life which exist beyond the tradition-regulated church and chapel. People no longer feel obliged to heed the boundaries of the religions of modernity. Instead, they are positively encouraged to exercise their 'autonomy' to draw on what has diffused through the culture. Somewhat revising James Beckford's second point, they show a 'willingness to combine symbols from (previously) disparate codes or frameworks of meaning'. They – so to speak – raid the world, drawing on whatever is felt desirable: the religious (perhaps shamanism and Christianity); the religious and the non-religious (perhaps yoga and champagne). Sometimes this is done sequentially, in the case of Prince Charles, moving from hunting foxes (traditionalism) to talking to trees (New Age) to hunting foxes again. And sometimes this is done by fusing the previously marked off: and hence the popularity of the term 'hybridity' among postmodern theorists. (My favourite example is Zennis, a fusion of Zen and tennis.)

A related way in which it can be argued that this kind of religion is postmodern is by pointing to the fact that it would often appear to be associated with forms of pragmatism and relativism: ethics associated with postmodernity through the work, for example, of Richard Rorty and Ernest Gellner. Instead of authoritative narratives or other forms of knowledge providing truth, 'truth' is seen in terms of 'what works for me'. People have what they *take* to be 'spiritual' experiences without having to hold religious *beliefs*. (Indeed, it is precisely because of this outlook that those concerned can draw on beliefs or rituals which the modernist would keep apart.) And this results in a form of relativism: religion beyond belief is religion where 'truth' is relative to what one takes to be involved in satisfying one's requirements.

A final consideration to be borne in mind when claiming that individualized, deregulated religion is postmodern is that it belongs to postmodern consumer culture. This culture, writes Zygmunt Bauman is 'dominated by the postmodern values of novelty, of rapid (preferably inconsequential and episodic) change, of individual enjoyment and consumer choice'. And, as Mike Featherstone puts it, the culture is one with 'a strong emphasis . . . upon the sensory overload, the aesthetic immersion, the dreamlike perceptions of de-centred subjects, in which people open themselves up to a wider range of sensations and emotional experiences'. The argument can then run that [such] religion – precisely because it is deregulated, operating apart from the disciplines of the church and the chapel as a cultural resource – can serve as a vehicle for acts of consumption. The products on offer are powerful experiences; the venues are spiritual Disneylands.

Difference: examples

Example: gendered difference

2.64 Pius XI: women's difference

Pope Pius XI, 1930: Casti Connubii (On Christian Marriage). In *Selected Papal Encyclicals and Letters 1939. Volume 1, 1896–1931*. London: Catholic Truth Society, pp. 1–67 (pp. 13–14).

Many religions of difference have been characterized by a strong, prescriptive insistence on difference between the sexes. Such difference is patriarchal, not least in the sense that it is men who articulate and attempt to enforce it. It is, however, common for such prescriptive difference to celebrate and exalt women – so long that is as they keep their proper place in the order of things. In modern times such teachings remain potent in many religions of difference, especially in religions of heightened difference. In the following extract Pope Pius XI insists that women should be subordinate to men, and forbids 'that exaggerated liberty which cares not for the good of the family'. Many of John Paul II's pronouncements on women echo the same themes.

Domestic society being confirmed, therefore, by this bond of love, there should flourish in it that 'order of love,' as St. Augustine calls it. This order includes both the primacy of the husband with regard to the wife and children, the ready subjection of the wife and her willing obedience, which the Apostle commends in these words: 'Let women be subject to their husbands as to the Lord, because the husband is the head of the wife, as Christ is the head of the church' (Eph. 5: 22, 23).

This subjection, however, does not deny or take away the liberty which fully belongs to the woman both in view of her dignity as a human person, and in view of her most noble office as wife and mother and companion; nor does it bid her obey her husband's every request if not in harmony with right reason or with the dignity due to a wife; nor, in fine, does it imply that the wife should be put on a level with those persons who in law are called minors, to whom it is not customary to allow free exercise of their rights on account of their lack of mature judgment, or of their ignorance of human affairs.

But it forbids that exaggerated liberty which cares not for the good of the family; it forbids that in this body which is the family, the heart be separated from the head to the great detriment of the whole body and the proximate danger of ruin. For if the man is the head, the woman is the heart, and as he occupies the chief place in ruling, so she may and ought to claim herself the chief place in love.

2.65 Khomeni: 'honourable women'

Ayatollah Khomeni, 1979: Speech on the occasion of Fatima's Birthday. In Azar Tabari and Nahid Yeganeh (eds) 1982: *In the Shadow of Islam. The Women's Movement in Iran.* London: Zed Press, pp. 100–2 (pp. 100–1).

The following extract from a speech by the Iranian leader Ayatollah Khomeni provides another example of a religion of difference prescribing difference between the sexes. Unlike Pius XI in the previous extract, however, Khomeni acknowledges that women can play important public and political roles, citing the example of women's role in the overthrow of the Shah of Iran. In the same speech, however, Khomeni speaks of women's domestic role, and contrasts the true freedom which Islam offers with the false freedoms offered by the westernizing regime of the Shah.

Woman is the instructor of the society. From the lap of woman human beings emerge. The first stage of being true men and women is the lap of the woman. The happiness and wealth of the country depends on woman.

It is woman who, with her correct education, produces humanity, who, with her correct education, cultivates the country. The origin of all happiness arises from the lap of the woman. Woman must accompany all happiness. [. . .]

Woman is the origin of all goodnesses. You saw, we saw, what woman did in this movement. History witnesses what women have been in the world and who is woman. History has witnessed and we have witnessed what women Islam has fostered, women who have revolted in this present era. And those who have revolted are the modest women of the south of the city [the poor sector of Tehran] and of other Islamic towns. Those who have been educated in the Aryamehri manner [reference to the Shah] were not at all involved. They were educated in a corrupt way, kept away from Islamic education.

Those who had Islamic bringing up gave their blood, gave martyrs, poured into the streets and made the movement victorious. We owe the movement to women. It was for women that men poured into the streets. Women encouraged men. Women were themselves in the front ranks. Woman is such a being. With limitless power she can defeat a satanic power. It was this woman who was lowered from her position in the era of Reza Shah and Mohammad Reza Shah.

[. . .] You honourable women wake up, be careful, do not be deceived. Do not be deceived by these devils who want you to come to the streets.

They want to deceive you just the way the cursed Shah used to do. Take refuge in Islam. Islam provides you with happiness.

2.66 Daly: post-Christian insistence on women's difference

Mary Daly, 1978: *Gyn/Ecology: The Metaethics of Radical Feminism.* In Charlene Spretnak (ed.) 1994: *The Politics of Women's Spirituality. Essays by the Founding Mothers of the Movement.* New York: Anchor/Doubleday, pp. 207–12 (pp. 211–12).

In reaction to religions which subordinate women, some feminists attempted a reform which downplayed difference and emphasized those elements of a tradition which stress the equality of the sexes. Such 'liberal feminism' has itself attracted feminist criticism in recent times, however. In an essay entitled 'Equal to whom?' (1997), for example, the feminist Luce Irigaray criticized the leading liberal feminist theologian Rosemary Radford Ruether, and argued that the liberal desire to claim equality with men should give way to a confident and positive assertion of women's difference. Some recent forms of feminist spirituality like Mary Daly's put such a strategy into practice by proposing new forms of religiosity which develop a truly feminist symbolic. The feminist assertion of gendered difference in relation to religion is also manifest in the recent rise of interest in various forms of goddess religion – see Carol Christ, reading **1.67**, Starhawk, reading **2.83**, and, for a succinct history and analysis of the movement, Neitz (1991).

Sparking is making possible Female Friendship, which is totally Other from male comradeship. Hence, the Spinster will examine male comradeship/fraternity, in order to avoid the trap of confusing sisterhood with brotherhood, of thinking (even in some small dusty corner of the mind) of sisterhood as if it were simply a gender-correlative of brotherhood. She will come to see that the term *bonding*, as it applies to Hags/Harpies/Furies/Crones is as thoroughly Other from 'male bonding' as Hags are the Other in relation to patriarchy. Male comradeship/bonding depends upon energy drained from women (its secret glue), since women are generators of energy. The bonding of Hags in friendship *for* women is not draining but rather energizing/

gynergizing. It is the opposite of brotherhood, not essentially because Self-centering women oppose and fight patriarchy in a reactive way, but because we are/act for our Selves. [...]

At first, it is hard to generate enough sparks for building the fires of Female Friendship. This is particularly the case since patriarchal males, sensing the ultimate threat of Female Sparking, make every effort to put out women's fires whenever we start them. They try to steal the fire of Furies in order to destroy us in their perpetual witchcraze. Like Cinderellas, Hags stand among the cinders, but we know that they are cinders of our burned foresisters. We know that the cinders still Spark.

Sparking means building the fires of gynergetic communication and confidence. As a result, each Sparking Hag not only begins to live in a lighted and warm room of her own; she prepares a place for a loom of her own. In this space she can begin to weave the tapestries of her own creation. With her increasing fire and force, she can begin to Spin. As she and her sisters Spin together, we create The Network of our time/space.

2.67   Jacquelyn Grant: 'black women's Jesus'

Jacquelyn Grant, 1989: *White Women's Christ and Black Women's Jesus. Feminist Christology and Womanist Response*. Georgia, Atlanta: Scholars Press (pp. 199–202; 205).

Taking the emphasis on the importance of religion respecting difference to an extreme, some feminist writers argue that every woman or group of women must create and follow a religion or spirituality true to their own experience. For example, as Jacquelyn Grant argues in the following extract, black women's theology must reflect their unique experience of ethnic, social and gender discrimination. Borrowing a term from the novelist Alice Walker, Grant refers to such theology as 'womanist'. Having as its basis individual experience rather than a common tradition, community, scripture or ideology, such differentiated religion naturally shades into a personalized religion of life.

Even if some individual feminists are not racists, the movement has been so structured, and therefore takes on a racist character. In a racist society, the oppressor assumes the power of definition and control while the oppressed is objectified and personified as a thing. As such, White women have defined the movement and presumed to do so not only for themselves but also for non-White women. They have misnamed themselves by calling themselves feminists when in fact they are White feminists, and by appealing to women's experience

when in fact they appeal almost exclusively to their own experience.
[. . .]

In spite of the negative responses of Black Women to the White
women's liberation movement described, there has been a growing
feminist consciousness among them, coupled with the increased willingness to do an independent analysis of sexism. This is creating an
emerging Black perspective on feminism. Black feminism grows out
of Black women's tri-dimensional reality of race/sex/class. It holds
that full human liberation cannot be achieved simply by the elimination of any one form of oppression. Consequently, real oppression must
be 'broad in the concrete'; it must be based upon a multi-dimensional
analysis. Recent writings by secular Black feminists have challenged
White feminist analysis and Black race analysis, particularly by introducing data from Black women's experience that has been historically
ignored by White feminists and Black male liberationists. [. . .]

A womanist is one who has developed survival strategies in spite
of the oppression of her race and sex in order to save her family and
her people. Walker's womanist notion suggests not 'the feminist,' but
the active struggle of Black women that makes them who they are. For
some Black women that may involve being feminine as traditionally
defined, and for others it involves being masculine as stereotypically
defined. In either case, womanist just means *being* and *acting* out who
you are. It is to the womanist tradition that Black women must
appeal for the doing of theology. [. . .]

Womanist theology begins with the experiences of Black women
as its point of departure.

2.68   Davidman on Jewish women seeking 'traditional' differentiated gender roles

Lyn Davidman, 1991: *Tradition in a Rootless World: Women Turn to Orthodox Judaism*. Berkeley,
Los Angeles, Oxford: University of California Press (pp. 198–9).

Despite feminists' criticisms of the prescriptive roles ascribed to women by many
religions of difference, significant numbers of women continue to be attracted
to such religions. Researchers like Davidman are interested in exploring the
reasons for this. The study from which this extract is taken was of socially and
culturally advantaged North American women converting to Orthodox Judaism.
Davidman's conclusion is that it is precisely because such religion maintains a
clear distinction between the sexes that it becomes attractive to women who, in
a dislocating world, value traditional domesticity and their role as wives and
mothers.

These groups offered models of gender, sexuality, and family that competed with those prescribed by most feminists. Instead of the feminist program of broader gender definitions and options, sexual liberation, an emphasis on careers, and the acceptance of a variety of family patterns, Orthodox Judaism proposed clearly circumscribed gender norms, the control of sexuality, assistance in finding partners, and explicit guidelines for nuclear family life.

Both religious communities [in this study] offered their own version of a distinct alternative to the liberal feminist goal of equality: that of equity, the idea of separate but equal roles. The religious groups were attractive to some contemporary women precisely because they legitimated the women's desires for the 'traditional' identity of wives and mothers in nuclear families. The rabbis told the recruits that woman's role was highly valued in Orthodoxy and that woman's primary place in the home, where a majority of the rituals took place, gave her special status within the Jewish religious world. In addition, Orthodox Judaism's emphasis on the nuclear family and women's place in it actually provided the women with an additional benefit: they gained support for a conception of men's roles that placed great stress on men's involvement in the home and with their families.

2.69 Ahmed: the return to the veil as a source of empowerment

Leila Ahmed, 1992: *Women and Gender in Islam. Historical Roots of a Modern Debate*. New Haven and London: Yale University Press (pp. 223–5).

Continuing the theme of women's empowerment through prescriptive difference and the manipulation of traditional religious symbols, Leila Ahmed argues that the recent 'return to the veil' in Islamic countries is not a capitulation to patriarchy but a means of class and gender assertion.

In adopting Islamic dress, then, women are in effect 'carving out legitimate public space for themselves,' as one analyst of the phenomenon put it, and public space is by this means being redefined to accommodate women. The adoption of the dress does not declare women's place to be in the home but, on the contrary, legitimizes their presence outside it. Consequently, it appears that the prevalence of the Islamic mode among women coming of age in the 1970s and 1980s – women of the second phase – cannot be seen as a retreat from the affirmations of female autonomy and subjectivity made by the generation of women who immediately preceded them. Although the voice of overt feminism and perhaps even feminist consciousness may be absent, the entry of women into the university, the professions, and public space in unprecedentedly large numbers and the availability of education and professional occupations to women from a far broader segment of the population than before cannot be construed as regressive, however apparently conservative the uniform they wear to accomplish these moves comfortably.

Moreover, it appears that the particular language adopted in pursuit of goals of female autonomy and subjectivity, be this the idiom of 'feminism' and 'Western' dress or that of 'Islam' and the 'veil,' is to an important degree, in these two recent generations as in past generations, a function of class and the urban-rural divisions of society. The pursuit of these goals in terms of the language of Western dress, secularism, and explicit 'feminism' was evidently typical predominantly of the urban middle classes – and consequently 'feminism' as a political movement may perhaps justly be described as 'elitist or sectional, and cut off from the grass roots of society.' [. . .]

One way of describing the process that has led in recent decades to the emergence of Islamic dress and affiliations with Islamism as a dominant discourse of social being is in terms of its marking a broad demographic change – a change that has democratized mainstream culture and mores and led to the rise and gradual predominance of a vocabulary of dress and social being defined from below, by the emergent middle classes, rather than by the formerly culturally dominant upper and middle classes. This change to a sociocultural vernacular is facilitating the assimilation of the newly urban, newly educated middle classes to modernity and to a sexually integrated social reality. From this perspective Islamic dress can be seen as the uniform, not of reaction, but of transition; it can be seen, not as a return to traditional dress, but as the adoption of Western dress – with modifications to make it acceptable to the wearer's notions of propriety. Far from indicating that the wearers remain fixed in the world of tradition and the past, then, Islamic dress is the uniform of arrival, signaling entrance into, and determination to move forward in, modernity.

2.70   Cucchiari: Pentecostalism and the domestication of men

Salvatore Cucchiari, 1991: Between Shame and Sanctification: Patriarchy and its Transformation in Sicilian Pentecostalism. *American Ethnologist*, November: 687–707 (pp. 688–93).

Religions may prove attractive to women not only because they change their lives, but because they change men's. Here Salvatore Cucchiari argues that Charismatic Christianity is radically revisionary of male–female relations. On the one hand it empowers women, offering them access to the divine and new roles and ministries; on the other hand, it domesticates both men and the Father God by valuing love, compassion and other tender virtues. In this way it undermines macho models of masculinity in the Sicilian context in which Cucchiari's fieldwork took place. Other researchers have noted the same phenomenon: David Martin (1990) in relation to Latin American Pentecostalism; Steven Tipton (1982) in relation to the Pacific Zen (Buddhist) Center in California; and Charles Keyes in relation to Thai Buddhism (1986).

There is no question that Pentecostal church communities are male-dominant in both organization and ideology. Indeed, at one level Sicilian Pentecostalism may be viewed as a conservative or nativistic response to stresses in the prevailing system of gender relations – that is, as an attempt to reestablish a stable patriarchal order within the boundaries of the church community. Yet ironically, in seeking to achieve this conservative goal, Sicilian Pentecostals actually undermine it. Despite formal limitations, Pentecostal women play major roles in the community and even dominate some religious ministries, and, in addition, Pentecostal religious discourse contains nonpatriarchal models and symbols of gender. In short, Pentecostalism constitutes a more complex and contradictory patriarchy than the hegemonic system, and for this reason may be a less viable vehicle for male dominance, one that in fact shifts power and opportunities for liberating struggle toward women. I shall discuss this shift not merely as a power struggle but as a fundamental transformation in the way Pentecostal men and women constitute their humanity, or what Burridge calls their 'integrity.' [. . .]

In the *culto*, or main worship service held three times weekly in most communities, the Pentecostal God is invariably referred to in prayer, prophecy, sermons, and testimonies in masculine terms; God is 'He,' 'Father,' 'Son,' 'Lord,' or 'Lord Jesus.' However, when one looks past the explicit masculine reference of the text to the symbolic content of the subtext, a more androgynous, cross-gender figure is clearly visible – a figure not easily fit into Sicilian gender categories.

There is no single theme more prevalent in the *culto* than this. The human heart, seat of 'our freedom' and emotional life, is never assaulted or taken 'by force' by the Pentecostal God. Over and over again the *culto* leader or other participants – both men and women – will admonish the congregation to 'open your hearts' to a courting God, thus thrusting the 'heart' and threshold images to the center of *culto* discourse. Sicilian Pentecostal salvation is the mystical union of hearts, a kind of soteriological romance, in which the individual willingly and joyfully surrenders his or her autonomy to God, and God in turn envelops the individual in loving forgiveness. For believers this union is also a sensual experience, as the Holy Spirit takes possession of the convert, who is said to be 'vanquished' by God's love. At the same time, this courting God is a God who suffers from a perpetual broken heart because his 'thirst' for human love, as one preacher suggests, is so often answered with nothing but the 'vinegar' of human rejection.

What kind of gender images do these romantic texts and themes suggest? Despite the masculine pronouns, they do not often project an idealized image of the Sicilian father – aloof, judgmental, punishing. In one text the divine pursuer is a seductress, but more often than not the divine lover is not only a seductress but also a seductive mother. God is frequently portrayed as a loving parent, and on occasion the maternal image is explicitly invoked, as in the following excerpt from a sermon by Umberto, in which God's love, in the person of Jesus, is compared to a mother's love:

> How marvelous that look of Christ's must have been. He was looking at the man, not with hostility, not with severity, but with a look full or grace. A look . . . like that of a mother at her child, a defenseless small child. She will never look at it with a severe or cruel look. She will look upon it with all her love.

In this text, Jesus the son clearly melds into the mother, the soft and enveloping protector who, unlike the severe father, looks indulgently on the child, but who nevertheless wants to possess it. Surely not coincidentally, this same text echoes the words of the Catholic prayer *Hail Mary* in describing the feminine Jesus' look as 'full of grace.'
[. . .]

I maintain that the cross-gender God is a gender prototype that opens up possibilities for gender redefinition within the Pentecostal community. It is still a patriarchal model, to be sure. God is still exclusively male at the explicit level, and other aspects of Pentecostal religious experience suggest that the Word contains or takes symbolic precedence over the Spirit. Nevertheless, the cross-gender God is a cultural crucible in which new models of masculinity/femininity are being forged. These new gender models are from the point of view of the hegemonic system relatively androgynous in nature – embodying a more active and powerful femininity, a softer and more emotionally open masculinity. The feature that makes the Pentecostal godhead an effective crucible for new forms is its very lack of definition: the unitary and fluid nature of its gender characteristics, the linguistic masking of the subtextual images. Conversely, it is the clear symbolic definition and sharp structural opposition that render the Celestial Family a powerful legitimating symbol for hegemonic gender relations.

2.71   Marler: family breakdown/church breakdown

Penny Long Marler, 1995: Lost in the Fifties: The Changing Family and the Nostalgic Church. In Nancy Tatom Ammerman and Wade Clark Roof (eds), *Work, Family and Religion in Contemporary Society*. New York and London: Routledge, pp. 23–60 (pp. 49–52).

Whilst women continue to be attracted to religions of difference for reasons like those explored in the readings by Davidman, Ahmed and Cucchiari above, the rise of feminism and changes in women's role and status in modern societies seem also to have had the effect of alienating some from such religion. Here Penny Long Marler suggests that the breakdown of the stable nuclear family can undermine churches which sanctify domesticity. It is interesting to compare her findings with those of Andrew Greeley (1990) who discovered that college-educated women who had been influenced by feminism and whose mothers had been confined to domestic roles during their daughter's childhood were likely to reject the Catholic faith in which they were raised, since they seemed to associate it with an image of womanhood which they had rejected (pp. 230–1). Reflections like these led William Swatos (1994) to write, 'I would be willing to offer the hypothesis that virtually the entire "decline" of "the churches" in American society can be "explained" by the entrance of women into the workforce, certainly much more so than by anything like a "crisis of belief"' (p. xi).

The good news is that something about Protestant churches draws traditional families; the bad news is that as their market share of the U.S. population decreases, it is very likely that a similar pattern will be reflected in the churches.

[. . .] *the family structure of the Protestant church is primarily composed of two rather complimentary cohorts: people who are in traditional families and those who used to be.* Older empty-nesters and widowed persons largely make up a fifties' *family residue.* This very visible segment in many white Protestant churches maintains a sentimentalized familial identity and a related commitment to the traditional family in the church. In addition, this ex-family cohort maintains considerable institutional loyalty: they support the church for the church's sake. 'New' traditional family members share older members' commitment to the traditional family. However, they are less likely to view the church itself as an extended traditional family. These traditional families choose the church for their sake and the sake of their children.

[. . .] *while the traditional family cohort is a very homogeneous group, younger families seem to be the most avid consumers – and the most reluctant producers.* These data underline the fact that younger traditional families expect to be served by the church rather than to serve. To some degree, this may be a function of having younger children on top of juggling dual careers.

[. . .] *the primary groups that are left out of the contemporary Protestant church are those that are gaining increasing shares of the family household market.* Singles, especially younger singles, and younger to middle-aged couples without children are gravely underrepresented in the white Protestant church. Some might well argue that this has always been the case. Yet, even if that is true, the lack of these nontraditional family types in the church is a serious issue. Indeed, it might be argued that in its nostalgia for the traditional family, the Protestant church has claimed a narrowly circumscribed market niche for itself, almost by default. [. . .]

This research offers hope and a warning. Change is occurring in the church, as witnessed by the continued inclusion of traditional families with very contemporary tastes – and the commitment to those families exhibited by the older, loyal family residue. Unfortunately, the 'missing families' – mostly nontraditional – continue to 'take their business elsewhere.' Clearly, while bowing to the critical contributions of traditional families, past and present, congregations must cast their nets farther and more conscientiously. Otherwise, contemporary white Protestantism may be forever 'lost in the fifties.' Given the realities of an aging population and a shrinking traditional family base, it is clear that a future mired in the past is really no future at all.

2.72 Lehman: differences between women and men in ministry

Edward C. Lehman, Jr., 1993: Gender and Ministry Style: Things Not What They Seem.
In William H. Swatos, Jr. (ed.) 1994: *Gender and Religion*. New Brunswick and London:
Transaction Publishers, pp. 3–13 (p. 10).

In relation to religious leadership, does gender difference make a difference? It
is only in modern times (in most cases, the twentieth century) that women have
been ordained in some of the Christian Churches, and this transformation is only
just beginning to be investigated. Here Edward Lehman finds that the 'maximalist'
hypothesis that men and women would have different styles of ministry is less
supported by the evidence than the 'minimalist' hypothesis that there would be
more similarities than differences between male and female ministry. Lehman
found that gender was only one of a number of other, more important variables
affecting ministry style. By contrast, Ruth A. Wallace's (1994) research on women
lay Catholic parish leaders discovered that they exercised a more collaborative
and empowering ministry than male priests.

The general *empirical* conclusions of the study are that:

1 There *are* some gender-specific approaches to pastoral ministry
  among female and male Protestant pastors, more than the min-
  imalists say but clearly less than proposed by the maximalists. It
  depends on which dimension is under consideration.
2 The *strength* of those differences tends to be *weak*, suggesting that
  the differences that do exist in ministry style of men and women
  are not as great as has been argued.
3 Whether *any* differences in women's and men's ministry style
  appeared at all was dependent on identifiable cultural, structural,
  and biographical conditions.

2.73 Comaroff and Comaroff: women as 'signs and ciphers' in Africa

Jean Comaroff and John Comaroff, 1993: Introduction. In Jean Comaroff and John Comaroff
(eds), *Modernity and Its Malcontents. Ritual and Power in Postcolonial Africa*. Chicago and London: The University of Chicago Press (pp. xi–xxxvii) (pp. xxviii–xxix).

Many of the readings above make it clear that debates about gender difference
are not 'merely' about gender. Gender opens out into issues of the body, sexuality, the family, and society. Gender, like religion, is often a key element within
an entire social and symbolic structure. To re-envision gender and/or religion is
thus to re-envision society. In this powerful passage Jean Comaroff and John
Comaroff discuss witchcraft in Africa, and note how women become symbols

and ciphers of wider social pressures and fears – particularly those engendered by the transition to capitalism.

As feudal communities felt the impact of merchant capital, women, marginalized as 'unproductive,' became sites of the conflict in a new social order.

There has, in this respect, been a wealth of recent work on the objectification of women's persons and bodies with the development of capitalism; especially of industrial capitalism, whose culture rests on asymmetric, often gendered contrasts between such things as the public and the domestic, production and reproduction, the city and the country, reason and intuition, work and leisure. Alongside this, there is growing evidence to show that the ideologies associated with the concomitant rise of 'modernity' grouped their counterimages under feminized signs: the rural, the preindustrial, the ritualistic, the irrational, the primitive. The old witch in the attic with her deadly spinning wheel was an apt icon of social inequities engendered by intensified market production in early modern Europe. Her kinship with the old Ngoni woman of the 1980s, who hid a medicine horn in her roof thatch, is striking. For Africa has been drawn inexorably into the world of capitalist production. And while it has hardly been made over entirely in European image, it *has* been subjected to forceful social change – of which the marginalization of the domestic, the rural, the 'primitive,' and the female has been a crucial, if complex component. This process of marginalization has many sides to it. Perhaps most poignant is the fact that those displaced along the way tend quickly to become signs and ciphers with which others make meaning. A final point here: lest we think that such phenomena belong merely to the early beginnings, or to the exotic fringes, of the 'modern' European world, let us remind ourselves of contemporary forms of Western witchcraft, witchcraft that addresses the contradictions of advanced capitalist societies. A clutch of images in the recent popular culture of North America are especially revealing in this respect: the 'Fatal Attraction' of the corporate harridan who would use sexual and professional wiles to destroy home, husband, and family – and will not die; the dangerous market woman of Wall Street, a trader in the vortex of voodoo economics, who will consume all before her, including the honest 'Working Girl'; the standardized nightmare of child abuse, embodied in the callous babyminder, whose 'Hand . . . Rocks the Cradle' and aborts social reproduction.

Although African witchcraft clearly predates colonialism, it is not the intention here to reconstruct or recuperate its earlier forms. As it happens, there is clear evidence that, in precolonial polities, it also gave human expression to structural contradictions; but probably less is known about its 'traditional' workings than anthropologists often suppose. In its late twentieth century guise, however, witchcraft is a finely calibrated gauge of the impact of global cultural and economic forces on local relations, on perceptions of money and markets, on the abstraction and alienation of 'indigenous' values and meanings. Witches are modernity's prototypical malcontents. They provide – like the grotesques of a previous age – disconcertingly full-bodied images of a world in which humans seem in constant danger of turning into commodities, of losing their life blood to the market and to the destructive desires it evokes. But make no mistake: these desires are eminently real and mortal. And some people are indeed more vulnerable than others to their magic allure. Nor, it should be stressed again, are witches advocates of 'tradition,' of a life beyond the universe of commodities. They embody all the contradictions of the experience of modernity itself, of its inescapable enticements, its self-consuming passions, its discriminatory tactics, its devastating social costs.

2.74 van der Veer: women as 'signs and ciphers' in Pakistan

Peter van der Veer, 1994: *Religious Nationalism: Hindus and Muslims in India*. Berkeley, Los Angeles and London: University of California Press (pp. 99–103).

The phenomenon discussed by Comaroff and Comaroff above whereby women become ciphers and symbols seems common in many religions and societies. In religions of heightened difference which consciously reject modern culture and seek a return to 'fundamentals', for example, the return of women to the domestic sphere and to the control of men becomes a powerful and central symbol of the integrity which is sought (likewise the ordination of women in the Christian churches became a symbol for conservatives of the loss of tradition and integrity). To put it another way: the reassertion of prescriptive gender difference goes hand in hand with the general reassertion of national and religious difference. Here Peter van der Veer discusses the symbolic role played by women in Pakistan, whose integrity comes to symbolize the integrity of religion and the nation. (Maududi was the chief theorist of the Islamic movement in Pakistan. His works, translated into Arabic in the 1950s, have been a major influence on resurgent Islam.)

When Pakistan emerged from the independence struggle, it was declared to be an Islamic state. What I want to argue here is that one of the key images of the nation-state became that of patriarchal power (authority and protection) exercised over female bodies. As in the Hindu case, however, this image was complicated by the dialectic of femininity and masculinity. It is the institution of female seclusion and veiling (*purdah*) that, as a ritual system of communication, becomes the sign of a society ordered by Islam.

Purdah exists among both Muslims and Hindus in South Asia but operates entirely differently among them. While Hindu purdah is related to relations of respect between affines, Muslim purdah is related to the unity of the kindred vis-à-vis the outside, nonkindred world. Different ideologies of the family appear to account for these differences in purdah. Since purdah in the Muslim case involves seclusion from the public sphere, it is closely bound up with the status of the family, which Hindu purdah is not. Families that can afford to keep women in seclusion, and thus uninvolved in economic activity outside the home, have a relatively high status. As Patricia Jeffery expresses it, the seclusion of women is a function of a family's worth, in an economic sense, but also becomes indicative of their social worth, of their honor. At the same time there are also important similarities between Hindu and Muslim purdah. Purdah is a means to protect women against their own sexual desires and against sexual advances by outsiders. The connected concepts of honor (*izzat*) and shame or modesty (*sharam*) are relevant here. [. . .]

It was only after the emergence of Pakistan, and especially in the last two decades, that religious nationalists tried to use purdah as a discursive tool to define the Islamic nature of Pakistan. In that context it also became an issue of state policy. Using the idiom of the family, nationalism makes the modesty (*sharam*) of women come to signify the honor (*izzat*) of the nation, safeguarded by a patriarchal state. [. . .]

In Maududi's view the ideal Muslim society should be ordered according to the example of the Prophet and the ordinance of the law. Such an enterprise would require an authoritarian, centralized state to guide the people along the right path. According to Maududi, an ordered society can only be maintained if there are safeguards preventing the arousal of sexual urges, except between a married couple. Therefore, purdah is an Islamic way of ordering social life. Within purdah, women's role is an inferior one: 'Islam effects a functional distribution of the sexes and sets different spheres of activity for both of them. Women should in the main devote themselves to their household duties in their homes and men should attend to their jobs in the socio-economic spheres'. Sayyid Asad Gilani, chairman of the Lahore branch of the Jama'at, made the point very clearly in a 1983 pamphlet entitled *Three Women, Three Cultures*: '1. There is no mixed society. 2. Women avoid going out of the home. 3. If they need to go out, they do not adorn themselves and use a veil. 4. They avoid conversation with men who are not related to them. 5. If they must speak, they speak briefly and directly, not gently and sweetly.' [. . .]

Not only in Pakistan but also in India the legal position of Muslim women has become an issue around which the nature of Muslim community can be asserted.

Example: ethnic difference

2.75 Hobsbawm on interrelations between religion and ethnicity

E. J. Hobsbawm, 1995: *Nations and Nationalism Since 1780: Programme, Myth, Reality*. Cambridge: Cambridge University Press, (pp. 69–70).

Ethnic difference tends to be produced by a combination of shared language, customs, and institutions which serve to distinguish one social group from another. 'Ethnicity', says Stuart Hall (1992), 'is the term we give to cultural features – language, religion, custom, traditions, feeling for "place" – which are shared by a people' (p. 297). Ethnicity also has to do with boundary-constructing processes which function as cultural markers between groups. Previously the term often embraced racial distinctiveness, a use which has been discredited by advances in genetics which have revealed that ethnic and racial groups are not in fact coterminous (but see reading **2.78** below). As Hobsbawm shows in the following extract, religious difference interacts with ethnic difference in complex ways. In some cases religion may reinforce a group's pre-existent sense of separate identity, in some it may help establish that identity, and in others it may have little or no bearing on ethnic or national identity at all.

But what exactly does religio-ethnic identification mean, where it occurs? Clearly in some cases an ethnic religion is chosen because a people feels different from neighbouring peoples or states in the first place. Iran, it would appear, has gone its own divine way both as a Zoroastrian country and, since its conversion to Islam, or at any rate since the Safavids, as a Shite one. The Irish only came to be identified with Catholicism when they failed, or perhaps refused, to follow the English into the Reformation, and massive colonization of part of their country by Protestant settlers who took away their best land was not likely to convert them. The Churches of England and Scotland are politically defined, even though the latter represents orthodox Calvinism. Perhaps the people of Wales, not till then much given to going a separate religious way, converted *en masse* to Protestant dissent in the first half of the nineteenth century as part of that acquisition of a national consciousness which has recently been the subject of some perceptive research. On the other hand it is equally clear that conversion to different religions can help to create two different nationalities, for it is certainly Roman Catholicism (and its by-product, the Latin script) and Orthodoxy (with its by-product, the Cyrillic script) which has most obviously divided Croats from Serbs, with whom they share a single language of culture. But, then again, there are peoples which clearly possessed some proto-national consciousness, such as the Albanians, while divided by more religious differences than are usually found in a territory the size of Wales (various forms of Islam, Orthodoxy, Roman Catholicism).

2.76 Voll: ethnicity and Islam

John O. Voll, 1982: *Islam. Continuity and Change in the Modern World*. Boulder, Colorado: Westview Press; Harlow: Longman (p. 280).

Here John Voll illustrates the complexity of the interplays between religious and ethnic difference in relation to Islam in modern times.

One of the complex elements of the modern Islamic experience is the relationship between faith and ethnic loyalties. In the central parts of the Islamic world, the Middle Eastern countries, society has often been described as a mosaic of peoples and cultures, with the smaller units maintaining special identities while being integrated into a larger social framework. Because of the universal implications and aspirations of the Islamic message, Islam is often considered to be an opponent of ethnicity, and it is possible to see the recent revival of ethnic loyalties and the resurgence of Islam as competing forces. As one analyst said, 'The coincidence of Islamic revival and ethnic consciousness in the context of the present crisis phase of the dialectical process pits Islam against ethnicity in virtually every Islamic country.'

The relationship is, however, more complex than that. For most major ethnic groups in the Islamic world, religion is one of the key features in the definition of a special ethnic identity. No Kurd, Malay, Azeri, Turk, or member of any of the many groups would envisage a definition of their special identity that would exclude Islam. When reformers like Ataturk, Reza Shah, or Muhammad Shah attempted such a definition, the majority of the population simply ignored their efforts. A revival of ethnic consciousness, such as that in Malaysia, thus involves a revival of religion rather than its negation. What is in conflict is not Islam and ethnic loyalty but, rather, differing identifications and interpretations of Islam. Kurds opposing the Khomeini regime in Iran may be opposing a particular form and interpretation of Islam, but they remain vigorously Islamic, and their faith plays an important role in the assertion of their special ethnic identity. In specific terms, the competing pattern is a univeralized Islam opposed to a pluralist Islam.

2.77 Mullins: religio-ethnic mobilization in Korea

Mark R. Mulllins, 1994: The Empire Strikes Back: Korean Pentecostal Mission to Japan. In Karla Poewe (ed.), *Charismatic Christianity as a Global Culture*. Columbia: University of South Carolina Press, pp. 87–102 (pp. 92–3).

Religion may be used to establish ethnic identity against a dominant imperial power and its legitimating religion(s). An obvious example is the revitalization of Islam, Sikhism, Hinduism and Buddhism in the Indian sub-continent in response to British domination. Here Mark Mullins draws attention to a less widely cited example: the growth of Pentecostalism in Korea in response to Japanese imperial domination. This is a good example of Steve Bruce's general point in reading **3.91** that sacralization often occurs when religion is used to help reinforce the identity of a threatened group.

[The expansion of Korean Pentecostalism] is clearly a case study of the 'Empire Striking Back.' Korea was colonized by Japan and was a part of the Japanese Empire from 1910 to 1945. During this period the Japanese language became the medium of instruction in public schools and Koreans were forced to adopt Japanese names and worship at Shinto Shrines (the state religion of Japan after the Meiji Restoration). Since the end of World War II, Christianity has been closely related to the development of Korean national identity. This is rooted in the colonial period, when many Korean Christians were involved in movements for independence and resisted (to the point of martyrdom) Japanese government orders that all Koreans, including church members and pupils in Christian schools, participate in Shinto Shrine ceremonies. It is not an overstatement to say that Christianity is positively related to Korean cultural identity largely due to the ruthless policies of the Japanese colonial government. Today many Korean Christians regard themselves as the 'new Israel,' with a special mission to Christianize Asia, including their former colonizer.

2.78 Gardell on race ideology and religious nationalism

Mattias Gardell, 1996: *Countdown to Armageddon. Louis Farrakhan and the Nation of Islam.* London: Hurst and Company (pp. 12–13).

Race has often been treated as the defining element of ethnic difference. The discovery that biology has little to do with ethnicity has not yet undermined the 'myth' of racial identity, nor attempts to build religions around race. Here Matthias Gardell considers how race became the basis of a number of African American religions (such as the Nation of Islam), and how pseudo-scientific nineteenth-century racial theories fed such religions (albeit in inverted forms – here blacks not whites were regarded as the superior race). The passage also reveals how racial, ethnic, religious and national difference became intertwined within such movements and their ideologies.

In the black nationalist usage, the distinction between race and nation was frequently blurred, due in part to the unique situation of the African Americans. Descendants from a wide variety of African peoples and cultures merged into a 'nation' during the centuries of slavery. Over time a pan–African American identity was formed based on a shared social history commenced in the holds of trans-Atlantic and inter-American cargo ships. As race became a factor determining social, economic, and political status, it also became a criterion for the black nation in America.

Black nationalists were influenced by the nineteenth century's scientific and romantic European, especially German, discourse on race, Prior to the rediscovery of the work of the biologist Gregor Johann Mendel, founder of the modern theory of genetics, race had a wider meaning. Its definitions were generally in line with the German *Volk* and owed much to the Pan-German *völkisch* tradition. The race transcended biology and acquired national romantic meanings of a spiritual, psychological, and cultural kind. Race solidarity was organic, and by 'nature' members of a race were believed to share mental and spiritual qualities, from which shared ambitions and a common destiny were derived. [. . .]

Black nationalism offered solutions to the problem of identity so crucial for post-Emancipation black discourse. Caught up in the peculiar position of being American but not American, African but not African, black nationalists suggested various concepts for their own national identity, none of which so far has been received with universal agreement. The heated debate over whether or not they should be called Negroes, Colored or Blacks, Negro-Saxons, Anglo-Africans, Euro-Africans, Afro-Americans, African-Americans, or, most recently, African Americans, highlights the emotional significance of the dilemma. [. . .]

Black religious nationalists advance the race-organism thesis by adding divine intention to the meaning of its existence. Generally, the African American is said to be of the 'chosen people,' created in His likeness. The aboriginal African culture is seen as the cradle of civilization, where it all began. For various reasons, not infrequently due to past transgressions against God's will, blacks lost their leading position among other races. Colonization and slavery are presented as hard but necessary parts of a greater divine plan in which blacks are predestined to reascend as the guides of mankind. Black religious nationalists have championed alternative concepts for their own people that reflect the perceived divine meaning of existence. In the United States movements can be found that advocate that African Americans properly should be named *Ethiopians* (African Orthodox Church, Rastafarians, and others), *Moors* (the Moorish Science Temple), *Jews* (various black Hebrew organizations), *Nubians* (the Ansaaru Allah Community), and *Bilalians* (the American Muslim Mission). The Nation of Islam, which argues that they are *the original black Asiatic man*, is an early proponent of this tradition.

2.79 Danzger on difference and Jewish identity

M. Herbert Danzger, 1989: *Returning to Tradition. The Contemporary Revival of Orthodox Judaism.* New Haven and London: Yale University Press (pp. 73–4).

Jewish identity is constituted by a complex overlap and interplay of ethnic, religious, and national differences. In *Returning to Tradition* Herbert Danzger shows how Jews in America from the nineteenth century onwards were forced by racialist theories of Jewish inferiority to develop universalizing narratives which stressed Jewish equality. In the 1960s, Jews in America often made common cause with blacks in the struggle for equal rights. As Danzger shows in the extract below, however, since the passing of the Civil Rights Acts in 1964, Jews and blacks have drawn apart as they have abandoned liberal universalism in favour of a stress on ethnic difference. The resurgence of Native American Culture and politics in the same period seems to be a related phenomenon (see Cornell, 1988).

> The radical change in the relationship between blacks and Jews in the mid-1960s had broad consequences for the relationship between the various Jewish denominations and society. As universalistic ethics had placed Orthodoxy on the defensive, the new emphasis on ethnic identity and uniqueness shifted the balance toward Orthodoxy. Secularist, socialist, and Reform Jewish philosophies that emphasized equality and the 'sameness of all' were in retreat before a worldview that emphasized differences. Granting legitimacy to ethnicity for blacks implied granting it as well to Jews. If so, then Orthodox Judaism won a measure of respect. If blacks could display symbols of their ethnicity proudly, could not Jews do the same? If one could war a dashiki in public and eat soul food, why could one not wear a kippah and eat kosher 'soul' food?

2.80   Trigano on the Holocaust and Jewish identity

Shmuel Trigano, 1997: The Jews and the Spirit of Europe: A Morphological Approach. In Alvin H. Rosenfeld (ed.), *Thinking about the Holocaust After Half a Century*. Bloomington and Indianapolis: Indiana University Press, pp. 300–18 (pp. 312–14).

Here Shmuel Trigano argues that the Shoah (Holocaust/mass extermination of Jews in Nazi Germany), has become central to the construction of Jewish identity in the post-war period. This furnishes an interesting example of the way in which a political event may come to undergird an ethnic identity when the original religious basis of that identity begins to fade.

> During [the 1980s], the memory of the Shoah took another turn and with it the meaning of the community changed. The Shoah became progressively the center of Jewish and even public debate. [. . .]
> The Jews sought for the European recognition of the Jewish specificity of Auschwitz. They no longer felt morally obligated by the Shoah. Europe now had to be. This change of attitude might explain why the victimization of the Jews became for the Jews the new way to the universal, a lachrymose universal. The belated recognition of Jewish suffering by the gentiles became for many Jews more important than their own positive existence, which the elevation of Auschwitz to a place of centrality obliterated. [. . .]

Auschwitz represents a place in Eastern Europe where the Jewish condition was always a collective, non-individual one. The sacralization of this space by secular Jews is most interesting. Their claim that this area will be dedicated to silence (i.e., the unthinkable) generates a sort of transcendence, a sense of sacredness. And, indeed, the memory of the Jewish martyrdom is apprehended here as a form of transcendence. It becomes a cause of repeated invocation, of ritual and ceremony, rather than of historical thinking. This transcendence, interpreted in a particularistic way, takes the Shoah (grasped as a coerced withdrawal from the modern condition of Jewish individualism and as a paradigm of Jewish collective fate) out of history and sacralizes it, this even as a Jewish collective identity remains unthinkable in modern Europe.

The paradox is that this sacredness became the basis for a new Jewish secular identity. From the time of the rise of the Israeli political right, the identification with Israel and Zionism of this sizable circle of people became vexed, so much so that it attenuated its Zionist 'civil religion.' The 'memory of the Shoah,' specific to secular Judaism, is a sort of return to (a secular) religion and to a new collective identity.

Difference: prospects

2.81   Hunwick: post-colonial reassertion of religious difference

John Hunwick, 1997: Sub-Saharan Africa and the Wider World of Islam. In Eva Evers Rosander and David Westerlund (eds) *African Islam and Islam in Africa. Encounters between Sufis and Islamists*. London: Hurst & Company, pp. 28–54 (pp. 28–9).

The twentieth century has witnessed old and new forms of political, ethnic and religious difference spring up in the fertile ground left by the receding tide of western imperial domination. The whole rhetoric of postmodern, post-colonial discourse tends to be directed favourably towards such difference, and can even supply legitimation for such difference. The difference it has in mind, however, is open difference. It is not entirely clear how it will respond to the rise of more assertive forms of prescriptive difference – such as those displayed by some varieties of resurgent Islam. Here John Hunwick discusses Islamic resurgence in general, and African Muslim resurgence in particular, and argues that it can only be properly understood in its relation to western imperialism. The collapse of totalizing communist regimes in the former USSR and Yugoslavia has also had the effect of allowing post-colonial religio-ethnic identities to emerge – in some cases with violent consequences. See also Juergensmeyer (2.59).

In the Muslim world of the late twentieth century, there is a sense of urgency about the need to restate Islamic values in the face of pervasive external influences inimical to them, such as has not, perhaps, been manifested since the late mediaeval period when it was perceived as necessary to batten down the hatches against the subversive influence of the legacy of Greek philosophy and science. That such a sense of urgency, expressed in discussion, debate and often militant action, should come about at a time when Muslim lands have been freed of the direct physical pressure of European colonialism, but are still reeling from its effects, is not surprising. During the 'colonial century' (roughly 1860–1960) it was not possible for Muslims to take stock of this situation. The parameters of a relationship with the non-Muslim world of Europe which had been forced on them with great suddenness, and often great violence, were still being negotiated under conditions of subservience. Muslims and non-Muslims under colonial conditions saw their principal goal, both jointly and severally, as the elimination of direct political and economic dominance and the assumption upon independence of the mantle of the colonial powers through the chosen framework of the nation-state.

After political independence was achieved, African Muslims became more clearly aware of what the colonial 'interlude' had cost them: notably, the disruption of long-nurtured institutions and the relative isolation of African Muslims from wider Islamic currents, the injection into their intellectual horizons of larger or smaller doses of western secular thought and 'methodological atheism', the political realignment of Muslim communities in a way that in many cases inextricably linked their futures with those of non-Muslims, and an economic reorientation towards Europe that entailed in West Africa a reorientation towards the non-Muslim (and eventually extensively Christianized) coastal lands.

Now, as we move towards the end of the twentieth century, it is clear that African Muslims, in common with most Muslims elsewhere, are still seeking to redefine their identity and their relationship to 'Western' values and cultural norms and to rethink the political and social frameworks within which they wish to live. Not only is this natural as Muslim peoples recover from the colonial experience and assess its impact upon them, but as other global, regional and local institutions – the United Nations Organization, the Organization of African Unity and the nation-state – often seem unequal to the challenges posed by communal and international strife, gross inequities in the distribution of wealth, environmental catastrophes, severe public health crises, unemployment, violent crime, and in many countries the virtual breakdown of state educational systems, it is natural that Muslims should seek solutions for themselves within the frame of reference of their own culture, which is at once global and local.

2.82   Wuthnow: diversity in small group spirituality

Robert Wuthnow, 1996: *Sharing the Journey. Support Groups and America's New Quest for Community.* New York, London, Toronto, Sydney and Singapore: The Free Press (pp. 355–6).

The previous reading suggests that the assertion of strong difference by religio-ethnic groups may continue to be a feature of the religious landscape into the future. Here Robert Wuthnow describes the growth of another sort of difference in post-war America: the rise of small groups as the locus of religious belief and practice. Wuthnow's research in the USA revealed that 40 per cent of Americans claim to be currently involved in some kind of small group, and that 61 per cent of these say they were in a group that focused on religious or spiritual matters. As in earlier books like *The Restructuring of American Religion* (1988), Wuthnow traces a shift in post-war American religion from more settled denominational and ethnic patterns of difference to increasingly diverse and voluntaristic ones. The move, in other words, is towards ever greater plurality. Far from engendering exclusivistic strong difference, Wuthnow shows how this shift tends to give rise to more open and even relativistic forms of religiosity. We are reminded of Giddens's vision of the rise of a politics of 'choice', 'lift-style', and self actualization' in reading **2.60**.

Spirituality within small groups themselves is extraordinarily diverse. [. . .]

Diversity is clearly one of the reasons why the small-group movement has been so successful. American religion has long been known for its denominational and confessional pluralism. Small groups take this pluralism one step further. A person is no longer limited simply to deciding whether to be a Baptist, a Lutheran, or a Catholic. Indeed, making the transition from one to the other might be so uprooting that it would be easier to stay at home on Sunday mornings. With dozens of small groups meeting in their neighbourhoods, individuals trying to identify a comfortable spiritual niche can shop around more easily. Perhaps another group in the Baptist church takes its denominational heritage less seriously. Perhaps an ecumenical group at another church focuses on prayer and Bible study and dismisses the importance of denominational distinctions entirely. To join a new group, you do not have to go through a new members class, study church history, undergo rebaptism, or incur a moral obligation to help pay the pastor's salary. You simply have to show up, meet a few friendly individuals, and then quit attending a few weeks or months later if the chemistry hasn't been right. In short, diversity helps religious organizations adapt to a more competitive market situation. Small groups are like product lines. The American automobile industry would have folded shop long ago had it continued to make only the family sedan. Sports cars, pick-ups, and minivans helped retain consumer interest. Small groups, offering diverse definitions of spirituality, do the same thing for the religious market.

The negative, flip side of this diversity is also worth emphasizing, however. Respect for diversity easily can lead to a Milquetoast religion in which any view is regarded as highly as any other view. The danger of this happening is even greater in the spiritual marketplace than it is in the automobile industry. [. . .] Small groups are not like dealerships that transmit prefabricated goods from factory to consumer. They are more like customizing shops, creating their own versions of spirituality. Moreover, each member of the group can walk away with an individualized, distinctive version – largely because spirituality remains personal and subjective. Even when group members discuss their religious beliefs, they may link them so closely with personal experience that it becomes difficult for anyone else to disagree. Heretical or half-baked views can be the result, as well as religious orientations that are self-congratulatory and self-justifying. What can counter this tendency, of course, is the more intensive spiritual mentoring and theological training that members receive in their churches and synagogues. Some of this training influences small groups directly – through clergy involvement, the study guides used, and the input of knowledgeable members. But diversity can become the prevailing value. And ideas about spirituality can as easily be influenced by television, the latest movies, popular writers, the neighborhood gossip, personal moods, and the dynamics of group interaction.

2.83   Starhawk on inventing religion without absolutes

Starhawk, 1989: *The Spiral Dance. A Rebirth of the Ancient Religion of the Great Goddess.* 10th Anniversary Edition. San Francisco: HaprerCollins (pp. 199–202; 207).

The following extract by Starhawk (an advocate of the revival of witchcraft in modern times) illustrates how the assertion of pluralism and open difference in religion may be taken to an extreme. Here religion becomes a matter of pure individual choice and self-expression. Since the embrace of open difference makes claims to universal truth impossible, Starhawk abandons any 'absolutism'. Difference and diversity themselves become her gods.

In thinking about the future of religion and of culture, we need to look at the present through the acrostic eye. That slightly skewed vision reveals those underlying mind sets I think of as the scabies of consciousness – because they cause us extreme discomfort and yet we can't ordinarily see them. They are embedded in us, under the skin. In this chapter, I want to examine the destructive forces, as well as the creative forces that are influencing the direction of our evolution as a society. Only when we understand the currents of the present can we clearly envision the future.

If we accept the responsibility of claiming the future for life, than we must engage in the demanding task of recreating culture. A deep and profound change is needed in our attitude toward the world and the life on it, toward each other, and in our conceptions of what is human. Somehow, we must win clear of the roles we have been taught, of strictures on mind and self that are learned before speech and are buried so deep that they cannot be seen. Today women are creating new myths, singing a new liturgy, painting our own icons, and drawing strength from the new-old symbols of the Goddess, of the 'legitimacy and beneficence of female power.' [. . .]

Witchcraft is indeed the Old Religion, but it is undergoing so much change and development at present that, in essence, it is being recreated rather than revived. The feminist religion of the future is presently being formed. Those of us who are involved in this reformation must look closely at the cultural context in which our own ideas about religion were formed, and examine the many regressive tendencies present in society today. Otherwise, the new incarnation of the Goddess will be subtly molded on the very forms we are working to transcend. [. . .]

The Judeo-Christian heritage has left us with the view of a universe composed of warring opposites, which are valued as either good or evil. They cannot coexist. A valuable insight of Witchcraft, shared by many earth-based religions, is that polarities are in balance, not at war. [. . .]

Dualism slides over into what I call the 'Righteousness Syndrome.' When there is One Right True and Only Way – Ours! – and everybody else is wrong, then those who are wrong are damned, and the damned are evil. We are excused from recognizing their humanness and from treating them according to the ethics with which we treat each other. Generally, the Righteous set about the task of purifying themselves from any contact with the carriers of evil. When they are in power, they institute inquisitions, Witchhunts, pogroms, executions, censorship, and concentration camps. [. . .]

A matrifocal culture, based on nature, celebrates diversity, because diversity assures survival and continuing evolution. Nature creates thousands of species, not just one; and each is different, fitted for a different ecological niche. When a species becomes overspecialized, too narrow in its range of adaptations, it is more likely to become extinct. When political and spiritual movements become too narrow, they are also likely to die out. The strength of the women's movement lies in its diversity, as old and young women, lesbian and straight, welfare mothers and aspiring bank presidents discover common interests, common needs, and common sisterhood. If our culture as a whole is to evolve toward life, we need to foster diversity, to create and maintain a wide range of differences in lifestyle, theory, and tactics. We need to win clear of the self-righteousness that comes from seeing ourselves as Chosen People, and need to create a religion of heretics, who refuse to toe any ideological lines or give their allegiance to any doctrines of exclusivity. [. . .]

To *will* does not mean that the world will conform to our desires – it means that *we* will: We will make our own choices and act so as to bring them about, even knowing we may fail. Feminist spirituality values the courage to take risks, to make mistakes, to be our own authorities.

2.84   Martin: the idea of unity as *the* big idea

David Martin, 1998: Christianity: Converting and Converted (Unpublished paper) (pp. 2–4).

In the face of the contemporary rise and celebration of pluralism, David Martin reminds us that nearly all the world's religions assert their possession of universal truth, and that this is 'the big idea' of human history. In explanation of the rise of difference, Martin notes how the universal ideal easily gives rise to violence and disillusionment. Martin's remarks prompt the thought that there may be a cyclical swing between the rise of universal narratives and the assertion of difference.

I am going to proceed as follows. First the question to be answered: how does a faith based on a voluntary change of heart and on the hope of a coming peaceable kingdom [Christianity] come to be implicated in violent expansive empires which convert by decree and deny choice? Then the first step in considering the answer. I am going to suggest that this inward change and this hope are rooted in four further ideas: the unity of God, the unity of humanity, the unity of the church, and the all-embracing unifying character of commitment, so that faith informs every aspect of life. These ideas further imply the notions of light and truth and hence the removal of idols and the defeat of darkness. I will suggest that such ideas, good in themselves and fundamental, can be very costly. Given a change of social context, as when Christianity is adopted as an imperial faith, they can easily lead to compulsion and the extirpation of idolatries. [. . .]

What of this speculative point about the dangerous potentials lying within the idea of one God, one humanity, one fraternity (the church), one truth, and an all-embracing, unified commitment? Perhaps the first thing to notice is that such an idea of unity lies at the root of the idea of a mass movement of people across ethnic, territorial and status barriers. So it is not confined to Christianity but presents a kind of model, exemplified also in Islam, and the ideologies of the Enlightenment, including Marxism. It is, if you like, *the* 'big idea'. However, once the 'big idea' is put into established practice it begins to turn into its opposite. All the great endeavours of humanity, which in their hopes elicit total commitment, in their concrete realisation are accused of treason and are hated for their betrayal of hope itself. In other words the mass movements embodying hopes of unity actually generate an animus against themselves once those hopes are scaled down and reversed by realities.

2.85 Clarke: the tension between universalism and difference

J. J. Clarke, 1997: *Oriental Enlightenment. The Encounter between Asian and Western Thought.* London: Routledge (pp. 215–17).

Here J. J. Clarke reflects on contemporary tensions between universalism and pluralism in relation to religion, orientalism, and politics. He remains optimistic that ultimately universalism and difference may exist in complementary harmony. On orientalism see also Said in reading **2.62**.

[Orientalism] is in many respects undergoing major changes which reflect a wider cultural metamorphosis in which there has been a remarkable world-wide multiplication of channels of communication and interaction, leading to the rejection of the old ideals of Western hegemony, and of its global pretensions, and the recognition of the claims of diversity and difference. Old boundaries are dissolving, and there are genuine attempts to bring about a 'fusion of horizons'. [. . .]

Inevitably this is a slow and uneven development in which optimism . . . must be set against the stubborn persistence of old Eurocentric attitudes, for a number of factors are clearly working in quite the opposite direction. Amongst the most obvious of these factors are the resurgence of nationalism after the end of the Cold War, the revival of extreme right-wing politics in Europe and America, and the ominous growth of religious fundamentalisms, a phenomenon which is now evident amongst Hindus and Buddhists as well as in the Abrahamic traditions. There is, furthermore, an ambivalence arising from the liberating energies of orientalist discourse itself. One of the consequences associated with the latter – though many other factors enter into the equation – is the increasingly aggressive assertion of multiple ethnocentric identities, which, though clearly in reaction against the process of Europeanisation, may turn out to be an almost deliberately formed mirror image of it, and to this extent orientalism may have encouraged the very divisiveness that it so often appears to have wished to transcend. As critics such as Sara Suleri have pointed out, the very 'alterism' (as she calls it) of some postcolonial discourse, aimed at the re-empowerment of the colonised 'other', tends to perpetuate 'the fallacy of the totality of otherness' and thereby reinforce the old binary essentialism of East and West. Moreover, the demand for recognition and respect by or on behalf of minority groups and interests has sometimes given rise to a new form of intolerance that goes under the popular title of 'political correctness'. The issues surrounding political correctness clearly go much wider than orientalism, but since the publication of Said's book in 1978, orientalism has often been associated with 'Third Worldism', namely an attitude of mind which encourages the West's sense of postcolonial guilt and self-contempt, its 'self-laceration for the crimes of colonization', as Ferenc Feher puts it, leading to 'the zeal of anti-ethnocentrism', a new 'political fundamentalism with a religious coloring'. The attitude of self-recrimination encourages not only an exaggerated and unhelpful sense of the West's supposed degeneracy, but also an overly-elevated and a-historical vision of the East's moral and spiritual purity, a process in which old myths are demolished only to be replaced by new ones.

This paradoxical situation is connected with the fact that orientalism is often caught in a dialectical tension between the extremes of universalism and pluralism: it tends towards a universalistic outlook which transcends cultural boundaries and encourages an inter-cultural perspective, yet increasingly it also seeks to affirm local and regional differences and to nurture the unique particularity of cultures; globalisation and parochialisation thus appear as equal yet opposite allurements. Looked at in a wider perspective, this situation clearly reflects the tensions involved in all hermeneutical encounters, which typically circulate from the particular to the general and back again, a circularity which is not necessarily vicious. Such a process does indeed seem peculiarly apt for the needs of the contemporary world. Nationalist and ethnic aspirations are not necessarily intolerant and aggressively chauvinistic; globalism is not necessarily blind to local and regional demands. There is no reason why orientalism should not be able to point the way towards the mediation between these two positions. After all, the East–West dialogue has at one and the same time helped to recover and revive indigenous traditions, while at the same time opening up minds to wider and more universal sympathies. Readers do not need to be reminded that the world today abounds in conflict, and that the creation of communities of understanding, able to recognise the demands of both the universal and the particular, are urgently needed. An enlightened orientalism has an important contribution to make to the creation of such a community of understanding. Its history, however chequered, is one of attempted crossings of boundaries, of dialogues between remote cultures, of the sharing of horizons, and most especially of critical reflexiveness. It has the capacity, at its best, to widen sympathies, enrich the imagination, encourage openness and multiculturalism, and enhance toleration between peoples. It may even contribute to the attainment of a new world order.

part three

trends

introduction to
part three

Whereas **Part One** concentrated on varieties of religion, and **Part Two** on religions in social contexts, the emphasis now is on the more general. Dwelling on widespread trends, including those which are bound up with more specific circumstances, **Part Three** is also more theoretical. It engages the reader with theories which claim to discern powerful developments within modern culture and society, and to link them with what is happening in religious life. Such theories, in their strongest form, posit comprehensive and unilinear processes: they claim that *all* religion in modern times has moved in certain directions – disappearing or gaining in strength, for example. Other theories, though, are more alert to the varieties and complexities of religion, culture and society. Distinguishing between different kinds of religion, they too specify trends: but these are seen as taking place under particular conditions, involving particular types of religion. As such they are clearly neither comprehensive or unilinear.

Given the importance of 'modernity' in modern times, it is not surprising that the majority of the extracts which follow theorize religion by reference to those institutions and forces which – in varying ways – are taken to be constitutive of modernity: capitalism, democracy, bureaucracy, consumer culture, the exercise of reason, and the role played by the autonomous self, to name but a few of the constitutive components which are introduced.

Part Three is divided into four chapters – Secularization, Detraditionalization, Universalization and Sacralization. The first and the fourth concern the relationship between modern times and the *amount* of religion to be found in social, cultural and personal spheres. In one regard, we are in the land of numbers, with researchers attempting to establish whether those who are (somehow) religious are declining or increasing in number, and theorizing accordingly. Equally importantly, though, these two chapters also dwell on the *significance* of religion for social, cultural and personal affairs. In this regard, we are in the land of 'impact', theorists attempting to establish the difference which religion might – or might not – be making, and theorizing accordingly.

In the second and third chapters of **Part Three**, attention turns to the relationship between modern times, specifically modernity, and changes *within* the religious domain per se. Whereas the topic of secularization has for long been high on the academic (and, at least in northern Europe) public agenda, with the topic of sacralization currently coming into prominence, the processes of detraditionalization and universalization have received relatively scant attention. Yet they are of very considerable importance, affecting the *nature* of what is taking place in religion in modern times. Thus among many other things, detraditionalization involves a shift from the authority of an external, supra-individual and traditional source of sacrality to the authority of the self, at its conclusion a self that is *the* Self (that is sacred). This shift clearly involves a radical transformation of what religion is all about – from obeying an Other to living out of and in terms of one Self. An equally, if not more important shift, now with regard to universalization, concerns the shift from the exclusive to the inclusive. The radical transformation here is from religion as something which (to varying degrees) damns all other religions, to religion as something which (also to varying degrees) finds 'the same' in all – or most – varieties of the religious life. There is clearly a huge difference in being religious in terms of these two extremes: from being an 'insider', locked into one's own superior religion, to being an integral component of a global religious whole. The political implications of these different positions are immense.

As in the rest of this volume, we do not merely introduce existing literature and language, but develop themes and suggest new approaches. Of particular note, in **Part Three** we help develop the ideas of 'detraditionalization' and 'universalization' – ideas which are emerging in the literature but which are not yet greatly explored.

CHAPTER NINE

secularization

Introduction

Among academics, secularization theory has for long dominated discussion about the relationship between religion and modern times. Advocates of the idea that modernity has had a corrosive effect on religion fall into two main camps. On the one hand, there are those who argue that religion is on course to fade away. Evidence for what can be called the *disappearance thesis* is provided by those – like Peter Berger (1969) – who claim that 'the modern West has produced an increasing number of individuals who look upon the world and their own lives without the benefit of religious interpretations'; indeed, that 'we have enough data to indicate the massive presence of . . . [the secularization of consciousness] in the contemporary West' (p. 108). On the other hand, there are those somewhat more cautious theorists who claim that religion might remain, but in a privatized form with very little cultural or social significance. What can be called the *differentiation thesis* thus holds that religion gets pushed out of social domains whilst remaining (of some) significance in private life. As Bryan Wilson (1985) makes the point, 'Nor does the model [of secularization] predict the disappearance of religiosity, nor even of organized religion; it merely indicates the decline in the significance of religion in the operation of the social system, its diminished significance in social consciousness, and its reduced command over the resources (time, energy, skill, intellect, imagination, and accumulated wealth) of mankind' (p. 14).

There are two other, less common, varieties of the secularization approach. One can be thought of as *de-intensification theory*, the idea being that religion remains but in a 'weak', insubstantial form. The readings on 'the turn to consumerized experience' at the end of this chapter serve to illustrate the point, the idea being that 'religion' has lost most of its religious attributes (such as providing ways to obtain salvation), instead serving as a consumer product. Another illustration concerns the argument that liberal religions of humanity, being detraditionalized versions of religions of difference, have little substance: a point made by Bruce in reading **1.51** in the course of explaining why liberal Protestantism is in decline. (See also Bruce, 1996, pp. 85–91.) As for the second variety, which might be thought of as *coexistence theory*, the idea is that whilst secularization takes place in particular circumstances, in other contexts religions retain their vitality, even grow. David Martin (**3.5**) provides an illustration of this, breaking with comprehensive and unilinear versions of secularization theory. (See also the reading by Hefner (**3.70**), as well as readings in the chapter on Sacralization for more on this kind of theorizing.)

Secularization theorists also differ in what they consider to be the most important reasons for the process. As will be seen from the readings, suggested processes include the development of the authority of secular reason, sociocultural differentiation (where religion is driven from various institutional domains, such as the economic and political), pluralization (the loss of faith in the face of multiplicity), and the consumerization (or trivialization) of religion.

What follows can usefully be read in conjunction with the chapter on the counter-argument: see Sacralization, later in **Part Three**. Related readings are also to be found in **Part One**. In particular sections entitled 'explanations' and 'prospects' in each of the main chapters on religions of difference, religions of humanity and spiritualities of life explore whether these types of religion are suffering from secularization. Material on the differentiation thesis (including counter-evidence) is to be found in all three chapters of **Part Two** as well as the chapter on Universalization in **Part Three**, where several readings explore the idea that states have become secularized in order to handle potentially disruptive pluralism.

That the literature on secularization is so large is due to the fact that much highly influential writing, dating back to the last century and influenced by Enlightenment thought, has come out of northern Europe – where secularization would appear to be most in evidence. Academics elsewhere in the world – especially in countries like India – are not attracted by the theory because religion where they live is alive and well. The amount of the literature, however, suggests that it is advisable to mention further reading: see, for example, the two-volume collection, *The Sociology of Religion* (1995a) edited by Bruce; *Religion and Modernization* (1992) also edited by Bruce; and Hammond's edited volume, *The Sacred in a Secular Age* (1985).

Secularization: overviews

3.1 Hammond summarizing secularization as a one-directional process

Philip E. Hammond, 1985: Introduction. In Philip E. Hammond (ed.), *The Sacred in a Secular Age. Toward Revision in the Scientific Study of Religion*. Berkeley, Los Angeles and London: University of California Press, pp. 1–8 (p. 1).

Philip Hammond outlines the main characteristics of the stronger (disappearance) rendering of the thesis, drawing attention to its unilinear, 'one-dimensional' character, as well as drawing attention to some of the factors which have been invoked to explain the process.

A linear image dominates Western thought about society. Even cyclical views are cast in spiral form, thus helping to maintain the notion that social life is systematically coming from somewhere and going elsewhere. Social science, born in nineteenth-century evolutionism, matured with this perspective almost exclusively, indeed contributing to it many of the master terms used in contemporary discourse about social change: *industrialization, modernization, rationalization, bureaucratization,* and *urbanization*, to name but a few. All imply one-directional processes.

In the social scientific study of religion this dominant linear image is expressed chiefly in the term *secularization*, the idea that society moves from some sacred condition to successively secular conditions in which the sacred evermore recedes. In fact, so much has the secularization thesis dominated the social scientific study of religious change that it is now conventional wisdom.

3.2 Bell and 'Enlightened thinkers'

Daniel Bell, 1977: The Return of the Sacred? The argument on the future of religion. *British Journal of Sociology* 28 (4): 419–49 (pp. 420–3).

Daniel Bell sets the disappearance rendering of the secularization thesis – a rendering forcefully advocated by 'Enlightened thinkers' during the last century and before – in historical perspective. Bell also serves to introduce one of the most influential secularization theorists, Bryan Wilson, to whom we return in extract **3.4**.

At the end of the eighteenth and to the middle of the nineteenth century, almost every Enlightened thinker expected religion to disappear in the twentieth century. The belief was based on the power of Reason. Religion was associated with superstition, fetishism, unprovable beliefs, a form of fear which was used as protection against other fears – a form of security one might associate with the behaviour of children – and which they believed, in fact, had arisen in the 'childhood' of the human race.

Religion, in this view, arose out of the fears of nature, both the physical terrors of the environment and the dangers lurking in the inner psyche which were released at night or conjured up by special diviners. The more rational answer – we owe the start, of course, to the Greeks – was philosophy, whose task was to uncover *physis* or the hidden order of nature. The *leitmotif* was the phrase which occurs first in Aristotle and is resurrected later by Hegel and Marx, 'the realization of philosophy'. For Aristotle, nature had a *telos*, and within it man would realize his perfected form. For Hegel, this *telos* lay in history, in the *marche générale* of human consciousness which was wiping away the fogs of illusion and allowing men to see the world more clearly.

The 'realization of philosophy' would be the overcoming of all the dualities that had divided consciousness, and made it so unhappy. In the Christian parable, man had been at one with God, there had been a Fall, and the expectation ever since was that there would be a *parousia*, the end of time, when there would be a reunification of man with God. In Hegel's philosophical substitution of philosophy for parable, there was an original cosmic consciousness which became 'dirempted' into the dualities of spirit and matter, nature and history, subject and object, but through the reflexiveness of self-consciousness, the *Begriff*, the anima of consciousness would fuse into the Absolute. And in Marx's naturalism, the original unity of primitive communism which became divided into the dualities of exploiter and exploited, mental and physical labour, town and country, would once again be attained, at a higher level of man's technical powers, in the realm of Man. 'The criticism of religion,' Marx said, 'ends with the precept that the supreme being for man is man. . . .'

The end of History would come in the 'leap' from 'the kingdom of necessity to the kingdom of freedom'. The end of History would be the unbinding of Prometheus, and Man stepping onto the mountain top to take his place with him among the Titans. As Shelley proclaimed:

The painted veil . . . is torn aside;
The loathsome mask has fallen, the man remains
Sceptreless, free, uncircumscribed, but man
Equal, unclassed, tribeless, and nationless,
Exempt from awe, worship, degree, the king
Over himself. . . .

What is striking in all this, in the poetry of Revolution which is heir to these hopes, is that Historical Reason passed over into a kind of romanticism, a romanticism which produced more cruel illusions and blacker veils than the religious naïvete and fanaticism it was designed to replace.

From the end of the nineteenth century to the middle of the twentieth century, almost every sociological thinker – I exempt Scheler and a few others – expected religion to disappear by the onset of the twenty-first century. If the belief no longer lay in Reason (though in Durkheim there remained a lingering hope, and in a book he expected to write after the *Elementary Forms of Religious Life*, but never did, he planned to sketch the forms of a new moral universalism that he thought might arise by the end of the century), it now lay in the idea of Rationalization. Reason is the uncovering – the underlying structure – of the natural order. Rationalization is the substitution of a technical order for a natural order – in the rhythms of work, in the functional adaptation of means to ends, in the criteria for use of objects, the principal criterion being efficiency – and the imposition of bureaucratic structures of organization to replace the ties of kinship and primordial relations. It is the world of technical rules and bureaucratic roles. And since, as most sociologists believe, men are largely shaped by the institutions in which they live, the world has become, in Max Weber's terrifying phrase, 'an iron cage'. As summed up by Weber:

> With the progress of science and technology, man has stopped believing in magic powers, in spirits and demons; he has lost his sense of prophecy and, above all, his sense of the sacred. Reality has become dreary, flat and utilitarian, leaving a great void in the souls of men which they seek to fill by furious activity and through various devices and substitutes.

This is the view, I dare say, of most sociologists today, though much of the poignancy has been drained away and replaced, if not by jargon, then by bare utilitarian prose – as if the language itself has become the proof of the proposition.

I take as an adherent of this Weberian belief – and he is the best, which is why we have to take him seriously – Mr Bryan Wilson, and as a text his recent 1976 *Contemporary Transformations of Religion*. Mr Wilson writes:

> For the sociologist it is axiomatic that the sources of change in religion should be looked for primarily in the social system. . . .

> The most powerful trend [accounting for the decline in belief] is secularization, which occurs as our social organization becomes increasingly dominated by technical procedures and rational planning. . . . Secularization is associated with the structural differentiation of the social system – separation of different areas of social activity into more specialized forms. . . . Instead of work activity, family life, education, religious practice, the operation of law and custom and recreation, all being part of each other, and affecting everyone in more or less self-sufficient close-knit small communities, as occurred in large measure in all pre-modern societies, we have highly specialized places, times, resources, and personnel involved in each of these areas of social life, and their efficiency and viability has depended on this process of specialization. . . .

> In the past religion was a primary socializing agency of men teaching them not only new rituals but something of the seriousness of eternal verities. . . . [Today] Religion has come to be associated much more as one among a number of leisure activities, it exists in the area of free choice of the use of time, energy, and wealth in which the end products of the economy are marketed for consumers. . . .

[And, as a result]

> Contemporary transformations of religion appear to me to be of a kind, an extent, and a rapidity previously unknown in human history . . . whereas in 1970 some polls discovered that 88 per cent of people in Britain professed to believe in God, and 45 per cent thought of God as a personal being, in the most recent survey only 64 per cent professed to believe in God – 29 per cent saying that God was a person, and 35 per cent saying he was some sort of spirit or Life Force. . . . All the evidence is towards the decline of belief in the supernatural, and the rejection of the idea that the supernatural has any significant influence in the everyday life of modern man.

3.3 Jameson: the disappearance thesis that religion is already dead

Fredric Jameson, 1991: *Postmodernism, or, The Cultural Logic of Late Capitalism.* London and New York: Verso (p. 67).

The short extract by Fredric Jameson which follows provides a good, albeit highly controversial, illustration of the belief that capitalistic modernity has already succeeded in killing religion.

Capitalism, and the modern age, is a period in which, with the extinction of the sacred and the spiritual, the deep underlying materiality of all things has finally risen dripping and convulsive into the light of day; and it is clear that culture itself is one of those things whose fundamental materiality is now for us not merely evident but quite inescapable.

3.4 Wilson: the differentiation thesis that religion has lost its public significance

Bryan Wilson, 1982: *Religion in Sociological Perspective.* Oxford and New York: Oxford University Press (pp. 149–151).

In contrast to the first three readings, which focus on the disappearance thesis, attention is now turned to differentiation. For Bryan Wilson, secularization is the process whereby '. . . religion ceases to be significant in the working of the social system'. This leaves open the possibility that people nevertheless remain interested in religion for personal reasons; that religion continues to exist in a privatized fashion. Having made the point that 'the thesis itself implies that there are processes of society "becoming more secular" which extend backward in time over the long course of human history' (p. 148), the historical dimension of the secularization thesis is further elaborated here, comparison being made with the supposedly much more profoundly religious life of 'simple' or 'traditional' societies. (See also Wilson (1985, pp. 16–20) for another good summary of secularization theory, including how it relates to 'resacralization'.)

Secularization relates to the diminution in the social significance of religion. Its application covers such things as, the sequestration by political powers of the property and facilities of religious agencies; the shift from religious to secular control of various of the erstwhile activities and functions of religion; the decline in the proportion of their time, energy, and resources which men devote to super-empirical concerns; the decay of religious institutions; the supplanting, in matters of behaviour, of religious precepts by demands that accord with strictly technical criteria; and the gradual replacement of a specifically religious consciousness (which might range from dependence on charms, rites, spells, or prayers, to a broadly spiritually-inspired ethical concern) by an empirical, rational, instrumental orientation; the abandonment of mythical, poetic, and artistic interpretations of nature and society in favour of matter-of-fact description and, with it, the rigorous separation of evaluative and emotive dispositions from cognitive and positivistic orientations.

These phenomena are likely to be causally linked, and yet they occur in varying order, and with different degrees of rapidity. In what measure, or in what priority they occur, is an empirical question for each specific case, and cannot be settled, *a priori*. The complexity of social life demands that allowance be made for innumerable contingent factors and an inextricable tissues of causes; but the impossibility of ever laying bare every causal influence in proper sequence should not occasion us to abandon our conception of broad social processes, reference to which at least offers us an interpretative comprehension of reality. If I may, for purposes of clarity, resort to a definition of secularization that I first used some years ago, and which I have found no reason to modify, let me say that, by the term *secularization*, I mean that process by which religious institutions, actions, and consciousness, lose their social significance. What such a definition does *not* imply is that all men have acquired a secularized consciousness. It does not even suggest that most individuals have relinquished all their interest in religion, even though that may be the case. It maintains no more than that religion ceases to be significant in the working of the social system. Clearly, that that should be so, may release many individuals from religious obligations and involvements that they might otherwise have found it necessary to sustain: religion's loss of social significance may cause men to gain psychological or individual independence of it, but that is a matter to be investigated, since there may be other non-religious constraints which operate to hold men to religious institutions or to persuade them to go through the motions of religious rituals. The definition that I have used is intended to cover any or all of the various applications of the concept that I have indicated above. We may see them as related phenomena, even if we cannot always state the terms of that relationship.

It is sometimes objected that the process implicit in the concept of secularization concedes at once the idea of an earlier condition of social life that was not secular, or that was at least much less secular than that of our own times. We can readily make that concession, even though it must be clear that by no means all men, even in the great ages of faith, were devoutly religious, and that, at the time of its most effective organization, the church in Europe, for example, was bedevilled by internal heresy and external heathenism, and by laxness, lassitude, and corruption. None the less, by most criteria, the social significance of religion for the conduct of human life was greater than than it is now. If we go back to earlier times, the evidence becomes even more overwhelming. Simpler cultures, traditional societies, and past communities, as revealed by their archaeological remains, appear to have been profoundly preoccupied with the supernatural (even though they may not have distinguished it by that name). Simpler peoples appear to have taken cognizance of themselves, of their origins, social arrangements, and destiny, by reference to a projected sphere of the supernatural. Their ultimate concerns, expressed perhaps most cogently with regard to death, were super-empirical, and such ideas, beings, objects, or conditions, commanded solemn attention and perhaps dedication. Everyday life was deeply influenced, and sometimes completely organized, with respect to a realm of transcendental suppositions.

3.5 Martin and the coexistence approach: secularization *and* vitality

David Martin, 1990: *Tongues of Fire. The Explosion of Protestantism in Latin America.* Oxford and Cambridge, Mass.: Basil Blackwell (pp. 4; 294–5).

The final 'overview' on the theory of secularization is designed to make the point that it is perfectly possible to combine this theory with the reverse claim, namely that some religions are also flourishing. How religion is faring, that is to say, depends on particular circumstances rather than on unilinear processes. In the extract which follows David Martin argues that European secularization is somewhat exceptional, religion having been associated with (often reactionary) elites and states, and therefore having been ill-suited for serving as a vehicle for social change. Elsewhere, however, the situation is very different. (See also Martin, 1978.)

Up to now the proponents of universal secularization have seen all Catholic societies as prefigured by France and all Protestant societies as prefigured by Sweden. But maybe Europe does not provide the universal model, and maybe Europe only illustrates what happens when social change occurs in states where religion has been tied to governments and to old elites. In the United States that tie was broken and religion floated free of the particular entanglements of status and power. Perhaps what is happening now in South America is a complicated dance in which both Catholicism and Protestantism are floating free and breaking out of the bounds set by the last two centuries. [. . .]

Theories of secularization indicate how religion, and specifically Christianity, relinquishes (and/or is deprived of) its hold on the central structures of power. It ceased to be the symbolic keystone in mechanical solidarity and is released from the centripetal pull which aligns it with elite interests and explicit party attachments. Theories of secularization also specify a complementary process whereby the state takes over and develops all kinds of organizations and functions, especially in education and social welfare, which were previously under religious aegis. This advance of the omnicompetent state is associated with the growth of professions whose interests come to lie in the extension of state action, and with the propagation of ideologies which define the religious contribution as irrelevant to the efficient running of society. As Bryan Wilson has argued, a net of rational bureaucratic regulation can supplant the moral densities, the conscientious sensitivities and the commitments once generated by communities of faith.

The question then becomes whether this process is contingent, i.e. dependent on specific circumstances, notably those which have obtained in Europe, or is a necessary and inevitable part of social development. Clearly if the latter is the case then a certain estimate of the significance and future of the phenomena discussed in this book follows. It is simply that temporary efflorescence of voluntary religiosity which accompanies a stage in industrialization and/or urbanization. As Methodism flourished during just such a period in Britain so Pentecostalism flourishes today in Latin America. The problematic stemming from Halévy applies to them both as parallel moments in a story which will end as they shrivel at the cold touch of rationalization and the omnicompetent state.

This may, of course, be the case. But there is the alternative view based on the notion that the European experience is contingent and fails to provide the universal paradigm to which all other societies must in time approximate. According to that alternative view the effect of establishment and religious monopoly such as existed in Europe has been to inhibit the adaptability of religion to social change, above all to the industrial city. However, the North American paradigm seems to show that once religion is no longer a matter of a relation of a particular body to the elite and to the state, religion adapts quite successfully to a changing world. In all the *proper* senses of the word it becomes popular. Indeed, it shows itself endlessly inventive and actually succeeds in assuaging the anomie and combatting the chaos of the megacity.

It may well be that the inventiveness displayed in North America has now been transferred to Latin America and the cycle of spirals derived from Europe thereby slowed or halted, even maybe reversed. If that is so, then secularization as understood in the European context is a particular kind of episode. If there is a universal element to it, that is restricted to the shift from structural location to cultural influence discussed earlier. Should that restricted and episodic view of secularization turn out to be correct then the crossing of the 'Anglo' and Hispanic patterns currently observed in Latin America is not a repeat performance of a sequence already played through and played out in Britain, but a new moment with new possibilities.

Secularization: examples

3.6 Brierley and Wraight on declining church membership

Peter Brierley and Heather Wraight, 1995: *UK Christian Handbook. 96/97 Edition.* London: Christian Research Association (p. 240).

The table of church members in the United Kingdom shows overall decline since 1975, from 18.5 per cent of the adult population (aged 15 and over) to a (projected) 10.8 per cent in 2010. It will be noted that the decline is progressive. The only sign of such decline being arrested is that the 'Free Churches' (comprised of the Baptists, Independent Churches, Methodists, New Churches, Other Churches and Pentecostals) have increased in numbers; so has the Orthodox Church. Although the evidence cannot be presented here, decline in attendance is also in evidence in other countries, especially in northern Europe.

Church members

	1975	1980	1985	1990	1992	1994	2000	2005	2010
Anglican	2,297,871	2,179,458	2,016,943	1,871,977	1,812,492	1,760,070	1,604,450	1,491,550	1,353,550
Baptist	235,884	239,780	243,051	230,858	228,199	229,276	230,010	229,275	228,65
Roman Catholic	2,605,255	2,454,253	2,279,065	2,198,694	2,087,511	2,002,758	1,830,865	1,685,650	1,546,430
Independent	240,200	227,782	225,634	221,444	214,246	210,200	201,300	194,250	188,885
Methodist	576,791	520,557	474,290	443,323	434,606	420,836	379,825	355,550	325,425
New Churches	12,060	25,250	80,494	125,869	149,556	164,317	200,300	233,000	270,800
Orthodox	196,850	203,165	223,721	265,968	276,080	283,897	309,565	331,960	354,050
Other Churches	137,083	131,510	126,127	121,681	120,609	119,453	115,988	113,970	112,725
Pentecostal	101,648	126,343	136,582	158,505	169,071	183,109	210,600	232,000	252,850
Presbyterian	1,589,085	1,437,775	1,322,029	1,213,920	1,172,011	1,120,383	995,496	889,174	788,587
TOTAL of which	7,992,727	7,545,873	7,127,936	6,852,239	6,664,381	6,494,299	6,078,399	5,756,890	5,421,952
Free Churches	1,303,666	1,270,862	1,286,178	1,301,680	1,316,287	1,327,191	1,338,023	1,358,056	1,379,335
Percentage total is of adult population	18.5	16.9	15.5	14.7	14.3	13.9	12.8	12.2	10.8

3.7 Hadaway, Marler and Chaves on halving church attendance in the United States

C. Kirk Hadaway, Penny Long Marler and Mark Chaves, 1993: What the Polls don't Show: a Closer Look at U.S. Church Attendance. *American Sociological Review* 58 (December): 741–52 (pp. 741, 748).

Church attendance varies very considerably from country to country (and region to region), monthly church attendance in Iceland being 9 per cent, in Ireland 87 per cent (see Barker, Halman and Vloet, 1993). C. Kirk Hadaway, Penny Marler and Mark Chaves report that 'approximately 40 per cent of the population of the United States is said to attend church weekly' (p. 741) – a figure considerably higher than most European countries. However, the 40 per cent figure is derived from what people say they do; and according to Hadaway, Marler and Chaves, the percentage is considerably lower if it is based on actual body counts of those who go to church. If they are right, the USA is not so 'exceptional' and it does not count against the secularization claim that advanced modernity is incompatible with relatively high levels of attendance.

Characterizations of religious life in the United States typically reference poll data on church attendance. Consistently high levels of participation reported in these data suggest an exceptionally religious population, little affected by secularizing trends. This picture of vitality, however, contradicts other empirical evidence indicating declining strength among many religious institutions. Using a variety of data sources and data collection procedures, we estimate that church attendance rates for Protestants and Catholics are, in fact, approximately one-half the generally accepted levels.

Percent age attending mass weekly, based on self-reports and actual counts of attendance: selected dioceses, 1990

	Percent age attending mass weekly	
Diocese	Self-report (95% Confidence Interval)	Actual count
Chicago	45.7 —— 51.3	25.7 —— 28.9
New York	37.8 —— 51.8	19.4 —— 21.5
Cincinnati	54.0 —— 64.6	35.5 —— 42.4
San Francisco	33.2 —— 44.6	29.9 —— 36.5

3.8   Hunter and the fortunes of Evangelicalism

James Davison Hunter, 1987: *Evangelicalism. The Coming Generation*. Chicago and London: The University of Chicago Press (pp. 4–5).

In this extract, James Davison Hunter provides evidence from across the world to show that after a promising nineteenth-century period of expansion, theologically conservative Protestantism has fared much less well this century. His conclusion – 'Its future remains justifiably in question' – can be compared with reading **3.86**, in the chapter on Sacralization, where Hunter shows that Evangelicalism is doing well in North America.

Since the turn of the century, substantial demographic changes have taken place within the ranks of conservative Protestants worldwide. Nineteenth-century confidence was, in many respects, short-lived for in all of the industrial powers of the West there were sharp decreases: in North America the percentage of conservative Protestants has decreased by one-fourth from what it was in 1900; in Oceania there was almost a 50 per cent decrease; in the United Kingdom and Western Europe there was a drop of over 4 per cent – to 10.2 per cent of the population. Only marginal increases were made in Latin America and in the countries of East and South Asia. The only significant growth has been in the less economically developed countries of Africa, where the percentage of conservative Protestants is presently more than five times what it was in 1900. Even so, only 8 per cent of the African population is under this religious umbrella. While it is true that much of the speculation about the demise of this expression of Christianity in the world has been based upon wishful thinking, there has been, in brief, some empirical grounding for these pessimistic forecasts. Its future remains justifiably in question.

Evangelical Christianity in the world (percentage of total population)

	North America	Western Europe	USSR and E. Europe	Oceania	Latin America	East Asia	South Asia	Africa
1900	41.0	14.5	2.0	34.5	1.2	0.1	0.2	1.5
1980	31.7	10.2	3.3	19.1	4.3	1.4	1.1	8.0

Secularization: explanations

Explanation: the triumph of secular reason

3.9 Kant on the 'courage to use your *own* understanding'

Immanuel Kant, 1996 (orig. 1784): An Answer to the Question: What is Enlightenment? In Lawrence E. Cahoone, From Modernism to Postmodernism: An Anthology. Oxford and Cambridge, Mass.: Blackwell, pp. 51–7 (pp. 51–2).

Enlightenment thought, attributing ultimate authority to human-cum-secular reason, fuelled the process of secularization and theorizing about it. The Enlightenment thinkers, that is to say, played a key role in developing the assumption – in the words of Kant – that all people have a 'duty . . . to think for themselves'; a duty which, by virtue of its individualism, has to contest the control of authoritative, collective, traditions.

Enlightenment is man's emergence from his self-incurred immaturity. Immaturity is the inability to use one's own understanding without the guidance of another. This immaturity is *self-incurred* if its cause is not lack of understanding, but lack of resolution and courage to use it without the guidance of another. The motto of enlightenment is therefore: *Sapere aude*! Have courage to use your *own* understanding!

Laziness and cowardice are the reasons why such a large proportion of men, even when nature has long emancipated them from alien guidance (*naturaliter maiorennes*), nevertheless gladly remain immature for life. For the same reasons, it is all too easy for others to set themselves up as their guardians. It is so convenient to be immature! If I have a book to have understanding in place of me, a spiritual adviser to have a conscience for me, a doctor to judge my diet for me, and so on, I need not make any efforts at all. I need not think, so long as I can pay; others will soon enough take the tiresome job over for me. The guardians who have kindly taken upon themselves the work of supervision will soon see to it that by far the largest part of mankind (including the entire fair sex) should consider the step forward to maturity not only as difficult but also as highly dangerous. Having first infatuated their domesticated animals, and carefully prevented the docile creatures from daring to take a single step without the leading-strings to which they are tied, they next show them the danger which threatens them if they try to walk unaided. Now this danger is not in fact so very great, for they would certainly learn to walk eventually after a few falls. But an example of this kind is intimidating, and usually frightens them off from further attempts.

Thus it is difficult for each separate individual to work his way out of the immaturity which has become almost second nature to him. He has even grown fond of it and is really incapable for the time being of using his own understanding, because he was never allowed to make the attempt. Dogmas and formulas, those mechanical instruments for rational use (or rather misuse) of his natural endowments, are the ball and chain of his permanent immaturity.

3.10   Gerth and Mills summarizing Weber on rationalization and disenchantment

H. H. Gerth and C. Wright Mills, 1991: The Man and his Work. In H. H. Gerth and C. Wright Mills (eds), *From Max Weber. Essays in Sociology*. London: Routledge & Kegan Paul, pp. 3–74 (pp. 51–2).

In line with Enlightenment philosophy, but grounded in social and cultural analysis, Weber argued that the exercise of reason – 'intellectualization and rationalization' – has meant that 'there are no mysterious incalculable forces that come into play, but rather that one can, in principle, master all things by calculation' (p. 139). Empirical science provides a good illustration. So does bureaucracy, H. H. Gerth and C. Wright Mills explaining that 'Weber . . . identifies bureaucracy with rationality, and the process of rationalization with mechanism, depersonalization, and oppressive routine' (p. 50).

The principle of rationalization is the most general element in Weber's philosophy of history. For the rise and fall of institutional structures, the ups and downs of classes, parties, and rulers implement the general drift of secular rationalization. In thinking of the change of human attitudes and mentalities that this process occasions, Weber liked to quote Friedrich Schiller's phrase, the 'disenchantment of the world.' The extent and direction of 'rationalization' is thus measured negatively in terms of the degree to which magical elements of thought are displaced, or positively by the extent to which ideas gain in systematic coherence and naturalistic consistency.

The urge towards such a comprehensive and meaningful interpretation of the universe is ascribed to groups of intellectuals, to religious prophets and teachers, to sages and philosophers, to jurists and experimental artists, and finally, to the empirical scientist. 'Rationalization,' socially and historically differentiated, thus comes to have a variety of meanings. In this connection Weber makes a masterful contribution to what has come to be known as the 'sociology of knowledge.'

Weber's view of 'disenchantment' embodies an element of liberalism and of the enlightenment philosophy that construed man's history as a unilinear 'progress' towards moral perfection (sublimation), or towards cumulative technological rationalization. Yet his skeptical aversion to any 'philosophical' element in empirical science precluded any explicit constructions of historical time in terms of 'cycles' or 'unilinear' evolution. 'Thus far the continuum of European culture development has known neither completed cyclical movements nor an unambiguously oriented "unilinear development."' We nevertheless feel justified in holding that a unilinear construction is clearly implied in Weber's idea of the bureaucratic trend.

3.11 Wilson and the role played by science

Bryan Wilson, 1996: *Religion in Secular Society. A Sociological Comment.* London: C. A. Watts (pp. 47–8).

Much in the fashion of Weber, Bryan Wilson explores the consequences of what is taken to be the increasing intellectual prestige of science over religion. Of particular note, for it paves the way for the next reading, Wilson shows how the application of science to the organization and management of the workplace has eroded the role once played by religion. (See also Owen Chadwick (1975) on the role played by historical science in undermining religious beliefs; Giddens (1991, pp. 175–7) dwells on the impact of the reflexive nature of modern knowledge in undermining traditions.)

The real danger of science to religion . . . was rather in the increased prestige of science and the decline in the intellectual prestige of religion. Since science had answers, and had positive and tangible fruits, it came increasingly to command respect and approval. As governments became less concerned with the promotion of religion, so they became increasingly disposed to sponsor science, at first by prizes and awards, and later by every-increasing endowments to scientific inquiry and scientific education. In earlier periods the men credited with knowledge, the 'wise' men of society, had necessarily been religionists, since the Church maintained virtually an intellectual stratum whose principal obligations had become the maintenance of cultured, civilized and educational values. But increasingly intellectual concerns passed beyond the knowledge and the ability of clergymen.

Even if from among their numbers many of the early scientists had come, as science became more specialized, and as specifically scientific education developed, so the possibility for the cleric to be a scientist diminished. Science grew up outside the control of the religious intellectual strata, and a new professional grouping came gradually into being.

Reflected in this process is also the shifting reliance to science for economic advance. Whereas nineteenth-century business men in the early period of industrialization relied on religion as an agency of social control, which helped to instil a sense of discipline and order into the work force, which was still the primary factor of production, in the twentieth century, as industry became more capitalized, so machinery increasingly 'controlled' labour, and that control could now be specifically adjusted for the particular task in hand without implications for controlling men in their private lives outside the work situation. The old control, with its 'letters of testimony' ('characters' as the working class knew them) relied on a man's general dispositions to industriousness, punctuality, thrift, sobriety, willingness and reliability: the new control demand nothing of his 'character' – the conveyer-belt could exact from him all the control that was needed. Industry has thus passed from internalized 'character' values, to mechanical manipulation. Thus it has turned from religious socialization to technical devices for the means of regulating the work situation and the productive process.

Eventually, for this imperative need to control men, industry has turned to new so-called sciences, of 'management' and 'industrial relations'. In economic terms it is wasteful to demand that the whole man, in all his facets should be self-disciplined when a more specific method of manipulation can be evolved of just that part of the man which is needed for the job. Industry has thus rejected the blanket control of religio-moral socialization of men, for methods which control men very much more as if they were mechanical instruments of production.

3.12   Weber's 'iron cage'

Max Weber, 1985 (orig. 1904–5): *The Protestant Ethic and the Spirit of Capitalism*. London, Boston and Sydney: Unwin (pp. 181–2).

The central argument of *The Protestant Ethic and the Spirit of Capitalism* is that the development of the capitalistic workplace – in particular in northern Europe and North America – owed a great deal to a Puritan ethic of duty to God and God's work. (see reading **2.6** for more on this thesis). In the closing pages of his work, however, Weber argues that the workplace has become an iron cage. The application of scientific reason to the workplace has turned it into a domain of 'mechanized petrification'; the 'pursuit of wealth', associated with that consumer culture which had to be developed for capitalism to work, means that 'we are forced' to work in a disenchanted realm.

> The Puritan wanted to work in a calling; we are forced to do so. For when asceticism was carried out of monastic cells into everyday life, and began to dominate worldly morality, it did its part in building the tremendous cosmos of the modern economic order. This order is now bound to the technical and economic conditions of machine production which to-day determine the lives of all the individuals who are born into this mechanism, not only those directly concerned with economic acquisition, with irresistible force. Perhaps it will so determine them until the last ton of fossilized coal is burnt. In Baxter's view the care for external goods should only lie on the shoulders of the 'saint like a light cloak, which can be thrown aside at any moment.' But fate decreed that the cloak should become an iron cage.
>
> Since asceticism undertook to remodel the world and to work out its ideals in the world, material goods have gained an increasing and finally an inexorable power over the lives of men as at no previous period in history. To-day the spirit of religious asceticism – whether finally, who knows? – has escaped from the cage. But victorious capitalism, since it rests on mechanical foundations, needs its support no longer. The rosy blush of its laughing heir, the Enlightenment, seems also to be irretrievably fading, and the idea of duty in one's calling prowls about in our lives like the ghost of dead religious beliefs. Where the fulfilment of the calling cannot directly be related to the highest spiritual and cultural values, or when, on the other hand, it need not be felt simply as economic compulsion, the individual generally abandons the attempt to justify it at all. In the field of its highest development, in the United States, the pursuit of wealth, stripped of its religious and ethical meaning, tends to become associated with purely mundane passions, which often actually give it the character of sport.
>
> No one knows who will live in this cage in the future, or whether at the end of this tremendous development entirely new prophets will arise, or there will be a great rebirth of old ideas and ideals, or, if neither, mechanized petrification, embellished with a sort of

convulsive self-importance. For of the last stage of this cultural development, it might well be truly said: 'Specialists without spirit, sensualists
without heart; this nullity imagines that it has attained a level of
civilization never before achieved.'

3.13   Marx's 'All that is solid melts into air'

Karl Marx, 1977 (orig. 1848): *The Communist Manifesto*. In David McLellan (ed.), *Karl Marx.
Selected Writings*. Oxford: Oxford University Press (pp. 223–4).

Also dwelling on the sphere of production, and providing an equally powerful
passage, Marx presents a complementary account of the impact of capitalistic
modernity on religion. If anything, it is even more pessimistic. The 'icy water of
egotistical calculation', Hobbesian 'naked self-interest', have become the order of
the day. (See **1.2** for Tipton's analysis of this kind of utilitarian individualism.)
All that matters is defined by the bourgeois-capitalist nexus; anything restrictive,
such as religious traditions, that stands in the way of constant quest to find new
ways of making money is swept away. (Compare the reading by Gehlen, **3.41**.)

The bourgeoisie, historically, has played a most revolutionary part.

The bourgeoisie, wherever it has got the upper hand, has put an end
to all feudal, patriarchal, idyllic relations. It has pitilessly torn asunder
the motley feudal ties that bound man to his 'natural superiors', and
has left remaining no other nexus between man and man than naked
self-interest, than callous 'cash payment'. It has drowned the most
heavenly ecstasies of religious fervour, of chivalrous enthusiasm, of
philistine sentimentalism, in the icy water of egotistical calculation. It
has resolved personal worth into exchange value, and in place of the
numberless indefeasible chartered freedoms, has set up that single,
unconscionable freedom – Free Trade. In one word, for exploitation, veiled by religious and political illusions, it has substituted naked,
shameless, direct, brutal exploitation.

The bourgeoisie has stripped of its halo every occupation hitherto
honoured and looked up to with reverent awe. It has converted the
physician, the lawyer, the priest, the poet, the man of science into its
paid wage-labourers.

The bourgeoisie has torn away from the family its sentimental veil,
and has reduced the family relation to a mere money relation.

The bourgeoisie has disclosed how it came to pass that the brutal
display of vigour in the Middle Ages, which Reactionists so much
admire, found its fitting complement in the most slothful indolence.
It has been the first to show what man's activity can bring about. It

has accomplished wonders far surpassing Egyptian pyramids, Roman aqueducts, and Gothic cathedrals; it has conducted expeditions that put in the shade all former Exoduses of nations and crusades.

The bourgeoisie cannot exist without constantly revolutionizing the instruments of production, and thereby the relations of production, and with them the whole relations of society. Conservation of the old modes of production in unaltered form, was, on the contrary, the first condition of existence for all earlier industrial classes. Constant revolutionizing of production, uninterrupted disturbance of all social conditions, everlasting uncertainty and agitation distinguish the bourgeois epoch from all earlier ones. All fixed, fast-frozen relations, with their train of ancient and venerable prejudices and opinions, are swept away, all new-formed ones become antiquated before they can ossify. All that is solid melts into air, all that is holy is profaned, and man is at last compelled to face with sober senses, his real conditions of life, and his relations with his kind.

Explanation: functional differentiation

3.14   Wilson explaining secularization

Bryan Wilson, 1985: Secularization: The Inherited Model. In Philip Hammond (ed.), *The Sacred in a Secular Age. Toward Revision in the Scientific Study of Religion*. Berkeley, Los Angeles and London: University of California Press, pp. 9–20 (pp. 12–15).

The argument is that 'the process of the structural differentiation of society', involving the development of autonomous spheres of procedure and value, means that religion 'has lost its presidency over other institutions', in particular the political, legal and economic. (See also Wilson, reading **3.4**.) The key explanatory theme is that modernity has seen more and more importance, authority and value attributed to the powers of human reason and self-determination: an authority which has wrested agency from religion towards those rational principles thought to be most effective with regard to particular domains of activity. (For more on the significance of secularization for morality, see Wilson (1966) where he writes of its generation of 'moral *laissez faire*' (p. 64).)

In particular, the secularization model has been taken as referring to the shift in the location of decision making in human groups from elites claiming special access to supernatural ordinances to elites legitimating their authority by reference to other bases of power. Political authority is, however, only the most conspicuous arena in which this transfer from agencies representing the supernatural has occurred.

Perhaps more basic has been the transformation of work activities by the development of new economic techniques and procedures that are increasingly dictated by more and more rational application of scarce resources and which, in consequence, more regularly ignore or abrogate rules of sacrality. To contrast North American Indian attitudes to the soil and agriculture with those of white men, or medieval codes of moral economic behavior with those of subsequent times, illustrates the steady transcendence of rational methods. Consequent on changes such as these, the reward structures of society change in commensurate ways, with diminished rewards and status accorded to those who manipulate supernatural 'explanations' and legitimations, and increased rewards to those whose work is directed to materialistic, empirically validated productivity. Human ecology and population distribution, following changes in economic technique and (to some extent) political organization, have further secularizing implications. Religion had its basis in the local social group and in the solemnization and sacralization of interpersonal relationships. New methods of social organization and economic activity permitted, and at times necessitated, a new distribution of wealth and of people, as the surplus productivity of the countryside facilitated consumption in cities, the growth of tertiary industry, and perhaps now – with the growth of entertainment – one might say in quaternary industry.

The increasing awareness that rules were not absolute and heaven-sent but were amenable to changing need, and that even the most sacred norms of society could be renegotiated, altered, and perhaps even superseded, challenged assumptions about the will of higher beings in favour of the more conscious purposes of man himself. The shift, which might be most dramatically documented in the area of law, led to the steady modification of those absolute decrees and transcendent social norms in which individual well-being was always sacrificed to community cohesion. The steady accumulation of empirical knowledge, the increasing application of logic, and the rational coordination of human purposes established an alternative vision and interpretation of life. Steadily, the good of man displaced what was once seen as the 'will of providence' (or such other supernatural categories) and, in such areas as health, the dispositions of the supernatural were no longer regarded as adequate explanation for man's experience. Sanitation, diet, and experimental pharmacology displaced prayer, supplication, and resignation as the appropriate responses to disease and death. Man ceased to be solely at the disposition of the gods. Change in the character of knowledge implied change in the method of its transmission, and the consequent amendment of the institutions concerned with the socialization and education of the young. And, finally, the shifting awareness of man's potential – and thus his freedom – diminished the sense of the need for responsibility and, indeed, responsiveness toward superhuman agencies. Man acquired greater control of wide areas of his own experience; mankind attained a sense of self-determination, and employed new criteria of human happiness – the latter particularly in the use of leisure time.

All of the foregoing processes have been documented, in varying terms, by sociologists, whether they explicitly recognized them as aspects of secularization or not. Most conspicuously in Weber's documentation of the processes of rationalization, the political and economic changes are discussed, while Marx sets forth the economic causes of changes in social stratification. Toennies's analysis of basic transformations in social organization, following from changing distributive and ecological patterns of human population, has strong implications for man's conception of the sacred. Durkheim documented the difference between retributive and restitutive justice, even though he only gradually perceived the implications for the character of moral norms, and even though the consequential shift in the basis of social cohesion was more radical than he recognized. Comte had already indicated the methodology of the natural sciences as the model for a new methodology in interpreting society. Hobhouse, among others, saw the possibilities for the growth of self-determining societies, and Freud provided a mode of analysis which related man's irrational psychology to his supernaturalist pre-dispositions and which promised new conceptions of moral judgment and individual responsibility.

The shift from primary preoccupation with the superempirical to the empirical; from transcendent entities to naturalism; from other-worldly goals to this-worldly possibilities; from an orientation to the past as a determining power in life to increasing preoccupation with a planned and determined future; from speculative and 'revealed' knowledge to practical concerns, and from dogmas to falsifiable propositions; from the acceptance of the incidental, spasmodic, random, and charismatic manifestations of the divine to the systematic, structured, planned, and routinized management of the human – all of these are implicit in the model of secularization which, in various strands, constitute the inheritance not only of the sociology of religion but of sociology per se. [. . .]

An alternative way of formulating the implications of the secularizing process to the one already given is to indicate the loss of
functionality of religion, in the process of the structural differentiation
of society. There is no need here to set forth in these, somewhat
different, terms the points already made with respect to various social
institutions. All that need be said is that – whereas legitimate authority once depended on religious sanctions; whereas social control once
relied heavily on religiously defined rewards and punishments;
whereas social policies, conspicuously including warfare, at one time
needed supernatural endorsement, or at least the endorsement of
those who were recognized as the agents of the supernatural; and
whereas revealed faith once specified the boundaries of true learning
– now, all of these functions have been superseded. Authority is now
established by constitutions. Social control is increasingly a matter
for law rather than for a consensual moral code, and law becomes
increasingly technical and decreasingly moral (even theologians now
draw a sharp line between sin and crime), while effective sanctions
are physical and fiscal rather than threats or blandishments about the
afterlife. Social policies increasingly require the approval of an elect-
orate, which endorses a manifesto. Revelation is a distrusted source
of knowledge, and the methodology of modern learning puts a pre-
mium on doubt rather than on faith, on critical scepticism rather
than on unquestioning belief. The erstwhile functions of religion have
been superseded, and this constitutes a process of the secularization
of society. Religion has lost its presidency over other institutions.

Explanation: differentiation and the growth of
the secular state

3.15   de Tocqueville and equality

Alexis de Tocqueville, 1965 (orig. 1835, 1840): *Democracy in America*. London: Oxford
University Press (pp. 305–6).

Although Alexis de Tocqueville, the nineteenth-century commentator on American religion, clearly thought that religion remains important to the liberal-cum-
secular state, he equally clearly thought that powerful, ritualized, state-supported
religion is incompatible with democracy and its underlying values: freedom and
equality. Equality, in particular with regard to all being equally free, means that
'nothing is more repugnant to the human mind . . . than the idea of subjection
to [religious] forms'. If citizens are to be free and equal, no particular religion can
be allowed to set the political agenda. (See also reading **3.48** by de Tocqueville.)

Another truth is no less clear – that religions ought to assume fewer external observances in democratic periods than at any others. In speaking of philosophical method among the Americans, I have shown that nothing is more repugnant to the human mind in an age of equality than the idea of subjection to forms. Men living at such times are impatient of figures; to their eyes symbols appear to be the puerile artifice which is used to conceal or to set off truths, which should more naturally be bared to the light of open day: they are unmoved by ceremonial observances, and they are predisposed to attach a secondary importance to the details of public worship. Those whose care it is to regulate the external forms of religion in a democratic age should pay a close attention to these natural propensities of the human mind, in order not unnecessarily to run counter to them. I firmly believe in the necessity of forms, which fix the human mind in the contemplation of abstract truths, and stimulate its ardour in the pursuit of them, while they invigorate its powers of retaining them steadfastly. Nor do I suppose that it is possible to maintain a religion without external observances; but, on the other hand, I am persuaded that, in the ages upon which we are entering, it would be peculiarly dangerous to multiply them beyond measure; and that they ought rather to be limited to as much as is absolutely necessary to perpetuate the doctrine itself, which is the substance of religions of which the ritual is only the form. A religion which should become more minute, more peremptory, and more surcharged with small observances at a time in which men are becoming more equal, would soon find itself reduced to a band of fanatical zealots in the midst of an infidel people.

3.16 Casanova on the privatization of religion as constitutive of western modernity

José Casanova, 1994: *Public Religions in the Modern World*. Chicago and London: The University of Chicago Press (pp. 40; 55; 56).

In José Casanova's (1994) summary he comments, 'It is a central claim of this study . . . that established churches are incompatible with modern differentiated states and that the fusion of the religious and political community is incompatible with the modern principle of citizenship' (p. 213). As he also puts it, 'disestablishment and separation are necessary to guarantee the freedom of religion from the state, the freedom of the state from religion, and the freedom of the individual conscience from both state and religion' (p. 57). These points are further developed in the following extract, one especially interesting hypothesis

being that 'From religion itself came the sectarian demand for "religious freedom"'. Religious pluralism, that is to say, encourages the view that all religions
must be allowed the freedom to flourish rather than any particular one coming
to dominate public polity, curtailing the activities of others. However much the
religions of earlier modernity might have wanted to dominate, the logic of their
circumstances prompted withdrawal from what has become an increasingly
'neutral' public arena. (On the role of religion in the rise of democracy and the
modern state, see also the readings in the chapter entitled Political, **2.44** and
2.45. As the reading by Casanova in **2.29** makes clear, he does not believe that
the differentiation of religion implies its loss of public and political significance;
see also reading **3.80** in the chapter on Sacralization.)

The private/public distinction is crucial to all conceptions of the modern social order and religion itself is intrinsically connected with the
modern historical differentiation of private and public spheres. As
inaccurate as it may be as an empirical statement, to say that 'religion
is a private affair' is nonetheless constitutive of Western modernity in
a dual sense. First, it points to the fact that religious freedom, in the
sense of freedom of conscience, is chronologically 'the first freedom'
as well as the precondition of all modern freedoms. Insofar as freedom
of conscience is intrinsically related to 'the right to privacy' – to the
modern institutionalization of a private sphere free from governmental
intrusion as well as free from ecclesiastical control – and inasmuch as
'the right to privacy' serves as the very foundation of modern liberalism and of modern individualism, then indeed the privatization of
religion is essential to modernity.

There is yet another sense in which the privatization of religion is
intrinsically related to the emergence of the modern social order. To
say that in the modern world 'religion becomes private' refers also to
the very process of institutional differentiation which is constitutive
of modernity, namely, to the modern historical process whereby the
secular spheres emancipated themselves from ecclesiastical control as
well as from religious norms. Religion was progressively forced to
withdraw from the modern secular state and the modern capitalist
economy and to find refuge in the newly found private sphere. Like
modern science, capitalist markets and modern state bureaucracies
manage to function 'as if' God would not exist. This forms the un-
assailable core of modern theories of secularization, a core which
remains unaffected by the frequent assertions of critics who rightly
point out that most people in the modern world still, or yet again,
believe in God and that religions of all kinds, old and new, manage
to thrive in the modern world. [. . .]

Within the liberal political tradition the distinction between private and public religions has always been clearly drawn in terms of the constitutional separation of church and state. In accordance with the liberal tendency to limit the public sphere to the governmental public sector with all the rest lumped into a great 'private' sector, established state churches are designated as 'public' religions whereas all other religions are considered to be 'private.' Since the liberal conception tends to conflate and confuse state, public, and political, the disestablishment of religion is understood and prescribed as a simultaneous process of privatization and depoliticization. In the liberal conception religion is and ought to remain a private affair. The liberal fear of the politicization of religion is simultaneously the fear of an establishment which could endanger the individual freedom of conscience and the fear of a deprivatized ethical religion which could bring extraneous conceptions of justice, of the public interest, of the common good, and of solidarity into the 'neutral' deliberations of the liberal public sphere. [. . .]

The liberal rationale for disestablishment is as valid and unimpeachable today as it always has been. Historical pressures for the separation of church and state emerged from the dual dynamics of internal religious rationalization and the secular state's emancipation from religion. From religion itself came the sectarian demand for 'religious freedom.' As Georg Jellinek showed conclusively, the modern principle of inalienable human rights originated with the radical sects and was first institutionalized constitutionally in the Bills of Rights of the various American states. Without this religious sectarian input one may reach the principle of religious 'toleration,' but not necessarily the principle of religious 'freedom.' Indeed, before becoming the enlightened liberal principle of 'freedom of thought,' the pressure for toleration more often than not found its historical source in *raison d'état*, in the modern state's exigency to emancipate itself from religion.

Explanation: pluralization

3.17 Berger: 'certainty is hard to come by'

Peter Berger, 1980: *The Heretical Imperative. Contemporary Possibilities of Religious Affirmation.* London: Collins (pp. 17–19).

In Durkheimian fashion, Peter Berger argues that when people are embedded in a particular form of life, 'social confirmation' sustains plausibility. However, people of the pluralized (or differentiated) world of modernity have to live with and choose between many different forms of belief or ways of life. Consequently, no one way of living receives strong 'social confirmation'. Although Berger does not develop the point here, it may also be argued that pluralism encourages questioning and suspicion: with all these options, how do I know which is right? (See also Berger et al., 1974, pp. 75–7 on the secularizing effect of pluralization with regard to individual consciousness; Berger also makes a similiar point in reading **1.24**.)

Modernity pluralizes both institutions and plausibility structures. The last phrase represents a central concept for an understanding of the relationship between society and consciousness. For the present purpose, its import can be stated quite simply. With the possible exception of a few areas of direct personal experience, human beings require social confirmation for their beliefs about reality. Thus the individual probably does not require others to convince him that he has a toothache, but he does require such social support for the whole range of his moral beliefs. Put differently, physical pain imposes its own plausibility without any social mediations, while morality requires particular social circumstances in order to become and remain plausible to the individual. It is precisely these social circumstances that constitute the plausibility structure for the morality at issue. For example, moral values of honor, courage, and loyalty are commonly characteristic of military institutions. As long as an individual is within such an institutional context, it is very likely that these values will be plausible to him in an unquestioned and taken-for-granted manner. If, however, this individual should find himself transposed into a quite different institutional context (say, there is no more need for many soldiers in his particular society, and he is forced by economic necessity to take up a civilian occupation), then it is very likely that he will begin to question the military values. Such a loss of plausibility is also the result of social processes – indeed, of the same kind of social processes that previously established and maintained the plausibility of the martial virtues. In the earlier situation other human beings provided social support for one set of moral values, as in the later situation social support is given to different moral values. Biographically, the individual may be seen as having migrated from one plausibility structure to another.

It follows from this that there is a direct relation between the cohesion of institutions and the subjective cohesiveness of beliefs, values, and worldviews. In a social situation in which everyone with whom the individual has significant ties is a soldier, it is not surprising that the soldier's view of the world, with all that this implies, will be massively plausible. Conversely, it is very difficult to be a soldier in a social situation where this makes little or no sense to everyone else. It may be added that this relation between social context and consciousness is not absolute. There are always exceptions – deviants or mavericks, individuals who maintain a view of the world and of themselves even in the absence of social support. These exceptions are always interesting, but they do not falsify the sociological generalization that human beliefs and values depend upon specific plausibility structures. In other words, this generalization is probabilistic – but the probability is very high indeed.

It further follows that the institutional pluralization of modernity had to carry in its wake a fragmentation and *ipso facto* a weakening of every conceivable belief and value dependent upon social support. The typical situation in which the individual finds himself in a traditional society is one where there are highly reliable plausibility structures. Conversely, modern societies are characterized by unstable, incohesive, unreliable plausibility structures. Put differently, in the modern situation certainty is hard to come by. It cannot be stressed enough that this fact is rooted in pretheoretical experience – that is, in ordinary, everyday social life. This experience is common to the proverbial man in the street and to the intellectual who spins out elaborate theories about the universe. The built-in uncertainty is common to both as well. This basic sociological insight is crucial for an understanding of the competition between worldviews and the resultant crisis of belief that has been characteristic of modernity.

The modern individual, then, lives in a world of choice, in sharp contrast with the world of fate inhabited by traditional man. He must choose in innumerable situations of everyday life.

3.18 Martin: 'the breaking of bonds in general'

David Martin, 1978: *A General Theory of Secularization*. Oxford: Basil Blackwell (pp. 87–8).

Also in Durkheimian fashion, David Martin sees religion being undermined by the collapse of sustaining communities. Religions which have to do 'with social and personal identity and their coherent relation to a whole' find it difficult to speak to those whose lives have become fragmented, atomized, depersonalized.

This is the point at which to emphasize and analyse the most specific consequence of the second industrial revolution [of which the typical instance might be the advent of electronic media]: the breaking of bonds in general. The institutions congruent with modern industry, with bureaucracy and technical rationality, are large, impersonal, and mechanical in their operation. The intimate bonds of horizontal community, working class of otherwise, are broken up; the ecology of the city encourages fragmentation; the small shop gives way to the supermarket; the family firm enters the international consortium; the small farm is rationalized into larger units run by scientific agriculture; the moderate-sized office is swallowed up in large-scale bureaucracy; the community of school is wrecked by education factories operated by mobile teachers. And overall the urban style associated with these developments englobes a yet larger proportion of the population.

Characteristically the horizontal bonds remain only in the form of interest groupings, united by instrumental rather than intrinsic motives. Trade unions cease to operate on the basis of local cohesion and participation but purely as vehicles of sectional advantage. They are built into the impersonal grid of the corporate state. The old rhetoric of community, equality and solidarity simply serves as the convenient cover under which such sectional advantages can be pressed. Leaders may be followed not because they are ideologically representative but because leaders with a particular form of intransigent secular ideology can more easily deliver the goods. The interdependent character of modern society makes it increasingly easy to press such demands, particularly in certain key industries, and a secular metaphysic of a Marxist kind then becomes the most useful way in which those in such industries can extract the maximum from the wider society.

Where cities are mere agglomerations of fragmented groupings and where atomization has become the most prevalent social mode even social control has to shift from intrinsic symbols to an appeal based on interest. Each private individual constructs an interested calculus that makes social loyalty simply dependent on how that calculus works out. Thus the religious symbols of community and the notion of an intrinsic morality (which is rooted in religion though not exclusively religious) are both downgraded. There is little consciousness of kind governing the reciprocities of neighbourliness and solidarity at the local level, and civic religion operates less powerfully at the national level. At the expanding centres of modern societies the symbols of national belonging, and the religious symbols partly encapsulated within them, have diminished resonance. At the same time the impersonal nature of the social process and the mechanical character of production jointly make a personal image of the cosmos less easy to attain. Moreover people are constantly thrown from one depersonalized sphere to another: office block to tower block, vast school to large factory, and so cannot easily acquire a coherent approach to living. Hence the world is as incoherent as it is depersonalized. Since religion has to do with social and personal identity and with their coherent relation to a whole it finds its resonance much restricted. Indeed, even quasi-mechanistic but rather individualistic cults like astrology can seem more congruent and relevant than traditional religion, and in any case they fit in with the residual superstition that informs 'religion-in-general'.

Explanation: the turn to consumerized experience

3.19 Byron's 'Sensation'

Byron, 1974: *Byron's Letters and Journals*, ed. Leslie A. Marchand. Cambridge: Harvard University Press, Belknap, vol. 3 (p. 109).

Given the argument that religion has been marginalized with regard to public life, what is left of privatized religion? Consideration is now paid to the role played by capitalistic consumer culture, the argument being that religion, especially spiritualities of life with their ability to provide intense experiences, has come to be treated as a mere consumer resource. To set the scene, Byron provides an excellent summation of what distinguishes a central feature of constemption: imbibing 'Sensation', the experience of existence. Interestingly, given that Byron was a Romantic, Campbell (1987) argues that Romanticism, 'a castle of Romantic dreams' (p. 227), played a key role in the construction of that consumer culture which is now arguably engulfing on religion.

The great object of life is Sensation – to feel that we exist – even though in pain – it is this 'craving void' which drives us to Gaming – to Battle – to Travel – to intemperate but keenly felt pursuits of every description whose principal attraction is the agitation inseparable from their accomplishment.

3.20   Lasch and 'orgiastic, ecstatic religiosity'

Christopher Lasch, 1980: *The Culture of Narcissism. American Life in an Age of Diminishing Expectations*. London: Abacus (pp. 4–5).

According to Christopher Lasch, 'People nowadays complain of an inability to feel. They cultivate more vivid experiences, seek to beat sluggish flesh to life, attempt to revive jaded appetites' (p. 11). The argument in the extract which follows is that the sixties played a role in encouraging people to turn to spiritualities of life (and cognates) simply to satisfy the desire to 'live for the moment in the prevailing passion'. (See also MacIntyre (1985) on 'emotivist' culture; Bell's (1976) claim that 'experience in and of itself' has become 'the supreme value' (p. 19); see also Baudrillard, 1988, pp. 12–13.)

After the political turmoil of the sixties, Americans have retreated to purely personal preoccupations. Having no hope of improving their lives in any of the ways that matter, people have convinced themselves that what matters is psychic self-improvement: getting in touch with their feelings, eating health food, taking lessons in ballet or belly-dancing, immersing themselves in the wisdom of the East, jogging, learning how to 'relate,' overcoming the 'fear of pleasure.' Harmless in themselves, these pursuits, elevated to a program and wrapped in the rhetoric of authenticity and awareness, signify a retreat from politics and a repudiation of the recent past. Indeed Americans seem to wish to forget not only the sixties, the riots, the new left, the disruptions on college campuses, Vietnam, Watergate, and the Nixon presidency, but their entire collective past, even in the antiseptic form in which it was celebrated during the Bicentennial. Woody Allen's movie *Sleeper*, issued in 1973, accurately caught the mood of the seventies. Appropriately cast in the form of a parody of futuristic science fiction, the film finds a great many ways to convey the message that 'political solutions don't work,' as Allen flatly announces at one point. When asked what he believes in, Allen, having ruled out politics, religion, and science, declares: 'I believe in sex and death – two experiences that come once in a lifetime'.

To live for the moment is the prevailing passion – to live for your-self, not for your predecessors or posterity. We are fast losing the sense of historical continuity, the sense of belonging to a succession of generations originating in the past and stretching into the future. It is the waning of the sense of historical time – in particular, the erosion of any strong concern for posterity – that distinguishes the spiritual crisis of the seventies from earlier outbreaks of millenarian religion, to which it bears a superficial resemblance. Many commentators have seized on this resemblance as a means of understanding the contemporary 'cultural revolution,' ignoring the features that distinguish it from the religions of the past. A few years ago, Leslie Fiedler proclaimed a 'New Age of Faith.' More recently, Tom Wolfe has interpreted the new narcissism as a 'third great awakening,' an outbreak of orgiastic, ecstatic religiosity. Jim Hougan, in a book that seems to present itself simultaneously as a critique and a celebration of contemporary decadence, compares the current mood to the millennialism of the waning Middle Ages. 'The anxieties of the Middle Ages are not much different from those of the present,' he writes. Then as now, social upheaval gave rise to 'millenarian sects.'

3.21 Wilson and 'pushpin, poetry, or popcorn'

Bryan Wilson, 1979: *Contemporary Transformations of Religion*. Oxford: Clarendon Press (p. 96).

Bryan Wilson, discussing the relatively recent development of new 'cults' and the claim that they count against the secularization thesis, dismisses them as merely a symptom of the consumeristic (certainly pushpin and popcorn, although poetry is more debatable). Such privatized religion, it appears, is for mere gratification, and is only religion by name.

> The scope, scale, and pervasiveness of secularization make it the more serious challenge to traditional religion, but there are sociologists who profess to see in the growth of new cults important evidence that controverts the hypothesis that has become known as 'the secularization thesis'. For them, the new cults represent religious revival. In contrast, I regard them as a confirmation of the process of secularization. They indicate the extent to which religion has become inconsequential for modern society. The cults represent, in the American phrase, 'the religion of your choice', the highly privatized preference that reduces religion to the significance of pushpin, poetry, or popcorns. They have no real consequence for other social institutions, for political power structures, for technological constraints and controls. They add nothing to any prospective reintegration of society, and contribute nothing towards the culture by which a society might live.

3.22   Bauman's 'perfect consumers'

Zygmunt Bauman, 1998: Postmodern Religion? In Paul Heelas (ed.) with the assistance of David Martin and Paul Morris, *Religion, Modernity and Postmodernity*. Oxford and Malden, Mass.: Blackwell (pp. 70–2).

Claiming that 'Postmodern men and women do need the alchemist able, or claiming to be able, to transmogrify base uncertainty into precious self-assurance' (p. 68), the argument in this extract even more explicitly states that various forms of (putative) religiosity – in particular those which can be thought of as spiritualities of life – are in fact reducible to the merely sensational or experiential. (Compare the spiritual role accorded to experience in the following chapter, Detraditionalization.)

[Can one] legitimately recognize the orgasmic experience of the postmodern sensation-gatherers as essentially religious?

I propose that the postmodern cultural pressures, while intensifying the search for 'peak-experiences', have at the same time uncoupled the search from religion-prone interests and concerns, privatized it, and cast mainly non-religious institutions in the role of purveyors of relevant services. The 'whole experience' of revelation, ecstasy, breaking the boundaries of the self and total transcendence – once the privilege of the selected 'aristocracy of culture' (saints, hermits, mystics, ascetic monks, *tsadiks* or *dervishes*) and coming either as an unsolicited miracle, in no obvious fashion related to what the receiver of grace has done to earn it, or as an act of grace rewarding the life of self-immolation and denial – has been put by postmodern culture within every individual's reach, recast as a realistic target and plausible prospect of each individual's self-training, and relocated as the product of a life devoted to the art of consumer self-indulgence. What distinguishes the postmodern strategy of peak-experience from one promoted by religions, is that far from celebrating the assumed human insufficiency and weakness, it appeals to the full development of human inner psychological and bodily resources and presumes infinite human potency. Paraphrasing Weber, one may call the postmodern, lay version of peak-experience the realm of 'this worldly ecstasy'. [. . .]

It goes without saying that any similarity between such [self-improvement] movements and religious churches or sects is purely superficial, reduced at best to their organizational patterns. Rather than sharing their character with religious institutions, they are products and integral parts of the 'counselling boom' – though they are not, like other branches of counselling, meant to serve directly the consumer choices of assumedly fully-fledged consumers, but are aimed rather at the training of *'perfect consumers'*; at developing to the full the capacities which the experience-seeking and sensation-gathering life of the consumer/chooser demands.

CHAPTER TEN

detraditionalization

Introduction

As Robert Bellah (1991) notes, 'one aspect of the great modern transformation [of religion] involves *the internalization of authority* . . . and this
has profound consequences for religion' (p. 223). The key to the process
of detraditionalization lies precisely with this internalization of authority, from 'without to within'. The change is from an authoritative realm
which exists over and above the individual or whatever the individual
might aspire to be, to the authority of the first hand spiritually-informed
experience of the self.

What can be thought of as *strongly traditionalized* religion involves faith
in knowledge and wisdom taken to be transmitted from the transcendent and authoritative past. The past informs the present and the future,
indicating what has to be done to achieve the perfect society or salvation.
As Theodore Bozeman (1988) writes of that Puritanism which existed
towards the beginning of modern times in the West: 'To move forward
was to strive without rest for reconnection with the paradigmatic events
and utterances of ancient and unspoiled times' (p. 11). Providing the
pathway to salvation, the traditional and the transcendent are necessarily
seen as being superior to life as it currently is. Strongly traditionalized
religion thus sees the self (to varying degrees) in negative light – as
fallen, as in need of salvation.

Rejecting what the past has to say and all that is merely 'external',
strongly detraditionalized religion turns elsewhere for authority. Faith is
placed in a knowledge and wisdom obtainable by each individual in the
here-and-now, without the benefit of some 'higher' – as self transcendent
– authority. Truth is found in direct experience rather than 'second-hand'
reception. The divine is found within the individual or the natural order,
and provides the basis for life. Only thus can one be liberated from the
anti-spiritual (capitalistic, consumeristic) tendencies of the modern world.

For detraditionalized religion, whatever is transmitted from without (whether that be religious traditions, beliefs, even gurus) is only to heeded if it has been tested by way of one's own, spiritually informed, experience. What Steven Tipton (reading **1.2**) calls the 'expressive ethic' replaces the 'authoritative' ethic of tradition. The fact that the authority ascribed to one's own 'true' experience is so great is bound up with the fact that the 'Self' itself is sacred. In contrast to strongly traditionalized religion, where the self is (relatively) devalued, the Self here becomes God, Goddess, divine.

Whilst strongly traditionalized religion is characterized by institutional forms, beliefs and rituals, the strongly detraditionalized by contrast looks very 'empty'. It is not simply that such religiosities do not contain the doctrines, dogmas, ethical commandments and narratives associated with tradition. They also lack the institutional arrangements of the traditionalized. The church, chapel or mosque, which serve to organize peoples' worship from 'without', are replaced by more informal or ad hoc encounters. Authoritative religious leaders are replaced by non-directive facilitators. Rather than belonging to particular religious organizations and following prescribed forms of worship, the authority which lies within leaves one free to choose which rituals or myths to follow in order to make contact with the spiritual realm. Whilst strongly detraditionalized religion *can* operate within church, chapel or mosque (participants experiencing what is on offer in these contexts in terms of the test of their inner spirituality), it is therefore much more commonly found in the realm of the (relatively) de-institutionalized: the workshop; the healing session; the training or event; or, in the sixties, the 'happening'.

Another point of contrast between strongly traditionalized and detraditionalized religion is that the former is bound up with the belief that religious traditions are far from equal. Any particular tradition, that is to say, will assume that it, and it alone, provides the best path to the truth. Other traditions are judged accordingly. By definition, however, strongly detraditionalized religion rejects the differences (and associated evaluations) made by the traditionalized order. It assumes that there is one interconnected or interfusing spirituality running through all religions as well as the self and the natural order as a whole.

In order to understand detraditionalized religion it is necessary to think in terms of interlocking forces and transformations. These include: a wider cultural turn from transcendence to immanence; from an external locus of authority to an internal one; from fate to choice; from ethical principles to ethical experiences; from test by way of text to test by way of experience; from negative evaluations of human nature to positive; from living in terms of what the established religious order announces (or imposes) to living out one's own spirituality; from differentiated religion to de-differentiated; from happiness by way of sacrifice to happiness by way of realization; from salvation by following tradition to enlightenment through self-chosen rituals (including those informed by technology (**1.69**; **1.70**)); and, very importantly, from looking to the future in terms of the past to experiencing 'life' itself in the here-and-now.

As should be apparent to the reader who has already dipped into this volume, strongly traditionalized religion is best exemplified by religions of difference (see chapter two in **Part One**). It should also be apparent, given that they break with a transcendent frame of reference, that the strongly detraditionalized (if not post-traditional) is best exemplified by spiritualities of life (see chapter four in **Part One**). Detraditionalization, however, also takes place *within* traditions, traditions being detraditionalized or traditionalized to varying *degrees*. Thus religions of humanity tend to be quite strongly detraditionalized (see chapter three in **Part One**). Likewise, experiential religions of difference seem to be characterized by the coexistence of the traditionalized and the detraditionalized, tradition being rejected insofar as authority is provided by immediate experience of the Holy Spirit, but retained insofar as institutional structure, scriptural authority, strong leadership and clear moral prescription remain. (See chapter five, Combinations in **Part One**.)

In this chapter we isolate five main varieties of detraditionalization. First, the 'weakening' of tradition, as in religions of humanity. Second, the sacralization of the self, as in spiritualities of life. Third, the 'individualization of religion', namely the shift from commitment to particular religions to the exercise of one's own authority in constructing personal spiritualities. (Although individualized religion can involve traditionalized components, as when individuals decide to be guided by both the Bible and the Koran, individualized religion is more typically associated with detraditionalized spiritualities of life which cater for the self and reject the formally institutionalized.) Fourth, there is the consumerization and instrumentalization of religion, consumerization involving detraditionalization (or secularization?) insofar as religion serves largely (entirely?) to satisfy and pleasure the self, instrumentalization involving the reduction of religion to serve largely (entirely?) as a means to the end of obtaining prosperity. And fifth, there is the universalization of religion, in which the traditions and externals which serve to differentiate religions are discarded in favour of what they hold in common.

These five different varieties (or processes) of detraditionalization can be explained in different ways. The first involves such factors as the development of the ethic of humanity and the application of critical reason to 'traditional' truths formerly held sacred. (These explanations are not explored in detail in this chapter, since they are covered elsewhere in the volume: see in particular chapter three, Religions of Humanity, in **Part One**, and chapter eleven, on Universalization.) Regarding the second variety of detraditionalization, that involving the development of spiritualities of life, the key explanatory factor here seems to be the wider cultural 'turn to the self' characteristic of modernity. Whether because people have been 'thrown back' on themselves and so have to seek 'meaning' from within, or because of the cultural elevation of the self as a source of value, the argument here is that the turn to the self can lead to self-sacralization. In this case, detraditionalization leads not to secularization and atheism: precisely because people are 'thrown' back on themselves, religiosity is (sometimes) regenerated. (As well as being explored in the readings which follow, this argument is also explored in chapter four in **Part One** on Spiritualities of Life; for more on the self-limiting thesis, see Sacralization in **Part Three**.)

The third type of detraditionalization, involving the individualization of religion, critically involves the development in modern times of what might be called 'the culture of choice'. Not only because of the turn to the self, but also because of the development of consumer culture, people come to believe that they have the right to choose and devise their own 'religions'. (As well as being explored in readings below, this line of argument is also found in readings in Sacralization.) As for the fourth kind of detraditionalization, involving the consumerization and instrumentalization of religion, here too the turn to the self and consumer culture can be seen to play an important role. The self in its 'utilitarian' rather than 'expressive' guise (Tipton, **1.2**) – that is, the self intent on gratifying itself in terms of what is offered by capitalistic modernity – detraditionalizes (or secularizes?) by accommodating religion to its own desires. (For reasons given in a moment, this process is not discussed in this chapter.) Finally, the fifth type of detraditionalization, involving the universalization of religion, can be explained by reference to such factors as pluralization. Thus one response to the potentially divisive pluralism characteristic of modern times is to move beyond differences to find what is held in common. (This process of universalization is discussed at the end of the current chapter; it is more comprehensively covered in chapter eleven.)

What is the relationship between detraditionalization and secularization? The two are *not* the same. Secularization necessarily involves the disappearance of religion (from public or private life, or both), or a loss of its significance (for public or private life, or both). In contrast, detraditionalization has a very different end point. It has to do with the transformation not the disappearance of religion, and leads (ultimately) not to atheism but to (the rise of) spiritualities of life. And whilst it might be true that detraditionalization will sometimes involve the de-intensification of religion and the spread of a precarious, privatized religiosity (see, for example, reading **3.28**), this *need* not be the case: there are plenty of publically and politically potent spiritualities of life around, both in the West and in India (amongst other places) – see for example readings **2.54** and **3.31**.

These points notwithstanding, there are significant overlaps and interplays between secularization and detraditionalization. Thus they both involve the disappearance of religion (although in the case of the latter only of certain – that is traditionalized – forms of belief and practice); and accordingly they both can involve similar (if not identical) processes, such as the application of reason to reject traditional beliefs, and the impact of pluralism. It can also be noted that the turn to the self – the crucial factor in fueling detraditionalization – is also bound up with secularization, the latter involving the erosion of traditions with their frames for the past and the future, and thus throwing the self back on itself (see reading 72 as well as below). Furthermore, the turn to the self may also contribute to secularization, the exercise of the authority of reason, for example, playing a role here (see readings **3.9–3.11** in Secularization). And although it cannot be explored here the argument that the Protestant Reformation contributed to secularization can also be noted (see Troeltsch in reading **1.46**). The relevant point in this regard is that the Reformation involved detraditionalization through a shift to individual authority and experience, thus contributing to the weakening of religion in the face of secularizing forces. (For more on this argument, see Casanova, 1994, pp. 21–2.) Here detraditionalization and secularization work hand-in-hand.

Should the consumerization and instrumentalization of religion be treated as involving detraditionalization or secularization? Although this is an ill-explored topic, our hunch is that both may be involved. Bearing in mind that we are defining detraditionalization as change *within* religion, consumerization and instrumentalization do not involve detraditionalization so long as 'religion' remains in evidence. When traditional Christianity is tailored to suit consumers, for example, it might lose aspects of tradition but it clearly remains 'religious'. (See the reading by Miller, **3.87**, **3.97**, and that by Hatch, **3.49**.) However, when 'religion' is merely treated as a means of pleasuring or empowering the self and is fully accommodated to the desires of the person, consumerization and instrumentalization do seem to lead to secularization. For present purposes, given that this is an ill-researched topic, we do not go into this here. (See, though, readings **3.20–3.22** in Secularization, and readings on magical empowerment in Economic, pp. 187–92.)

It would seem apparent, given what follows, that an increasing number of people seek freedom from tradition; do not want to be bound by the past; and wish religion to enhance life now. Given this, detraditionalization would indeed appear to be a significant trend within religions of modern times. And given the fact that detraditionalization crucially involves the authorization of the Self, the importance of the 'turn to the self' cannot be over-emphasized. One cannot have religions of humanity without faith in *human reason*; one cannot have spiritualities of life without faith in *human experience* or without enough faith in what it is to be human to *sacralize humanity*. It should be emphasized, however, that we do not for one moment think that detraditionalization is an across-the-board process. We do not agree with those – such as Giddens (1991, p. 106) – who see modernity as a whole having become 'post-traditional'. Modernity involves tradition-maintenance, tradition-invention, and retraditionalization, as well as detraditionalization. As such, the latter coexists with these other processes in the realm of religion. (See Heelas et al. (eds) 1996.)

Detraditionalization: overviews

3.23   Troeltsch: on the value of 'this present life'

Ernst Troeltsch, 1912: *Protestantism and Progress*. London: Crown Theological Library (pp. 22–3).

As well as summarizing key aspects of the process of detraditionalization, this short reading from Ernst Troeltsch serves to make the point that the removal of the frame provided by tradition – linking the present with both the past and the future – goes together with ever-increased attention to what the present has to offer.

If the absolute authority has fallen which, in its absoluteness, made the antithesis of the divine and human equally absolute, if in man an autonomous principle is recognized as the source of truth and moral conduct, then all conceptions of the world which were especially designed to maintain that gulf between the human and the divine, fall along with it. With it falls the doctrine of the absolute corruption of mankind through original sin, and the transference of the ends of life to the heavenly world in which there will be deliverance from this corruption. In consequence, all the factors of this present life acquire an enhanced value and a higher impressiveness, and the ends of life fall more and more within the realm of the present world with its ideal of transformation.

3.24 Simmel: 'this wholly formless mysticism'

Georg Simmel, 1976 (orig. 1917): The Crisis of Culture. In P. A. Lawrence, *Georg Simmel: Sociologist and European*. Middlesex: Nelson, pp. 253–66 (pp. 258–9).

Writing at the beginning of this century, Georg Simmel sees 'large social groups' turning away from organized religion, namely Christianity, to adopt 'all sorts of exotic, far-fetched and bizzare new doctrines'. The authority of individual choice is very much in evidence, many adopting a strongly detraditionalized 'religion of the soul'.

We all know the great polarization that has split the religious life of our times, affecting everyone except Christians of convenience and people with absolutely no religious sense at all: the split between Christianity and a religion which repudiates any historical content, whether it be undogmatic monotheism, or pantheism, or a purely inward spiritual condition not entailing any specific beliefs. The age, with its universal religious tolerance, exerted no pressures on men to choose. [. . .]

  In the religious sphere, . . . real Christians, in obedience to some intellectual quirk, adopt an undogmatic pantheistic stance, while decided unbelievers talk themselves into a kind of Christianity by 'symbolically' adapting basic Christian teachings. Any person of some maturity will presumably have long since made his decision – except that because of the peculiar cultural broadmindedness which our situation seemed to permit, or even demand, that decision was often intermingled with, or concealed by, its opposite. This is, however, no longer possible in a period of radical eruption of man's religious depths. No matter how far either attitude is visible to the outside world: within men's souls, what is ripe for supremacy will come into its own.

In our present context the essential fact is the existence of large social groups who, in pursuit of their religious needs, are turning away from Christianity. The fact that they are turning to all sorts of exotic, far-fetched and bizarre new doctrines appears to be of no importance whatsoever. Nowhere among them, except in isolated individual cases, can I discern any genuinely viable belief providing an adequate and precise expression of the religious life. On the other hand, the widespread rejection of any fixed form of religious life is in keeping with our general cultural situation. Thus supra-denominational mysticism has by far the strongest appeal to these groups. For the religious soul hopes to find here direct spontaneous fulfilment, whether in standing naked and alone, as it were, before its God, without the mediation of dogma in any shape or form, or in rejecting the very idea of God as a petrefaction and an obstacle, and in feeling that the true religion of the soul can only be its own inmost metaphysical life not moulded by any forms of faith whatever. Like the manifestations of futurism touched on above, this wholly formless mysticism marks the historical moment when inner life can no longer be accommodated in the forms it has occupied hitherto, and because it is unable to create other, adequate forms, concludes that it must exist without any form at all.

3.25 Bellah: '. . . without imposing . . . a prefabricated set of answers'

Robert N. Bellah, 1964: Religious Evolution. *American Sociological Review* 29: 358–74 (pp. 372–4).

What Robert Bellah calls 'modern religion' is that which 'is beginning to understand the laws of the self's own existence and so help man take responsibility for his own fate'. In the language we are using in this volume, Bellah is primarily talking about religions of humanity, although there are distinct signs of spiritualities of life coming into evidence. Bellah is talking about (relatively) detraditionalized religiosity, one encouraging 'each individual [to] work out his own ultimate solutions', and one which increasingly involves people moving beyond the church (as Paine says, 'My mind is my church').

Behind the 96 per cent of Americans who claim to believe in God there are many instances of a massive reinterpretation that leaves Tillich, Bultmann and Bonhoeffer far behind. In fact, for many churchgoers the obligation of doctrinal orthodoxy sits lightly indeed, and the idea that all creedal statements must receive a personal reinterpretation is widely accepted. The dualistic world view certainly persists in the minds of many of the devout, but just as surely many others have developed elaborate and often psuedo-scientific rationalizations to bring their faith in its experienced validity into some kind of cognitive harmony with the 20th century world. The wave of popular response that some of the newer theology seems to be eliciting is another indication that not only the intellectuals find themselves in a new religious situation.

To concentrate on the church in a discussion of the modern religious situation is already misleading, for it is precisely the characteristic of the new situation that the great problem of religion as I have defined it, the symbolization of man's relation to the ultimate conditions of his existence, is no longer the monopoly of any groups explicitly labeled religious. However much the development of Western Christianity may have led up to and in a sense created the modern religious situation, it just as obviously is no longer in control of it. Not only has any obligation of doctrinal orthodoxy been abandoned by the leading edge of modern culture, but every fixed position has become open to question in the process of making sense out of man and his situation. This involves a profounder commitment to the process I have been calling religious symbolization than ever before. The historic religions discovered the self; the early modern religion found a doctrinal basis on which to accept the self in all its empirical ambiguity; modern religion is beginning to understand the laws of the self's own existence and so to help man take responsibility for his own fate.

This statement is not intended to imply a simple liberal optimism, for the modern analysis of man has also disclosed the depths of the limitations imposed by man's situation. Nevertheless, the fundamental symbolization of modern man and his situation is that of a dynamic multi-dimensional self capable, within limits, of continual self-transformation and capable, again within limits, of remaking the world including the very symbolic forms with which he deals with it, even the forms that state the unalterable conditions of his own existence. Such a statement should not be taken to mean that I expect, even less that I advocate, some ghastly religion of social science. Rather I expect traditional religious symbolism to be maintained and developed in new directions, but with growing awareness that it is symbolism and that man in the last analysis is responsible for the choice of his symbolism. Naturally, continuation of the symbolization characteristic of earlier stages without any reinterpretation is to be expected among many in the modern world, just as it has occurred in every previous period.

Religious action in the modern period is, I think, clearly a continuation of tendencies already evident in the early modern stage. Now less than ever can man's search for meaning be confined to the church. But with the collapse of a clearly defined doctrinal orthodoxy and a religiously supported objective system of moral standards, religious action in the world becomes more demanding than ever. The search for adequate standards of action, which is at the same time a search for personal maturity and social relevance, is in itself the heart of the modern quest for salvation, if I may divest that word of its dualistic associations. How the specifically religious bodies are to adjust their time honored practices of worship and devotion to modern conditions is of growing concern in religious circles. Such diverse movements as the liturgical revival, pastoral psychology and renewed emphasis on social action are all efforts to meet the present need. Few of these trends have gotten much beyond the experimental but we can expect the experiments to continue.

In the modern situation as I have defined it, one might almost be tempted to see in Thomas Paine's 'My mind is my church,' or Thomas Jefferson's 'I am a sect myself' the typical expression of *religious, organization* in the near future. Nonetheless it seems unlikely that collective symbolization of the great inescapabilities of life will soon disappear. Of course the 'free intellectual' will continue to exist as he has for millenia but such a solution can hardly be very general. Private voluntary religious association in the West achieved full legitimation for the first time in the early modern situation, but in the early stages especially, discipline and control within these groups was very intense. The tendency in more recent periods has been to continue the basic pattern but with a much more open and flexible pattern of membership. In accord with general trends I have already discussed, standards of doctrinal orthodoxy and attempts to enforce moral purity have largely been dropped. The assumption in most of the major Protestant denominations is that the church member can be considered responsible for himself. This trend seems likely to continue, with an increasingly fluid type of organization in which many special purpose sub-groups form and disband. Rather than interpreting these trends as significant of indifference and secularization, I see in them the increasing acceptance of the notion that each individual must work out his own ultimate solutions and that the most the church can do is provide him a favorable environment for doing so, without imposing on him a prefabricated set of answers. And it will be increasingly realized that answers to religious questions can validly be sought in various spheres of 'secular' art and thought.

Here I can only suggest what I take to be the main *social implication* of the modern religious situation. Early modern society, to a considerable degree under religious pressure, developed . . . the notion of a self-revising social system in the form of a democratic society. But at least in the early phase of that development social flexibility was balanced against doctrinal (Protestant orthodoxy) and characterological (Puritan personality) rigidities. In a sense those rigidities were necessary to allow the flexibility to emerge in the social system, but it is the chief characteristic of the more recent modern phase that culture and personality themselves have come to be viewed as endlessly revisable. This has been characterized as a collapse of meaning and a failure of moral standards. No doubt the possibilities for pathological distortion in the modern situation are enormous. It remains to be seen whether the freedom modern society implies at the cultural and personality as well as the social level can be stably institutionalized in large-scale societies. Yet the vary situation that has been characterized as one of the collapse of meaning and the failure of moral standards can also, and I would argue more fruitfully, be viewed as one offering unprecedented opportunities for creative innovation in every sphere of human action.

The schematic presentation of the stages of religious evolution just concluded is based on the proposition that at each stage the freedom of personality and society has increased relative to the environing conditions. Freedom has increased because at each successive stage the relation of man to the conditions of his existence has been conceived as more complex, more open and more subject to change and development.

3.26   Bellah et al.: 'Sheilaism'

Robert N. Bellah, Richard Madsen, William M. Sullivan, Ann Swidler and Steven M. Tipton, 1985: *Habits of the Heart. Individualism and Commitment in American Life.* Berkeley, Los Angeles and London: University of California Press (pp. 220–1; 235).

In a widely cited passage, the authors of *Habits of the Heart* provide a classic description – broadly in the camp of spiritualities of life – of what the deistic/

rationalistic Paine (in the preceding extract) describes as his 'church'. Sheila really seems to be de-institutionalized! It can be added, though, that it is highly unlikely that there will ever be anything approaching '200 million American religions'. For in reality, people like Sheila are institutionalized in that they share much the same spiritual culture or 'church' (sustained by books, films, like-minded friends and so on). Accordingly, there is much in common between 'different' Sheilaisms.

> One person we interviewed has actually named her religion (she calls it her 'faith') after herself. This suggests the logical possibility of over 220 million American religions, one for each of us. Sheila Larson is a young nurse who has received a good deal of therapy and who describes her faith as 'Sheilaism.' 'I believe in God. I'm not a religious fanatic. I can't remember the last time I went to church. My faith has carried me a long way. It's Sheilaism. Just my own little voice.' Sheila's faith has some tenets beyond belief in God, though not many. In defining 'my own Sheilaism,' she said: 'It's just try to love yourself and be gentle with yourself. You know, I guess, take care of each other. I think He would want us to take care of each other.' Like many others, Sheila would be willing to endorse few more specific injunctions. [. . .]
>
> Radically individualistic religion, particularly when it takes the form of a belief in cosmic selfhood, may seem to be in a different world from conservative or fundamentalist religion. Yet these are the two poles that organize much of American religious life. To the first, God is simply the self magnified; to the second, God confronts man from outside the universe. One seeks a self that is finally identical with the world; the other seeks an external God who will provide order in the world. Both value personal religious experience as the basis of their belief. Shifts from one pole to the other are not as rare as one might think.
>
> Sheila Larson is, in part, trying to find a center in herself after liberating herself from an oppressively conformist early family life. Her 'Sheilaism' is rooted in the effort to transform external authority into internal meaning. The two experiences that define her faith took a similar form. One occurred just before she was about to undergo major surgery. God spoke to her to reassure her that all would be well, but the voice was her own. [. . .]
>
> The other experience occurred when, as a nurse, she was caring for a dying woman whose husband was not able to handle the situation. Taking over care in the final hours, Sheila had the experience that 'if she looked in the mirror' she 'would see Jesus Christ.' Tim

Eichelberger's mystical beliefs and the 'nonrestrictive' nature of his yoga practices allowed him to 'transcend' his family and ethnic culture and define a self free of external constraint.

3.27 Radhakrishnan: mysticism as the escape from tradition

Radhakrishnan, 1960 (orig. 1927): *The Hindu View of Life*. London: Unwin (pp. 24–5).

This extract by Radhakrishnan makes the important point that detraditionalization can take place within religious traditions. Mystics are typically – especially in the East – detraditionalizers, dropping beliefs as they approach the ultimate. Whilst on the topic of mysticism, it can be added that mystical 'traditions', generally speaking, are not really traditions. As Paul Valliere (1987) points out, mysticism is about 'experience': 'mysticism is not a matter of tradition, since experience cannot be received from or handed or to others' (p. 11).

Hindu thought believes in the evolution of our knowledge of of God. We have to vary continually our notions of God until we pass beyond all notions into the heart of the reality itself, which our ideas endeavour to report. Hinduism does not distinguish ideas of God as true and false, adopting one particular idea as the standard for the whole human race. It accepts the obvious fact that mankind seeks its goal of God at various levels and in various directions, and feels sympathy with every stage of the search. The same God expresses itself at one stage as power, at another as personality, at a third as all-comprehensive spirit, just as the same forces which put forth the green leaves also cause the crimson flowers to grow. We do not say that the crimson flowers are all the truth and the green leaves are all false. Hinduism accepts all religious notions as facts and arranges them in the order of their more or less intrinsic significance. The bewildering polytheism of the masses and the uncompromising montheism of the classes are for the Hindu the expressions of one and the same force at different levels. Hinduism insists on our working steadily upwards and improving our knowledge of God. 'The worshippers of the Absolute are the highest in rank; second to them are the worshippers of the personal God; then come the worshippers of the incarnations like Rāma, Kṛṣṇa, Buddha; below them are those who worship ancestors, deities and sages, and lowest of all are the worshippers of the petty forces and spirits.' Again, 'The deities of some men are in water (i.e. bathing-places), those of the more advanced are in the heavens, those of the children (in religion) are in images of wood and stone, but the sage finds his God in his deeper self.' 'The man of action finds his God in fire, the man of feeling in the heart, and the feeble-minded in the idol, but the strong in spirit find God every-where.' The seers see the Supreme in the self, and not in images.

It is, however, unfortunately the case that the majority of the Hindus do not insist on this graduated scale but acquiesce in admit-tedly unsatisfactory conceptions of God. The cultivated tolerate popu-lar notions as inadequate signs and shadows of the incomprehensible, but the people at large believe them to be justified and authorized. It is true that the thinking Hindu desires to escape from the con-fusion of the gods into the silence of the Supreme, but the crowd still stands gazing at the heavens.

3.28   Beckford on postmodern religion

James A. Beckford, 1992: Religion, Modernity and Post-Modernity. In B. R. Wilson (ed.), *Religion: Contemporary Issues*. London: Bellew (pp. 11–23) (pp. 19–20).

As this extract by James Beckford points out, much of what is discussed under the heading 'postmodernity' involves detraditionalization (including loss of alle-giance to 'frameworks of knowledge' and a shift to individualized religion). In this sense some New Age (spiritualities of life) religion might be thought of as postmodern. However, we can add, it is not postmodern insofar as it provides an essentialized, experiential metanarrative.

It seems to me that the following are most commonly associated with post-modernity:

1   A refusal to regard positivistic, rationalistic, instrumental criteria as the sole or exclusive standard of worthwhile knowledge.
2   A willingness to combine symbols from disparate codes or frame-works of meaning, even at the cost of disjunctions and eclecticism.
3   A celebration of spontaneity, fragmentation, superficiality, irony and playfulness.
4   A willingness to abandon the search for over-arching or triumphalist myths, narratives or frameworks of knowledge.

If these characteristics are the hallmarks of the post-modern sens-ibility in general, then one might expect, on the analogy with post-modern fine arts, architecture and literature, that it would receive a distinctive expression in religion. My expectation would be that putatively post-modern forms of religion would embrace diversity of discourse and the abandonment of unitary meaning systems; cross-references between, and pastiches of, different religious traditions; collapse of the boundary between high and popular forms of religion; and an accent on playfulness or cynicism.

It would be no exaggeration to describe a few New Age groups and new religious movements as post-modern in these terms. The Neo-Sannyas movement of the Bhagwan Shree Rajneesh, for example, epitomizes anti-rationalism, pastiche, populism and playfulness. Some Buddhist spiritualities 'deconstruct' identity into experiences of fragmentation. And an avowedly post-modern theologian like Robert Bellah celebrates the fact that monks and guests at a Benedictine retreat in California contemplated the sacrament of the Eucharist 'in the posture of zazen'. But these examples are purely illustrative: not representative. More to the point, they are definitely rare and marginal to most forms of present-day religion in the UK. This raises the point that *many* examples of post-modernism are precisely rare and of élitist concern. They may 'quote' from mass-cultural styles but they do not represent mass products. Perhaps they attract a disproportionate amount of attention not only because of their sheer exoticism but also because the majority of British adults have become illiterate or 'deskilled' in matters of religion. As a result, there are fewer standards and fixed points of reference by which to place novelties such as NRMs in any wider perspective.

Detraditionalization: examples

Example: the radically detraditionalized

3.29 Adams and Haaken: 'anticultural culture'

Richard Adams and Janice Haaken, 1987: Anticultural Culture: Lifespring's Ideology and Its Roots in Humanistic Psychology. *Journal of Humanistic Psychology*, 27 (4) Fall: 501–17 (pp. 502–3).

Writing about Lifespring, a large enlightenment seminar which has been active in North America, Richard Adams and Janice Haaken emphasize the extent to which external, supra-self sources of authority are rejected. This apparently post-traditional organization also illustrates how freedom or 'omnipotence' is associated with liberation from the external.

Anticultural culture refers to any meaning system or set of values that deny the legitimacy of meaning systems or values having their origin outside of the individual. Thus when we use the term we are not referring to sets of values that simply deny the legitimacy of any other particular set of values. We do not mean, for example, a 'counterculture' or revolutionary movement that clearly sets out to oppose one set of values with another. Rather, those participating in an anticultural culture do not believe that legitimate values exist outside of themselves. Thus the prescriptions of others, of tradition, of experts, of religious texts, and all such external sources are not considered to be legitimate.

This anticultural stance need not involve separating oneself off from the society. Indeed, what is of interest about the anticultural aspect of LIFESPRING is that it offers a means of achieving a sense of personal omnipotence while being fully and uncritically involved in the society.

The particular mode of anticultural culture we will be discussing here is characterized by a highly individualistic subjectivism. From this perspective what is true or right for an individual can be known only by an awareness of 'inner' potential, needs, drives, and so on. That which is 'inner' is seen to be presocial and precultural; knowledge precedes experience. The inner self is thus set in distinction from the outer world. And to the extent to which the outer world is seen as restricting or repressing the inner self, culture is considered the enemy of the self.

3.30 Kopp: 'Killing the Buddha'

Sheldon Kopp, 1974: *If You Meet the Buddha on the Road, Kill Him!* London: Sheldon Press (p. 140).

Really radical detraditionalization, as this passage from Sheldon Kopp shows, involves the rejection of the idea that any source of external significance should be heeded, even that of the Buddha. True meaning can only come from oneself, from one's mastery.

The Zen Master warns: 'If you meet the Buddha on the road, kill him!' This admonition points up that no meaning that comes from outside of ourselves is real. The Buddhahood of each of us has already been obtained. We need only recognize it. Philosophy, religion, patriotism, all are empty idols. The only meaning in our lives is what we each bring to them. Killing the Buddha on the road means destroying the hope that anything outside of ourselves can be our master. No one is any bigger than anyone else. There are no mothers or fathers for grown-ups, only sisters and brothers.

3.31   Jayakar: Krishnamurti and 'Truth is a pathless land'

Popul Jayakar, 1986: *J. Krishnamurti. A Biography*. Harmondsworth: Penguin/Arkana (pp. 78–9).

Speaking in 1929 to announce his determination to dissolve the (Theosophical) Order of the Star, of which he was the Head, 'you and you alone can find the truth' is the message from Krishnamurti. The spiritual quest cannot take place within any institutionalized framework. (See also Harding, **1.62** and Gillman, **3.60**.)

I [Krishnamurti] maintain that Truth is a pathless land, and you cannot approach it by any path whatsoever, by any religion, by any sect. That is my point of view, and I adhere to that absolutely and unconditionally. Truth, being limitless, unconditioned, unapproachable by any path whatsoever, cannot be organized; nor should any organization be formed to lead or to coerce people along any particular path. If you first understand that, then you will see how impossible it is to organize a belief. A belief is purely an individual matter, and you cannot and must not organize it. If you do, it becomes dead, crystalized; it becomes a creed, a sect, a religion, to be imposed on others. Truth is narrowed down and made a plaything for those who are weak, for those who are only momentarily discontented. Truth cannot be brought down, rather the individual must make the effort to ascend to it. You cannot bring the mountain-top to the valley. If you would attain to the mountain-top you must pass through the valley, climb the steeps, unafraid of the dangerous precipices. You must climb towards the Truth, it cannot be stepped down or organized for you. I do not want to belong to any organization of a spiritual kind, please understand this. Again, I maintain that no organization can lead man to spirituality. If an organization be created for this purpose, it becomes a crutch, a weakness, a bondage, and must cripple the individual, and prevent him from growing, from establishing his uniqueness, which lies in the discovery for himself of that absolute, unconditioned Truth. So that is another reason why I have decided, as I happen to be the Head of the Order, to dissolve it. No one has persuaded me to this decision.

3.32 Christ, Starhawk and the nature of the Goddess

Carol P. Christ, 1992: Why Women Need the Goddess. In Carol P. Christ and Judith Plaskow (eds), *Womanspirit Rising: A Feminist Reader in Religion*. San Francisco: HarperCollins, 273–87 (pp. 278–9).

As Carol Christ shows, for Starhawk (a leading spirituality of life Pagan), the Goddess herself is detraditionalized in that She is Self-dependent. She has no separate existence apart from those who realize themselves through her.

> Others seem quite comfortable with the notion of Goddess as a divine female protector and creator and would find their experience of Goddess limited by the assertion that she is not *also* out there as well as within themselves and in all natural processes. When asked what the symbol of Goddess means, feminist priestess Starhawk replied, 'It all depends on how I feel. When I feel weak, she is someone who can help and protect me. When I feel strong, she is the symbol of my own power. At other times I feel her as the natural energy in my body and the world.' How are we to evaluate such a statement? Theologians might call these the words of a sloppy thinker. But my deepest intuition tells me they contain a wisdom that Western theological thought has lost.

Example: the less radically detraditionalized

3.33 Stanton: 'the golden rule'

Elizabeth Cady Stanton, 1985 (orig. 1895, 1887): *The Woman's Bible. The Original Feminist Attack on the Bible*. Edinburgh: Polygon Books (pp. 12–13).

Elizabeth Stanton accepts only those aspects of traditions which conform to what she calls 'the golden rule'. Other aspects are rejected – detraditionalization takes place as the authority of the text gives way to the authority of an interpretation according to the standards found in the religion of humanity.

> There are some general principles in the holy books of all religions that teach love, charity, liberty, justice and equality for all the human family, there are many grand and beautiful passages, the golden rule has been echoed and re-echoed around the world. There are lofty examples of good and true men and women, all worthy our acceptance and example whose lustre cannot be dimmed by the false

sentiments and vicious characters bound up in the same volume. The Bible cannot be accepted or rejected as a whole, its teachings are varied and its lessons differ widely from each other. In criticising the peccadilloes of Sarah, Rebecca and Rachel, we would not shadow the virtues of Deborah, Huldah and Vashti. In criticising the Mosaic code we would not question the wisdom of the golden rule and the fifth Commandment. Again the church claims special consecration for its cathedrals and priesthood, parts of these aristocratic churches are too holy for women to enter, boys were early introduced into the choirs for this reason, woman singing in an obscure corner closely veiled. A few of the more democratic denominations accord women some privileges, but invidious discriminations of sex are found in all religious organizations, and the most bitter outspoken enemies of woman are found among clergymen and bishops of the Protestant religion.

The canon law, the Scriptures, the creeds and codes and church discipline of the leading religions bear the impress of fallible man, and not of our ideal great first cause, 'the Spirit of all Good,' that set the universe of matter and mind in motion, and by immutable law holds the land, the sea, the planets, revolving round the great centre of light and heat, each in its own elliptic, with millions of stars in harmony all singing together, the glory of creation forever and ever.

3.34 Miller and the New Paradigm churches and 'a middle course'

Donald E. Miller, 1997: *Reinventing American Protestantism. Christianity in the New Millennium.* Berkeley, Los Angeles and London: University of California Press (pp. 127–9).

New Paradigm churches, sometimes known as megachurches, postdenominational churches, or, as elsewhere in Donald E. Miller's study, 'postmodern traditionalist', combine features more commonly associated with religions of difference (Miller refers to the fact that clergy 'insist on Biblical literalism' (p. 184)) with characteristics more reminiscent of spiritualities of life (Miller writes of the fact that 'purity of heart is more important than purity of doctrine' (pp. 127–8)). His study is of the Calvary Chapel, Vineyard Christian Fellowship and Hope Chapel. It shows how this form of experiential religion of difference is detraditionalized insofar as personal conviction, one's experienced relationship with God, is considerably more important than doctrine and theology. The reading also provides an example of how detraditionalization accompanies tolerance. For more on New Paradigm churches, see extracts by Miller in the Sacralization chapter of **Part Three** (**3.87**, **3.97**).

A Vineyard Fellowship pastor echoed this sentiment, saying that purity of heart is more important than purity of doctrine. Another Vineyard pastor cogently stated this view: 'The apostles didn't know theology. They just knew Jesus.' And a Hope Chapel pastor claimed to welcome different theological views, in marked contrast to many of his colleagues in other churches who, he says, follow the 'party line' in an effort to produce 'theological clones.'

In commenting on Chuck Smith's teaching, a Calvary Chapel pastor said that he was amazed while listening to various taped Bible studies at how Smith avoids talking about divisive doctrinal issues such as election, predestination, and various views of the return of Christ and the end of the world. 'The average student listening to Chuck will never even be faced with that stuff.' Reflecting on the experience of sitting in Calvary Bible studies, he emphasized: 'You may not come out a theologian, but you'll be excited about God's love, you'll be excited about the reality, the possibility of a relationship with God, and you'll want to serve the Lord.' In other words, new paradigm Christianity is not primarily a matter of cognitive assent; it is an attitude and a relationship between the individual and God.

In this regard, new paradigm churches differ from older-style fundamentalism, in which doctrinal orthodoxy was the hallmark of who was 'saved' and who was 'lost.' Using the metaphor of a circle, Chuck Smith told us that fundamentalists know exactly who is inside and who is outside the circle. In contrast, he said, you are in the Calvary circle if you are present and 'fellowshipping' (in relationship with others in the movement). 'We don't have the distinct lines of definition that they draw,' he stressed, implying that new paradigm churches are not sectarian, that they do not create doctrinal boundaries distinguishing one group from another.

Many new paradigm Christians indicate that it is a sign of Christian maturity to be tolerant of denominational pluralism. After admitting, 'I used to do a lot of denominational bashing,' one pastor explained that he now sees denominational differences as being primarily a matter of temperament: 'Some people really like a high Episcopal type thing, and other people like to swing from chandeliers and leap out of windows.' Chuck Smith reflected the same view: 'I see the place of denominations. I don't think that everyone should worship in a free way like we do, nor should everyone worship in a liturgical way. I see the place for liturgy. I see people who need liturgy. I see people who need the extreme emotionalism that they find within the Pentecostal church. And so I am not opposed to that emotionalism.' He sees himself as offering a middle course, what he calls a 'casual' approach to worship. 'If you want to be emotional,' he says, 'go down to the Assemblies [of God]. If you want to be liturgical, then go on down to the Presbyterian church. God uses them and God blesses them and they have their place in the Body of Christ as I have my place.' [. . .]

Over and over, new paradigm Christians express their emphasis on personal conviction over doctrine. A representative from a Calvary ministry that was ecumenical in its outreach to youth offered this formula for participation in the program: 'If you love Jesus Christ, if he's your personal Lord and Savior, and you love kids, then you're in.' A Vineyard pastor we interviewed said, 'I think we need to find out what we need to do in our dad's house [i.e., for God's kingdom] and be tolerant of others. Unless there is a clear theological wrong-doing, or biblical wrongdoing of some kind, I think we should be tolerant and give people some room. I don't want to go to heaven being "Mr. Right." Do you want to go to heaven as the "Scripture Answer Man"? Is that what it is? God help us!'

Example: individualized religion

3.35 Durkheim on 'a free private, optional religion, fashioned according to one's own needs'

Emile Durkheim, in W. S. F. Pickering, 1975: *Durkheim on Religion. A Selection of Readings with Bibliographies*. London and Boston: Routledge & Kegan Paul (p. 96).

Detraditionalization is so bound up with the authority of the self, an authority which manifests itself by way of the exercise of choice, that it is hardly surprising that it is bound up with individualized (therefore de-institutionalized) religion. People exercise choice, that is to say, to draw on traditions as they will; indeed, to construct their own religious beliefs and activities. No doubt individualized religion can take a (relatively) traditionalized form, but this cannot be the case when – as Durkheim puts it – religion 'is fashioned according to one's own needs and understanding'. What can be thought of as 'mild' detraditionalization takes place when people individualize religion in traditional societies whilst retaining some of the beliefs of tradition (Durkheim's 'private totems'). Strong detraditionalization takes place when what is drawn on is itself detraditionalized.

There are beliefs and practices which indeed seem to be religious and which are however partly the result of individual spontaneity. In fact, there are no religious societies where, as well as the gods whom everybody is compelled to worship, there are not also others which anyone can freely create for his own personal use. From the very beginning, in addition to the collective totem venerated by the whole clan, there have been the private totems that everyone chooses as he wishes and which nevertheless are the objects of a true cult. Similarly today there is hardly a believer who does not view more or less in his own way the God commonly worshipped, and who does not modify traditional concepts on some point or other. There are even some people who refuse to recognize any other deity than the one which free meditation has led them to believe exists; and in this case they are the real legislators of the cult to which they adhere. Finally, even when the believer addresses himself to the God worshipped by the community, he does not always confine himself to the practices rigorously prescribed. He takes others upon himself and he forces himself to make sacrifices or to undergo disciplines which religious law does not positively demand. But if all these facts are undeniable, and no matter what the relationship they may have to those we have discussed so far, they require none the less to be distinguished from them. If one does not want to be open to grave misunderstanding, it is necessary to be aware of confusing a free, private, optional religion, fashioned according to one's own needs and understanding, with a religion handed down by tradition, formulated for a whole group and which it is obligatory to practise. The two disciplines which are so different cannot meet the same needs: one is completely orientated towards the individual, the other towards society.

3.36 Casanova and 'the cult of the individual'

José Casanova, 1994: *Public Religions in the Modern World*. Chicago and London: The University of Chicago Press (pp. 52–3).

Contrary to those academics who seek what Weber called 'the polytheism of modern values' at the level of structural differentiation, José Casanova portrays an internalized 'polytheism': 'the temple of modern polytheism is the mind of the individual self'. With the 'temple' inside, it can be added, there is a strong tendency to reject external religious institutions. (See Krishnamurti (**3.31**) for an example of the radical rejection of the institutionalized.)

One could distinguish between private individual religiosity, the religion of the private self, and all the public forms of associational religion. This distinction corresponds roughly to the one drawn by Thomas Luckmann between invisible religion and church religion, as well as to the typological distinction between what Ernst Troeltsch called 'individual mysticism,' or 'spiritual religion,' and the typically modern form of voluntary, individualistic, and pluralistic religious association, 'the denomination.' [. . .]

It is a commonplace of sociological analysis that the modern differentiation of autonomous spheres leads irremediably to a pluralism of norms, values, and worldviews. Max Weber attributed 'the polytheism of modern values' to this differentiation. Undoubtedly, the differentiation of the spheres leads to conflicts between the various gods (Eros, Logos, Nomos, Mars, Leviathan, Mammon, the Muses, etc.). But this conflict can be institutionalized and contained through systemic functional differentiation. In any case, this is not the true source of modern polytheism. If the temple of ancient polytheism was the Pantheon, a place where all known and even unknown gods could be worshiped simultaneously, the temple of modern polytheism is the mind of the individual self. Indeed, modern individuals do not tend to believe in the existence of various gods. On the contrary, they tend to believe that all religions and all individuals worship the same god under different names and languages, only modern individuals reserve to themselves the right to denominate this god and to worship him/her/it in their own peculiar language. Rousseau's 'religion of man . . . without temples, altars or rituals,' Thomas Paine's 'my mind is my church,' and Thomas Jefferson's 'I am a sect myself' are paradigmatic 'high culture' expressions of the modern form of individual religiosity. Deism, the typical fusion of individual mysticism and enlightenment rationalism, is recognizable in all three expressions. 'Sheilaism' is the name Robert Bellah et al. have given to the contemporary 'low culture' expression, after one of the people they interviewed actually named her own 'faith' after herself. . . . The interviewers add, 'This suggests the logical possibility of over 220 million American religions, one for each of us.' The cultic form of modern polytheism is not idolatry but human narcissism. In this particular sense, the cult of the individual has indeed become, as foreseen by Durkheim, the religion of modernity.

3.37 Wuthnow on privatization

Robert Wuthnow, 1989: *The Struggle for America's Soul. Evangelicals, Liberals, and Secularism.* Grand Rapids, Michigan: Williams B. Eerdmans (p. 116).

The point of this brief extract is simply to introduce the relationship between what we are calling the individualization (and detraditionalization) of religion and the widely used concept of 'privatization'. As should be clear from the following extract from Wuthnow, only the first and third connotations of the term can involve detraditionalization (although they might also involve the traditional). (See also Bellah et al. (1985) on 'religious individualism' (pp. 222–5) – individualized religion in the USA, almost entirely about the self, and dating back to the eighteenth century.)

One of the most frequently advanced characterizations of American religion is that it is becoming increasingly 'privatized.' That is, the public, corporate, communal quality of religion is said to be declining, leaving individuals with their own highly subjective and idiosyncratic expressions of faith. The terms 'private' or 'privatized' actually carry several connotations in this context.

One connotation suggests that the religion practiced by an increasing number of Americans may be entirely of their own manufacture – a kind of eclectic synthesis of Christianity, popular psychology, *Reader's Digest* folklore, and personal superstitions, all wrapped up in the anecdotes of the individual's biography.

A different connotation suggests that religious practices remain subject to much more orthodox influences, namely, the churches and synagogues; they have no influence on public affairs in the world of business and politics. According to this conception, religion has withdrawn into the 'private sphere' to function much in the same manner as leisure activities, voluntary gatherings, and family relations.

Still another connotation focuses on the possibility that even within the private sector religious expression may have become less public, less organized, less relational, leaving individuals radically alone in their experience of the divine. All three of these connotations bear some resemblance to popular images of American religion.

3.38 Beckford: 'Religion has come adrift from its former points of anchorage'

James A. Beckford, 1989: *Religion and Advanced Industrial Society.* London, Boston, Sydney and Wellington: Unwin Hyman (pp. 170–2).

James Beckford advances our understanding of individualized religion by arguing that religion has come to be treated as a 'cultural resource'. In this 'deregulated' mode, it is put to use to serve a wide variety of purposes. Given that it is 'deregulated', religion is detraditionalized in that it is no longer under the control of traditionalized religious institutions. This cultural resource, it can be added, is by no means necessarily privatized in that it may be deployed for social and cultural purposes. (See also Hoover and Lundby (1997) on religion in the culture and extract **2.54**.)

It is becoming clear that religion can still convey symbols of newly perceived social realities. It can serve as a language for representing powerful inspirations, perceptions, sufferings and aspirations even though the users of this language may not necessarily associate with any religious organization. In some cases, religion conveys conservative ideas of national, tribal, or cultural integrity. In other cases, it conveys new and challenging ideas of personhood, wholeness, peace and justice. In all cases, however, it is apparent that the *use* of religious symbols is likely to be controversial and contested because they are no longer necessarily tied to age-old communities or other so-called natural groupings. It can no longer be taken for granted that most uses of religion will, by definition, be for the straightforward benefit of the whole community. Religion has come adrift from its former points of anchorage but is no less potentially powerful as a result. It remains a potent cultural resource or form which may act as the vehicle of change, challenge, or conservation. Consequently, religion has become less predictable. The capacity to mobilize people and material resources remains strong, but it is likely to be mobilized in unexpected places and in ways which may be in tension with 'establishment' practices and public policy.

This argument about what Simmel might have called the 'autonomization' of religion amounts to much more than the claim that religion can nowadays be marketed in a quasi-commercial fashion. This is only part of the picture. The partial freeing of religion from its points of anchorage in communities and natural social groupings has also turned it into a resource which may be invested with highly diverse meanings and used for a wide variety of purposes. Religion can now be put to varied uses both within and outside the framework of religious organizations and, where they exist, state religions. Civil religions, for example, are best thought of as symbolic resources employed by politicians independently of religious organizations. Religious symbols frequently serve the interests of revolutionaries and political radicals as well. Health care, movements for the protection of the environment or the promotion of peace, and the institutions of human rights are other spheres in which religious symbolism is increasingly being appropriated. The post-Second World War transformation of the kinds of industrial society envisaged by sociologists in the early twentieth century has tended to undermine the communal, familial and organizational bases of religion. But religious forms of sentiment, belief and action have survived as relatively autonomous resources. They retain the capacity to symbolize, for example, ultimate meaning, infinite power, supreme indignation and sublime compassion. And they can be deployed in the service of virtually any interest group or ideal: not just organizations with specifically religious objectives. This presents obvious advantages in states which offer constitutional protections for religious activity. But it also leads to problems if the 'protected' use of religion falls foul of public opinion or government policy.

This can all be summarized in the statement that, from a sociological point of view, it is nowadays better to conceptualize religion as a cultural resource or form than as a social institution. As such, it is characterized by a greater degree of flexibility and unpredictability. For the decline of the great religious monopolies in the West has been accompanied by the sporadic deployment of religion for a great variety of new purposes. Religion can be combined with virtually any other set of ideas or values. And the chances that religion will be controversial are increased by the fact that it may be used by people having little or no connection with formal religious organizations. The deregulation of religion is one of the hidden ironies of secularization. It helps to make religion sociologically problematic in ways which are virtually inconceivable in the terms of the sociological classics.

Detraditionalization: explanations

Explanation: the turn to the detraditionalized self

3.39 Heelas summarizing the 'standard' history of the turn to the self

Paul Heelas, 1996: Cultural Studies and Business Cultures. In Andrew Godley and Oliver M. Westall (eds), *Business History and Business Culture*. Manchester and New York: Manchester University Press pp. 77–98 (pp. 78–81).

Detraditionalization takes place when the self exercises its authority, as when reason is applied to discard (**1.34**) or demythologize (**1.35**) traditional beliefs. Detraditionalization is also facilitated when the self comes to be highly valued, this making it possible to locate the sacred within. Detraditionalization must therefore be explained by reference to the development of the autonomous and 'elevated' self (on the last, see **1.38**). Drawing on a variety of scholars, but especially influenced by the work of Robert Bellah and Steven Tipton, Paul Heelas provides an overview of how the self has developed in many contexts in modern times. It can be added that the expressive self, with its interests in delving within, is the most likely to be involved with detraditionalized spiritualities of life, at least those which are not prosperity inclined (see the readings in the explanations section of Spiritualities of Life for more on this point, e.g. **1.75**). It should be added that this extract offers what might be called the 'standard' history of the turn to the self in that alternative histories are now being published. (See, for example, Porter, 1977.)

It may be helpful to summarise what amounts to the standard account of key aspects of the cultural history of modernity. Jacob Burckhardt, Emile Durkheim and contemporary scholars like Bellah et al., Berger et al. and Richard Sennett are among those who have dwelt on the fall of what can be thought of as 'the traditional self'. Such scholars also dwell on the associated elaboration of discourses and practices concerning what it is to be an autonomous individual, a way of being which, it is maintained, has increasingly come into prominence.

The traditional self is that which is embedded in the established order of things. Tradition-informed ways of life are those in which the person thinks in terms of 'external' (supra-individual) voices of authority, control and destiny. Living the good life, solving problems, seeking advancement or obtaining salvation are a matter of heeding social, cultural or religious duties and obligations. Constituted by position in the established order as a whole, there is little scope or incentive (culturally speaking) for the person to exercise autonomy or freedom of expression. By definition – for the person here thinks in terms of others – this order of the self is collectivistic. The person is primarily other-informed or sociocentric rather than self-informed or individualistic. Durkheim makes the point, 'the individual personality is lost in the depths of the social mass'. Although it is highly doubtful that traditions, however powerful or authoritative, have ever managed to swamp the exercise of individual autonomy to quite this extent, Durkheim's observation graphically conveys the thrust of the supra-individual mode of existence.

From the time of the Renaissance, if not earlier, the standard account under consideration maintains that a variety of factors have served to weaken the hold of the cultural domain as an external order of authority. Increasingly, especially during the last couple of centuries, people have ceased to think of themselves as belonging to, or as informed by, overarching systems. Such disembedded or de-traditionalised selves, the argument goes, have adopted cultural assumptions and values that articulate what it is to stand 'alone' – as individuals – in the world. Such people consider themselves to be autonomous agents, relying on their own – or inner – sources of authority, control and responsibility. In anthropologist Clifford Geertz's formulations, 'the Western conception of the person' is of a 'bounded, unique, more or less integrated motivational and cognitive universe, a dynamic centre of awareness, emotion, judgement, and action organised into a distinctive whole and set contrastingly both against other such wholes and against its social and natural background'.

The shift to the self, it is then often claimed, has taken two directions. Following Steven Tipton's analysis, one involves the language of utilitarian individualism. As Tipton puts it, 'utilitarianism begins with the individual person as an agent seeking to satisfy his own wants or interests':

> The utilitarian first asks, 'What do I want?' or 'What are my interests?' His answer to this first question defines the goodness of consequences. This, in turn, determines the answer to his second question, 'Which act will produce the most good consequences, that is, will most satisfy my wants?' Utilitarianism is quite clear about which acts are right: those that produce the greatest amount of good consequences. It is less clear about what consequences are good, usually taking wants or interests as given or self-evident in a way that suggests notions like happiness, pleasure or self-preservation to define what is good in itself.

The utilitarian individualist – calculating the best ways of maximising one's own material interest in the fashion of that 'economic man' favoured by rational choice theorists – is a familiar figure in the contemporary West. Bellah et al.'s analysis of the culture of the United States continually highlights this mode of being, one in which the self is 'separated from family, religion, and calling as sources of authority, duty, and moral example' and which instead 'seeks to work out its own form of action by autonomously pursuing happiness and satisfying its wants'. Its significance is also proclaimed by portrayals of the consumer culture, including, for example, that provided by Christopher Lasch in his influential account of 'the culture of narcissism'. Another index of significance is seen in the fact that there is a strong utilitarian tone to much of the discourse of the Thatcherite – and Majorite – enterprise culture.

Turning to the second version of the shift to the self, the expressive individualist supposes that there is much more to being a person than merely satisfying the 'wants' which one happens to have in accord with the capitalistic emphasis on wealth creation and materialistic consumption. Expressivists think in terms of what they take to be a much richer account of what it is to be human. They are intent on discovering and cultivating their 'true' nature, delving within to experience the wealth of life itself. Utilitarian pursuits are dismissed on the grounds that they encourage all that is bad in human life – greed, selfishness, envy, crude satiation and so on – being replaced by the quest for authenticity, creativity, personal 'growth', 'meaningful' relationships, and the experience of harmony or 'holism'. Furthermore, the expressivist rejects the calculative, rational ethicality of the utilitarian in favour of an ethic based on the assumption that good acts are those which best manifest one's true nature. As Tipton makes the point, the assumption is that 'everyone ought to act in any given situation and moment in a way that fully expresses himself, specifically his inner feelings and his experience of the situation'.

Some theorists conclude that de-traditionalised selves – whether utilitarian, expressive or an amalgam of the two – have very largely (if not entirely, it is sometimes suggested) usurped the traditional version. Anthony Giddens, with the importance he attaches to the monitoring or self-steering individual, provides an example, writing that 'The individual no longer lives primarily by extrinsic moral precepts but by means of the reflexive organisation of the self'. And so does Alasdair MacIntyre, complaining that the contemporary West has turned from traditions to 'emotivism', namely 'the doctrine that all evaluative judgements and more specifically all moral judgements are nothing but expressions of preference, expressions of attitude or feeling, insofar as they are moral or evaluative in character'.

Although it is generally accepted that the autonomous self has come into greater prominence with the course of modernity, theorists differ in the extent to which they see the balance shifting away from the tradition-informed mode of being. Much suggests that Giddens and MacIntyre, not to speak of the even more radical claims made by advocates of 'the post-modern condition', underestimate the continuing hold of the traditional. Accordingly, it can be argued that traditional systems, involving sustained voices of authorities which examine, judge and regulate their subjects, remain of considerable importance. Theistic – God or Bible-directed – Christianity remains a potent source of self-understanding in countries such as the United States. And the significance of the 'say' of the collectivity – where, by definition, the person is imbued with the spirit of belonging to, and being informed by, others – is seen in any number of forms of life. People heed supra-individual authorities, legitimated in canonical ways, when, for example, they go to university, become a barrister or join the armed forces. Of particular note, it might be argued that evidence provided by corporate (business) cultures counts against those who stress de-traditionalisation. Defined as those 'systems' which emphasise the collectivity, the vision of public purpose and the importance of working for the company, such cultures effect the rule of tradition.

All things considered, although the shift to individualism has long been associated with the weakening of traditional formations, the continuing significance of extrinsic, structured modes of adjudication should not be underestimated. It follows that contemporary culture is best seen as dispersed into what Charles Taylor describes as different 'sources of the self' (see also the portrayal provided by Bellah *et al.*). The creation of identity and its articulation and control through the expectations and condemnations of established orders competes with discourses and practices which dwell on the freedom, desires and expressivity of the agent.

3.40 Simmel: 'The subjectivism of modern personal life . . .'

Georg Simmel, 1976 (orig. 1909): The Future of Our Culture. In P. A. Lawrence, *Georg Simmel: Sociologist and European*. Middlesex: Nelson pp. 250–2 (pp. 250–1).

In this extract Georg Simmel seeks to explain why 'the modern age' is so preoccupied with the inner life. His answer, in his pioneering work, is that people have become estranged from 'objective culture', and have thus been forced to turn to themselves as a source of significance. For Simmel (1997), it can be added, detraditionalization is self-limiting and does not result in the disappearance of religion because the experience of the resources of the self generates a spiritual response. (See also reading **1.71** in which Peter Berger draws on this kind of theory to explain the development of inner spiritualities.)

> As far as I can see, the reason for the apparent pessimism of the majority of philosphical minds regarding the present state of culture is the widening gulf between the culture of things and personal culture. As a result of the division of labour during the last few centuries, the technology at our service and the knowledge, arts, life-styles and interests at our disposal have expanded to an unprecedented variety. But the individual's capacity to use this increased raw material as means of personal culture increases only very slowly and lags further and further behind. We can no longer absorb into our lives all those things, which multiply as if in obedience to an inexorable fate indifferent to us. They develop their own purely objective life, which we are almost entirely unable even to understand.
>
> What the Ancient Greeks created in politics and science, strategy and scope for pleasure, had a sufficiently consistent style and simple structure to be grasped to some extent by any educated man. He could, without difficulty, make use of the sum total of objective culture to build up his own subjective culture. Thus they could both evolve in a harmony which, in the modern age, has been destroyed as they have become independent of each other. In our indescribably complex culture, individual ideas and achievements leave behind permanent forms in which the fruits of individual lives become independent of those lives. There are too many of them for the individual to absorb them all: their inevitable lack of a common style is enough to make this profoundly impossible. The subjectivism of modern personal life, its rootless, arbitrary character, is merely the expression of this fact: the vast, intricate, sophisticated culture of things, of institutions, of objectified ideas robs the individual of any consistent inner relationship to culture as a whole, and casts him back again on his *own* resources.

3.41   Gehlen and the development *'of the psyche itself'*

Arnold Gehlen, 1980: *Man in the Age of Technology*. New York: Columbia University Press (pp. 74–7).

In many respects Arnold Gehlen's effort to explain the 'psychologization' of the modern world complements that of Simmel. '. . . even religion', he writes, 'become[s] subjectivized'.

Any individual transplanted into our own times from the vigorously concrete cultures of antiquity, of the Middle Ages, or even of the baroque era, would find most astonishing the conditions of physical proximity, and the lack of structure and form, in which the people of our time are forced to vegetate; and would wonder at the elusiveness and abstractness of our institutions, which are mostly 'immaterial states of affairs.' Because of this we seem to possess practically no patterns of conduct whereby men can exist *with one another*; even sport has turned into a show supplying stimuli to passive masses. The family remains as the sole 'symbiotic' social form, and owes its stability to this monopoly position, a stability astonishing in so changing a culture. The family appears as the true counterpart to the public realm, as a refuge of privacy. As public life loses its deeper, symbolic import, as institutions devolve into statutes and statutes into traffic regulations, the private sphere separates itself wholly from this context. However, it becomes a sphere wholly given over to immediacy, where individuals interact in the whole range of their strengths and weaknesses; [. . .]

With the decay of solid social orderings is associated the development not just of psychology, but *of the psyche itself.* [. . .]

All instincts which no longer find an external outlet, turn inward: hence the growth within man of what was later to be called 'soul,' writes Nietzsche. [. . .]

As we have already argued elsewhere, one cannot seriously doubt that modern subjectivism is rooted in the wider cultural situation; in the presence of a flood of stimuli that overtax our capacity for emotional response, an emphasis on inner elaboration and 'psychologization' represents an attempt to keep things under control; external determinants are vital, though unacknowledged. Emotional reactions can no longer be invested in an external world which has become so reified and deprived of symbolic undertones; raw nature no longer opposes us with a felt resistance, the exertion of bodily effort has become largely dispensable. How could this not have as a consequence a continuous flow of internal experiences, which must be monitored through unceasing awareness and reflection? It is here that art, law, even religion become subjectivized and weakened. 'Ideas' bud forth everywhere, and one can only deal with them by discussion, this being the appropriate form of external elaboration. This intellectualization and subjectivization of a culture screened away from action is a novelty of our own historical era; it is a component of the very air we breathe. Those who cannot see this must be refusing to look. [. . .]

Let us try to grasp the logic of the relationship between inner and outer experience. The lack of stable institutions, which at bottom are nothing but preformed and customary decisions, makes heavy demands upon man's ability and willingness to deliberate; and, by demolishing the bulwarks of habit, exposes him defenseless to the casual flow of stimuli. These stimuli give rise to interests, gains, and needs which attain a more or less stable equilibrium within the individual.

3.42 Hunter, Evangelicalism and 'fascination with the self'

James Davison Hunter, 1987: *Evangelicalism. The Coming Generation*. Chicago and London: The University of Chicago Press (pp. 65–6; 69–71).

Strong evidence that the turn to the self is widespread and plays a major role in the detraditionalization of religion is provided by James Hunter's analysis of what is happening to conservative religion. What he describes as a 'dramatic turnabout' in North American culture, 'entailing an accentuation of subjectivity and the virtual veneration of the self', has been associated with quite radical changes in the Evangelical camp. 'Traditional assumptions about the self', not least its sinful leanings (portrayed elsewhere in Hunter's volume), 'have undergone a fundamental assault'. If Hunter is correct, Evangelicalism in the USA would appear to be moving in the direction of what we are calling detraditionalized spiritualities of life. (See also Miller, **3.87** and **3.97**; see also Berger, extract **1.37** and Witten (1993, p. 105) on the turn to the self and liberal theology.)

Both popular and more serious academic scholarship have documented a dramatic turnabout within the larger American culture on this count from the mid-1960s. It was a turnabout entailing an accentuation of subjectivity and the virtual veneration of the self, exhibited in deliberate efforts to achieve self-understanding, self-improvement, and self-fulfillment. Though it might be supposed that Evangelicalism would be most resistant to change along these lines, traditional assumptions about the self appear to have weakened substantially here as well. There are, in fact, strong indications that a total reversal has taken place in the Evangelical conception of the nature and value of the self. As one might expect, this is particularly prominent within the coming generation of Evangelicals. For example, nearly nine out of every ten Evangelical students (roughly paralleling the number of public university students) agreed that 'self-improvement is important to me and I work hard at it'. Likewise most (collegians, 68%;

seminarians, 52%) agreed that they felt a 'strong need for new experiences.' The relative significance of these responses is highlighted when they are compared to a national survey of adult Americans conducted by Yankelovich in 1979. The percentage of Evangelical students agreeing with these statements far exceeded the corresponding percentage of the general population on both the importance of self-improvement and the need for new experiences. On the former, only 39 percent of the general population agreed; on the latter, only 22 percent agreed. But there is more. In this general population survey, Yankelovich statistically isolated a special minority. This minority (17% of the adult, working population) manifested and was distinguished by a particularly strong orientation toward self-fulfillment, self-expression, and personal freedom. These were the dominant values upon which they shaped their lives. Yet only 66 percent of this group agreed with the statement that 'self-improvement is important to me and I work hard at it,' and only 46 percent agreed with the statement that they felt a strong personal need for new experiences. Evangelical students, then, more uniformly endorsed these values than did Yankelovich's 'strong-formers.' [...]

The fascination with the self and with human subjectivity has then become a well-established cultural feature of Evangelicalism generally in the latter part of the twentieth century, not simply an ephemeral fashion among the younger generation. [...]

The self and human subjectivity have not only gained attention but have gained legitimacy as well. They have attained a positive value in Evangelical culture. Logically, any discussion of self-improvement, self-fulfillment, and 'self-actualization' presupposes that the self can be and is worth being improved, fulfilled, and actualized; any discussion of human potentiality and emotional and psychological maturity presupposes these as legitimate and worthwhile goals. Indeed, the self would seem to achieve ultimate significance and ultimate value when these concerns are framed within biblical and Christian symbolism. Not only is there a moral imperative to seek one's full potential as a human being but there is a divine imperative as well. It is God's will for every Christian. This has been suggested by the comments of students, but it is also precisely the message of such books as *Mental Health: A Christian Approach* (Cosgrove and Mallory), *The Psychology of Jesus and Mental Health* (Cramer), *The Art of Understanding Yourself* (Osborne), *The Undivided Self: Bringing Your Whole Life in Line with God's Will* (Wilson), *You Can Become the Person You Want to Be*

(Schuller), *The Healthy Personality and the Christian Life* (Hooker), *You Count—You Really Do*! (Miller), *Christo-Psychology* (Kelsey), *How to Become Your Own Best Self* (Grimes), and *Self-Esteem: The New Reformation* (Schuller). The self, as the repository of human emotions and subjectivity, has intrinsic and ultimate worth and significance. [. . .]

The place, value, and meaning of the self have then altered in the culture of American Evangelicalism. And as expected, these cultural innovations are especially prominent in the world of the coming generation. Charmed by it as opposed to being oblivious to it, absorbed in it rather than being (spiritually) repelled by it, modern Evangelicals have accorded the self a level of attention and legitimacy unknown in previous generations. Traditional assumptions about the self have undergone a fundamental assault.

Explanation: freedom and choice

3.43 Bell: 'all is to be explored'

Daniel Bell, 1979: *The Cultural Contradictions of Capitalism*. London: Heinemann (pp. 13–4).

As has already been suggested in this chapter, the development of individualized religion is associated with the development of a self authoritative and confident enough to exercise its freedom to choose: to the point of making 'ultimate' choices with regard to devising one's own religion. Here, Daniel Bell provides a powerful characterization of a self-focused culture of choice.

Modern culture is defined by this extraordinary freedom to ransack the world storehouse and to engorge any and every style it comes upon. Such freedom comes from the fact that the axial principle of modern culture is the expression and remaking of the 'self' in order to achieve self-realization and self-fulfillment. And in its search, there is a denial of any limits or boundaries to experience. It is a reaching out for all experience; nothing is forbidden, all is to be explored.

3.44 Bloom: not 'Don't do that!'

William Bloom (ed.), 1991: Introduction. *The New Age. An Anthology of Essential Writing.* London: Rider, pp. xv–xix (p. xvi).

The purpose of including this extract by New Age advocate William Bloom is to emphasize the point that detraditionalized spiritualities of life appear to appeal to detraditionalized selves. They cater for the authoritative, authorial, freedom-loving self; those who value being free to develop what they truly are and who want their religion to be an articulation of themselves. To derive an expression taken from Daniel Bell's (1979) term 'the untrammeled self' (p. 16), untrammeled selves seek out 'untrammeled religion'. (Evidence for this is provided in the 'explanations' section of Spiritualities of Life; see also Bellah et al. 1985, pp. 235–7; Hammond, 1992; Roof, 1993; and Roof and McKinney, 1987.)

> The great beauty of the New Age movement is that if someone in it is approached by someone else looking for insight or counselling about the inner or religious dimension, he or she will not be told: *'Believe this! Do this! Don't do that!'* but rather: *'There are a thousand different ways of exploring inner reality. Go where your intelligence and intuition lead you. Trust yourself.'* New Age attitudes are the antithesis of fundamentalism.

3.45 Wuthnow and 'religious populism' in the USA

Robert Wuthnow, 1989: *The Struggle for America's Soul. Evangelicals, Liberals, and Secularism.* Grand Rapids, Michigan: Williams B. Eerdmans (pp. 116–17; 180).

Thinking of the USA, Robert Wuthnow explores the idea that 'religious expression is becoming increasingly the product of individual biographies'. No doubt people draw on traditionalized as well as detraditionalized religions to help construct their biographical religiosity, but all of this is detraditionalized in that it is (apparently) largely taking place beyond the authority of particular traditions. (For more material on the USA, see also Roof and Gesch, 1995; Hammond, 1992; and Bellah et al. 1985, pp. 235–7; see also Bellah et al. (1985, ch. 9) on the coexistence of traditional and detraditionalized components in how people have put together their own religious paths.)

> The idea that religious expression is becoming increasingly the product of individual biographies is supported by the very fact of America's pluralistic religious culture. With several hundred different denominations, sects, and cults to choose from, every individual can pretty much tailor his or her religious views to personal taste. As individuals are increasingly exposed to the teachings of different faiths through books, television, travel, and geographic mobility, eclecticism becomes the likely result. This tendency is also reinforced by the highly individualistic ethos in American culture which asserts the individual's freedom of conscience in matters of religion. We believe that individuals should make up their own minds about what they

believe, drawing on whatever sources of inspiration they may find. Thus, it is not uncommon to find public expressions – President Eisenhower's famous remark uttered in the 1950s, for example – that faith is important, but we do not care what that faith is. [. . .]

Some time ago I wrote about a development in American society which I called 'religious populism.' It was comparable in religious circles to what social analysts saw happening in modern societies more generally. With the extension of mass media and a breakdown of institutional authority, people were becoming undifferentiated consumers – inhabitants of the proverbial 'mass society.' At the grass roots, this development meant that people increasingly chose their own private forms of religious expression rather than relying on the authority of a tradition or a religious community. Equally significant was a tendency for leaders to lose important protections from the pressures brought to bear on them by their constituencies. Rather than being able to draw on the authority of their office, their calling, or even their specialized knowledge, clergy were thrust into the harsh glare of public criticism. They had to play to the media, fill large auditoriums, and speak the words that seemed most relevant at the moment. The result was that meeker souls lost out.

3.46 Berger: 'the necessity to make choices as to . . . beliefs'

Peter Berger, 1980: *The Heretical Imperative. Contemporary Possibilities of Religious Affirmation*. London: Collins (pp. 28–31).

This reading by Peter Berger begins with a time when the heretic was the person who consciously decided to deviate from tradition. Today, however, pluralization means that we are all forced to be heretics and 'make choices' as to our beliefs. Although Berger does not dwell on the development of individualized religion, his argument concerning pluralism could well help explain the development of that culture of choice which favours religiosity beyond the regulation of tradition.

The heretic denied this authority, refused to accept the tradition *in toto*. Instead, he picked and chose from the contents of the tradition, and from these pickings and choosings constructed his own deviant opinion. One may suppose that this possibility of heresy has always existed in human communities, as one may suppose that there have always been rebels and innovators. And, surely, those who represented the authority of a tradition must always have been troubled by the possibility. Yet the social context of this phenomenon has changed radically with the coming of modernity: *In premodern situations there is a world of religious certainty, occasionally ruptured by heretical deviations. By contrast, the modern situation is a world of religious uncertainty, occasionally staved off by more or less precarious constructions of religious affirmation.* Indeed, one could put this change even more sharply: *For premodern man, heresy is a possibility – usually a rather remote one; for modern man, heresy typically becomes a necessity.* Or again, *modernity creates a new situation in which picking and choosing becomes an imperative.*

Now, suddenly, heresy no longer stands out against a clear background of authoritative tradition. The background has become dim or even disappeared. As long as that background was still there, individuals had the possibility of *not* picking and choosing – they could simply surrender to the taken-for-granted consensus that surrounded them on all sides, and that is what most individuals did. But now this possibility itself becomes dim or disappears: How can one surrender to a consensus that is socially unavailable? Any affirmation must first create the consensus, even if this can only be done in some small quasi-sectarian community. In other words, individuals now *must* pick and choose. Having done so, it is very difficult to forget the fact. There remains the memory of the deliberate construction of a community of consent, and with this a haunting sense of the *constructedness* of that which the community affirms. Inevitably, the affirmations will be fragile and this fragility will not be very far from consciousness. [. . .]

The weight of the peculiarly American phrase 'religious preference' may now have become apparent. It contains within itself the whole crisis into which pluralism has plunged religion. It points to a built-in condition of cognitive dissonance – and to the heretical imperative as a root phenomenon of modernity.

To sum up the argument thus far: Modernity multiplies choices and concomitantly reduces the scope of what is experienced as destiny. In the matter of religion, as indeed in other areas of human life and thought, this means that the modern individual is faced not just with the opportunity but with the necessity to make choices as to his beliefs. This fact constitutes the heretical imperative in the contemporary situation. Thus heresy, once the occupation of marginal and eccentric types, has become a much more general condition; indeed, heresy has become universalized.

3.47 Voyé and Dobbelaere: bricolage 'beyond secularization'

Lilliane Voyé and Karel Dobbelaere, 1993: Roman Catholicism: Universalism at Stake. In Roberto Cipriani (ed.), *Religions sans Frontières? Present and Future Trends of Migration, Culture, and Communication*. Rome: Dipartimento per L'Informazione e L'Editoria pp. 83–111 (pp. 95–6).

Lilliane Voyé and Karel Dobbelaere, dwelling on the development of (relatively) de-institutionalized, (certainly) individualized religion, argue that the secularization of traditional religion – at least in northern Europe – means that it no longer has the power to regulate how people go about doing their religion. And degregulated religion is fuelled by the cultural value attached to choice, exercised by those who approach religion – of any kind – in the detraditionalized spirit of 'what works?'. (See also Beckford, **3.38**, on deregulated religion.)

The diminution of the influence and control capacity of collective belonging (the family and local community in particular) favours the affirmation of the individual as the master of his own affairs and the locus of choice, decision and responsibility. This process of autonomization of the individual shows up in all domains. In politics, where the parties' 'captive clientele' shrinks in favour of a floating mass and 'à la carte' votes, depending on the moment, the problems and the people involved. In the family domain, where cohabitation has developed, divorce rates have grown, the term 'serial marriage' has been coined, birthrates have declined, and family-roles have become quasi-permanently negotiable. The religious field has not escaped this same process. Here, as elsewhere, the individual himself claims to define in what way he is religious and the content he lends to his religiosity. To do this, he draws from the reservoir of rites, practices and beliefs he is most familiar with and which he considers available without responding to any institutional prerequisites or their consequences. He retains what seems to respond to his needs and combines it with elements foreign to this religion, borrowed from other religions or philosophies, or even from other fields – ranging from psychology to the occult sciences. This explains the acceleration of the sharp decline in mass attendance on weekends during the late sixties and early seventies, which, however, is not matched by a similar steep decline in participation in the rites of passage. Along these same lines, one observes that the contemporary individual's knowledge of Church doctrine is usually vague and superficial; moreover, he hardly feels himself constrained by its prescriptions. As for the Church's moral edicts, rather than simply accepting the general and universal rules, the contemporary individual generally tries to attune them to the concrete situations he encounters in terms of his own evaluation of them.

The institution's ability to impose its rules has consequently become weaker and it lacks the power to check the heterodox uses which individuals, as well as various collective agents, make of its rites, practices and beliefs. Thus it has become commonplace to see certain political figures having recourse to images that are related to the religious heritage to establish the self-presentation they wish to project; for example, during the last presidential campaign in France, Mitterand had himself photographed with a village dominated by a church in the background to affirm his 'tranquil strength'. There is also no lack of publicity which makes similar recourse to religious narratives or figures, just as its promoters incorporate elements of folktales, folklore and show business personalities, thereby reducing religion to the same level. [. . .]

Such things seem to show clearly the extent to which a whole series of religious elements are an intrinsic part of the collective memory but, at the same time, the extent to which they are out of the ecclesiastical institution's control, not only in becoming objects picked out for individual constructions but also in being re-invested in other concerns and thus alienated from their primary significance and proper scope. The later clearly indicates that, at least in Europe, we are in a period 'beyond secularization'.

Explanation: the impact of democratization and universalization

3.48 de Tocqueville, democracy and religion

Alexis de Tocqueville, 1965 (orig. 1835, 1840): *Democracy in America*. London: Oxford University Press (pp. 307).

Alexis de Tocqueville's basic point is that '. . . nothing is more repugnant to the human mind in an age of equality than the idea of subjection to forms' (see reading **3.15**). Consequently democracies are incompatible with religions, in pluralistic societies, threatening peoples' freedom by attempting to specify how they should behave. In the language we are using, religions should therefore detraditionalize, losing those elements which threaten democratic freedom. If de Tocqueville is right, the key values of modernity drive detraditionalization. (See also readings on differentiation **3.15** and **3.16**, in the chapter on Secularization, and readings **3.73–3.75** in Universalization.)

The more the conditions of men are equalized and assimilated to each other, the more important is it for religions, while they carefully abstain from the daily turmoil of secular affairs, not needlessly to run counter to the ideas which generally prevail, and the permanent interests which exist in the mass of the people. For as public opinion grows to be more and more evidently the first and most irresistible of existing powers, the religious principle has no external support strong enough to enable it long to resist its attacks.

3.49   Hatch, democracy and religion

Nathan O. Hatch, 1989: *The Democratization of American Christianity.* New Haven and London: Yale University Press (pp. 6; 7; 9–10; 14; 213).

Very much in the spirit of de Tocqueville, but with a much closer eye on empirical evidence, Nathan Hatch explores some of the ways in which religion in the USA was democratized. 'The passion for equality during these [post-Revolution] years equalled the passionate rejection of the past', writes Hatch: a clear sign that quite radical detraditionalization was taking place within the Christianity he describes.

Above all, the [American] Revolution dramatically expanded the circle of people who considered themselves capable of thinking for themselves about issues of freedom, equality, sovereignty, and representation. Respect for authority, tradition, station, and education eroded. Ordinary people moved toward these new horizons aided by a powerful new vocabulary, a rhetoric of liberty that would not have occurred to them were it not for the Revolution. In time, the issue of the well-being of ordinary people became central to the definition of being American, public opinion came to assume normative significance, and leaders could not survive who would not, to use Patrick Henry's phrase, 'bow with utmost deference to the majesty of the people.' The correct solution to any important problem, political, legal, or religious, would have to appear to be the people's choice. [. . .]

   At the same time, Americans who espoused evangelical and egalitarian convictions, in whatever combination, were free to experiment with new forms of organization and belief. Within a few years of Jefferson's election in 1800, it became anachronistic to speak of dissent in America – as if there were still a commonly recognized center against which new or emerging groups defined themselves. [. . .]

The democratization of Christianity, then, has less to do with the specifics of polity and governance and more with the incarnation of the church into popular culture. In at least three respects the popular religious movements of the early republic articulated a profoundly democratic spirit. First, they denied the age-old distinction that set the clergy apart as a separate order of men, and they refused to defer to learned theologians and traditional orthodoxies. All were democratic or populist in the way they instinctively associated virtue with ordinary people rather than with elites, exalted the vernacular in word and song as the hallowed channel for communicating with and about God, and freely turned over the reigns of power. These groups also shared with the Jeffersonian Republicans an overt rejection of the past as a repository of wisdom. By redefining leadership itself, these movements reconstructed the foundations of religion in keeping with the values and priorities of ordinary people. [. . .]

This story also provides new insight into how America became a liberal, competitive, and market-driven society. In an age when most ordinary Americans expected almost nothing from government institutions and almost everything from religious ones, popular religious ideologies were perhaps the most important bellwethers of shifting worldviews. The passion for equality during these years equaled the passionate rejection of the past. Rather than looking backward and clinging to an older moral economy, insurgent religious leaders espoused convictions that were essentially modern and individualistic. These convictions defied elite privilege and vested interests and anticipated a millennial dawn of equality and justice. Yet, to achieve these visions of the common good, they favored means inseparable from the individual's pursuit of spiritual and temporal well-being. They assumed that the leveling of aristocracy, root and branch, would naturally draw people together in harmony and equality. In this way, religious movements eager to preserve the supernatural in everyday life had the ironic effect of accelerating the break-up of traditional society and the advent of a social order of competition, self-expression, and free enterprise. [. . .]

What then is the driving force behind American Christianity if it is not the quality of its organization, the status of its clergy, or the power of its intellectual life? I have suggested that a central force has been its democratic or populist orientation. America has lived in the shadow of a democratic revolution and the liberal, competitive culture that followed in its wake. Forms of popular religion characteristic of

that cultural system bound paradoxical extremes together: a reassertion of the reality of the supernatural in everyday life linked to the
quintessentially modern values of autonomy and popular sovereignty.
American Christians reveled in freedom of expression, refused to
bow to tradition or hierarchy, jumped at opportunities for innovative
communication, and propounded popular theologies tied to modern
notions of historical development. No less than Tom Paine or Thomas
Jefferson, populist Christians of the early republic sought to start the
world over again.

3.50   Casanova: Catholicism and 'a universalistic language'

José Casanova, 1994: *Public Religions in the Modern World*. Chicago and London: The
University of Chicago Press (p. 223).

A major theme, supported by several readings in the next chapter on Universalization, is that detraditionalization is often very much bound up with the search
to find ways of handling potentially, if not actually, divisive forms of pluralism.
The search is to find what is (supposedly) held in common by – say – different
religions in a particular nation, the commonality then serving as a basis for
adjudicating between the different religions. To find what is (supposedly) held
in common involves detraditionalization in that it involves moving beyond all
those traditional features which make the religions significantly (divisively) different. In the following extract, José Casanova argues that in order to handle
pluralism the Catholic Church has to work with a 'universalistic language' – a
language which, as Casanova implies, owes a great deal to the ethic of humanity
(see more on this in the reading by the Pope, **3.69**.) The adoption of this ethic
means that the Catholic Church has moved in a 'non-denominational' direction:
only possible if distinctive elements of tradition are left behind.

Given modern structural conditions, if the Catholic church wants to
maintain its universalist claims as a church, it will have to learn to
live with social and cultural pluralism both outside and specially
inside the church. This means that to maintain its viability as a private religion it will have to cater to the various pastoral needs of
increasingly diverse Catholic groups, while to maintain its effectiveness as a public religion its public interventions will have to be and
appear nonpartisan and non-denominational; that is, they will have
to be framed in a universalistic language. This by no means precludes
a 'preferential option for the poor' or a continuation of the traditional
Catholic opposition to abortion. On the contrary, it is the moral

obligation to protect human life and to demand universal access to discourse, justice, and welfare that requires that the Universal Church take such a position or such an option. But most important, whichever position or option it takes, the church will have to justify it through open, public, rational discourse in the public sphere of civil society. Moreover, as the lesson of American Catholicism indicates, the church will have to learn to let all the faithful participate in the constant elaboration and reformulation of its normative teachings and allow for different practical judgments as to how to interpret those normative teachings in concrete circumstances.

CHAPTER ELEVEN

universalization

Introduction

Modern times have witnessed the assertion of various forms of 'difference'. (See many readings elsewhere in this volume, in particular in chapter eight on Difference in **Part Two**.) At the same time, however, modern times have also witnessed increased attention being paid to the quest for 'the same': the quest for those universals which differences only serve to mask. Of special note, one can think of the development of the ethic of humanity: that ethicality which is premised on the idea that ethnic, gendered or national differences should not be allowed to disguise the fact that – essentially – we are all humans. (See chapter three, Religions of Humanity, in **Part One** for more on the development of 'humanity'.)

A primary aim in the readings which follow is to explore the idea that a major trend in religions in modern times has involved a shift from religions stressing difference to religions stressing the universal. The shift in emphasis regarding the degree to which differences maintain their significance can be thought of in terms of a spectrum. At one end we find 'strong' traditions, strong in that they promise *the* truth. Religions which transmit other beliefs and values are accordingly judged to be in error. From the point of view of religions *of* difference, such religions are engaged in the transmission of falsehoods. At the other end of the spectrum, we find the assumption that all (virtually all or a great many) religions are essentially the same. Differences in beliefs, virtues, experiences and practices are taken to be adventitious. There is but one religious source. It might not always be 'received' as well as it could be, but its operation is not limited to any particular society. Religious truths, in other words, belong to the realm of the perennial. Religious cultures and practices simply play out variations on the constant, the universal, the 'timeless truths'. The same really does prevail over diversity. Finally, and beyond the spectrum as it is laid out here, one can also think of postmodern religions of difference, embracing diversity as a good in itself.

As for what takes place between these two poles, and moving from emphasis on exclusivity to emphasis on inclusivity, one can think (for example) of those who tolerate or 'put up with' other religions whilst judging them wrong; those who respect participants of other religions whilst judging their beliefs to be mistaken; those who take other beliefs to be partially true; those who see other beliefs as providing different truths or different glimpses of the one truth (one reading of the Gandhian cry that 'All Religions are True', given his prioritization of India); and those who judge other religions as being essentially the same as their own, albeit providing inferior renderings of the perennial.

The universalization of religion is a relatively ill-explored topic. At the empirical level there is enough evidence (introduced in the readings below) to suggest that modern times, at least in western contexts, have favoured universalization. Evidence is also provided by readings in chapter three on Religions of Humanity in **Part One**, such liberal, other-respecting forms of religiosity having grown up with modernity; and by readings in chapter four on Spiritualities of Life (also in **Part One**), which are even more markedly universalistic. However, the process of universalization is nowhere nearly as well documented as it should be.

At the theoretical level, study is even less advanced. Consider the fact that all religions, of whatever variety, have to respond to the challenge of difference. That is to say, they have to handle the fact that other religions espouse (apparently different) truths. Why is it that an increasing number of religions, in many countries, handle difference by finding the same? How does this response link up with more general sociocultural processes in favour of the universal, 'the same'? What are these socio-cultural processes? Furthermore, why is it that religions of difference – with their exclusivistic, remaining resolutely different, response to the challenge of difference – remain very much in evidence, in western contexts and even more so elsewhere? (On this last issue, see chapter two on Religions of Difference in **Part One** and chapter twelve on Sacralization in **Part Three**.)

Although answers to the questions raised above are rather few and far between, this chapter attempts to draw together relevant scholarly reflection. In the attempt to explain universalization, attention is directed to various trends in modern times. One concerns the rise of democracy and of the ethic of humanity. The values associated with these developments, it can then be argued, become more and more important within religious life and thought. Since these values include 'equality' and 'respecting others', it follows that the (exclusivistic) significance of difference is weakened in the religious sphere. (It can be noted that some have also argued that capitalism has a bearing on these cultural developments – a point illustrated by readings **3.76** and **3.77**, below.) Another major consideration is that universalization has taken place as a reponse to pluralism: detraditionalization takes place in order to find 'the same' beyond the differentiations of tradition, thereby to bring unity out of potentially disruptive plurality (see especially the readings below by Gandhi and Hefner).

Because of its concentration on the significance of economic and political factors in the shift towards universalization, this section meshes closely with readings on Economic and Political contexts in **Part Two**. There are also close links with the Detraditionalization chapter of **Part Three**. Virtually by definition, strong traditions negatively evaluate other forms of religion. The 'weaker' a tradition, that is, the more it is detraditionalized, the less there is to serve to differentiate it from other religions. Given this, the development of detraditionalized forms of religion is closely bound up with universalization; and, it can be added, the development of universalization is closely bound up with detraditionalization in that people with a universalistic outlook are likely to ignore all those traditional components which serve to differentiate beliefs. Above all, however, this section should be read in connection with the chapter on Difference in **Part Two**.

Finally, and to help avoid confusion, it should be noted that this chapter does not include any entries on another way in which universalization operates in religious life. We are thinking, in particular, of religions of difference which typically maintain that the truths which they embody should be universally adopted. The aim here is to eradicate difference by converting people to the one truth. This kind of universalization is not discussed because it is premised on the importance of one particular form of difference rather than seeking the universal beyond difference.

Universalization: overviews

3.51 Herberg's 'American Way of Life'

Will Herberg, 1960 (orig. 1955): *Protestant–Catholic–Jew. An Essay in American Religious Sociology*. New York: Doubleday & Company (pp. 36–7; 38–9).

In a classic early statement on universalization, albeit within the confines of a particular nation (the USA), Will Herberg notes that 'A century or even half a century ago, the question, "What are they?", would have been answered in terms of ethnic-immigrant origin' (p. 36). As he goes on to claim, however, increasingly broadly conceived religious formations – ending with just 'Protestant–Catholic–Jew' – have taken over as identifiers. Furthermore, and this is where universalization, or totalization really bites, Herberg claims that these three religiosities have come to serve as the 'diverse representations of the same "spiritual values"'. Herberg wrote in 1955, so it is useful to compare his account with the readings on ethnic and national difference in modern times – in Difference and Political chapters of **Part Two** – which paint a very different picture of the situation today, highlighting how immigrant or ethnic religions now serve to sustain cultural differences; it is also interesting to compare Herberg's account of 'spiritual values' with Bellah's civil religion (**2.42**).

By and large, in the America that has emerged with the third generation [of immigrants], the principle by which men identify themselves and are identified, locate themselves and are located, in the social whole is neither 'race' (except for Negroes and those of Oriental origin) nor ethnic-immigrant background (except for recent arrivals) but religious community. Increasingly the great mass of Americans understand themselves and their place in society in terms of the religious community with which they are identified. And 'religious community' in this usage refers not so much to the particular denominations, of which there are scores in this country, but to the three great divisions, Catholics, Protestants, and Jews. America is indeed, in Mrs. Kennedy's terminology, the land of the 'triple melting pot,' for it is within these three religious communities that the process of ethnic and cultural integration so characteristic of American life takes place. Only, as we have noted, 'transmuting pot' would perhaps be more appropriate than 'melting pot,' since in each of these communities what emerges is a 'new man' cast and recast along the same 'American' ideal type. It is general conformity to this ideal type that makes us all Americans, just as it is the diversity of religious community that gives us our distinctive place in American society. And in the basic diversity of religious community most other diversities tend to be defined and expressed.

We can restate all this by saying that, while the unity of American life is indeed a unity in multiplicity, the pluralism that this implies is of a very special kind. America recognizes no permanent national or cultural minorities; what Europe knows under this head are in this country regarded as foreign-language or foreign-culture groups whose separateness is merely temporary, the consequence of recent immigration, destined to be overcome with increasing integration into American life. [. . .]

For all its wide variety of regional, ethnic, and other differences, America today may be conceived, as it is indeed conceived by most Americans, as one great community divided into three big sub-communities religiously defined, all equally American in their iden-tification with the 'American Way of Life.' [. . .]

Just as sociologically we may describe the emerging social structure of America as one great community divided into three big sub-communities religiously defined, all equally American, so from another angle we might describe Protestantism, Catholicism, and Judaism in America as three great branches or divisions of 'American religion.' The assumption underlying the view shared by most Americans, at least at moments when they think in 'non-sectarian' terms, is not so much that the three religious communities possess an underlying theological unity, which of course they do, but rather that they are three diverse representations of the same 'spiritual values,' the 'spiritual values' American democracy is presumed to stand for (the fatherhood of God and brotherhood of man, the dignity of the individual human being, etc.). That is, at bottom, why no one is expected to change his reli-gion as he becomes American; since each of the religions is equally and authentically American, the American is expected to express his religious affirmation in that form which has come to him with his family and ethnic heritage. Particular denominational affiliations and loyalties within each of the communities (only Protestantism and Judaism come into question here, since Catholicism has no inner denominational lines) are not necessarily denied, or even depreciated, but they are held to be distinctly secondary. With some important exceptions, it is becoming more and more true that the American, when he thinks of religion, thinks of it primarily in terms of the three categories we have designated as religious communities.

All this has far-reaching consequences for the place of religion in the totality of American life. With the religious community as the primary context of self-identification and social location, and with Protestantism, Catholicism, and Judaism as three culturally diverse representations of the same 'spiritual values,' it becomes virtually mandatory for the American to place himself in one or another of these groups. It is not external pressure but inner necessity that compels him. For being a Protestant, a Catholic, or a Jew is understood as the specific way, and increasingly perhaps the only way, of being an American and locating oneself in American society.

3.52 Wuthnow and declining 'tensions'

Robert Wuthnow, 1989: *The Struggle for America's Soul: Evangelicals, Liberals and Secularism.* Grand Rapids, Michigan: Eerdmans (p. 15).

Remaining with the USA, Robert Wuthnow draws on a considerable amount of evidence concerning 'denominational switching' to provide a summary which backs up Herberg's account in that it suggests that universalization is growing in importance. The reading also serves to introduce several explanatory considerations, including the impact of the ecumenical movement and (liberal) higher education. (For more on the importance of the ecumenical movement, see Kinnaman and Cope (eds), 1997.)

One of the most important, albeit gradual, changes that has taken place in American religion since World War II has been a decline in the tensions between Protestants and Catholics, between Christians and Jews, and between different Protestant denominations. In the immediate postwar years, these tensions gave American religion its internal structure and influenced many of the activities of the major religious bodies. By the end of the 1960s, however, and even to a greater extent by the end of the 1970s, the effects of the ecumenical movement, of the more general attitudes of toleration being promoted by higher education, and of regional migration, intermarriage, and other forms of social mixing were having notable effects. Traditional organizational lines were still there, but these lines meant far less than they had only a few decades before. People switched denominations with alacrity, married across faith boundaries with increasing ease, and generally saw little reason to revere the distinctive traditions of their own faith – or at least to let these loyalties interfere with social interaction.

3.53 Wilson on Britain and the 'marginally different'

Bryan R. Wilson, 1989: Sects and Society in Tension. In Paul Badham (ed.), *Religion, State, and Society in Modern Britain.* Lewiston, Queenston, Lampeter: Edwin Mellon Press, pp. 159–84 (pp. 159–60).

Turning to Britain, Bryan Wilson draws attention to the way in which Christianity has become 'generalised, and perhaps increasingly colourless'. Explanations are introduced, in particular the relativizing effect of the development of 'more markedly alien religions' such as Islam.

It is commonplace to refer to the cultural situation in Britain as one of religious pluralism, in which a notional and pervasive orthodoxy has been fragmented by various currents of diversified religious belief and practice. In some measure that pluralism has existed for centuries, of course, but it may be important to note that two divergent tendencies have been at work. Whilst new and exotic religions have been introduced, certain older forms of religious diversity have lost their distinctiveness. The terms in which we have become accustomed to think of religions other than orthodoxy – 'nonconformity' and 'dissent' – have become anachronisms, not only because we have largely abandoned the idea of religious conformity as a norm, but also because bodies once seen as radical departures from the norm have gradually come to be regarded as only marginally different. (This has occurred as a consequence of secularization, changes in social structure, amalgamations, and the general effect on Christianity of the introduction of much more markedly alien religions.) The social bases and the theological import of those old religious differences have been largely eroded as more radical departures have relativized the position of the erstwhile 'dissenters,' as Muslims, Sikhs and Hindus have moved into British society. What once were challenging and even dangerous rivals to orthodox faith have become more or less acceptable variants within a generalized, and perhaps increasingly colourless, Christianity. 'Non-conformity' and 'dissent' have virtually dropped out of the nation's (non-legal) vocabulary. The reality of such divergent 'nonconformity' persists only in minority sectarian movements.

3.54 Huxley's 'perennial philosophy'

Aldous Huxley, 1946: *The Perennial Philosophy*. London: Chatto & Windus (p. 1).

Turning now to spiritualities of life, where 'holistic' themes are dominant, one of the most influential formulations of the idea that the same wisdom lies embedded in all religions, past and present, is found in the opening lines of Aldous Huxley's book. Many of the eastern traditions which Huxley goes on to discuss, it can be noted, have for long been strongly universalisitic: the quest for the same, it would seem, predates modern times.

Philosophia perennis – the phrase was coined by Leibniz; but the thing – the metaphysic that recognizes a divine Reality substantial to the world of things and lives and minds; the psychology that finds in the soul something similar to, or even identical with, divine Reality; the ethic that places man's final end in the knowledge of the immanent and transcendent Ground of all being – the thing is immemorial and universal. Rudiments of the Perennial Philosophy may be found among the traditionary lore of primitive peoples in every region of the world, and in its fully developed forms it has a place in every one of the higher religions. A version of this Highest Common Factor in all preceding and subsequent theologies was first committed to writing more than twenty-five centuries ago, and since that time the inexhaustible theme has been treated again and again, from the standpoint of every religious tradition and in all the principal languages of Asia and Europe.

3.55 Heelas summarizing differentiation and dedifferentiation

Paul Heelas, 1998: Introduction: on Differentiation and Dedifferentiation. In Paul Heelas (ed.) with the assistance of David Martin and Paul Morris, *Religion, Modernity and Postmodernity*. Oxford and Malden, Mass.: Blackwell, pp. 1–18 (pp. 2–4).

This reading aims to locate universalization within modernity. Paul Heelas summarizes evidence which shows that modernity has been driven by both the forces of differentiation (involving exclusivization) and dedifferentiation (involving inclusivization). It is argued that neither process can 'win', the reason being that they call up each other. (See also Clarke (**2.85**) on the tension and oscillation between differentiation and universalization.)

Let us start with modernity. There is absolutely no doubting the fact that differentiation has taken place. Whether it be the intensification of premodern, Medieval differences, or the development of new ones, modernity has emphasized a whole range of contrasts: to do with the division of labour; the division between work (belonging to public life) and the home (the private realm); the construction of national or 'tribal' identities. Or one might think of contrasts which have developed within the ethical culture, the turn to the self existing in tension with traditionalist collectivism, expressivism with utilitarian individualism. To use Daniel Bell's phrase, modernity is riddled with 'cultural contradictions'. And from a more abstract point of view, modernity is characterized by the attempt to 'pin down': to establish the determinate; to find order by way of classification; to explain how things work by distinguishing between essences and finding relevant mechanisms of operation.

As for religion, the evidence might well begin with the Reformation. The gulf between God and the person became more radically articulated, as did the gulf between God and nature. Exclusivistic sects rapidly proliferated. Then there was that early fracture line, between Protestantism and Roman Catholicism, which resulted in the Thirty Years War. As for later fracture lines, we can think of that functional differentiation which occurred with regard to religion and politics (or the secular state); or that which has taken place as science separated itself off from the religious life. Then there is the consideration that religion has become more internally differentiated, very considerable contrasts now existing between traditional, authoritative religions of the text, liberal teachings with a strong dose of humanism, prosperity teachings stamped with the mark of utilitarian individualism, and all those alternative spiritualities or New Age teachings with their emphasis on the expressive.

DEDIFFERENTIATION

Despite the importance of differentiating processes, however, there is also no doubting the fact that modernity has witnessed powerful countervailing tendencies – now in favour of dedifferentiation. The search has been for the unifying or the unitary; for the same; for the transcendental, in the Kantian sense of the necessary and the universal. With regard to morality, Kantians have sought unconditional or categorical imperatives, serving as laws for everyone; and on the ground, human rights legislation has spread throughout the world. With regard to what it is to be human, modernity has seen the construction of 'humanity' – the acknowledgement that, in a fundamental sense, all people are the same and that cultural (etc.) differences are (relatively) unimportant. And with regard to nature, Romantics – and their successors – have thought in terms of a unifying soul of the world.

Indeed, the Romantics and their (expressivist) successors serve to highlight the process of dedifferentiation. In the words of Abrams, 'what was most distinctive in Romantic thought was the normative emphasis on . . . an organized unity in which all individuation and diversity survive . . . as distinctions without division'. The quest was for the unitary which lies 'within' or 'behind' (relatively) insignificant differences. The quest was to articulate the whole, namely that which runs through the human, the natural and the divine.

Looking more generally at dedifferentiation with regard to religion, just as modernity has seen the development of the ethic of humanity, so has it witnessed the – interplaying – development of the spirituality of the perennial. Religious exclusivism has, in measure, given way to religious inclusivism. Denominations – by definition less exclusivistic than sects – have come to dominate mainstream religious life. Increasing numbers of people are prepared to move from denomination to denomination, finding much the same truth behind differences. The ecumenical movement has waxed. Prince Charles speaks of becoming 'Defender of Faith', reflecting the views of all those inclined to find much the same spirituality at the heart of all religious traditions. And on a somewhat different note, it might be added, it is arguably the case that dedifferentiation has also taken place with regard to the secular–sacred boundary. In measure, the religious has become less obviously religious, the secular less obviously secular. This can be considered, for example, in connection with expressive individualism. An estimated 10 per cent or more of Western populations now speak the language of 'authenticity', of 'being true to oneself': and this is to operate in some sort of indeterminate zone, the language being humanistic, the ontology smacking of the Immanent. Rain forests are treated *as if* they were sacred; the boundary between the sacred and the secular loses its hold in many alternative therapies and healing provisions.

Modernity, we have seen, can be thought of as an amalgam of various differentiations and dedifferentiations. Furthermore, differentiation can never be total: boundaries, if they were to become too strong, would make social life impossible. Equally, dedifferentiation can never be comprehensive: for the same or the whole to exist there must be something different. And each process elicits the other. Stephen Toulmin, in *Cosmopolis: The Hidden Agenda of Modernity*, claims that the Enlightenment search for the universal was elicited by the Thirty Years War – an event which served to highlight the dangers of difference. Conversely, it might be argued, the weight of uniformity can encourage the proliferation of particular individual and cultural identities.

Universalization: examples

Example: religions of difference

3.56   Otto's 'unnamed Something'

Rudolf Otto, 1958 (orig. 1917): *The Idea of the Holy. An Inquiry into the Non-rational Factor in the Idea of the Divine and Its Relation to the Rational.* London, Oxford and New York: Oxford University Press (pp. 1; 6).

Although religions of difference, with their specific transcendent or theistic sources of authority and bounded communities, are generally exclusivistic, attempts have been made to introduce the all-encompassing. Although the question as to whether or not the theologian Rudolf Otto's endeavour is successful cannot be discussed here, his classic *The Idea of the Holy* is clearly informed by the coexistence of the specific and the universal.

> It is essential to every theistic conception of God, and most of all to the Christian, that it designates and precisely characterizes deity by the attributes spirit, reason, purpose, good will, supreme power, unity, selfhood. [. . .]
>   Christianity not only possesses such conceptions but possesses them in unique clarity and abundance, and this is, though not the sole or even the chief, yet a very real sign of its superiority over religions of other forms and at other levels. This must be asserted at the outset and with the most positive emphasis. [. . .]
>   It will be useful, at least for the temporary purpose of the investigation, to invent a special term to stand for 'the holy' *minus* its moral factor or 'moment', and, as we can now add, minus its 'rational' aspect altogether.
>   It will be our endeavour to suggest this unnamed Something [the 'numinous'] to the reader as far as we may, so that he may himself feel it. There is no religion in which it does not live as the real innermost core, and without it no religion would be worthy of the name. It is pre-eminently a living force in the Semitic religions, and of these again in none has it such vigour as in that of the Bible.

3.57   Bahr on shifts to the more liberal in Middletown

Howard M. Bahr, 1982: Shifts in the Denominational Demography of Middletown, 1924–1977. *Journal for the Scientific Study of Religion* 21 (2): 99–114 (p. 113).

Leaving the realms of theology, and entering everyday life, religions of difference in modern times have not infrequently lost much of their difference, developing into more moderate, accommodating forms of religiosity, akin to – if not becoming – religions of humanity. Assessing the situation in 'Middletown' (a pseudonym for a typical US community) some 50 years after the pioneering study by the Lynds (1929; 1937), Bahr provides the evidence for such a development, evidence – it can be noted – which supports Wuthnow's claims in reading **3.52**. (See also Caplow et al., 1983; and, on universalization within the North American evangelical camp, see Hunter, 1987, pp. 162–3.)

A comparison of the religious preferences of today's adults and their parents suggests that there has been a quite striking stability in the overall distribution of the city's population among the major denominational categories. Even more striking, however, is the *lack* of stability that shows up when we ask whether people belong to the same churches that their parents belonged to. There is much switching; as many as 40 per cent of the city's adults now claim a different religious preference from that claimed by their parents.

Although religious identities are at least as strong as they were one or two generations ago, the Christianity of Middletown is less bristling, strident, sharp-edged than it once was. As the increase in interfaith marriages and the common denominational switching might suggest, Middletown people are less likely to define their particular brand of Christianity as the *one* solution to everyone's problems.

In demographic character – education, income, marital statues – Middletown's congregations are more alike than they were 50 years ago. The maintenance or increase in the people's identification with organized religion has been accompanied by a clear trend toward convergence. Denominational differences are muted, and it would seem that religion is therefore a greater force for community solidarity today than it was when the Lynds said that a 'militant Protestantism' was one of the forces dividing the city.

Example: religions of humanity

3.58 Bonney: The World's Parliament of Religions and the 'golden rule'

Charles Carroll Bonney, Opening Address. Cited in John Henry Barrows (ed.), 1894: *The World's Parliament of Religions: An Illustrated and Popular Story of the World's First Parliament of Religions, Held in Chicago in Connection with the Columbian Exposition of 1893*, 2 vols. London: The Review of Reviews Office, vol. 1, pp. 67–72 (pp. 68; 72).

In his Presidential address to the 1983 The World's Parliament of Religions, Swedenborgian Charles Bonney explains why God is understood in various ways. Although by no means denying difference *in toto*, 'substantial unity' between the world faiths is located in ethicality, specifically the 'golden rule'. (See Ammerman, reading **1.33** for more on the liberal emphasis on ethicality and the 'golden rule' and Seager, **1.49**, on the World's Parliament.)

As the finite can never fully comprehend the infinite, nor perfectly express its own view of the divine, it necessarily follows that individual opinions of the divine nature and attributes will differ. But, properly understood, these varieties of view are not causes of discord and strife, but rather incentives to deeper interest and examination. Necessarily God reveals himself differently to a child than to a man: to a philosopher than to one who cannot read. Each must see God with the eyes of his own soul. Each must behold him through the colored glasses of his own nature. Each one must receive him according to his own capacity of reception. The fraternal union of the religions of the world will come when each seeks truly to know how God has revealed himself in the other, and remembers the inexorable law that with what judgment it judges it shall itself be judged. [. . .]

In this Congress each system of Religion stands by itself in its own perfect integrity, uncompromised, in any degree, by its relation to any other. In the language of the preliminary publication in the Department of Religion, we seek in this Congress 'to unite all Religion against all irreligion; to make the golden rule the basis of this union; and to present to the world the substantial unity of many religions in the good deeds of the religious life.' Without controversy, or any attempt to pronounce judgment upon any matter of faith or worship or religious opinion, we seek a better knowledge of the religious condition of all mankind, with an earnest desire to be useful to each other and to all others who love truth and righteousness.

This day the sun of a new era of religious peace and progress rises over the world, dispelling the dark clouds of sectarian strife.

This day a new flower blooms in the gardens of religious thought, filling the air with its exquisite perfume.

This day a new fraternity is born into the world of human progress, to aid in the upbuilding of the kingdom of God in the hearts of men.

Era and flower and fraternity bear one name. It is a name which will gladden the hearts of those who worship God and love man in every clime. Those who hear its music joyfully echo it back to sun and flower.

IT IS THE BROTHERHOOD OF EELIGIONS.

In this name I welcome the first Parliament of the Religions of the World.

3.59 Küng: 'True religion is the fulfilment of true humanity'

Hans Küng, 1991: *Global Responsibility. In Search of a New World Ethic.* London: SCM Press (pp. 90; 91; 92).

The highly influential Christian theologian Hans Küng draws attention to the crucial fact that religions of humanity are intimately bound up with that great cultural universal of modern times, 'true humanity'. Küng thinks that the *humanum* is to be found in the obviously traditional features of the major religions, rather than having to probe below to find the esoteric by way of one's own experience (in the fashion of spiritualities of life). Küng sees the ethicality of true humanity as the universal touchstone for discerning the authentically religious and as the basis of a 'global ethic' to unite the world.

Should it not be possible for all religions to agree at least on this basic question of criteria: what is good for human beings is what helps them truly to be human? According to this basic norm of authentic humanity, it is possible to distinguish between good and evil, true and false. So it is also possible to distinguish between what is basically good and bad, true and false, in an individual religion. One can formulate this criterion positively or – often more effectively – negatively in respect of religion:

- Put positively: a religion is true and good to the degree that it serves humanity, to the degree that in its doctrine of faith and morals, its rites and institutions, it advances men and women in their identity, sense of meaning and sense of dignity, and allows them to attain to a meaningful and fruitful existence.
- Put negatively: a religion is false and bad to the degree that it disseminates inhumanity, to the degree that in its doctrine of faith and morals, its rites and institutions, it hinders men and women in their identity, sense of meaning and sense of dignity, and thus does not allow them to attain to a meaningful and fruitful existence. [...]

- True humanity is the presupposition for true religion. That means that the *humanum* (respect for human dignity and basic values) is a minimal requirement of any religion: where authentic religious feeling is to be realized, there must at least be humanity (that is a minimal criterion). But in that case why religion?
- True religion is the fulfilment of true humanity. That means that religion (as the expression of all-embracing meaning, supreme values, unconditional obligation) is an optimal presupposition for the realization of the *humanum*: there must be religion, in particular (that is a maximal criterion) where humanity is to be realized and made concrete as a truly unconditioned and universal obligation. [. . .]

So humanity was not regarded as an 'invention' of the West. Quite the opposite. From the Jewish side one could hear that 'Judaism undoubtedly has a classical religious basis for affirming a universal ethical reality.' The Muslim spoke of the Qur'an as the 'ideal codex of human rights' and referred to a very recent official Muslim declaration on human rights of 1988. The representative of Hinduism spoke of a close connection between morality and religious feeling and of the need for resistance against the self-destructive forces in the world. Even the Buddhist said that the recognition of the trans-anthropocentric and cosmological dimension of human beings in Buddhism did not exclude their specific human significance in the universe or make it impossible. Precisely the wisdom of Buddhism with its strong stress on 'compassion' implied 'the recognition and affirmation of each and all in their difference and in their uniqueness'. The Confucian went furthest, being able to stress from the great humanistic tradition of Confucianism: 'The quest for ecumenical criteria poses no problem for the Confucian tradition. The *humanum* has always been the central concern of Confucianism.' All this might support the considerations that I put forward in the first part of my plea for a world ethic.

3.60 Gillman: Quakers and 'Why have membership at all?'

Harvey Gillman, 1994: *A Light that is Shining. An Introduction to the Quakers.* London: Quaker Home Service (p. 79).

When God is found within all religions, there is no pressing need to belong to any particular one. As well as making this point, Harvey Gillman also illustrates how universalists justify and explain the practice of belonging to a particular body of worshippers, in this instance the Friends. (Compare Harding's 'Headless Way', **1.62**.)

> If you go to meeting you will be hard pressed to tell who is the Friend and who the attender. (It really troubles me when I hear people saying 'I'm only an attender', no-one is 'only' anything). If there is no spiritual distinction between member and attender, the question is asked, Why have membership at all?
>
> Among the early Friends membership was seen as commitment to the promptings of the voice of Christ or the inward light as expressed in daily life. The universalist tendency among many Quakers, which stresses that all religions are illuminated with God's light, has led some to assert that there is no point in identifying too closely with one particular group. Quakers today would not dream of saying that truth was alive only among Friends. To become a Quaker is not a matter of saying here alone is all truth. It is to say: 'This is where I as an individual feel at home. Here I can worship in a way that leads me to fulfillment. Here I can find others who share my seeking and my finding. This is my community'. It is not a matter of being 'good enough' or 'intellectual enough', or even having this or that exact view about Jesus of Nazareth. It is a matter of believing that the relationship between the self, the community, and God are best expressed for you among these people. This is not to say that this relationship cannot be expressed elsewhere; a number of Quakers do worship in other places as well as in the meeting house. Membership does not lead Quakers to live only in the Quaker compound, as it were, but is a matter of making a public witness to the truth as you see it.

3.61   Tagore and 'messengers of Man'

Rabindranath Tagore, 1961 (orig. 1931): *The Religion of Man*. London: Unwin Books (pp. 71–2).

This extract from Rabindranath Tagore provides a strongly universalized – 'God in Man' – interpretation of the 'messengers' who founded 'all great religions'. The fact that Tagore ignores the theistic nature of religions of humanity, only emphasizing 'the inner heart of humanity', is bound up with the fact that his interpretation is from the perspective of a strongly humanistic spirituality. (See also Tagore in **1.85**.)

It is significant that all great religions have their historic origin in persons who represented in their life a truth which was not cosmic and unmoral, but human and good. They rescued religion from the magic stronghold of demon force and brought it into the inner heart of humanity, into a fulfilment not confined to some exclusive good fortune of the individual but to the welfare of all-men. This was not for the spiritual ecstasy of lonely souls, but for the spiritual emancipation of all races. They came as the messengers of Man to men of all countries and spoke of the salvation that could only be reached by the perfecting of our relationship with Man the Eternal, Man the Divine. Whatever might be their doctrines of God, or some dogmas that they borrowed from their own time and tradition, their life and teaching had the deeper implication of a Being who is the infinite in Man, the Father, the Friend, the Lover, whose service must be realized through serving all mankind. For the God in Man depends upon men's service and men's love for his own love's fulfilment.

Example: spiritualities of life

3.62   Emerson and the 'beatitude of man'

Ralph Waldo Emerson, 1983: *Essays & Lectures. An Address to the Senior Class in Divinity College, Cambridge, July 15, 1838.* Cambridge: The Press Syndicate of the University of Cambridge (pp. 77–9).

Emerson explores the ethical, experiential and transformative aspects of the underlying metaphysical universal he calls 'one mind' – a universal, it will be seen, which is far from limited to the depths of the human self. Emerson here serves to represent the Romantic Movement as a whole, which strongly emphasized – and helped popularize – universalized spirituality.

The sublime creed, that the world is not the product of manifold power, but of one will, of one mind; and that one mind is everywhere active, in each ray of the star, in each wavelet of the pool; and whatever opposes that will, is everywhere balked and baffled, because things are made so, and not otherwise. Good is positive. Evil is merely privative, not absolute: it is like cold, which is the privation of heat. All evil is so much death or nonentity. Benevolence is absolute and real. So much benevolence as a man hath, so much life hath he. For all things proceed out of this same spirit, which is differently named love, justice, temperance, in its different applications, just as the ocean receives different names on the several shores which it washes. All things proceed out of the same spirit, and all things conspire with it. Whilst a man seeks good ends, he is strong by the whole strength of nature. In so far as he roves from these ends, he bereaves himself of power, of auxiliaries; his being shrinks out of all remote channels, he becomes less and less, a mote, a point, until absolute badness is absolute death.

The perception of this law of laws awakens in the mind a sentiment which we call the religious sentiment, and which makes our highest happiness. Wonderful is its power to charm and to command. It is a mountain air. It is the embalmer of the world. It is myrrh and storax, and chlorine and rosemary. It makes the sky and the hills sublime, and the silent song of the stars is it. By it, is the universe made safe and habitable, not by science or power. Thought may work cold and intransitive in things, and find no end or unity; but the dawn of the sentiment of virtue on the heart, gives and is the assurance that Law is sovereign over all natures; and the worlds, time, space, eternity, do seem to break out into joy.

This sentiment is divine and deifying. It is the beatitude of man. It makes him illimitable. Through it, the soul first knows itself. It corrects the capital mistake of the infant man, who seeks to be great by following the great, and hopes to derive advantages *from another*, – by showing the fountain of all good to be in himself, and that he, equally with every man, is an inlet into the deeps of Reason. When he says, 'I ought'; when love warms him; when he chooses, warned from on high, the good and great deed; then, deep melodies wander through his soul from Supreme Wisdom. Then he can worship, and be enlarged by his worship; for he can never go behind this sentiment. In the sublimest flights of the soul, rectitude is never surmounted, love is never outgrown.

This sentiment lies at the foundation of society, and successively creates all forms of worship. The principle of veneration never dies out. Man fallen into superstition, into sensuality, is never quite without the visions of the moral sentiment. In like manner, all the expressions of this sentiment are sacred and permanent in proportion to their purity. The expressions of this sentiment affect us more than all other compositions. The sentences of the oldest time, which ejaculate this picty, are still fresh and fragrant. This thought dwelled always deepest in the minds of men in the devout and contemplative

East; not alone in Palestine, where it reached its purest expression, but in Egypt, in Persia, in India, in China. Europe has always owed to oriental genius, its divine impulses. What these holy bards said, all sane men found agreeable and true. And the unique impression of Jesus upon mankind, whose name is not so much written as ploughed into the history of this world, is proof of the subtle virtue of this infusion.

3.63 Beckford and holistic spirituality

James A. Beckford, 1992: Religion, Modernity and Post-modernity. In B. R. Wilson (ed.), *Religion: Contemporary Issues*. London: Bellew, pp. 11–23 (p. 18).

Concentrating on western societies, James Beckford argues that holistic spirituality – a central aspect of what we are calling spiritualities of life – is becoming increasingly important in many quarters. The theme of 'inter-connectedness' entails universalization in that the same spirituality is taken to be running through whatever is inter-connected. Certainly those who have adopted the holistic premise are typically strongly universalistic with regard to how they see 'other' religions.

I am not suggesting that a wave of holism is threatening to sweep away patterns of religious culture which have been sedimented over centuries. My claim is the more modest one that a relatively new sensibility to holistic considerations is working its way into organized religion and other social spheres. I am thinking particularly about the recent evolution of some ways of thinking about medicine, sport, leisure, education, peace, ecology, dying and grieving, self-help, gender, relations with non-human animals, social work, and even management training. There is a growing recognition in each of these spheres of the strengths that can be derived from emphasizing the wholeness of the human person, the inter-connectedness of the human/non-human environment, and the essentially global nature of social and natural processes. The thrust is towards a transcendent, but not necessarily supernatural, point of reference. An echo of this 'transcendent humanism' has been detected even in the rural French Catholic Church.

Now, there will no doubt be objections (i) that this holistic current is confined to a tiny proportion of the population, and (ii) that spirituality is not the same as religion. On the first point, I have to admit that the number of activists and true believers deliberately pursuing or cultivating holism may still be relatively small. But I contend that holistic consciousness has already made inroads deep into public thinking about ecology, peace, gender and health. On the second point, it seems to me that there is far more overlap than difference between 'religion' and 'spirituality' in so far as they both denote ways of thinking, feeling and acting which are oriented towards the highest sources of meaning and value. If spirituality lacks the sense of communal obligation and collective ritual attaching to public religion, it is only appropriate that it should expand at a time when personal choice seems to be the criterion of well-being in so many areas of life.

3.64 Gandhi and 'the permanent element in human nature'

M. K. Gandhi, cited in Stephen Hay (ed.), 1991: *Sources Of Indian Tradition. Volume Two: Modern India and Pakistan*, 2nd edn. New Delhi: Penguin Books India. (p. 250).

Gandhi here points to the political implications of immanentist holism. Differences between traditions are seen in terms of the quest for 'prestige' which is likened to mere 'furniture'. (See also the reading from Gandhi later in this chapter.)

Quite selfishly, as I wish to live in peace in the midst of a bellowing storm howling around me, I have been experimenting with myself and my friends by introducing religion into politics. Let me explain what I mean by religion. It is not the Hindu religion, which I certainly prize above all religions, but the religion which transcends Hinduism, which changes one's very nature, which binds one indissolubly to the truth within and which ever purifies. It is the permanent element in human nature which counts no cost too great in order to find full expression and which leaves the soul utterly restless until it has found itself, known its Maker and appreciated the true correspondence between the Maker and itself.

The fact is, I have no desire for prestige anywhere. It is furniture required in courts of kings. I am a servant of Mussalmans [Muslims], Christians, Parsis and Jews, as I am of Hindus. And a servant is in need of love, not prestige. That is assured to me so long as I remain a faithful servant.

Universalization: explanations

Explanation: detraditionalization and the turn to humanity

3.65 Heelas explaining links between detraditionalization and the ethic of humanity

Paul Heelas, 1996: On Things not being Worse, and the Ethic of Humanity. In Paul Heelas, Scott Lash and Paul Morris (eds), *Detraditionalization. Critical Reflections on Authority and Identity*. Oxford and Cambridge, Mass.: Blackwell, pp. 200–22 (pp. 211–14).

Given the immense significance of 'humanity' for modern times, and given the importance of this notion within universalized religion, there is little doubt that the development of the notion that humans are essentially the same provides the cultural key to explaining universalizing trends within the religious domain, in particular religions of humanity and spiritualities of life. 'Humanity', that is to say, together with its values (equality, respect, dignity and value of life), has shaped religious thought. Given this argument, explaining universalization within the religious domain involves explaining the development of 'humanity'. Beginning with the role played by detraditionalization, Heelas discusses some of the ways in which the development of 'the ethic of humanity' can be explained. (See also Bellah (1964) for the role played by Christianity in the development of democratic humanism; and see the chapter on Detraditionalization in **Part Three** for explanations as to why many traditions have been eroded during modern times.)

> Detraditionalization involves loss of faith in established orders. For this to happen, a person has to become disengaged, that is, has to cease to be dominated by authoritative 'others'. More exactly, detraditionalization involves a shift to the authority of the 'individual' because the person has to acquire new 'individualistic' values – different from those provided by established orders – in order to lose faith in what has been on offer.... Most accounts of detraditionalization suppose that these values are of a self-centred, utilitarian, relativistic variety. However, it can also be argued that detraditionalization provides something approaching the necessary – although not necessary and sufficient – condition for the construction of the ethic of humanity.
>
> In an especially significant passage, which will therefore be cited in its entirety, Durkheim states:
>
> > Originally society is everything, the individual nothing. Consequently, the strongest social feelings are those connecting the individual with the collectivity; society is its own aim. Man is considered only an

instrument in its hands; he seems to draw all his rights from it and has no counter-prerogative, because nothing higher than it exists. But gradually things change. As societies become greater in volume and density, they increase in complexity, work is divided, individual differences multiply, and the moment approaches when the only remaining bond among members of a single human group will be that they are all men. Under such conditions the body of collective sentiments inevitably attaches itself with all its strength to its single remaining object, communicating to this object an incomparable value by so doing. Since human personality is the only thing that appeals unanimously to all hearts, since its enhancement is the only aim that can be collectively pursued, it inevitably acquires exceptional value in the eyes of all. It thus rises far above all human aims, assuming a religious nature.

An initial observation derives from the claim that 'the individual' is 'nothing' in societies where the 'collectivity' is all-important. However exaggerated this might be, a considerable amount of evidence suggests that embeddedness is associated with exclusivistic outlooks. Many socio-cultural orders, that is to say, serve to value their occupants so as to generate contextualized inequalities. To the extent that people are defined – or constituted – in terms of a particular socio-cultural formation, that formation serves to characterize their true way of being. Other socio-cultural formations, with their different ways of life, are accordingly seen to be associated with alien – and therefore invalid – modes of being. Such perceptions, it naturally follows, count against those experiences which might serve as the basis for holding a notion of the human which transcends socio-cultural differentiations.

To the extent that 'strong' traditions serve to exclusivize what counts as human nature, the inclusivistic outlook can only develop under circumstances of detraditionalization. By definition, it goes without saying, the ethic is incompatible with strong tribal or national identities. Hence the importance Durkheim attaches to the claim that 'the moment approaches when *the only remaining bond* among the members of a single human group will be that they are all men' (my emphasis). But does detraditionalization provide something akin to the necessary *and sufficient* conditions for the construction of the ethic of humanity? Why should it not simply result in egoistical individualism? Durkheim argues, it will be recalled, that 'Since human personality is the only thing that appeals unanimously to all hearts, since its enhancement is the only aim that can be collectively pursued, it inevitably acquires exceptional value in the eyes of all.' Unfortunately, the argument is patently circular or tautological. What is supposedly being explained, namely the exceptional value ascribed to the human personality, is actually explained by the same thing, namely the unanimous appeal of human personality.

Durkheim's explanation hangs on an ontological commitment; a commitment even more clearly seen in such passages as 'The obligations laid upon us by both the one and the other arise *solely* from our intrinsic human nature or those with whom we find ourselves in relation'. Detraditionalization thus serves to reveal an authentic human nature, an inner 'voice' which can direct detraditionalized selves in the right direction; whose virtues explain the construction, form and authority of the religion of humanity. And, it can be noted, such a Romantic or expressivist approach has played an important role among other theorists of the development of human values. One might think of the work of Peter Berger et al. on the expressivist-orientated 'homeless mind', David Harvey on 'ecosocialism' and Marx's 'species being', Charles Taylor on the 'ethic of authenticity' or Victor Turner on 'communitas'. Or one might think of Zygmunt Bauman, arguing that 'the end of morality as we know it' has enabled 'the moral capacity of the self' to come into its own.

Detraditionalization has clearly played a role in paving the way for the construction of the tradition of humanity. The degree of value attributed to the self *qua* self is surely incompatible with socially-dominated views of personhood. The idea that there is a self 'above society' (as Durkheim puts it) is surely incompatible with those selves generated by socio-cultural differentiations. And it is certainly safe to conclude that detraditionalization has played a crucial role in facilitating the operation of the ethic: human rights, for example, have only been able to come to serve as a virtually universal ethical standard – possessing validity across states and therefore entitling intervention – because the self-determining authority of nations has become weaker. But appeal to 'intrinsic human nature' or a 'moral self' – to provide that inner authority which explains why detraditionalization has not simply led to egotistical, anarchical individualism – will only convince the converted.

What precisely has fuelled the ideology, in the West let alone elsewhere, that the 'non-social' self – belonging to humanity rather than to the differentiated cultural realm – is of primary value, constitutes a formidable task for intellectual inquiry. Indeed, rather than there being anything demonstrably 'natural' or self-evident about the notion of intrinsic human nature, the historical record of ideologies of inequality shows that much has counted against the idea. There are no easy answers as to what has served to fuel a somewhat exceptional feature of cultural life. Christianity, for example, might appear to provide a ready solution, it being argued that the ethic has been inspired by relevant Biblical passages and subsequent teaching. However, the Bible can be read in many different ways (including those of an exclusivistic variety). Indeed, as John Passmore has argued, Christianity has very often taken an 'Augustinian' form, emphasizing the difference between those who are saved and those who are not. Considerations of this kind, together with the fact that the ethic of humanity did not become significant until relatively recently, suggest that widespread adoption of the 'humankind' interpretation of the Bible has almost certainly been determined by other factors.

To complicate matters further, theorization of those processes which have fuelled the ethic of humanity cannot ignore all those other processes affecting moral beliefs. The ethic cannot be understood in isolation from all that it has to contend with. Exclusivizing tendencies are widespread in the West, let alone elsewhere. What counts as 'being properly human' is defined contextually, in terms of strong tradition-informed religious or ethnic criteria. The 'I am a man' slogans of the civil rights movement of the 1960s have in measure been replaced with the slogans – to do with 'Black consciousness' and 'Black nature' – of the radical, differentiating multiculturalist. Then there are those tendencies involving another kind of contextualism, the self-referentiality of egoistic individualists taking precedence over humanistic values. In addition, and recalling the kind of claim made by Bloom, there are also tendencies encouraging that form of relativistic liberalism which emphasizes 'respect for the other'.

Furthermore, 'the problem of solidarity' has to be handled. As Durkheim argued forcefully, morality thrives when people *belong* to collectivities. Assemblies, rituals, a diverse range of group activities and communal practices, serve to generate and enhance commitment to moral values. Communitarians today argue along much the same lines. As Richard Bellamy puts it, 'They point out that we only acquire the capacity for judgement through living in real societies embodying those conceptions of the good which give our lives their particular purpose, meaning and character'. Bearing in mind that the ethic of humanity is associated with detraditionalized circumstances, the problem is thus one of identifying what has served to fuel its ethic of solidarity. The only answer, it would seem, is that its *own* practices – for example those taking place in schools – suffice to account for its potency.

Explanation: handling difference

3.66   Toulmin and the 'Religious Wars'

Stephen Toulmin, 1992: *Cosmopolis. The Hidden Agenda of Modernity*. Chicago: The University of Chicago Press (p. 89).

Focusing on the seventeenth century, Stephen Toulmin (1992) argues that 'The more acute the differences between Protestant and Catholic zealots, the more dogmatically they denounced one another, and the more urgently did cooler heads embrace the project for a "rational" method to establish truths whose certainty was clear to reflective thinkers of any denomination' (pp. 82–3). The Enlightenment and theological search for universals, that is to say, is seen as a reaction to the violent disturbances associated with tradition-inspired difference. (See also Bauman (1993, pp. 25–8) on the role of reason and law in the search for universals to handle differences.)

After 1650, the peoples of Northern and Western Europe faced grave problems of political and intellectual reconstruction. For fifty years, religious fervor and ideological denunciation had undermined the arts of diplomacy, and Europeans had lost the arts of living together in mutual respect. Both sets of arts now had to be restored. Domestically, the years of the Religious Wars saw the power of the landed nobility diluted, as the influence of professional men and city merchants grew. This new historical situation required the countries of Western Europe to develop fresh social structures and modes of solidarity.

Both social tasks had intellectual counterparts. The breakdown of diplomatic communication in the previous half-century was rationalized as a by-product of theological antagonisms: serious-minded men on both sides of the barricades now had to hammer out fresh modes of discussion that would let them circumvent (if not overcome) earlier disagreements. For those who survived into the years after the Religious Wars, the dream of logically necessary arguments whose 'certainty' could go beyond the 'certitude' of any theological position kept its charm in both modes of reasoning and language. Half a century of confrontation and head-butting made Rationalism look all the more enticing. In the long run, might it not also help to bind up the wounds in Cosmopolis, and restore the lost harmony between the natural and social orders?

3.67 Niebuhr on 'the road to unity'

H. Richard Niebuhr, 1957 (orig. 1929): *The Social Sources of Denominationalism*. New York and London: Henry Holt and Company (pp. 278–9; 280–1; 284).

For theologian Richard Niebuhr, Christianity has become embroiled in the divisions of the world. As he writes, 'Denominational Christianity, that is a Christianity which surrenders its leadership to the social forces of national and economic life, offers no hope to the divided world' (1957, p. 275). His solution is to attempt to reactivate what he believes to be the Christianity of the gospels: a universalized Christianity which can attend to 'the common interests of mankind'. Here he describes such Christianity.

Its purpose is not the foundation of an ecclesiastical institution or the proclamation of a metaphysical creed, though it seeks the formation of a divine society and presupposes the metaphysics of a Christlike God. Its purpose is the revelation to men of their potential childhood to the Father and their possible brotherhood with each other. That revelation is made not in terms of dogma but of life, above all in the life of Christ. His son-ship and his brotherhood, as delineated in the gospel, are not the example which men are asked to follow if they will, but rather the demonstration of that character of ultimate reality which they can ignore only at the cost of their souls. The *summum bonum* which this faith sets before men is nothing less than the eternal harmony of love, in which each individual can realize the full potentiality of an eternal life in self-sacrificing devotion to the Beloved Community of the Father and all the brethren. [. . .]

For the proclamation of this Christianity of Christ and the Gospels a church is needed which has transcended the divisions of the world and has adjusted itself not to the local interests and needs of classes, races, or nations but to the common interests of mankind and to the constitution of the unrealized kingdom of God. No denominational Christianity, no matter how broad its scope, suffices for the task. The church which can proclaim this gospel must be one in which no national allegiance will be suffered to infringe upon the unity of an international fellowship. In it the vow of love of enemy and neighbor and the practice of non-resistance will need to take their place beside the confession of faith and the rites. For without complete abstention from nationalist ethics the universal fellowship of this church would inevitably fall apart into nationalist groups at the threat of war or under the influence of jingoistic propaganda. In such a church distinctions between rich and poor will be abrogated by the kind of communism of love which prevailed in the early Jerusalem community. This communism differs as radically from the dictatorship of the proletariat as it does from the dictatorship of capitalism. The principle of harmony and love upon which it alone can be established requires that each contribute to the community according to his ability and receive from it according to his need, not according to some predetermined principles of quantitative equality or of privilege. Furthermore, this church of love will need to bridge the chasm between the races, not only by practising complete fellowship within the house of God but by extending that practice into all the relationships of life. It will need to mediate the differences of culture by supplying equality of opportunity to tutored and untutored alike and by giving each their share in the common task and in the common love. [. . .]

The road to unity which love requires denominations, nations, classes, and races to take is no easy way. There is no short cut even to the union of the churches. The way to the organic, active peace of brotherhood leads through the hearts of peacemakers who will knit together, with patience and self-sacrifice, the shorn and tangled fibers of human aspirations, faiths, and hopes, who will transcend the fears and dangers of an adventure of trust. The road to unity is the road of repentance. It demands a resolute turning away from all those loyalties to the lesser values of the self, the denomination, and the nation, which deny the inclusiveness of divine love. It requires that Christians learn to look upon their separate establishments and exclusive creeds with contrition rather than with pride. The road to unity is the road of sacrifice which asks of churches as of individuals that they lose their lives in order that they may find the fulfilment of their better selves. But it is also the road to the eternal values of a Kingdom of God that is among us.

3.68 Rolland reacting to 'this shameful world war'

Francis Dore and Marie-Laure Prevost (eds), 1990: *Selected Letters of Romain Rolland*. Oxford, New York and Delhi: Oxford University Press (p. 13).

In a letter to Tagore, sent in 1919, Romain Rolland proposes another kind of solution to the problem of diversity and conflict, drawing not on Christianity but on 'Asia's thought'. As another letter in the volume spells out, Rolland believes that this involves 'Asian faculties of concentration, which finally achieve identity at the depths of that universal Being whom everyone carries in him' (p. 84). Rolland does not, however, believe that Asian thought alone will bring peace and harmony to the world. What is needed is a complementary view of East and West on this issue. (See also Clarke, reading **2.85**.)

I was glad to receive your friendly letter, dated 24 June, and two of your books which were sent by your publisher, Macmillan: *Nationalism* and *The Home and the World*. I cordially thank you for them. The reading of *Nationalism* has been a great joy for me; for I entirely agree with your thoughts, and I love them even more now that I have heard them expressed by you with this noble and harmonious wisdom which – being your own – is so dear to us. It gives me profound pain (and, I might say, remorse, if I did not consider myself a human being rather than a European) when I consider the monstrous abuses which Europe makes of her power, this havoc of the universe, the destruction and debasement of so much material and moral wealth of the greatest forces on earth which it would have been in her interest to defend and to make strong by uniting them to her own. The time has come to react. It is not only a question of justice, it is a question of saving humanity.

After the disaster of this shameful world war which marked Europe's failure, it has become evident that Europe alone cannot save herself. Her thought is in need of Asia's thought, just as the latter has profited from contact with European thought. These are the two hemispheres of the brain of mankind. It is necessary to re-establish their union and their healthy development.

3.69 John Paul II responding to difference

John Paul II, 1995: The Fabric of Relations among Peoples. *Origins* 25 (18): 293, 295–9 (pp. 295; 299).

During an Address to the UN General Assembly, John Paul II (1995) first extols 'freedom', going on to note that 'the quest from freedom in our time has its basis in those universal rights which humans enjoy by the very fact of their humanity' (p. 295). The point is then made – in the extract which follows – that such rights are vital for an 'international politics of persuasion'; that is, for handling abuses of freedom. The last paragraph of the extract shows, however, that the Pope has not simply capitulated to the UN ethic of humanity: this is a sacralized, Catholic form of universalization and part of the 'natural law' tradition dating back to Aquinas and before. In sum, the Pope sees ethics and politics as grounded in a moral logic built into human life, itself a divine creation. (See also Casanova, 1994, p. 191.)

It is important for us to grasp what might be called the inner structure of this world-wide movement [the UN]. It is precisely its global character which offers us its first and fundamental 'key' and confirms that there are indeed universal human rights rooted in the nature of the person, rights which reflect the objective and inviolable demands of a universal moral law. These are not abstract points; rather, these rights tell us something important about the actual life of every individual and of every social group. They also remind us that we do not live in an irrational or meaningless world. On the contrary, there is a moral logic which is built into human life and which makes possible dialogue between individuals and peoples. If we want a century of violent coercion to be succeeded by a century of persuasion, we must find a way to discuss the human future intelligibly. The universal moral law written on the human heart is precisely that kind of 'grammar' which is needed if the world is to engage this discussion of its future.

In this sense, it is a matter for serious concern that some people today deny the universality of human rights, just as they deny that there is a human nature shared by everyone. To be sure, there is no single model for organizing the politics and economics of human freedom; different cultures and different historical experiences give rise to different institutional forms of public life in a free and responsible society. But it is one thing to affirm a legitimate pluralism of 'forms of freedom' and another to deny any universality or intelligibility to the nature of man or to the human experience. The latter makes the international politics of persuasion extremely difficult, if not impossible. [. . .]

We must not be afraid of the future. We must not be afraid of man. It is no accident that we are here. Each and every human person has been created in the 'image and likeness' of the One who is the origin of all that is. We have within us the capacities for wisdom and virtue. With these gifts, and with the help of God's grace, we can build in the next century and the next millennium a civilization worthy of the human person, a true culture of freedom. We can and must do so! And in doing so, we shall see that the tears of this century have prepared the ground for a new springtime of the human spirit.

3.70 Hefner and a 'shared national culture' in Indonesia

Robert W. Hefner, 1998: Secularization and Citizenship in Muslim Indonesia. In Paul Heelas (ed.), with the assistance of David Martin and Paul Morris, *Religion, Modernity and Postmodernity*. Oxford and Malden: Blackwell, pp. 147–68 (pp. 149; 156; 159).

Robert Hefner argues that liberal Indonesian Muslim reformers (of whom the best-known is Madjid) have responded to pluralism in the region by encouraging the desacralization of those beliefs and practices which have traditionally served to differentiate communities. Although Hefner calls this a 'soft' version of secularization, it is perhaps best seen as the detraditionalization of those beliefs and practices which threaten the unity of the nation. The reason for this is that it is very much bound up with the development of forms of belief able to exercise 'unitary appeal'.

> Over the past fifteen years, there has been a far-reaching Islamic revival, and its projects have included the extirpation of heterodox folk traditions and the 'Islamization' of areas of everyday life previously regulated by non-Islamic norms. At a deeper level, however, these developments are less exceptional relative to the Western experience [of secularization] than might first appear to be the case. In particular, I will suggest, a basic challenge to religion in both regions has been, and remains, the question of how simultaneously to develop a shared national culture, with its associated ideals of cultural citizenship, while still being responsive to the nation's pluralism. A key issue for Muslims attempting to devise such a response has been the question of whether Islam provides fixed ethical formulae for such a project, or values of a more generalized sort. [. . .]
>
> Though, by comparison with other Muslim societies, Javanese Islam remains vigorously pluralistic, there can be no question that reformist Muslims have carried out nothing less than a great transformation, bringing popular religion into closer conformity with Islam's monotheistic ideals.
>
> Is this secularization? Clearly if our ideas on secularization are based on the 'hard' version of the thesis . . . , this is not secularization at all, but simply a delegitimation of old religious practices and the sacralization of others. Religion has not been banisher to the realm of the personal, exposed as 'essentially irrational', or pushed down a slippery slope towards extinction. On the contrary, while attacking spirit cults and shamans, Muslim reformers promote daily prayer, mosque attendance, payment of alms, and other expressions of Islamic piety. From a normative Islamic perspective, the Javanese appear more religious than ever.
>
> If, however, what we mean by secularization is more the 'soft' version to which I earlier referred, with its desacralization of the concrete in favour of an abstraction of the divine, I think it is clear that the efforts of Islamic reformers contain elements similar to what

is conventionally known as secularization. In attacking guardian spirits, belittling the spiritual efficacy of ancestors, and contesting the morality of magic, Muslim reformers have desacralized domains that previously fell under the spell of magical and spiritist technique, and relocated divinity to a higher or more abstract plane. In so doing, the reformers have enacted an ethic consistent with the Islamic emphasis on God's absolute oneness (*tauhid*). At the same time, they have brought popular religion in line with more general notions of spiritual agency, displacing the immediate, manipulable spiritualism of animist cults with a unitary appeal to Allah. [. . .]

In the aftermath of several anti-Christian incidents (including church burnings) in 1991–2, Madjid and his supporters launched a bold appeal for religious tolerance, basing it on, among other things, the highly controversial argument that people of other faiths could and should be properly regarded as 'Muslim' when professing faith in God. More recently, civil pluralist Muslims have been at the centre of efforts to promote the democratization of Indonesia's still tightly controlled political system, calling for, among other things, a loosening of controls on the press, an end to government manipulation of elections, and official tolerance of a political 'opposition' (a policy the government rejects on the grounds that it is contrary to Indonesian cultural tradition).

3.71   Parel: Gandhi's search for 'national integration'

Anthony J. Parel, 1995: The Doctrine of *Swaraj* in Gandhi's Philosophy. In Upendra Baxi and Bhikhu Parekh (eds), *Crisis and Change in Contemporary India*. New Delhi, Thousand Oaks and London: Sage, pp. 57–81 (pp. 76–7).

Whereas Madjid (in the previous extract) uses the word 'Muslim' in connection with those of any faith who profess belief in God, Gandhi never wanted to impose the term 'Hindu' in this fashion. But his response to diversity – and the associated threat of violence – was much the same as that found among the liberal reformers in Indonesia and elsewhere. Essentially, he taught that the unitary – the 'religion which underlies all religions' – is much more significant than the different. (See also Gandhi earlier in this chapter.) As in the previous reading, the general point is that universalized religion is of great importance in countries facing pluralistic dissolution, differentiated and dedifferentiated religion coexisting with the former trying to hold things together.

He [Gandhi] attempted to adapt modern nationalism to two principles of Indian civilisation – unity in diversity and assimilation of disparate elements. He paid special attention to the two issues that affected Indian nationalism most – the Hindu–Muslim conflict and the linguistic conflict. The implementation of the above two principles, he believed, would make India a genuinely multi-religious, multilingual nation:

> India cannot cease to be one nation because people belonging to different religions live in it. The introduction of foreigners does not destroy the nation, they merge in it. A country is one nation only when such a condition obtains in it. That country must have a faculty for assimilation. India has ever been such a country.

He revived two other principles of Indian civilisation which he thought would contribute to national integration. They also give us a preview, as it were, of what later would come to be known as ecumenism. The first is that 'religions are different roads converging to the same point', and the second, that there is such a thing as 'religion which underlies all religions.' If organised religions can comport themselves along these principles, a multi-religious nation can flourish and the average citizen would be able to avoid, he believed, the Scylla of scepticism and the Charybdis of fundamentalism in religious matters.

3.72 Berger and responses to competition in the market

Peter Berger, 1963: A Market Model for the Analysis of Ecumenicity. *Social Research* (Spring): 77–93 (pp. 85–7).

A reading from Peter Berger now provides an illustration of a very different way in which difference can contribute to universalization. In the USA, it is argued, one way that religious organizations – specifically denominations – have responded to the pluralism associated with the separation of religion and state, is by way of 'cartelization'. 'Ecclesiastical mergers', it goes without saying, are highly likely to encourage the spread of similar beliefs and practices.

Ecumenicity in the American situation functions to rationalize competition. This competition, for a variety of well-known historical reasons, is given in the pattern of denominational pluralism. The individual denominations cannot count on special favors from the state, although they all benefit equally from certain political privileges such as the economic bonanza of the tax exemption laws. Therefore, they must compete with each other for the interest, allegiance, and financial support of their potential clientele. We are thus faced here with the classic picture of competition between a large number of units in a free market. The way in which this competition operated before the coming of ecumenical cooperation can, indeed, be described as falling in one of the fairly brutal categories of *laissez-faire* economics. [. . .]

Such untrammelled competition becomes increasingly impractical and expensive for those denominations largely dependent on the middle-class, suburban market. Their bureaucracies are forced to rationalize their operations. In view of the fundamental economic pressures at work here, it should not surprise us that the methods of this rationalization bear close resemblance to those employed in the secular economy to make free enterprise a more civilized affair. Essentially, we have here the well-known process of cartelization, facilitated in the ecclesiastical case by the absence of a Sherman Act. This absence, incidentally, points to an interesting consequence of the separation of church and state. While the state continues to interfere in the secular economy in ways that often are economically irrational – although they may be perfectly rational in political or moral terms – the state is constitutionally unable to interfere in the inner affairs of the church. Thus the process of rationalization in the religious economy occurs free of political interference. To put this pointedly, the separation of church and state guarantees the dominance of economic over political factors in the shaping of church affairs. . . .

Suffice it to repeat that the denominational bureaucracies find themselves in a situation in which cartelization is the logical course of conduct, and that they are free to follow this course both as a result of the absence of state controls, given in the constitution, and their increasing independence *vis-à-vis* their constituency; the latter produced by the inevitable entrenchment of bureaucratic forms of administration, but further reinforced by the fiscal factor referred to in connection with denominational investments.

Cartelization rationalizes competition by reducing the number of competing units by amalgamation and also by dividing up the market between the larger units that remain. This is precisely what has happened in the market under discussion; the number of competing units has been steadily reduced through ecclesiastical mergers.

Explanation: democracy and equality

3.73   de Tocqueville: equality and 'the unity of the Creator'

Alexis de Tocqueville, 1965 (orig. 1835, 1840): *Democracy in America*. London: Oxford University Press (p. 305).

There is no doubting the fact that the development of democracy, with its assumptions and values, has been a major influence on religious thought. Here, Alexis de Tocqueville looks at how a key democratic (and human) value – equality – has made its mark. (See also de Tocqueville, **3.15** and **3.48**; notice also the 'opposite' argument that religion has been a major influence on democracies (**2.44** and **2.45**).)

> I find that in order for religions to maintain their authority, humanly speaking, in democratic ages, they must not only confine themselves strictly within the circle of spiritual matters: their power also depends very much on the nature of the belief they inculcate, on the external forms they assume, and on the obligations they impose. . . . [T]hat equality leads men to very general and very extensive notions, is principally to be understood as applied to the question of religion. Men living in a similar and equal condition in the world readily conceive the idea of the one God, governing every man by the same laws, and granting to every man future happiness on the same conditions. The idea of the unity of mankind constantly leads them back to the idea of the unity of the Creator; while, on the contrary, in a state of society where men are broken up into very unequal ranks, they are apt to devise as many deities as there are nations, castes, classes, or families, and to trace a thousand private roads to Heaven.

3.74   Bloom and 'openness'

Allan Bloom, 1987: *The Closing of the American Mind*. New York: Simon and Schuster (pp. 25–6).

Those who attach high value to equality and freedom more or less necessarily attach equally high value to toleration and openness. Although Allan Bloom does not explicitly address the point, toleration is an important step towards inclusivity: from being intolerant towards respecting others and seeing their truths as 'equal' to one's own. (The process can even be taken as far as relativism.) This way of evaluating others, it can then be argued, paves the cultural way for the belief that – at some deep level – all religions are essentially equal in that they are the same.

There is one thing a professor can be absolutely certain of: almost every student entering the university believes, or says he believes, that truth is relative. If this belief is put to the test, one can count on the students' reaction: they will be uncomprehending. That anyone should regard the proposition as not self-evident astonishes them, as though he were calling into question 2 + 2 = 4. These are things you don't think about. The students' backgrounds are as various as America can provide. Some are religious, some atheists; some are to the Left, some to the Right; some intend to be scientists, some humanists or professionals or businessmen; some are poor, some rich. They are unified only in their relativism and in their allegiance to equality. And the two are related in a moral intention. The relativity of truth is not a theoretical insight but a moral postulate, the condition of a free society, or so they see it. They have all been equipped with this framework early on, and it is the modern replacement for the inalienable natural rights that used to be the traditional American grounds for a free society. That it is a moral issue for students is revealed by the character of their response when challenged – a combination of disbelief and indignation: 'Are you an absolutist?,' the only alternative they know, uttered in the same tone as 'Are you a monarchist?' or 'Do you really believe in witches?' This latter leads into the indignation, for someone who believes in witches might well be a witchhunter or a Salem judge. The danger they have been taught to fear from absolutism is not error but intolerance. Relativism is necessary to openness; and this is the virtue, the only virtue, which all primary education for more than fifty years has dedicated itself to inculcating. Openness – and the relativism that makes it the only plausible stance in the face of various claims to truth and various ways of life and kinds of human beings – is the great insight of our times. The true believer is the real danger. The study of history and of culture teaches that all the world was mad in the past; men always thought they were right, and that led to wars, persecutions, slavery, xenophobia, racism, and chauvinism. The point is not to correct the mistakes and really be right; rather it is not to think you are right at all.

The students, of course, cannot defend their opinion. It is something with which they have been indoctrinated. The best they can do is point out all the opinions and cultures there are and have been.

3.75 Wuthnow, toleration and college education

Robert Wuthnow, 1989: *The Struggle for America's Soul: Evangelicals, Liberals and Secularism.*
Grand Rapids, Michigan: Eerdmans (p. 35).

Like Bloom, Robert Wuthnow accords considerable importance to the role of liberal college education in encouraging (relatively) positive assessments of other forms of life. Indeed, the fact that (some of) the college-educated are reported as being interested in experimenting with new religions suggests that they are prepared to look for truth in other religions, not simply tolerate them. (See also the reading from Wuthnow, **3.52** earlier in this chapter.)

[A] consequence of the turmoil of the 1960s that stands out is the increasing role of higher education in differentiating styles of religious commitment. In the 1950s, perhaps surprisingly so in retrospect, those who had been to college and those who had not were remarkably similar on most items of religious belief and practice. By the early 1970s, a considerable education gap had emerged between the two.

The college educated were much less likely, even than the college educated of the previous decade, to attend religious services regularly. Their belief in a literal interpretation of the Bible had eroded dramatically. They were more tolerant of other religions, and they were more interested in experimenting with the so-called new religions, such as Zen, Transcendental Meditation, Hare Krishna, and the human potential movement. Those who had not been to college remained more committed to traditional views of the Bible, were more strongly interested in religion in general, continued to attend religious services regularly, and expressed doubt about other faiths, including the new religions.

In short, educational differences were becoming more significant for religion, just as they were being emphasized more generally in the society. Higher education was becoming a more significant basis for creating social and cultural distinctions. In regard to religion, education was beginning to reinforce the cleavage between religious liberals and religious conservatives.

Explanation: the role played by capitalism

3.76 Gellner and the egalitarian outlook

Ernest Gellner, 1983: *Nations and Nationalism.* Oxford: Basil Blackwell (pp. 24–5).

Although the universalization of religion may owe relatively little to capitalism *per se*, it can readily be argued that the development of capitalism goes together with the development of a cultural 'climate' conducive to the erosion of the evaluative significance of differences. Ernst Gellner here concentrates on a differentiating process – the division of labour – and explains how this can lead to the development of the egalitarian outlook. Although he does not address the matter, this outlook surely helps explain why it is not coincidental that capitalism, democracy and the ethic of humanity have grown up together in many countries. (See Berger (1987), Moore (1967) and Novak (1991) on links between capitalism and liberal, egalitarian democracy.)

High productivity, as Adam Smith insisted so much, requires a complex and refined division of labour. Perpetually growing productivity requires that this division be not merely complex, but also perpetually, and often rapidly, changing. This rapid and continuous change both of the economic role system itself and of the occupancy of places within it, has certain immediate and profoundly important consequences. Men located within it cannot generally rest in the same niches all their lives; and they can only seldom rest in them, so to speak, over generations. Positions are seldom (for this and other reasons) transmitted from father to son. Adam Smith noted the precariousness of bourgeois fortunes, though he erroneously attributed stability of social station to pastoralists, mistaking their genealogical myths for reality.

The immediate consequence of this new kind of mobility is a certain kind of egalitarianism. Modern society is not mobile because it is egalitarian; it is egalitarian because it is mobile. Moreover, it has to be mobile whether it wishes to be so or not, because this is required by the satisfaction of its terrible and overwhelming thirst for economic growth.

A society which is destined to a permanent game of musical chairs cannot erect deep barriers of rank, of caste or estate, between the various sets of chairs which it possesses. That would hamper the mobility, and, given the mobility, would indeed lead to intolerable tensions. Men can tolerate terrible inequalities, if they are stable and hallowed by custom. But in a hectically mobile society, custom has no time to hallow anything. A rolling stone gathers no aura, and a mobile population does not allow any aura to attach to its stratification. Stratification and inequality do exist, and sometimes in extreme form; nevertheless they have a muted and discreet quality, attenuated by a kind of gradualness of the distinctions of wealth and standing, a lack of social distance and a convergence of life-styles, a kind of statistical or probabilistic quality of the differences (as opposed to the rigid, absolutized, chasm-like differences typical of agrarian society), and by the illusion or reality of social mobility.

3.77 Bruce: 'modernization' and 'fundamental egalitarianism'

Steve Bruce, 1998: Cathedrals to Cults: the Evolving Forms of the Religious Life. In Paul Heelas (ed.). with the assistance of David Martin and Paul Morris, *Religion, Modernity and Postmodernity*. Oxford and Malden, Mass.: Blackwell, pp. 19–35 (pp. 23–8).

Steve Bruce's general thesis, best formulated in his *Religion in the Modern World* (1996), is that 'if the church was the dominant form of religion in the pre-Reformation world, the sect its embodiment in the early modern period, and the denomination its classic form in the twentieth century, the emblem of religion for the twenty-first century is the cult' (p. 4). For Bruce the church and the sect are exclusivistic (in that they judge those outside their boundaries wrong), the denomination liberal (respecting and finding some truth in others), and the 'cult' inclusivistic (in this reading, Bruce writes of the typical cultic belief that 'all is one'). Drawing on Gellner and others, Bruce supplies a battery of ideas to help explain the shift towards the inclusive. Changes in cultural values, associated with institutional modernization, provide a key theme. (See also Bruce, 1996, pp. 41–3; 75–7. On the question of how globalizing processes have affected religion, see Robertson and Chirico, 1985.)

The point of introducing these distinctions [between church, sect, denomination and cult] is to offer a very simple way of describing the major changes in the religious climate of the Western world. We can observe the possibility and popularity of the four forms of religion in different sorts of society. I am not suggesting that sects were unknown prior to the Reformation, and that denominations and cults were unknown prior to the last quarter of the nineteenth century; would that history were so simple! Even within the massive consensus of the Holy Roman Empire one had Christian humanists (of whom the young Erasmus would be a good example) who searched for some common values to unite the range of religious expression they confronted. However, I am suggesting that there is a crucial difference in the number, size and popularity of the exemplars of the various forms. Further, I am suggesting that close inspection of what may at first sight appear to be cases out of time and place will often reinforce the point.

The key to the shift between these four forms is *modernization*. With no suggestion of claiming the intellectual status of Max Weber, I want to be clear that I am using the term in the manner of the sadly often misunderstood Protestant ethic thesis. By modernization, I refer to a *historically and geographically specific* package of major social, political and economic changes that came with urbanization and industrialization in western Europe, and to the form of consciousness associated with those changes. I am not at this point making any universal claims or offering observations about societies that have more recently been affected by some of those changes. The extent to which the patterns may be repeated will depend on the extent to which new circumstances match the old.

Modernization makes the church form of religion impossible. The church requires either cultural homogeneity or an elite sufficiently powerful to enforce conformity. Societies expand to encompass ever larger numbers of religious, ethnic and linguistic groups and improved communication brings increased knowledge of that diversity. Modernization also undermines the hierarchical and rigid social structures which permit the maintenance of monocultures. What at first sight might appear to be paradoxical changes combine to encourage and legitimate diversity.

First, as Durkheim notes in his distinction between mechanical and organic solidarity, the increased division of labour and growth of economies creates ever greater social diversity and social distance. The feudal estate and closed village become the town and the city. The medieval old town of Edinburgh, where people of very different 'stations' lived on different floors of the same tenement and threw their excrement into the same street, was replaced with the New Town, inhabited by the bourgeoisie and their servants, separated from the trades and the factories. Increasingly, different social circumstances created increasingly different cultures, and that expressed itself in religious diversity as different social groups reworked the dominant religious tradition in ways that made sense from their position in the world.

At the same time, as Gellner in his theory of nationalism persuasively argues, modernization produced a basic egalitarianism. A division of labour need not undermine a hierarchical society (the caste system of India is profoundly hierarchical and the castes are defined by their occupations) but economic development also brought change and the expectation of further change. And it brought occupational mobility. People no longer did the job they always did because their family always did that job. Occupational mobility made it hard for people to internalize visions of themselves that suppose permanent inferiority. One cannot have people improving themselves and their class position while thinking of themselves as fixed in a station or a degree or a caste in an unchanging hierarchical world. Modern societies are thus inherently egalitarian.

Economic expansion increased contact with strangers. Profound inequalities of status are tolerable and can work well when the ranking system is well known and widely accepted as legitimate. Soldiers can move from one regiment to another and still know their place because there is a uniform ranking system and one's rank is displayed on one's uniform. Economic innovation and expansion means constant change in the nature of occupations, and increased mobility, both of which in their different ways mean that we have trouble placing people. There is no way of ensuring that we know whether we are superior or subordinate to this or that new person.

The separation of work and home, of the public and the private, further makes for equality. 'Serf' and 'peasant' were not job descriptions; they were enveloping social, legal and political statuses. One cannot be a serf during working hours and an autonomous individual for the evenings and at weekends. A temporary work-role is not a full identity and though work-roles may be ranked in a hierarchy, they can no longer structure the whole worldview. In the absence of a shared belief system which would sanction inequality and subjection (and the decline of religion usually removes that), egalitarianism becomes the default position.

The precondition of employability, dignity, full moral citizenship and an acceptable social identity is a certain level of education, which must include literacy – and literacy in a single language common throughout the economy. Once this was recognized, socialization became standardized and placed in the hands of a central agency; not a family, clan or guild but a society-wide education system. It required a single cultural and linguistic medium through which people could be instructed.

Gellner is not, of course, saying that in modern societies everyone is equal. His point is that the profound and fixed division of rights one finds in traditional and feudal societies is incompatible with economic development. Modernization and the development of the capitalist economy require the end of the old world.

The fundamental egalitarianism that came with modernization meant that, at the political level, the costs of coercing religious conformity were no longer acceptable: the state was no longer willing to accept the price in social conflict and adopted a position of neutrality on the competing claims of various religious bodies. In some settings, the neutrality was explicit (as in the Constitution of the United States); in others, it was implicit (as in the fudge which left the Established Churches of England and Scotland with notional advantages over their competitors but removed their real privileges). At the level of individual consciousness, it made it ever more difficult (though, of course, still possible) to dismiss religious views at odds with one's own as being of entirely no account.

Let us go back and pick up another thread of change to follow. In some countries, where the Lutheran influence predominated, the religious upheavals of the Reformation were largely contained within the church form. In others, religious dissent, accelerated by the social changes of the early modern period, created a profusion of 'sects', most of which initially tried to establish themselves as the church. It was only after failing to achieve power, either through becoming the majority religion or by effecting a minority coup, that many of them discovered the principle of toleration and evolved into denominations.

At the same time as external relations with other religious organizations and with the state were giving the sect good reason to moderate its claims, there were a variety of internal pressures in the same direction. This is the well-known Niebuhr thesis. For millenarian sects, the failure of the world to end is one problem that must be faced. For almost all sects the position of the children of the sectarians calls into question the initial hard demarcation between the saved and the unregenerate. It is natural for sectarians to suppose that their children, who have been raised in the faith, are not quite the same as the children of outsiders.

Gradually the strict membership tests are relaxed. Survival for any length of time brings assets (buildings, publishing houses, and capital) which require to be managed. The creation of a bureaucratic structure in turn brings officials whose interests are to a degree at odds with the original radical impetus of the sect. The asceticism of the sect may well result in upward social mobility. Even if there is no independent 'Protestant ethic' effect, most sects have endured in circumstances of general economic growth. Increasing prosperity means that the sacrifices inherent in asceticism are proportionately ever larger. When coupled with the lower levels of commitment found among those generations which have inherited their sectarianism rather than acquired it through choice, the result is a gradual relaxation of Puritanism and a gradual accoummodation to the ways of the world.
[. . .]

Thus far in what must be a massively simplified view of the history of religion in the West, we have seen first the church form faced with competition from the sect and then both churches and sects tending to become denominations. Where does the cult come into this account? First with the new religious movements of the 1960s and 1970s and then with the New Age religion of the 1980s, we have seen a flowering of alternative religions, some re-workings for the Western mind of traditional Eastern religions, others spiritualized versions of lay psychotherapies that are the bastard children of Freud and Jung. In terms of numbers, new religious movements and New Age religiosity are insignificant. Field sports are more popular than alternative religions. There are more train spotters than white witches, magicians, and pagans. However, the cult form of religion is, I would argue, emblematic.

First, there is the point that the decline in the main religious traditions leaves ever larger numbers of people free to experiment; free because they are not personally tied to an older form and free because the decline of that older form reduces its ability to stigmatize cultic alternatives as 'deviant'. Secondly, there is the core belief of New Age religion in the divinity of the self. Grounded in some variant of the Hindu and Buddhist view that the apparent diversity of matter disguises a fundamental unity and hence that 'all is one', it argues that we should no longer seek God outside ourselves but within. For we are both all God's children and all God. I want to suggest that this substantive proposition is, like the interdenominational position of the liberal denominations and the ecumenical movement, both an article of faith and a necessary adjustment to the fact of minority status. Just as most conservative schismatic sects came to love the principle of toleration once they had failed to achieve a position of power in which they could enforce conformity to their own beliefs, so the purveyors of the cultic world have found a happy match of principle and expedience in eclecticism and relativism.

Finally, the cultic milieu is emblematic of modern religion in openly laying claim to what for the last half-century has been an implicit principle of much involvement in traditional religion: the right of the sovereign individual to determine what is truth and what is falsity.

Individualism used to mean the freedom to dissent; now it means the right to determine, not simply what one likes to do, but what is the case. It has grown from being a political and behavioural principle to being an ontological device.

Just to clarify the argument, I will briefly deal with two common objections to this sociological gloss of history. It is certainly true that something like the profusion of religious beliefs we now see in the New Age milieu could also be found during the English Civil War and Commonwealth periods. However, the range of beliefs was considerably narrower; they were all Protestant Christian. But more important for the sociologist is the fact that most of the alternatives available during the Commonwealth were *competing sects*, each certain of its unique grasp of the truth and of the falsity of the positions of the Church of England. In the New Age we see a cultic milieu, a world in which individuals select from a diverse range of beliefs and supernaturalisms, very few of the purveyors of which claim to be uniquely legitimate. Even if the promoting organization is supported by an inner circle of full-time officials who claim a unique grasp of the truth, such claims are routinely rejected by the consumers of their product and the awareness that such a fate can hardly be avoided is daily reflected in them moderating their claims for public consumption. Whatever those in the inner circle of Transcendental Meditators privately think, their newspaper advertisements stress that 'no change of belief is required'. To put it simply, we have previously had alternatives but they have been competing sects, not co-operating and complementary cults.

Similarly, early premodern spokesmen for toleration will usually turn out on close inspection to have in mind a considerably narrower range of what is permissible than the average liberal Christian. Those Congregationalists and Presbyterians of the English Civil War period who argued for toleration (and there were many who opposed it) wished it to include themselves and the state church but did not allow Roman Catholics or Quakers the privilege.

CHAPTER TWELVE

sacralization

Introduction

Secularization theory, at least in its strongest form, maintains that modernization inevitably involves the withering away of religion. In stark contrast, sacralization theory focuses attention on religion gaining in strength in modern times. Another way of putting the contrast is to ask: which is exceptional – the United State with (apparently) high levels of religious involvement, or Europe with (apparently) much lower levels? Secularization theorists would see America as being exceptional, whereas sacralization theorists would view Europe as the exception.

Until recently, the academy was noticeably quiet on the topic of sacralization. Now, however, sacralization theory has become influential enough for José Casanova (**3.78**) to raise the question as to whether secularization is a 'myth'. Could it be the case that the 'hold' of secularization theory blinded earlier thinkers to contrary evidence? Has religion itself gained enough power during recent decades to demand the development of the sacralization approach? What is to be made of (journalistic?) claims of the 'Islam set to invade Europe' variety? However such questions might be answered, one thing is clear: a quite fundamental change has taken place whereby many scholars now believe that religion is far from incompatible with modernization.

Just as we introduced the chapter on Secularization by identifying three sub-theses – disappearance, differentiation, deintensification – so we introduce this section by identifying three sub-theses which emphasise the reverse: growth (by way of conversion), dedifferentiation (or deprivatization) and intensification. (Coexistence theory, also introduced in the chapter on Sacralization, is also introduced here: as the name implies, it does not belong to either camp.)

First – and perhaps most obviously – sacralization involves the *growth* of religion, due to conversion and related processes, with the numerical significance of religion increasing as non-religious people join the ranks.

Second, sacralization can involve what Casanova (reading **3.80**) calls *deprivatization*. Here what might be thought of as the 'conversion' of the public realm takes place, with secular institutions (political, workplace, gendered) previously evacuated of religion by modernity coming to be re-enchanted by religion. Religion, that is to say, finds roles to play in generating policy decisions, mobilizing moral commitments, defending human rights, legitimating ethnic or national identities, instilling work ethics, and otherwise influencing sociocultural affairs. As for the third way in which sacralization can operate, one can think of the process as one of *intensification*: that is, people who are 'weakly' or nominally religious come to adopt 'stronger', more potent, vital, time-consuming, efficacious, life-influencing forms of religiosity; forms of applied religiosity, it can be observed, which can also serve to intensify the process of deprivatization by motivating people to act in the public sphere.

Although growth by way of conversion, the first of these trends, is (perhaps) the most obvious way in which sacralization can take place, it is rarely claimed that the process is of much importance. There are two main reasons for this. Much of the world's population – in India, the United States or Africa, for example – is already religious, which means that it does not make sense to talk of people becoming believers. (Evidence for conversion, in the sense that the term is being used here, is not provided when particular religions expand by drawing people from other religions.) And second, in those parts of the world such as northern Europe, where there are significant numbers of atheists and agnostics, there are no signs of religions making real inroads into the realms of the unconverted or unconvinced.

As will become clear from the readings which follow, most sacralization theorists concentrate on the second and third trends, deprivatization and intensification. They argue, against secularization theory, that religion has not retreated from public life, and/or that those who remain religious are deeply committed. Many of those who defend sacralization, however, view it (by analogy with secularization theory) as a general, unilinear trend. By contrast, we have organized this current chapter in order to illustrate what we take to be the variety rather than the uniformity of sacralization. In particular, we relate sacralization to the different varieties of religions introduced in **Part One**.

Viewed from this perspective, it would appear that religions of difference, experiential religions of difference, and spiritualities of life are faring particularly well in modern times. The former, with their emphasis on making a difference, would appear to thrive when they help accomplish a cultural, social or existential job (undergirding identities and mobilizing communities, for example). By contrast, experiential religions of difference appear to be flourishing because they cater so well for the widespread cultural turn to the self, whilst at the same time providing clear authority, moral depth and structure. The ability to cater for the turn to the self is even more in evidence in spiritualities of life which, with their stong emphasis on freedom, appear to appeal to many in the western world. Generally they appear to be expanding; they may even to attracting the previously non-religious. It might also be argued that such spiritualities are doing well because they deal with the immanent, the here-and-now, the this-worldly and everyday – particular areas of concern for the many who have turned away from tradition and a belief in a transcendent realm. Regarding religions of humanity, however, a consensus seems to have developed that they are in decline (see, for example, readings **1.51** and **1.52**; although for counter consideration, see Ammerman, reading **1.33**). For this reason we do not dwell on this variety of religion here.

Reinforcing once more this volume's emphasis on the coexistence approach, it is surely the case that both trends, secularization *and* sacralization, are operative in the modern world. Given the powerful claims found in the relevant chapters in favour of both, it would be rash indeed to assert that either secularization or sacralization are 'across-the-board' trends. In Britain, for example, although many religions are waning, some are waxing (see reading **3.6**). It is also perfectly possible for the same religion to be doing well in one part of the world but not in another. Institutionalized Christianity might be waning in northern Europe, but this goes together with the fact that the numerical significance of those who are (somehow) religious, but who rarely if ever go to church, is increasing here (see **3.89**). The location of religion, it appears, has changed, from church and chapel to the culture at large: something very different from comprehensive secularization. Faced with such complexity, it would seem clear that a great deal more research is required in order to specify – on a local and global scale – the *particular* circumstances (and dynamics) under which *particular* forms of religion are waxing or waning.

Remaining with the coexistence approach, but now from a more theoretical point of view, we can briefly introduce the theory found at the end of this chapter. The *'self-limiting'* thesis, as it can be called, holds that the greater the amount of secularization the greater the likelihood – indeed, in some versions of the theory, the necessity – for the return of religion. This thesis, found below in readings from Berger, Stark and Bell, holds that there are basic anthropological needs which have to be met. When secularization means that they are not met by old religious traditions, new religious forms emerge. (See also readings in Detraditionalization, in particular Simmel, **3.40**.)

Just as more research is needed to explore coexistence, so is it required to settle another aspect of the debate between advocates of secularization and sacralization. This concerns the difficult matter of gauging the extent to which religions – especially religions of humanity and spiritualities of life – make a difference to people's lives. Are theorists correct in concluding that liberal religions of humanity are a weak, largely secularized form of religion? (See **1.51**.) How widely applicable is the very different portrayal provided by Ammerman (**1.33**), who notes that 51 per cent of church goers in North America are of the liberal persuasion, many with strong commitment? What is to be made of those (for example Bauman (**3.22**) who claim that spiritualities of life are merely consumeristic and therefore secularized? What is to be made of the very different claims of many participants? (see reading **1.56**). Given our present state of knowledge, all that can be said is that it would be incautious in the extreme to conclude that religions of humanity and spiritualities of life are *necessarily* 'de-intensified' or weak; or that they *necessarily* fail to resist secular expectations and values.

As well as the obvious benefit of reading this chapter together with the readings in Secularization, there are many points of contact with the readings on 'explanations' and 'prospects' of religion introduced in **Part One**. (See also Combinations at the end of **Part One**.) **Part Two** reinforces the point – especially pertaining to the coexistence thesis – that the growth or decline of religion is very much due to different concrete circumstances. (See, for example, readings **2.31–2.33**) on the success of religion when addressing or undergirding ethnic or national identity; see also readings in Economic (chapter six) concerning the resacralization of work.) As for **Part Three**, material on why detraditionalized religion – largely beyond church and chapel – could well be increasing in numerical significance can be found in the chapter on Detraditionalization. Finally, it might be observed that much sacralization theory fails to engage with the evidence and theories of secularization. Perhaps sacralization theorists should explore the possibility of becoming more coexistent!

Sacralization: overviews

3.78 Casanova on 'a radical change in intellectual climate'

José Casanova, 1994: *Public Religions in the Modern World*. Chicago and London: The University of Chicago Press (p. 11).

Although José Casanova, with his deprivatization thesis (see reading **3.80** below) is himself an advocate of sacralization theory, he also accepts that secularization 'still has much explanatory value'. His concern in what follows is that the 'majority' of sociologists of religion have *uncritically* shifted their allegiance from one 'paradigm', secularization, to its converse.

Who still believes in the *myth* of secularization? Recent debates within the sociology of religion would indicate this to be the appropriate question with which to start any current discussion of the theory of secularization. There are still a few 'old believers,' such as Bryan Wilson and Karel Dobbelaere, who insist, rightly, that the theory of secularization still has much explanatory value in attempting to account for modern historical processes. But the majority of sociologists of religion will not listen, for they have abandoned the paradigm with the same uncritical haste with which they previously embraced it. Indeed, some are mocking the rationalists, who made so many false prophecies about the future of religion, in the same way the philosophes before them mocked religious visionaries and obscurantist priests. Armed with 'scientific' evidence, sociologists of religion now feel confident to predict bright futures for religion. The reversal is astounding when one thinks that only some twenty years ago practically nobody was ready to listen when, in the first 'secularization debate,' the first voices were raised by David Martin and Andrew Greeley questioning the concept and the empirical evidence, or lack thereof, behind the theory of secularization. But how could anybody listen attentively then, when even the theologians were proclaiming the death of God and celebrating the coming of the secular city?

How can one explain this reversal? How could there have been so much myth before and so much light now? It is true that much empirical counterevidence has been accumulated against the theory since the 1960s, but similar counterevidence had existed all along and yet the evidence remained unseen or was explained away as irrelevant. The answer has to be that it is not reality itself which has changed, as much as our perception of it, and that we must be witnessing a typical Kuhnian revolution in scientific paradigms. Some may object to the use of the word 'scientific' in this particular context. But there can be no doubt that we are dealing with a radical change in intellectual climate and in the background worldviews which normally sustain much of our social-scientific consensus.

3.79 Berger: secularization theory as 'essentially mistaken'

Peter L. Berger (forthcoming): The Desecularization of the World. A Global Overview. In Peter L. Berger (ed.), *The Desecularization of the World. Essays on the Resurgence of Religion in World Politics*. Washington: Ethics and Public Policy Center; Grand Rapids: William B. Eerdmans.

Without wishing to imply that Peter Berger is one of those whom Casanova in the preceding reading has in mind when he writes of 'uncritical haste' in changing from the secularization to the sacralization paradigm, the fact remains that there are two Peter Bergers: the earlier, advocating secularization theory (see Berger, 1969), and the later, advocating sacralization. In the article from which the following is taken, Berger writes, 'One prediction . . . can be made with some assurance: there is no reason to think that the world of the twenty-first century will be any less religious than the world is today'. Indeed, in the reading – which also serves to specify three ways in which religion operates in powerful fashion – Berger indicates that he expects some increases in the 'furiously religious'. Finally, the reading serves to introduce what Berger takes to be 'what are arguably the two most dynamic religious upsurges in the world today', namely 'the Islamic and the Evangelical ones'. (See also **1.84**.)

The assumption that we live in a secularized world is false. The world today, with some exceptions . . . is as furiously religious as it ever was, and in some places more so than ever. This means that a whole body of literature by historians and social scientists loosely labeled 'secularization theory' is essentially mistaken. In my early work I contributed to this literature. I was in good company – most sociologists of religion had similar views, and we had good reasons for holding them. Some of the writings we produced still stand up. . . .

Although the term 'secularization theory' refers to works from the 1950s and 1960s, the key idea of the theory can indeed be traced to the Enlightenment. That idea is simple: Modernization necessarily leads to a decline of religion, both in society and in the minds of individuals. And it is precisely this key idea that has turned out to be wrong. To be sure, modernization has had some secularizing effects, more in some places than in others. But it has also provoked powerful movements of counter-secularization. Also, secularization on the societal level is not necessarily linked to secularization on the level of individual consciousness. Certain religious institutions have lost power and influence in many societies, but both old and new religious beliefs and practices have nevertheless continued in the lives of individuals, sometimes taking new institutional forms and sometimes leading to great explosions of religious fervor. Conversely, religiously identified institutions can play social or political roles even when very few people believe or practice the religion that the institutions represent. To say the least, the relation between religion and modernity is rather complicated.[. . .]

The Islamic upsurge, because of its more immediately obvious political ramifications, is better known [than the Evangelical]. Yet it would be a serious error to see it only through a political lens. It is an impressive revival of emphatically *religious* commitments. And it is of vast geographical scope, affecting every single Muslim country from North Africa to Southeast Asia. It continues to gain converts, especially in sub-Saharan Africa (where it is often in head-on competition with Christianity). It is becoming very visible in the burgeoning Muslim communities in Europe and, to a much lesser extent, in North America. Everywhere it is bringing about a restoration, not only of Islamic beliefs but of distinctively Islamic life-styles, which in many ways directly contradict modern ideas – such as ideas about the relation of religion and the state, the role of women, moral codes of everyday behavior, and the boundaries of religious and moral tolerance. The Islamic revival is by no means restricted to the less modernized or 'backward' sectors of society, as progressive intellectuals still like to think. On the contrary, it is very strong in cities with a high degree of modernization, and in a number of countries it is particularly visible among people with Western-style higher education – in Egypt and Turkey, for example, many daughters of secularized professionals are putting on the veil and other accoutrements of Islamic modesty.

Yet there are also great differences within the movement. Even within the Middle East, the Islamic heartland, there are both religiously and politically important differences between Sunni and Shi'ite revivals – Islamic conservatism means very different things in, say, Saudi Arabia and Iran. Away from the Middle East, the differences become even greater. Thus in Indonesia, the most populous Muslim country in the world, a very powerful revival movement, the Nudhat'ul-Ulama, is avowedly pro-democracy and pro-pluralism, the very opposite of what is commonly viewed as Muslim 'fundamentalism.' Where the political circumstances allow this, there is in many places a lively discussion about the relation of Islam to various modern realities, and there are sharp disagreements among individuals who are equally committed to a revitalized Islam. Still, for reasons deeply grounded in the core of the tradition, it is probably fair to say that, on the whole, Islam has had a difficult time coming to terms with key modern institutions, such as pluralism, democracy, and the market economy.

The Evangelical upsurge is just as breathtaking in scope. Geographically that scope is even wider. It has gained huge numbers of converts in East Asia – in all the Chinese communities (including, despite severe persecution, mainland China) and in South Korea, the Philippines, across the South Pacific, throughout sub-Saharan Africa (where it is often synthetized with elements of traditional African religion), apparently in parts of ex-Communist Europe. But the most remarkable success has occurred in Latin America; there are now thought to be between forty and fifty million Evangelical Protestants south of the U.S. border, the great majority of them first-generation Protestants. The most numerous component within the Evangelical upsurge is Pentecostalism, which combines biblical orthodoxy and a rigorous morality with an ecstatic form of worship and an emphasis on spiritual healing. Especially in Latin America, conversion to Protestantism brings about a cultural transformation – new attitudes toward work and consumption, a new educational ethos, a violent rejection of traditional *machismo* (women play a key role in the Evangelical churches).[. . .]

Let me, then, repeat what I said a while back: The world today is massively religious, is *anything but* the secularized world that had been predicted (be it joyfully or despondently) by so many analysts of modernity.

3.80 Casanova: religion and 'the ongoing construction of the modern world'

José Casanova, 1994: *Public Religions in the Modern World*. Chicago and London: The University of Chicago Press (pp. 3–6).

Accepting that 'the core of the theory of secularization, the thesis of the differentiation and emancipation of the secular spheres from religious institutions and norms, remains valid', José Casanova nevertheless claims that 'we are witnessing the "deprivatization" of religion in the modern world' (see also Casanova, **2.29**.) Religions, that is to say, have come to play 'important public roles in the ongoing construction of the modern world', not least the negotiation of conflicts between power blocs, and the quest for liberation among the deprived. What we are calling spiritualities of life, it will be noted, are seen as secularized in that they are taken to have little or no significance for the 'dominant structures' of the public realm.

Religion in the 1980s 'went public' in a dual sense. It entered the 'public sphere' and gained, thereby, 'publicity.' Various 'publics' – the mass media, social scientists, professional politicians, and the 'public at large' – suddenly began to pay attention to religion. The unexpected public interest derived from the fact that religion, leaving its assigned place in the private sphere, had thrust itself into the public arena of moral and political contestation. Above all, four seemingly unrelated yet almost simultaneously unfolding developments gave religion the kind of global publicity which forced a reassessment of its place and role in the modern world. These four developments were the Islamic revolution in Iran; the rise of the Solidarity movement in Poland; the role of Catholicism in the Sandinista revolution and in other political conflicts throughout Latin America; and the public reemergence of Protestant fundamentalism as a force in American politics.

During the entire decade of the 1980s it was hard to find any serious political conflict anywhere in the world that did not show behind it the not-so-hidden hand of religion. In the Middle East, all the religions and fundamentalisms of the region – Jewish, Christian, and Muslim – fed by old power struggles, were meeting each other in civil and uncivil wars. Old feuds between the various world religions and between branches of the same religions were flaring up again from Northern Ireland to Yugoslavia, from India to the Soviet Union. Simultaneously, religious activists and churches were becoming deeply involved in struggles for liberation, justice, and democracy throughout the world. Liberation theologies were spreading beyond Latin America, acquiring new forms and names, African and Asian, Protestant and Jewish, black and feminist. With the collapse of socialism, liberation theology seemed the only 'International' that was left.

The decade, which began in 1979 with the Iranian and Nicaraguan revolutions, the visit of the Polish pope to Poland, and the establishment of the 'Moral Majority,' ended as dramatically and as ambiguously as it had begun, with the Salman Rushdie 'affair,' the death of Ayatollah Khomeini, the final triumph of Solidarity reverberating throughout Eastern Europe, and Gorbachev's visit to the pope. It was symbolically fitting that even the Romanian Revolution was sparked by a Hungarian Reformed pastor. No less telling was the fact that in El Salvador the decade which had opened with the assassination of Archbishop Romero closed with the murder of yet six more Jesuits by state terror.

Throughout the decade religion showed its Janus face, as the carrier not only of exclusive, particularist, and primordial identities but also of inclusive, universalist, and transcending ones. The religious revival signaled simultaneously the rise of fundamentalism and of its role in the resistance of the oppressed and the rise of the 'powerless.' Ali Shariati, the intellectual father of the Islamic revolution, in translating Franz Fanon's *Les Damnés de la Terre*, chose the resonant Koranic term *mostaz'afin* (the disinherited). The term 'the disinherited of the earth' was to occupy a central place in the rhetoric of the Islamic revolution. Gustavo Gutiérrez, the father of liberation theology, effected a similar transvaluation from secular back to religious categories when he turned the proletariat into the biblical *los pobres*. 'The eruption of the poor in history' became one of the central categories of Gutiérrez's eschatological theology. A similar term, 'the power of the powerless,' was coined by Vaclav Havel, the father of the 'velvet' revolution. It all looked like modernization in reverse, from rational collective action back to primitive rebellion.

It is unlikely that these are mere historical coincidences. They can be seen rather as examples of biblical prophetic politics linking the Middel East, Latin America, and Eastern Europe. The transvaluation of values which, according to Nietzsche, biblical slave morality had introduced into the dynamics of classical aristocratic civilization was apparently still at work. The archetypal dream of a liberating Exodus from enslavement had not yet lost its utopian, eschatological force.

I have selectively left out of my account of religion in the 1980s many other religious phenomena which also gained wide publicity throughout the decade and certainly had public and political significance, but which were not in themselves varieties of what I call 'public' religion. I have in mind such phenomena as 'New Age' spirituality; the growth of cults and the ensuing controversies surrounding them; televangelism with all its peccadillos; the collective suicide of the residents of the People's Temple in Jonestown; the spread of evangelical Protestantism in Latin America; the rapid growth of Islam in the United States; the seriousness with which so many people in modern secular societies – including Nancy Reagan while at the White House – took astrology; the fact that Manuel Noriega may have practiced voodoo; or the fact that most people everywhere continued to practice, or not to practice, religion in the 1980s in the same way they had in the 1970s.

Those were significant religious phenomena, and any comprehensive history of religion in the 1980s would have to include them. It is likely that quantitative surveys would select precisely those phenomena as being the typical, normal, and relevant ones. Nevertheless, one could still argue that they were not particularly relevant either for the social sciences or for the self-understanding of modernity, at least insofar as they do not present major problems of interpretation. They fit within expectations and can be interpreted within the framework of established theories of secularization. As bizarre and as new as they may be, they can nonetheless be taken for granted as typical or normal phenomena in the modern world. They can be classified as instances of 'private' or of what Thomas Luckmann called 'invisible' religion. Such religious phenomena per se do not challenge either the dominant structures or the dominant paradigms.

What was new and unexpected in the 1980s was not the emergence of 'new religious movements,' 'religious experimentation' and 'new religious consciousness' – all phenomena which caught the imagination of social scientists and the public in the 1960s and 1970s – but rather the revitalization and the assumption of public roles by precisely those religious traditions which both theories of secularization and cyclical theories of religious revival had assumed were becoming ever more marginal and irrelevant in the modern world. Indeed, as Mary Douglas has rightly pointed out, 'No one credited the traditional religions with enough vitality to inspire large-scale political revolt.'

The central thesis of the present study is that we are witnessing the 'deprivatization' of religion in the modern world. By deprivatization I mean the fact that religious traditions throughout the world are refusing to accept the marginal and privatized role which theories of modernity as well as theories of secularization had reserved for them. Social movements have appeared which either are religious in nature or are challenging in the name of religion the legitimacy and autonomy of the primary secular spheres, the state and the market economy. Similarly, religious institutions and organizations refuse to restrict themselves to the pastoral care of individual souls and continue to raise questions about the interconnections of private and public morality and to challenge the claims of the subsystems, particularly states and markets, to be exempt from extraneous normative considerations. One of the results of this ongoing contestation is a dual, interrelated process of repoliticization of the private religious and moral spheres and renormativization of the public economic and political spheres. This is what I call, for lack of a better term, the 'deprivatization' of religion.

I do not mean to imply that the deprivatization of religion is something altogether new. Most religious traditions have resisted all along the process of secularization as well as the privatization and marginalization which tend to accompany this process. If at the end they accepted the process and accommodated themselves to the differentiated structures of the modern world, they often did so only grudgingly. What was new and became 'news' in the 1980s was the widespread and simultaneous character of the refusal to be restricted to the private sphere of religious traditions as different as Judaism and Islam, Catholicism and Protestantism, Hinduism and Buddhism, in all 'three worlds of development.'

The inelegant neologism 'deprivatization' has a dual purpose, polemical and descriptive. It is meant, first, to call into question those theories of secularization which have tended not only to assume but also to prescribe the privatization of religion in the modern world. Yet, while I agree with many of the criticisms that have been raised lately against the dominant theories of secularization, I do not share the view that secularization was, or is, a myth. The core of the theory of secularization, the thesis of the differentiation and emancipation of the secular spheres from religious institutions and norms, remains valid. But the term 'deprivatization' is also meant to signify the emergence of new historical developments which, at least qualitatively, amount to a certain reversal of what appeared to be secular trends. Religions throughout the world are entering the public sphere and the arena of political contestation not only to defend their traditional turf, as they have done in the past, but also to participate in the very struggles to define and set the modern boundaries between the private and public spheres, between system and life-world, between legality and morality, between individual and society, between family, civil society, and state, between nations, states, civilizations, and the world system.

Basically, one can draw two lessons from religion in the 1980s. The first is that religions are here to stay, thus putting to rest one of the cherished dreams of the Enlightenment. The second and more important lesson is that religions are likely to continue playing important public roles in the ongoing construction of the modern world. This second lesson in particular compels us to rethink systematically the relationship of religion and modernity and, more important, the possible roles religions may play in the public sphere of modern societies.

3.81   Haynes, deprivatization and the discontents of modernity

Jeff Haynes, 1998: *Religion in Global Politics*. London and New York: Longman (p. 19).

Complementing the previous extract by Casanova, Jeff Haynes draws attention to two – linked – dynamics behind deprivatization. Both involve religion being drawn upon to handle the discontents of modernization.

My main argument is that the political impact of religion will fall into two main – not necessarily mutually exclusive – categories. First, if the mass of people are not especially religious, organized religion will often seek a public role as a result of the belief that society has taken a wrong turn and needs an injection of religious values to put it back on the straight and narrow. Religion will try to deprivatize itself, so that it has a voice in contemporary debates about social and political direction. The aim is to be a significant factor in political deliberation so that religion's voice is taken into account. Religious leaders seek support from ordinary people by addressing certain crucial issues, including not only the perceived decline in public and private morality but also the insecurities of life in an undependable market where 'greed and luck appear as effective as work and rational choice'

(Comaroff). In sum, in the West religion's return to the public sphere is moulded by a range of factors, including the proportion of religious believers in society and the extent to which religious organizations perceive a decline in public standards of morality and compassion.

In Third World societies, on the other hand, most people are already religious believers. Following widespread disappointment at the outcomes of modernizing policies, however, religion often focuses and coordinates opposition, especially – but not exclusively – the poor and ethnic minorities. Attempts by political leaders to pursue modernization leads religious traditions to respond. What this amounts to is that in the Third World in particular religion is often well placed to benefit from any strong societal backlash against the perceived malign effects of modernization.

3.82   Warner and 'American exceptionalism'

R. Stephen Warner, 1993. Work in Progress toward a New Paradigm for the Sociological Study of Religion in the United States. *American Journal of Sociology* 98 (5), March: 1044–93 (pp. 1048–50; 1081–2).

Earlier in his article, R. Stephen Warner notes that 'much of secularization theory's best evidence and most forceful advocacy comes from Europe, where secularization is arguably a historical fact as well as a theory' (p. 1048). From the point of view of sacralization theory, Europe is exceptional. In contrast, and now from the perspective of secularization theory, the USA – with its 'all round vitality . . . in religion' (p. 1048) – is the exception. As well as providing evidence of the growth of religion in the USA, Warner plans to 'demystify the concept of American exceptionalism', by showing that there is nothing unusual about religion flourishing in the North American context. (Compare Warner's portrayal of religion in the USA with that provided by Hadaway, Marler and Chaves in the chapter on Secularization, **3.7**.) The 'crux' of the 'emerging paradigm', it can be noted, 'is that organized religion thrives in the United States in an open market system' (p. 1044). (For more on Stark's contribution, mentioned in the reading, see below, **3.96**.)

The emerging paradigm begins with theoretical reflection on a fact of U.S. religious history highly inconvenient to secularization theory: the proportion of the population enrolled in churches grew hugely throughout the 19th century and the first half of the 20th century, which, by any measure, were times of rapid modernization. Whereas about 10% of the population were church members at the time of the American Revolution, about 60% are so today, with particularly rapid growth registered in the 50 years preceding the Civil War and the

Great Depression. One naive glance at the numbers is bound to give the impression that, in the experience of the United States, societal modernization went hand in hand with religious mobilization. The end result is that, with the exception of 'a few agrarian states such as Ireland and Poland,' 'the Unites States has been the most God-believing and religion-adhering, fundamentalist, and religiously traditional country in Christendom' as well as the 'most religiously fecund country' where 'more new religions have been born . . . than in any other society' (Lipset).

In default of census data on individual religious affiliation, which the government may not inquire into, sociologists of religion employ what can be called 'poll' data (sample surveys done by Gallup, NORC, etc.) and 'roll' data (reports of internal counts by religious bodies themselves). Measured in terms of poll data, the current rate of adult church membership is between 69%; in roll data terms, the figure is 59%. While mainline Protestant denominations have lost members since peaking in the mid-1960s and individually reported church membership has declined four or five percentage points from the 73% registered in polls at that time, it stretches these points mightily to see this slight and uneven decline over three decades as evidence for secularization theory, in view of about 10 previous decades of strong and positive zero-order correlations between church membership and industrialization, urbanization, immigration, and most of the other processes that are thought to cause secularization. [. . .]

. . . Attempts to specify the determinants of the American religious system. Is the key to American religious vitality given in Tocqueville's analysis of the historically apolitical stance of most U.S. religious groups, the notion that American religion has largely stayed out of politics? Or is religious pluralism the key, as Finke and Stark would have it, the sheer variety of religious choices? Or is it deregulation, the lack of either subsidy or state oversight of religious organizations? Comparative institutional research, unburdened of the secularization expectations of the older paradigm, will serve to demystify the concept of American exceptionalism. Until that has been accomplished, the exception may well be taken as the rule.

3.83 Hoover summarizing the growth of religion in Middletown

Dwight W. Hoover, 1991: Middletown. A Case Study of Religious Development, 1827–1982. *Social Compass* 38 (3): 273–84 (p. 275).

Middletown – already encountered in reading **3.57** – is the representative middle-American community first studied by the Lynds in the 1920s, and more recently by Caplow and associates (see in particular their *All Faithful People. Change and Continuity in Middletown's Religion,* 1983). In the following short reading Hoover summarizes all the kinds of evidence which show that religion has both grown numerically and become stronger. It can be added that this includes working-class religion.

> In a recent book, *All Faithful People,* the scholars who returned to Middletown fifty years after the Lynds arrived conclude that, by every objective indicator – church attendance, church membership, and church support, among others – and by such subjective indicators as an expressed need for religious faith, the residents of Middletown are more religious than were their grandparents. Fifty years of life in an industrial community seem only to have strengthened the bonds of religion instead of loosing them.

Sacralization: examples

Example: religions of difference vs. religions of humanity

3.84　Berger and the rise of religions 'dripping with reactionary supernaturalism'

Peter L. Berger (forthcoming): The Desecularization of the World. A Global Overview. In Peter L. Berger (ed.), *The Desecularization of the World. Essays on the Resurgence of Religion in World Politics.* Washington: Ethics and Public Policy Center; Grand Rapids: William B. Eerdmans.

Peter Berger here lists some of the conservative, orthodox or traditionalist movements – what we are calling religions of difference – which, it is claimed, 'are on the rise almost everywhere'. Religions of humanity (Berger's 'mainline Protestantism') which attempt to conform to modernity, rather than making a stand and providing a difference, are seen as being 'almost everywhere in decline'. (See also the graph provided by Roof and McKinney in reading **1.26**.)

> Interestingly, secularization theory has . . . been falsified by the results of adaptation strategies by religious institutions. If we really lived in a highly secularized world, then religious institutions could be expected to survive to the degree that they manage to adapt to secularity. That has been the empirical assumption of adaptation strategies. What has in fact occurred is that, by and large, religious communities have survived and even flourished to the degree that they have *not* tried

to adapt themselves to the alleged requirements of a secularized world. To put it simply, experiments with secularized religion have generally failed; religious movements with beliefs and practices dripping with reactionary supernaturalism (the kind utterly beyond the pale at self-respecting faculty parties) have widely succeeded. [. . .]

On the international religious scene, it is conservative or orthodox or traditionalist movements that are on the rise almost everywhere. These movements are precisely the ones that rejected an *aggiornamento* with modernity as defined by progressive intellectuals. Conversely, religious movements and institutions that have made great efforts to conform to a perceived modernity are almost everywhere on the decline. In the United States this has been a much commented upon fact, exemplified by the decline of so-called mainline Protestantism and the concomitant rise of Evangelicalism; but the United States is by no means unusual in this.

Nor is Protestantism. The conservative thrust in the Roman Catholic Church under John Paul II has borne fruit in both number of con-verts and renewed enthusiasm among native Catholics, especially in non-Western countries. Following the collapse of the Soviet Union there occurred a remarkable revival of the Orthodox Church in Russia. The most rapidly growing Jewish groups, both in Israel and in the Diaspora, are Orthodox. There have been similarly vigorous upsurges of conservative religion in all the other major religious communities – Islam, Hinduism, Buddhism – as well as revival movements in smaller communities (such as Shinto in Japan and Sikhism in India). These developments differ greatly in their social and political implica-tions. What they have in common is their unambiguously *religious* inspiration. Consequently, taken together they provide a massive falsification of the idea that modernization and secularization are cognate phenomena. At the very least they show that *counter-*secularization is at least as important a phenomenon in the contem-porary world as secularization.

3.85 Voll and dynamic Islam

John Obert Voll, 1982: *Islam. Continuity and Change in the Modern World*. Boulder: Westview (pp. 1–2).

As well as reminding us of the dynamism of Islam, a point already made by Berger in reading **3.79** earlier in this section, John Voll introduces some of the ways in which Islam is contributing to the construction of the 'special identities' of modern Islamic states. A clear-cut religion of difference is seen as making a real difference. (See also reading **3.92** by Hefner, below.) It can be added that Islamic religions of humanity – with noticeable exceptions such as Islam in Indonesia (see Hefner, reading **3.70**) – also seem not to be faring very well. (Gardell (1996), it can be noted, claims that 'Islam is . . . well on its way to surpassing Judaism as the second largest religion in the United States' (p. 4).)

Islam is a dynamic force in the contemporary world, and in the 1980s, at the beginning of the fifteenth Islamic century, movements of Muslim revival have increasing visibility and influence. From the Islamic revolution in Iran to Southeast Asia and West Africa, the entire world of Islam is in active motion. Previously unnoticed currents of religious conviction have come to the surface and appear to be major elements in determining the course of events. [. . .]

The resurgence of Islam in the final third of the twentieth century creates a need for a reexamination of the modern history of the Islamic world. Perhaps, in the long run, the predictions of the demise of religion will be accurate. However, the assumptions and conclusions of such theories can no longer be accepted as readily as they once were. In a world in which a growing number of states are reexamining their legal structures in the light of the Quran and the requirements of traditional Islamic law, Islamic law cannot be described simply as an anachronism whose jurisdiction is being progressively limited. In a world in which radical Islamic social programs are being defined, it is no longer possible to state without significant qualifications that the secularization of the polity is in many respects a prerequisite for significant social change. In a world of militant Islamic activism, one cannot say quite so confidently that in recent years Islam has so declined in authority and vitality that it has become a mere instrument for state policy, although it is still active as a folk religion.

This book is based on the assumption that the currently visible resurgence of Islam is not simply the last gasp of a dying religious tradition. The general basis for this assumption results from an examination of the experience of the Islamic community in modern history, which broadly concludes that the Islamic world, like other societies in the contemporary world, is in the process of a major transformation. However, the result of that process will not be identically modernized, secularized societies. The shape of global, postmodern society is only beginning to emerge, but it seems clear that the special identities provided by the major religious traditions of the world will have an important role to play in that unfolding social order.

Example: experiential religions of difference

3.86 Hunter: Evangelicalism in the USA as 'far from pale and lifeless'

James Davison Hunter, 1987: *Evangelicalism. The Coming Generation.* Chicago and London: The University of Chicago Press (pp. 6–7).

Without wishing to imply that all the religions discussed by Hunter under the rubric 'Evangelicalism' are experiential religions of difference, many are. As James Davison Hunter shows, in contrast to the post-1965 decline of liberal Protestantism, conservative Protestantism is alive and well in North America. (Compare reading **3.8**, also by Hunter, on the less favourable picture for Evangelical religion elsewhere in the world.)

The position of theologically conservative Protestantism as a global phenomenon may depend in large part on how it fares in North America. For in spite of an overall shrinking demographic base, it is here, under the name of Evangelicalism, that it has its greatest force and vitality. Consider the following:

While virtually all Protestant denominations show increased membership growth between 1955 and 1965, it has only been the traditionally Evangelical denominations that continued this trend from 1965 to the present. Since 1965, membership in liberal denominations has *declined* at an average five-year rate of 4.6 per cent. By contrast, Evangelical denominations have *increased* their membership at an average five-year rate of 8 per cent.

Conservative Protestants have increased their per capita annual church donations every five years since the end of World War II as measured in constant 1970 dollars. Since 1965, the average five-year increase has been 3 per cent. Liberal Protestants, however, have decreased their per capita annual giving since 1965 at an average five-year rate of 1.6 per cent. What is perhaps even more striking is the fact that Evangelicals give the church on average 44 per cent more than do liberals. In 1983, for example, each Evangelical church member on average donated $535 per year while mainstream Protestants only donated $301.

Private Evangelical primary and secondary schools have increased in number by 47 per cent between 1971 and 1978, with a 95 per cent increase in student enrollment. As of 1985, estimates rate the total number of such schools to be between 17,000 and 18,000, representing roughly two and a half million students. This growth is occurring in a climate of sharply declining educational enrollment – where between 1970 and 1980, overall enrollment in elementary and high schools of all kinds in the United States dropped by approximately 13.6 per cent.

Conservative Protestant publishing has also grown prodigiously in the post-World War II era. In this time, the number of periodicals associated with the Evangelical Press Association has grown to 310 and at present shows a net gain of 20 to 25 new member-periodicals per year. Likewise in Evangelical book publishing, the total number of specifically Evangelical publishing houses presently exceeds 70. Marketing a large share of the books published by these houses are independently owned and operated Christian bookstores, of which there are approximately 6,000. Close to 3,500 of these belong to the Christian Booksellers Association. In 1984 these stores alone accounted for one and a quarter billion dollars in gross sales per year.

As of 1985, the 1,180 members and affiliated stations of the National Religious Broadcasters (an affiliate of the National Association of Evangelicals) handled 85 per cent of all Protestant religious broadcasts in the United States and 75 per cent of all Protestant religious broadcasts in the world.

As of 1975, North America accounted for 70 per cent of the free and subsidized Bible distribution in the world. Evangelical organizations dominated this activity.

In 1980, the United States sent abroad thirty thousand Evangelical nationals as missionaries, constituting nearly eleven times the number of American liberal Protestant missionaries and twice as many as the combined number of Protestant nationals sent abroad from all of the countries of the world.

Together these facts point to a movement that is far from pale and lifeless.

3.87   Miller: 'a new era of postdenominational Christianity in America'

Donald E. Miller, 1977: *Reinventing American Protestantism. Christianity in the New Millennium.* Berkeley, Los Angeles and London: University of California Press (p.1).

New Paradigm churches, introduced earlier (**3.34**), are doing well. Donald Miller's study concentrates on the Calvary Chapel, Vineyard Christian Fellowship and Hope Chapel, which together number over one thousand congregations, and are growing rapidly. This is a clear example of the success of experiential religions of difference in the contemporary setting.

A revolution is transforming American Protestantism. While many of the mainline churches are losing membership, overall church attendance is not declining. Instead, a new style of Christianity is being born in the United States, one that responds to fundamental cultural changes that began in the mid-1960s. These new paradigm churches, as I call them in this book, are changing the way Christianity looks and is experienced. Like upstart religious groups of the past, they have discarded many of the attributes of establishment religion. Appropriating contemporary cultural forms, these churches are creating a new genre of worship music; they are restructuring the organizational character of institutional religion; and they are democratizing access to the sacred by radicalizing the Protestant principle of the priesthood of all believers.

The new paradigm can be found in many places. One of its most typical sites is within the numerous independent churches that have proliferated in recent years. These churches are contributing to what has been called a new era of postdenominational Christianity in America, reflecting a general disillusionment with bureaucratic hierarchies and organizational oversight. Other new paradigm churches remain within existing denominations, but their worship and organizational style differ decidedly from those of the more *institutionalized* churches in their denominations. Indeed, some of these new paradigm churches disguise that fact that they even have a denominational affiliation.

Example: spiritualities of life

3.88   Lewis on a 'significant cultural shift'

James R. Lewis, 1992: Approaches to the Study of the New Age Movement. In James R. Lewis and J. Gordon Melton (eds), *Perspectives on the New Age*. Albany: State University of New York Press, pp. 1–12 (pp. 4–5).

In a reading (**1.77**) in the Spiritualties of Life chapter of **Part One**, Thomas Luckmann claims that 'Modern religious themes such as "self-realization", personal autonomy, and self-expression have become dominant'. If true, the West has witnessed a true religious revolution, traditional theistic Christianity having been overtaken by inner spiritualities and cognates. Measured by way of sales of relevant (spiritual) commodities, it is perfectly clear that interest in spiritualities of life has indeed been increasing: for example, in Britain publications classified as 'New Age/occult' have increased by 75.5 per cent between 1993 and 1997; and in the San Francisco area, *Common Ground* – advertising courses and events – shows an increase in activities from some 300 in 1979 to some 1,500 in 1997. Furthermore, as other extracts in the 'explanations' and 'prospects' parts of the spiritualities of life section show, the turn to the expressive self is of considerable cultural importance, and is associated with *quasi* or explicitly spiritual concerns. It is to be doubted, though, that the quest within has become dominant. This said, however, there are (arguable) exceptions, one being Finland where Harri Heino (1997, p. 21) reports that the greatest numbers (69 per cent) of a Gallup national survey say that they 'get in touch with God' by 'listening to one's own conscience' and 63 per cent find God 'among or in nature': figures which add up to a stronger immanentist picture than the Christian route ('by praying' attracting 64 per cent and 'by living according to the commandments' a relatively small 50 per cent). In the following reading, and turning to the USA, James R. Lewis argues that the New Age, in the USA, is but the tip of a much larger 'occult-metaphysical' (p. 3), holistic, subculture.

The question of distinguishing the New Age from the spiritual subculture out of which the movement emerged should cause us to ask certain other kinds of questions, such as, Just how extensive is this larger subculture? My impressionistic sense of the New Age is that it is merely the most visible part of a more significant cultural shift. While the popularity of phenomena like channeling and crystals may well be on the decline, the larger spiritual subculture which gave birth to these more particular phenomena is growing steadily. These impressions are reinforced by Gallup Poll statistics which indicate that one out of every four Americans believes in astrology, and that one out of five Americans believes in reincarnation. Similar surveys taken in the United Kingdom turn up the interesting statistic that 30–35 per cent of the British population hold a belief in reincarnation.

Statistics of this magnitude indicate that we are no longer talking about a marginal phenomenon. Rather, we appear to be witnessing the birth of a new, truly pluralistic mainstream. This especially seems to be the case in northern California where a recent newspaper survey found that roughly 25 per cent of San Francisco Bay area residents agree with certain key New Age ideas, such as the notion that 'nature, or Mother Earth, has its own kind of wisdom, a planetary consciousness of its own.' While it might be inaccurate to conclude from this survey that 25 per cent of all Bay area residents should be regarded as New Agers, it would not be inaccurate to assert that approximately 25 per cent of Bay area Californians adhere to certain holistic, ecological, and metaphysical points of view that depart significantly from traditional perspectives.

Example: vitality beyond institutionalized religion

3.89 Heelas on growth beyond church and chapel

Paul Heelas, 1999/2000: Expressive Spirituality and Humanistic Expressivism. Sources of Significance beyond Church and Chapel. In Steven Sutcliffe and Marion Bowman (eds), *Beyond the New Age. Alternative Spirituality in Britain*. Edinburgh: Edinburgh University Press.

In northern Europe, and almost certainly in other parts of the world, declining participation in institutionalized religion, specifically the churches and chapels of Christianity, does not go together with commensurate increases in the numbers of atheists and agnostics. As Paul Heelas argues with regard to Britain, the conclusion to be drawn is that there has been an increase in the numbers of those who are religious (in an apparently wide variety of ways) without (or rarely) going to church or chapel. Certainly such people now greatly outnumber regular attenders. (See also readings on individualized religion in the chapter on Detraditionalization.)

Some thirty-five years ago, Thomas Luckmann wrote that the 'sociology of religion is exclusively concerned with church-oriented religiosity'. Today, there is a much greater awareness of what lies beyond church and chapel: those beliefs which are religious, spiritual, supernatural, paranormal or supra-empirical in that they transgress what the secular frame of reference takes to be 'obviously' factual, rational, reasonable, sensible, and convincing; in that they are not 'readily' demonstrable to the public in general.

More specifically, but without aiming to be comprehensive or unduly systematic, such beliefs include: orthodox, theistic Christianity (Islam, etc.), associated with private Bible study or prayer (for example); less conventional and/or attenuated forms of traditional teachings; 'alternative' (and cognate) spiritualities, envisaging the ultimate as integral to the person and/or the natural order as a whole; magical or occult powers, found in connection with astrology, card-reading, palmistry, clairvoyance, mediumship, parapsychology, and in connection with many superstitions; out-of-the ordinary states of affairs, like Atlantis, ley lines, crop circles, Mayan mysteries, angels, alien life-forms, the mysterious happenings of X-file culture; out-of-the-ordinary or uncanny experiences, taken to be of religious, spiritual or supernatural significance; and the relatively inchoate, as with 'there must be something more, a "Higher Power", out there' or of the Shakespearean 'There are more things in Heaven and Earth . . . than were ever dreamt of in your philosophy' variety. [. . .]

Is (relatively broadly conceived) 'religion' beyond church and chapel in decline, or does it show signs of sustainability, even vitality? It is simply not possible, in the present context, to address the evidence pertaining to all kinds of beliefs. Neither is it possible to explore the significance of beliefs for the lives of adherents. Instead, our aim is limited to drawing on a few claims and indices to argue that very considerable numbers of people are involved.

Among others, the case has been made by David Martin and Grace Davie. Martin writes, 'Whatever we are we are *not* a secular society, particularly if by that omnibus adjective we mean an increasing approximation of average thinking to the norms of natural and social science', continuing, 'There is a luxuriant theological undergrowth which provides the working core of belief more often than is realized', and concluding, 'our society remains deeply imbued with every type of superstition and metaphysic'. Turning to Davie, the claim is that 'some sort of religiosity persists despite the obvious drop in [institutionalized] practice. The sacred does not disappear – indeed in many ways *it is becoming more rather than less prevalent in contemporary society*'.

In some contrast, however, Steve Bruce argues that '. . . in so far as we can measure *any* aspect of religious interest, belief or action and can compare 1995 with 1895, the only description for the change between the two points is "decline" '. Explicitly addressing Davie, the argument runs: 'Davie sees . . . [latent or implicit religion] as a compensating alternative [with regard to the decline of institutionalized religion]. Given that such measures of latent religiosity as are available show the same decline as those of involvement in formal religion (starting from a higher point but heading in the same direction), it seems more plausible to view them as evidence not of a compensating alternative, but of a residue'.

What is to be made of these contrasting assessments? First, it can be argued that religion beyond church and chapel is a growth area relative to what has been taking place within the traditional, institutionalized frame of reference in the UK. Dwelling on developments since the Second World War, institutionalized religion might indeed be argued to have shown very considerable decline: from some 40 per cent of the adult population attending church in England and

Wales in 1950 to some 10 per cent in 1990 (Bruce). But during roughly the same period, belief in '. . . a personal God' and '. . . some sort of spiritual or vital Force which controls life' only declined from 84 (in 1947) to 79 per cent (in 1987) in Britain (see Bruce). Clearly, this strongly suggests that religious belief, showing only a small decline (or dip?), is considerably more durable than church attendance. Furthermore, and taking into account the fact that the 84 per cent of 'believers' of 1947 presumably includes the (approximately) 40 per cent attending Church, it appears that 44 per cent then believed without attending (84 minus 40 per cent), the equivalent figure for the late 1980s being 69 per cent (79 minus 10 per cent). By this way of reckoning the matter, in other words, religious belief beyond church and chapel has become progressively more significant relative to numbers going to the traditional institutions.

And second, it is also possible to draw on statistics to argue that the numbers of those who have some kind of 'religion' without being involved in institutionalized worship has actually been increasing. The argument, in this regard, runs as follows. Again citing figures provided by Bruce, 10 per cent in Britain were atheists in 1991, 14 per cent being agnostics (totalling 24 per cent). Assuming, as is perhaps reasonable, that figures for 1950 were half this, 5 per cent were then atheists, 7 per cent agnostics (totalling 12 per cent). Then think of the decline in church attendance in England and Wales – from 40 (1950) to 10 per cent (1990), it will be recalled. With all these figures in mind, it seems that more people (30 per cent) have left church and chapel than have rejected religion or become agnostic (12 per cent). And this entails that those who are (somehow) religious without attending church or chapel have been increasing in number.

To emphasise a crucial point: it would be misleading in the extreme to conclude that everything going on beyond the frame of institutionalized worship is of great 'religious' (or spiritual, paranormal, etc.) significance. It is highly likely that much is trivial or tucked away for occasional or nominal use. But the fact remains that *many* more people are (somehow) 'religious' without going to church on anything approaching a regular basis than are attendees, one set of figures indicating that the difference is between some 70 per cent (for those believers in a personal God and a spiritual/vital Force who are not attendees) and 10 per cent (for the regulars). In short, there is much to commend Luckmann's claim concerning 'the replacement of the institutional specialization of religion by a new *social* [that is, beyond church and chapel] form of religion'.

Sacralization: explanations

Explanation: religions of difference

3.90   Casanova, deprivatization and the critique of modernity

José Casanova, 1994: *Public Religions in the Modern World*. Chicago and London: The University of Chicago Press (pp. 228–30).

Religions of difference, precisely because they are in the position to make a difference, are at the forefront of the deprivatization process. José Casanova here summarizes three ways in which religions are encouraged to engage in 'public interventions', all involving 'critiques of particular forms of institutionalization of modernity from a modern normative perspective'. (See also Casanova, 1994, pp. 57–8; and the chapters entitled Economic and Political in **Part Two**, for example **2.5** and **2.38**.)

Looking particularly at those forms of religious intervention in the public sphere which have emerged in an advanced modern society like the United States, one could say that the deprivatization of modern religion has assumed three main forms. There is, first, the religious mobilization in defense of the traditional lifeworld against various forms of state or market penetration. The mobilization of Protestant fundamentalism and, to a certain extent, the Catholic mobilization against abortion can be seen as examples of this first form of deprivatization.

The argument presented here has been that even in those cases in which religious mobilization could be explained simply as a traditionalist response to modern processes of universalization, which are promoted or protected by state juridical interventions and which disrupt, for instance, the traditional patriarchal family or established patterns of racial or gender discrimination, the deprivation of religion may have an important public function. By entering the public sphere and forcing the public discussion or contestation of certain issues, religions force modern societies to reflect publicly and collectively upon their normative structures. Naturally, one should not minimize the dangers a traditionalist backlash or a fundamentalist project of restoration may pose to modern normative structures. But in the very process of entering the modern public sphere, religions and normative traditions are also forced to confront and possibly come to terms with modern normative structures. Such a public encounter may permit the reflexive rationalization of the lifeworld and may open the way for the institutionalization of processes of practical rationalization.

A second form of deprivatization is manifested in those cases in which religions enter the public sphere of modern societies to question and contest the claims of the two major societal systems, states and markets, to function according to their own intrinsic functionalist norms without regard to extrinsic traditional moral norms. By questioning the morality of national security doctrines and the inhuman premises of nuclear defense policies, based on MAD scenarios, ready to sacrifice immeasurable numbers of human beings for the sake of state sovereignty and superpower supremacy, religions remind both states and their citizens of the human need to subordinate the logic of state formation to 'the common good.' Similarly, by questioning the inhuman claims of capitalist markets to function in accordance with impersonal and amoral self-regulating mechanisms, religions may remind individuals and societies of the need to check and regulate those impersonal market mechanisms to ensure that they are accountable for the human, social, and ecological damage they may cost and that they may become more responsible to human needs. Moreover, transnational religions are in a particularly advantageous position to remind all individuals and all societies that under modern conditions of globalization 'the common good' can increasingly be defined only in global, universal, human terms and that, consequently, the public sphere of modern civil societies cannot have national or state boundaries.

There is moreover a third form of deprivatization of religion connected with the obstinate insistence of traditional religions on maintaining the very principle of a 'common good' against individualist modern liberal theories which would reduce the common good to the aggregated sum of individual choices. As long as they respect the ultimate right and duty of the individual conscience to make moral decisions, by bringing into the public sphere issues which liberal theories have decreed to be private affairs, religions remind individuals and modern societies that morality can only exist as an intersubjective normative structure and that individual choices only attain a 'moral' dimension when they are guided or informed by intersubjective, interpersonal norms. Reduced to the private sphere of the individual self, morality must necessarily dissolve into arbitrary decisionism. By bringing publicity into the private moral sphere and by bringing into the public sphere issues of private morality, religions force modern societies to confront the task of reconstructing reflexively and collect-ively their own normative foundations. By doing so, they aid in the process of practical rationalization of the traditional lifeworld and of their own normative traditions.

If the thesis presented so far is correct, the recent transformations of religion analyzed in this study are qualitatively different from what is usually understood as 'the return of the sacred.' The deprivatization of religion cannot be understood either as an antimodern or as a postmodern phenomenon. None of the religious phenomena pre-sented here can be viewed meaningfully as instances of the kind of modern privatized religiosity which, in my view, is the true harbinger of the postmodern condition. All are grounded in that founda-tional tradition which Richard Niebuhr called radical monotheism. All still publicly uphold universalistic normative and truth claims. The critique of Enlightenment rationalism and of the teleological grand narratives of progress and secular redemption – a critique usually associated with postmodern discourse – may have legitimated and facilitated, at least indirectly, the rehabilitation of those religious traditions which had usually been the target of rationalist critique. Nevertheless, it would be difficult to find either direct links or elect-ive affinities between postmodernity and the public resurgence of religion. As already indicated, it would seem more appropriate to view the public interventions of religion analyzed here as immanent critiques of particular forms of institutionalization of modernity from a modern normative perspective.

3.91 Bruce: religion, cultural defence and transition

Steve Bruce, 1996: *Religion in the Modern World. From Cathedrals to Cults.* Oxford and New York: Oxford University Press (p. 96).

In much the same vein as Casanova, Bruce argues that secularization is resisted when religion finds itself having a public job to do: defending a culture, or assisting people 'to cope with the shift from one [sociocultural] world to another'. (See also readings in the chapters entitled Economic and Political.)

Modernity undermines religion except when it finds some major social role to play other than mediating the natural and supernatural worlds. Most of those social roles can be grouped under the two headings of cultural defence and cultural transition.

The role of religion in cultural defence can be described like this. Where there are two (or more) communities in conflict and they are of different religions (for example, Protestants and Catholics in Ulster, or Serbs, Croats, and Bosnian Muslims in what used to be Yugoslavia), then the religious identity of each can acquire a new significance and call forth a new loyalty as religious identity becomes a way of asserting ethnic pride and laying claim to what Max Weber called 'ethnic honour': the sense of 'the excellence of one's own customs and the inferiority of alien ones'. Similarly when there is a people with a common religion dominated by an external force (of either a different religion or none at all), then religious institutions acquire an additional purpose as defenders of the culture and identity of the people.

The role of religion in cultural transition involves religion acquiring an enhanced importance because of the assistance it can give in helping people to cope with the shift from one world to another. It might be that the people in question have migrated; it might be that they remain in the same place while that place changes under their feet.

3.92 Hefner: Gellner, Islam and the nation-state

Robert W. Hefner, 1977: Introduction. Islam in an Era of Nation-States: Politics and Religious Renewal in Muslim Southeast Asia. In Robert W. Hefner (ed.), *Politics and Religious Renewal in Muslim South East Asia*. Honolulu: University of Hawaii Press, pp. 1–40 (pp. 19–20).

Robert Hefner here provides a summary of Ernest Gellner's argument as to why the secularization thesis (apparently) does not apply to the Muslim world. The key to the argument – which is in tune with the two preceding readings – is that Islamic tradition has been able to play an important role in the construction of the modern nation-state.

Some observers, such as the philosopher and anthropologist Ernest Gellner, have been . . . adamant in rejecting the relevance of the secularization thesis for the Muslim world. . . . Gellner attributes this exceptionalism not to Islam's antimodernizing dispositions, but to its uniqueness in adapting to the modern nation-state. The key, Gellner argues, is that Islam has been able to play a role in the nation-state functionally (but not substantively) equivalent to that of nationalism in the West. In the West, nineteenth- and early-twentieth-century nationalists revived and idealized popular ethnic culture, using it as an instrument of nation building. This change in political culture was facilitated by the social dislocation reshaping Europe, as the vertical allegiances of the feudal era were undermined and replaced by new lateral ones. Nationalism seized on the realities of vernacular language, folk customs, and myths of national origin to respond to this crisis and forge a new basis for the political order, one founded on the sovereignty of a 'people' defined by common culture. In this manner, nationalism displaced Christianity as the key idiom of European political identity and, along the way, accelerated the secularization of modern European politics.

Gellner points out that a similar detraditionalization has altered social ties in the Muslim world. However, he argues that for several reasons Islam has been able to respond to the change while avoiding the secularist juggernaut. Islam, Gellner notes, had long been divided between an elite and a popular variant. The high tradition was associated with the transethnic and transferential clerisy, the *ulama*, who were responsible first and foremost for preserving and implementing the law, the master institution in Islamic tradition. By contrast, the low or folk tradition in Islam was grounded on tribal organizations, kinship politics, and the veneration of living Muslim saints. While paying homage to the high tradition of scholarship and law, popular Islam had an only intermittent interest, at best, in its casuistic detail. Throughout history the two traditions flowed into and influenced each other. Periodically, however, they also erupted into conflict, when reformers 'revived the alleged pristine zeal of the high culture, and united tribesmen in the interests of purification and of their own enrichment and political advancement' (Gellner). For a while thereafter, a purified Islam would dominate the political scene, but eventually it too would succumb to the twin corruptions of urban decadence and tribal parochialism.

With its industries, education, and, above all, powerful state, the modern era has irreversibly altered this 'flux and reflux' in the life of Islam, shifting the historical advantage to the supporters of the clerisy-sustained high tradition. Modernizing reformists have blamed folk Islam for the Muslim world's backwardness. In reformers' eyes, the twin challenges of modernization and Western dominance demand that this backward tradition be replaced once and for all with a purified, high Islam. Only through such a total-cultural revolution can the Muslim world restore its lost glory and propel itself into the modern era. With the machinery of the modern state at their disposal, Gellner suggests, Muslim reformists can for the first time implement their programs of total-cultural revolution on a societywide scale. For Gellner, Islam is unique among the world's historic religions in being able to pull off this feat, using 'a pre-industrial great tradition of a clerisy as the national, socially pervasive idiom and belief of a new style community'.

3.93 Elphick: rapid change in South Africa

Richard Elphick, 1977: Introduction. Christianity in South African History. In Richard Elphick and Rodney Davenport (eds), *Christianity in South Africa. A Political, Social and Cultural History*. Berkeley: University of California Press, pp 1–15 (pp. 1; 7–8).

Having made the point that there has been a veritable explosion of Christianity in South Africa, Richard Elphick illustrates the kind of very practical work which religion can do, and which therefore makes it popular.

About 72.6 per cent of South Africans now claim to be Christian, up from about 46 per cent in 1911. Over the twentieth century Christianity has grown most dramatically among Africans – the largest, fastest growing, and now politically dominant sector of the South African population – up from 26 per cent of Africans in 1911 to 76 per cent in 1990. In addition, by 1990, 92.1 per cent of South African whites, 86 per cent of Coloureds, and 13 per cent of Indians called themselves Christians.[...]

This explosion of Christian adherence coincided with massive social, economic, and intellectual transformations that some theorists call 'modernization,' while others, especially those influenced by Marxism, see as products of 'industrial capitalism.' Three aspects of these transformations were of particular importance to the churches: urbanization, secularization, and a closely related intellectual current, theological liberalism.

In the early twentieth century, Afrikaans-speaking whites and Africans flooded to the cities in the wake of the mining boom, the subsequent growth of secondary industries, and the deterioration of life in the countryside. Most middle-class members of English-speaking churches had little empathy for the white and black workers, who began to press the demands of organized labour on South African politicians, or for the black peasant populations left behind in the deteriorating rural reserves. By contrast, the Afrikaner Reformed churches, acutely aware of economic and spiritual dangers the cities posed to Afrikaans-speaking whites, undertook to alleviate the 'poor-white problem' with work colonies, boarding houses for the poor, hostels in town for rural school children, industrial schools, orphanages, and hospitals. Similarly, many missionaries of all denominations thought that the urbanization of Africans would lead to crime, sexual immorality, and religious indifference, and from this concern arose an influential body of South African Christian social thought, often called 'Social Christianity'.

The churches whose members had little political power often responded to urbanization by aggressively planting new churches in the cities. Thus, new forms of Zionist Christianity emerged that offered physical healing, a supportive community, and spiritual solace to newly urbanized Africans. As a consequence of such vigorous evangelization, the majority of urbanized whites and blacks became members of Christian churches. In this respect the history of South African Christianity more closely resembles the pattern of the United States than that of European countries; in Britain, for example, the church failed to implant itself in the working-class culture of nineteenth-century cities and went into decisive decline.

3.94   Kelley and 'the essential function of religion'

Dean M. Kelley, 1978: Why the Conservative Churches are still Growing. *Journal for the Scientific Study of Religion* 17(2): 165–72 (pp. 170–1).

Early in his article, Dean M. Kelley distinguishes between mainline, ecumenical (more liberal) religious bodies in the USA and those which he calls 'non-ecumenical'. The former are in decline; the latter – including the Southern Baptist Convention, the Church of Jesus Christ of Latter-Day Saints, the Jehovah's Witnesses, and the Seventh-Day Adventists – are 'rapidly growing' (pp. 165, 166). Why? Kelley's answer, based on a North American Interchurch Study involving interviews with over 3,500 church people, is that the latter are much better at doing a particular job: 'the denominations which grow are, by and large, those which do a better job at the essential function of religion, which I characterized as "making life meaningful in ultimate terms"' (p. 166). Religions of difference, with their emphasis on obedience, worship and seriousness appeal precisely because they are doing the work which people expect from religion; conversely, ecumenical religions are in trouble because they do not focus adequately on the Ultimate. (See Hefner, **1.23** for another statement of the importance of the Ultimate; see Bibby (1978) for the additional point that the development of conservative religion owes much to socialization.)

The purpose of the church is not, and should not be, to 'comfort' or to 'challenge,' 'to meet people's religious needs' or 'to explain the ultimate meaning of life,' but to 'preach the Gospel' and 'win others to Christ.' If it does that effectively, it will both comfort and challenge, it will meet people's religious needs by making life meaningful in ultimate terms, and – sooner or later – it will attract new members as well as retaining present members: it will grow.

In four years of giving talks around the country, reading reviews and correspondence, I have not encountered much disagreement with the first main point . . . : that the basic business of religion is to explain the ultimate meaning of life. The second main point has not been as fortunate: that the quality which makes one system of ultimate meaning more convincing is not its content but its seriousness/ costliness/strictness. That is an ungracious notion that falls discordantly upon the debonair, modern 'liberal' churchperson, producing such prodigies of Humpty-dymptyism as the Unitarian who declared that, 'we are very strict about permitting individual diversity!' – thus substituting for the object of strictness its functional opposite. [. . .]

Could not a modern congregation sit down together and search the Scriptures and ask themselves: What is it we are prepared – in obedience to God – to be serious about – if anything? What are we prepared – in obedience to God – to die for – if anything? If nothing, then the air would be cleared, and they would realize that theirs was not really a church but a clubhouse-with-a-steeple, and they could quit pretending to be religious, and everyone would be much relieved, including God, who could then turn her/his attention to more serious devotees. It should not require any very profound insight to suspect that people interested in religious help would be more drawn to a congregation or a denomination that was trying to be serious about its task than to one that was merely playing at it.

3.95 Berger on the quest for certainty

Peter L. Berger (forthcoming): The Desecularization of the World. A Global Overview. In Peter L. Berger (ed.), *The Desecularization of the World. Essays on the Resurgence of Religion in World Politics.* Washington: Ethics and Public Policy Center; Grand Rapids: William B. Eerdamans.

Closely related to Kelley's argument, Peter Berger summarizes his view that people need certainty (later in his article he writes that 'for many' lack of certainty is 'intolerable'), that modernity undermines certainty (among other things because of the impact of pluralism (**1.71 3.17**), and that religions of a fundamentalistic variety therefore appeal because they can provide certainty. (For a classic account of how modernity can operate to undermine certainty, see the reading from Marx, **3.13**.)

> It [the term fundamentalism] suggests a combination of several features – great religious passion, a defiance of what others have defined as the *Zeitegeist*, and a return to traditional sources of religious authority. These are indeed common features across cultural boundaries. And they do reflect the presence of secularizing forces, since they must be understood as a reaction *against* those forces. (In that sense, at least, something of the old secularization theory may be said to hold up, in a rather back-handed way.) This interplay of secularizing and counter-secularizing forces is, I would contend, one of the most important topics for a sociology of contemporary religion, but far too large to consider here. I can only drop a hint: Modernity, for fully understandable reasons, undermines all the old certainties; uncertainty is a condition that many people find very hard to bear; therefore, any movement (not only a religious one) that promises to provide or to renew certainty has a ready market.

3.96   Stark: pluralism and 'creating a demand'

Rodney Start, 1997: Bringing Theory Back In. In Lawrence A. Young (ed.), *Rational Choice Theory and Religion*. New York and London: Routledge, pp. 3–24 (pp. 17–18).

In stark contrast to Berger – who sees pluralization as a secularizing force (**3.17**) – Rodney Stark argues that pluralization encourages growth. Specialized religions (which, it is safe to say, include religions of difference), catering for the specific needs of a pluralistic society, 'create a demand' (p. 17); by virtue of being in a competitive market environment, they are encouraged to engage in 'vigorous [and appealing] marketing activity'. It can also be argued that pluralism can benefit religion just because there are more religions to do different jobs, including the maintenance of sociocultural identities (see Martin, 1978). (For more on the debate about the significance of pluralism for religion, see Bruce (1992) and Warner (1993).) The first two propositions of the theory now presented it should be noted, can be ignored for present purposes.

> *Pluralism* refers to the number of firms active in the economy: the more firms having a significant market-share, the greater the degree of pluralism.

I shall not deal here with why pluralism must arise in free markets. Rather I shall focus on my realization that competitive pluralism is not the evil force that saps the vigor from religion. To the contrary, where there is greater pluralism and competition, religious organizations are stronger, and the overall level of religious participation is higher. This led me to formulate the next two propositions:

Proposition 3: *To the degree that a religious economy is pluralistic, firms will specialize.*

To *specialize*, a firm caters to the special needs and tastes of specific market segments.

Proposition 4: *To the degree that a religious economy is competitive and pluralistic, overall levels of religious participation will tend to be high. Conversely, to the degree that a religious economy is monopolized by one or two state-supported firms, overall levels of participation will tend to be low.*

Economists take it for granted that a set of specialized firms will, together, be able to appeal to a far greater proportion of consumers than can a solitary unspecialized firm. The same principle applies to religion. Moreover, because so much of the religious product necessarily is intangible and concerns the far distant future, vigorous marketing activity is needed to achieve high levels of consumption. But that is not how state-supported monopoly firms function. It is a major proposition of economics that such firms tend to be inefficient. Writing in 1776 about established religions in general and the Church of England in particular, Adam Smith noted their lack of 'exertion' and 'zeal':

[T]he clergy, reposing themselves upon their benefices, had neglected to keep up the fervour of faith and devotion of the great body of the people; and having given themselves up to indolence, were incapable of making vigorous exertion in defence even of their own establishment.

Explanation: experiential religions of difference

3.97 Miller: why are the New Paradigm churches growing?

Donald E. Miller, 1977: *Reinventing American Protestantism. Christianity in the New Millennium.* Berkeley, Los Angeles and London: University of California Press (pp. 182–3).

Introduced earlier in this chapter (**3.87**; and see **3.34**), the argument here is that the – relatively detraditionalized and deinstitutionalized – New Paradigm churches 'have responded to the *therapeutic, individualistic*, and *anti-establishment themes* of the counterculture' (p. 21). As Donald E. Miller shows throughout his book, these churches cater for the values and expectations of many baby boomers: 'the importance of *feeling* the presence of God during worship' (p. 23); 'it is a sign of Christianity to be *tolerant* of denominational pluralism' (p. 128); the importance of the experience of the Holy Spirit in arriving at moral judgement (p. 130); the value ascribed to self-empowerment (pp. 178–9). These religions of the 'heart' (p. 180) serve to bring religion alive, validate belief and contribute to therapeutic growth. They differ from spiritualities of life, however, in that they combine all the above characteristics with what Miller, in the reading which follows, describes as 'the first century model of Christianity'. The Bible, in particular, provides a source of (experienced) authority to ensure that the New Paradigm churches have enough structure to appeal to those 'dissatisf[ied] with aspects of countercultural values'. On the one hand catering for the turn to the self and experience, on the other providing order (and, it can be added, community): hence the appeal of these churches. (For more on what babyboomers are looking for in religion, see **1.75**; see also Tipton's study of the Living World Fellowship (**1.82**), an important precursor of Miller's work.)

The 1960s were a watershed era in American culture with important ramifications for people's current religious choices. Whatever one may think of the political events of this period, many individuals developed a deep cynicism toward public institutions as well as an inclination to make autonomous decisions irrespective of tradition and conventional mores. With this revolution in consciousness, individuals no longer felt compelled to follow the religious tradition of their parents, and churchgoing was no longer a matter of social obligation. Conventional religious practices (such as confession for Catholics) were viewed as optional, as were many of the moral dictates of religion. A deep layer of distrust surrounded all forms of institutional religion.

Research on the religious attitudes of baby boomers reveals that many people make a distinction between 'religion' and 'spirituality.' Religion is seen as institutional and man-made; thus defined, it is of marginal interest to many people. Spirituality represents individual attempts to connect with the larger mysteries of the universe. While many critics have argued that the sixties led to narcissistic expressions of individualism, this is only one result. New paradigm churches are another, embodying numerous values of the 1960s while rejecting many of the social pathologies that the counterculture spawned. Indeed, many people who joined new paradigm churches did so because of their dissatisfaction with aspects of countercultural values, although their aesthetic tastes and understanding of institutional life were products of the sixties.

It is not surprising that baby boomers opted to attend churches that did not look religious, to worship in a home, a civic center, a converted warehouse, or a storefront. Since spirituality was the goal, not public conformity, little virtue was associated with 'dressing up' to go to church. Because authority was distrusted, pastors were viewed with suspicion if they dressed differently from the congregation. Furthermore, pastors were expected to share reflections from their meditation on scripture rather than to preach from some authoritative position.

Given this cultural shift in values, the worship of new paradigm churches evolved in very different ways. In place of the rituals of what was viewed as man-made religion, relatively simple services emerged. [...]

To summarize: new paradigm churches eliminated many of the inefficiencies of bureaucratized religion by an appeal to the first-century model of Christianity; this 'purged' form of religion corresponded to the countercultural worldview of baby boomers, who rejected institutionalized religion; with their bureaucratically lean, lay-oriented organizational structure, new paradigm churches developed programs sensitive to the needs of their constituency; new paradigm churches offered a style of worship that was attractive to people alienated from establishment religion because it was in their own idiom; this worship and the corresponding message provided direct access to an experience of the sacred, which had the potential of transforming people's lives by addressing their deepest personal needs.

Explanation: spiritualities of life

3.98 Berger: 'modernization and subjectivization are cognate processes'

Peter Berger, 1979: *The Heretical Imperative. Contemporary Possibilities of Religious Affirmation.* New York: Anchor Press/Doubleday (pp. 20–1).

Various aspects of the development of spiritualities of life have already been explored: in the readings on 'explanations' and 'prospects' in the chapter on

Spiritualities of Life in **Part One**, in a number of readings to do with the resacral-ization of work in the Economic chapter of **Part Two**, and in the Detraditional-ization chapter of **Part Three**. A key theme, here explored by Peter Berger, concerns the turn to the self. In some contrast to the earlier reading from Berger in this section (**3.95**), where he links uncertainty with pluralism and the appeal of quite strong religions of difference, he argues in the following extract that the erosion of 'objectivity' with regard to the 'plausibility structures' of the lifeworld (associated, it can be added, with pluralism) compels people to 'turn inward.'

Modernization has brought with it a strong accentuation of the sub-jective side of human existence; indeed, it may be said that moderni-zation and subjectivization are cognate processes. This has often been remarked upon as far as theoretical thought, especially philosophy, is concerned. Thus, Western philosophy since Descartes has been characterized as a turning toward subjectivity. Epistemology, of course, expresses this by asking over and over again the question 'What can I know?' It is very important to understand that this question not only is asked by philosophers but, under certain circumstances, becomes an urgent concern for the ordinary man in the street. Modernity produces such circumstances. But even under more reliable conditions human beings must have available some sort of answer to this question, if only because every new generation of children asks it in one way or another – and the adults must be in a position to reply. In a society with stable, coherent plausibility structures the answers can be given in a tone of great assurance. That is, the socially defined reality has a very high degree of objectivity: 'This is what the world is like; it is this and no other; it could not be any different; so stop asking silly questions.' It is precisely this type of objectivity that comes to be eroded by the forces of modernization. In consequence, the answers to the perennial human question 'What can I know?' become uncertain, hesitating, anxious. Yet the individual must have some answers, because he must have some sort of meaningful order to live in and live by. If answers are not provided objectively by his society, he is compelled to turn *inward*, toward his own subjectivity, to dredge up from there whatever certainties he can manage. This inward turning is subjectivization, a process that embraces both Descartes and the man-in-the-street who is puzzled about the proper course of action in this or that area of everyday life.

If this point is understood, it should not be surprising that modern Western culture has been marked by an ever-increasing attention to subjectivity. Philosophy is only one small part of this. There is modern literature (the novel is the prime example here), modern art, and, last but not least, the astronomic proliferation of modern psychologies and psychotherapies.

3.99 Luckmann: a 'profound change in the "location" of religion in society'

Thomas Luckmann, 1990: Shrinking Transcendence, Expanding Religion? *Sociological Analysis*, 50(2): 127–38 (pp. 132–5).

Thomas Luckmann's thesis is that whereas religions of ' "great" transcendences' – of over-arching canopies of meaning – are well-suited for relatively integrated societies, 'There seems to be a powerful "elective affinity" between the structural privatization of individual life and the "sacralization" of subjectivity that is celebrated in much of modern consciousness'. Putting it in a nutshell, the autonomous individual is looking for a spirituality *for* him or herself.

The long-range consequences of institutional specialization of religion have been customarily interpreted as a process of secularization, of the shrinking and eventual disappearance of religion from the modern world. This notion stems from an etiological myth of modernity. In my view, the consequences of institutional specialization of religion are more appropriately described as leading to another profound change in the 'location' of religion in society. This process may be described as *privatization* of religion. [...]

The functional segmentation of modern social structure proved to be highly unfavorable to the social construction of a taken-for-granted, obligatory model of transcendent reality. The specifically religious representations pointing to the 'great' transcendences of life were integrated into the 'official' traditional Christian model of religion. The monopoly of the Christian churches in the matter of religious socialization was broken in Europe with the French Revolution. In no modern industrial society are Christian themes the only specifically religious representations offered on the newly formed 'market' of 'transcendence.' Traditionally religious views of Christian origin compete with religious orientations pertaining to the various levels of transcendence that stem from the most diverse sources. They are disseminated by the mass media in books and by television, and by prophets and teachers in public and private places, *e.g.*, in the burgeoning 'seminar' industry.

The 'sacred cosmos' of modern industrial societies no longer has one obligatory hierarchy, and it is no longer articulated as a consistent thematic whole. It consists of assortments of social reconstructions of transcendence. The term 'assortment' points out a significant distinction between the modern sacred cosmos and the sacred cosmos of a traditional society. The latter contains well-articulated themes that form a universe of 'ultimate' significance that is reasonably consistent in terms of its own logic. The former also contains themes that may be legitimately defined as religious; they are capable of being internalized by potential consumers as significant reconstructions of experiences of transcendence. These themes, however, do not form a coherent universe. The assortment of religious representations – a sacred cosmos in a loose sense of the term only – is not internalized by potential consumers as a whole. The 'autonomous consumer selects, instead, certain religious themes from the available assortment and builds them into a somewhat precarious private system of 'ultimate' significance. Individual religiosity is thus no longer a replica or approximation of an 'official' model. [. . .]

Specifically and explicitly religious orientations refering to the 'great' transcendences of subjective experience (which are generally derived from one of the traditional 'sacred universes') now offered on the religious market not only compete among themselves; they also compete with models of socialization and of the 'good life' that contain no specifically religious representations although they consist of reconstructions of this worldly transcendences and thus also contain distinct views of a moral order.

The social basis of the newly emerging religion is to be found in the 'private sphere.' The themes that have come to occupy a dominant position in the sacred cosmos today originate in and refer to an area of individual existence in modern society that is removed from primary social institutions. But, as already indicated, not all the themes that are available in the sacred cosmos today originate in the 'private sphere.' Some can be traced to the traditional Christian cosmos, while others originated in the 'secular' institutional ideologies of the eighteenth and nineteenth centuries. But in recent decades concern with the minimal transcendence symbolized by notions such as self-fulfillment and the like has become widespread, if not dominant. (Their derivation from romanticism, certain branches of philosophic idealism, and the more recent 'depth-psychologies' is obvious. But what were marginal phenomena then seem to have become mass phenomena now, broadly characteristic of modern consciousness.)

The tendency to shift intersubjective reconstructions and social constructions away from the 'great' other-worldly transcendences to the 'intermediate' and, more and more, also to the minimal transcendences of modern solipsism may be considered as the 'thematic' (cultural) correlate of (social) 'structural' privatization. There seems to be a powerful 'elective affinity' between the structural privatization of individual life and the 'sacralization' of subjectivity that is celebrated in much of modern consciousness.

3.100 Stark and secularization as 'self-limiting'

Rodney Stark, 1985: Europe's Receptivity to Religious Movements. In Rodney Stark (ed.), *Religious Movements: Genesis, Exodus, and Numbers*. New York: Paragon House, pp. 301–39 (pp. 302; 303; 305–6).

What follows in this reading has to be approached by way of Rodney Stark's use of deprivation–compensation theory. As he writes elsewhere (1985), 'When we examine human desires, we see that people often seek rewards of such magnitude and apparent unavailability [such as the meaning of life and what happens after death] that only by assuming the existence of an active supernatural can credible compensators be created' (p. 7). When mainstream religion – for whatever reason – loses its authority, religious movements (including those to do with inner spirituality) come to serve as compensators. In what now follows, Stark claims that he can show that Europe is far from exceptional (as secular) in that it has compensated for the decline in mainstream denominations by developing cults (and sects), which include spiritualities of life.

Secularization *does not bring the end of religion*. Rather, secularization is self-limiting in that it stimulates significant processes of reaction in other sectors of any religious economy. The first of these is the familiar feature of conventional church-sect theory: As secularization weakens particular religious organizations, schisms result and new organizations appear. We call this process *revival* – sects break away to revive the original vigor of the conventional religious tradition. But secularization prompts more than revival, it also stimulates *innovation* – rather than being only new organizations of an old faith, groups also appear that constitute *new faiths*. We identify these as cult movements. The greater the degree of secularization experienced by a conventional religious tradition, the more cult movements that will appear, and the greater the probability that one or more of them will successfully supplant the old tradition of faith. For example, it was the excessive secularization of the pagan faiths of the Roman world that gave Christianity its opening to triumph in that religious economy. In effect, we argue that secularization causes shifts in the *sources* of religion within a society, while the *amount* of religion remains relatively constant. [. . .]

From the beginning, I have been fully aware (and colleagues often have pointed out) that the theory appears to fail when applied to Europe. Since many nations in Western Europe would appear to be considerably more affected by secularization than is the United States, other things being equal, they ought to have developed or attracted more cult movements. [. . .]

In this essay I will attempt to show that expert opinion is wrong. It is true that in much of Europe the long dominant and established denominations have fallen on bad times – as have the highest status and most liberal Protestant bodies in America. However fully in accord with our theory, secularization produces religious revival and innovation in Europe as well as in North America. That is, I intend to demonstrate, that the United States is not especially prolific of cult and sect movements; that many European nations are even more receptive to such movements than is America. Indeed, I shall show that many distinctively American cult and sect movements are doing better across the Atlantic (and the South Pacific as well) than they have ever done back home.

Explanation: significance beyond institutionalized religion

3.101 Heelas and constructing autobiographies

Paul Heelas, 1998: Beyond New Religious Movements – Towards Spiritual Shopping. Paper delivered to the American Academy of Religion Annual Conference.

Many points have already been made, in other readings and links, which pertain to the theme of the significance of religiosity beyond church and chapel. Of particular note, since spiritualities of life could well be an important aspect of growth beyond church and chapel, the reader is directed to relevant readings in the chapters on Spiritualities of Life, Detraditionalization and, for prosperity spiritualities, the Economic chapter; see also the preceding three readings. The following reading draws attention to just one more aspect of growth beyond church and chapel. It is argued that 'new spiritual outlets' – all those (relatively non-authoritative) events, courses, rituals, healings, shops which provide spirituality, typically for a payment – are the place to go if one wants spirituality to contribute to the construction of one's autobiography.

> As Madeleine Bunting, Religious Affairs Correspondent for The *Guardian* suggests, 'The sacred narrative has moved from the Cosmic – as in the Jews' beliefs of God's Chosen People, or Christianity's belief in the Redemption through God's Son, Jesus – to the individual's life journey. We each develop a narrative, heavily influenced by psycho-therapeutic concepts, in which we explain and seek to understand the twists and turns of our lives. Self-knowledge has replaced knowledge of God as the ultimate objective'. This marvellous formulation alerts us to another aspect of the increasing popularity of new spiritual outlets, especially for expressivists. The argument is that people are looking for spiritualities to help construct their autobiographies. As they move through life – through health and sickness, good and bad fortune, marriage and divorce, job and retirement, and so on – people want different spiritual provisions. The 'twists and turns' – if not fragmentations – of their lives call for different forms of resourcing. New spiritual outlets are the obvious place to turn: one can select what is right for one's autobiography at any particular point in time; one can select and utilize without any worries about being drawn into long-term commitments; without having to adopt some grand 'sacred narrative' (to recall Bunting).

Explanation: the need for religion, and the future

3.102 Bell and the return of the Sacred

Daniel Bell, 1977: The Return of the Sacred? The Argument on the Future of Religion. *British Journal of Sociology*, 28(4): 419–49 (pp. 442, 444–7).

Berger (in reading **3.98** above) and Stark (reading **3.100**, also above) respectively draw attention to two different aspects of why people have an anthropological need for religion: certainty and meaning. In one of the best-known essays on the theme of sacralization, Daniel Bell argues in similar fashion, although attaching more importance to the experience of the basic anthropological condition. Fully accepting that secularization has taken place, it is claimed that it is self-limiting: 'that very destruction [of 'aura'] – and the realization of that fact – is itself the starting point of a new response'. Spelling this out, the claim is that 'The ground of religion is existential: the awareness of men of their finiteness and the inexorable limits to their powers, and the consequent effort to find a coherent answer to reconcile them to that human condition'. For Bell the secularization of religion and the increasing barenness of modernity *reveals* this awareness, this need: hence sacralization. Perhaps, it might be added, this is why so few of the global population are atheists. (In many regards, it can be noted, Bell's argument is very similar to that proponded by Simmel (1997) at the beginning of this century; see also Simmel, **3.40**).

Will there be a return of the sacred, the rise of new religious modes? Of that I have no doubt. Religion is not an ideology, or a regulative or integrative feature of society – though in its institutional forms it has, at different times, functioned in this way. It is a constitutive aspect of human experience because it is a response to the existential predicaments which are the *ricorsi* of human culture. That complex German writer Walter Benjamin maintained that 'the concrete totality of experience is religion', and he gave to this form of authentic experience the word 'aura'. It is akin to Rudolf Otto's conception of the 'numinous' or to the Biblical conception of 'awe'. The age of mechanical reproduction, Benjamin thought, had stripped art of its uniqueness and the 'aura' of unbridgeable distance has been destroyed. I think – as I have argued elsewhere – that this 'eclipse of distance' is the common syntax of Modernism itself: in its emphasis on simultaneity, immediacy, sensation and shock. And it is this destruction of 'aura' (to use Benjamin's word) in the high culture which opened the way for that destruction in the mass culture. But that very destruction – and the realization of that fact – is itself the starting point for new responses. [. . .]

If there are to be new religions – and I think they will arise – they will, contrary to previous experience, return to the past, to seek for tradition and to search for those threads which can give a person a set of ties that place him in the continuity of the dead and the living and those still to be born. Unlike romanticism, it will not be a turn to nature, and unlike modernity it will not be the involuted self; it will be the resurrection of Memory.

I do not know how these will arise, but I have some dim perception of the forms they may take. I would be bold enough to say that in the West they would be of three kinds.

The first I would call *moralizing* religion. Its roots and strength are in a Fundamentalist faith, evangelical and scourging, emphasizing sin and the turning away from the Whore of Babylon. In the United States, in recent years, the largest-growing voluntary associations have been the Fundamentalist churches. To some extent this is an aggressive reaction on the part of the 'silent majority', so to speak, against the carryover of modernist impulses into politics – especially the claims of complete personal freedom in sexual areas (e.g. Gay rights), morals, abortion and the like. But that is too simple an explanation. I think, given the history of Western culture, that a large substratum of society has always felt the need for simple pieties, direct homilies, reassurances against their own secret impulses (such as in Nathaniel Hawthorne's powerful story 'Young Goodman Brown'), but that until recently these people have been derided by the predominantly liberal *culture* (not society) and, more importantly, abandoned by the clergy, who, coming from the educated classes and subject to the conformist pressures of the liberal culture, had lost their own nerve, and often, as well, their belief in God. The exhaustion of Modernism and the emptiness of contemporary culture mitigate that social pressure, and Fundamentalist ministers can step forward, with less fear of derision from their cultured despisers. These groups, traditionally, have been farmers, lower-middle class, small-town artisans, and the like. In the long-run occupational sense, they are in the decline. Yet in the more immediate future they may be the strongest element in a religious revival.

The second – which I think will find its adherents in the intellectual and professional classes – I would call *redemptive*, and derives, I think, from two sources. One is the retreat from the excesses of modernity. One can face death, perhaps, not by seeking to be self-infinitizing, but by looking back. Human culture is a construction by men to maintain *continuity*, to maintain the 'un-animal life'. Animals seeing each other die do not imagine it of themselves; men alone know their fate and create rituals not just to ward off mortality (the pretty stories of heaven and hell), but to maintain a 'consciousness of kind', which is a mediation of fate. In this sense, religion is the awareness of a space of transcendence, the passage out of the past from which one has come, and to which one is bound, to a new conception of the self as a moral agent, freely accepting one's past (rather than just being shaped by it) and stepping back into tradition in order to maintain the continuity of moral meanings. It is a redemptive process (in Kenelm Burridge's terms), whereby individuals seek to discharge their obligations – and if one claims *rights*, at some point there has to be recognition of *obligations* as well – to the moral imperatives of the community: the debts in being nurtured, the debts to the institutions that maintain moral awareness. Religion, then, begins, as it must, in the mutual redemption of fathers and sons. It involves, in Yeat's phrase, becoming 'the blessed who can bless', the laying on of hands.

There is a second, more direct sociological source of the redemptive. This is in the growth, as I believe it will come, of what Peter Berger has called 'mediating institutions'. In the reaction against central government, of large-scale bureaucracy and the mega-structures of organization, there is a desire to reinstate a private sphere – of family, church, neighbourhood and voluntary association – to take back the function which it has lost of *caring*: of caring for the afflicated and the ill, of caring for welfare, of caring for each other. For Hegel, mediation was the central concept which explained how the universal became concrete. Mediation for Hegel 'is nothing but self-identity working itself out through an active self-directed process', the act of reflection which balances the immediacy of existence with the idea of universality.

The mediating institutions, centred as they will be on the idea of caring, resurrect the idea of *caritas*, one of the oldest sources of human attachments, a form of love that has been crushed between rationalized *eros* and profaned *agape* and superseded by the welfare state. They may arise, to use an older theological term, in the *koinonia*, the primary groups where people live and work. There have always been utopian colonies, but these fled from the world. There was – and is – more recently, the *kibbutzim*, but they were too secular, they swallowed up their members in the whole of their lives, and they are being crushed by the economic forces of a larger world. Yet they did, in their earliest years, transform a society and a people, and made the desert bloom. Whether the mediating institutions that I think will arise become the cenacles of a new religion remains to be seen.

The third religion, more diffuse, will be a return to some mythic and mystical modes of thought. The world has become too scientistic and drab. Men want a sense of wonder and mystery. There is a persistent need to overcome the dualisms that prize apart the tendrils of self which yearn for unification of being. There is also the temptation to walk along the knife-edge of the abyss. As Rilke began his *Duino Elegies*: 'For Beauty's nothing but the beginning of Terror. . . .' Yet myth tames the terror and allows us to look at the Medusa's head without turning to stone. Myth returns us to what Goethe called the *Urphänomene*, the *ricorsi* of the existential predicaments. [. . .]

To sum up my argument. The ground of religion is not regulative, a functional property of society, serving, as Marx or Durkheim argued, as a component of social control or integration. Nor is religion constitutive, a property of human nature, as argued by Schleirmacher, Rudolf Otto and religious phenomenologists such as Max Scheler. The ground of religion is existential: the awareness of men of their finiteness and the inexorable limits to their powers, and the consequent effort to find a coherent answer to reconcile them to that human condition.

conclusion

It would be hard to read this book without being struck by the quality of the readings which are gathered here. The first part of this Conclusion reviews some of their main themes and findings, before going on to consider the broader picture of religion in modern times which emerges. The Conclusion ends with suggestions about possible priorities for future research and, more riskily, with some predictions about the future of religion.

Themes and Conclusions from the Literature

Of all the topics covered in this book, the one which has stimulated the greatest amount of scholarly time and energy has undoubtedly been *secularization theory*. Contemporaneous in its origins with the rise of sociology itself, its powerful influence has been felt in almost all subsequent studies of religion in modern times.

Whilst secularization theory has much to do with numbers, the sheer quantity of those engaged in – or disengaged from – religious belief and practice, the empirical data are still incomplete and imperfect (see, for example, Hadaway, Marler and Chaves' findings about the inaccuracy of polled church attendance figures for the United States, reading **3.7**). In truth, much secularization theory seems to be driven not so much by the data but by theoretical reflection on the nature of the interaction between religion and modernity.

For much of the twentieth century, the dominance of secularization theory went virtually unquestioned. Challenges to the theory have now gathered such momentum that it is possible to speak of the new and developing counter-theory of 'sacralization'. The debate between secularization and sacralization theory seems set to run for some time. Whilst it is hard to dispute the figures of religious decline throughout the course of the twentieth century, particularly since the 1960s, and particularly in northern Europe, the evidence of continuing religious vitality in other parts of the world may give strength to the sacralizationists' arguments. Equally, whilst it is hard to dispute differentiation theory and the observation that specialization in modernized countries has increasingly pushed religion out of key public areas like politics, education and welfare, sacralization theory has usefully directed attention to the newly important roles of religion in the public square in the West (see Casanova, reading **3.80**), and to the central socio-political roles religion continues to play in many other parts of the world.

The *political mobilization* of religion is thus a second area which has attracted a great deal of attention in recent times. To a large extent this interest appears to have been driven not so much by theory (such developments being contrary to what secularization theory would have expected), but by the sheer force of events. The revolution in Iran in 1979; the mobilization of Islam from Algeria to Afghanistan; the rise of Hindu militancy in India and Sri Lanka; the role of Christian churches in the collapse of communism in eastern Europe at the end of the 1980s; the wars in the former Yugoslavia – as we have seen in **Part Two**, these and similar events have drawn the attention of scholars of religion as well as politics. A clear conclusion emerging from the literature is that religion continues to play a key role in undergirding threatened political, ethnic and national identities; in providing a stimulus for political militancy and mobilization; in providing a basis for resistance; and in shaping and inspiring the political imagination.

The literature pays similar, and related, attention to the continuing role of religion in providing *social, economic and cultural capital*. Indeed, so many of the readings in this volume deal with this topic that it has proved impossible to cross-reference them all. We have seen, for example, how Charismatic Christianity in Latin America serves, in a way analogous to Methodism in the eighteenth- and nineteenth-century West, as a force for social and economic development by providing opportunities for education, social advancement, and a training in the proto-capitalist virtues of discipline, hard-work and frugality (see readings **2.23** and **2.53** by Bernice Martin and David Martin). Likewise, we have seen that many explanations of the success of religions of difference and heightened difference appeal to their ability to provide social and moral capital in times of turmoil, change, uncertainty, and social fragmentation (anomie). Such explanations may be compared with once-popular functionalist approaches to religion. The latter fell out of favour because they came to be seen as unhelpfully reductionist insofar as they ignored the 'thick' social and cultural reality of religions in their eagerness to discover 'deeper' social functions. Whilst sharing something of the same approach, most of the theorists of 'capital religions' cited here display much greater ethnographic sensitivity than did their predecessors, and balance description of the internal discourses, logics and self-descriptions of religion with analysis of its social functions.

Mention of anomie and social fragmentation brings us to another area of concentration in the literature: *pluralization*. This topic includes both social and religious pluralization and – most importantly – the interactions between the two. Whilst there is a great deal of work in this area, it is possible to identify at least three different clusters of theorizing. All can be found in the work of the single most influential writer in this area, Peter Berger. Berger is best known for drawing attention to the importance of pluralization in the social and cultural realms, and for arguing that such pluralization leads to secularization by undermining the plausibility of religion (see readings **1.24** and **3.46**). Berger also argues, however, that pluralization leads to the assertion of strongly differentiated forms of religion (see reading **3.95**), thus highlighting a second widely-agreed conclusion in this area: that the fragmentation and anomie which accompany modernization can lead to a revitalization of religions of heightened difference. His explanation is that the latter are able to maintain plausibility in a pluralized world through their tightly bounded and separatist social forms and their tightly-controlled common rituals and doctrines. The third line of argument in relation to pluralization is that pluralization leads to the privatization and even trivialization of religion. Here it is suggested that social and cultural pluralization force religion to retreat to the purely private realm and to surrender its wider public and political functions. Finally, a fourth cluster of theorizing about pluralization, most commonly associated with the work of Rodney Stark, argues (against Berger) that religious pluralism leads not to decline but to growth in religion as a free market is better able to deliver the products which customers seek (see reading **3.96**).

Privatization theory is bound up with another area of some consensus in the literature: that religion in modern times is decisively influenced by the *turn to the self*. Thomas Luckmann's work has been influential here, as has that of many other scholars from Europe and America, including importantly (and perhaps not surprisingly!) many who have a strong association with California – from Wade Clark Roof to Steven Tipton. The turn to the self refers to a widespread shift in modernity away from deference to external sources of authority towards a reliance on individual capacities and capabilities. Much of the literature reviewed in this book claims that this trend is as powerful in the religious sphere as it is in the modern political, domestic or economic realms. In relation to religion the turn to the self is claimed to involve not only suspicion towards scripture, tradition, priests and institutionalized religion more generally, but also a turn away from an external, transcendent God to the immanent 'god within' definitive of spiritualities of life.

New Approaches, Emerging Themes

Whilst this volume draws together a wide selection of literature on religion in modern times, it also seeks to frame and approach it in a new way. As explained in the Introduction, a general aim of the book is to understand the diversity of both religion and modern times, and of the interplays between them. Its approach has been based on the recognition that neither religion nor modernity is one thing. Consequently, it is suspicious of the very language of modernity, postmodernity and pre-modernity insofar as this tends to suggest uniform and homogeneous periods. By the same token, it is suspicious of generalizing theories, which postulate unilinear trends running through all religion in all places and all (modern) times. Often such theories are bound up with a pre-modern/ modern periodization, since they assume an inexorable, unidirectional, irreversible evolutionary movement in which religion advances from one stage of development to another.

Suspicion of unilinear theories and uniform accounts of religion is by no means unique to the authors of this volume. Indeed it could be viewed as part of the widespread suspicion of metanarratives which currently affects many disciplines. More importantly, it is shared by many others involved in the study of religion, some of whom have greatly influenced us, and whose work we have presented in the preceding pages. Writing recently about new directions in the study of religion, the ever-perceptive Robert Wuthnow (1997) notes that:

> the one feature that most clearly distinguishes contemporary scholarship from, say, the 1950s or 1960s is its rejection of . . . 'linear narratives of disembodied trends'. Recent studies not only dispute the claims of theories that emphasize, for instance, secularization and modernization; they also reject the value of such theories, preferring instead to talk about gender differences, multiple vocabularies, local cultures, contradictory impulses, negotiation, and the construction of meaning. (p. 248)

What Wuthnow primarily has in mind is a shift from grand theorizing to detailed ethnographic study. The approach taken in this book is somewhat less extreme. We agree with Wuthnow when he goes on to say that an exclusive emphasis on the idiosyncratic details of the specific case can rob the human sciences of the ability to generate cumulative knowledge. Instead of abandoning theory and the attempt to making meaningful empirical generalizations altogether, we have therefore tried to theorize the diversity of religion in modern times. The volume therefore attempts to give an account of the *variety* of religion in modern times, of its interaction with *various* social contexts, and of the *varied* ways in which different trends play out in relation to the varieties of religion and context. To many, such theorizing will no doubt still appear to be on much too grand a scale. Our defence would be that what might be called 'intermediate theory' (intermediate between macro-level unilinear theory and micro-level empirical research) can still be of value in making sense of religion in modern times.

The debate about secularization furnishes a useful example of what is at stake here, and helps illustrate some of the new directions in which intermediate theory of the sort we are advocating may lead. Until now, most secularization theory has been couched in undifferentiated terms: religion (one thing) inevitably affected by modernity/modernization (one thing) in one unvaried direction (privatization, differentiation, inevitable decline). We are not alone in thinking that this may no longer be the most fruitful way of approaching the topic. In relation to a more differentiated approach to secularization, one must mention first of all the pioneering work of David Martin whose somewhat confusingly titled *General Theory of Secularisation* (1978) actually undermined grand theory by considering the variables affecting secularization in western Europe, most notably the political variables (see reading **3.5**). More recently, José Casanova (1994), for example, has pointed out that the factors most commonly identified as the carriers of secularization (namely the Protestant Reformation; the formation of modern states; the growth of modern capitalism; and the scientific revolution) are variables not constants. He suggests that it would therefore be interesting to examine the different historical patterns of secularization which have developed as each of these carriers developed different dynamics in different places and at different times (pp. 19–25).

In terms of the particular version of intermediate theory advocated in this book, secularization theory might be taken in still other, more differentiated, directions. As well as continuing Martin's work by investigating the ways in which political and economic contexts affect religion, it would be fruitful to consider secularization in relation to the different varieties of religion in modern times – religions of difference and experiential religions of difference, religions of humanity and experiential religions of humanity, and spiritualities of life. In the preceding pages an attempt has been made to indicate the ways in which such an approach will reveal significant variations in the vitality and numerical significance of different types of religion in modern times. As the chapter on Sacralization in **Part Three** makes clean, religions of humanity seem to be shrinking fastest. By comparison, religions of difference, spiritualities of life and experiential religions of difference appear to be faring well. And (to add in the political and economic complexities), religions of difference (for example) appear to be doing particularly well when they are helping to define and undergird other forms of difference, both ethnic and national, or to provide social capital.

In short, a more differentiated approach to secularization results in a rather different picture of religion in modern times than the one which has been generated by unilinear theories. This book has, we hope, conveyed something of this. The picture which emerges is not of a uniformly disenchanted world, but of a world in which vibrant and growing varieties of religion coexist with stagnant or declining ones.

'Coexistence' is a word which crops up several times in this volume as it attempts to characterize the state of religion in modern times. In many ways it sums up the book's findings. Different varieties of religion coexist, and different trends coexist, in different contexts. Sometimes this coexistence may be harmonious, at other times conflictual. (In the chapter on Combinations at the end of **Part One** we attempted to develop a vocabulary for describing some of these different forms of coexistence.) But what appears as a contradiction at the logical and theoretical level may not be a contradiction at the empirical level. It may simply be an example of coexistence. Thus both sacralization and secularization seem evident in modern times, and the theories which attempt to describe and explain them may not be as incompatible as a monolithic and totalizing theoretical approach necessarily assumes.

Another form of coexistence which emerges from this book is that between different varieties of religion, and in particular between those at the 'triangle' and the 'blob' ends of the spectrum illustrated in the Introduction. Where the former stress difference, the latter stress the universal; where the former are exclusive, the latter are inclusive; and where the former worship a transcendent God, the latter strive to realize the god within. Yet both appear to be doing well. At present they coexist. When this coexistence takes place within the same religion, it may lead to conflict. Equally, the two may coexist harmoniously in different sites, and even within the same religion, without troubling one another. In yet other examples, some form of synthesis and rapprochement between the two may be attempted, as in experiential religions of difference.

Another closely related form of coexistence in religion in modern times is that between universalism and difference. Both are themes which are only just emerging in the literature, and which have been highlighted and developed in this book. As the chapter on Universalization in **Part Three** illustrates, the collapse of strong, prescriptive forms of difference is a powerful trend in many forms of religion in modern times. Thus almost all spiritualities of life involve the claim that different religions give access to the one perennial truth; most religions of humanity seek a single, rational, humanitarian religion behind the diversity of historical religion; and ecumenical endeavour and the universalist defence of 'human dignity' has been influential even within religions of difference. As the chapters entitled Political (chapter seven) and Difference (chapter eight) in **Part Two** illustrate, however, the apparently contradictory process of differentiation has been equally important. In the wake of communism and western imperialism, for example, we have seen religion playing a major role in the assertion of ethnic and national difference. The success of religions of heightened difference across the world testifies to the continuing force of an exclusivist difference which sometimes leads to serious conflict and even violence. Equally, we have seen religion playing a part in the construction and maintenance of separatist sects, prescribed gender differences, and strict moral codes.

The conclusion must be that the processes of univeralization and differentiation coexist in modern times. Religions have always had to cope with the fact that there are other, significantly different, religions. For reasons discussed in the main body of the text, the need to make sense of this difference has become pressing and inescapable for religions in modern times. Whilst some religions react by asserting their difference and superiority, others respond in more inclusive and universalist fashion. The interactions and tensions between these trends will no doubt continue to be a source of both vitality and conflict. Of particular note, perhaps, are the many attempts to hold together universalism and difference. In the neo-Vedantic tradition in Hinduism, for example, it is common to find the claim that difference (for example the worship of different gods) is necessary and good at the lower stages of the spiritual life, even though the truly enlightened move beyond difference (*nama-rupa*, name and form) to an undifferentiated experience of the formless. A very different example can be found in the pronouncements of Pope John Paul II, or of a number of the intellectual leaders of modern Islam such as Maududi, where we find the exclusivistic claim that the Catholic church (or Islam) is the sole guardian of God's truth, alongside an insistence that this truth is a universal truth about 'humanity' and human flourishing. Finally, recent attempts to forge postmodern forms of religion seem powerfully motivated by the desire to embrace, affirm and narrate difference without denying the right of others to do the same.

A further form of coexistence which emerges clearly in this book concerns the private and public manifestations of religion. Again, the differentiated approach we are advocating allows us to see that universal unilinear claims about the privatization or deprivatization of religion, and about its political insignificance or political resurgence, may not be incompatible. The claim that religion is inexorably shrinking from the public to the private realm ('social differentiation') seems to describe what is happening in relation to modern democratic states. Yet it is also true that religion continues to play important public and political roles in modern secular polities. In the United States, for example, besides more striking developments associated with the rise of the New Right, presidents and politicians continue to parade their Christian credentials, and the survival of the entire 'American way of life' is seen by many to depend upon the future vitality of 'civil religion' (see reading **2.57**).

Having been chased from the public square in many modern polities, some forms of religion seem to be developing new, less direct (and probably less influential) ways of continuing to influence public and political life. In other parts of the world, however, something very different has been happening as religion has displayed its continuing power for political mobilization. As scholars like Mark Juergensmeyer remind us, the rise of religious nationalisms in places like India, the Middle East, and the former USSR has been one of the most surprising features of the late twentieth century for those who believed that secularization and differentiation were universal trends (see reading **2.31**). The continuing power and vitality of religion in defending political identity against assimilation or destruction (as in the case of Sufi Islam in the USSR), in opposing political regimes (as in the case of the churches in eastern Europe), or in constructing and defending ethnic identities (as in India), is certainly as striking as its retreat from the political sphere in other parts of the world.

The coexistence of religion in and out of politics does not only take place on a global scale, of course. It can also take place within particular nations or communities. The UK furnishes one example of this, with the political militancy of northern Irish religion contrasting strikingly with the political marginalization of 'established' Anglicanism in England. Equally, the United States is the site of both highly privatized forms of religion, and of politically resurgent forms – a coexistence which quite often leads to conflict of various sorts. The vast amount of literature currently generated by the debate about 'church and state' in America is one obvious sign of the tense coexistence of religion in and out of politics in that country.

Another striking example of the coexistence of religion in and out of the public realm is furnished by the interplay between religion and economics. Again, this is a rather under-researched theme which we have tried to develop and highlight in this volume. What emerges most clearly from the chapter on Economic contexts in **Part Two** are the many instances in which religion continues to play a huge role in relation to economic activity in modern times, entering into the workplace through work ethics and techniques of 'magical empowerment'. This is not what unilinear theories of secularization and differentiation would have led us to expect. Indeed, what seems to be the huge importance of prosperity religion world-wide constitutes one of the largest challenges to unilinear theories of secularization insofar as it appears to disprove in a very striking way the idea that rationalization and disenchantment are inexorable processes. Prosperity religion flourishes in bizarre coexistence with rationalized forms of life, and a single individual is able to combine perfectly rational and perfectly magical behaviour in relation to the workplace and economic success. Likewise, the heartlands of economic activity, which differentiation theory might have expected to be empty of religion, continue to happily combine religion with money making (the large number of churches which serve the City of London's financial community, for example, or the popularity of Lakshmi, goddess of prosperity, throughout Indian society).

Overall, then, this book presents a picture of the coexistence of many different trends and types of religion in modern times. This conclusion is not dogma, but discovery. Coexistence may continue, or it may disappear if one of two opposite trends overwhelms the other. In some cases such an imbalance is already evident. In others it is so strong that it is probably better to speak of a straightforward trend rather than coexistence. The evidence accumulated in this book would suggest that the clearest example of such a trend in religion in modern times is detraditionalization. As we have defined and developed the notion in **Part Three**, detraditionalization embraces a number of inter-connected processes. Essentially it involves a shift away from overarching sacred canopies towards a spirituality taken to be integral to the self, its relationships, and the natural order. It is a shift from the given to the chosen, the external to the internal, the transcendent to the here-and-now.

Detraditionalization seems to have affected religion in all modernized or modernizing societies – the rise of religions of heightened difference like Christian Fundamentalism notwithstanding. In pre-modern differentiated religion – from popular Buddhism to Christianity – the aim is to abolish the self and the will, or to tame and conform them to God's will. For some this is achieved most perfectly through monastic disciplines. For others it can be attempted through a life in which one submits to the disciplines of powerful and authoritative monopolistic religious institutions, their scriptures, traditions and priestly representatives, and abandons any claim to be able to discover the truth for oneself.

Today such traditionally differentiated religion is under severe pressure. One of the clearest signs of this is the way in which monasticism has declined in nearly every one of the world's religions. Another is a widespread scepticism about the authority of tradition – a scepticism evident not only in religions of humanity and spiritualities of life, but even in so-called conservative religions like Evangelicalism and resurgent Islam (which both privilege scripture over tradition). Across the whole spectrum of religious types, the religions which seem to be doing well (particularly in modernized western societies) are those which make room for individual participation, self-expression, experience and relationality. By contrast, those which are more traditional, impersonal, hierarchical and formal, which allow little or no room for participation and choice, and which encourage rejection of this life in favour of the next, are either detraditionalizing fast or losing numbers. To illustrate this shift, one need only compare a Roman Catholic mass in the first half of the twentieth century with its equivalent today – or with one of the charismatic services to which many Roman Catholics have defected.

As the chapter on Detraditionalization in **Part Three** illustrates, the force of detraditionalization is testimony to some of the most powerful cultural and social trends in modern times: the elevation of the self; the triumph of the ideals of freedom and equality; the spread of democracy; the influence of liberal education; the flight from deference, heteronomy, and authority; the collapse of stable, hierarchical societies; and the economic and political enfranchisement of more and more of the world's population. Religion, it seems, has been unable to withstand such forces. In some cases, as we have also seen, it has been a powerful factor in unleashing them (see, for example, Ernst Troeltsch and Talcott Parsons in readings **2.44** and **2.45**).

Discussion of detraditionalization leads us to an area which merits more discussion than has been possible in this volume, namely trends and changes in the forms of religious institutions themselves. (As mentioned in the introduction to **Part Two**, we would liked to have examined a fourth context of religion in modern times, had we had more space – the small-scale context, constituted by secondary and intermediate institutions like religious communities, educational institutions, families and the workplace, as well as by the whole arena of 'personal life'.) In relation to religious institutions and communities it is possible to discern a detraditionalizing and de-institutionalizing trend in modern times away from Troeltsch's church type (see reading **1.9**) to more informal, intimate, less hierarchical, more participatory and less tradition-determined religious institutions. Even though very large communities have not been abandoned ('mega-churches' for example), they are highly relational and often spawn smaller groups (Bible study; creche; prayer groups). Robert Wuthnow (1996) has been particularly influential in drawing attention to the rise of such small groups – and to their detraditionalizing effects at the level of belief as well as practice (see reading **2.82**). The effect of such small groups, he suggests, is to domesticate religious belief, to turn the divine Judge into friend and helper. It would be interesting to consider whether a parallel process is operative in other traditions.

A final question this volume raises is simply whether there is anything new under the sun. A stock strategy employed by audiences facing a scholar intent on outlining some unique aspect of modernity is to find examples of the same phenomenon in earlier times (often ancient Greece!). Whilst scholars may become tetchy at this point, and argue that what they describe is more widespread in modern times, or unique in certain important respects, the historical observation is not without point. In particular it is important because it draws attention to the fact that catch-all periodizations really are too simplistic, and that they often have an extremely loose purchase on historical reality (this is *particularly* true of the category 'pre-modernity', encompassing as it does all human culture and society prior to the Enlightenment).

So is there really anything new or distinctive about the phenomena discussed here under the heading of religion in modern times? Without attempting to answer this question in any detail, it is possible to point out that the differentiated approach we have been commending is at least open to the question and does not try to foreclose on the answer. For by speaking of modern times rather than modernity, and by trying to view these times in terms of variety rather than uniformity, the possibility that they are shaped and formed by the forces of the past as well as the present is kept open. Just as different types, contexts and trends interplay in religion in modern times, so too do different social and cultural traditions, some of them very old indeed. Just as tradition is constantly modernized, so modernity is constantly traditionalized. Consequently, one very important aspect of the approach advocated here is a strong and sophisticated historical awareness. The work of Ernst Troeltsch might be cited as exemplary in this respect.

Priorities for Future Research

By gathering together the literature on religion in modern times, this volume also exposes some major research gaps. Extensive on some topics, the literature thins considerably in relation to others.

Most surprisingly, frustrating gaps (or wonderful opportunites) are revealed even in relation to the secularization debate. A great deal of the literature here is theoretical rather than empirical. Whilst there is extensive quantitative data from polling in relation to North America and Europe, such data is patchy or non-existent for other parts of the world. Equally, some of its more common questions (Do you have a soul?; Do you believe in a Higher Power?) are so question-begging that they cry out to be taken further by more qualitative and in-depth forms of research.

Another ill-explored area in relation to both secularization and sacralization concerns religion (particularly in the West) 'beyond church, chapel and mosque' – beyond visible, institutional religious groups. Claims about such religion range from the extravagant – 'a luxuriant undergrowth' – to the dismissive. By its very nature, such religion is hard to quantify. Again, there seems a need for methodologically innovative forms of research to be brought to bear on this area.

This volume approaches the issues of secularization and sacralization in terms of different varieties of religion and their different trajectories and contexts. Here too it would seem that there is a great deal more work to be done at both the theoretical and the empirical levels. As indicated above, there is an emerging consensus in the literature that the two forms of religion which are doing best are religions of difference (particularly of heightened difference) and spiritualities of life. Even here, however, there is a lack of hard evidence. World-wide, it is reasonable to guess that the former vastly outweigh the latter (not least because Christianity and Islam are the world's largest religions, and because the majority of Christians and Muslims possibly belong to some form of religion of difference). However, it is also important to remember that spiritualities of life are not confined to the middle classes and the margins of the West (California, Scandinavia) as is sometimes assumed, but are also influential in places as far-flung as India, Brazil, and Japan.

The related area of consensus in the literature is that religions of humanity are faring relatively badly. Here the evidence to which appeal is made is almost exclusively the relative decline of 'mainline' churches in the West. Some more recent evidence suggests that there may, however, be more to be said. Most importantly, Nancy Ammerman's extensive research on American congregations revealed that 51 per cent of those questioned fall into the category of 'Golden Rule Christians', who embrace many of the key tenets of a religion of humanity, and who significantly outnumber Evangelicals (see reading **1.33**). Even if decline of liberal denominations has taken place, one can hazard a guess that there are still large numbers of liberals (even a majority?) in many of the large Christian denominations, not least the Roman Catholic church. Will further research on this topic reveal that rumours of the death of religions of humanity have been greatly exaggerated?

Another equally important reason for questioning the consensus that only religions of difference and spiritualities of life are doing well in modern times is that it is clear that more is flourishing in the middle ground than this allows. This middle ground is inhabited not only by religions of humanity, but also by experiential religions of difference and experiential religions of humanity. As a number of readings show, the first, in the guise of the Charismatic upsurge, has a good claim to be the most vibrant and quickly growing of all forms of late twentieth-century religion (alongside resurgent Islam). This upsurge, most particularly in Latin America, and increasingly in Africa, is an area which has attracted a great deal of extremely high quality research. One thing which this has revealed is that such religion is not a straightforward example of a religion of difference – and certainly not of 'Fundamentalism' – because it is characterised by such features as a measure of individualism and a stress on the authority of experience. It would be extremely interesting to see if examples of experiential religions of difference are also to be found in other religious traditions.

By contrast, experiential religions of humanity have obviously been less well studied, since the category is not yet established in the literature. As we have seen, this trajectory displays some features of a religion of humanity, including a 'humanitarian' emphasis, but also places value on experience and self-expression. A key feature of such religiosity is its strongly *relational* emphasis. This is another example of detraditionalization, but one in which the turn is not just to the self, but to the relational self and relationships. The goal of self-realization is qualified by the goal of perfected relationality – both in relation to the divine and the human. The religiosity espoused by Princess Diana and many who paid tribute to her furnishes an excellent example (see Woodhead in reading **1.87**). (It may be that this strong relational emphasis also qualifies some contemporary religions of difference – as in the strong stress placed by Evangelical religion on 'personal relationship' with Jesus Christ.)

Whilst both secularization and sacralization thus present many opportunities for further research, they have attracted a great deal more scholarly interest than has universalization. Whilst Chapter Eleven offers many examples of this trend, there is still no reliable data on how many people believe, à la Prince Charles or Aldous Huxley, that there is a perennial truth at the heart of all religions. Likewise there is a dearth of theoretical reflection on this topic: why, for example, does universalization appear to have gained pace in the last one hundred years, and how does it relate to the forces of modernization?

What of our final trend, detraditionalization? As indicated above, this is an area which has already been relatively well explored, particularly under the guiding rubrics of 'subjectivization', 'the turn to the self', and the 'expressive turn'. Though detraditionalization has been investigated primarily in relation to spiritualities of life, research has also been undertaken on the extent to which it is evident in other forms of religion (see, for example James Davison Hunter's work on Evangelicalism, extracts **1.27** and **3.86**). More work remains to be done. It would be interesting, for example, to carry out ethnographic work on the many forms of traditionalized religion which still exist world-wide (including monasticism) in order to see how far, and in what ways, the processes we have described are at work. It would also be interesting to broaden the investigation from the turn to the self and subjectivization to consider the spiritualization of everyday life in the West. The popularity of spiritual self-help manuals, and the current vogue for Feng Shui (the spirituality of interior decoration) suggest that the enchantment of the everyday is a major unexplored aspect of detraditionalization.

Further research is also needed on the different contexts of religion in modern times. The topic of religion and politics is quite well researched by contrast with that of religion and economics. It would be interesting to discover more about what, if anything religious, undergirds work ethics in the modernized world. Equally, whilst some fascinating research has been carried out on prosperity religion in various places, not least by anthropologists, much still remains to be done. For example, it would be interesting simply to determine how prevalent prosperity religion really is, and to investigate whether it really does flourish in every part of the world, irrespective of the state and form of economic development. Another intriguing empirical and theoretical topic concerns the strange coexistence noted in Chapter Six between quasi-magical forms of prosperity religion and otherwise rationalized forms of life.

The whole area of gender and religion is likewise surprisingly under-researched. Even in relation to research on secularization, where statistics on gender and religious affiliation may be available, the gender variable is relatively unexplored. The most obvious question remains unanswered (and often unasked): are more women religious than men, and if so why? If the answer is yes, as it seems to be in relation to the Christian churches at least, then the implications for secularization theory are hugely important. It might, for example, be possible to explain secularization in relation to the mainline churches solely in terms of the defection of women. Equally, women's loyalty or dissatisfaction with the churches (or their death) may be the single most important factor determining the fate of these institutions in the years ahead. It would also be interesting to learn more about how gender relates to the trends and varieties of religion which are explored in this volume. Are women, for example, more attracted to certain types of religion than others? At the moment we have little idea.

In some ways, however, these startling gaps in relation to research on religion and gender seem to be merely symptomatic of what seems to be the most gaping hole of all in the study of religion in modern times. To put it simply: we just do not know much about what people believe. Thanks to modern polling techniques, we now have an idea of how many atheists, agnostics, and believers in a personal God and a Higher Power there are in many western societies. Thanks to some excellent qualitative and ethnographic studies we are have some idea about what men and women in certain specific religious communities believe (particularly in religions of difference and experiential difference like Orthodox Judaism, Fundamentalist Christianity, Evangelicalism and

Pentecostalism; we have less empirical data on the beliefs of those in spiritualities of life and religions of humanity). And we have next to no idea about the beliefs of those who have no active or institutional religious affiliation. Evidence from publishers' catalogues and book sales enables us to guess that religious belief is not confined to the institutionally affiliated, but we still have little idea about its scale or the nature of commitment.*

Finally, it may be worth mentioning how, in the course of producing this book, it has also become apparent that in geographical terms the distribution of research on religion is patchy. Whilst there are many studies of religion outside the West in modern times, these are often purely text-based in their research and/or constrained by a framework of 'world religions' and 'traditions'. Often they fail to engage with theoretical or empirical studies of religion, or with wider debates about the nature of modernity and modern times. We found this to be most true in relation to studies of Islam and Hinduism (partly because of a colonial legacy?). Where religion is concerned, the most and best studied part of the world is undoubtedly North America, with Latin America probably coming second. This is not surprising, given that the academic study of religion is more strongly established, more extensive, and better funded in North America than anywhere else in the world. Whilst Europe has also produced much significant work in this area, religion there has been less extensively studied, particularly at the empirical level. But the most understudied part of the world in relation to religion in modern times is almost certainly China, with India coming a close second. It seems that we know just enough about religion in India to know how much there is that we do not know. For from the point of view of religion in modern times, India must surely be one of the most fascinating nations on earth, not least because of the meeting there of tradition

---

* Three of us at Lancaster – Paul Heelas, Bronislaw Szersysznski and Linda Woodhead – are currently preparing to study a small English town in depth in order to learn more about its inhabitants' 'sources of significance'. Theoretically and methodologically this is extremely challenging. It raises huge questions; not least, how much significance can one attach to people's 'attitudes' or to what they say they believe? We have begun to devise some strategies for research, including ethnographic work in church communities, street surveys, focus groups, immersion in various communities, analysis of newsagent and bookstore sales, of obituaries and epitaphs, and in-depth interviewing along with observation of peoples' homes, books, records and prized possessions. Gender will also be an important 'variable' which will help inform this research. We would be very interested to hear of similar projects, and hope that more work of this kind can help extend and test our knowledge of religion in modern times.

with modernization, but also because of the sub-continent's huge variety of religion. India has powerful religions of difference, increasingly associated with political and ethnic mobilization. It has a huge variety of spiritualities of life, many of them related to ancient traditions. And it is home to highly influential religions of humanity, articulated with great force by many of those who shaped independent India and its so-called 'secularist' (in truth more spiritually-informed humanistic) ideology. The story of how a largely traditional and polytheistic country came to be ruled by an spiritual ideology of human unity is surely one of the great untold stories of religion in modern times.

Predicting Religion

This volume has attempted to address three questions: What is happening to religion? Why is it happening? What might happen next? The last question is the trickiest. In some ways it is also the most entertaining, involving as it does a great deal of speculation and imagination (spiced with a measure of personal preference and prejudice).

The literature makes many, often contradictory, predictions. Secularization theorists predict that religion will wither away altogether or become simply a matter of personal and private concern. Sacralization theorists predict the opposite (or do they? it is not entirely clear whether they predict growth, or continuity in an already religious world). Something of a consensus has developed that religions of humanity are the most likely to wane, religions of difference the least likely. Many predict that the turn to the self will continue – and that the spiritualities of life which cater so well for this turn will therefore fare well. On the other hand, some believe that such 'formless', self-centred, unstructured, and 'trendy' religiosity is bound to have a short shelf-life.

Our own predictions are similar in some respects, different in others. They are based on the premise that the varieties of religion which will do best are (a) those which go with rather than against the grain(s) of modern times and (b) those which have jobs to do – in particular in relation to economic and/or political life.

On this basis, and sticking our necks out as far as they will go, we predict the following:

- Across the globe, religions which can accommodate democratic aspirations, including aspirations to greater personal freedom, autonomy and empowerment, will do well.

- Religious of difference, including Catholicism and Islam, will fare well in modernizing countries developing democratic modern states when they integrate elements drawn from religions of humanity, in particular the ethic of humanity and human rights, and thereby serve to represent and articulate the interests of the disenfranchised (as in eastern Europe, Bangladesh and Indonesia).
- Religions which are able to accommodate a degree of detraditionalization by abandoning institutional hierarchies perceived to be oppressive, allowing participation of all their members (including women), and by adding value to people's lives in the here-and-now, will do well. The process of detraditionalization will, however, be checked by a continuing desire for structured religion which can link present with past and future.
- Religions – particularly religions of heightened difference – will continue to do well in areas where they serve to undergird emerging or endangered local, ethnic, or national identities.
- Particularly outside the West, 'modernizing religions' will do well. Such religions enable individuals, communities and nations to find ways of adapting to a global capitalist economy without following a westernizing and secularizing model and so losing their distinctive traditions, identities and faiths. (Pentecostal Christianity and Islam provide good examples.)
- Religion affiliated with established power-structures and social elites will continue to fare badly (as has been the fate of the Roman Catholic church in many parts of modern Europe, and the Church of England).
- Religions that wish to retain widespread public influence in the developed world will continue to accommodate themselves to the modern state and find ways of tailoring their 'difference' and distinctive message to a democratic civil ethos (as in the Pope's strategy of defending democracy and human rights).
- The hegemony of the libertarian democratic civil ethos in the developed world will also continue to stimulate the growth of more radical, counter-cultural and separatist religious groups and tendencies (albeit on a fairly small scale and with only sporadic disruption to the mainstream).
- Social dislocation due to high mobility which characterizes modern and modernizing societies will lead not only to individualism, but to a counterbalancing desire for strong and supportive community: 'Relational religions' which offer a sense of belonging and a focus for local community will therefore fare well. The dislocations of modern

society will also favour those religions which offer moral depth and a structure for living, and which put people in touch with a God who is higher than self.

- De-essentialized postmodern religions that attempt to deconstruct the categories of self, God, and religion are unlikely to have a great influence outside the academy. Religions outside such circles are strongly essentialized; it is hard to see how they could perform social, political, salvific and moral tasks if they were not.
- The religions which do best will be those which are able to mobilize the most resources, both financial and human. The accumulation of wealth over long periods is a definite advantage possessed by some older faiths that may sustain an existence that would otherwise have been precarious.

In terms of the analysis of different varieties of religion with which this book began, these predictions can also be stated in the following terms:

- Spiritualities of life will not fare as well as many have predicted, because of their inability to sustain anything more than adventitious and instrumental communities, and their failure to provide a clear framework for living. The 'Self', we feel, may not always prove strong enough to sustain itself in complex and testing times. Furthermore, we predict that spiritualities of life will face increasing competition from experiential religions of difference and humanity, both of which cater better for the self *and* the relational, the universal *and* the different.
- In the West, religions of heightened difference will continue as counter-cultural pockets of protest and witness. They will continue to fare well everywhere they have a job to do undergirding ethnic and national differences.
- Experiential religions of difference will fare particularly well because of (a) their ability to cater both for an expressive turn *and* for structure and transcendence and (b) their ability to: help followers cope with the modernizing process by socializing them into democratic and capitalistic virtues; empower and guide; offer support and community in a world of rapid change. (This range of abilities means that such religions will flourish in both modern *and* modernizing societies.)
- Long-established religions of difference will become increasingly internally plural, with some followers stressing difference, others a

universal civil ethos, and others travelling in a more experiential direction.

- Religions of humanity will also find their followers pulled in different directions, either towards religions of difference or more experiential and expressive forms of religion. In the West it is likely some people will continue to occupy the middle ground and to articulate some version of the creed of 'human values'. Different forms of experiential religions of humanity may fare particularly well. In countries where pluralism threatens to become divisive the strong universalism characteristic of religions of humanity will also prove advantageous.

- Finally, we predict that coexistence will continue. Whilst religions of experiential difference may grow most quickly in the coming years, religions of difference, religions of humanity and spiritualities of life will not fade away (we are not, in other words, predicting significant secularization; worldwide there are surprisingly few atheists today and we do not expect that there will be many more tomorrow). Equally, the different trends we have outlined will probably coexist, and continue to generate tensions both creative and conflictual.

In short, we predict that a wide variety of religions will continue to coexist, but that the winners will be those which put people in touch with a God beyond self, make a difference, sustain supportive and affective communities, emphasize experience, have a political or economic job to do, and empower.

Time will tell.

references

This reference list details all works cited in the editorial passages in this volume.

Albanese, Catherine L. 1977: *Corresponding Motion. Transcendental Religion and the New America*. Philadelphia: Temple University Press.

Albanese, Catherine L. 1990: *Nature Religion in America. From the Algonkian Indians to the New Age*. Chicago and London: Chicago University Press.

Ammerman, Nancy 1997: *Congregation and Community*. New Brunswick: Rutgers University Press.

Anderson, Benedict 1991: *Imagined Communities*. London: Verso.

Arjomand, Said Amir (ed.) 1984: *From Nationalism to Revolutionary Islam*. London and Basingstoke: Macmillan.

Asad, Talal 1993: *Genealogies of Religion. Discipline and Reasons for Power in Christianity and Islam*. Baltimore and London: Johns Hopkins University Press.

Ayubi, N. 1991: *Political Islam. Religion and Politics in the Arab World*. London: Routledge.

Barker, David, Lock Halman and Astrid Vloet 1993: *The European Value Study 1981–1990*. London: The Gordon Cook Foundation.

Baudrillard, Jean 1981: *For a Critique of the Political Economy of the Sign*. St Louis: Mo.

Baudrillard, Jean 1988: *Selected Writings*. Cambridge: Polity.

Bauman, Zygmunt 1993: *Postmodern Ethics*. Oxford and Cambridge, Mass.: Blackwell.

Bell, Daniel 1979: *The Cultural Contradictions of Capitalism*. London: Heinemann.

Bellah, Robert 1964: Religious Evolution. *American Sociological Review*, 29: 358–74.

Bellah, Robert 1975: *The Broken Covenant. American Civil Religion in Time of Trial*. New York: The Seabury Press/Crossroad.

Bellah, Robert 1991: *Beyond Belief*. Oxford: University of California Press.

Bellah, Robert N., Richard Madsen, William M. Sullivan, Ann Swidler, and Steven M. Tipton 1985: *Habits of the Heart. Individualism and Commitment in American Life*. Berkeley, Los Angeles and London: University of California Press.

Berger, Peter L. 1969: *The Sacred Canopy. Elements of a Sociological Theory of Religion*. New York: Anchor Books.

Berger, Peter L. 1987: *The Capitalist Revolution. Fifty Propositions about Prosperity, Equality and Liberty*. Aldershot: Wildwood House.

Berger, Peter L., Brigitte Berger and Hansfried Kellner 1974: *The Homeless Mind. Modernization and Consciousness*. Harmondsworth: Penguin.

Berman, Marshall 1992: Why Modernism Still Matters. In Scott Lash and Jonathan Friedman (eds), *Modernity and Identity*. Oxford and Cambridge, Mass.: Blackwell.

Bibby, Reginald W. 1978: Why the Conservative Churches *Really* are Growing. Kelly Revisited. *Journal for the Scientific Study of Religion*, 17 (2): 129–37.

Bozeman, Theodore Dwight 1988: *To Live Ancient Lives. The Primitivist Dimension in Puritanism*. Chapel Hill and London: University of North Carolina Press.

Brierley, Peter 1991: *Christian England*. London: MARC.

Bruce, Steve (ed.) 1992: *Religion and Modernization. Sociologists and Historians Debate the Secularization Thesis*. Oxford: Clarendon Press.

Bruce, Steve (ed.) 1995a: *The Sociology of Religion*, 2 vol. Cheltenham: Edward Elgar.

Bruce, Steve 1995b: *Religion in Modern Britain*. Oxford: Oxford University Press.

Bruce, Steve 1996: *Religion in the Modern World. From Cathedrals to Cults*. Oxford and New York: Oxford University Press.

Burdick, John 1996: *Looking for God in Brazil. The Progressive Catholic Church in Brazil's Religious Arena*. Berkeley: University of California Press.

Campbell, Colin 1987: *The Romantic Ethic and the Spirit of Modern Consumerism*. Oxford and New York: Basil Blackwell.

Caplow, Theodore, Howard M. Bahr, Bruce A. Chadwick et al. 1983: *All Faithful People. Change and Continuity in Middletown's Religion*. Minneapolis: University of Minnesota Press.

Casanova, José 1994: *Public Religions in the Modern World*. Chicago and London: University of Chicago Press.

Chadwick, Owen 1975: *The Secularization of the European Mind in the Nineteenth Century*. Cambridge: Cambridge University Press.

Cornell, Stephen 1988: *The Return of the Native. American Indian Political Resurgence*. Oxford: Oxford University Press.

Cucchiari, Salvatore 1991: Between Shame and Sanctification: Patriarchy and its Transformation in Sicilian Pentecostalism. *American Ethnologist*, November, 687–707.

Daly, Mary 1973: *Beyond God the Father. Towards a Philosophy of Women's Liberation*. Boston: Beacon Press.

Esposito, John L. (ed.) 1983: *Voices of Resurgent Islam*. New York and Oxford: Oxford University Press.

Fenn, Richard K. 1978: *A Theory of Secularization*. Storrs. Com.: Society for the Scientific Study of Religion.

Fisher, Mary Pat 1997: *Living Religions: An Encyclopaedia of the World's Faiths*. London: I. B. Tauris.

Fukuyama, Francis 1992: *The End of History and the Last Man*. London and New York: Penguin Books.

Gardell, Mattias 1996: *Countdown to Armagedon. Louis Farrakhan and the Nation of Islam*. London: Hurst.

Gay, Peter 1968: *Deism: An Anthology*. Princeton, Toronto, Melbourne and London: D. Van Nostrand Co.

Gerth, H. H. and C. Wright Mills (eds) 1970: *From Max Weber: Essays in Sociology*. London, Boston, Melbourne and Henley: Routledge and Kegan Paul.

Giddens, Anthony 1990: *The Consequences of Modernity*. Cambridge: Polity.

Giddens, Anthony 1991: *Modernity and Self-Identity. Self and Society in the Late Modern Age*. Cambridge: Polity.

Greeley, Andrew M. 1990: *The Catholic Myth. The Behaviour and Beliefs of American Catholics*. New York: Charles Scribner's Sons.

Hadden, Jeffrey K. 1969: *The Gathering Storm in the Churches*. Garden City, NY: Doubleday.

Hall, Stuart, David Held and Tony McGrew (eds) 1992: *Modernity and Its Futures*. Cambridge: Polity Press/The Open University.

Hammond, Phillip E. 1992: *Religion and Personal Autonomy. The Third Disestablishment in America*. South Carolina: University of South California Press.

Hammond, Phillip E. (ed.) 1985: *The Sacred in a Secular Age, Toward Revision in the Scientific Study of Religion*. Berkeley, Los Angeles and London: University of California Press.

Hanegraaff, Wouter J. 1996: *New Age Religion and Western Culture. Esotericism in the Mirror of Secular Thought*. Leiden, New York and Koln: E. J. Brill.

Hannigan, John A. 1990: Apples and Oranges or Varieties of the Same Fruit? The New Religious Movements and the New Social Movements Compared. *Review of Religious Research*, 31 (3): 246–58.

Hannigan, John A. 1991: Social Movement Theory and the Sociology of Religion: Toward a New Synthesis. *Sociological Analysis*, 52 (4): 311–31.

Harris, Marvin 1981: *America Now*. New York: Simon & Schuster.

Harvey, David 1990: *The Condition of Postmodernity*. Oxford and Cambridge, Mass.: Blackwell.

Hauerwas, Stanley and Will Willimon 1989: *Resident Aliens*. Nashville: Abingdon Press.

Haynes, Jeff 1998: *Religion in Global Politics*. London and New York: Longman.

Heelas, Paul 1992: God's Company: New Age Ethics and The Bank of Credit and Commerce International. *Religion Today*, 8 (1): 1–4.

Heelas, Paul 1996: *The New Age Movement. The Celebration of the Self and the Sacralization of Modernity*. Oxford and Cambridge, Mass.: Blackwell.

Heelas, Paul (ed.) 1998: *Religion, Modernity and Postmodernity*. Oxford and Malden, Mass.: Blackwell.

Heelas, Paul, Scott Lash and Paul Morris (eds) 1996: *Detraditionalization. Critical Reflections on Authority and Identity*. Oxford and Cambridge, Mass.: Blackwell.

Heino, Harri 1997: *Mihin Suomi Tanaa Uskoo*. Juva and Helsinki: WSOY.

Hill, Michael 1973: *A Sociology of Religion*. New York: Basic Books.

Hinnells, John R. (ed.) 1997: *A New Handbook of Living Religions*. London: Penguin.

Hofstadter, Richard 1962: *Anti-Intellectualism in American Life*. New York: Cape.

Hoover, Stewart M. and Knut Lundby 1997: *Rethinking Media, Religion and Culture*. Thousand Oaks, London and New Delhi: Sage.

Hunter, James Davison 1987: *Evangelicalism. The Coming Generation*. Chicago and London: The University of Chicago Press.

Irigaray, Luce 1997 (orig. 1983): Equal to Whom? In Graham Ward (ed.), *The Postmodern God. A Theological Reader*. Malden, Mass. and Oxford: Blackwell, pp. 198–214.

Jellinek, George 1979: *The Declaration of the Rights of Man and of the Citizen*. Westport, Conn.: Hyperion Press.

Kelley, Dean 1977: *Why Conservative Churches are Growing*, 2nd edn. San Francisco: Harper and Row.

Keyes, Charles F. 1986: Ambiguous Gender. Male Initiation in a Northern Thai Buddhist Society. In Caroline Walker Bynum, Stevan Harrell and Paul Richman (eds), *Religion and Gender. On the Complexity of Symbols*. Boston: Beacon Press, pp. 66–96.

Kinnaman, Michael and Brian Cope (eds) 1997: *The Ecumenical Movement. An Anthology of Key Texts*. Grand Rapids, MI: William B. Eerdmans.

Kohn, Hans 1955: *Nationalism: Its Meaning and History*. Princeton, NJ: D. Van Nostrand Lawrence.

Lash, Scott and John Urry 1987: *The End of Organized Capitalism*. Cambridge: Polity Press.

Lawrence, Bruce 1995: *Defenders of the Faith. The Fundamentalist Revolt Against the Modern Age*. South Carolina: University of South Carolina Press.

Levine, Daniel H. (ed.) 1985: *Churches and Politics in Latin America*. Beverly Hills and London: Sage Publications.

Levine, Daniel H. (ed.) 1992: *Popular Voices in Latin American Catholicism*. Princeton, NJ: Princeton University Press.

Lyotard, J.-F. 1979: *The Post-Modern Condition: A Report on Knowledge*. Manchester: Manchester University Press.

Lynd, Robert S. and Helen Merrel Lynd 1929: *Middletown*. New York: Harcourt, Brace & World.

Lynd, Robert S. and Helen Merrel Lynd 1937: *Middletown in Transition*. New York: Harcourt, Brace, & World.

MacIntyre, Alasdair 1985: *After Virtue. A Study in Moral Theory*. London: Duckworth.

Madan, T. N. 1997: *Modern Myths, Locked Minds. Secularism and Fundamentalism in India*. Delhi: Oxford University Press.

Martin, David 1969: *The Religious and The Secular. Studies in Secularisation*. London: Routledge and Kegan Paul.

Martin, David 1978: *A General Theory of Secularisation*. London: Basil Blackwell.

Martin, David 1983: Received Dogma and New Cult. In Mary Douglas and Steven Tipton (eds), *Religion and America. Spiritual Life in a Secular Age.* Boston: Beacon Press, pp. 111–29.

Martin, David 1990: *Tongues of Fire. The Explosion of Protestantism in Latin America.* Oxford and Cambridge, Mass.: Basil Blackwell.

Martin, David 1996: *Forbidden Revolutions. Pentecostalism in Latin America and Catholicism in Eastern Europe.* London: SPCK.

Martin, David 1997: *Does Christianity Cause War?* London: Clarendon Press.

Marty, Martin E. 1970: *Righteous Empire. The Protestant Experience in America.* New York: The Dial Press.

Marty, Martin E. and R. Scott Appleby (eds) 1991: *Fundamentalisms Observed.* Chicago: University of Chicago Press.

Marty, Martin E. and R. Scott Appleby (eds) 1993a: *Fundamentalisms and Society: Reclaiming the Sciences, the Family, and Education.* Chicago: University of Chicago Press.

Marty, Martin E. and R. Scott Appleby (eds) 1993b: *Fundamentalisms and the State. Remaking Polities, Economies, and Militance.* Chicago: University of Chicago Press.

Marty, Martin E. and R. Scott Appleby (eds) 1994: *Accounting for Fundamentalisms. The Dynamic Character of Movements.* Chicago: University of Chicago Press.

Marty, Martin E. and R. Scott Appleby (eds) 1995: *Fundamentalisms Comprehended.* Chicago: University of Chicago Press.

Maslow, Abraham H. 1965: *Eupsychian Management. A Journal.* Homewood, Ill.: Richard D. Irwin and The Dorsey Press.

Meyer, Thomas 1989: *Fundamentalismus: Aufstand gegen die Moderne.* Reinbek bei Hamburg: Rowohlt.

McGuire, Meredith B. 1997: *Religion. The Social Context,* 4th edn. Belmont: Wadsworth.

McKean, Lise 1996: *Divine Enterprise. Gurus and the Hindu Nationalist Movement.* Chicago and London: The University of Chicago Press.

Moore, Barrington 1967: *Social Origins of Dictatorship and Democracy. Lord and Peasant in the Making of the Modern World.* Harmondsworth: Penguin.

Neitz, Mary Jo 1991: In Goddess We Trust. In Thomas Robbins and Dick Anthony (eds), *In Gods We Trust: New Patterns of Religious Pluralism in America,* 2nd edn. New Brunswick and London: Transaction, pp. 353–72.

Novak, Michael 1991: *The Spirit of Democratic Capitalism.* London: The IEA Health and Welfare Unit.

Owen, R. 1992: *State, Power and Politics in the Making of the Modern Middle East.* London: Routledge.

Parsons, Talcott 1968: *The Structure of Social Action. Volume 1.* New York: The Free Press; London: Collier-Macmillan.

Piscatori, James 1986: *Islam in a World of Nation-States.* Cambridge: Cambridge University Press.

Porter, Roy 1977: Introduction. In Roy Porter (ed.), *Rewriting the Self. Histories from the Renaissance to the Present.* London and New York: Routledge, pp. 1–14.

Prothero, Stephen 1996: *The White Buddhist. The Asian Odyssey of Henry Steel Olcott.* Bloomington and Indianapolis: Indiana University Press.

Ray, Larry 1987: The Protestant Ethic Debate. In R. J. Anderson, J. A. Hughes and W. W. Sharrock (eds), *Classic Disputes in Sociology.* London, Boston, Sydney, Wellington: Allen & Unwin, pp. 97–125.

Richards, Jeffrey, Scott Wilson and Linda Woodhead (eds) 1999: *Diana. The Making of a Media Saint.* London: I. B. Tauris.

Robertson, Roland and JoAnn Chirico 1985: Humanity, Globalization, and World-wide Religious Resurgence. A Theoretical Explanation. *Sociological Analysis,* 40 (3): 219–42.

Robinson, John A. T. 1963: *Honest to God.* London: SCM.

Roof, Wade Clark 1978: *Community and Commitment: Religious Plausibility in a Liberal Protestant Church.* New York: Elsevier.

Roof, Wade Clark 1993: *A Generation of Seekers. The Spiritual Journeys of the Baby Boom Generation.* New York: HarperCollins.

Roof, Wade Clark and Lyn Gesch 1995: Boomers and the Culture of Choice. Changing Patterns of Work, Family, and Religion. In Nancy Ammerman and Wade Clark Roof (eds), *Work, Family, and Religion in Contemporary America.* New York and London: Routledge, pp. 61–80.

Roof, Wade Clark and William McKinney 1987: *American Mainline Religion. Its Changing Shape and Future.* New Brunswick and London: Rutgers University Press.

Roszak, Theodore 1979: *Person-Planet: The Creative Destruction of Industrial Society.* London: Gollancz.

Rushkoff, Douglas 1997: *The Ecstasy Club.* London: Hodder and Stoughton.

Said, Edward 1985: *Orientalism.* Harmondsworth: Penguin.

Schumacher, E. F. 1980: *Good Work.* London: Sphere Books.

Shanks, Andrew 1995: *Civil Society, Civil Religion.* Oxford: Blackwell.

Simmel, Georg 1976 (orig. 1909): The Future in Our Culture. In P. A. Lawrence, *Georg Simmel. Sociologist and European.* Middlesex: Thomas Nelson, pp. 250–2.

Simmel, Georg 1997: *Essays on Religion.* New Haven and London: Yale University Press.

Sisk, Timothy D. 1992: *Islam and Democracy. Religion, Politics and Power in the Middle East.* Washington, D.C.: United States Institute of Peace Press.

Sivan, Emmanuel 1985: *Radical Islam, Medieval Theology and Modern Politics.* New Haven and London: Yale University Press.

Smart, Ninian 1998: *The World's Religions,* 2nd edn. Cambridge: Cambridge University Press.

Stark, Rodney and William Sims Bainbridge 1985: *The Future of Religion. Secularization, Revival and Cult Formation.* Berkeley, Los Angeles and London: University of California Press.

Stephan, Alfred 1988: *Rethinking Military Politics*. Princeton: Princeton University Press.

Swatos, William H. (ed.) 1994: *Gender and Religion*. New Brunswick and London: Transaction Publishers.

Taylor, Charles 1989: *Sources of the Self. The Making of Modern Identity*. Cambridge: Cambridge University Press.

Taylor, Mark C. 1984: *Erring. A Postmodern A/Theology*. Chicago: University of Chicago Press.

Tipton, Steven 1982: *Getting Saved from the Sixties. Moral Meaning in Conversion and Cultural Change*. Berkeley, Los Angeles and London: University of California Press.

Valliere, Paul 1987: Tradition. In Mircea Eliade (ed.), *The Encyclopedia of Religion*, Vol. 15. New York: Macmillan, pp. 1–16.

Wallace, Ruth A. 1994: The Social Construction of a New Leadership Role. Catholic Women Pastors. In William H. Swatos (ed.), *Gender and Religion*. New Brunswick and London: Transaction Publishers, pp. 15–26.

Warner, R. Stephen 1990: *New Wine in Old Wineskins. Evangelicals and Liberals in a Small-Town Church*. Berkeley, Los Angeles and London: University of California Press

Warner, R. Stephen 1993: Work in Progress toward a New Paradigm for the Sociological Study of Religion in the United States. *American Journal of Sociology* 98 (5), March: 1044–93.

Weber, Max 1991 (orig. 1915): The Social Psychology of the World Religions. In H. H. Gerth and C. Wright Mills (eds), *From Max Weber: Essays in Sociology*. London: Routledge, pp. 267–301.

Wessinger, Catherine (ed.) 1996: *Religious Institutions and Women's Leadership. New Roles inside the Mainstream*. Columbia: University of South Carolina Press.

Wiener, Martin J. 1985: *English Culture and the Decline of the Industrial Spirit, 1850–1980*. Harmondsworth: Penguin.

Wilson, Bryan 1966: *Religion in Secular Society*. London: C. A. Watts.

Wilson, Bryan 1985: Secularization: The Inherited Model. In Philip Hammond (ed.), *The Sacred in a Secular Age. Toward Revision in the Scientific Study of Religion*. Berkeley, Los Angeles and London: University of California Press, pp. 9–20.

Wilson, Bryan and Karel Dobbelaere 1994: *A Time to Chant. The Soka Gakkai Buddhists in Britain*. Oxford and New York: Clarendon Press.

Witten, Marsha G. 1993: *All is Forgiven. The Secular Message in American Protestantism*. Princeton: Princeton University Press.

Witten, Marsha G. 1995: 'Where Your Treasure Is': Popular Evangelical Views of Work, Money, and Materialism. In Robert Wuthnow (ed.), *Rethinking Materialism. Perspectives on the Spiritual Dimension of Economic Behavior*. Michigan: William B. Eerdmans, pp. 117–44.

Wuthnow, Robert 1988: *The Restructuring of American Religion*. Princeton, NJ: Princeton University Press.

Wuthnow, Robert 1996: *Sharing the Journey. Support Groups and America's New Quest for Community*. New York, London, Toronto, Sydney, Singapore: The Free Press.

Wuthnow, Robert (ed.) 1995: *Rethinking Materialism. Perspectives on the Spiritual Dimension of Economic Behavior*. Michigan: William B. Eerdmans.

Wuthnow, Robert 1997: The Cultural Turn. Studies, Logic, and the Quest for Identity in American Religion. In Penny Edgell Becker and Nancy L. Eisland (eds), *Contemporary American Religion. An Ethnographic Reader*. Walnut Creek, London and New Delhi: AltaMira, pp. 245–65.

index of names